Delmar
HEALTH CARE

A GUIDE TO HEALTH INSURANCE BILLING

FOURTH EDITION

D0642381

MARIE A. MOISIO
MA, RHIA

DELMAR
CENGAGE Learning·

Australia • Brazil • Japan • Korea • Mexico • Singapore • Spain • United Kingdom • United States

DELMAR
CENGAGE Learning·

A Guide to Health Insurance Billing, Fourth Edition
Marie A. Moisio, MA, RHIA

Vice President, Careers & Computing:
Dave Garza

Healthcare Publisher: Steve Helba

Executive Editor: Rhonda Dearborn

Director, Development-Career and Computing:
Marah Bellegarde

Product Development Manager: Juliet Steiner

Product Manager: Amy Wetsel

Editorial Assistant: Courtney Cozzy

Brand Manager: Wendy Mapstone

Market Development Manager: Nancy Bradshaw

Senior Production Director: Wendy Troeger

Production Manager: Andrew Crouth

Senior Content Project Manager:
Kathryn B. Kucharek

Senior Art Director: Jack Pendleton

Media Editor: Bill Overrocker

Cover image: www.Shutterstock.com

The 2013 versions of CPT, ICD-9-CM, ICD-10-CM, and ICD-10-PCS were used in preparation of this product.

CPT copyright 2012 American Medical Association. All rights reserved. CPT is a registered trademark of the American Medical Association. Applicable FARS/DFARS Restrictions Apply to Government Use. Fee schedules, relative value units, conversion factors and/or related components are not assigned by the AMA, are not part of CPT, and the AMA is not recommending their use. The AMA does not directly or indirectly practice medicine or dispense medical services. The AMA assumes no liability for data contained or not contained herein.

For product information and technology assistance, contact us at
Cengage Learning Customer & Sales Support, 1-800-354-9706

For permission to use material from this text or product,
submit all requests online at **www.cengage.com/permissions.**
Further permissions questions can be e-mailed to
permissionrequest@cengage.com

Library of Congress Control Number: 2012949441
Book Only ISBN-13: 978-1-285-19358-8
Package ISBN-13: 978-1-285-19359-5

Delmar
5 Maxwell Drive
Clifton Park, NY 12065-2919
USA

Cengage Learning is a leading provider of customized learning solutions with office locations around the globe, including Singapore, the United Kingdom, Australia, Mexico, Brazil, and Japan. Locate your local office at:
international.cengage.com/region

Cengage Learning products are represented in Canada by Nelson Education, Ltd.

To learn more about Delmar, visit **www.cengage.com/delmar**

Purchase any of our products at your local college store or at our preferred online store **www.cengagebrain.com**

Notice to the Reader
Publisher does not warrant or guarantee any of the products described herein or perform any independent analysis in connection with any of the product information contained herein. Publisher does not assume, and expressly disclaims, any obligation to obtain and include information other than that provided to it by the manufacturer. The reader is expressly warned to consider and adopt all safety precautions that might be indicated by the activities described herein and to avoid all potential hazards. By following the instructions contained herein, the reader willingly assumes all risks in connection with such instructions. The publisher makes no representations or warranties of any kind, including but not limited to, the warranties of fitness for particular purpose or merchantability, nor are any such representations implied with respect to the material set forth herein, and the publisher takes no responsibility with respect to such material. The publisher shall not be liable for any special, consequential, or exemplary damages resulting, in whole or part, from the readers' use of, or reliance upon, this material.

Printed in the United States of America
8 9 10 11 12 13 14 23 22 21 20 19

Table of Contents

Preface   **xxiii**

CHAPTER 1: **The Insurance Billing Specialist**   **1**

Learning Objectives   1
Key Terms   1
Overview   2
Insurance Billing Specialist   2
    Personal Qualifications   2
    Technical Qualifications   4
Employment Opportunities   6
Educational, Certification, and Career Opportunities   10
Abbreviations   13
Summary   14
Review Exercises   15
Comprehension Exercises   16
Critical Thinking Exercises   17
Websites   17

CHAPTER 2: **Legal Aspects of Insurance Billing**   **19**

Learning Objectives   19
Key Terms   19
Overview   20
Origin of Legal Issues   20
General Legal Terms   21
    Emancipated Minor   22
    Embezzlement   22
    Employer Liability   22
    Guardianship and Power of Attorney   22
    Malpractice   23
    Negligence   24
    Statute of Limitations   24
    Subpoena of Records   24

Confidential Information   26

   Health Insurance Portability and Accountability Act of 1996 (HIPAA)   26

      HIPAA Security Rule   28

   Release of Information (ROI)   30

      Release of Information for HIV, AIDS, or Alcohol and Drug Abuse   32

      Telephone Release of Information   32

      Facsimile Release of Information   32

      Internet and Electronic Release of Information   33

Insurance Fraud and Abuse Laws   37

   Fraud   37

      Fraud Prevention and Reporting Incentives   39

      Penalties for Fraud   40

   Abuse   42

      Abuse Prevention and Reporting Incentives   42

      Penalties for Abuse   44

Patient Protection and Affordable Care Act   45

Abbreviations   48

Summary   48

Review Exercises   49

Comprehension Exercises   52

Internet Exercise   53

Critical Thinking Exercises   53

Websites   53

CHAPTER 3: **Introduction to Health Insurance**   **55**

Learning Objectives   55

Key Terms   55

Overview   56

Defining Health Insurance   56

   Health Insurance: Then and Now   56

Managed Care   60

Managed Care Organizations   62

   Health Maintenance Organization Models   63

      Staff Model   63

      Independent Practice Association (IPA)   63

      Group Model   63

      Network Model   63

   Preferred Provider Organization (PPO)   63

   Exclusive Provider Organization (EPO)   64

Integrated Delivery System   64

Point-of-Service Plan (POS)   64

Health Insurance Terminology   65

Health Insurance Policy Terms   65

Terms for Insurance Policy Purchasers and Insurance Companies   65

Terms Related to the Policy   67

Terms Related to Payment   71

Health Care Provider Terms   75

Paying the Bill with Health Insurance   78

Fee-for-Service   78

Episode-of-Care Reimbursement   78

Capitation   79

Abbreviations   81

Summary   81

Review Exercises   82

Critical Thinking Exercises   85

Website   87

CHAPTER 4: **International Classification of Diseases, Tenth Revision**   **89**

Learning Objectives   89

Key Terms   89

Overview   90

International Classification of Diseases, Tenth Revision, Clinical Modification (ICD-10-CM)   90

ICD-10-CM Components   93

Tabular List   93

Chapter 15: Pregnancy, Childbirth, and the Puerperium   94

Chapter 16: Certain Conditions Originating in the Perinatal Period   94

Chapter 17: Congenital Malformations, Deformations, and Chromosomal Abnormalities   95

Chapter 18: Symptoms, Signs, and Abnormal Clinical and Laboratory Findings, Not Elsewhere Classified   95

Chapter 19: Injury, Poisoning, and Certain Other Consequences of External Causes   96

Chapter 20: External Causes of Morbidity   96

Chapter 21: Factors Influencing Health Status and Contact with Health Services   97

Tabular List *Format*   97

Alphabetic Index   99

Index to Diseases and Injuries   99

External Cause of Injuries Index   101

Table of Drugs and Chemicals   102

IDC-10-CM Coding Conventions 103

    Punctuation 103

    Instructional Notes 104

    General Notes 105

    Includes Notes 105

    Excludes Notes 105

    Etiology and Manifestation Notes 107

    "Code Also" Note 107

    Cross-references 108

    Connecting Words 108

    Abbreviations 108

ICD-10-CM Official Guidelines for Coding and Reporting 110

    Section I.B. General Coding Guidelines 111

        Symptoms and Signs 111

        Acute and Chronic Conditions 111

        Combination Codes 111

        Late Effects (Sequela) 111

        Laterality 111

    Section IV. Diagnostic Coding and Reporting Guidelines for Outpatient Services 112

        Guideline IV. A. Selection of First-Listed Condition (Diagnosis) 112

        Guideline IV.B. Codes from A00.0 through T88.9, Z00-Z99 112

        Guideline IV.C. Accurate Reporting of ICD-10-CM Diagnosis Codes 113

        Guideline IV.D. Codes That Describe Symptoms and Signs 113

        Guideline IV.E. Encounters for Circumstances Other Than a Disease or Injury 113

        Guideline IV.F. Level of Detail in Coding 113

        Guideline IV.G. ICD-10-CM Code for the Diagnosis, Condition, Problem, or Other Reason for Encounter/Visit 114

        Guideline IV.H. Uncertain Diagnosis 114

        Guideline IV.I. Chronic Diseases 114

        Guideline IV.J. Code All Documented Conditions That Coexist 114

        Guideline IV.K. Patients Receiving Diagnostic Services Only 114

        Guideline IV.L. Patients Receiving Therapeutic Services Only 115

        Guideline IV.M. Patients Receiving Preoperative Evaluations Only 116

        Guideline IV.N. Ambulatory Surgery 116

        Guideline IV.O. Routine Outpatient Prenatal Visits 116

        Guideline IV.P. Encounters for General Medical Examinations with Abnormal Findings 116

        Guideline IV.Q. Encounters for Routine Health Screening 116

    Section II. Selection of Principal Diagnosis 117

        Guideline II.A. Codes for Symptoms, Signs, and Ill-Defined Conditions 117

        Guideline II.B. Two or More Interrelated Conditions, Each Potentially Meeting the Definition for Principal Diagnosis 118

Guideline II.C. Two or More Diagnoses That Equally Meet the Definition for Principal Diagnosis 118

Guideline II.D. Two or More Comparative or Contrasting Conditions 118

Guideline II.E. A Symptom(s) Followed by Contrasting/ Comparative Diagnoses 118

Guideline II.F. Original Treatment Plan Not Carried Out 119

Guideline II.G. Complications of Surgery and Other Medical Care 119

Guideline II.H: Uncertain Diagnosis 119

Guideline II.I. Admission from Observation Unit 120

Guideline II.J. Admission from Outpatient Surgery 120

Assigning ICD-10-CM Diagnoses Codes 122

Selecting Diagnoses Codes 122

Sequencing Diagnoses Codes 123

International Classification of Diseases, Tenth Revision, Procedure Coding System (ICD-10-PCS) 125

ICD-10-PCS Components 126

ICD-10-PCS Sections 126

ICD-10-PCS Alphabetic Index 128

ICD-10-PCS Tables 129

ICD-10-PCS Code Structure 132

Character 1: Section 132

Character 2: Body System 132

Character 3: Root Operation, Type, Modality 132

Character 4: Body Part, Body System/Region, Treatment Site, Qualifier 137

Character 5: Approach, Duration, Contrast, Radionuclide, Modality Qualifier, Type Qualifier, and Qualifier 138

Character 6: Device, Equipment, Function, Isotope, Method, Substance, and Qualifier 141

Character 7: Qualifier 143

ICD-10-PCS Coding Guidelines 147

General Guidelines 147

Body System Guidelines 147

Root Operation Guidelines 147

Assigning ICD-10-PCS Procedure Codes 150

Abbreviations 151

Summary 152

Review Exercises 152

ICD-10-CM Coding Practice Sets 153

Coding Challenge 156

Websites 158

CHAPTER 5: **International Classification of Diseases, Ninth Revision, Clinical Modification (ICD-9-CM)** **159**

Learning Objectives 159

Key Terms 159

Overview 160

International Classification of Diseases, Ninth Revision, Clinical Modification (ICD-9-CM) 160

ICD-9-CM Components 162

   Volume 1: Tabular List of Diseases and Injuries 162

      Chapter 11: Complications of Pregnancy, Childbirth, and the Puerperium 163

      Chapter 14: Congenital Anomalies 164

      Chapter 15: Certain Conditions Originating in the Perinatal Period 164

      Chapter 16: Symptoms, Signs, and Ill-Defined Conditions 164

      Chapter 17: Injury and Poisoning 164

      Tabular List Format 164

      Supplementary Classifications 167

      Appendices 167

   Volume 2: Alphabetic Index of Diseases and Injuries 171

      Indentation Patterns 172

      Alphabetization Rules 173

      Tables 175

      Hypertension Table 176

      Neoplasm Table 177

      Table of Drugs and Chemicals 178

   ICD-9-CM Coding Conventions 181

      Cross-References 181

      Instructional Notes 181

      Connecting Words 184

      Abbreviations 185

      Punctuation 185

ICD-9-CM Official Guidelines for Coding and Reporting 188

   Section IV. Diagnostic Coding and Reporting Guidelines for Outpatient Services 189

      Guideline IV.A. Selection of First-Listed Condition (Diagnosis) 189

      Guideline IV.B. Codes from 001.0 through V91.99 189

      Guideline IV.C. Accurate Reporting of ICD-9-CM Diagnosis Codes 189

      Guideline IV.D. Selection of Codes 001.0 through 999.9 189

      Guideline IV.E. Codes that Describe Symptoms and Signs 189

      Guideline IV.F. Encounters for Circumstances Other Than Disease or Injury 189

      Guideline IV.G. Level of Detail in Coding 190

      Guideline IV.H. Code for the Diagnosis, Condition, Problem, or Other Reason for Encounter/Visit 190

Guideline IV.I. Uncertain Diagnosis 190

Guideline IV.J. Chronic Diseases 190

Guideline IV.K. Code All Documented Conditions That Coexist 190

Guideline IV.L. Patients Receiving Diagnostic Services Only 191

Guideline IV.M. Patients Receiving Therapeutic Services Only 191

Guideline IV.N. Patients Receiving Preoperative Evaluations Only 191

Guideline IV.O. Ambulatory Surgery 192

Guideline IV.P. Routine Outpatient Prenatal Visits 192

Section II. Selection of Principal Diagnosis 192

Guideline II.A. Codes for Symptoms, Signs, and Ill-Defined Conditions 192

Guideline II.B. Two or More Interrelated Conditions, Each Potentially Meeting the Definition for Principal Diagnosis 192

Guideline II.C. Two or More Diagnoses That Equally Meet the Definition for Principal Diagnosis 193

Guideline II.D. Two or More Comparative or Contrasting Conditions 193

Guideline II.E. A Symptom(s) Followed by Contrasting/ Comparative Diagnoses 193

Guideline II.F. Original Treatment Plan Not Carried Out 193

Guideline II.G. Complications of Surgery and Other Medical Care 194

Guideline II.H. Uncertain Diagnosis 194

Guideline II.I. Admission from Observation Unit 194

Guideline II.J. Admission from Outpatient Surgery 195

Assigning ICD-9-CM Diagnostic Codes 196

Selecting the Diagnostic Codes 196

Sequencing Diagnostic Codes 198

Supplementary Classifications 200

V Codes 200

Categories V01–V06: Persons with Health Hazards Related to Communicable Diseases 201

Categories V07–V09: Persons with Need for Isolation, Other Potential Health Hazards and Prophylactic Measures 201

Categories V10–V19: Persons with Potential Health Hazards Related to Personal and Family History 202

Categories V20–V29: Persons Encountering Health Services in Circumstances Related to Reproduction and Development 203

Categories V30–V39: Liveborn Infants according to Type of Birth 207

Categories V40–V49: Persons with a Condition Influencing Their Health Status 208

Categories V50–V59: Persons Encountering Health Services for Specific Procedures and Aftercare 208

Categories V60–V69: Persons Encountering Health Services in Other Circumstances 209

Categories V70–V82: Persons Without Reported Diagnosis Encountered During Examination and Investigation of Individuals and Populations 211

E Codes 215

Miscellaneous Coding Guidelines   216

    Late Effects   216

    Burns   216

    HIV/AIDS   217

    Volume 3: Tabular List and Alphabetic Index of Procedures   218

        Alphabetic Index   218

        Tabular List   219

        Volume 3 *Coding Conventions*   219

Assigning ICD-9-CM Procedure Codes   221

    Identifying the Principal Procedure   222

    Selecting and Sequencing Procedure Codes   222

Miscellaneous Coding Guidelines for Procedures and Biopsies   224

    Bilateral Procedures   224

    Canceled, Incomplete, and Failed Procedures   224

    Biopsy Coding   226

Abbreviations   228

Summary   229

Review Exercises   230

ICD-9-CM Coding Practice Sets   231

Coding Challenge   239

Websites   242

CHAPTER 6: **Current Procedural Terminology (CPT) and Healthcare Common Procedure Coding System (HCPCS)**   **243**

Learning Objectives   243

Key Terms   243

Overview   244

Current Procedural Terminology   244

    CPT Components   245

        CPT Main Sections   245

        CPT Appendices   246

    CPT Alphabetic Index   247

    CPT Coding Conventions   249

        Semicolon   249

        Bullets and Triangles   251

        Facing Triangles   251

        Plus Sign   251

        Circle   252

        Circled Bullets   252

        Null Zero or Universal No Code   252

Flash Symbol	252
Number Symbol	252
See and See Also	252
Instructional Notes	253
Heading Notes	253
Notes Before/After CPT Codes	253
Section Guidelines	253
Evaluation and Management Section (99201–99499)	255
Commonly Used Terms	255
E/M Categories	255
Levels of Service	258
History	262
Examination	263
Medical Decision Making	264
Documentation Requirements	267
Selecting Evaluation and Management Codes	272
Evaluation and Management Modifiers	274
Anesthesia Section (00100–01999)	275
Anesthesia Modifiers	276
Anesthesia Add-On Codes	278
Anesthesia Code Selection and Reporting	279
Surgery Section (10021–69990)	280
Surgical Package	281
Separate Procedures	284
Modifiers	285
Ambulatory Surgery Center Modifiers	288
Radiology Section (70010–79999)	290
Radiological Supervision and Interpretation	290
Pathology and Laboratory Section (80047–89398)	291
Medicine Section (90281–99607)	291
Healthcare Common Procedure Coding System (HCPCS)	296
HCPCS Level II: National Codes	296
HCPCS Level II: Modifiers	296
Selecting HCPCS Level II Codes	299
Abbreviations	299
Summary	300
Review Exercises	301
Coding Challenge	303
Challenge Exercise	306
Websites	306

CHAPTER 7: **Developing and Processing an Insurance Claim** — 307

Learning Objectives	307
Key Terms	307
Overview	308
Developing an Insurance Claim	308
New Patient Procedures	309
Patient Registration Form and Authorizations: New Patient	310
Established Patient Procedures	313
Primary and Secondary Insurance Policies	314
Clinical Assessment and Treatment	318
Patient Departure Procedures: New and Established Patients	318
Scheduling and Billing	318
Posting Charges and Payments	319
Assigning Numeric Codes	321
Insurance Claims Processing	323
Insurance Carrier Procedures	323
Posting Insurance Payments	324
Insurance Claim Follow-Up	326
State Insurance Commission	328
Credit and Collections	330
Abbreviations	334
Summary	334
Review Exercises	335
Challenge Exercises	337
Website	337

CHAPTER 8: **CMS-1500 Completion Guidelines: Private and Commercial Insurance Claims** — 339

Learning Objectives	339
Key Terms	339
Overview	339
Optical Scanning Guidelines	341
CMS-1500 Guidelines	342
CMS-1500 Patient Information	342
Block 1: Insurance Plan	342
Block 1a: Insured's I.D. Number	342
Block 2: Patient's Name	342
Block 3: Patient's Birth Date and Sex (Gender)	343
Block 4: Insured's Name	343

Block 5: Patient's Address 343

Block 6: Patient Relationship to Insured 343

Block 7: Insured's Address 343

Block 8: Patient Status 343

Blocks 9–11: Other Insured's Name; Is Patient Condition Related To; Insured's Policy Group or FECA Number 343

Blocks 9–9d: Other Insured's Name; Policy Number; Date of Birth; Employer's or School Name; Insurance Plan Name or Program Name 344

Block 9: Other Insured's Name 344

Block 9a: Other Insured's Policy or Group Number 344

Block 9b: Other Insured's Birth Date 344

Block 9c: Employer's Name or School Name 344

Block 9d: Insurance Plan Name or Program Name 344

Blocks 10–10d: Is Patient's Condition Related To 344

Block 10a: Employment? (Current or Previous) 344

Block 10b: Auto Accident? Place (State) 344

Block 10c: Other Accident 344

Block 10d: Reserved for Local Use 345

Blocks 11–11d: Insured's Policy Group Number or FECA Number; Insured's Date of Birth; Employer's Name or School Name; Insurance Plan Name or Program; Is There Another Health Benefit Plan? 345

Block 11: Insured's Policy Group or FECA Number 345

Block 11a: Insured's Date of Birth 345

Block 11b: Employer Name or School Name 345

Block 11c: Insurance Plan Name or Program 345

Block 11d: Is There Another Health Benefit Plan? 345

Blocks 12 and 13: Patient Authorization 346

Block 12: Patients or Authorized Persons Signature 346

Block 13: Insured's or Authorized Person's Signature 346

CMS-1500 Treatment and Provider Information 348

Block 14: Date of Current: Illness (First symptom) OR Injury (Accident) OR Pregnancy (LMP) 348

Block 15: If Patient Has Had Same or Similar Illness, Give First Date 348

Block 16: Dates Patient Unable to Work in Current Occupation 348

Block 18: Hospitalization Dates Related to Current Services 349

Blocks 17, 19, and 20 349

Block 17: Name of Referring Provider or Other Source 349

Block 17a (no title, shaded): 349

Block 17b: NPI (unshaded) 349

Block 19: Reserved for Local Use 349

Block 20: Outside Lab? 349

Block 21: Diagnosis or Nature of Illness or Injury (Relate Items 1, 2, 3, or 4 to Item 24E by Line) 349

Block 22: Medicaid Resubmission Code 350

Block 23: Prior Authorization Number 350

Blocks 24A–J: Dates of Service; Procedures; Charges; Miscellaneous 351

    Block 24A: Dates of Service 351

    Block 24B: Place of Service 351

    Block 24C: EMG 351

    Block 24D: Procedures, Services, or Supplies 351

    Block 24E: Diagnosis Code 351

    Block 24F: Charges 353

    Block 24G: Days or Units 353

    Block 24H: EPSDT Family Plan (Early and Periodic Screening for Diagnosis and Treatment) 354

    Block 24I: ID. QUAL. (shaded area) 354

    Block 24J: Rendering Provider ID # (shaded area) 354

    Block 24J: Rendering Provider ID # NPI (unshaded area) 354

Blocks 25–33: Provider and Billing Entity Identification; Charges 354

Block 25: Federal Tax I.D. Number 355

Block 26: Patient's Account No. 355

Block 27: Accept Assignment? 355

Block 28: Total Charges 355

Block 29: Amount Paid 355

Block 30: Balance Due 355

Block 31: Signature of Physician or Supplier 356

Blocks 32–32b: Name and Address of Facility Where Services Were Rendered 356

    Block 32a (unshaded) 356

    Block 32b (shaded) 356

Block 33: Billing Provider Info & PH # 356

    Block 33a (unshaded) 356

    Block 33b (shaded) 356

Common Errors Made When Completing the CMS-1500 357

Abbreviations 359

Summary 359

Review Exercises 359

Challenge Exercise 360

Website 360

CHAPTER 9: **Electronic Claims Submission** **361**

Learning Objectives 361

Key Terms 361

Overview	361
Electronic Claims Submission Options	363
Carrier-Direct Claims Submission	363
Clearinghouse Claims Submission	364
Interactive Communication	365
Processing Electronic Health Insurance Claims	366
Retrieving, Editing, and Submitting Insurance Claims	367
Patient and Physician Signature Requirements	368
Clearinghouse/Insurance Carrier Error-Edit Messages	369
Confidentiality and Electronic Claims Processing	371
Electronic Record Management	372
Abbreviations	374
Summary	374
Review Exercises	375
Challenge Activity	377
Website	377

CHAPTER 10: Common UB-04 (CMS-1450) Completion Guidelines — 379

Learning Objectives	379
Key Terms	379
Overview	380
Hospital Reimbursement	381
Developing the Insurance Claim	383
Patient Registration	383
Capturing Charges for Services Rendered	384
Assigning Diagnosis and Procedure Codes	386
UB-04 Completion Guidelines	389
UB-04 Patient and Provider Information (FL 1–17)	390
FL 1: Provider Name, Address, and Telephone Number (Untitled)	390
FL 2: Pay-to Name, Address, (Untitled)	391
FL 3a: Patient Control Number (PAT CNTL #)	391
FL 3b: Medical Record Number	391
FL 4: Type of Bill (TOB)	391
FL 5: Federal Tax Number	393
FL 6: Statement Covers Period	393
FL 7: Untitled	393
FL 8: Patient Name	393
FL 9: Patient Address	393
FL 10: Patient's Birth Date	393
FL 11: Sex	394

FL 12: Admission Date   395

FL 13: Admission Hour   395

FL 14: Type of Admission   395

FL 15: Source of Admission (SRC)   395

FL 16: Discharge Hour (DHR)   395

FL 17: Patient Status (STAT)   396

UB-04 Condition and Event Information (FL 18–41)   398

FL 18–28: Condition Codes   398

FL 29: Accident State (ACDT STATE)   399

FL 30: (Untitled)   399

FL 31–34: Occurrence Codes and Dates   399

FL 35 and 36: Occurrence Span   399

FL 37: (Untitled)   399

FL 38: Responsible Party (Untitled)   400

FL 39–41: Value Codes   400

FL 42 and FL 43: Revenue Code (REV. CD.) and Description   403

FL 44: HCPCS/Rates   405

FL 45: Service Date (SERV. DATE)   406

FL 46: Service Units (SERV. UNITS)   406

FL 47: Total Charges   406

FL 48: Noncovered Charges   406

FL 49: Untitled   406

Insurance and Employer Information (FL 50–65)   406

FL 50: Payer Name   407

FL 51: Health Plan No.   407

FL 52: Release of Information (REL INFO)   407

FL 53: Assignment of Benefits (ASG BEN)   407

FL 54: Prior Payments   407

FL 55: Estimated Amount Due   408

FL 56: NPI   408

FL 57: Other Provider ID   408

FL 58: Insured's Name   408

FL 59: Patient's Relationship to Insured (P. REL)   408

FL 60: Insured's Unique ID   408

FL 61, 62: Group Name, Insurance Group Number   408

FL 63: Treatment Authorization Codes   409

FL 64: Document Control Number   409

FL 65: Employer Name   409

Medical Codes and Physician Identification (FL 66–81)   410

FL 66: DX (Diagnosis and Procedure Code Qualifier)   411

FL 67: Preprinted 67 (Principle Diagnosis Code) — 411

FL 67A–Q: Preprinted (Other Diagnosis Codes) — 412

FL 68: Untitled — 412

FL 69: Admitting Diagnosis (Admit Dx) — 412

FL 70a–c: Patient's Reason for Visit (Patient Reason Dx) — 412

FL 71: Prospective Payment System Code (PPS Code) — 412

FL 72: External Cause of Injury Code (ECI) — 412

FL 73: Untitled — 412

FL 74: Principal Procedure Code and Date — 412

FL 74a–e: Other Procedure Code and Date — 413

FL 75: Untitled — 413

FL 76: Attending Physician (Provider) Name and Identification (Attending NPI; QUAL) — 413

FL 77: Operating Provider Name and Identification Number (Operating) — 413

FL 78–79: Other Provider Name and Identification Number (Other) — 413

FL 80: Remarks — 414

FL 81a–d: Code-Code (CC) — 414

Submitting the Insurance Claim — 416

Abbreviations — 418

Summary — 419

Review Exercises — 419

Application Exercise — 425

Challenge Exercises — 425

Websites — 425

CHAPTER 11: **Blue Cross/Blue Shield** — **427**

Learning Objectives — 427

Key Terms — 427

Overview — 427

Blue Cross/Blue Shield General Information — 429

Blue Cross/Blue Shield Health Insurance Plans — 430

Blue Cross/Blue Shield Individual Plans — 430

Medigap Plans — 431

Blue Cross/Blue Shield Group Plans — 432

Employer-Sponsored Health Insurance Plans — 432

Other Group Health Insurance Plans — 433

Participating and Nonparticipating Providers — 433

Provider Reimbursement — 434

Usual, Customary, and Reasonable (UCR) Fees — 434

Relative Value Scale (RVS) Amount — 436

Blue Cross/Blue Shield Claims Submission — 438

Abbreviations	443
Summary	443
Review Exercises	444
Challenge Activity	446
Website	446

CHAPTER 12: **Medicare**   **447**

Learning Objectives	447
Key Terms	447
Overview	448
Medicare Part A	449
Medicare Part A: Covered Services	450
Medicare Part A: Deductibles and Co-payments	450
Lifetime Reserve Days	451
Medicare Part B	454
Medicare Part B: Covered Services	454
Medicare Part B: Providers	458
Participating Providers	458
Nonparticipating Providers (NonPARs)	461
Medicare Part C	464
Medicare Advantage Health Maintenance Organizations and Preferred Provider Organizations	464
Medicare Private Fee-for-Service (PFFS) Plans	465
Medicare Part D: Prescription Drug Benefit	465
Prescription Coverage	465
Prescription Drug Plan Enrollment	466
Prescription Drug Plan Premiums, Deductibles, and Co-Payments	466
Other Medicare Health Plan Choices	467
Medicare Fee Schedule (MFS)	469
National Correct Coding Initiative (NCCI)	470
Medicare Claims Submission	473
General Guidelines for Medicare Claims Submission	474
Medicare as Primary Payer	475
Completing the CMS-1500: Medicare as Primary Payer	477
Medicare as Primary with Supplemental Insurance	482
Medigap Insurance Plans	482
Processing Medigap Claims	484
Completing the CMS-1500: Medicare Primary with Medigap	484
Employer-Sponsored Medicare Supplemental Plans	486
Medicare-Medicaid Crossover Program	486

Processing Medicare-Medicaid Crossover Claims 487

Completing the CMS-1500: Medicare-Medicaid Crossover Claims 487

Medicare as Secondary Payer (MSP) 488

Completing the CMS-1500: Medicare Secondary 491

Processing Medicare Payments 493

Abbreviations 495

Summary 497

Review Exercises 498

Challenge Activities 502

Websites 502

CHAPTER 13: Medicaid **503**

Learning Objectives 503

Key Terms 503

Overview 503

Medicaid Coverage 504

Medicaid Billing 507

Medicaid Claims Submission 507

Medicaid Secondary Payer 511

Medicare/Medicaid Crossover Program 513

Processing Medicaid Payments 514

Abbreviations 516

Summary 517

Review Exercises 517

Challenge Activities 520

Websites 520

CHAPTER 14: TRICARE and CHAMPVA **521**

Learning Objectives 521

Key Terms 521

Overview 522

TRICARE Health Benefits Programs 523

TRICARE Prime 523

TRICARE Standard 524

TRICARE Extra 524

TRICARE for Life 524

Deers Enrollment and Tricare Reimbursement 526

Participating and Nonparticipating Providers 526

Covered and Noncovered Services 527

Preauthorization   528

Durable Medical Equipment (DME)   529

TRICARE Billing   531

Deductibles, Cost Sharing, and Allowable Charges   532

Estimating TRICARE Payment   533

CMS-1500 Completion for TRICARE   535

TRICARE as Secondary Payer   539

Fraud and Abuse   539

CHAMPVA   541

Covered and Noncovered Services   542

Providers, Deductibles, and Cost Sharing   542

CHAMPVA Billing   543

CMS-1500 Guidelines for CHAMPVA   543

Abbreviations   547

Summary   548

Review Exercises   549

Challenge Activities   552

Websites   552

CHAPTER 15: **Workers' Compensation**   **553**

Learning Objectives   553

Key Terms   553

Overview   554

Federal Workers' Compensation Programs   554

Occupational Safety and Health   558

State-Sponsored Workers' Compensation Programs   559

Workers' Compensation Basics   560

Eligibility   560

Classification of Work-Related Injuries   560

Medical Claims With No Disability   560

Temporary Disability   560

Permanent Disability   560

Vocational Rehabilitation   562

Work-Related Death   562

Workers' Compensation Documentation Requirements   564

Progress Reports   564

Reimbursement and CMS-1500 Completion   566

Abbreviations   569

Summary   570

Review Exercises   571

Challenge Activities   573

Websites   573

APPENDIX A: **Superiorland Clinic Practice Manual**   **574**

How to Access Appendix A: Superiorland Clinic Practice Manual and SimClaim™   574

General Instructions and Hints for SimClaim   574

APPENDIX B: **References**   **575**

Books   575

Periodicals   575

Newsletters   575

Websites   575

APPENDIX C: **Abbreviations**   **577**

Glossary   **581**

Index   **595**

Preface

INTRODUCTION

Insurance billing is an excellent career choice in the health care industry. Employment opportunities are available in physicians' offices, rural hospitals, regional medical centers, ambulatory surgery centers, specialty clinics, and other health-related agencies. *A Guide to Health Insurance Billing* covers introductory information, examples, and application exercises that develop a foundation for becoming an insurance billing specialist.

OBJECTIVES

The primary objective of *A Guide to Health Insurance Billing* is to expose students to health insurance billing topics. The text is intended to provide students with opportunities to become familiar with health insurance terminology; understand the legal implications of insurance billing; develop a basic understanding of medical coding systems; and accurately complete health insurance claims.

FEATURES OF THE TEXT

The features and benefits of this text are designed to encourage student success. They are as follows:

- Learning objectives and key terms, abbreviations, and phrases help identify essential information in each chapter.
- Diagnosis and procedure coding exercises include several degrees of difficulty—from simple to complex.
- Reinforcement exercises allow students to check their progress throughout each chapter.
- Practical examples provide clarification of health insurance terms, procedures, and regulations associated with health insurance billing.
- Separate chapters cover details on electronic claims submission and insurance payers.
- The coding chapters cover the *International Classification of Diseases, Clinical Modification, Ninth Revision* (ICD-9-CM), the *International Classification of Diseases, Clinical Modification, Ninth Revision* (ICD-10-CM), and the ICD-10 Procedure Coding System (ICD-10-PCS); and *Current Procedural Terminology* (CPT). Coding exercises and challenges include diagnoses and procedure coding that require the student to read and interpret medical documentation.
- End-of-chapter reviews and challenge exercises include objective and subjective measures of student comprehension.
- The Superiorland Clinic Practice Manual (Appendix A), housed on this text's Premium Website, is an extensive application exercise that features 20 case studies that provide practice completing CMS-1500 claims, encounter forms, coding from office notes, and UB-04 claim forms.
- Internet links in each chapter provide resources for locating the most current information about key topics.

NEW TO THE FOURTH EDITION

- Fully updated to the most current guidelines, billing forms, and code sets.
- Revised coverage for electronic claims submission with new figures and examples.
- Review of the Patient Protection and Affordable Care Act's key provisions.
- Features a new and improved SimClaim student practice software, housed on this text's Premium Website, paired with 20 case studies in Appendix A.
- 59-day trial of OptumInsight's™ EncoderPro.com Expert.

SUPPLEMENTS

The following supplements accompany the text:

Instructor's Manual

The *Instructor's Manual* provides sample course syllabi, additional chapter quizzes and exams, complete answer keys for all exercises and activities, and blank forms that can be used to create additional billing exercises.
ISBN-13: 978-1-285-19360-1

Instructor Resources

The Instructor Resources are available on CD-ROM and online. The Instructor Resources provide many aids to help the instructor plan and implement a course for health insurance specialists.

The Instructor Resources include the following:

- **Computerized Test Bank in ExamView** makes generating tests and quizzes a snap. With more than 900 questions and different styles to choose from, you can create customized assessments for your students with the click of a button. Add your own unique questions and print rationales for easy class preparation.
- Customizable instructor support **slide presentations in PowerPoint** format focus on key points for each chapter.
- The *Instructor's Manual* contains various resources and answers for each textbook chapter.

ISBN-13: 978-1-285-19361-8

Premium Website

Additional textbook resources for students and instructors can be found online by following the instructions that follow.

Student Resources on the Premium Website

Some resources located on the Premium Website to accompany *A Guide to Health Insurance Billing, Fourth Edition* are free, whereas others (such as SimClaim™) will require passcode entry. To access passcode-protected content, follow the instructions on the printed access card bound into this textbook.

Student Resources

- Blank forms
- SimClaim claims completion software (available as both online and downloadable versions)

- Code updates as they become available
- Appendix A Superiorland Clinic Practice Manual

Instructor Resources

- All the Instructor Resources are provided including the *Instructor's Manual*, computerized test bank, and chapter presentations in PowerPoint.
- Answer keys to the Appendix A SimClaim cases
- Access to all free student supplements

About the Author

Marie A. Moisio, MA, RHIA

Marie Moisio has over 25 years of experience in health information management. She was an Associate Professor at Northern Michigan University (retired in 2003). Ms. Moisio has 15 years of teaching experience in medical billing, medical coding, and health information processing. In addition, she was also the director of a health information department at a 400-bed regional medical center and a 450-bed regional psychiatric treatment facility. She was a consultant for several long-term care facilities and physician offices. Her knowledge and experience include health information management, compliance, coding practices, and auditing insurance claims and documentation. She has offered several workshops about the legal aspects of health information management and documentation. Ms. Moisio's other books for Delmar, Cengage Learning, include *Medical Terminology for Insurance and Coding, Medical Terminology: A Student Centered Approach,* and *Understanding Laboratory and Diagnostic Tests.*

REVIEWERS AND CONTRIBUTORS

The publisher and the author would like to extend a special thank-you to the reviewers and contributors who gave recommendations and suggestions throughout the development of this textbook. Their experience and knowledge were valuable resources for the author. A special thank you to Judith E. Fields, our Technical Reviewer. We appreciate your hard work and expertise!

Judith Fields, CCS, CCS-P has successfully completed Training and Assessment for the AHIMA Academy for ICD-10. She is an accomplished coding educator at Southeast Kentucky Community & Technical College, Cumberland, Kentucky, where she has been on the faculty since 2005. She has taught keyboarding, medical terminology, medical billing, and medical coding classes. Her focus is currently medical coding classes for ICD-9-CM and CPT/HCPCS. She is a member of the Adjunct Faculty Council and Office System Technology Advisory Council at Southeast Kentucky. She is employed full-time for a large, nationally recognized hospital as a medical coder. She is also a member of AHIMA and AAPC. She has 21 years of experience in various health care roles as a HIM medical coding supervisor, coding consultant, medical coding and billing for both physician and hospital-based offices, and medical assisting. Judith loves her career and enjoys teaching her students and seeing them excel in their health care career.

Reviewers

Katherine E. Baus, RHIA, CCS-P
Program Manager, Health Information Management
Southwest Florida College
Ft. Myers, Florida

Diane Roche Benson, CMA (AAMA), BSHCA, MSA, CFP, CMRS, CPC, CDE, NSC-SCFAT, ASE, AHA BCLS/First Aid-Instructor, PALS, CAAM-I, ACLS, CCT, NCI-I Professor
Wake Technical Community College;
Also University of Phoenix
Raleigh, North Carolina

Laurie Dennis, CBCS
HIBC Instructor
Florida Career College
Clearwater, Florida

Rashmi Gaonkar, BS, MS
Senior Instructor
ASA Institute
Brooklyn, New York

Misty Hamilton, MBA, RHIT
Director/instructor HIM Program
Zane State College
Zanesville, Ohio

Annette Jackson, MBA, CMRS
Subject Area Coordinator
Medical Administrative Assistant (Billing
Emphasis) Program
Bryant & Stratton College
Eastlake, Ohio

Joshua Maywalt, NCICS, NCMOA
MBC Instructor
City College
Casselberry, Florida

Lezlie McHenry, CBCS, MA, BS
Adjunct Professor for HITT/POFM
LoneStar-North Harris and Kingwood
College
Houston, Texas

Jean Mosley, BS, CMA(AAMA)
Medical Assisting Program Director
Surry Community College
Dobson, North Carolina

Lynne Padilla, CPC, CHI
Medical Curriculum Developer, Medical
Editor
Allied Business Schools
Laguna Hills, California

Agnes Pucillo, LPN, RHCE, AHI, CMBCS
Medical Billing and Coding Instructor
Prism Career Institute
Cherry Hill, New Jersey

Beverly A. Ramsey, CMA, CPC, CHBC
Instructor
Asheville-Buncombe Technical Community
College
Asheville, North Carolina

Tonia A. Seay-Josephina, CPAR, RMC,
RMM, CPC
Medical Billing and Coding Instructor
Advanced Career Training
Atlanta, Georgia

Sharon Skonieczki, BS MA, CMA (AAMA)
Academic Dean, Medical Program Director
Elmira Business Institute
Elmira and Vestal, New York

Marta E. Urdaneta, PhD
Chair, Healthcare Management
South University
Savannah, Georgia

Joshua J. VanDusen
Medical Assisting Instructor
Miller Motte Technical College
Chattanooga, Tennessee

Acknowledgments

Amy Wetsel, Kathy Kucharek, and Tania Andrabi, provided me with exemplary editorial and professional advice and support. Elmer Moisio, my husband of 40 years, continued with his unwavering encouragement and willingness to "take care of everything else" so that I had the time to work on this revision.

How to Use this Text

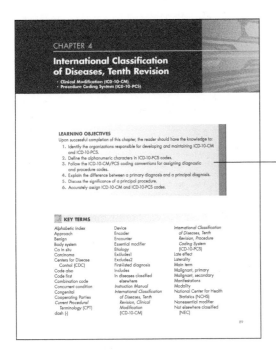

Objectives and Key Terms

The Objectives lists the expected learning outcomes for the chapter. Review the objectives before and after studying the chapter. Key Terms give an overview of the new vocabulary in each chapter. Each term is highlighted in the chapter and defined on first usage. A complete definition of each term appears in the glossary at the back of the book.

Overview

Each chapter begins with an Overview that provides a brief synopsis of the topics covered in the chapter. The Objectives and Overview together provide a framework for studying the chapter content.

OVERVIEW

As mentioned in Chapter 1, the two main coding systems associated with health insurance claims processing are the *International Classification of Diseases, Ninth Revision, Clinical Modification* (ICD-9-CM) for medical diagnoses and procedures and *Current Procedural Terminology* (CPT) for physician and other provider services and procedures. This chapter covers ICD-9-CM, which remains in effect until the *International Classification of Diseases, Tenth Revision* (ICD-10) is adopted.

Accurate coding is crucial to reimbursement and the avoidance of fraud and abuse charges. Insurance billing specialists need at least a basic understanding of medical coding. The purpose of this chapter is to provide the student with a foundation for ICD-9-CM coding. Topics presented include the following:

- Unique characteristics of *Volumes 1, 2,* and 3
- Coding conventions, such as special instructional notes and the meaning of punctuation marks
- Sections of each volume that apply to physician office coding
- Coding guidelines from Sections II and IV of the ICD-9-CM *Official Guidelines for Coding and Reporting*

To gain the most from this chapter, have ICD-9-CM *Volumes 1, 2,* and 3 readily available as references. Some exercises provide opportunities to practice using the code books. This chapter also includes several figures and tables adapted from the 2013 official version of ICD-9-CM. The figures and tables allow the student to complete some of the review exercises if the code books are not available.

EXAMPLE: CONGENITAL CONDITION
Jenny, a 16-year-old high school sophomore, just received the results of her kidney scan. The physician tells Jenny that she has polycystic kidneys and explains that she was "born with" this condition. Even though Jenny is 16, the diagnosis of polycystic kidneys is coded as a congenital anomaly.

Chapter 15: Certain Conditions Originating in the Perinatal Period

Chapter 15 codes classify conditions specific to a newborn. The condition must be associated with the perinatal period, which begins before birth and lasts through the 28th day of life. Most perinatal conditions are resolved by time, treatment, or death. However, some conditions manifest themselves later in life.

EXAMPLE: CONDITION ORIGINATING IN THE PERINATAL PERIOD
Rachel is being treated for vaginal cancer. Rachel's health history reveals that her mother took the antinausea medication DES (diethylstilbestrol) during her pregnancy with Rachel. The physician explains to Rachel that her current condition could be a result of intrauterine exposure to DES.

In this case, the vaginal cancer is assigned the appropriate malignant neoplasm code. Intrauterine DES exposure is a significant factor in the development of vaginal cancer. Therefore, the code for vaginal cancer is selected, and the code for DES from Chapter 15 is also assigned.

Examples

Examples appear throughout the text and serve to provide further explanation of key concepts.

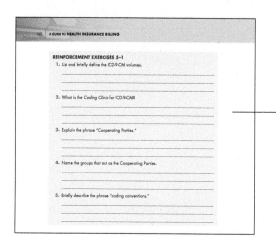

Reinforcement Exercises

Reinforcement Exercises appear throughout the chapters and allow for immediate practice with concepts.

Summary

The Summary at the end of each chapter recaps key concepts and can serve as a review aid when preparing for tests.

SUMMARY

The *International Classification of Diseases, Tenth Revision, Clinical Modification* (ICD-10-CM) is used in all health care settings for coding and reporting diagnoses. The National Center for Health Statistics (NCHS), a division of the Centers for Disease Control (CDC), was responsible for developing ICD-10-CM. The classification system is updated annually by the Cooperating Parties, which include the American Hospital Association (AHA), the American Health Information Management Association (AHIMA), the Centers for Medicare and Medicaid Services (CMS), and the NCHS. In addition, the AHA publishes the quarterly *Coding Clinic*, the official publication for ICD-10-CM guidelines.

The ICD-10-CM has 21 chapters organized by body system and related conditions, diseases, and interactions with health care agencies. Codes consist of three to seven alphabetic and numeric characters. Coding conventions are part of the ICD-10-CM and provide billing specialists and medical coders direction for code assignment. The annual *ICD-10-CM Official Guidelines for Coding and Reporting* is available on the CDC website: http://www.cdc.gov/nchs/. These guidelines include information from the *Coding Clinic* and other updates from the Cooperating Parties.

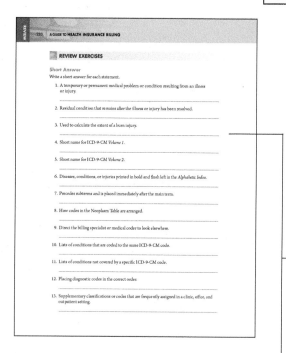

Review Exercises and Coding Challenges

At the end of each chapter, there are Review Exercises to test your understanding of content and critical thinking ability.

The coding chapters feature Coding Challenge exercises that provide practice coding from medical reports.

SimClaim is an educational tool designed to familiarize you with the basics of claim form completion. Because in the real world there are many rules that can vary by payer, facility, and state, every effort has been made to make SimClaim generically correct in order to provide you with the broadest understanding of claim form completion.

How to Access SimClaim

To access the SimClaim software program, refer to the information on the printed access card bound into this textbook. SimClaim for *A Guide to Health Insurance Billing,* Fourth Edition, is designed for use with the case studies found in Appendix A, the "Superiorland Practice Manual." The Appendix A case studies posted on the Premium Website are also provided in the SimClaim software.

Main Menu

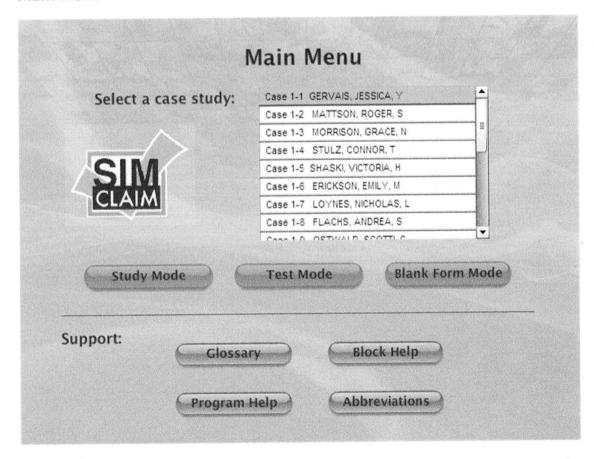

From the Main Menu, you can access the SimClaim program three different ways: Study Mode, Test Mode, and Blank Form Mode.

- Click on **Study Mode** if you want feedback as you fill out claim forms for the Appendix A case studies.
- Click on **Test Mode** to fill out claim forms for the Appendix A case studies if you are ready to test yourself. There is no feedback in this mode, and your completed claim form(s) is graded and can be printed and e-mailed to your instructor.
- Use **Blank Form Mode** if you wish to use the SimClaim program to fill out a blank CMS or UB-04 form with another case study provided by your instructor.

Please note that while a blank, editable, printable UB-04 form is provided in SimClaim, there is no grading provided for the UB-04. You will need to complete it, print it to PDF, and then submit it to your instructor for grading.

SimClaim Support

You may also access SimClaim support documentation from the Main Menu. Support includes Block Help videos, a glossary, and a list of common abbreviations. While using SimClaim in any mode, if you need help entering information in a particular block, simply click on Block Help for instructions.

General Instructions and Hints for Completing CMS-1500 Claim Forms in SimClaim

Please read through the following general guidelines before beginning work in the SimClaim program:

- **Turn on Caps Lock:** All data entered into SimClaim must be in ALL CAPS.
- **Do not abbreviate:** Spell out street, drive, avenue, signature on file, Blue Cross/Blue Shield, and so forth. No abbreviations (other than state abbreviations) will be accepted by the program.
- **Do not use "Same As" or "None" in any block:** If patient information is the same as insured information, you must enter that information again on the claim.
- **There may be more than one Diagnosis Pointer in Block 24E:** For SimClaim case studies, more than one diagnosis pointer may be required in block 24E.
- **Amount Paid:** If there is no amount paid indicated on the case study, you must enter "0 00" in block 29.
- Follow accepted form guidelines on punctuation use in the form. The NUCC CMS-1500 claim form instruction manual may be downloaded from www.nucc.org.
- For additional help, refer to the Block Help documentation within the SimClaim program.

How to Access the EncoderPro.com— Expert 59-Day Trial

OptumInsight's *www.EncoderPro.com Expert* is a powerful medical coding software solution that allows you to locate CPT, HCPCS level II, ICD-9-CM, ICD-10-CM, and ICD-10-PCS codes. The software provides users with fast searching capabilities across all code sets, greatly reduces the time needed to build or review an insurance claim, and helps improve overall coding accuracy. The software includes additional features such as ICD-10-CM and ICD-10-PCS crosswalks for ICD-9-CM codes and coding guidance (e.g., 1995 E&M guidelines). This software can be used to assign codes to any of the exercises in the *A Guide to Health Insurance Billing Fourth Edition* textbook.

EncoderPro.com Video-based Autodemo

View OptumInsight's online EncoderPro.com video-based Autodemo at www.optumcoding.com by scrolling your mouse over Products and eSolutions, and clicking on the eSolution Online Demos link. Then, click on the EncoderPro.com link to start the Autodemo, which is approximately five minutes in length. The EncoderPro.com features are described and using the encoder to locate a code is demonstrated.

How to Access the Free Trial of www.EncoderPro.com

Information about how to access your 59-day trial of www.EncoderPro.com (Expert version) is included on the printed tear-out card located in the back cover of this textbook. The card contains a unique user access code and password. Once you log in, scroll down to the bottom of the License Agreement page, and click the I Accept link. Then, click the I Accept link on the Terms of Use page. Be sure to check with your instructor before beginning your free trial because it will expire 59 days after your initial login.

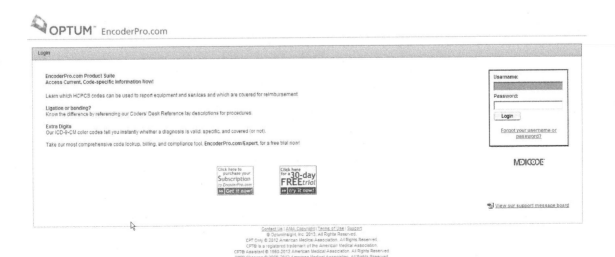

Features and Benefits of EncoderPro.com

EncoderPro.com is the essential code-lookup software for CPT, HCPCS (level II), ICD-9-CM Vol. 1, ICD-9-CM Vol. 3, ICD-10-CM, and ICD-10-PCS code sets from OptumInsight. It gives users fast searching capabilities across all code sets. EncoderPro.com can greatly reduce the time it takes to build or review a claim and helps improve overall coding accuracy.

During your free trial period of EncoderPro.com Expert, the following tools are available to you:

- **Powerful CodeLogic search engine.** Search all four code sets simultaneously by using lay terms, acronyms, abbreviations, and even misspelled words.
- **Lay descriptions for thousands of CPT codes.** Enhance your understanding of procedures with easy-to-understand descriptions.
- **Color-coded edits.** Understand whether a code carries an age or sex edit, is covered by Medicare, or contains bundled procedures.
- **ICD-10 Mapping Tool.** Crosswalk from ICD-9-CM codes to the appropriate ICD-10 code quickly and easily.
- **Great value.** Get the content from over 20 code and reference books in one powerful solution.

For more on EncoderPro.com or to become a subscriber beyond the free trial, email us at **esales@ cengage.com**.

CHAPTER 1

The Insurance Billing Specialist

LEARNING OBJECTIVES

Upon successful completion of this chapter, the reader should have the knowledge to:

1. Describe at least 10 responsibilities of an insurance billing specialist.
2. Identify at least five personal qualifications and five technical qualifications associated with insurance billing specialist positions.
3. Provide three examples that illustrate the importance of medical terminology to insurance billing activities.
4. Describe five different job opportunities related to the insurance billing process.

 ## KEY TERMS

American Academy of Professional Coders (AAPC)

American Health Information Management Association (AHIMA)

American Medical Billing Association (AMBA)

Certification

Certified coding associate (CCA)

Certified coding specialist (CCS)

Certified coding specialist–physician-based (CCS-P)

Certified healthcare reimbursement specialist (CHRS)

Certified medical billing specialist (CMBS)

Certified medical billing specialist–chiropractic assistant (CMBS-CA)

Certified medical billing specialist–hospital (CMBS-H)

Certified medical reimbursement specialist (CMRS)

Certified professional coder (CPC)

Certified professional coder–hospital (CPC-H)

Certified professional coder–payer (CPC-P)

Claims assistance professional (CAP)

Insurance billing specialist

Insurance collection specialist

Insurance counselor

Medical Association of Billers (MAB)

Medical coder

Medical coding

Medical terminology

National Electronic Billers Alliance (NEBA)

Patient account representative

Personal qualifications

Technical qualifications

OVERVIEW

The health care industry offers employment opportunities in clinical careers such as medicine, nursing, physical therapy, medical assisting, physician's assistant, and other patient-contact jobs. Clinical professionals and the health care industry as a whole rely on a large nonclinical workforce, which is collectively known as support staff.

Picture the health care industry like a pyramid. Clinical professions are at the top of the pyramid, and support staff represent the foundation. Figure 1–1 illustrates some job titles for support staff employees. The position of each title does not reflect the importance or value of the profession. This book focuses on the roles and responsibilities of the insurance billing specialist.

INSURANCE BILLING SPECIALIST

An insurance billing specialist is an individual who processes health insurance claims in accordance with legal, professional, and insurance company guidelines and regulations. Insurance billing specialists work closely with the financial and managerial areas of a health care agency. The insurance billing specialist is a key player in the financial operations of an agency or medical office.

Tasks assigned to an insurance billing specialist can range from collecting patient insurance information to resolving billing problems between the office, patient, and insurance company. Anyone who works in this dynamic field must possess certain personal and technical qualifications. Both types of qualifications are important, and the degree of emphasis placed on each depends on the individual employer.

Personal Qualifications

Personal qualifications are behaviors that define the character or personality of an individual. Personal qualifications include terms such as *aggressive, aloof, assertive, cooperative, ethical,*

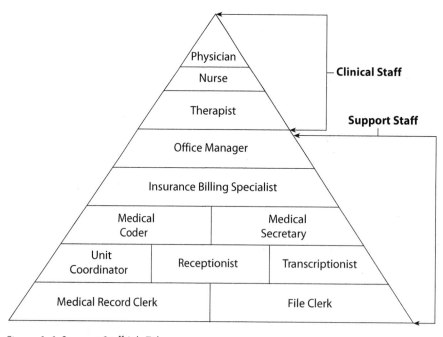

Figure 1–1 Support Staff Job Titles

hardworking, reliable, and *self-motivated.* These qualifications are difficult to measure and are often based on an observer's interpretation. Qualities you identify as assertive and hardworking could be considered by others as aggressive.

Employers try to quantify personal qualifications by describing behaviors that exemplify the qualification. For example, *cooperative* is described as the ability to work with others; *assertive* is described as an ability to communicate with others; *reliable* is measured by attendance and task completion; and *ethical* is described as the ability to maintain confidential information and adhere to rules and regulations. These types of descriptions are part of (or should be part of) the job description.

Personality inventory tests can identify personal qualifications. A personality inventory is a series of questions designed to identify aspects of an individual's personality or personal characteristics. Personality inventory tests have become a routine part of the employment application process.

Office managers and personnel directors identify the highest-rated personal qualifications as assertive, honest, reliable, self-motivated, ethical, detail-oriented, and adaptable to change. Table 1–1 lists key personal qualifications and examples of behaviors that demonstrate each qualification.

Most people believe they are honest, reliable, ethical, and able to maintain confidentiality. Assessing your ability to adapt to change and your attention to detail is more difficult. Professional, legal, and insurance company regulations that govern health insurance billing practices are continually revised. A simple clerical or data entry oversight might delay or deny payments for services provided. Success as an insurance billing specialist depends on the ability to accurately complete and submit insurance claims.

TABLE 1–1

Personal Qualifications	
Personal Qualification	**Behavioral Examples**
Adaptable	Accepts shift and holiday rotation schedule; willing to learn new software features; interested in cross-training
Assertive; confident	Speaks clearly with eye contact; asks questions; describes goals; answers questions directly
Cooperative	Works or has worked on group projects; interested in learning overall office workflow
Detail-oriented	Accurately alphabetizes a list of names; accurately organizes a list of numbers; accurately completes health insurance billing forms
Ethical	Adheres to insurance billing guidelines; refrains from negative comments about current and previous coworkers and employers
Honest	Leaves office supplies at the office; uses sick time according to agency policy
Maintains confidentiality	Maintains professional confidences (e.g., patient information); does not contribute to rumors or gossip
Reliable	Is ready to work at the beginning of the shift; completes tasks within assigned deadlines
Self-motivated	Initiates work assignments; organizes work area

REINFORCEMENT EXERCISES 1–1

Write the name of the personal qualification described in each statement.

1. Olivia is at her desk and ready to tackle her assignments when the workday begins.

_____

_____

2. Linda refuses to answer her fiancé's questions about his boss, a recent patient at Linda's office.

_____

_____

3. Brian tells his supervisor that he used the wrong insurance code on the claims he sent out yesterday.

_____

_____

4. Tawanda calls Dr. Shaski and asks for clarification concerning the diagnosis for Mrs. Gervais.

_____

_____

5. Hank reviews the new instructions for electronic claims submission before submitting Medicare insurance claims.

_____

_____

6. Monroe reviews Mrs. Mattson's insurance form and discovers that "vasectomy follow-up" was noted as the reason for the office visit. He flags the insurance form for determination of the correct reason for Mrs. Mattson's office visit.

_____

_____

Technical Qualifications

Technical qualifications are measurable abilities and skills that one can learn through education and experience. Basic skills include the ability to keyboard (data entry), read, complete simple math functions, use correct grammar in written and oral communications, accurately record telephone or voice mail messages, and follow directions. Table 1–2 lists these basic skills and application examples.

TABLE 1–2

Technical Qualifications	
Technical Qualification	**Application Examples**
Data entry (keyboarding)	Updates computerized patient records and financial and insurance records
Documenting messages	Retrieves voice mail messages; accurately takes and routes telephone messages
Math skills	Updates patient accounts; calculates charges for billing; reconciles amount paid with amount owed
Oral communication skills	Answers questions and telephone inquiries by using complete sentences and correct grammar
Ability to follow directions	Reviews and implements new procedures related to insurance billing tasks
Written communication skills	Formats memos; composes letters, fax, and e-mail messages; uses correct grammar, punctuation, and spelling

In addition to basic skills, the insurance billing specialist must have a working knowledge of medical terminology and be familiar with medical coding protocols. Virtually all financial aspects of a medical practice depend on thorough documentation of the patient's condition and accurate medical coding of diagnostic and treatment terms.

Medical terminology is the language of the health care industry. A working knowledge of medical terminology is more than memorizing lists of words. The insurance billing specialist must be able to:

- Read and understand medical reports.
- Recognize the relationship between diagnostic statements and treatments provided.
- Identify discrepancies in medical documentation.

Example A illustrates the ability to recognize the relationship between diagnostic statements and the treatments provided. Example B illustrates the ability to identify discrepancies in medical documentation.

EXAMPLE A
The diagnosis and subsequent treatment of strep throat should be supported by a throat culture test result that identified the streptococcus bacteria.

EXAMPLE B
The diagnosis prostatitis (inflammation of the prostate gland) should not appear in the medical record of a female patient.

Medical coding is the process of documenting medical information as numeric codes. Two major coding systems apply to medical information: the International Classification of Diseases (ICD) and *Current Procedural Terminology* (CPT). Chapter 4, Chapter 5, and Chapter 6 discuss these two coding systems.

Both coding systems are revised annually. The insurance billing specialist must remain current with coding practices. This is accomplished by attending workshops, seminars, and other continuing education (CE) events. Insurance billing specialists and medical coders who are certified by a professional association are often required to attain a specific number of CE credits within a given time frame. Failure to fulfill CE requirements may lead to the revocation of credentials and the loss of employment.

REINFORCEMENT EXERCISES 1–2

Write the name of the technical qualification described in each statement.

1. Martha entered patient insurance files into the financial database.

_____

_____

2. Roger completed several letters of inquiry and sent them to different insurance companies.

_____

_____

3. Lisa's first job every morning is to scan the office voice mail system for priority messages.

_____

_____

4. Per office policy, Rosa updates her insurance billing manual as soon as she receives new guidelines.

_____

_____

5. Lucy provided Mrs. Washington with an estimate of her out-of-pocket expenses for her scheduled mammography.

_____

_____

EMPLOYMENT OPPORTUNITIES

Employment opportunities in the medical insurance billing field range from hourly entry-level billing clerk positions to five-figure management positions. Jobs are available in medical offices, hospitals, clinics, insurance companies, government agencies, medical suppliers, and

JOB DESCRIPTION

POSITION TITLE: Insurance Billing Specialist

SUMMARY: Accurately completes and submits health insurance claims following legal, professional, and insurance company guidelines. The work is detail-oriented, repetitive, and involves extensive communication with others.

RESPONSIBILITIES: The listed responsibilities are intended to be representative rather than all-inclusive.

1. Abstracts identification, health insurance plan, and diagnoses and treatment information from the patient record.
2. Uses abstracted information to accurately complete health insurance claim form(s).
3. Follows applicable coding conventions to accurately assign numeric codes to each diagnosis and treatment statement.
4. Reviews policy and guideline bulletins (updates) from health insurance companies and organizations.
5. Applies updated regulations and guidelines to all insurance claim completion activities.
6. Monitors denied or rejected claims to identify the clerical mistakes or clinical omission that generated the rejection.
7. Notifies clinical and support staff of changes in insurance regulations and guidelines that affect documentation of patient information and insurance billing procedures.
8. Assists clinical and support staff in resolving documentation problems related to insurance claims.
9. Posts insurance payments and adjustments to patients' financial records.
10. Keeps patient information confidential.
11. Adheres to office policy and procedures related to work attendance, breaks, vacation, and sick leave.

MINIMUM QUALIFICATIONS
1. High-school diploma, or equivalent, and one year experience as an insurance billing specialist OR graduate of an insurance billing specialist education program.
2. Demonstrated knowledge of medical terminology, including names of diseases, clinical procedures, basic anatomy, and physiology.
3. Keyboarding skills, including data entry, updating databases, word processing, and other related skills.
4. Familiarity with at least one major word-processing software program, such as Microsoft Word or WordPerfect.
5. Ability to work cooperatively and independently as necessary.

DESIRABLE QUALIFICATIONS
1. Demonstrated knowledge of current procedural and diagnostic coding conventions.
2. Certified Medical Billing Specialist (CMBS) or Certified Medical Reimbursement Specialist (CMRS) credentials.

Figure 1–2 Insurance Billing Specialist Job Description

consulting firms. An insurance billing specialist with extensive experience can own and operate a successful insurance claim processing business. Figure 1–2 is a generic job description for an insurance billing specialist.

Job titles such as billing clerk, medical biller, insurance claims processor, and reimbursement specialist are sometimes used in place of insurance billing specialist. Larger group practices and hospital billing departments often employ individuals who specialize in specific types of health insurance billing.

> **EXAMPLE**
> Segway Physicians, Inc., a 15-physician group practice, has a large insurance billing department. The department includes a Medicare billing specialist, a Medicaid billing specialist, and a Blue Cross/Blue Shield billing specialist. These specialists develop insurance billing expertise in their assigned areas.

Other job opportunities related to the insurance billing process include:

- Claims assistance professional (CAP): He or she assists patients in completing the paperwork necessary to obtain insurance payments. CAPs can work for health care agencies or operate their own businesses.
- Insurance collection specialist: He or she works with insurance companies to resolve billing and payment problems.
- Patient account representative: He or she helps the patient identify the amount that health insurance pays for a given service and how much the patient must pay. A patient account representative is also called an insurance counselor.
- Medical coder: He or she assigns numeric codes to diagnostic, procedure, and treatment information.

Health insurance billing positions have a common group of responsibilities and tasks in addition to the specific duties associated with the individual position. Common tasks and responsibilities for all positions include the ability to:

- Abstract information from patient records.
- Communicate via fax, e-mail, telephone, letters, and memos.
- Demonstrate an understanding of insurance billing legal and ethical issues.
- Follow office policies and procedures.
- Maintain a positive working relationship with patients, staff, and visitors.
- Operate word-processing equipment.
- Participate in CE activities.

Specific duties related to each health insurance billing position depend on the job and employer preference. Table 1–3 lists each position and gives examples of additional responsibilities for that position.

In addition to the specific duties listed in Table 1–3, each health insurance billing position is associated with a particular employment setting. CAPs usually work directly for the client or patient and are often self-employed. Insurance collection specialists usually work for medium-to-large health care agencies, such as physician group practices or hospitals. These specialists represent the interest of the health care agency when any problems with insurance payments occur. Patient account representatives, who are employed by large multispecialty clinics or hospitals, work to establish payment options before services are provided.

TABLE 1–3

Insurance Billing Position Responsibilities	
Position	**Responsibilities**
Claims assistance professional	• Helps individuals, clients, or patients submit medical bills to insurance companies • Explains the content of insurance company documents to the client, individual, or patient • Communicates with medical office and insurance company staff on behalf of the client
Insurance collection specialist	• Works with patients, insurance companies, and employer health benefits representatives to resolve insurance billing or payment problems • Reviews insurance forms to identify patterns of errors that result in unpaid or rejected claims • Monitors medical coding accuracy • Provides insurance form completion training to medical office staff • Maintains knowledge of regulations related to insurance collection practices
Patient account representative	• Discusses insurance coverage with the patient • Contacts the insurance company to verify the patient's eligibility and the amount to be paid by insurance • Helps establish a payment plan for the patient

REINFORCEMENT EXERCISES 1–3

1. List three job titles that are synonymous with *insurance billing specialist.*

_____

_____

_____

2. The _____ helps clients complete the paperwork necessary to obtain insurance payments for medical bills.

3. Melinda met with the _____ in order to find out the amount insurance would pay for her impending surgery.

4. List three minimum qualifications that are often listed on an insurance billing specialist job description.

_____

_____

_____

continued on the next page

continued from the previous page

5. Identify five common tasks associated with insurance billing positions.

_____

_____

_____

_____

_____

EDUCATIONAL, CERTIFICATION, AND CAREER OPPORTUNITIES

Medical insurance billing has become increasingly complex, and most employers now require successful completion of some kind of formal education. Insurance billing specialist programs include courses such as medical terminology, anatomy and physiology, medical insurance processing, medical coding, word processing, and English. These programs are usually between one and two years long. A one-year program is known as a certificate or diploma program, and a two-year program usually results in an associate degree. These programs allow you the opportunity to acquire the technical qualifications discussed earlier in this chapter.

Certification involves successful completion of a professionally recognized exam. Employers know that education and/or experience are needed to pass national or professional exams. Professional credential exams are viewed as objective measures of an individual's expertise in a given field. Several professional associations offer certification or credentialing exams related to medical billing and medical coding. Table 1–4 lists the name and website of medical billing professional associations, the exams offered by the association, the requirements to take the exam, and the title associated with successful completion of the exam. The exams include questions related to insurance billing, medical terminology, and medical coding.

Certification specifically related to medical coding significantly increases career opportunities for an insurance specialist. Table 1–5 lists the name and website of professional associations that offer medical coding certification exams, the requirements to take the exam, and the title associated with successful completion of the exam.

Each professional association's website has the most current information about credentials, certification exams, and member services.

Career opportunities differ from employment opportunities in that the word *career* brings to mind professional growth and development. A career ladder or career path indicates that the individual is moving toward a higher goal. Advancement along a career path is accompanied by an increase in status, responsibility, and pay. Career advancement is accomplished through acquiring additional education and experience. Once career goals are met, the individual must stay current in all aspects of his or her chosen field.

Beginning your career path as an insurance billing specialist can provide opportunities for advancement. Experience, education, and certification can lead to positions such as claims or billing department supervisor, medical office manager, collections manager, and medical practice manager. Insurance billing specialists with extensive insurance claims processing experience can establish a successful medical billing service. Table 1–6 provides information about these positions.

TABLE 1–4

Medical Billing Certification Exams	
Professional Association	**Certification Exams**
American Medical Billing Association (AMBA): http://www.ambanet.net	• **Certified Medical Reimbursement Specialist (CMRS):** Individuals with medical billing experience in various health care settings
Medical Association of Billers (MAB): http://www.physicianswebsites.com	• **Certified Medical Billing Specialist (CMBS):** Individuals currently working in a medical office, a health insurance company, or an insurance billing agency; an entry-level billing and coding exam • **Certified Medical Billing Specialist–Chiropractic Assistant (CMBS-CA):** Individuals working in a chiropractic agency; an intermediate level exam • **Certified Medical Billing Specialist–Hospital (CMBS-H):** Individuals working in a hospital; an intermediate-level exam covering the differences between inpatient and outpatient billing
National Electronic Billers Alliance (NEBA): http://www.nebazone.com	• **Certified Healthcare Reimbursement Specialist (CHRS):** Individuals with experience in all areas of the medical billing profession

TABLE 1–5

Medical Coding Certification Exams	
Professional Association	**Certification Exams**
American Academy of Professional Coders (AAPC): http://www.aapc.com	• **Certified Professional Coder (CPC):** Current experience working in home health, ambulatory surgery centers, physician office, or group practice • **Certified Professional Coder–Hospital (CPC-H):** Current experience working in hospital-based outpatient departments or ambulatory surgery centers • **Certified Professional Coder–Payer (CPC-P):** Current experience working for insurance companies or insurance billing services • Specialty Certifications: Various medical coding certifications related to specific medical specialties; associate degree recommended
American Health Information Management Association (AHIMA): http://www.ahima.org	• **Certified Coding Associate (CCA):** An entry-level exam; six months of medical coding experience or completion of a medical coding training program • **Certified Coding Specialist (CCS):** Three or more years of current experience in a hospital (inpatient) setting strongly recommended; demonstrated knowledge of anatomy, physiology, pathophysiology, and pharmacology • **Certified Coding Specialist–Physician-based (CCS-P):** Three or more years of current experience in physician office settings strongly recommended; demonstrated knowledge of anatomy, physiology, pathophysiology, and pharmacology

TABLE 1–6

Career Positions

Billing Department Supervisor

- Two or more years of current experience in all areas of health insurance billing
- Medical billing certification highly recommended
- Supervises insurance billing specialist
- Communicates with physicians, patients, and insurance companies to resolve insurance processing problems

Collection Manager

- Two or more years of current experience in all areas of health insurance billing, including resolving problems related to collecting payment for services
- Medical billing certification highly recommended
- Communicates with patients, insurance companies, and collection agencies to secure payment for overdue or past due accounts

Medical Office Manager

- Two years of current experience in a medical office
- Medical office manager certification highly recommended
- Associate's degree in office management or business administration recommended
- Establishes procedures for overall office functions
- Performs duties associated with staffing the office
- Communicates with physicians, office supervisors and staff, patients, and sales representatives

Medical Practice Manager

- Associate's degree in accounting, business, or management required
- Bachelor's degree highly recommended
- Three or more years of accounting or business management experience in health care
- Communicates with physicians, hospital administrators, vendors, regulatory agencies, and other external agencies in matters related to the business and financial functions of the medical practice
- Responsible for all financial and business functions of the medical practice
- Establishes and implements policies that comply with state and federal laws and regulatory agency requirements

Owner, Medical Billing Service

- Five or more years current experience in all areas of health insurance billing
- Two years of supervisory or management experience
- Associate's degree in business, management, accounting, or health care administration
- Communicates with physicians, medical office managers, medical practice managers, insurance companies, and sales representatives
- Establishes medical billing (insurance claims submission) contracts with health care providers
- Establishes and implements policies and procedures that comply with state and federal laws and regulatory agency requirements

REINFORCEMENT EXERCISES 1–4

1. List three courses that are essential to an insurance billing specialist education program.

_____

_____

_____

_____

2. Spell out each abbreviation and then name the professional association that offers each credential.

CMBS

_____

CMBS-H

_____

CMRS

_____

3. Briefly describe the differences between the three medical coding certification exams offered by AHIMA.

_____

_____

_____

4. Spell out and briefly describe CPC and CPC-H. Name the professional association that offers these credentials.

_____

_____

_____

ABBREVIATIONS

Abbreviations are a fact of life in the health care industry. Table 1–7 lists the abbreviations presented in this chapter.

TABLE 1–7

Abbreviations and Meanings	
Abbreviation	Meaning
AAPC	American Academy of Professional Coders
AHIMA	American Health Information Management Association
AMBA	American Medical Billing Association
CAP	claims assistance professional
CCA	certified coding associate
CCS	certified coding specialist
CCS-P	certified coding specialist–physician-based
CE	continuing education
CHRS	certified healthcare reimbursement specialist
CMBS	certified medical billing specialist
CMBS-CA	certified medical billing specialist–chiropractic assistant
CMBS-H	certified medical billing specialist–hospital
CMRS	certified medical reimbursement specialist
CPC	certified professional coder
CPC-H	certified professional coder–hospital
CPC-P	certified professional coder–payer
CPT	*Current Procedural Terminology*
ICD	International Classification of Diseases
MAB	Medical Association of Billers
NEBA	National Electronic Billers Alliance

SUMMARY

An insurance billing specialist is a key player in the financial operation of health care agencies. This individual processes health insurance claims in accordance with legal, professional, and insurance company guidelines and regulations. By observing an individual's behavior and by using personality inventory tests, one can identify personal qualifications. Technical qualifications are measurable skills that one can learn through education and experience. Employment and career opportunities for insurance billing specialists are readily available.

REVIEW EXERCISES

Short Answer

1. Describe the different types of jobs that represent clinical and nonclinical career choices.

   _____

   _____

   _____

2. Briefly define *insurance billing specialist.*

   _____

   _____

   _____

3. List the office staff who work closely with the insurance billing specialist.

   _____

   _____

   _____

Definition of Terms

Fill in the blank beneath each definition with the appropriate term from the following list: certification, certified coding specialist, certified professional coder, claims assistance professional, insurance billing specialist, insurance collection specialist, insurance counselor, medical coding, medical terminology, patient account representative, personal qualifications, technical qualifications.

1. Credential offered by the American Health Information Management Association.

   _____

2. Individual who processes health insurance claims in accordance with legal and professional guidelines and regulations.

   _____

3. Behaviors that identify the character or personality of an individual.

   _____

4. Documenting medical information as numeric codes.

   _____

5. An individual who helps clients complete health insurance paperwork.

   _____

6. Language of the health care industry.

_____

7. Measurable abilities and skills.

_____

8. Helps resolve billing and payment problems between the medical office and the insurance company.

_____

9. Establishes payment options before services are provided.

_____

10. Successful completion of a professionally recognized exam.

_____

11. Credential offered by the American Academy of Professional Coders.

_____

Matching

Match each term in Column A with the appropriate item in Column B.

Column A	Column B	
a. self-motivated	1. interested in cross-training	_____
b. reliable	2. works well with others	_____
c. ethical	3. adheres to attendance policies	_____
d. detail-oriented	4. initiates work assignments	_____
e. data entry	5. maintains confidentiality	_____
f. cooperative	6. updates financial records	_____
g. communication skills	7. verifies diagnosis codes	_____
h. adaptable	8. uses correct grammar and spelling	_____

COMPREHENSION EXERCISES

1. Why does the insurance billing specialist need a working knowledge of medical terminology?

_____

_____

2. Select the three personal qualifications that you believe are most important. Write a brief report explaining why you chose each of them.

_____

_____

_____

_____

_____

_____

 CRITICAL THINKING EXERCISES

1. Review the personal and technical qualifications listed in Table 1–1 and Table 1–2. Compare the qualifications with the information in the Insurance Billing Specialist Job Description (Figure 1–2). Are the qualifications addressed in the job description? Match the qualification(s) with the corresponding statement(s).

2. Access the Medical Association of Billers website to review the sample certification exam questions.

WEBSITES

American Academy of Professional Coders: http://www.aapc.com
American Health Information Management Association: http://www.ahima.org
American Medical Billing Association: http://www.ambanet.net
Medical Association of Billers: http://www.physicianswebsites.com
National Electronic Billiers Alliance: http://www.nebazone.com

CHAPTER 2

Legal Aspects of Insurance Billing

LEARNING OBJECTIVES

Upon successful completion of this chapter, the reader should have the knowledge to:

1. Briefly define all general medical-legal terms presented in the chapter.
2. Identify six key components of an authorization to release information form.
3. Discuss the advantages and disadvantages of the electronic release of information.
4. Provide 10 examples of fraudulent activities and 8 examples of abuse activities.
5. Explain abbreviations for the six government agencies associated with fraud and abuse prevention.
6. Describe six steps associated with fraud protection and prevention.
7. Discuss the Privacy Rule and the Security Rule enacted under the Health Insurance Portability and Accountability Act of 1996.

KEY TERMS

Abuse
Affordable Care Act
Centers for Medicare and Medicaid Services (CMS)
Confidential information
Confidentiality
Covered entities
Department of Health and Human Services (HHS)
Department of Justice (DOJ)
Durable power of attorney
Electronic protected health information (EPHI)
Emancipated minor
Embezzlement
Employer liability

Federal Bureau of Investigation (FBI)
Fraud
Guardian
Guardianship
Guardianship of the estate
Guardianship of the person
Health care fraud
Health Insurance Portability and Accountability Act of 1996 (HIPAA)
HIPAA Privacy Rule
HIPAA Security Rule
Malfeasance
Malpractice
Minimum necessary
Misfeasance

Negligence
Nonfeasance
Office of Civil Rights (OCR)
Office of the Inspector General (OIG)
Patient Protection and Affordable Care Act
Power of attorney
Privacy officer
Protected health information (PHI)
Release of information (ROI)
Respondeat superior
Statute of limitations
Subpoena
Subpoena duces tecum
Workforce members

OVERVIEW

Health care is a heavily regulated industry. Clinical staff must be licensed or certified as required by state law. Health care organizations must follow strict local, state, and federal regulations that govern everything from building size to the types of services offered. In addition to governmental regulations, the health care industry is affected by the code of ethics associated with clinical and support staff occupations. The combination of governmental regulations and occupational codes of ethics contributes to the legal aspects of the health care industry.

Health insurance organizations and practices are not exempt from the legal requirements of the health care industry. Legal issues range from the obvious confidentiality of patient information to the more obscure areas of billing fraud and abuse regulations. Physicians, nurses, business managers, and accountants have always been subject to and concerned about the legal and ethical implications of their work. However, legal and ethical issues apply to every individual who works in a health care job.

Many governmental regulations and occupational codes of ethics directly affect the insurance billing specialist. The insurance billing specialist has access to confidential and sensitive information. Patient medical and financial information, business and billing practice information, physician and clinical staff documentation patterns, and information related to payments received from government-sponsored insurance programs are essential for insurance billing activities.

This chapter provides an overview of the basic legal issues associated with the health care industry. Issues such as confidentiality, the release of information, and guardianship are covered. Legal issues directly related to insurance billing practices, such as fraud and abuse, are also presented. The insurance billing specialist should know that just like the clinical and administrative staff, the insurance specialist is accountable for his or her own actions in regard to these legal issues.

 ## ORIGIN OF LEGAL ISSUES

Legal regulations originate from three primary sources: local, state, and federal government organizations and agencies. Each governmental unit has a restricted scope of influence. Township building codes may vary within a county but may not contradict state and federal laws. In some areas, the federal government has left regulation to the states, as in clinical staff licensure and certification. Some federal laws, such as civil rights laws, cannot be overturned by any governmental unit. Health care agencies must comply with regulations from all levels of government. These regulations cover everything from building codes to health care provider licensure. Examples A, B, and C illustrate county, state, and federal laws or regulations associated with the health care industry.

EXAMPLE A: COUNTY REGULATION
County building codes may require that the clinic or hospital have a certain number of ramped entrances. The county, however, cannot pass laws governing health care provider licensure.

EXAMPLE B: STATE LAW
State licensing laws for clinical staff ensure that individuals involved in direct patient care meet certain practice standards. However, state laws cannot change Medicare regulations.

EXAMPLE C: FEDERAL LAW
The federal government establishes regulations related Medicare eligibility, reimbursement, and covered services.

 ## GENERAL LEGAL TERMS

Several general legal terms and concepts apply to the business practices of the health care industry. Laws that address the emancipated minor, embezzlement, employer liability, guardianship, malpractice, negligence, statute of limitations, and subpoena of records affect the clinical and administrative functions of physicians' practices. The insurance billing specialist may be directly or indirectly affected by these general legal principles. Table 2–1 lists and summarizes the general legal terms. Each term or phrase is then discussed in the text.

TABLE 2–1

General Legal Terms and Definitions	
Term	**Definition**
Durable power of attorney	Power of attorney that remains in effect after the individual who grants the power of attorney dies or is declared incompetent
Emancipated minor	An individual who has not reached the age of majority, usually 18, who lives independently
Embezzlement	Stealing money
Employer liability	Employer's responsibility for employee job-related actions; known as respondeat (reh-SPON-dee-at) superior, which literally means "let the master respond"
Guardian	Individual legally designated to act on behalf of a minor or an incompetent adult
Guardianship	Legal authority to act on behalf of a minor or an incompetent adult
Guardianship of the estate	Legal authority over financial resources and other assets
Guardianship of the person	Legal authority over personal and medical decisions
Malpractice	Any professional behavior of one individual that results in damages to another individual; bad practice
Negligence	Failure to exercise the appropriate standard of care, resulting in injury
Power of attorney	Voluntary transfer of decision-making authority from one competent individual to another competent individual
Statute of limitations	Period of time associated with legal liability
Subpoena	A legal document requesting an individual to appear in court; literally means "under penalty"
Subpoena duces tecum	A legal document requesting an individual to bring records to court

Emancipated Minor

An emancipated minor is an individual who has not reached the age of majority as established by state law but who lives independently, is self-supporting, and has decision-making rights. An emancipated minor is usually younger than 18 years old. Emancipation is usually accomplished by petitioning the appropriate court and providing documentation or other evidence of self-sufficiency, by entering into a legal marriage, or by joining the armed forces. An emancipated minor makes all decisions without parental or guardian approval and is responsible for his or her own debts. Keep in mind that not all states recognize emancipated minors.

Many states allow individuals who are younger than 18 and who have not been emancipated to agree to certain types of medical care. The types of care allowed range from birth control counseling to receiving emergency treatment for a sports injury.

Embezzlement

Embezzlement is briefly defined as stealing money that an individual has access to but does not have any legal claim to take, keep, or spend. Common examples of embezzlement are found in accounting practices and trust fund management. The insurance billing specialist does not routinely have access to or responsibility for the actual money associated with a specific medical practice. However, if your job description includes posting payments and depositing funds, you should take steps to protect yourself from accusations of embezzlement.

Employer Liability

Employer liability means that the employer is responsible for the actions of employees that are within the context of employment. The Latin phrase respondeat superior ("let the master answer") is a legal description of employer liability. Although it may be comforting to believe that the employer is accountable for the employees' behavior, in reality, accountability rests with each individual.

The insurance billing specialist is accountable for the results of his or her actions related to health insurance claims submission. In fact, the Medicare definition of fraud states that the "violator may be an employee of any provider, billing service ... or any person in a position to file a claim for Medicare benefits." Insurance billing specialists cannot excuse employment-related actions by saying, "I was only doing what I was taught (or told) to do." As individuals in support staff positions achieve both professional and financial recognition, they assume more responsibility for their actions.

Guardianship and Power of Attorney

A guardian is as an individual who is legally designated to act on behalf of a minor or an incompetent adult. Guardianship is the legal authority to act as an individual's guardian. For example, a child may have a court-appointed guardian because the parents are absent or deceased. The guardian can be given different types of authority, such as guardianship of the child's financial resources—known as guardianship of the estate—or guardianship of the child's personal and medical decisions—known as guardianship of the person.

Each type of guardianship can involve specific or limited areas of control or can be fairly broad in scope. The guardian may have the authority to give consent for medical treatment but may not have authority to use the individual's assets to pay the medical bill. Likewise, a guardian with control of financial decisions may not have authority for medical treatment.

In divorce situations, issues of custodial rights and decision-making rights are similar to guardianship issues. Although one parent may have custody, the divorce decree may allow joint decision making. Without joint decision-making rights, the noncustodial parent has few if any rights to deny or authorize treatment. Either the custodial or the noncustodial parent may be responsible for the medical bills. Divorce decrees often address this responsibility by naming which parent has medical financial responsibility for the minor. The courts usually assign medical financial responsibility to the parent, custodial or not, who has health insurance.

Guardianship and custodianship can be problematic issues for both clinical and support staff. Clinical staff must be certain that the person authorizing treatment has the authority to do so. The insurance billing specialist must make a good-faith effort to have accurate information regarding medical financial responsibility when submitting insurance claims.

Power of attorney is the voluntary transfer of decision-making authority from one competent individual to another competent individual. The individual who has granted the power of attorney can revoke the power of attorney at any time. The power of attorney automatically ends when the person granting the power of attorney dies or is declared incompetent. A durable power of attorney is identical to a standard power of attorney—with one important exception: A durable power of attorney remains in effect even after the individual granting the power of attorney dies or is unable to make decisions. A good example of a health-related durable power of attorney is the document used to designate a specific person to make medical decisions if the competent individual is unable to communicate on his or her own behalf.

EXAMPLE

Mrs. Smith is scheduled for triple coronary bypass surgery. Her risk factor is very high. Mrs. Smith asks her son John to complete the durable power of attorney form that the surgeon gave her. When properly executed, this document gives John the power to authorize or refuse medical treatment in accordance with his mother's wishes if she is unable to do so herself.

A patient does not have to grant the durable power of attorney to a blood relative; he or she can select any competent individual as the designee. The individual selected as designee must agree to accept the power of attorney, cannot benefit from the death of the patient, and cannot be associated with the health agency providing care to the patient.

Malpractice

Malpractice is defined as any professional behavior of one individual that results in damages to another individual. Malpractice simply means "bad practice" and is usually applied to the conduct of the physician. Malpractice has three categories: (1) malfeasance, which means that the wrong action was taken; (2) misfeasance, which means that the correct action was done incorrectly; and (3) nonfeasance, which means that no action was taken when action was necessary.

EXAMPLES

Malfeasance: removing a healthy uterus because a patient has uncomfortable menstrual periods.
Misfeasance: incomplete removal of a malignant uterus.
Nonfeasance: failure to remove a malignant uterus.

Insurance billing specialists are seldom accused of professional malpractice. Insurance processing errors are covered by fraud and abuse laws, which are discussed later in this chapter.

Negligence

Negligence is the failure to exercise the standard of care that a reasonable person would exercise in similar circumstances. Negligence occurs when failure to exercise the standard of care results in injury. Physicians and other health care providers are the usual targets of malpractice lawsuits based on negligence. Examples of negligence include failure to notify the patient of an abnormal test result; failure to provide coverage for patients when the physician is on vacation (abandonment); and failure to explain the side effects of a medication.

Statute of Limitations

Statute of limitations is the period of time during which an agency, business, or individual is vulnerable to civil or criminal proceedings. Statutes of limitations vary from state to state. Clinical and support staff should have a working knowledge of the statute of limitations related to their professional conduct. Statutes of limitations are often described in state laws that govern business practices, health or medical treatments, and corporate or individual liability.

Insurance billing specialists are affected by statutes of limitations that govern the business practices of the medical office. For example, a medical practice has a limited time period in which to initiate legal action against an insurance company for payment delays, against an individual for nonpayment, and for resubmitting rejected claims. Because the billing specialist knows about these time frames, legal actions can be taken as necessary. The insurance billing specialist must also know the time limits associated with claims submission.

> **EXAMPLE**
>
> The insurance billing specialist at Northern Clinic fails to submit an insurance claim in a timely manner. The insurance company denies payment because the claim was not received within the prescribed time frame. The billing specialist informs the patient that legal action is necessary to obtain payment from the insurance company.

Subpoena of Records

A subpoena is a legal document signed by a judge or an attorney that requires an individual to appear in court as a witness. The word *subpoena* is Latin for "under penalty." Subpoena duces tecum means that the individual should appear and "bring records with you." A subpoena is served to a specific individual, and the individual can only bring records within the scope of his or her responsibility.

In a medical office, a subpoena is usually served to the physician, the business manager, or the medical records professional. Most medical offices designate one employee as the keeper of the medical records. Only that employee can legally accept a subpoena duces tecum related to patient records. Because the billing specialist is not the usual keeper of medical records, the specialist cannot accept such a subpoena.

In order to be enforceable, a subpoena must be properly served by being handed directly to the prospective witness. Once a subpoena is delivered, the individual is obligated, under penalty of law, to appear at the proceedings as directed. Deliberate disregard for a subpoena is considered contempt of court and is punishable by a fine, imprisonment, or both.

REINFORCEMENT EXERCISES 2–1

Write the correct legal term for each description.

1. Stealing money from an employer.

_____

2. Designated to act on behalf of a minor or an incompetent adult.

_____

3. Legal authority to act on behalf of an individual.

_____

4. Authority to authorize medical treatment.

_____

5. Failure to provide appropriate services at the appropriate time.

_____

6. Under penalty of law, bring the records with you.

_____

7. A minor who lives independently, is self-supporting, or is a part of a legal marriage.

_____

8. Let the master answer.

_____

9. Employer responsibility for employee actions within the scope of employment.

_____

10. Authority over financial resources.

_____

11. Failure to act as expected.

_____

12. Bad practice resulting in damage or injury.

_____

13. Authority to act on behalf of a competent individual.

_____

CONFIDENTIAL INFORMATION

Confidential information is information that is not open to public inspection. The principle of confidentiality presumes that certain information is not shared with others. State and federal laws affirm that an individual's medical, financial, and educational information is confidential. Confidentiality belongs to the individual and not to the information itself. For example, health care statistics are the end product of information taken from patient medical records. The information is gathered and analyzed without including patients' names, so confidentiality is maintained.

Topics related to confidentiality include the Health Insurance Portability and Accountability Act of 1996; release of information guidelines; special considerations related to positive human immunodeficiency virus (HIV) test results; acquired immunodeficiency syndrome (AIDS), alcohol, and substance abuse records; requests for information by telephone; and guidelines for facsimile (fax), e-mail, and Internet transmissions.

Insurance billing specialists are directly involved in releasing patient diagnosis and treatment information by mail and electronic means. The billing specialist also responds to telephone inquiries concerning the status of insurance claims. Calls come from insurance company representatives, employer benefits representatives, and patients.

As a general rule, it is poor practice to release any patient information on the telephone, via fax, or by e-mail. It is difficult to verify the identity of the caller, to know who retrieves fax reports, and to ensure the security of e-mail messages. However, electronic communication is a fact of life, and it is legal to use these tools. Policies and procedures that govern the release of confidential information should describe confidentiality safeguards related to telephone, fax, and Internet activities.

Health Insurance Portability and Accountability Act of 1996 (HIPAA)

In 1996, the U.S. Congress enacted the Health Insurance Portability and Accountability Act, commonly known as HIPAA (HIP-ah). This law established a set of national standards for the protection of certain health information. Under HIPAA, the U.S. Department of Health and Human Services (HHS) issued the Standards for Privacy of Individually Identifiable Health Information, commonly known as the HIPAA Privacy Rule. The Office of Civil Rights (OCR), which is part of HHS, is responsible for implementing and enforcing the Privacy Rule. The HIPAA Privacy Rule has been in effect since 2003 and has had a profound effect on the confidentiality and release of information policies and procedures for the entire health care industry. Simply put, the HIPAA Privacy Rule gives individuals a federally protected right to control the use and release of their health information.

The information in this chapter is a very brief summary of the Privacy Rule and is based on the *Office of Civil Rights Privacy Rule Summary*. Because the Privacy Rule has been and continues to be modified, the most current information is available on the OCR website at http://www.hhs.gov/ocr/privacy. In addition, professional associations, such as the American Health Information Management Association (AHIMA), are excellent resources for information about complying with the Privacy Rule.

The HIPAA Privacy Rule applies to covered entities—that is, health plans, health care clearinghouses, and any health care providers who transmit health information in electronic form. Table 2–2 gives a brief definition and some examples of covered entities.

TABLE 2–2

HIPAA Privacy Rule Covered Entities		
Entity	Definition	Examples
Health plans	Individual or group that pays for medical services	Health, dental, vision, and prescription medication insurers; HMOs; employer-sponsored group health plans; government and church-sponsored health plans; multiemployer health plans
Health care providers	Institutions or individuals that provide health care services; any other person or organization that furnishes, bills, or is paid for health care services	Hospitals; long-term care facilities; medical offices; ambulatory health offices/facilities; physicians; dentists; nurses; allied health professionals
Health care clearinghouses	Organizations that process information for health plans	Billing services; community health management information systems

The HIPAA Privacy Rule defines and limits the circumstances under which an individual's protected health information (PHI) is used or disclosed. Protected health information is individually identifiable health information that relates to a person's past, present, or future physical or mental health condition; the health care services provided to the person; or the past, present, or future payment for health care services provided to the person. In general, protected health information can be released only with the written authorization or consent of the individual. A parent or legal guardian may give consent on behalf of a minor child or an incompetent adult. The Privacy Rule allows the release of protected health information without written consent when:

- The information is subpoenaed.
- The information is needed to defend the health care provider or agency in a lawsuit.
- The information is necessary for life-saving emergency treatment.
- The patient is covered by Medicaid or workers' compensation health insurance programs.
- The information is needed to comply with another law—for example, to report suspected child abuse.

The Privacy Rule limits the use of, disclosure of, and request for protected health information to the minimum necessary. Minimum necessary is only that amount of information needed to accomplish the intended use, disclosure, or request. For example, the billing specialist may release only the information necessary to obtain payment for services provided; nursing students may access only the records of patients assigned to them; and maintenance staff may not access any protected health information.

In order to comply with the provisions of the Privacy Rule, the covered entity must:

- Develop and implement written privacy policies and procedures for the use of, release or distribution of, and request for protected health information.
- Designate an individual, often called a privacy officer, who is responsible for enforcing the policies and procedures.
- Develop and implement policies and procedures that limit access to and use of protected health information based on the specific roles of workforce members, defined as employees, volunteers, trainees, and other persons under direct control of the agency.

- Train all workforce members in its privacy policies and procedures.
- Apply appropriate sanctions against workforce members who violate privacy policies and procedures.
- Maintain reasonable and appropriate safeguards to prevent violations of privacy policies and procedures—for example, securing medical records with lock and key or pass code.
- Provide a written notice of the agency's privacy practices related to the use and disclosure of protected health information to individuals who receive services from the agency.
- Develop procedures that tell an individual how to submit a complaint related to violations or suspected violations of privacy policies and procedures.
- Identify the contact person or office that is responsible for receiving the complaints.
- Develop policies and procedures that tell an individual how to review, obtain a copy of, and amend his or her protected health information.

Billing specialists work with protected health information and are responsible for maintaining the privacy of PHI according to the written policies and procedures of their employers. Self-employed billing specialists must establish and maintain business practices that comply with the Privacy Rule. Failure to comply with a Privacy Rule requirement is a civil offense and may result in monetary penalties of $100 per failure, not to exceed $25,000 for multiple violations of the same Privacy Rule requirement in a calendar year.

HIPAA Security Rule

Ensuring the security of patient information is not a new concept. Patient information must be protected against damage, loss, theft, and unauthorized access. Paper, microfilm, or microfiche patient information can be stored in locked cabinets and file areas equipped with a sprinkler system. Access can be controlled by assigning to the file area staff members who are responsible for retrieving patient records and by providing keys to a limited number of individuals for times when the file area is not staffed. In today's environment, patient information is often stored electronically, which presents unique challenges for security.

In February 2003, HHS adopted standards for the security of electronic protected health information (EPHI). EPHI is protected health information maintained or transmitted in electronic form. These standards are commonly called the HIPAA Security Rule. The Security Rule, which is part of HIPAA, describes federally mandated patient information security regulations. The Security Rule became effective in April 2003. All covered entities—which include health plans, health care clearinghouses, and any health care provider—were required to comply with the requirements of the Security Rule by April 21, 2006. The Centers for Medicare and Medicaid Services (CMS), a division of HHS, is responsible for administering the Security Rule.

The information presented here is a very brief summary of the Security Rule and is based on the final rule published in *Health Insurance Reform: Security Standards* by Fed. Reg. (February 20, 2003). The most current information related to the Security Rule is available on the Department of Health and Human Services (HHS), Office of Civil Rights (OCR) website at http://www.hhs .gov/ocr. The search term is HIPAA Security Rule. Health care professional associations are also excellent resources for information about complying with the Security Rule.

While the HIPAA Privacy Rule covers all protected health information, the Security Rule only applies to protected health information that is electronically stored and transmitted. Electronic storage includes but may not be limited to computer hard drives, digital memory cards, magnetic tapes or disks, optical disks, and servers. Electronic media transmission includes but may not be limited to the Internet, leased lines, private computer networks, dial-up lines, and the physical movement of removable/transportable electronic storage media (e.g., disks, CDs, and magnetic tapes). The Security Rule did not include paper-to-paper fax and telephone transmissions in the definition of electronic media transmission.

The HIPAA Security Rule standards are grouped into five categories: administrative safeguards, physical safeguards, technical safeguards, organizational requirements, and policies and procedures and documentation requirements. Although it is beyond the scope of this text to include a detailed review of all standards, Table 2–3 briefly summarizes the standards for each of the five categories.

TABLE 2–3

Summary of HIPAA Security Rule Standards

Administrative Safeguards

- Analyze risks to security.
- Implement policies/procedures to prevent, detect, and correct security violations.
- Provide security awareness training for all employees.
- Identify a security official/officer.
- Limit access to EPHI as appropriate to a specific position, job, or function.
- Develop procedures to create and maintain retrievable exact copies of EPHI and/or restore any lost data.
- Apply appropriate sanctions against employees who fail to comply with security policies and procedures.

Physical Safeguards

- Implement policies and procedures to limit physical access to electronic information systems.
- Provide physical protection against unauthorized users for all workstations that access EPHI.
- Implement procedures to protect the physical safety of hardware and electronic media that is moved into, out of, and within the facility.
- Implement procedures to remove EPHI from electronic media before the media are made available for reuse.
- Implement procedures regarding the final disposition (destruction, archiving, retention) of EPHI and/or the hardware or electronic media on which it is stored.

Technical Safeguards

- Assign a unique identifier for all authorized users.
- Establish procedures for obtaining EPHI during an emergency.
- Implement policies and procedures to protect EPHI from improper destruction or alteration.
- Implement security measures that protect EPHI against unauthorized access during transmission via an electronic communications network.

Organizational Requirements

- Contracts with business associates (individuals or agencies that provide contractual services to the covered entity—e.g., billing services) must include provisions that direct the business associate to implement administrative, physical, and technical safeguards that protect EPHI and comply with the HIPAA Security Rule.
- Group health plans must implement administrative, physical, and technical safeguards that protect EPHI and comply with the HIPAA Security Rule.

continued on the next page

continued from the previous page

Summary of HIPAA Security Rule Standards

Policies and Procedures and Documentation Requirements

- Implement reasonable and appropriate policies and procedures necessary to comply with the HIPAA Security Rule.
- Maintain policies and procedures in written (including electronic) form.
- Retain policies and procedures for six years from the date created or last in effect, whichever is later.
- Review and update policies and procedures as needed.

Billing specialists are involved in the electronic transmission of EPHI and are responsible for maintaining the security of EPHI according to the written policies and procedures of their employers. Self-employed billing specialists must establish and maintain business practices that comply with the Security Rule. Failure to comply with a Security Rule requirement is a civil offense and may result in monetary penalties of $100 per failure, not to exceed $25,000 for multiple violations of the same requirement in a calendar year.

Release of Information (ROI)

Because confidentiality belongs to the individual, the individual has the right to authorize the release or distribution of his or her confidential information. Authorization is accomplished with a **release of information (ROI)** form. In nearly all circumstances, confidential information can be released only with the written authorization or consent of the individual. A parent or legal guardian may give consent on behalf of a minor or an incompetent adult.

The release of information authorization form must contain the items listed in Table 2–4. All items should be filled in before the patient is asked to sign the form. Figure 2–1 is an example of a properly completed release of information form. Note that conditions related to HIV status, AIDS, and alcohol and drug abuse have separate statements authorizing release of that information.

TABLE 2–4

Release of Information Items

Term	Definition
Identification	Physician or agency name(s) and patient name, address, and date of birth
Time frame	Date of service, office visit, or hospital admission and discharge dates
Information to be released	Checklist of reports and special authorization statements
Purpose of disclosure	Self-explanatory
Date(s)	Date signed and expiration date
Signature(s)	Patient or legal representative

MOISIO MEDICAL GROUP
714 HENNEPIN ROAD
MARQUETTE, MICHIGAN 49855

AUTHORIZATION FOR RELEASE OF INFORMATION

<u>Moisio Medical Group</u> is authorized to release the following
(Name of Agency)
information from the health record of <u>Erik William Mattson</u>,
(Patient name)
<u>06/30/1972</u>, for the period covering <u>March 199x</u>
(Date of Birth)   (Beginning date)
to <u>April 20xx</u>.
(Ending date)
The information is to be released to <u>Maria Gervais, MD,</u>

<u>999 West College Road, Marquette Michigan 49855,</u> for the
(Name and Address)
purpose of <u>continued patient care</u>.

Information to be released includes (check all that apply, cross out non-applicable items):

✔ Complete health record   ✔ History and Physical Exam

✔ Procedure Report   ✔ Laboratory Test Results

✔ Progress/Office Notes   ✔ Other test results

Other Reports: _____N/A_____

_____.

I authorize the release of health records related to:

NO   HIV status

NO   Acquired Immunodeficiency Syndrome (AIDS) and/or AIDS

     related complex (ARC)

NO   Alcohol and substance abuse treatment records.

This authorization expires on   ____6/12/20xx____.
                                  (Expiration Date)
Erik Mattson   *3/12/20xx*
(Patient/Legal Representative)   (Date Signed)

Figure 2–1 Authorization for Release of Information

Under the HIPAA Privacy Rule, patient information can be released without written authorization when:

- The patient record is subpoenaed.
- The information is needed to defend the physician in a lawsuit.
- There is a question of child abuse and, in some states, elder abuse.
- The patient is covered by Medicaid or workers' compensation health insurance programs.

In emergency situations, which is defined in most states as life-threatening, information may be released without authorization. When these circumstances exist, only enough information to satisfy the need for emergency treatment can be released.

Release of Information for HIV, AIDS, or Alcohol and Drug Abuse

Information related to AIDS, positive HIV test results, and alcohol and drug or substance abuse can be highly prejudicial. Federal and state laws exist to provide an individual with additional safeguards concerning the release of such information. The patient must provide written authorization before the release of AIDS, HIV status, or alcohol or drug abuse information. Even the diagnostic and treatment codes for these conditions cannot be released unless the patient gives written consent.

The ROI authorization form in Figure 2–1 includes a section that gives the patient the opportunity to authorize the release of sensitive information. Before submitting claims that contain HIV, AIDS, or substance abuse information, the insurance billing specialist must be certain that the patient has signed a valid authorization.

Telephone Release of Information

The billing specialist receives phone calls related to the status of insurance claims. Telephone inquiries can come from the insurance company, the patient, or someone acting on behalf of the patient. Before releasing any information over the phone, the billing specialist must identify the caller. Caller identification may be enough to satisfy this requirement.

If the office does not have caller identification or if the caller's identification is blocked, reasonable steps must be taken to verify the identity of the caller. Ask the caller to identify the date of service, the type of service, and the nature of the problem. When the caller is not the patient or insurance company representative, ask for a written request. Another option is to take the caller's name and phone number. Return the call *only* when you are certain that the caller has a right to the information.

Any information given over the phone must be documented and kept in the patient's record. Include the date and time of the call, a summary of the information given, the name of the caller, and the name or initials of the insurance billing specialist.

When the caller is an attorney, *never* reveal any patient information via the telephone. Inform the attorney that he or she must submit the request in writing and accompany it with a valid release of information authorization signed by the patient or the patient's legal representative. Electronic requests submitted by or in the name of an attorney should be handled like a telephone request. Always respond to an attorney's request in writing with a copy of the communication filed in the patient's record.

Facsimile Release of Information

Facsimile (fax) machines are an efficient and effective way to move information from one location to another. Fax transmissions are particularly useful in a health care setting when a need arises to immediately communicate with other health care providers.

> **EXAMPLE**
> For a patient scheduled to see several physicians in a large group practice whose offices are in different locations, each physician can fax his or her findings as the patient moves from one appointment to the next.
> The billing specialist can fax information to the insurance carrier in order to resolve reimbursement problems. Using fax transmissions, insurance carriers can quickly notify billing specialists about changes in coverage or claims-processing procedures.

Fax transmissions present unique confidentiality challenges. Questions such as who actually receives the fax, where the fax machine is located, and who has access to fax messages must be

1. Before sending patient information via fax:

   - You must have a written authorization from the patient.

   - Call/ask the person who is requesting the information these questions:

     a. Do you have direct access to the fax messages?

     b. Where is the fax machine located?

     c. Is the fax machine location open to all employees, passersby, or others?

     d. How often are fax messages retrieved?

     e. Who distributes fax messages?

2. If you are satisfied with the security of the fax message, continue with Step 3. If you are not satisfied, call/ask the individual requesting the information to send a request in writing.

3. Complete the fax transmittal cover sheet.

   - In the Remarks section note the information sent.

   - Recheck all fax numbers before transmittal.

4. Enter the fax number and documents and wait until transmission is complete.

5. Retrieve the fax cover sheet when it is returned with the completed statement of receipt.

6. File the returned fax cover sheet in the patient's record.

Figure 2–2 Procedure for Faxing Patient Information

considered. Before faxing patient information, the insurance billing specialist should find answers to those questions. Figure 2–2 is a sample procedure for faxing patient information.

The fax cover sheet for all health care agencies must include a confidentiality statement. Figure 2–3 is a sample cover sheet that addresses the challenges of faxing patient information.

The American Health Information Management Association (AHIMA) has developed a practice brief that covers faxing patient information. This document is an excellent resource for billing specialists and other health professionals who transmit information via fax. To access the practice brief, go to the AHIMA website (http://www.ahima.org) and then search for the practice brief titled *Facsimile Transmission of Health Information.*

Internet and Electronic Release of Information

Electronic release of patient information includes Internet and e-mail communications. The HIPAA Privacy Rule and Security Rule *do not* expressly prohibit the use of either of these methods. Both rules do require that health care agencies implement policies and procedures that protect against any tampering with and unauthorized disclosure of (or access to) protected health information.

```
                    NORTHERN CLINIC, INC.
                      714 Hennepin Road
                 Marquette, Rhode Island 55555
                    Telephone: (505)555-5555
                      FAX NO. 055—005-5555


  TO: _____      DATE: _____
        (Receiver's Name)

                                          TIME: _____
      _____             (AM or PM)
        (Receiver's Address)

  FAX NUMBER: _____

  FROM: _____
        (Your Name and Department)

  REMARKS: _____

           _____


  TO THE RECIPIENT: PLEASE FAX THIS COMPLETED STATEMENT TO
  THE SENDER. FAX NUMBER: 055-005-5555. THANK YOU.


  I, _____, received _____
                                   (pages with cover sheet)

  from_____ on _____ at _____.
                                (date)        (time) AM/PM


  IF YOU HAVE RECEIVED THIS TRANSMITTAL IN ERROR, PLEASE
  NOTIFY THE SENDER IMMEDIATELY. PHONE: (505) 555-5555.

  RETURN THE INFORMATION BY FAX: 055-005-5555.

  THE INFORMATION IN THIS TRANSMISSION IS CONFIDENTIAL AND
  LEGALLY PRIVILEGED. THIS INFORMATION IS INTENDED ONLY FOR
  THE USE OF THE INDIVIDUAL OR ENTITY NAMED ABOVE.

  IF YOU ARE NOT THE INTENDED RECIPIENT, ANY DISCLOSURE,
  COPYING, DISTRIBUTION, OR ACTION TAKEN ON THE BASIS OF
  THIS INFORMATION IS STRICTLY PROHIBITED.
```

Figure 2–3 Fax Transmittal Cover Sheet

The benefits of processing insurance claims via the Internet and other electronic methods are evident. The billing specialist can submit claims directly to insurance company data files. Billing software can be equipped with validation capabilities that flag an insurance claim when information is missing or inconsistent. To use the Internet for any patient-related applications, security safeguards must be in place. Table 2–5 identifies and describes Internet security measures. These precautions allow the insurance billing specialist to take advantage of this communication tool.

Billing specialists who send and receive patient information by e-mail must take the following actions to ensure that e-mails are secure:

- Protect his or her password.
- Never leave a message onscreen when the terminal is unattended.
- Double-check and verify the e-mail address of the intended recipient.
- Limit the content of the e-mail to the minimum information needed to achieve the purpose of the communication.
- Obtain automatic confirmation that the recipient received the e-mail.

TABLE 2–5

Internet Security Measures	
Security Measure	**Description**
Access report(s)	Maintains an ongoing record of Internet communication of patient billing/medical information
Encryption	Transforms information into a form that is unreadable by unauthorized users
Firewalls	Hardware and software applications that control incoming and outgoing Internet transactions; they prevent unauthorized Internet access to the office's computer files while allowing office staff to use the Internet
User authentication	Assigning a unique identifier to individuals who communicate via the Internet
Written policies	Implementing and enforcing policies and procedures that address Internet transmissions of patient billing and medical information

Billing specialists must stay current with the standards, regulations, and laws that cover access to and the use and disclosure of patient information. The professional associations noted in Chapter 1 are excellent resources. In addition, HHS websites, including those for the CMS and the OCR, provide a wealth of information about the privacy and security of protected health information.

REINFORCEMENT EXERCISES 2–2

Provide a short answer for each statement or question.

1. List three general categories of confidential information.

_____

_____

_____

2. Briefly describe the HIPAA Privacy Rule.

_____

_____

_____

3. What is the meaning of the Privacy Rule phrase "minimum necessary"?

_____

_____

_____

continued on the next page

continued from the previous page

4. Discuss the difference(s) between the Privacy Rule and the Security Rule.

_____

_____

_____

5. What do the initials ROI mean in the context of medical billing?

_____

_____

_____

6. Which types of patient medical information require special consideration prior to release?

_____

_____

_____

7. What steps can be taken to verify caller identity prior to releasing information over the telephone?

_____

_____

_____

8. When is it permissible to release patient information to an attorney?

_____

_____

_____

9. Identify confidentiality challenges associated with fax transmissions.

_____

_____

_____

10. Briefly describe encryption, firewalls, and user authentication as Internet security measures.

_____

_____

_____

INSURANCE FRAUD AND ABUSE LAWS

HIPAA made health care insurance billing fraud a federal offense. Federal law enforcement agencies are available to seek, find, prosecute, and punish any individual involved in insurance fraud or abuse. HIPAA also established a Fraud and Abuse Control Program. Under this program, three major federal agencies have active roles in investigating fraud and abuse. These federal agencies are the Office of the Inspector General (OIG), which is part of HHS; the Federal Bureau of Investigation (FBI); and the Department of Justice (DOJ).

The OIG is responsible for cases associated with Medicare, Medicaid, workers' compensation, and other federal health care insurance programs. The OIG can levy fines on and exclude violators from receiving payment from federal programs. The FBI investigates fraud cases that involve either federal or private health insurance programs but does not take disciplinary action. The OIG and FBI refer fraud and abuse cases that fall under federal criminal law to the DOJ.

To help all sectors of the health care industry comply with HIPAA antifraud provisions, the OIG has issued compliance program guidelines. A billing compliance program allows physician offices to monitor the entire health insurance billing process. The purpose of a compliance program is to eliminate billing and coding errors. As an essential player in the billing process, the insurance billing specialist has a definite stake in eliminating errors and participating in the compliance program. Figure 2–4 shows an insurance billing specialist with visions of legal abbreviations dancing in her head.

Fraud

Although fraud and abuse are often used in the same context, they have different meanings and carry different penalties. The difference between fraud and abuse is the person's intent. Fraud is deliberate, and the person knows his or her actions are deceptive. Abuse presumes that there was no intent to be deceptive and that the errors are unplanned.

Medicare defines fraud as "the intentional deception or misrepresentation that an individual knows to be false or does not believe to be true and makes, knowing that the deception could

Figure 2–4 Abbreviations Spoken Here!

result in some unauthorized benefit to himself/herself or some other person." HIPAA defines health care fraud as "knowingly and willfully [executing], or [attempting] to execute, a scheme or artifice—(1) to defraud any health care benefit program; or (2) to obtain, by means of false or fraudulent pretenses, representations, or promises, any of the money or property owned by, or under the custody or control of, a health care benefit program." Simply stated, fraud is an attempt to obtain something you are not entitled to have. Keep in mind that the attempt itself is fraud, regardless of whether any gain or benefit is realized.

Health insurance billing fraud usually means that someone is illegally attempting to collect insurance payments from government health insurance programs. Most health insurance billing fraud is targeted at the Medicare program. The CMS is part of HHS. The CMS is responsible for managing Medicare. According to CMS guidelines, the person attempting fraud includes:

- A physician or other practitioner, a hospital or other institutional provider;
- A clinical laboratory or other supplier, an employee of any provider;
- A billing service;
- A beneficiary(patient);
- A Medicare carrier employee (insurance company employee); or
- Any person in a position to file a claim for Medicare benefits.

The insurance billing specialist qualifies as "any person in a position to file a claim for Medicare benefits."

Health insurance fraud activities fall under three main categories: fraudulent diagnoses, billing for services not rendered, and medical coding errors. Table 2–6 presents examples of fraudulent practices within each category.

TABLE 2–6

Fraudulent Activities
Fraudulent Diagnoses
• Falsifying the diagnosis
• Misrepresenting the diagnosis
• Selecting a diagnosis based on reimbursement
Billing for Services Not Rendered
• Equipment such as crutches and dressing changes
• Hospital visits
• Laboratory or other diagnostic tests
• Cancelled or missed appointments
• Phantom billing and billing for services rendered to patients who do not exist or who are deceased
Medical Coding Errors
• Upcoding: selecting a diagnostic code based on reimbursement
• Leveling: using the same code for all office visits
• Unbundling: assigning individual medical or office visit codes to services or diagnoses that are covered by a single code

The insurance billing specialist is responsible for submitting information about services provided, diagnoses, and medical codes to the appropriate insurance program. The billing specialist has a legal and ethical obligation to verify the accuracy of that information. The following scenarios illustrate this obligation.

EXAMPLE

Services Provided

Mrs. Yoha's bill lists charges for an office visit, six lab tests, and an EKG. "Sore throat" is the reason for the office visit. It appears that there were more tests than needed for a "sore throat." The billing specialist reviews the record for documentation that supports the lab tests and EKG. If there is no supporting documentation, the billing specialist (or supervisor) alerts the physician that the claim cannot be submitted until the documentation is available.

Accurate Diagnosis

The physician writes ulcerative colitis as the diagnosis for a new patient. The only test done was a complete blood count (CBC). Diarrhea is listed as the reason for the office visit. Because ulcerative colitis cannot be diagnosed with a CBC and a complaint of diarrhea, the billing specialist reviews the patient record for additional documentation that verifies the diagnosis. If no other supporting information is available, the physician either provides the information or changes the diagnostic statement. The billing specialist does not submit an insurance claim with a questionable diagnosis.

Medical Coding

The physician has circled cholecystitis (inflamed gallbladder) as the patient's diagnosis. The office manager has provided the insurance billing specialist with a list of physician-approved, frequently used medical codes. Cholecystitis with obstruction is the only listed cholecystitis code. Because there is a significant difference in the payment for treating an inflamed gallbladder with obstruction versus one without obstruction, the insurance billing specialist reviews the patient record or asks the physician for clarification. The billing specialist does not submit an insurance claim unless the selected medical code is supported by the documentation in the patient record.

Fraud Prevention and Reporting Incentives

Insurance billing specialists can actively participate in fraud prevention as well as protect themselves from being drawn into any fraudulent behavior. Table 2–7 summarizes fraud prevention and protection strategies.

Under federal law, insurance companies and billing services are expected to report fraudulent billing practices. Any employee of an insurance company, billing service, health care agency, or the patient can report fraudulent activities. The federal government provides monetary incentives and rewards to help reduce or eliminate fraudulent practices.

The Federal False Claims Act provides financial incentives when suspected fraudulent activities are proven true. Any individual who reports the fraud may receive 15 to 25% of any judgment.

TABLE 2–7

Fraud Prevention Strategies
Six Steps to Fraud Protection and Prevention
1. *Never* alter information in a patient medical record.
2. *Never* add a diagnosis to an insurance claim form that is not documented in the patient medical record.
3. *Never* add a procedure to an insurance claim form that is not documented in the patient medical record.
4. *Always* follow current billing and coding practices.
5. *Always* complete insurance claim forms fully and accurately.
6. *Always* ask for clarification when the documentation does not support the diagnosis or procedure.

EXAMPLE

In an actual case, a provider paid $500,000 in fines for submitting fraudulent claims to Medicare. The individual who reported the fraudulent claims scheme received between 15 and 25% of that $500,000 fine.

HHS has implemented a program that rewards anyone who alerts Medicare to possible acts of fraud and abuse. Individuals who report fraud and abuse in the Medicare program are eligible for rewards of up to $1000. The reward is paid when the information is not already a part of an ongoing investigation and when the information helps recover Medicare funds. Billing practices are monitored at every level—from the individual patient to government-sponsored fraud and abuse investigation agencies.

Penalties for Fraud

The civil, criminal, and administrative penalties associated with fraud are intended to punish and prevent fraud. These penalties range from requiring an office to implement an insurance billing compliance program to extensive fines and, in the worst cases, imprisonment. Health care providers, insurance companies, and billing services can also be excluded from all federally funded health care programs. Table 2–8 summarizes the administrative, civil, and criminal penalties connected with fraud.

TABLE 2–8

Penalties for Fraud
Administrative Penalties
• Coding and billing educational activities
• Exclusion from participation in Medicare and Medicaid programs
Civil Penalties
• Monetary penalties, without imprisonment
• $2000 to $10,000 for each item or service of a fraudulent claim
• Fine of three times the amount of a fraudulent claim

continued on the next page

continued from the previous page

Criminal Penalties

- Monetary penalties and/or imprisonment
- No limits for monetary fines
- Up to 10 years in prison for knowingly and willingly carrying out or attempting to carry out a fraudulent scheme
- Twenty years in prison if the fraudulent scheme results in serious bodily harm to a patient
- Life in prison if the fraudulent scheme results in the death of a patient

---

REINFORCEMENT EXERCISES 2–3

Provide a short answer for each statement.

1. Briefly define fraud.

   _____

   _____

   _____

2. Give two examples of health insurance fraud.

   _____

   _____

   _____

3. List and describe the three types of information the insurance billing specialist should review for accuracy.

   _____

   _____

   _____

Spell out these abbreviations.

1. HIPAA

   _____

2. OIG

   _____

continued on the next page

continued from the previous page

3. HHS

_____

4. FBI

_____

5. DOJ

_____

6. CMS

_____

Abuse

The Medicare definition of abuse states, "Abuse involves actions that are inconsistent with accepted, sound medical, business, or fiscal practices…that directly or indirectly result in unnecessary costs to the [Medicare] program through improper payments." The difference between fraud and abuse is the person's intent. However, both fraud and abuse have the same result: They take money from the Medicare insurance program. Fraud is an intentional act; abuse is not.

> EXAMPLES
>
> Fraud: A physician orders an EKG on every Medicare patient solely to increase his or her income.
>
> In this example, the physician is engaged in a deliberate attempt to make more money from Medicare.
>
> Abuse: A physician consistently bills for the highest level of office visit based solely on the amount of time spent with the patient, and not on the patient's diagnosis or problem.
>
> In this example, the physician is using the wrong criteria for the level of service. Office visit reimbursement is based on the nature of the problem, not solely on the time spent with the patient.

Health insurance abuse activities fall under three main categories: inadvertent billing and coding errors; excessive charges for services, equipment, or supplies; and billing for services that are not medically necessary. Table 2–9 presents examples of abusive insurance practices for each category. The insurance billing specialist is at higher risk for abuse than for fraud. Unintentional coding and billing errors that result in overpayment by Medicare or any insurance company may qualify as abuse.

Abuse Prevention and Reporting Incentives

The insurance billing specialist can protect him- or herself from charges of insurance abuse by following current billing and coding guidelines. Outdated insurance billing and coding references increase the risk of abuse. The insurance billing specialist is well-advised to keep current on the yearly changes in ICD and CPT codes.

TABLE 2–9

Health Insurance Abuse Activities

Billing and Coding Errors

- Billing errors that result in overpayment
- Billing Medicare for services covered by another insurance program
- Medical coding errors that result in overpayment
- Submitting claims for medically unnecessary services
- Using outdated criteria for selecting medical codes

Excessive Charges

- Billing for prescription refills
- Billing for telephone conversations with the patient
- Charging Medicare patients more than other patients

Unnecessary Services

- Excessive referrals to other health care practitioners
- Performing more tests than necessary to reach a diagnosis
- Scheduling follow-up visits that may not be necessary

Insurance companies provide bulletins that describe acceptable and up-to-date insurance billing practices. Professional associations offer workshops and seminars that address changes in medical coding procedures. Government insurance programs routinely alert physicians' offices about changes that affect the insurance billing process. This information should be made available to the insurance billing specialist. If the employer does not routinely share these bulletins and updates, the insurance billing specialist must take the initiative and ask for the information.

The insurance billing specialist is in a unique position to help administrators and physicians identify potentially abusive practices. The following example illustrates this point.

EXAMPLE

The insurance billing specialist alerts the office manager that Medicare patients have more laboratory tests done than other patients. The office manager reviews the patients' records to identify reasons for the difference. The reasons could include the following:

- Medicare patients' problems are more complex.
- Tests are necessary to rule out various diagnoses.
- Physicians are ordering all tests covered by Medicare.

If the documentation in the patients' medical records supports the medical necessity of all lab tests, there is no cause for concern. However, if it appears that the tests are done because Medicare pays for them, the office manager discusses the situation with the physicians. The physicians must either provide documentation that supports the medical necessity of the lab tests or reduce the number of tests. In either event, the potential problem is resolved internally before it draws the attention of external reviewers.

The financial incentives for reporting abuse are more limited than the incentives for reporting fraud. Individuals who report suspected abusive practices are eligible for rewards of up to $1000. The reward is paid when the information is not already a part of an ongoing investigation and when the information helps recover Medicare funds. Because the Federal False Claims Act addresses fraudulent activities, the reporting rewards identified in that act do not apply to abuse.

Penalties for Abuse

The penalties associated with abuse are intended to educate rather than punish. Administrative remedies are used to correct abusive practices. The usual penalties include educational sessions, recovering insurance overpayments, and withholding further insurance payments.

Educational sessions may focus on insurance billing practices, medical coding activities, or Medicare guidelines. Recovering insurance overpayments simply means that the organization must return all money received as a result of the abusive practice. Insurance payments can also be withheld or delayed until the abusive practice is discontinued.

REINFORCEMENT EXERCISES 2–4

Provide a short answer for each statement or question.

1. Briefly define abuse.

_____

_____

_____

2. What are the three main health insurance abuse categories?

_____

_____

_____

3. Name the usual penalties associated with abuse.

_____

_____

_____

4. What is the key difference between fraud and abuse?

_____

_____

_____

PATIENT PROTECTION AND AFFORDABLE CARE ACT

The Patient Protection and Affordable Care Act, commonly called the Affordable Care Act, was signed into law in March, 2010. The act is intended to:

- Provide access to health insurance for individuals, families, and small business owners;
- Reduce health insurance premium costs; and
- Limit the ability of insurance companies to deny, rescind, or restrict coverage.

The provisions of the Affordable Care Act are implemented over a six-year period, from 2010 to 2015. Provisions of the act are organized by three main categories: consumer protection, improving quality and lowering costs, and increasing access to affordable care. It is well beyond the scope of this text to cover the entire act. Table 2–10 summarizes the main provisions by category and implementation date. The effective date is noted in parentheses.

TABLE 2–10

Provisions of the Patient Protection and Affordable Care Act

2010 Consumer Protections

- Establish a website for consumers to compare health insurance options (July 1, 2010)
- Prohibit denying coverage for children under age 19 due to a preexisting condition (September 23, 2010)
- Eliminate lifetime limits on insurance coverage for essential benefits, such as hospital stays, for health plans (beginning on or after September 23, 2010)
- Restrict annual dollar limits on insurance coverage for health plans (beginning on or after September 23, 2010)
- Provide and establish a consumer appeal process for insurance company decisions for health plans (beginning on or after September 23, 2010)
- Award grants to states that establish or expand consumer assistance programs related to health insurance (awarded in October 2010)

2010 Improving Quality and Lowering Costs

- Small business health insurance tax credit (March 2010)
- Tax-free, one-time rebate for seniors who reach the gap in Medicare prescription drug coverage (June 2010)
- Eliminate deductible, co-pay, or coinsurance for preventive services such as mammograms for health plans (beginning on or after September 23, 2010)
- Establish a Prevention and Public Health Fund for programs that promote health, such as smoking cessation (funding begins in 2010)
- Establish new policies for reducing fraud and waste in Medicare, Medicaid, Children's Health Insurance Programs (2010)

2010 Increasing Access to Affordable Care

- Provide access to health insurance for uninsured Americans with pre-existing conditions, state or national programs (national program effective July 1, 2010)
- Allow young adults, under the age of 26, to stay on their parents' health insurance plan (beginning on or after September 23, 2010)

continued on the next page

continued from the previous page

Provisions of the Patient Protection and Affordable Care Act

- Provide funds for employers to continue health insurance coverage for early retirees (ages 55–65), their spouses and dependents (applications for employers available June 1, 2010)

- Improve scholarships and loan repayment provisions for primary care physicians and nurses in underserved areas (2010)

- Provide grants to states that have or plan to have measures that require insurance companies to justify premium cost increases (2010)

- Provide federal matching funds to states that increase Medicaid coverage (April 1, 2010)

- Increase payments to rural health care providers (2010)

- New funding for construction and expansion of community health centers (2010)

2011 Improving Quality and Lowering Costs

- 50% discount for Medicare covered brand-name prescriptions, available to seniors who reach the Medicare prescription drug coverage gap (January 1, 2011)

- Free prevention services, such as wellness visits and prevention plans for Medicare beneficiaries (January 1, 2011)

- Establish a Center for Medicare and Medicaid Innovation that tests new ways of delivering care to patients (January 1, 2011)

- Post-hospitalization Community Care Transitions Programs for high risk Medicare beneficiaries (January 1, 2011)

- Target waste, reduce costs, and improve health outcomes by extending the life of the Medicare Trust Fund (administrative funding available October 1, 2011)

2011 Increasing Access to Affordable Care

- Allow states to offer, through Medicaid, home- and community-based services to disabled individuals (October 1, 2011)

2011 Holding Insurance Companies Accountable

Note: This category is unique to the 2011 Affordable Care Act provisions.

- 85% of premium dollars collected by insurance companies from large employer health care plans *must* be spent on health care services and quality improvement (January 1, 2011)

- 80% of premium dollars collected by insurance companies from individuals and small employers *must* be spent on benefits and quality improvement (January 1, 2011)

- Requires insurance companies to provide rebates to consumers when these targets are not met (January 1, 2011)

- Eliminate discrepancy between payments to insurance companies that administer traditional and Medicare Advantage insurance plans (January 1, 2011)

2012 Improving Quality and Lowering Costs

- Provides financial incentives to hospitals to improve the quality of care (October 1, 2012)

- Provide incentives for physicians to form practices that emphasizes coordinated patient care (January 1, 2012)

- Require health plans to establish electronic exchange of health information (October 1, 2012)

- Identify health disparities based on race and ethnicity (March 2012)

continued on the next page

continued from the previous page

2013 Improving Quality and Lowering Costs

- Provide additional funding to state Medicaid programs that cover preventive services at little or no cost (January 1, 2013)

- Establish a flat rate for an episode of care, including physician, hospital, and other provider fees, for services provided to Medicare beneficiaries (January 1, 2013)

2013 Increasing Access to Affordable Care

- Increase Medicaid payment to primary care physicians (January 1, 2013)

- Provide additional funding for the Children's Health Insurance Program (CHIP) (October 1, 2013)

2014 Consumer Protections

- Prohibit insurance companies from refusing to sell coverage or renew policies due to an individual's pre-existing conditions (January 1, 2014)

- Prohibit insurance companies from charging higher rates based on gender or health status (January 1, 2014)

- Eliminate annual dollar limits on the amount of coverage an individual may receive (January 1, 2014)

- Require insurance companies to fully cover individuals participating in a clinical trial related to cancer or other life-threatening disease (January 1, 2014)

2014 Improving Quality and Lowering Costs

- Provide tax credits to moderate and middle income families for health insurance premium costs (January 1, 2014)

- Establish Affordable [Health] Insurance Exchanges (January 1, 2014)

- Increase the small business tax credit for small businesses and small nonprofit organizations that provide health insurance (January 1, 2014)

2014 Increasing Access to Affordable Care

- Increase Medicaid eligibility and provide federal funding for states that expand coverage (January 1, 2014)

- Require individuals, who can afford it, to obtain basic health insurance coverage or pay a fee to help offset the costs of caring for the uninsured (January 1, 2014)

- Allow employees to use the employer's contribution for insurance coverage to help purchase a more affordable health plan (January 1, 2014)

2015 Improving Quality and Lowering Costs

- Tie physician payment to the quality of care provided (January 1, 2015)

The Patient Protection and Affordable Care Act generated much controversy. At the time of publication, several states filed legal action intended to repeal many provisions of the act. Current information about the Affordable Care Act is available at HealthCare.gov (http://www .healthcare.gov), search term Affordable Care Act.

ABBREVIATIONS

Table 2–11 lists the abbreviations presented in this chapter.

TABLE 2–11

Abbreviations and Meanings	
Abbreviation	Meaning
CHIP	Children's Health Insurance Program
CMS	Centers for Medicare and Medicaid Services
DOJ	Department of Justice
EPHI	electronic protected health information
FBI	Federal Bureau of Investigation
HHS	Department of Health and Human Services
HIPAA	Health Insurance Portability and Accountability Act of 1996
OCR	Office of Civil Rights
OIG	Office of the Inspector General
PHI	protected health information
ROI	release of information

SUMMARY

The insurance billing specialist must be familiar with general medical-legal terms, ranging from confidentiality to fraud and abuse. Confidentiality is a principle that presumes that certain types of information are not shared with the public. The patient has control over the release of his or her confidential information. Release of information usually requires the patient's written authorization. The authorization form must clearly describe the information to be released. It is necessary to obtain the patient's written authorization in order to release alcohol and substance abuse, HIV, and AIDS information.

Health Insurance Portability and Accountability Act of 1996 (HIPAA) established a set of national standards for the protection of certain health information. The HIPAA Privacy Rule gives individuals a federally protected right to control the use and release of their health information. The HIPAA Security Rule applies only to protected health information that is electronically stored and transmitted.

Insurance fraud is intentional; abuse is not. HIPAA makes health care insurance billing fraud a federal offense. Three main categories of health insurance fraud are:

- Submission of fraudulent diagnoses
- Billing for services not rendered
- Medical coding errors

Fraudulent billing and coding practices can result in serious civil and criminal penalties, ranging from monetary fines to imprisonment. There are financial incentives for reporting health insurance fraud.

Abuse includes actions that directly or indirectly result in financial gain. Health insurance abuse falls into three categories:

- Inadvertent billing and coding errors
- Excessive charges for services, equipment, or supplies
- Billing for services that are not medically necessary

The insurance billing specialist is at a higher risk for abuse than fraud and is in a unique position to help identify potentially abusive billing practices.

The Patient Protection and Affordable Care Act was signed into law in March 2010. The purpose of this federal law is to provide better access to health insurance, reduce health insurance premium costs, improve the quality of health care, and limit the insurance companies' ability to deny, rescind, or restrict coverage.

 REVIEW EXERCISES

Definitions of Terms

Briefly define these legal terms and phrases.

1. Emancipated minor

   _____

   _____

   _____

2. Embezzlement

   _____

   _____

   _____

3. Subpoena

   _____

   _____

   _____

4. Subpoena duces tecum

   _____

   _____

   _____

5. Respondeat superior

   _____

   _____

   _____

6. Malpractice

_____

_____

_____

7. Covered entities

_____

_____

_____

8. Protected health information

_____

_____

_____

9. Workforce members

_____

_____

_____

10. Electronic protected health information

_____

_____

_____

Short Answer

1. List four examples of situations where patient information can be released without written authorization.

_____

_____

_____

2. Describe the differences and similarities between health insurance fraud and abuse.

_____

_____

_____

3. Give an example of or briefly describe how the insurance billing specialist can verify the accuracy of the services provided, diagnoses, and medical codes.

_____

_____

_____

4. What is individually identifiable health information, as described in the HIPAA Privacy Rule?

_____

_____

_____

5. Give three examples of physical safeguards and three examples of technical safeguards, as described in the HIPAA Security Rule standards.

_____

_____

_____

_____

_____

_____

6. List the three main categories of the Patient Protection and Affordable Care Act provisions.

_____

_____

_____

Abbreviations Review

Spell out these abbreviations.

1. FBI _____

2. CMS _____

3. HIPAA _____

4. OIG _____

5. ROI _____

Matching

Match each term in Column A with the appropriate item in Column B.

Column A	Column B	
a. civil penalty	1. billing fraud; federal offense	_____
b. HIPAA	2. manages the Medicare program	_____
c. criminal penalty	3. using medical codes to increase payments	_____
d. upcoding	4. fines; exclusion from programs	_____
e. CMS	5. fines; imprisonment	_____

COMPREHENSION EXERCISES

Identify each statement as an example of fraud or abuse.

1. Excessive charges for services, equipment, or supplies. _____

2. Billing for services never provided. _____

3. Unbundling charges for laboratory tests. _____

4. Scheduling frequent follow-up visits that may not be necessary. _____

5. Changing the date of service. _____

6. Using outdated criteria for selecting medical codes. _____

7. Upcoding. _____

8. Billing individual components of a treatment over several days when all treatment was provided in one visit. _____

9. Billing for calling in prescription refills. _____

True or False

Mark each statement as True or False.

1. Incentives for reporting abuse are the same as incentives for reporting fraud. _____

2. The Federal False Claims Act addresses fraudulent activities. _____

3. Insurance payments can be withheld until an abusive practice is discontinued. _____

4. Abuse is intended to take money from Medicare. _____

5. Criminal penalties are used to punish those who engage in abusive practices. _____

6. The insurance billing specialist may notice potentially abusive practices before the physician. _____

7. The Affordable Care Act allows young adults under the age of 26 to be covered by the parent's health insurance plan. _____

8. The provisions of the Affordable Care Act were fully implemented by January 1, 2013. _____

INTERNET EXERCISE

Locate the Office of Civil Rights (OCR) privacy page at http://www.hhs.gov/ocr/privacy and then click on How to File a Complaint.

1. List the languages available under the heading How to File a Health Information Privacy Complaint in Multiple Languages.

2. Click the Health Information Privacy Complaint Form Package and then find the address for the OCR's regional office in your state.

 CRITICAL THINKING EXERCISES

1. Develop a confidentiality in-service training session for new employees.

2. Write a procedure that covers nursing and allied health students' access to protected health information.

 WEBSITES

American Health Information Management Association: http://www.ahima.org
HealthCare.gov: http://www.healthcare.gov
Centers for Medicare and Medicaid Services: http://www.cms.hhs.gov
Office of Civil Rights: http://www.hhs.gov/ocr
Office of the Inspector General: http://www.oig.hhs.gov

CHAPTER 3

Introduction to Health Insurance

LEARNING OBJECTIVES

Upon successful completion of this chapter, the reader should have the knowledge to:

1. Describe and define health insurance and the health insurance industry.
2. Briefly explain all health insurance policy and health care provider terms and phrases presented in the chapter.
3. Differentiate between direct pay, indirect pay, and third-party reimbursement methods.
4. List and discuss the three third-party reimbursement methods presented in the chapter.
5. Differentiate between employer-sponsored health insurance plans, government-sponsored health care programs, and individual health insurance policies.
6. Describe the four government-sponsored health care programs presented in this chapter.
7. Identify similarities and differences among managed care organizations.

KEY TERMS

Accept assignment
Admitting physician
Assignment of benefits
Attending physician
Birthday rule
Capitation
Coordination of benefits (COB)
Co-payment (co-pay)
Coverage
Dependent
Direct pay
Employer-sponsored health insurance plan

Episode-of-care reimbursement
Exclusion
Exclusive provider organization (EPO)
Fee-for-service
Government-sponsored health care program
Group model
Health care provider
Health insurance
Health insurance policy
Health maintenance organization (HMO)

Independent practice association (IPA)
Indirect payer
Individual policy
Insurance policy
Integrated delivery system (IDS)
Managed care
Managed care organization (MCO)
Maximum allowable fee
Network model
Per capita
Point-of-service plan (POS)

Policyholder
Preferred provider
    organization (PPO)
Preauthorization
Precertification

Predetermination
Pre-existing condition
Premium
Prepaid health plan
Service provider

Staff model
Third-party payer
Third-party reimbursement
Waiver

 ## OVERVIEW

This chapter provides a basic review of the health insurance industry and the historical factors that influenced the growth of the industry. This chapter answers questions such as these:

- What is health insurance?
- How does someone get health insurance?
- Who pays for health insurance?
- What do all those health insurance terms mean?

The information covered in this chapter is the foundation for subsequent chapters. The concepts, terms, and definitions presented here are used repeatedly throughout the text.

 ## DEFINING HEALTH INSURANCE

Throughout our lives, we are exposed to all types of insurance: life insurance, which provides survivors with money in the event of our death; car insurance, which provides money to pay bills that arise from a car accident; and liability insurance, which provides money for bills that arise from our professional or personal actions. An insurance policy is the document that describes the situations covered by a particular type of insurance. An insurance policy is a legal contract between the individual and the company that provides the insurance. The policy sets forth the conditions of the contract and the cost of the contract. The cost of the contract, called a premium, is a fee paid at regular intervals by the policyholder.

In many ways, health insurance is no different. Health insurance provides money to pay bills generated by receiving health care–related services. Situations covered by health insurance are described in the health insurance policy; the policy is a legal contract, and the cost of the contract is called the premium. Health insurance, therefore, is defined as a contract that provides money to cover all or a portion of the cost of medically necessary care.

Health insurance differs from other types of insurance in one important area: While individuals are usually responsible for buying their own life, car, and liability insurance, health insurance is often provided as an employment benefit. The state and federal government also provide health insurance for certain populations: people over 65 years of age, individuals receiving public assistance (welfare), and individuals with certain conditions, such as blindness and end-stage renal disease.

Health Insurance: Then and Now

Prior to the 1940s, most Americans paid their own medical bills. People were treated and cared for in their homes and were expected to pay for that care and treatment. This type of payment is called direct pay, which means that the patient or individual pays the physician or health care practitioner for provided services. Figure 3–1 illustrates the direct pay concept.

Figure 3–1 Direct Pay

Individuals who could not afford to pay were given essential treatment at no charge. It was during this time that various religious and fraternal groups provided health care services to the poor.

Prior to the 1940s, only the most serious illnesses were treated by physicians. Babies were born at home, with or without a midwife in attendance; everyday scrapes, bruises, and uncomplicated broken limbs were treated with home remedies; and hospitals were viewed as the place to go when you were sick enough to die. The family doctor routinely made house calls and often cared for the citizens of a given community from birth to death.

Between the late 1920s and early 1940s, individuals began banding together to find ways to improve health care in local communities. As a result, contracts between a specific group of individuals and local hospitals and physicians were developed. Each member of the group paid a premium in order to be included in the contract. The contracts outlined the medical services available to group members and the fees that the physician or hospital would receive for providing the services. These contracts were known as prepaid health plans, the forerunners of current health maintenance organizations (HMOs). Prepaid health plans, including HMOs, are discussed in the "Managed Care" section of this chapter.

Beginning in the 1950s, rapid advances in medical care, technology, and medications set the stage for a more complex and costly health care environment. Hospitals became centers for disease treatment and surgical procedures as well as places to recover from illnesses. Physicians believed they could use their time more efficiently and treat more patients if the patients came to the physician rather than the physician going to the patients. As medical care became more centralized and costs increased, memberships in prepaid health insurance plans expanded.

Another factor influencing the growth of health insurance plans was the practice of employers offering health insurance coverage as a benefit of employment. This practice gave rise to employer-sponsored health insurance plans, wherein the employer pays all or part of the premium to purchase health insurance for employees and their dependents. The increase in employer-sponsored health insurance plans can be traced to World War II. Because many employers had to comply with government-enforced pay scales, paid health insurance plans were used to recruit and retain good employees. As a result of these and other factors, the responsibility of paying for health insurance shifted from the individual to the employer.

Between 1965 and 1966, federal and state governments entered the health insurance industry by establishing government-sponsored health care programs. These programs—the Civilian Health and Medical Program of the Veterans Administration (CHAMPVA), Medicare, Medicaid, and TRICARE—were designed to provide health insurance to specific populations. Table 3–1 describes the original intent of these programs. Each program is discussed in detail in subsequent chapters.

Under employer- and government-sponsored health insurance plans, the employer or government agency negotiates a contract with an insurance company and pays all or part of the premium needed to maintain the contract. The insurance contract describes the individuals included in the contract, the medical services covered by the contract, and the amount of money the physician or hospital receives for providing the services. When an individual receives a covered

TABLE 3–1

Government-Sponsored Health Care Programs	
Term	**Definition**
CHAMPVA	Federal health insurance program for spouses and dependents of veterans with service-connected disabilities or of veterans who died because of such disabilities
Medicaid	Combined federal/state health insurance program that covers people who meet specific financial need requirements; also called Medical Assistance Program
Medicare	Federal health insurance program for people aged 65 or older and retired on Social Security, railroad retirees, federal government retirees, individuals legally disabled for 24 months, and persons with end-stage renal disease (kidney failure)
TRICARE (CHAMPUS)	Civilian Health and Medical Program of the Uniformed Services; federal health insurance program for spouses and dependents of active-duty uniformed personnel and personnel who have died while on active duty and for retired personnel, including their spouses and dependents
Workers' Compensation	Health insurance program that requires employers to cover medical expenses and loss of wages for workers who develop job-related health problems; mandated by federal and state governments

Figure 3–2 Indirect Pay

service, the insurance company reimburses the physician or hospital. This is known as indirect or third-party payer.

Payment for medical services is often negotiated between the employer or government agency, the insurance company, and the physician or health care provider with the patient in the role of bystander. Figure 3–2 illustrates this point.

Employer- and government-sponsored health insurance plans remove the individual from the direct responsibility of either purchasing an individual policy or paying the full cost for health care services.

REINFORCEMENT EXERCISES 3–1

Provide a short answer for each statement.

1. List the similarities between health insurance and other types of insurance.

_____

_____

_____

continued on the next page

continued from the previous page

Provide the correct term for each insurance-related definition.

1. Fee paid to maintain the insurance contract _____

2. Document that describes the conditions of the insurance contract _____

3. Provides money to cover all or a portion of the cost of health care services _____

Write the correct term after each definition:

direct pay
indirect pay
individual policy
prepaid health plan

1. Forerunners of current health maintenance organizations.

_____

2. Patient pays for care.

_____

3. Self-provided health insurance.

_____

4. Another term for third-party payer.

_____

Briefly describe each phrase.

1. Employer-sponsored health insurance plan

_____

2. Government-sponsored health care program

_____

MANAGED CARE

Managed care is broadly defined as any method of organizing health care providers that gives people access to high-quality, cost-effective health care. Managed care can be traced to the early 1900s, when large industries—such as railroad, lumber, and mining—established prepaid medical plans to serve employee health care needs.

One of the first nonindustrial prepaid programs was the rural farmers' cooperative health plan established in 1929 by Michael Shadid. He sold shares for $50 each to build a new hospital, and each shareholder was entitled to receive discounted medical care. In addition, each member of the family paid annual dues to cover the cost of medical care, surgery, and house calls. The health plan grew, and in 1934, the cooperative's medical staff was partially supported by 600 family memberships.

In the 1930s and 1940s, a number of prepaid group plans were formed that served a broader population and were supported by the local business community. The plans prospered, even though they often faced opposition from the majority of physicians. These predecessors of today's HMO models included:

- Group Health Association in Washington, D.C. (1937)
- Kaiser Permanente Medical Care Program in California (1942)
- Group Health Cooperative of Puget Sound (1947)
- Health Insurance Plan of Greater New York (1947)
- Group Health Plan of Minneapolis (1957)

In these early prepaid group plans, physicians shared the risk of financing health care. Physicians took the chance that they could treat their patients within budgeted costs. If a patient's treatment exceeded the budget, the physician absorbed the extra costs.

Early prepaid group plans also reduced the incentive to hospitalize patients. Because a single premium covered inpatient and outpatient care, physicians treated patients on an outpatient basis when appropriate and avoided unnecessary and expensive hospitalizations.

During the 1970s, health maintenance organizations (HMOs) were the predominant type of managed care plan. An HMO is a prepaid group practice that can be sponsored and operated by the government, insurance companies, consumer groups, employers, labor unions, physicians, or hospitals. An HMO provides a specific range of inpatient and ambulatory health care services to its members. In 1973, President Richard Nixon signed the HMO Act, which made it easier to set up and operate an HMO. The HMO Act of 1973 attempted to support the development of HMOs and to ensure some degree of quality care.

During the 1980s, managed care programs were a small segment of the health insurance industry. In the 1990s, managed care became a dominant player, and today, industry estimates indicate that managed care programs handle approximately 90% of all medical bills.

The primary objective of managed health care programs is to control health care costs. Managed care programs try to achieve this goal by:

- Obtaining reduced fees for services provided to members of the managed care program
- Controlling patient access to specialized care
- Eliminating unnecessary services
- Integrating health care delivery and payment systems through prepaid fees
- Establishing fixed rates for provider (and hospital) services

Employers and patients usually benefit most from managed health care. Employers benefit because employee health insurance costs are less with managed care plans than with fee-for-service plans. Patients benefit because insurance co-payments are generally lower for managed care plans than for traditional health insurance plans. In addition, most managed care plans promote health education and preventive health care practices, such as well-child visits, regular physical exams, smoking cessation programs, and diabetes management classes. The education and prevention approach is intended to increase quality of life and lessen the demand for more expensive health-related services.

The disadvantages of managed care lie primarily in the area of choice. Choice is controlled by financial considerations because most managed care plans will only pay for services rendered by providers who are part of or contract with the plan. In addition to financial constraints, most managed care plans do not allow self-referral to specialists. If an individual wants to see a specialist, the family physician or internist must generate a referral. Because of these limitations, some patients believe they have little control over their treatment options. It is important to note that an individual does have the option of seeing any provider, as long as the individual is able and willing to pay for the services.

In today's health care environment, all prepaid health plans are called managed care organizations (MCOs) or managed care systems. This text uses *managed care organization* as the generic term for prepaid health plans.

 ## MANAGED CARE ORGANIZATIONS

MCOs are categorized by five models:

1. Health maintenance organization (HMO)
2. Preferred provider organization (PPO)
3. Exclusive provider organization (EPO)
4. Integrated delivery system (IDS)
5. Point-of-service plan (POS)

In the past, distinguishing one type of MCO from another was fairly easy. HMOs, PPOs, and traditional fee-for-service plans were distinct and mutually exclusive. Although these distinctions have become somewhat blurred, with each type of organization attempting to incorporate the best features of the others, differences do exist.

Providers who participate in or who are part of an MCO are reimbursed for services rendered to members of the managed care plan. There are four basic types of provider reimbursement: salaried, capitation, fee-for-service, and negotiated or discounted fee. Table 3–2 describes these reimbursement methods.

In all types of MCO models, the member pays a premium to the MCO and in return is eligible to receive services from providers who participate in the program. The premium may be paid by the individual, an employer, or a government agency.

TABLE 3–2

Provider Reimbursement Methods	
Method	Description
Salaried	Providers, including physicians, are employed by the MCO; benefits include malpractice insurance, life insurance, a retirement plan, and incentives for increased productivity
Capitation	Applies primarily to physician providers, who receive a set fee per month per enrolled member, regardless of the number of patient visits or frequency of services provided
Fee-for-service	Providers are reimbursed for each individual service
Negotiated or discounted fee	Similar to fee-for-service, except that providers agree to treat members (enrollees) of a managed care plan for a reduced fee

Health Maintenance Organization Models

There are four general types of HMO model: the staff model, the independent practice association (IPA), the group model, and the network model.

Staff Model

In a staff model HMO, the HMO operates and staffs the facility or facilities where members receive treatment. All premiums and other revenues accrue to the HMO. Physicians and other providers receive a salary and other incentives, which may include profit sharing. In addition to comprehensive medical coverage, staff model HMOs frequently offer preventive care and patient education programs to their members.

Independent Practice Association (IPA)

An independent practice association (IPA) is an HMO that contracts directly with physicians who continue to practice in their private offices. IPA physicians are compensated by various reimbursement methods, including capitation, fee-for-service, and discounted fee-for-service. Refer to Table 3–2 for a description of these reimbursement methods. The IPA also contracts with other providers, such as hospitals and laboratories, and pays them on a fee-for-service basis.

Unlike staff model HMOs, IPAs do not have the costs associated with maintaining a facility. Because IPAs usually have a large physician network, they have less control over physicians' practice patterns. However, IPA members have a greater choice of primary care physicians.

Group Model

A group model HMO establishes contracts with physicians who are organized as a partnership, professional corporation, or other association. The HMO reimburses the physician group for contracted services. The medical group is responsible for compensating its physician members and contracting with hospitals for patient care.

Network Model

A network model HMO contracts with more than one physician group, and it may contract with single- and multispecialty groups. Any number of group practices, IPAs, and staff models can be joined together by a management HMO to form a network model HMO. The different groups are coordinated to allow patients to use any physician within the network. Each physician works out of his or her own office and may provide care for individuals who are not part of the HMO.

Preferred Provider Organization (PPO)

A preferred provider organization (PPO) is an MCO that contracts with a group of providers, who are called preferred providers, to offer services to the MCO's members. The preferred providers are paid a maximum allowable fee, which is the most a PPO will pay the physician or other health care provider for a given service; a discounted fee-for-service; or a capitation fee. Providers are willing to accept a reduced payment in return for a high patient volume.

The PPO encourages members to seek services from the preferred providers by eliminating or reducing the member's co-payment. If a member elects to receive services from a nonparticipating provider, the member must pay a higher co-payment. PPOs have grown in popularity because members are allowed to choose a provider.

Exclusive Provider Organization (EPO)

An exclusive provider organization (EPO) is similar to a PPO in that the MCO contracts with health care providers to obtain services for members. However, EPOs restrict members to the participating providers for all health care services. If an EPO member receives services from a non-EPO provider, the member is responsible for paying the bill. Employers whose primary objective is to reduce health care benefit costs usually select an EPO managed care system. Employees are more likely to accept the restrictions of an EPO because the employer is paying for the health care benefit at little or no cost to the employee.

Integrated Delivery System

An integrated delivery system (IDS) is an MCO that brings together physicians, physician groups, hospitals, HMOs, PPOs, insurance companies, management services, and employers to integrate all aspects of patient care into one comprehensive system. In addition to basic health care services, the system may include physician services, hospitalization, dental care, vision care, prescription drugs, billing services, and workers' compensation.

Point-of-Service Plan (POS)

A point-of-service plan (POS) is an MCO, usually an HMO or a PPO, that gives members a choice to receive services from providers outside of the MCO. Under a POS, members can self-refer to a specialist or other provider. As with other MCOs, members who receive service from providers outside of the plan have higher out-of-pocket expenses.

REINFORCEMENT EXERCISES 3–2

Fill in the blank.

1. The primary objective of _____ is to control health care costs.

2. A(n) _____ is a prepaid group practice.

3. _____ is a generic term for prepaid health plans.

4. The _____ attempted to support the development of HMOs and ensure quality care.

5. The main disadvantage of managed care is in the area of _____.

6. Most managed care plans do not allow _____ to specialists.

continued on the next page

continued from the previous page

Briefly describe or define the listed HMOs.

1. group model

_____

2. independent practice association

_____

3. network model

_____

4. staff model

_____

HEALTH INSURANCE TERMINOLOGY

Like any other specialized industry, the health insurance industry has a unique vocabulary. Establishing a basic understanding of the more commonly used health insurance and billing terms and phrases is essential for developing a successful career in this dynamic field. Commonly used terms and phrases are categorized as health insurance policy terms and health care provider terms.

Health Insurance Policy Terms

A health insurance policy is a legal contract between an individual or a group of individuals and a company or government program that describes how the medical bills of the individual or group will be paid. As a legal document, a health insurance policy contains terms that are unique to this type of document. The health insurance policy affects the individual or group who purchases the policy, the company or governmental agency that sells or provides health insurance policies, and physicians and other providers who receive insurance payments.

Health insurance policy terms are organized and described as they apply to insurance policy purchasers, insurance companies, payment, and the insurance policy itself. Physician- and provider-related terms are discussed later in this chapter.

Terms for Insurance Policy Purchasers and Insurance Companies

In the retail/wholesale industry, individuals or groups who purchase something may be called buyers, customers, owners, or clients. The health care industry also has a variety of terms associated with those who purchase health insurance policies. These terms include designations for the actual purchaser of the health insurance policy—the policyholder—and designations for individuals who are allowed to use the insurance policy, such as dependents. Table 3–3 lists the health insurance policy terms associated with the purchase, ownership, and use of the policy.

TABLE 3-3

Terms Associated with the Purchase, Ownership, and Use of a Health Insurance Policy	
Term	Definition
Applicant	Individual applying for health insurance
Dependent	Person(s) financially supported by the insured (i.e., spouse, children, and others as described in the policy)
Group contract	Health insurance policy purchased by an organization or corporation that covers a defined group of individuals and eligible dependents (e.g., the employees of an organization/corporation or members of a union or professional association)
Individual contract	Health insurance purchased by an individual; usually includes dependents
Insured	Person or organization that purchases the health insurance and is protected against financial loss caused by illness
Member, policyholder, recipient, subscriber	Other terms for *insured*
Personal contract	Another name for *individual contract*

The insurance company or government program that sells or provides health insurance policies is also described by a variety of terms. The terms are listed and defined in Table 3–4. Note that the first three terms are used interchangeably.

TABLE 3-4

Health Insurance Company Terms	
Term	Definition
Insurance carrier	Insurance company that sells the health insurance policy and administers the terms of the policy
Insurance company	Organization that sells health insurance policies; also known as *insurance carrier* or *insurer*
Insurer	Another term for *insurance carrier*
Private insurance carrier	Nongovernmental insurance company (e.g., Aetna Insurance, Metropolitan Insurance, and Wausau Insurance); also known as a *commercial insurance carrier*
Third-party payer	Individual or corporation that pays all or part of a patient's medical bills; the insurance company/carrier

REINFORCEMENT EXERCISES 3–3

Provide a short answer for each statement or question.

1. Briefly describe the term "insured."

    _____

    _____

    _____

2. List three additional terms for "insured."

    _____

    _____

    _____

3. What is a dependent?

    _____

    _____

    _____

4. Briefly describe the term "insurance carrier."

    _____

    _____

    _____

5. List two additional terms for insurance carrier.

    _____

    _____

    _____

6. Aetna Insurance is an example of what type of insurance carrier?

    _____

    _____

    _____

Terms Related to the Policy

Health insurance policy terms include general terms such as premium (the fee paid to the insurance company for the health insurance policy) and terms related to coverage, which identifies the medical conditions that may or may not be included in the insurance policy. Coverage terms range from straightforward exclusions—conditions not covered by the policy—to pre-existing conditions, which are vaguely identified as problems the individual had before the insurance policy was in effect.

Every insurance policy has unique clauses and conditions defined in the policy, but some terms are commonly used in most insurance policy documents. General health insurance policy terms are described in Table 3–5. Terms related to coverage are listed in Table 3–6.

TABLE 3–5

Health Insurance Policy General Terms	
Term	**Definition**
Premium	Fee paid to the insurance company to keep the health insurance policy active; paid monthly, quarterly, or annually by the insured (individual) or group
Grace period	Number of days allowed between the premium due date and cancellation of health insurance coverage; usually 10 to 30 days
Guaranteed renewable	Insurance company must renew the health insurance policy as long as the premiums are paid; renewal may be limited by age or may be for life
Conditionally renewable	Insurance company may refuse to renew the health insurance policy at the end of a payment period; reasons stated in the policy often include age or employment status
Optionally renewable policy	Insurance company may or may not renew the health insurance policy on a specified date; may increase rates and decrease coverage
Cancelable policy	Insurance company may cancel the health insurance policy at any time for any reason
Noncancelable policy	Insurance company must renew the health insurance policy; the policy may have age-related limitations

TABLE 3–6

Health Insurance Coverage Terms	
Term	**Definition**
Benefit	Amount paid by the insurance company for covered medical expenses; either a percentage of the charge or a specific dollar amount; may be paid to the insured or to the health care provider
Hospital benefit	Amount paid by the insurance company for hospital expenses; either a percentage of the charge or a specific dollar amount; may be paid to the insured or to the hospital
Surgical benefit	Amount paid by the insurance company for expenses related to a surgical procedure; either a percentage of the charge or a specific dollar amount; may be paid to the insured or to the health care provider

continued on the next page

continued from the previous page

Major medical benefit	A fixed amount of money available for the lifetime of the insured and any dependent; pays for unusually large medical expenses resulting from continued illness or serious injury
Extended care benefit	Amount paid by the insurance company for nursing facility or long-term care expenses
Exclusions	Situations that are not covered by a health insurance policy; examples may include self-inflicted injury, work-related injury, and injuries suffered during military service; expenses arising from exclusions are not paid by the insurance company
Pre-existing conditions	Health conditions that were treated or existed before the individual was covered by the health insurance policy; expenses arising from pre-existing conditions are not usually paid by the insurance company
Waiting period	Period of time before specified illnesses or accidents are covered by the insurance policy; expenses arising from illnesses or accidents during the waiting period are not paid by the insurance company until the waiting period has expired; also known as an *elimination period*
Waiver	An attachment to the insurance policy that excludes conditions that would otherwise be covered by the insurance policy; expenses arising from conditions identified in a waiver are not paid by the insurance company

Exclusion, pre-existing condition, and waiver describe conditions not covered by the insurance policy. Each term applies to specific circumstances.

Exclusions are part of most health insurance policies and address conditions that are often covered by other types of insurance. Because work-related injuries are covered by workers' compensation insurance and military-service-related injuries are often covered by veterans' health insurance, most insurance companies exclude those injuries from coverage.

Pre-existing conditions are specific to the insured and are not usually listed in the insurance policy. The policy contains general language that indicates noncoverage of pre-existing conditions.

EXAMPLE

MaryAnn is a new employee of Erika Electric Company and is eligible for health insurance. Before (and since) joining the company, she has been treated for bleeding ulcers. Erika Electric's health insurance carrier may, under the pre-existing condition clause, deny coverage for treatment MaryAnn receives for her bleeding ulcer. Some insurance policies allow the pre-existing condition to be covered if the condition does not recur for a certain amount of time, such as one year.

A waiver (sometimes called a rider) is a specific attachment or addition to the health insurance policy that excludes covered conditions. The waiver may apply to a specific individual or specific group that is part of the insurance plan. Waivers are often used to protect the insurance company from paying out large claims.

EXAMPLE

Rodney is purchasing health insurance, and he has a strong family history of colon cancer. His current rectal exams are normal. The insurance agent tells Rodney that a waiver excluding coverage for colon cancer treatment lowers the monthly premiums.

REINFORCEMENT EXERCISES 3–4

Provide a short answer for each item.

1. The fee paid to keep the health insurance policy active.

_____

_____

2. The amount paid by the insurance company for a covered medical expense.

_____

_____

3. An attachment to the insurance policy that excludes conditions otherwise covered by the policy.

_____

_____

_____

4. Conditions not covered by the insurance policy.

_____

_____

5. Briefly describe the difference between grace period and waiting period.

_____

_____

_____

6. Define the phrase "major medical benefit."

_____

_____

_____

Terms Related to Payment

Health insurance policy terms associated with paying the medical bills are listed and defined in Table 3–7.

The phrase assignment of benefits identifies the individual or agency that actually receives insurance payment.

> **EXAMPLE**
>
> Juanita's physician's office submits insurance claims for the patients. The insurance clerk asks Juanita to sign an assignment of benefits authorization form. The clerk explains that by signing the authorization, Juanita's insurance company will send the insurance payment directly to the physician's office.

Juanita does not have to assign the insurance benefit to the physician. The insurance company will send the payment to Juanita unless she has assigned the benefit to the physician.

TABLE 3–7

Health Insurance Payment Terms	
Term	Definition
Assignment of benefits	Permission granted by the insured that allows the insurance company to send payments directly to the physician, health care provider, hospital, or nursing facility
Claim	Request for payment of a covered medical expense; sent to the insurance company; may be submitted by the insured or by the health care provider
Time limit	Number of days allowed to submit a claim
Deductible	Specified amount of money that the insured must pay for covered medical expenses before the insurance policy begins to pay; usually an annual amount per individual or family
Coordination of benefits	Health insurance policy clause that applies to an individual covered by more than one medical insurance policy; requires that the combined benefits paid by the policies do not exceed 100% of the medical expenses
Primary payer	Term used to describe which health insurance policy will pay first when an individual is covered by more than one health insurance policy
Secondary payer	Term used to describe which health insurance policy will pay second when an individual is covered by more than one health insurance policy
Preauthorization	Determination of whether a specific service or treatment is medically necessary and covered by the insurance policy; required by many insurance companies
Precertification	Determination of whether a specific treatment or service is covered by the insurance policy; required by many insurance companies
Predetermination	Determination of the potential dollar amount the insurance company will pay for a specific treatment or service
Reimbursement	Receiving payment for services rendered

Whether benefits are assigned to the provider or retained by the patient, the patient or his or her legal representative is responsible for ensuring that the medical bill is paid. Exceptions include prepaid health plans, such as those provided by HMOs, and capitation reimbursement, whereby the insurance company automatically sends the insurance payment directly to the provider.

The phrase accept assignment indicates that a physician or provider is willing to accept the amount the insurance company pays for a service *as payment in full*. If there is a difference between the insurance company's payment and the provider's charge, the patient does not have to pay that difference.

EXAMPLE

Medical Health Insurance, Inc., pays $45 for brief office visits for services such as follow-up care for a non-life-threatening condition (e.g., psoriasis). Sara has health insurance through this company, and her dermatologist charges $50 for a brief office visit. The dermatologist accepts the insurance company's benefit for brief office visits. When Sara assigns the insurance benefit to the dermatologist, the $45 is accepted as payment in full.

The birthday rule determines the primary payer when the patient is a child living with both parents and each parent carries health insurance. Under the birthday rule, the primary payer is the parent whose birth month and date comes earlier in a calendar year. Only the month and date are considered under the birthday rule. Therefore, a parent born in February takes precedence over a parent born in December. If both birthdays fall in the same month, the birth date is used to determine which insurance company is the primary payer. Therefore, a February 1st birth date takes precedence over a February 5th birth date. If both birthdays fall on exactly the same month and date, the policy that has been in effect the longest is considered primary.

Demographics show that most husbands are older than their wives. Therefore, the birth year is disregarded in order to prevent a disproportionate number of primary payer designations being assigned to men's insurance policies.

Coordination of benefits (COB) applies when the individual is covered by more than one insurance policy. Billing decisions are made so the total amount of money paid by all insurance companies does not exceed the total bill. Figure 3–3 illustrates COB.

EXAMPLE

Lisa has health insurance with her employer and is also covered by her husband's health plan. Both policies pay 80% of the bill. Lisa currently has a medical bill for $100. Submission of claims must be coordinated between Lisa's policy and her husband's policy so that only one company pays the 80%. If Lisa submitted the same bill to both companies and received 80% from each one, she would receive more money than the total bill.

Co-payment, also called co-pay, is defined as the dollar or percentage amount that the patient must pay the provider for each visit. The majority of insurance policies, including most issued by government-sponsored programs and HMOs, require some type of patient co-payment. If possible, it is good practice to collect the co-payment at the time of service.

WITH COORDINATION OF BENEFITS	WITHOUT COORDINATION OF BENEFITS
STATEMENT	STATEMENT
Balance Due...................$100.00	Balance Due...............................$100.00
Lisa's Insurance	Lisa's Insurance
80% of $100................$ 80.00	80% of $100............................$ 80.00
Balance Due...................$ 20.00	
Husband's Insurance	Husband's Insurance
100% of balance...........$ 20.00	80% of $100............................$ 80.00
TOTAL RECEIVED..............$100.00	TOTAL RECEIVED $160.00

Figure 3–3 Coordination of Benefits

A fixed dollar amount co-payment is exactly that: The patient must pay a fixed amount for each episode of service or office visit.

EXAMPLE

Victoria's private insurance company requires a $20 co-payment for every office visit. Her last appointment included four separate lab tests, and the total bill was $200. The insurance billing specialist collected the $20 co-payment from Victoria and then billed the remaining $180 to the insurance company.

With percentage co-payments, the patient pays a fixed percentage of the total bill.

EXAMPLE

Louis has health insurance with 80/20 coverage: The insurance company pays 80% of the bill, and Louis is responsible for the other 20%. Louis completes his annual visit, which costs $100. He stops at the insurance billing desk and assigns the benefit to the physician. The insurance billing specialist tells Louis that the insurance company pays $80 for the visit, and Louis is responsible for the remaining $20.

Other common percentage co-payments include 90/10—which means that the insurance company pays 90% and the patient pays 10%—and 50/50, with the insurance company and the patient paying an equal share of the medical bill.

Preauthorization, precertification, and predetermination are activities that help determine if the insurance company will pay the bill. Preauthorization determines the medical necessity of the treatment.

EXAMPLE

Ling's mother and sister died from ovarian cancer. She wants to have an oophorectomy (removal of the ovaries) as a preventive measure for ovarian cancer. Ling does not know if her health insurance covers oophorectomy as a preventive procedure. Ling or the billing specialist contacts the insurance company representative to find out if the procedure qualifies as an authorized medical necessity.

Precertification identifies whether a treatment is covered by an insurance policy.

EXAMPLE

Helen wants to have the bags under her eyes removed. She believes that this problem makes her look older and prevents career advancement. Helen meets with a surgeon who assures her that surgery will correct the problem. Helen or the billing specialist contacts the insurance company to verify whether the surgery is covered.

Many insurance companies require preauthorization or precertification. The term "preauthorization" is sometimes used to include the determination of medical necessity and insurance coverage for a specified treatment.

Predetermination, a function of the billing department, provides an estimated insurance payment for a given treatment. The insured is responsible for paying the balance.

EXAMPLE

Terrell is scheduled for a total hip replacement that costs about $8000. Prior to surgery, the billing specialist contacts the insurance company and learns that Terrell's insurance covers 90% ($7200) of the bill. Terrell is informed that he is responsible for the $800 balance.

REINFORCEMENT EXERCISES 3–5

Provide a short answer for each statement or question.

1. A request for payment of a covered expense is a(n) _____.

2. Determination of medical necessity and insurance coverage of a particular treatment is known as _____.

3. Determination of insurance policy coverage is called _____.

4. Determination of the potential dollar amount that will be paid for a particular treatment is known as _____.

5. Receiving payment for services rendered is called _____.

6. What is the difference between assignment of benefits and accepting assignment?

_____

_____

_____

continued on the next page

continued from the previous page

7. What is the difference between coordination of benefits and co-payment?

_____

_____

_____

8. What is the birthday rule? Give an example.

_____

_____

_____

Health Care Provider Terms

At one time, the physician was the primary (if not sole) provider of medical care to individuals, who were always called patients. Today, other professionals provide many health services to individuals, who are called patients, clients, residents, or recipients. Nurse practitioners, nurse midwives, physician assistants, dietitians, physical therapists, medical assistants, and pharmacists are just a few examples of other health care professionals now providing care or services. The phrase health care provider is the generic term for anyone who provides health or medical services to persons who need such services.

The health insurance industry uses a variety of titles and terms that refer to the health care provider. These terms range from the obvious "physician" and "surgeon" to the vague phrase service provider, which can be interpreted as anyone from an occupational therapist to a nursing facility aide. Health insurance may pay for services rendered by other health care professionals. Table 3–8 describes insurance policy terms that refer to health care providers. Terms and phrases that require additional explanation and examples are discussed in the following text.

TABLE 3–8

Health Insurance Payment Terms	
Term	Definition
Admitting physician	Physician who arranges the patient's hospital admission; may not be responsible for patient's care during the hospital stay
Attending physician	Physician responsible for the patient's care during the hospital stay
Case manager	Health care professional who coordinates the care of patients with long-term problems
Group practice	Three or more health care providers who share equipment, supplies, and personnel; usually refers to a physician group practice

continued on the next page

continued from the previous page

Health Insurance Payment Terms

Term	Definition
Health care specialist	Health care provider other than the primary care physician; may refer to physician specialist or others such as an optometrist, a podiatrist, or a chiropractor
In-network provider	A health care professional who provides services to individuals covered by a particular health insurance policy and who accepts the insurance company's approved fee for each service; also known as a participating provider
Limited license practitioner	Nonphysician health care professional licensed to perform specific services; examples include clinical social workers, clinical psychologists, and psychologists
Nonparticipating provider	A health care professional who does not contract with insurance companies and does not accept an insurance company's approved fee for services; also known as an out-of-network provider
Out-of-network provider	Another term for nonparticipating provider
Participating provider	Another term for in-network provider
Physician	Health care professional licensed to practice as a medical doctor (MD) or an osteopathic doctor (DO)
Physician specialist	Physician who provides health care services related to a specialty or subspecialty, such as cardiology, oncology/hematology, endocrinology, or gastroenterology
Physician extender	Nonphysician health care professional licensed by the state to perform specific health-related activities; includes physician assistants, nurse anesthetists, nurse practitioners, and nurse midwives
Primary care manager	TRICARE term for primary care physician
Primary care physician	Physician responsible for providing all routine health care and determining the need for referrals to physician specialists; usually includes family practice, internal medicine, and pediatric physicians
Referring physician	Physician who arranges for the patient to see another physician or health care provider

The insurance billing specialist must give careful attention to the terms "admitting physician" and "attending physician." The admitting physician arranges for the patient's admission to the hospital. The admitting physician is entitled to receive reimbursement for the services provided to the patient as part of the admission process. When the admitting physician *does not* treat the patient throughout the hospital stay, the admitting physician is not entitled to additional reimbursement.

The attending physician is the physician responsible for the patient's care during the hospital stay. If the attending physician *did not* provide services during the admission process, the attending physician should not bill for admission services.

REINFORCEMENT EXERCISES 3–6

Briefly define each term.

1. Case manager

_____

_____

_____

2. Health care specialist

_____

_____

_____

3. Primary care manager

_____

_____

_____

4. Primary care physician

_____

_____

_____

5. Admitting physician

_____

_____

_____

6. Attending physician

_____

_____

_____

7. Describe the difference between a participating provider and a nonparticipating provider.

_____

_____

_____

PAYING THE BILL WITH HEALTH INSURANCE

As previously defined, a health insurance policy is a contract that provides money to cover all or a portion of the cost of medically necessary care. The contract may be between the employer and the insurance company, the government program and the insurance company, or the individual and the insurance company. In order for a medical bill to be paid, someone must notify the insurance company that services have been rendered.

During the early days of health insurance, physicians and hospitals submitted the claims to the insurance company. Health care providers viewed this as a service to the patient and as a way to ensure that the medical bill would be paid. The patient would sign the appropriate document that allowed the insurance company to pay the provider. As previously defined, this is called assignment of benefits.

As more insurance companies entered the health insurance market and insurance policies became more complex, many health care providers stopped submitting claims for the patient. Physicians saw this as a way to reduce administrative costs. As a result, the number of unpaid medical bills increased. Patients could pay all or part of the medical bill at the time of service, submit the claim, receive payment from the insurance company, and keep the money.

In the late 1980s, in order to ensure reimbursement for services rendered, physicians and other health care providers resumed submitting claims to health insurance companies. Also, federal regulations mandated that providers must file claims for Medicare recipients. Receiving payment from someone other than the patient—that is, the insurance company—is called third-party reimbursement or third-party payment. Third-party reimbursement methods include fee-for-service, episode of care, and capitation.

Fee-for-Service

Fee-for-service, charging a price or fee for each individual service, is the traditional reimbursement method. Under this method, every service is itemized and charged to the patient's account (Figure 3–4).

> EXAMPLE
>
> During an annual physical examination, the physician also completes a Pap smear, removes the sutures from a laceration, and removes a wart from the patient's hand. The patient is charged for each individual service, even though the services were completed during one office visit.

Episode-of-Care Reimbursement

Episode-of-care reimbursement is charging a lump sum for all services associated with a particular problem, illness, condition, or procedure. Surgical care is often associated with the episode-of-care reimbursement method. A surgical episode-of-care fee would include preoperative visits, the actual surgery, and routine postoperative care. Obstetrical services are another example of this type of reimbursement method. An obstetrical episode-of-care fee would cover routine prenatal visits, physician attendance at the delivery, and routine postnatal care of the mother. Figure 3–5 illustrates episode-of-care reimbursement.

Services covered by an episode-of-care fee must be clearly identified to the patient. Additional or unexpected services or services related to complications are usually billed on a fee-for-service basis.

Figure 3–4 Illustration of Fee-for-Service Reimbursement Method

Figure 3–5 Episode of Care Reimbursement Method

Capitation

Fee-for-service and episode-of-care reimbursement methods depend on the number of services, individual or grouped, provided to the patient. Capitation is a reimbursement method that depends on the number of individuals covered by the health insurance contract.

Under capitation, the health care provider receives a fixed amount, or fee, on a per capita (per person) basis. The fee is paid at predetermined intervals, such as monthly, quarterly, semiannually, or annually. The number of services provided does not affect the fee. A simple instance of capitation reimbursement is described in the following example.

EXAMPLE

Erika Electric Company has 100 employees, and each employee has two dependents. The company provides health insurance for all 300 employees and dependents. Family Practice, Inc., a respected medical practice, has a reputation for providing thorough annual physicals to all age groups. Erika Electric provides full coverage for annual physical examinations as part of the company's wellness program. In order to manage the cost of this benefit, the company is interested in paying for the annual physical examinations on a per-person basis.

Representatives of Erika Electric Company or the company's insurance carrier and Family Practice, Inc., meet and establish a formal agreement. The agreement states that Family Practice, Inc. will provide annual physical examinations for the 300 employees and dependents of Erika Electric. Erika Electric will reimburse Family Practice, Inc. at the rate of $100 per employee and dependent for a total of $30,000, to be paid in semiannual installments.

Under the capitation reimbursement method, health care providers are reimbursed for the number of individuals in the contract rather than by the number of services provided. Therefore, if only 150 Erika Electric employees and dependents actually have an annual physical examination, Family Practice, Inc. still receives the full $30,000.

Capitation is commonly associated with prepaid health insurance plans, such as those offered by HMOs. However, any organization that provides health insurance can negotiate a capitation reimbursement method. This type of reimbursement may be used to cover selected services, as described in the example, or it may be expanded so that health care providers receive a fixed fee for providing comprehensive services.

REINFORCEMENT EXERCISES 3–7

Provide a short answer for each item.

1. What is third-party reimbursement?

_____

_____

_____

2. Describe the traditional reimbursement method.

_____

_____

_____

continued on the next page

continued from the previous page

3. Briefly define and provide one example of episode-of-care reimbursement.

_____

_____

_____

4. Describe capitation as a reimbursement method.

_____

_____

_____

 ## ABBREVIATIONS

Table 3–9 lists the abbreviations presented in this chapter.

TABLE 3–9

Abbreviations and Meanings	
Abbreviation	Meaning
COB	coordination of benefits
EPO	exclusive provider organization
HMO	health maintenance organization
IDS	integrated delivery system
IPA	independent practice association
MCO	managed care organization
POS	point-of-service plan
PPO	preferred provider organization

SUMMARY

This chapter provided a brief overview of the health insurance industry and some historical factors that influenced its growth. Terms associated with health insurance were presented and organized as health insurance policy terms and health care provider terms. Direct pay, indirect pay, and third-party reimbursement methods were defined and discussed.

Managed care organizations (MCOs) include all managed health care models and can be found in every state. The primary goal of all MCOs is to provide quality health care services while containing health care costs. Managed care affects all segments of the health care industry. Providers are under considerable pressure to offer services for reduced or negotiated fees, and consumers are encouraged to choose providers who participate in managed care plans.

REVIEW EXERCISES

Matching

Match the terms in Column A with the definitions in Column B.

Column A	Column B	
a. benefit	1. noncovered situation	_____
b. claim	2. payment for services	_____
c. coverage	3. policyholder	_____
d. dependent	4. amount paid by insurance company	_____
e. direct pay	5. request for payment	_____
f. exclusion	6. an attachment to the policy	_____
g. insured	7. cost of insurance policy	_____
h. premium	8. person supported by the insured	_____
i. reimbursement	9. patient pays the bill	_____
j. waiver	10. included and excluded conditions	_____

Fill in the Blank

Write the correct insurance term or phrase for each statement.

1. An HMO that contracts with physicians who continue to practice in their private offices is called a(n) _____.

2. A(n) _____ encourages members to receive services from participating providers by reducing the members' co-payment amount.

3. The most restrictive type of an MCO is a(n) _____.

4. An HMO that owns, operates, and hires personnel for its health care facilities is called a(n) _____.

5. The fee established by a PPO is called the _____.

6. Another term for indirect pay is _____.

7. The _____ is the number of days allowed between the premium due date and cancellation of the health insurance policy.

8. A _____ is the time that must pass before certain illnesses or accidents are covered by the health insurance policy.

9. The number of days allowed for submitting a claim is called the _____.

10. The _____ is responsible for providing all routine health care and determining the need for referrals to physician specialists.

Definitions

Briefly define the listed health insurance terms.

1. Accepts assignment

_____

_____

_____

2. Assignment of benefits

_____

_____

_____

3. Deductible

_____

_____

_____

4. Pre-existing condition

_____

_____

_____

5. Case manager

_____

_____

_____

6. Physician extender

_____

_____

_____

7. Group practice

_____

_____

_____

8. Co-payment

_____

_____

_____

9. Insurance carrier

_____

_____

_____

10. Birthday rule

_____

_____

_____

Identification

Identify the correct government-sponsored health care program associated with each statement: TRICARE, CHAMPVA, Medicaid, Medicare, workers' compensation.

1. Based on financial need _____

2. Job-related health problems _____

3. Covers people aged 65 and older _____

4. Uniformed personnel and dependents _____

5. Employers must provide this insurance _____

6. Uniformed services–related disabilities _____

7. Covers end-stage renal disease _____

8. Also called Medical Assistance Program _____

9. Active-duty and retired military personnel _____

10. Covers railroad retirees _____

Short Answer

1. Describe what is meant by the terms "preauthorization," "precertification," and "predetermination." How are these activities related?

_____

_____

_____

2. What is the difference between a primary payer and a secondary payer?

_____

_____

_____

3. Explain the terms "participating provider" and "nonparticipating provider." Include any alternate terms for each.

_____

_____

_____

Abbreviation Review

Write out and give a brief definition for each abbreviation.

1. IPA

_____

2. PPO

_____

3. EPO

_____

4. COB

_____

CRITICAL THINKING EXERCISES

Read each case summary and then answer the questions that follow.

Case Summary A

Towanda has health insurance through her employer. She recently visited her family physician. As she reviews her bill, she notices that each service has a separate fee. At the billing desk, Towanda signs a form that lets the insurance company pay the physician directly. She leaves the office feeling confident that the bill will be paid.

1. What type of insurance does Towanda have?

_____

_____

_____

2. Name the reimbursement method described in the case.

_____

_____

_____

3. Why can the insurance company pay the physician directly?

_____

_____

_____

Case Summary B

Roberto has just learned that his prostate must be removed. He is concerned about the cost, and his physician refers him to the billing specialist. Roberto is relieved when he learns that the preoperative office visit, surgery, and normal postoperative care are included in one fee. The billing specialist calls the insurance representative and finds out how much the insurance company will pay for Roberto's treatment. In addition, the billing specialist informs Roberto that his supplemental insurance can be billed for the remaining balance. Roberto is relieved that finances will not be a problem.

1. What type of reimbursement method is described in this case?

_____

_____

_____

2. Did the billing specialist do a predetermination for Roberto's treatment? How can you support your answer?

_____

_____

_____

3. Why does the billing specialist not submit the full claim to both of Roberto's insurance companies?

_____

_____

_____

Case Summary C

Elmer has been to his physician at least six times this year. At every visit, at least four blood tests are done, and he often has one other problem taken care of. Elmer's health insurance plan uses a reimbursement method that depends on the number of individuals covered by the insurance contract.

1. What type of reimbursement method is described in this case?

_____

_____

_____

2. Does the number of services affect the reimbursement amount?

_____

_____

_____

3. Could Elmer belong to a health maintenance organization?

_____

_____

_____

WEBSITE

Centers for Medicare and Medicaid Services: http://www.cms.hhs.gov

CHAPTER 4

International Classification of Diseases, Tenth Revision

- **Clinical Modification (ICD-10-CM)**
- **Procedure Coding System (ICD-10-PCS)**

LEARNING OBJECTIVES

Upon successful completion of this chapter, the reader should have the knowledge to:

1. Identify the organizations responsible for developing and maintaining ICD-10-CM and ICD-10-PCS.
2. Define the alphanumeric characters in ICD-10-PCS codes.
3. Follow the ICD-10-CM/PCS coding conventions for assigning diagnostic and procedure codes.
4. Explain the difference between a primary diagnosis and a principal diagnosis.
5. Discuss the significance of a principal procedure.
6. Accurately assign ICD-10-CM and ICD-10-PCS codes.

KEY TERMS

Alphabetic Index
Approach
Benign
Body system
Ca in situ
Carcinoma
Centers for Disease
  Control (CDC)
Code also
Code first
Combination code
Concurrent condition
Congenital
Cooperating Parties
*Current Procedural
  Terminology* (CPT)
dash (-)

Device
Encoder
Encounter
Essential modifier
Etiology
Excludes1
Excludes2
First-listed diagnosis
Includes
In diseases classified
  elsewhere
Instruction Manual
*International Classification
  of Diseases, Tenth
  Revision, Clinical
  Modification*
  (ICD-10-CM)

*International Classification
  of Diseases, Tenth
  Revision, Procedure
  Coding System*
  (ICD-10-PCS)
Late effect
Laterality
Main term
Malignant, primary
Malignant, secondary
Manifestations
Modality
National Center for Health
  Statistics (NCHS)
Nonessential modifier
Not elsewhere classified
  (NEC)

Not otherwise specified (NOS)
Parentheses ( )
Perinatal period
Placeholder *x*
Point dash (.-)
Present on admission (POA)
Primary diagnosis
Principal diagnosis
Principal procedure

Provider
Puerperium
Qualifier
Residual effects
Root operation
7th character extension
Secondary condition
Sections
See
See also
See condition

Sequela, sequelae
Sequencing
Slanted brackets *[ ]*
Square brackets [ ]
Subterm
Tables
Tabular List
Uncertain behavior
Unspecified behavior
Use additional code

 ## OVERVIEW

Two of the three main coding systems associated with health insurance claims processing are the *International Classification of Diseases, Tenth Revision, Clinical Modification* (ICD-10-CM) for medical diagnoses and the *International Classification of Diseases, Tenth Revision, Procedure Coding System* (ICD-10-PCS). The ICD-10-CM applies to all health care settings, and the ICD-10-PCS is used to code inpatient procedures. The third coding system is the *Current Procedural Terminology* (CPT), which applies to physician and other provider services performed in an ambulatory, office, or outpatient setting.

Accurate coding is critical to reimbursement and the avoidance of fraud and abuse charges. Insurance billing specialists need at least a basic understanding of medical coding. The purpose of this chapter is to cover ICD-10-CM in some detail and provide an overview of ICD-10-PCS. Topics presented include the following:

- Unique characteristics of ICD-10-CM's *Tabular List* and *Alphabetic Index*
- Coding conventions, such as instructional notes and the meaning of punctuation marks
- Coding guidelines from selected sections of the ICD-10-CM Official Guidelines for Coding and Reporting

To gain the most from this chapter, have the ICD-10-CM and ICD-10-PCS available as references.

 ## INTERNATIONAL CLASSIFICATION OF DISEASES, TENTH REVISION, CLINICAL MODIFICATION (ICD-10-CM)

The ICD-10-CM is the United States' adaptation of the World Health Organization's (WHO) *International Statistical Classification of Diseases and Related Health Problems, Tenth Revision* (ICD-10). ICD-10 was published between 1992 and 1994. Every country that participates in maintaining health care statistics has adopted ICD-10. In Figure 4–1, the author and Dr. Fedor Rosocha review ICD-10 codes at his clinic in Podhorod, Slovakia.

As published by the WHO, ICD-10 consists of three volumes:

- **Volume 1:** Tabular List—a list of alphanumeric codes, organized by diseases, conditions, disorders, external causes of diseases and conditions, and factors influencing health status
- **Volume 2:** Instruction Manual—a compilation of rules, guidelines, and coding conventions
- **Volume 3:** Alphabetic Index—an alphabetic index to the conditions in *Volume 1*

Figure 4–1 Reviewing ICD-10 in Podhorod, Slovakia (2004)

The National Center for Health Statistics (NCHS), a division of the Centers for Disease Control (CDC), is responsible for developing the clinical modification of ICD-10. Since 2003, NCHS has published updates of the *International Classification of Diseases, Tenth Revision, Clinical Modification* (ICD-10-CM). Information in this text is based on the 2012 ICD-10-CM Official Guidelines for Coding and Reporting. Current information about ICD-10-CM is available on the CDC website: http://www.cdc.gov/nchs/. At this CDC address, use ICD-10-CM as the search term.

The ICD-10-CM is used to classify diagnoses and reasons for visits or encounters in all health care settings. The ICD-10-CM is updated every year, and changes are effective October 1 of that year. Four organizations make up the Cooperating Parties that are responsible for maintaining and updating ICD-10-CM. The Cooperating Parties include:

- American Hospital Association (AHA)
- American Health Information Management Association (AHIMA)
- Centers for Medicare and Medicaid Services (CMS)
- National Center for Health Statistics (NCHS)

Table 4–1 describes the responsibilities of each party.

As noted in Table 4–1, the AHA publishes the *Coding Clinic for ICD-10-CM*. This valuable resource is released quarterly and is considered the official publication for ICD-10-CM. The information in the *Coding Clinic* is regarded as advice from the four Cooperating Parties. Billing specialists and medical coders in all health care settings can rely on the *Coding Clinic* for up-to-date coding advice.

ICD-10-CM and ICD-10-PCS coding products can be purchased from commercial sources. Electronic versions of the coding products, called encoders, are also available. Although each publisher may offer special editorial features, the codes are the same as those published in the official version.

TABLE 4–1

Cooperating Parties Responsibilities	
Party	Responsibilities
NCHS	Maintains and updates diagnoses in ICD-10-CM
CMS	Maintains and updates ICD-10-PCS, procedure codes
AHA	Maintains the ICD-10-CM Central Office for queries related to ICD-10-CM; publishes the *Coding Clinic for ICD-10-CM*, the official guidelines for ICD-10-CM usage
AHIMA	Provides training and certification for coding professionals; functions as an advisor to the Cooperating Parties

REINFORCEMENT EXERCISES 4–1

Spell out each abbreviation.

1. CDC

_____

2. CMS

_____

3. ICD-10-CM

_____

4. NCHS

_____

5. WHO

_____

Fill in the blank.

1. The _____ are responsible for maintaining and updating ICD-10-CM.

2. ICD-10 is published by the _____.

3. Published by _____, the *Coding Clinic for ICD-10-CM* is a valuable resource for billing specialists and medical coders.

4. The NCHS is a division of the _____, a government agency that maintains current information about ICD-10-CM.

5. _____ are electronic versions of ICD-CM-10 coding products.

ICD-10-CM COMPONENTS

The components of ICD-10-CM include the *Tabular List* and the *Alphabetic Index*. The *Alphabetic Index* is divided into three sections: the "Index to Diseases and Injuries"; the "External Cause of Injuries Index"; and the "Tables of Drugs and Chemicals."

Tabular List

The *Tabular List* consists of 21 chapters, which are listed in Table 4–2.

TABLE 4–2

ICD-10-CM Chapters with Code Ranges	
Chapter	**Title and Code Ranges**
Chapter 1	Certain Infectious and Parasitic Diseases (A00–B99)
Chapter 2	Neoplasms (C00–D49)
Chapter 3	Diseases of the Blood and Blood-Forming Organs and Certain Diseases Involving the Immune Mechanism (D50–D89)
Chapter 4	Endocrine, Nutritional, and Metabolic Diseases (E00–E89)
Chapter 5	Mental, Behavioral, and Neurodevelopmental Disorders (F01–F99)
Chapter 6	Diseases of the Nervous System (G00–G99)
Chapter 7	Diseases of the Eye and Adnexa (H00–H59)
Chapter 8	Diseases of the Ear and Mastoid Process (H60–H95)
Chapter 9	Diseases of the Circulatory System (I00–I99)
Chapter 10	Diseases of the Respiratory System (J00–J99)
Chapter 11	Diseases of the Digestive System (K00–K95)
Chapter 12	Diseases of the Skin and Subcutaneous Tissue (L00–L99)
Chapter 13	Diseases of the Musculoskeletal System and Connective Tissue (M00–M99)
Chapter 14	Diseases of the Genitourinary System (N00–N99)
Chapter 15	Pregnancy, Childbirth, and the Puerperium (O00–O9A)
Chapter 16	Certain Conditions Originating in the Perinatal Period (P00–P96)
Chapter 17	Congenital Malformations, Deformations, and Chromosomal Abnormalities (Q00–Q99)
Chapter 18	Symptoms, Signs, and Abnormal Clinical and Laboratory Findings, Not Elsewhere Classified (R00–R99)
Chapter 19	Injury, Poisoning, and Certain Other Consequences of External Causes (S00–T88)
Chapter 20	External Causes of Morbidity (V00–V99)
Chapter 21	Factors Influencing Health Status and Contact with Health Services (Z00–Z99)

O24.9   **Unspecified diabetes mellitus in pregnancy, childbirth, and the puerperium**
Use additional code for long-term (current) use of insulin (Z79.4)

    O24.91   **Unspecified diabetes mellitus in pregnancy**

        O24.911   **Unspecified diabetes mellitus in pregnancy, first trimester**

        O24.912   **Unspecified diabetes mellitus in pregnancy, second trimester**

        O24.913   **Unspecified diabetes mellitus in pregnancy, third trimester**

    O24.92   **Unspecified diabetes mellitus in childbirth**

    O24.93   **Unspecified diabetes mellitus in the puerperium**

Figure 4–2 ICD-10-CM Chapter 15 Pregnancy, Childbirth, and the Puerperium

Most of the ICD-10-CM chapter titles are self-explanatory. Chapter 15 through Chapter 21 need brief explanations. Figure 4–2 through Figure 4–8 are samples of the codes and conditions in these chapters.

Chapter 15: Pregnancy, Childbirth, and the Puerperium (Figure 4–2)

Chapter 15 codes classify conditions that affect the management of pregnancy, childbirth, and the puerperium. The puerperium is the period of time that begins at the end of the third stage of labor and continues for six weeks. Codes in this chapter cover conditions such as high-risk pregnancy, obstructed labor due to deformed pelvis, and maternal care for malpresentation of [the] fetus. Chapter 15 codes are assigned only to conditions affecting the mother, not the fetus or newborn.

Chapter 16: Certain Conditions Originating in the Perinatal Period (Figure 4–3)

Chapter 16 codes classify conditions specific to the newborn. The condition must be associated with the perinatal period, which begins before birth and lasts until the 28th day of life. Many perinatal conditions are resolved by time, treatment, or death. However, Chapter 16 codes may be

P03   **Newborn (suspected to be) affected by other complications of labor and delivery**
Code first any current condition in newborn

    P03.0   **Newborn (suspected to be) affected by breech delivery and extraction**

    P03.1   **Newborn (suspected to be) affected by other malpresentation, malposition and disproportion during labor and delivery**
Newborn (suspected to be) affected by contracted pelvis
Newborn (suspected to be) affected by conditions classifiable to O64–O66
Newborn (suspected to be) affected by persistent occipitoposterior
Newborn (suspected to be) affected by transverse lie

    P03.2   **Newborn (suspected to be) affected by forceps delivery**

    P03.3   **Newborn (suspected to be) affected by delivery by vacuum extractor [ventouse]**

Figure 4–3 ICD-10-CM Chapter 16 Certain Conditions Originating in the Perinatal Period

> **Q25** **Congenital malformations of great arteries**
>
> **Q25.0** **Patent ductus arteriosus**
> Patent ductus Botallo
> Persistent ductus arteriosus
>
> **Q25.1** **Coarctation of aorta**
> Coarctation of aorta (preductal) (postductal)
>
> **Q25.2** **Atresia of aorta**
>
> **Q25.3** **Supravalvular aortic stenosis**
>
> **Excludes1:** congenital aortic stenosis NOS (Q23.0)
> congenital aortic valve stenosis (Q23.0)

© 2014 Cengage Learning, All Rights Reserved.

Figure 4–4 ICD-10-CM Chapter 17 Congenital Malformations, Deformations, and Chromosomal Abnormalities

used throughout the life of the patient if the condition is still present. Codes from this chapter are never assigned to the maternal health record.

Chapter 17: Congenital Malformations, Deformations, and Chromosomal Abnormalities (Figure 4–4)

Chapter 17 codes classify conditions that are congenital, which means at or present since the time of birth. These codes are not for use in the maternal or fetal health record. Because congenital and chromosomal conditions often persist for the life of an individual, these codes may be assigned at any age.

Chapter 18: Symptoms, Signs, and Abnormal Clinical and Laboratory Findings, Not Elsewhere Classified (Figure 4–5)

Chapter 18 codes classify symptoms, signs, and abnormal findings that range from elevated blood glucose to vomiting. These codes are used *only* when a more specific diagnosis code cannot be assigned.

> **R78** **Findings of drugs and other substances, not normally found in blood**
> **Use additional** code to identify any retained foreign body, if applicable (Z18.-)
> **Excludes1:** mental or behavioral disorders due to psychoactive substance use (F10–F19)
>
> **R78.0** **Finding of alcohol in blood**
> **Use additional** external cause code (Y90.-), for detail regarding alcohol level.
>
> **R78.1** **Finding of opiate drug in blood**
>
> **R78.2** **Finding of cocaine in blood**
>
> **R78.3** **Finding of hallucinogen in blood**
>
> **R78.4** **Finding of other drugs of addictive potential in blood**
>
> **R78.5** **Finding of other psychotropic drug in blood**

© 2014 Cengage Learning, All Rights Reserved.

Figure 4–5 ICD-10-CM Chapter 18 Symptoms, Signs, and Abnormal Clinical and Laboratory Findings, Not Elsewhere Classified

T58 Toxic effect of carbon monoxide
Includes: asphyxiation from carbon monoxide
           toxic effect of carbon monoxide from all sources
The appropriate 7th character is to be added to each code from category T58
A   initial encounter
D   subsequent encounter
S   sequela

T58.0 Toxic effect of carbon monoxide from motor vehicle exhaust
      Toxic effect of exhaust gas from gas engine
      Toxic effect of exhaust gas from motor pump

   T58.01   Toxic effect of carbon monoxide from motor vehicle exhaust, accidental (unintentional)

   T58.02   Toxic effect of carbon monoxide from motor vehicle exhaust, intentional self-harm

   T58.03   Toxic effect of carbon monoxide from motor vehicle exhaust, assault

   T58.04   Toxic effect of carbon monoxide from motor vehicle exhaust, undetermined

Figure 4–6 ICD-10-CM Chapter 19 Injury, Poisoning, and Certain Other Consequences of External Causes

Chapter 19: Injury, Poisoning, and Certain Other Consequences of External Causes (Figure 4–6)

Chapter 19 codes classify conditions ranging from a black eye to shellfish poisoning. Burns, complications of care, stab wounds, and fractures are coded to Chapter 19. Codes from other chapters are often assigned with Chapter 19 codes.

Chapter 20: External Causes of Morbidity (Figure 4–7)

Chapter 20 codes classify environmental events and circumstances as the cause of injury and other problems. Environmental factors range from car accidents to sports-related injuries. These codes are used as secondary codes with conditions classifiable to other ICD-10-CM chapters. Chapter 20 codes are usually associated with codes from Chapter 19 Injury, Poisoning, and Certain Other Consequences of External Causes.

V03.9   Pedestrian injured in collision with car, pick-up truck or van, unspecified whether traffic or nontraffic accident

   V03.90   Pedestrian on foot injured in collision with car, pick-up truck or van, unspecified whether traffic or nontraffic accident
       Pedestrian NOS injured in collision with car, pick-up truck or van, unspecified whether traffic or nontraffic accident

   V03.91   Pedestrian on roller-skates injured in collision with car, pick-up truck or van, unspecified whether traffic or nontraffic accident

   V03.92   Pedestrian on skateboard injured in collision with car, pick-up truck or van, unspecified whether traffic or nontraffic accident

Figure 4–7 ICD-10-CM Chapter 20 External Causes of Morbidity

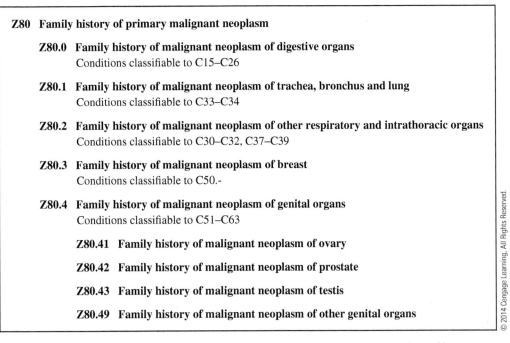

Z80 Family history of primary malignant neoplasm

  Z80.0 Family history of malignant neoplasm of digestive organs
    Conditions classifiable to C15–C26

  Z80.1 Family history of malignant neoplasm of trachea, bronchus and lung
    Conditions classifiable to C33–C34

  Z80.2 Family history of malignant neoplasm of other respiratory and intrathoracic organs
    Conditions classifiable to C30–C32, C37–C39

  Z80.3 Family history of malignant neoplasm of breast
    Conditions classifiable to C50.-

  Z80.4 Family history of malignant neoplasm of genital organs
    Conditions classifiable to C51–C63

    Z80.41 Family history of malignant neoplasm of ovary

    Z80.42 Family history of malignant neoplasm of prostate

    Z80.43 Family history of malignant neoplasm of testis

    Z80.49 Family history of malignant neoplasm of other genital organs

Figure 4–8 ICD-10-CM Chapter 21 Factors Influencing Health Status and Contact with Health Services

Chapter 21: Factors Influencing Health Status and Contact with Health Services (Figure 4–8)

Chapter 21 codes represent reasons or circumstances for health care encounters or visits other than disease, injury, or external cause. These codes range from routine childhood physical examinations to follow-up encounters related to organ transplants.

Tabular List Format

ICD-10-CM *Tabular List* chapters are organized into blocks of three-character categories that cover similar or closely related conditions. Each chapter begins with a summary of the category blocks contained in the chapter. Figure 4–9 illustrates this feature.

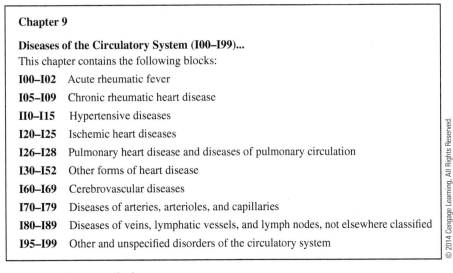

Chapter 9

Diseases of the Circulatory System (I00–I99)...
This chapter contains the following blocks:

I00–I02	Acute rheumatic fever
I05–I09	Chronic rheumatic heart disease
I10–I15	Hypertensive diseases
I20–I25	Ischemic heart diseases
I26–I28	Pulmonary heart disease and diseases of pulmonary circulation
I30–I52	Other forms of heart disease
I60–I69	Cerebrovascular diseases
I70–I79	Diseases of arteries, arterioles, and capillaries
I80–I89	Diseases of veins, lymphatic vessels, and lymph nodes, not elsewhere classified
I95–I99	Other and unspecified disorders of the circulatory system

Figure 4–9 Category Blocks

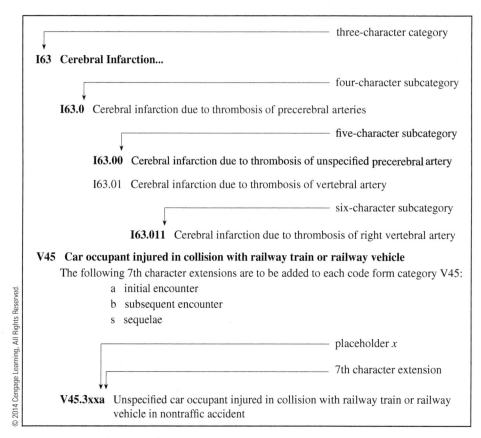

Figure 4–10 *Tabular List* Codes

Codes in the *Tabular List* may include up to seven alphanumeric characters, which include *three-character category* codes; *four-character subcategory* codes; *five-character subcategory* codes; *six-character subcategory* codes; 7th character extensions; and the placeholder *x*. The first character is always alphabetic. Refer to Figure 4–10 for examples of ICD-10-CM codes.

- *Three-character category (code):* A capital letter followed by two digits or one digit and one alphabetic character that represents a single disease or a group of closely related conditions. Although most three-character categories are further divided into four-character subcategories, some conditions are coded to a three-character category.
- *Four-character subcategory (code):* A three-character category followed by a period/decimal point and one numeric character or one alphabetic character. The fourth digit provides more information or specificity for the description of the condition. In most cases, the fourth digit 8 (.8) means that even though the diagnostic statement may include some specific information, there is no other code available for the condition. The fourth digit 9 (.9) usually means that the diagnostic statement does not include enough information to select a more specific code.
- *Five-character subcategory (code):* A three-character category followed by a period/decimal point and two additional characters. A five-character subcategory code is a subdivision of a four-character subcategory code.
- *Six-character subcategory (code):* A three-character category followed by a period/decimal point and three additional characters. A six-character subcategory code is a subdivision of a five-character subcategory code.

- *7th character extension:* Many ICD-10-CM codes require an additional character, called an "extension," to provide additional information about the patient's condition. An extension is always the seventh and final character in a code. Letters and numbers are used as 7th character extensions.
- *Placeholder x:* Also called the "dummy x," the placeholder *x* is used in conjunction with codes that require a 7th character extension. When a code with fewer than six characters requires a seventh character, the placeholder *x* is used to create a six-character code. Refer to entry V45 in Figure 4–10 for an example of the placeholder *x*.

REINFORCEMENT EXERCISES 4–2

Fill in the blank.

1. The _____ and _____ are the two main components of ICD-10-CM.

2. Twenty-one chapters make up the _____ of ICD-10-CM.

3. _____ codes are only assigned to conditions affecting the mother, never to the newborn.

4. _____ codes are only assigned to conditions affecting the newborn.

5. Encounters or visits for reasons other than disease or injury are often coded to _____.

Write a brief definition for each term.

1. placeholder x _____

2. 7th character extension _____

3. three-character code _____

Alphabetic Index

The ICD-10-CM *Alphabetic Index* is the key to locating codes in the *Tabular List*. Codes selected from the *Alphabetic Index* must be verified by reviewing the description of the code in the *Tabular List*. The *Alphabetic Index* is divided into three sections:

- "Index to Diseases and Injuries"
- "External Cause of Injuries Index"
- "Table of Drugs and Chemicals"

The *Alphabetic Index* is organized by main terms that are bolded and flush left.

Index to Diseases and Injuries

The "Index to Diseases and Injuries" is an alphabetical list of diseases, conditions, injuries, signs, symptoms, and reasons for encounters or services. Main terms for this section include words like bronchitis, failure, vomiting, examination, vaccination, and complications.

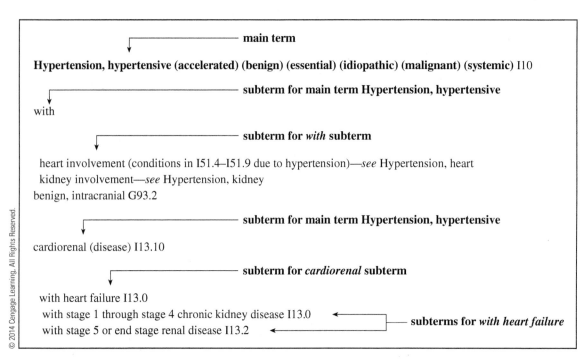

Figure 4–11 ICD-10-CM *Alphabetic Index* Entry

Main terms, which are printed in bold and flush left, are followed by words that further describe the main term. These words are called nonessential modifiers and essential modifiers. Nonessential modifiers are enclosed in parentheses and do not affect code assignment. Essential modifiers, usually called subterms, do affect code assignment and identify the site, etiology, or other clinical descriptions. Etiology is simply defined as the cause of a disease or condition.

Subterms are indented and listed below a main term or another subterm. Subterms are arranged alphabetically, *except* the subterm **with**. This subterm is always listed immediately after the main term. The main term *hypertension, hypertensive* in Figure 4–11 illustrates main term, subterm, and nonessential modifier arrangement. A dash or hyphen (-) at the end of some codes indicates that the code is incomplete and needs additional characters.

The "Index to Diseases and Injuries" includes the ICD-10-CM Table of Neoplasms. The main term *neoplasm, neoplastic* refers the billing specialist or medical coder to this table. The Table of Neoplasms is organized by anatomic site. Codes are categorized as:

- malignant, primary; the site where the cancerous neoplasm originated
- malignant, secondary; the site to which the cancerous neoplasm has spread
- Ca in situ; the carcinoma (Ca) is encapsulated in a specific location; carcinoma identifies a malignant neoplasm (tumor)
- benign; noncancerous
- uncertain behavior; the neoplasm cannot be identified as malignant or benign
- unspecified behavior; the diagnosis does not identify the neoplasm as malignant or benign

Figure 4–12 is a sample of the ICD-10-Table of Neoplasms.

	Malignant Primary	Malignant Secondary	Ca in situ	Benign	Uncertain Behavior	Unspecified Behavior
cervical region	C76.0	C79.89	D09.8	D36.7	D48.7	D49.89
cervix (cervical) (uteri) (uterus)	C53.9	C79.82	D06.9	D26.0	D39.0	D49.5
canal	C53.0	C79.82	D06.0	D26.0	D39.0	D49.5
endocervix (canal) (gland)	C53.0	C79.82	D06.0	D26.0	D39.0	D49.5
exocervix	C53.1	C79.82	D06.1	D26.0	D39.0	D49.5
external os	C53.1	C79.82	D06.1	D26.0	D39.0	D49.5
internal os	C53.0	C79.82	D06.0	D26.0	D39.0	D49.5
nabothian gland	C53.0	C79.82	D06.0	D26.0	D39.0	D49.5
overlapping lesion	C53.8	-	-	-	-	-
squamocolumnar junction	C53.8	C79.82	D06.7	D26.0	D39.0	D49.5
stump	C53.8	C79.82	D06.7	D26.0	D39.0	D49.5

Figure 4–12 ICD-10-CM Table of Neoplasms

External Cause of Injuries Index

The "External Cause of Injuries Index" is an alphabetical list of terms that describe accidents and acts of violence. Main terms in this index are words like assault, collision, and fall. These terms are associated with ICD-10-CM's Chapter 20: External Causes of Morbidity. Figure 4–13 illustrates this index.

Abandonment (causing exposure to weather conditions) (with intent to injure or kill) NEC X58
Abuse (adult) (child) (mental) (physical) (sexual) X58
Accident (to) X58
aircraft (in transit) (powered)—*see also* Accident, transport, aircraft
due to, caused by cataclysm—*see* Forces of nature, by type
…
bare foot water skiier V94.4

Bite, bitten by
alligator W58.01
arthropod (nonvenomous) NEC W57
bull W55.21
cat W55.01
cow W55.21
crocodile W58.11
dog W54.0

Terrorism (involving) Y38.80
biological weapons Y38.6x-
chemical weapons Y38.7x-
conflagration Y38.3x-
drowning and submersion Y38.89-
explosion Y38.2x-
destruction of aircraft Y38.1x-
marine weapons Y38.0x-

Figure 4–13 External Cause of Injuries Index

Substance	Poisoning Accidental	Poisoning Intentional	Poisoning Assault	Poisoning Undetermined	Adverse Effect	Underdosing
Black						
flag	T60.91	T60.92	T60.93	T60.94	-	-
henbane	T62.2×1	T62.2×2	T62.2×3	T62.2×4	-	-
leaf (40)	T60.91	T60.92	T60.93	T60.94	-	-
widow spider (bite)	T63.311	T63.312	T63.313	T63.314	-	-
Bleach	T54.91	T54.92	T54.93	T54.94	-	-
Eucalyptus oil	T49.7×1	T49.7×2	T49.7×3	T49.7×4	T49.7×5	T49.7×6
Window cleaning fluid	T65.891	T65.892	T65.893	T65.894	-	-

Figure 4–14 ICD-10-CM Table of Drugs and Chemicals

Table of Drugs and Chemicals

The "Table of Drugs and Chemicals" is an alphabetic list of all kinds of drugs and chemicals, from aspirin and ammonia to household and industrial products. This table also includes the diagnostic codes for poisoning, adverse affects, and underdosing of the listed products. Figure 4–14 is a sample section of the "Table of Drugs and Chemicals."

REINFORCEMENT EXERCISES 4–3

Briefly describe each component of ICD-10-CM's *Alphabetic Index.*

1. "Index to Diseases and Injuries" _____

2. "External Cause of Injuries Index" _____

3. "Table of Drugs and Chemicals" _____

Fill in the blank.

1. In the *Alphabetic Index,* _____ are bolded and flush left.

2. _____ further describe(s) a disease or condition and do not affect code assignment.

3. In the *Alphabetic Index,* the _____ is organized by anatomic site.

continued on the next page

continued from the previous page

4. _____ are also called subterms and do affect code assignment.

5. The cause of a disease or condition is a simple definition of the term _____.

6. A code for "accidental poisoning by drinking bleach" may be listed in the _____.

7. The _____ may list a code for an injury caused by a dog bite.

IDC-10-CM Coding Conventions

A thorough understanding of ICD-10-CM coding conventions is essential for accurate code assignment. Coding conventions are the "rules of the road" and are clearly defined in all ICD-10-CM coding products. Additional conventions are described in the *Official Guidelines for Coding and Reporting*. ICD-10-CM conventions are discussed first and a summary the *Official Guidelines* follows.

ICD-10-CM coding conventions, which are found in the *Tabular List* and the *Alphabetic Index*, include:

- Punctuation
- Instructional notes
- Cross-references
- Abbreviations
- Connecting words

Punctuation

Punctuation marks associated with coding conventions include: parentheses (); square brackets [ ]; slanted brackets [ ]; dash -; and point dash .-.

Parentheses ( ) are used in the *Tabular List* to enclose codes that apply to conditions that are excluded from a particular category and the range of codes included in a chapter or category block of codes. In the *Alphabetic Index*, parentheses enclose nonessential modifiers, words or statements in the diagnosis that do not affect the code. Example A illustrates this use in the *Tabular List*; Example B illustrates this use in the *Alphabetic Index*.

EXAMPLE A: *TABULAR LIST*
K63.3 Ulcer of intestine. Excludes1: duodenal ulcer (K28.-).
    In this example, parentheses enclose the category code for duodenal ulcer, which is excluded from K63.3 Ulcer of intestine.

EXAMPLE B: *ALPHABETIC INDEX*
Retinopathy (background) (Coats) H35.9.
    In this example, background and Coats do not affect code assignment for retinopathy.

Square brackets [ ] are used in the *Tabular List* to enclose synonyms, alternative wording or explanatory phrases.

EXAMPLE

B01 Varicella [chickenpox].

In this example, square brackets enclose a common name for varicella.

EXAMPLE

B02 Zoster [herpes zoster].

In this example, square brackets enclose alternative wording for the diagnosis zoster.

Slanted square brackets *[ ]* are used to identify codes for conditions that are manifestations of underlying conditions. Codes for underlying conditions must be listed first, before codes for the manifested condition.

EXAMPLE

Retinopathy—arteriosclerotic I70.8 *[H35.0-]*.

In this example the diagnostic statement is arteriosclerotic retinopathy. The slanted square brackets indicate that retinopathy is a manifestation of arteriosclerosis. Retinopathy is coded to category H35.0- retinal disorders in diseases classified elsewhere. As the underlying condition, arteriosclerosis is coded to I70.8 and listed before the retinopathy code.

The point dash .- is used in the *Tabular List* and indicates that the code is incomplete and an additional digit (or digits) is needed (Example A). In the *Alphabetic Index*, a dash - is used for the same purpose (Example B).

EXAMPLE A: *TABULAR LIST*

K63.3 Ulcer of intestine…**Excludes1**: duodenal ulcer (K26.-).

In this example, the point dash indicates that the code for duodenal ulcer is incomplete. The billing specialist or medical coder must go to category K26 to find the complete code.

EXAMPLE B: *ALPHABETIC INDEX*

Retinopathy (background) (Coats) H35.9—hypertensive H35.03-.

In this example, the dash indicates that the code for hypertensive retinopathy is incomplete. The billing specialist or medical coder must go to H35.03 to locate the complete code.

Table 4–3 summarizes ICD-10-CM punctuation conventions.

Instructional Notes

Instructional notes provide additional guidance for accurate code selection. These notes include:

- General notes
- Includes notes
- Excludes notes
- Etiology and manifestation notes
- "Code also" note

TABLE 4–3

ICD-10-CM Punctuation Conventions

Convention	Example
Dash (-)	Identifies incomplete codes that require additional digits (*Alphabetic Index*)
Parentheses ( )	Enclose nonessential modifiers Enclose codes excluded from a category Enclose the range of codes for a chapter or category block of codes
Point dash (.-)	Identifies incomplete codes that require additional digits (*Tabular List*)
Square brackets [ ]	Enclose synonyms, alternative wording, or explanatory phrases
Slanted square brackets *[ ]*	Identify codes for conditions that are manifestations of underlying conditions

© 2014 Cengage Learning, All Rights Reserved.

General Notes

General notes are found at the beginning of the *Tabular List* and each *Tabular List* chapter. The notes may include a brief description of the purpose of the chapter; a list of included and excluded diseases or conditions; and other chapter-specific information.

> **EXAMPLE**
> Chapter 17 Congenital malformations, deformations, and chromosomal abnormalities (Q00-Q99)

Note: Codes from this chapter are not for use on maternal or fetal records.

Includes Notes

Includes notes are used throughout the *Tabular List* either at the beginning of a chapter or immediately under a three-character code. As the name implies, includes notes describe information included in a specific category.

> **EXAMPLE**
> **Chapter 1 Certain infectious and parasitic diseases (A00-B99)**
> **Includes:** diseases generally recognized as communicable or transmissible
> **A38 Scarlet fever**
> **Includes:** scarlatina

Excludes Notes

The ICD-10-CM has two types of excludes notes, Excludes1 and Excludes2. **Excludes1** means "not coded here!" This note indicates that the excluded code should never be used at the same time as the code above the Excludes1 note. Excludes1 identifies two conditions that cannot occur together, such as a congenital and acquired form of the same condition. These notes are used extensively in the *Tabular List* at the chapter level (Example A) and the individual code level (Example B).

> EXAMPLE A: EXCLUDES1 NOTE, CHAPTER LEVEL
> **Chapter 4 Endocrine, nutritional and metabolic diseases (E00-E89)**
> **Excludes1:** transitory endocrine and metabolic disorders specific to newborn (P70-P74)

> EXAMPLE B: EXCLUDES1 NOTE, CODE SPECIFIC
> **K63.3   Ulcer of intestine:**
> Primary ulcer of small intestine
> **Excludes1:** duodenal ulcer (K26.-)

Excludes2 means "not included here." The excluded condition is not part of the condition represented by the code preceding the note. However, the patient may have both conditions at the same time. Therefore, both codes may be assigned. Excludes2 notes are used extensively in the *Tabular List* at the chapter code level (Example A) and the individual code level (Example B).

> EXAMPLE A: EXCLUDES2 NOTE, CHAPTER LEVEL
> **Chapter 8 Disease of the ear and mastoid process (H60-H95)**
> **Excludes2:** neoplasms (C00-D49)

> EXAMPLE B: EXCLUDES2 NOTE, CODE SPECIFIC
> **I12 Hypertensive chronic kidney disease**
> **Excludes2:** acute kidney failure (N17.-)

REINFORCEMENT EXERCISES 4–4

Match the convention in Column 1 with the definition in Column 2.

Column 1	Column 2
1. _____ dash -	a. enclose nonessential modifiers
2. _____ Excludes1	b. enclose synonyms, alternative wording, or phrases
3. _____ Excludes2	c. identifies an incomplete code in the *Alphabetic Index*
4. _____ parentheses ( )	d. identifies an incomplete code in the *Tabular List*
5. _____ point dash .-	e. identify codes for manifestations of underlying conditions or diseases
6. _____ square brackets [ ]	f. not included here
7. _____ slanted square brackets *[ ]*	g. not coded here

Etiology and Manifestation Notes

Some conditions have an underlying etiology (cause) and multiple body system manifestations due to the underlying etiology. A manifestation is a condition that is caused by or associated with another condition, disease, or problem. Diabetes is a good example of a disease that often presents several manifestations, such as diabetic retinopathy (disease of the retina of the eye). ICD-10-CM has a specific convention that requires assigning codes to the manifestation and the underlying condition. The underlying condition code must be listed before the manifestation code.

Code first, use additional code, and in diseases classified elsewhere are the notes that alert the billing specialist or medical coder that the diagnosis is a manifestation of an underlying condition. These notes are found in the *Tabular List*. "Use additional code" is noted at the etiology code and "code first" is noted at the manifestation code. In most cases, the manifestation code includes "in diseases classified elsewhere" in the title. Figure 4–15 illustrates *Tabular List* etiology and manifestation notes.

In the *Alphabetic Index*, the etiology and manifestation codes are listed together. The etiology code is given first followed by the manifestation code in slanted square brackets.

> EXAMPLE
> Glaucoma H40.9
> - in (due to)…
> -- endocrine disease NOS E34.9 *[H42]*…

In this example, endocrine disease NOS is the underlying condition or etiology related to glaucoma. The endocrine disease code (E34.9) is listed first. Glaucoma is a manifestation, as indicated by the slanted square brackets. Both codes must be verified in the *Tabular List*.

"Code Also" Note

The code also note is used in the *Tabular List* to alert the billing specialist or medical coder that two codes may be required to fully describe a condition. This note does not indicate which code is listed first.

> EXAMPLE
> N39.3   Stress incontinence (female) (male)
> **Code also** any associated overactive bladder (N32.81)

In this example, if overactive bladder is documented in the patient's record, both the stress incontinence and overactive bladder are coded.

H72   Perforation of tympanic membrane
        Code first any associated otitis media (H65.-, H66.1.-,…)

J01   Acute sinusitis
        Use additional code (B95–B97) to identify infectious agent

J17   Pneumonia **in diseases classified elsewhere**
        Code first   underlying disease, such as:
                Q fever (A78)
                rheumatic fever (I00)
                schistosomiasis (B65.0–B65.9)

Figure 4–15 *Tabular List* Etiology and Manifestation Notes

Conjunctiva—*see* **Condition**
Conjunctivitis (staphylococcal) (streptococcal) **NOS** H10.9
acute H10.3-
  atopic H10.1-
  chemical (*see also* Corrosion, cornea) H10.21-
...
  allergic (acute)
    viral—*see* Conjunctivitis, acute, atopic

Figure 4–16 *Alphabetic Index* Cross-Reference Notes

Cross-references

Cross-references "see," "see also," and "see condition" are found in the *Alphabetic Index* following a main term. See is a mandatory instruction. The billing specialist or medical coder must go to the referenced main term to locate the correct code. The see also instruction tells the billing specialist or medical coder that another referenced main term may be useful in locating the correct code. If the original main term leads to the accurate code, then it is not necessary to follow "see also." See condition indicates that an anatomic site or adjective rather than a condition or disease was used as a main term. The billing specialist or medical coder must refer to the diagnosis for the condition or disease. Figure 4–16 illustrates these *Alphabetic Index* cross-references.

Connecting Words

ICD-10-CM connecting words are "*and*" and "*with*." In the *Tabular List*, "and" means and/or to indicate that either of two conditions may be assigned to a given code.

> **EXAMPLE**
> N76.1 Subacute and chronic vaginitis.
> In this example, either subacute vaginitis or chronic vaginitis may be assigned to code N76.1.

When the word "with" appears in a code title, in the *Alphabetic Index* or the *Tabular List* (see Example), "with" means *associated with* or *due to*. "With" also indicates that more than one condition may be included in a given code.

> **EXAMPLE: *TABULAR LIST***
> N40.1 Enlarged prostate with lower urinary tract symptoms (LUTS).
> In this example, code N40.1 covers both an enlarged prostate and lower urinary tract symptoms. If specific urinary tract symptoms are noted in the patient's records, the code for the symptom is also assigned.

In the *Alphabetic Index* "with" is listed immediately after the associated main term or subterm. Other subterms are then listed in alphabetical order. Figure 4–17 illustrates "with" in the *Alphabetic Index*.

Abbreviations

The abbreviations NEC (not elsewhere classified) and NOS (not otherwise specified) are used in the *Tabular List* and *Alphabetic Index*. NEC means that a diagnosis or condition, no matter how specific, does not have a separate code. In the *Alphabetic Index*, NEC directs the billing specialist

```
"With" Following a Main Term Entry
Hearing examination Z01.10
 with abnormal findings NEC Z01.118
 following failed hearing screening Z01.110
 for hearing conservation and treatment Z01.12


"With" Following a Subterm Entry
Perforation...
 uterus
  with ectopic or molar pregnancy O08.6
  by intrauterine contraceptive device T83.39
  following ectopic or molar pregnancy O08.6
  obstetrical trauma O71.1
```

Figure 4–17 "With" in the ICD-10-CM *Alphabetic Index*

or medical coder to the "other specified" code in the *Tabular List*. Figure 4–18 illustrates an *Alphabetic Index* NEC entry and the corresponding *Tabular List* entry.

The abbreviation NOS means the same thing as unspecified. An NOS code is selected when the documentation does not provide enough detail to select a more specific code. NOS codes usually end in 9. Figure 4–19 illustrates *Alphabetic Index* NOS entries and the corresponding *Tabular List* entries.

```
Alphabetic Index

Hematoma (traumatic) (skin surface intact)—see also Contusion
birth injury NEC P15.8

Tabular List

P15  Other birth injuries...
     P15.8  Other specified birth injuries
```

Figure 4–18 NEC *Alphabetic Index* and *Tabular List* Entries

```
Alphabetic Index

Conjunctivitis (staphylococcal) (streptococcal) NOS H10.9
Disease, diseased—see also Syndrome
heart (organic) I51.9
 ischemic (chronic or with a stated duration of over 4 weeks) I25.9

Tabular List

H10.9  Unspecified conjunctivitis
I25.9  Chronic ischemic heart disease, unspecified
       Ischemic heart disease (chronic) NOS
```

Figure 4–19 NOS *Alphabetic Index* and *Tabular List* Entries

REINFORCEMENT EXERCISES 4–5

Match the convention in Column 1 with the description in Column 2.

Convention		Description
1. _____ code first		**a.** another main term may be helpful
2. _____ NEC		**b.** documentation does not support a more specific code
3. _____ NOS		**c.** indicates an adjective was used as the main term
4. _____ *see*		**d.** indicates associated or due to conditions
5. _____ *see also*		**e.** no code available for a specific diagnosis
6. _____ *see condition*		**f.** instruction associated with a manifestation code
7. _____ use additional code		**g.** instruction associated with an etiology code
8. _____ with		**h.** mandatory cross-reference

ICD-10-CM OFFICIAL GUIDELINES FOR CODING AND REPORTING

The CMS and the NCHS develop and update the ICD-10-CM *Official Guidelines for Coding and Reporting* the diagnosis and treatment of diseases, conditions, and other health-related encounters. The *Official Guidelines* provide coding instructions in situations not covered by ICD-10-CM Coding Conventions. *ICD-10-CM Coding Conventions always take precedence over the Official Guidelines.* The Cooperating Parties—CMS, NCHA, AHIMA, and AHA—approve the *Official Guidelines.* The guidelines are included in the official government version of ICD-10-CM, in the *Coding Clinic* for ICD-10-CM published by the AHA, and in commercial ICD-10-CM publications.

In the guidelines, the term encounter is used for all settings and the term provider means any physician or qualified health care practitioner who is legally accountable for establishing a patient's diagnosis. The guidelines are organized into the following sections:

- Section I. Conventions (general coding guidelines and chapter specific guidelines).
- Section II. Selection of Principal Diagnosis (non-outpatient settings).
- Section III. Reporting Additional Diagnoses (non-outpatient settings).
- Section IV. Diagnostic Coding and Reporting Guidelines for Outpatient Services.
- Appendix I. Present on Admission (POA) Reporting Guidelines.

It is beyond the scope of this text to review the entire contents of the guidelines, which are available on the CMS website at http://www.cms.gov. The search term or key word is ICD-10-CM Official Guidelines.

Section I.B. General Coding Guidelines; Section IV. Diagnostic Coding and Reporting Guidelines for Outpatient Services; and Section II. Selection of Principal Diagnosis are included here.

Section I.B. General Coding Guidelines

The general coding guidelines provide overall instructions for assigning ICD-10-CM diagnosis codes. All codes first located in the *Alphabetic Index* must be verified in the *Tabular List*. Billing specialists and medical coders should *never* code directly from the *Alphabetic Index*.

Symptoms and Signs

Codes related to symptoms and signs rather than diagnoses or conditions may be used *when a definitive diagnosis has not been established or confirmed* by the provider. Chapter 18 Symptoms, Signs, and Abnormal Clinical and Laboratory Findings, Not Elsewhere Classified contains many codes for symptoms.

Some symptoms and signs are routinely associated with a particular disease or condition. These symptoms or signs should not be assigned a separate code, unless ICD-10-CM coding conventions instruct otherwise. For example, nausea and vomiting often accompany gastroenteritis. Once a code is assigned to gastroenteritis, no additional codes are needed for the nausea and vomiting. On the other hand, if a patient is seen for nausea and vomiting, and no definitive diagnosis is identified, codes are assigned to nausea and vomiting.

Acute and Chronic Conditions

Some conditions are described as acute or chronic and should be coded according to the appropriate category. There are times when a condition is described as acute or subacute and chronic in the same diagnostic statement. When two codes exist for this situation, assign both codes and list the acute or subacute code first.

Combination Codes

A combination code is a single code used to classify two diagnoses, a diagnosis with an associated secondary condition (manifestation), or a diagnosis with an associated complication. When a combination code accurately represents the diagnostic conditions documented in the patient's record, assign *only* the combination code. When the combination code does not accurately represent the diagnostic conditions, assign additional or secondary codes as needed.

Late Effects (Sequela)

A late effect is a condition or problem that remains after the acute phase of an illness or injury. Late effects are also called residual effects or sequela. Paralysis is an example of a late effect of a stroke (cerebrovascular accident). There is no particular time period associated with a late effect or residual condition. The key factor is that the acute phase of an illness or injury must be over.

Late effects usually require two codes, one for the condition that represents the late effect, and one for the reason for the late effect. The condition code is listed first, followed by the code for the reason. Figure 4–20 is an example of an *Alphabetic List* late effect entry and the corresponding *Tabular List* entry. Note that *sequelae* is the *Alphabetic List* main term for late effects.

Laterality

Laterality indicates whether the condition affects one side of the body or another. The ICD-10-CM has many separate codes for right and left. The final character of the code identifies laterality. If no code exists for a bilateral condition, assign separate codes for the right and left side.

Alphabetic Index

Sequelae (of)—*see also* condition
hemorrhage…
  subarachnoid I69.00
  aphasia I69.020

Tabular List

I69   Sequelae of cerebrovascular disease
Note: Category I69 is to be used to indicate conditions in I60–I67 as the cause of the
          sequelae. The 'sequelae' include conditions specified as such or as residuals which
          may occur at any time after the onset of the causal condition. …

I69.02   Speech and language deficits following nontraumatic subarachnoid hemorrhage

   I69.020   Aphasia following nontraumatic subarachnoid hemorrhage

Figure 4–20 Late Effects (Sequelae) *Alphabetic Index* and *Tabular List* Entries

Section IV. Diagnostic Coding and Reporting Guidelines for Outpatient Services

The guidelines in Section IV are approved for hospital and provider-based outpatient services and office visits. Under the guidelines, *encounter* and *visit* are used interchangeably to describe outpatient service contacts. The reason for the encounter or visit is called the first-listed diagnosis (condition). Some providers also use the term primary diagnosis. As the name implies, the first-listed diagnosis code is listed first when submitting an insurance claim. A summary of the "Diagnostic Coding and Reporting Guidelines for Outpatient Services" is presented here and illustrated as needed.

Guideline IV. A. Selection of First-Listed Condition (Diagnosis)

In the outpatient setting, the first-listed diagnosis or condition is always the reason for the encounter. A definitive or final diagnosis may not be established during the initial encounter or visit. In these situations, the billing specialist or medical coder may assign symptom, sign, or abnormal finding codes. Always begin the search for code assignment through the *Alphabetic Index*. Never begin the initial search in the *Tabular List*. The ICD-10-CM coding conventions take precedence over the outpatient guidelines.

1. Outpatient surgery: When a patient presents for outpatient surgery, code the reason for the surgery as the first-listed diagnosis, even if the surgery is not performed due to a contraindication.
2. Observation stay: When a patient is admitted for observation for a medical condition, assign the code for the medical condition as the first-listed diagnosis. If a patient develops complications following outpatient surgery requiring admission for observation, code the reason for the surgery as the first-listed diagnosis, followed by codes for the complications as secondary diagnoses.

Guideline IV.B. Codes from A00.0 through T88.9, Z00-Z99

Appropriate ICD-10-CM codes from A00.0 through T88.9, Z00-Z99 must be used to identify diagnoses, symptoms, conditions, problems, complaints, or other reasons for an encounter or visit.

Guideline IV.C. Accurate Reporting of ICD-10-CM Diagnosis Codes

For accurate reporting of ICD-10-CM diagnosis codes, the documentation should describe the patient's condition, using terminology that includes specific diagnoses, as well as symptoms, problems, or reasons for the encounter.

REINFORCEMENT EXERCISES 4–6

Fill in the blank.

1. The _____ take precedence over the _____ when assigning ICD-10-CM diagnoses codes.

2. The term _____ is used to describe an interaction with a health care agency or setting.

3. A _____ is a physician or qualified health care practitioner who is legally accountable for establishing a patient's diagnosis.

4. Under the *Official Guidelines* the terms _____ and _____ are used interchangeably.

5. A _____ is a single code that covers two related or associated conditions or diagnoses.

Write a brief definition for each term.

1. late effect _____

2. first-listed diagnosis _____

3. laterality _____

4. residual effect _____

5. primary diagnosis _____

6. sequela _____

Guideline IV.D. Codes That Describe Symptoms and Signs

Codes that describe symptoms and signs, rather than diagnoses, are acceptable for reporting purposes when a diagnosis has not been established (confirmed) by the provider. Chapter 18 of the ICD-10-CM, Symptoms, Signs, and Abnormal Clinical and Laboratory Findings, Not Elsewhere Classified contains many but not all codes for symptoms.

Guideline IV.E. Encounters for Circumstances Other than a Disease or Injury

The ICD-10-CM provides codes when encounters are for circumstances or reasons other than disease or injury. Chapter 21, Factors Influencing Health Status and Contact with Health Services, codes Z00-Z99, are assigned in these circumstances.

Guideline IV.F. Level of Detail in Coding

ICD-10-CM is composed of codes with three to seven characters. A code is invalid if it does not have the full number of characters required for that code, including the 7th character extension, if applicable.

Guideline IV.G. ICD-10-CM Code for the Diagnosis, Condition, Problem, or Other Reason for Encounter/Visit

List first the ICD-10-CM code for the diagnosis, condition, problem, or other reason for the encounter shown in the medical record to be chiefly responsible for the services provided. Codes that describe any coexisting conditions are placed after the first-listed diagnosis code. In some cases the first-listed diagnosis may be a symptom when a diagnosis has not been established (confirmed) by the physician.

> **EXAMPLE**
>
> Mark is seen in the physician's office for heart palpitations. He also has non–insulin dependent diabetes mellitus, type II that is under control. The first-listed diagnosis is palpitations. The diabetes code is listed as an additional code for a coexisting condition.

Guideline IV.H. Uncertain Diagnosis

Do not code diagnoses documented as "probable," "suspected," "questionable," "rule out," or "working diagnosis" or other similar terms indicating uncertainty. Rather, code the condition(s) to the highest degree of certainty for that encounter, such as symptoms, signs, abnormal test results, or other reasons for the visit.

> **EXAMPLE**
>
> Selina was seen in the physician's office with complaints of vertigo, nausea, and a headache. Rule out inner ear infection. In this case, if the inner ear infection is not confirmed, code the vertigo, nausea, and headache. The physician should indicate which symptom is primary.

Note: This guideline differs from the coding practices used by short-term care, acute care, long-term care, and psychiatric hospitals.

Guideline IV.I. Chronic Diseases

Chronic disease treated on an ongoing basis may be coded and reported as many times as the patient receives treatment and care for the condition(s).

Guideline IV.J. Code All Documented Conditions That Coexist

Code all documented conditions that coexist at the time of the encounter, and require or affect patient care, treatment, or management. Do not code conditions that were previously treated and no longer exist. However, history codes (Z80-Z87) may be used as secondary codes if the historical condition or family history has an impact on current care or influences treatment.

Guideline IV.K. Patients Receiving Diagnostic Services Only

For patients receiving diagnostic services only during a visit, the first-listed diagnosis or condition is the diagnosis, condition, problem, or other reason for the visit documented as being chiefly responsible for the outpatient services provided during the visit. Codes for other diagnoses may be listed as additional diagnoses.

Encounters for routine laboratory/radiology testing in the absence of any signs, symptoms, or associated diagnosis are coded to Z01.89, Encounter for other specified special examination.

If routine testing is performed during the same encounter as a test to evaluate a sign, symptom, or diagnosis, it is appropriate to assign codes for both tests.

For outpatient encounters for diagnostic tests that have been interpreted by a physician, and a final report is available at the time of coding, code any confirmed or definitive diagnosis documented in the report. Do not code related signs and symptoms as additional diagnosis.

EXAMPLE

Joel is seen for a colonoscopy because of frequent rectal bleeding, with a probable diagnosis of ulcerative colitis. In this case, the billing specialist has two options:

A. Submit the insurance claim before the results of the colonoscopy are available. The first-listed diagnosis is rectal bleeding because that is the reason for the colonoscopy. The colonoscopy is coded to the appropriate CPT category.

B. Wait until the results of the colonoscopy are available and then submit the insurance claim. The diagnosis listed in the colonoscopy report is coded and reported as the first-listed diagnosis. The colonoscopy is coded to the appropriate CPT category.

Because the results of the colonoscopy should provide a more specific diagnosis than rectal bleeding, option B is the better choice.

Guideline IV.L. Patients Receiving Therapeutic Services Only

For patients receiving therapeutic services only during an encounter, the first-listed diagnosis is the diagnosis, condition, problem, or reason for the visit documented in the patient's record as the reason for the services provided. Codes for other diagnoses (e.g., chronic conditions) may be listed as additional diagnoses.

An exception to this guideline applies when the encounter is related to chemotherapy or radiation therapy. In these cases, the appropriate Z code for the service is listed first, and the diagnosis or problem for which the service is being performed is listed second. Figure 4–21 is a *Tabular List* entry for chemotherapy and radiation therapy.

Z51   **Encounter for other aftercare**
  Excludes1: follow-up examination after treatment (Z08–Z09)
  Code also: condition requiring care

  Z51.0   **Encounter for antineoplastic radiation therapy**

  Z51.1   **Encounter for antineoplastic chemotherapy and immunotherapy**
    Excludes2: encounter for chemotherapy and immunotherapy for nonneoplastic condition—code to condition

    Z51.11   **Encounter for antineoplastic chemotherapy**

    Z51.12   **Encounter for antineoplastic immunotherapy**

Figure 4–21 *Tabular List* Entry for Chemotherapy and Radiation Therapy

Guideline IV.M. Patients Receiving Preoperative Evaluations Only

For patients receiving preoperative evaluation only, list the code from subcategory Z01.81, Encounter for pre-procedural examinations that describes the preoperative consultation first. The reason for the procedure or surgery is coded as an additional diagnosis. Any findings related to the preoperative evaluation are also coded.

> **EXAMPLE**
>
> LaMar, whose medical treatment for an enlarged prostate has been unsuccessful, is seen for a preoperative evaluation prior to his scheduled TURP (transurethral resection of the prostate). The physician's note indicates that LaMar is diabetic and has hypertension.
>
> In this case, the Z code for the preoperative evaluation is assigned and listed first; the code for enlarged prostate is next; and codes for diabetes and hypertension are listed as additional diagnoses.

Guideline IV.N. Ambulatory Surgery

For ambulatory (outpatient) surgery, code the diagnosis for which the surgery was performed. If the postoperative diagnosis is different from the preoperative diagnosis, and confirmed and documented in the patient's record, code the postoperative as the reason for the procedure or surgery.

> **EXAMPLE**
>
> Maureen underwent a polypectomy for several polyps in her descending colon. Familial polyposis was the preoperative diagnosis. The physician's postoperative note states that five polyps were removed—four benign and one malignant. Colorectal cancer is the postoperative diagnosis.
>
> In this case, the postoperative diagnosis is more definitive than the preoperative diagnosis. Colorectal cancer is coded and listed first. Do not code familial polyposis. The procedure is coded to the appropriate CPT category.

Guideline IV.O. Routine Outpatient Prenatal Visits

For routine prenatal outpatient visits, when no complications are present, a code from category Z34, Encounter for supervision of normal pregnancy, should be used as the first-listed diagnosis. Codes from category Z34 should not be used in conjunction with codes from Chapter 15, Pregnancy, Childbirth, and the Puerperium.

For routine prenatal outpatient visits for patients with high-risk pregnancies, a code from category O09, Supervision of high-risk pregnancy, should be used as the first-listed diagnosis. Secondary codes from Chapter 15 may be used if appropriate.

Guideline IV.P. Encounters for General Medical Examinations with Abnormal Findings

The subcategories for encounters for general medical examinations, Z00.0-, provide codes for general medical examination encounters with or without abnormal findings. When the examination results in an abnormal finding, the code for the general medical examination with abnormal finding is listed first. Secondary codes for any abnormal findings are also assigned.

Guideline IV.Q. Encounters for Routine Health Screening

Codes from the ICD-10-CM Chapter 21, Factors influencing health status and contact with health services (Z00-Z99) are for use in any health care setting. Z codes may be used either as a first-listed diagnosis code or as a secondary code, depending on the circumstances of the encounter. Chapter 21 contains extensive instructional notes to ensure accurate code selection.

ICD-10-CM codes related to encounters for routine health screening are found primarily in categories Z00-Z13, Persons encountering health services for examinations. These codes cover services ranging from an adult general medical examination with or without abnormal findings (Z00.00 and Z00.01) to screening tests for various diseases and conditions (Z13). Any conditions, diseases, or problems identified by the screening examination are coded to the appropriate ICD-10-CM category.

REINFORCEMENT EXERCISES 4–7

Fill in the blank.

1. A symptom code may be listed first if a _____ has not been confirmed.

2. An ICD-10-CM diagnosis code is _____ if it does not have the full number of required characters.

3. _____ code diagnoses documented as *probable*, *suspected*, or *questionable*.

4. Once a diagnosis is confirmed, _____ code symptoms of the diagnosis.

5. When the encounter is for chemotherapy or radiation therapy, the Z code for the service is _____.

6. If the postoperative diagnosis differs from the preoperative diagnosis, the _____ is coded as the reason for the procedure or surgery.

7. Codes from ICD-10-CM Chapter 21, Factors influencing health status and contact with health services are sometimes called _____ codes.

8. _____ may be coded as many times as the patient receives treatment and care for the condition(s).

Section II. Selection of Principal Diagnosis

The guidelines in Section II, Selection of Principal Diagnosis, apply to services rendered in non-outpatient settings, such as acute care, short-term care, long-term care, and psychiatric hospitals; home health agencies; rehabilitation facilities; and nursing homes. In these settings, principal diagnosis is used instead of first-listed diagnosis. The principal diagnosis is defined as the condition established after study to be chiefly responsible for the patient's admission for care. The principal diagnosis code is listed (sequenced) first on the insurance claim.

In determining the principal diagnosis, ICD-10-CM coding conventions take precedence over the *Official Guidelines*. Accurate code assignment depends on consistent, complete, and accurate documentation in the medical record.

Guideline II.A. Codes for Symptoms, Signs, and Ill-Defined Conditions

Codes for symptoms, signs, and ill-defined conditions from ICD-10-CM's Chapter 18 are not used as principal diagnoses when a related definitive diagnosis has been established.

EXAMPLE

Lekeitia is admitted to the hospital for severe nausea, vomiting, headache, and a stiff neck. The laboratory workup confirms the diagnosis of bacterial meningitis. Lekeitia is hospitalized for six days and treated with intravenous antibiotics.

In this example, bacterial meningitis is selected and coded as the principal diagnosis. Codes are not assigned to the symptoms of the disease.

Guideline II.B. Two or More Interrelated Conditions, Each Potentially Meeting the Definition for Principal Diagnosis

When two or more interrelated conditions potentially meet the definition of principal diagnosis, either condition may be sequenced first, unless the circumstances of the admission, the therapy provided, or instructions in the *Tabular List* or *Alphabetic Index* indicate otherwise.

EXAMPLE

Following a car accident, Ramone underwent open reduction and internal fixation for fractures of the humerus and shaft of the ulna and radius. He spent two days in the hospital.

In this example, either fracture may be selected as the principal diagnosis.

Guideline II.C. Two or More Diagnoses That Equally Meet the Definition for Principal Diagnosis

In the unusual instance when two or more diagnoses equally meet the criteria for principal diagnosis, any one of the diagnoses may be selected as the principal diagnosis and sequenced first. The circumstances of the admission, diagnostic workup, treatment provided, and all coding guidelines must be considered in determining the principal diagnosis.

EXAMPLE

Wanda was admitted for elective surgery. A cystocele was repaired, and she also underwent a hemorrhoidectomy for prolapsed internal hemorrhoids.

In this example, either the cystocele or prolapsed internal hemorrhoids may be selected as the principal diagnosis.

Guideline II.D. Two or More Comparative or Contrasting Conditions

In those rare instances when two or more contrasting or comparative diagnoses are documented as "either/or" (or similar terminology), they are coded as if the diagnoses are confirmed. The diagnoses are sequenced according to the circumstances of the admission. If no further determination can be made as to which diagnosis should be principal, either diagnosis may be sequenced first.

EXAMPLE

Diagnoses: Irritable bowel syndrome or spastic colitis.

If neither diagnosis is confirmed, either may be selected as the principal diagnosis.

Guideline II.E. A Symptom(s) Followed by Contrasting/Comparative Diagnoses

When a symptom(s) is followed by contrasting/comparative diagnoses, the symptom(s) code is sequenced first. All contrasting/comparative diagnoses should be coded as additional diagnoses.

EXAMPLE

Chen was admitted with symptoms of periodic vomiting with blood present in the vomitus, indigestion, and a low-grade fever over the past two weeks. Following workup, Dr. Samuelson dictated the following diagnostic statement: "Vomiting with frank blood due to either bleeding gastric ulcer or bleeding esophageal ulcer."

In this example, the symptom "vomiting with frank blood" is selected as the principal diagnosis and sequenced first. "Bleeding gastric ulcer" and "bleeding esophageal ulcer" are coded as secondary diagnoses.

Guideline II.F. Original Treatment Plan Not Carried Out

Sequence as the principal diagnosis the condition that after study occasioned the admission to the hospital, even if treatment was not carried out because of unforeseen circumstances.

EXAMPLE

Travis was admitted for gastric bypass surgery. His diagnoses are morbid obesity and poorly controlled non–insulin-dependent diabetes mellitus, type II. Prior to the beginning of surgery, he exhibited an episode of hypotension and the surgery was cancelled.

In this example, morbid obesity is the principal diagnosis because it was the reason for the admission. Morbid obesity is coded and sequenced first. Non–insulin-dependent diabetes mellitus, type II, poorly controlled, is coded as a secondary or complicating diagnosis.

Guideline II.G. Complications of Surgery and Other Medical Care

When the admission is for treatment of a complication resulting from surgery or other medical care, the complication code is sequenced as the principal diagnosis. If the complication is classified to categories T80-T88 and the code lacks the necessary specificity in describing the complication, an additional code for the specific complication should be assigned.

EXAMPLE

Oksana was treated for peritonitis following recent gastrointestinal surgery. The peritonitis was caused by the presence of nonabsorbable suture material accidentally left in her abdominal cavity.

In this example, the complication code for a foreign body accidentally left during a procedure is coded as the principal diagnosis. An additional code for peritonitis is also assigned.

Guideline II.H: Uncertain Diagnosis

If the diagnosis documented at the time of discharge is qualified as "probable," "suspected," "likely," "questionable," "possible," "still to be ruled out," or other similar terms indicating uncertainty, code the condition as if it existed or was established. The bases for these guidelines are the diagnostic workup, arrangements for further workup or observation, and initial therapeutic approach that correspond most closely with the established diagnosis. This guideline applies only to inpatient admissions to short-term care, acute care, long-term care, and psychiatric hospitals.

EXAMPLE

Carla was admitted for acute onset of several episodes of explosive diarrhea and severe cramping within the past 24 hours. Patient described the stool as dark brown, "slimy," and foul-smelling. She was placed on a clear liquid diet and treated with intravenous hydrocortisone. Stool samples were taken for laboratory analysis. Colonoscopy was deferred pending resolution of acute symptoms. After three days, she was discharged on Prednisone. She is scheduled for a colonoscopy as an outpatient on Monday. Final diagnosis: probable ulcerative colitis.

Because the patient was admitted and treated for symptoms consistent with ulcerative colitis and an additional diagnostic procedure is scheduled, ulcerative colitis is the principal diagnosis and coded as if the condition existed.

Guideline II.I. Admission from Observation Unit

1. Admission following medical observation: When a patient is admitted to an observation unit for a medical condition, which either worsens or does not improve, and is subsequently admitted as an inpatient of the same hospital for the same medical condition, the principal diagnosis is the medical condition that led to the hospital admission.
2. Admission following postoperative observation: When a patient is admitted to an observation unit to monitor a condition (or complication) that develops following outpatient surgery and then is subsequently admitted as an inpatient of the same hospital, the principal diagnosis is the condition established after study to be chiefly responsible for the inpatient admission.

EXAMPLE

Elmer underwent a transurethral resection of the prostate (TURP) as an outpatient procedure. Following the procedure, he exhibited a fever and hematuria (blood in the urine). He was admitted to an observation unit, and his condition did not improve. Elmer was then admitted as an inpatient for further treatment for fever and hematuria.

If the condition causing the hematuria and fever is identified, that condition becomes the principal diagnosis. However, if a definitive diagnosis cannot be established or confirmed, hematuria is the principal diagnosis. Fever may also be coded as an additional problem.

Guideline II.J. Admission from Outpatient Surgery

When a patient receives surgery in the hospital's outpatient surgery department and is subsequently admitted for continuing inpatient care at the same hospital, the following guidelines should be followed in selecting the principal diagnosis for the inpatient admission:

- If the reason for the inpatient admission is a complication, the complication is the principal diagnosis.
- If no complication or other condition is documented as the reason for the inpatient admission, assign the reason for the outpatient surgery as the principal diagnosis.
- If the reason for the inpatient admission is another condition unrelated to the surgery, assign the unrelated condition as the principal diagnosis.

Diagnostic coding can be a challenge for any insurance billing specialist. ICD-10-CM coding conventions and official guidelines must be carefully followed. One final coding rule actually supersedes all others: Code only the conditions, problems, diagnoses, and procedures that are clearly documented in the patient's medical record.

REINFORCEMENT EXERCISES 4–8

Write a brief definition for each term.

1. principal diagnosis _____

2. non-outpatient settings _____

3. sequenced _____

4. hematuria _____

5. cystocele _____

Mark each statement as True (T) or False (F). If the statement is False, add the correction that makes the statement True.

1. Symptoms are sometimes used as a principal diagnosis. _____

2. ICD-10-CM coding conventions take precedence over the *Official Guidelines for Coding and Reporting.* _____

3. A principal diagnosis cannot be assigned when a procedure or treatment is cancelled. _____

4. At the time of discharge, diagnoses like *probable*, *likely*, and *still to be ruled out* are coded as if they existed. _____

5. A complication related to outpatient surgery may be a principal diagnosis for a subsequent inpatient admission. _____

6. The diagnosis associated with outpatient surgery may not be a principal diagnosis for a subsequent inpatient admission. _____

ASSIGNING ICD-10-CM DIAGNOSES CODES

Assigning ICD-10-CM diagnoses codes depends on three activities:

- Following ICD-10-CM coding conventions and the ICD-10-CM *Official Guidelines for Coding and Reporting*
- Selecting diagnoses codes
- Sequencing diagnoses codes

Only those diagnoses, conditions, or problems that are clearly documented in the patient's medical record are coded and submitted with the insurance claim.

Selecting Diagnoses Codes

The *Alphabetic Index* and the *Tabular List* are used for accurate coding. The steps for code selection are enumerated and described with examples.

1. Identify the main term(s) in the diagnostic statement. (In this example, the main term is in bold.)

    EXAMPLE
    Urinary tract **infection** due to *E. coli*.

2. Find the main term(s) in the *Alphabetic Index*.

    EXAMPLE
    Locate "Infection" in the Index.

3. Review the diagnostic statement for additional information concerning the main term.

    EXAMPLE
    "Urinary tract" identifies the anatomic location of the **infection**.

4. Review the subterms listed under the main term to determine whether an entry matches the additional information in the diagnostic statement.

    EXAMPLE
    "Urinary (tract)" is a subterm listed under *"Infection."* There is no mention of *"due to E. coli."*

5. Follow any cross-reference instructions such as "see" or "see also." If there are no cross-reference instructions, note the code listed with the subterm entry.

    EXAMPLE
    The code for *"Infection, urinary (tract) NEC"* is N39.0.

6. **Check the code listed in the *Alphabetic Index* with the description in the *Tabular List*.**

    EXAMPLE
    Code N39.0 in the *Tabular List* is described as "Urinary tract infection, site not specified." **Use additional** code (B95-B97) to identify infectious agent indicates the need for another code. **Excludes1:** lists several conditions not covered by this code.
    E. coli is identified in the diagnostic statement and is coded as B96.20 *Escherichia coli [E.coli]* as the cause of the infection.

7. Read and follow all inclusion, exclusion, and other instructional notes.

   EXAMPLE

   In the previous example, the instruction "use additional code (B95-B97) to identify infectious agent" requires a code for *E. coli*.

8. Assign the code(s) to the highest level of specificity.

   EXAMPLE

   N39.0 is the highest level of specificity for urinary tract infection due to *E. coli* because no five-, six-, or seven-character code is available. For the same reason, B96.20 is the highest level of specificity for the *E. coli* code.

9. Select and assign all codes that complete the diagnostic statement.

   EXAMPLE

   Urinary tract infection due to *E. coli* is coded N39.0, B96.20.

Step 6 is bolded for a very important reason. The *Tabular List* provides a complete description of conditions included and excluded under a particular code as well as important instructional notes. A competent insurance billing specialist *never* codes directly from the *Alphabetic Index*.

Sequencing Diagnoses Codes

To ensure that the health care agency receives appropriate reimbursement for services, diagnostic codes must be accurately listed on the insurance claim. Placing diagnostic codes in the correct order is called sequencing. Sequencing depends on the type of health care agency and on the definition of first-listed diagnosis and principal diagnosis.

The first-listed diagnosis is the condition noted as the reason for a specific encounter or visit. First-listed diagnosis criteria apply to outpatient settings, such as a physician's office.

   EXAMPLE

   A patient is seen in the office for strep throat. During the exam, the physician also reviews the current status of the patient's diabetes. The first-listed diagnosis in this case is strep throat (the reason for the visit) and is sequenced first on the insurance claim. Diabetes may be listed as a concurrent or secondary condition.

A concurrent condition is a problem that coexists with the first-listed diagnosis and complicates the treatment of the first-listed diagnosis. A secondary condition is a condition that coexists with the first-listed diagnosis but does not directly affect the outcome or treatment of the first-listed diagnosis.

The principal diagnosis is the diagnosis determined after study to be the reason for the patient's admission to a hospital or other non-outpatient setting.

   EXAMPLE

   A patient is admitted to the hospital for rectal bleeding. After the appropriate tests, colorectal cancer is identified as the diagnosis. The principal diagnosis in this case is colorectal cancer, even though the initial reason for hospitalization was rectal bleeding. The code for colorectal cancer is sequenced first on the insurance claim.

Improper sequencing of diagnostic codes can lead to inadequate reimbursement for services rendered; denied or delayed reimbursement for services rendered; and, in a worst-case scenario, charges of fraud or abuse. Strict adherence to ICD-10-CM coding conventions, sequencing guidelines, and the *Official Guidelines for Coding and Reporting* prevents reimbursement problems.

REINFORCEMENT EXERCISES 4–9

Rank each statement from 1 to 9. Place a 1 in front of the first step for selecting an ICD-10-CM diagnosis code and a 9 in front of the last step.

_____ Assign the code(s) to the highest level of specificity.

_____ Identify the main term(s) in the diagnosis statement.

_____ Follow any cross-reference instructions.

_____ Check the code listed in the *Alphabetic Index* with the description in the *Tabular List*.

_____ Find the main term in the *Alphabetic Index*.

_____ Select and assign all codes that complete the diagnostic statement.

_____ Review the subterms listed under the main term in the *Alphabetic Index*.

_____ Read and follow all inclusion, exclusion, and other instruction notes.

_____ Review the diagnostic statement for additional information concerning the main term.

Write a short answer for each statement.

1. Describe the difference between the first-listed diagnosis and the principal diagnosis.

_____

2. Briefly define the term *sequencing*.

_____

3. Describe the difference between a *concurrent condition* and a *secondary condition*.

_____

Write the main term and assign the correct ICD-10-CM code for each diagnosis.

1. Gastric influenza

Main Term: _____ Code: _____

2. Laceration of the eyeball

Main Term: _____ Code: _____

continued on the next page

continued from the previous page

3. Acute pyogenic thyroiditis

   Main Term: _____ Code: _____

4. Malaria with hepatitis

   Main Term: _____ Code: _____

5. Recurrent bleeding peptic ulcer

   Main Term: _____ Code: _____

6. Hypoglycemia

   Main Term: _____ Code: _____

7. Lymphangitis, acute

   Main Term: _____ Code: _____

8. Ectopic pregnancy

   Main Term: _____ Code: _____

9. Arthritis due to psoriasis

   Main Term: _____ Code: _____

10. Appendicitis with perforation

   Main Term: _____ Code:_____

INTERNATIONAL CLASSIFICATION OF DISEASES, TENTH REVISION, PROCEDURE CODING SYSTEM (ICD-10-PCS)

The ICD-10-PCS replaced *ICD-9-CM Volume 3* procedure codes. The ICD-10-PCS was developed by 3M Health Information Systems under contract with the CMS. The first draft was completed in 1996 and the final draft was completed in 1998. The ICD-10-PCS is updated annually. Information in this text is based on the 2012 ICD-10-PCS guidelines as published by the CMS. The most up-to-date information is available on the CMS website, http://www.cms.gov, using ICD-10-PCS as the search term.

The ICD-10-PCS manual is available from several commercial publishers. Although each publisher offers unique editing features, guidelines, conventions, and all information related to assigning codes must comply with the CMS version.

The ICD-10-PCS is used for coding and reporting treatments provided in hospital and other inpatient settings. The term *procedure* is used in the widest possible context and includes everything from chest x-rays to heart transplants. This coding system is detailed and complex.

It is well beyond the scope of this text to cover every ICD-10-PCS section. This chapter provides an overview of ICD-10-PCS and more detailed information from ICD-10-PCS Section 0, *Medical and Surgical*.

ICD-10-PCS Components

The ICD-10-PCS components are *Tables* and an *Alphabetic Index*. The *Tables* are organized into sections that include the codes associated with each section. The *Alphabetic Index* is an alphabetical list of entries that direct the billing specialist or medical coder to the applicable *Table* for code assignment.

ICD-10-PCS Sections

The ICD-10-PCS is divided into 16 sections according to the type of procedure performed. Each section is assigned a unique alphabetic or numeric character that is the initial or first character in every code associated with the section. Table 4–4 lists the ICD-10-PCS procedure sections with a brief description of the section's contents.

TABLE 4–4

ICD-10-PCS Sections	
Character	**Section**
0	Medical and Surgical *Body Systems*: Medical and Surgical section body systems are listed in Table 4–5 *Root Operations*: Alteration; Bypass; Change; Control; Creation; Destruction; Detachment; Dilation; Division; Drainage; Release; Removal; Repair; Replacement; Reposition; Resection; Restriction; Revision; Supplement; Transfer; Transplant
1	Obstetrics *Body System*: Pregnancy *Root Operations*: Abortion; Delivery
2	Placement *Body Systems*: Anatomical Regions; Anatomical Orifices *Root Operations*: Compression; Dressing; Immobilization; Packing; Traction; Change; Removal
3	Administration *Body Systems*: Physiological Systems and Anatomical Regions; Circulatory; Indwelling Device *Root Operations*: Introduction; Irrigation; Transfusion
4	Measurement and Monitoring *Body System*: Physiological Systems *Root Operations*: Measurement; Monitoring

continued on the next page

continued from the previous page

5	Extracorporeal Assistance and Performance
	Body System: Physiological Systems
	Root Operations: Assistance; Performance; Restoration
6	Extracorporeal Therapies
	Body System: Physiological Systems
	Root Operations: Atmospheric Control; Decompression; Electromagnetic Therapy; Hyperthermia; Hypothermia; Pheresis; Phototherapy; Ultrasound Therapy; Ultraviolet Light Therapy; Shock Wave Therapy
7	Osteopathic
	Body System: Anatomical Regions
	Root Operation: Treatment
8	Other Procedures
	Body Systems: Physiological Systems; Anatomical Regions
	Root Operation: Other Procedures—Methodologies that attempt to remediate or cure a disorder or disease
9	Chiropractic
	Body System: Anatomical Regions
	Root Operation: Manipulation
B	Imaging
	Body Systems: Central Nervous System; Heart; Upper Arteries; Lower Arteries; Veins; Lymphatic System; Eye; Ear, Nose, Mouth, and Throat; Respiratory System; Gastrointestinal System; Hepatobiliary System and Pancreas; Endocrine System; Skin, Subcutaneous Tissue, and Breast; Connective Tissue; Skull, and Facial Bones; Non-Axial Upper Bones; Non-Axial Lower Bones; Axial Skeleton, Except Skull and Facial Bones; Urinary System; Female Reproductive System; Male Reproductive System; Anatomical Regions; Fetus and Obstetrical
	*Type: Plain Radiography; Fluoroscopy; CT Scan; MRI; Ultrasound
	*Type is used in lieu of root operation.
C	Nuclear Medicine
	Body Systems: Central Nervous System; Heart; Veins; Lymphatic and Hematologic System; Eye; Ear, Nose, Mouth, and Throat; Respiratory System; Gastrointestinal System; Hepatobiliary System and Pancreas; Endocrine System; Skin, Subcutaneous Tissue, and Breast; Musculoskeletal System; Urinary System; Male Reproductive System; Anatomical Regions
	*Type: Planar Imaging; Tomographic (Tomo) Imaging; Tomographic (PET) Imaging; Nonimaging Uptake; Nonimaging Probe; Nonimaging Assay; Systemic Therapy
	*Type is used in lieu of root operation.

continued on the next page

continued from the previous page

ICD-10-PCS Sections	
Character	**Section**
D	Radiation Oncology *Body Systems*: Central Nervous System; Lymphatic and Hematologic System; Eye; Ear, Nose, Mouth, and Throat; Respiratory System; Gastrointestinal System; Hepatobiliary System and Pancreas; Endocrine System; Skin; Breast; Musculoskeletal System; Urinary System; Female Reproductive System; Male Reproductive System; Anatomical Regions *Modality: Beam Radiation; Brachytherapy; Stereotactic Radiosurgery; Other Radiation *Modality is used in lieu of root operation.
F	Physical Rehabilitation and Diagnostic Audiology *Section Qualifier: Rehabilitation; Diagnostic Audiology **Type: Treatment; Assessment; Fittings; Caregiver Training *Section Qualifier is used in lieu of body systems. ** Type is used in lieu of root operation.
G	Mental Health *Body Systems*: None *Type: Psychological Tests; Crisis Intervention; Medication Management; Individual Psychotherapy; Counseling; Family Psychotherapy; Electroconvulsive Therapy; Biofeedback; Hypnosis; Narcosynthesis; Group Psychotherapy; Light Therapy *Type is used in lieu of root operation.
H	Substance Abuse Treatment *Body Systems*: None *Type: Detoxification Services; Individual Counseling; Group Counseling; Individual Psychotherapy; Family Counseling; Medication Management; Pharmacotherapy *Type is used in lieu of root operation.

ICD-10-PCS *Alphabetic Index*

The ICD-10-PCS *Alphabetic Index* is the key to locating the correct *Table* for code assignment. *Main terms* in the *Index* are printed flush-left in bold. Main terms are names of procedures and treatments, anatomic sites, and specific body structures. *Subterms* are indented under main terms or other subterms and provide additional information for accurate code assignment.

In the *Alphabetic Index, see* and *use* are cross-references. "See" directs the billing specialist or medical coder to the correct procedure or treatment main entry (Example A). "Use" identifies the name of the body structure associated with the site of the procedure or treatment (Example B).

EXAMPLE A: "SEE"
Frank underwent an abdominoplasty to repair a work-related injury. The main term **Abdominoplasty** has three "see" cross-references: *see* Alteration, Abdominal Wall **0W0F**; *see* Repair, Abdominal Wall **0WQF**; *see* Supplement, Abdominal Wall **0WUF**. The billing specialist or medical coder selects repair and refers to *Table* 0WQF to complete the code.

EXAMPLE B: "USE"
Reba was admitted for *repair of a torn acromioclavicular ligament.* Acromioclavicular ligament is not listed as a subterm under the main term **Repair**. The billing specialist or medical coder checks the *Index* for acromioclavicular ligament. The cross-reference *"use* Bursa and Ligament, Shoulder (right or left)" identifies the correct subterm for this procedure. The billing specialist or medical coder locates *bursa and ligament* under the main term **Repair** and selects the appropriate *Table* to continue code assignment.

Figure 4–22 illustrates ICD-10-PCS *Alphabetic Index* entries and cross-references "see" and "use."

ICD-10-PCS *Tables*

The ICD-10-PCS codes have seven characters. Each section of the ICD-10-PCS consists of *Tables* that have the detailed information needed to assign an ICD-10-PCS code. Figure 4–23 illustrates a *Table* from Section 0, Medical and Surgical.

Abdominal aortic plexus *use* Nerve, Abdominal Sympathetic
Abdominal esophagus *use* Esophagus, Lower
Abdominohysterectomy
    see Excision, Uterus **0UB9**
    see Resection, Uterus **0UT9**

Abdominoplasty
    see Alteration, Abdominal Wall **0W0F**
    see Repair, Abdominal Wall **0WQF**
    see Supplement, Abdominal Wall **0WUF**

Abductor hallucis muscle
    use Muscle, Foot, Right
    use Muscle, Foot, Left

Ablation *see* Destruction

Figure 4–22 ICD-10-PCS *Alphabetic Index* Entries and Cross-References

Section	**0** Medical and Surgical
Body System	**D** Gastrointestinal
Operation	**B** Excision: Cutting out or off, without replacement, a portion of a body part

Body Part	*Approach*	*Device*	*Qualifier*
1 Esophagus, Upper **2** Esophagus, Middle **3** Esophagus, Lower **4** Esophagogastric Junction **5** Esophagus **6** Stomach **7** Stomach, Pylorus **8** Small Intestine **9** Duodenum **A** Jejunum **B** Ileum **C** Ileocecal Valve **E** Large Intestine **F** Large Intestine, Right **G** Large Intestine, Left **H** Cecum **J** Appendix **K** Ascending Colon **L** Transverse Colon **M** Descending Colon **N** Sigmoid Colon **P** Rectum	**0** Open **3** Percutaneous **4** Percutaneous Endoscopic **7** Via Natural or Artificial Opening **8** Via Natural or Artificial Opening Endoscopic	**Z** No Device	**X** Diagnostic **Z** No Qualifier
Q Anus	**0** Open **3** Percutaneous **4** Percutaneous Endoscopic **7** Via Natural or Artificial Opening	**Z** No Device	**X** Diagnostic
	8 Via Natural or Artificial Opening Endoscopic **X** External		**Z** No Qualifier
R Anal Sphincter **S** Greater Omentum **T** Lesser Omentum **V** Mesentery **W** Peritoneum	**0** Open **3** Percutaneous **4** Percutaneous Endoscopic	**Z** No Device	**X** Diagnostic **Z** No Qualifier

Figure 4–23 **Section 0, Medical and Surgical Table**

The top row of the *Table* gives the first three characters of a procedure code. Subsequent rows include four columns that provide options for the next four characters of a procedure code. Valid codes must be constructed using *only* the choices offered in the columns associated with each row.

EXAMPLE

The ICD-10-PCS code for a procedure involving the anus begins with the characters **0DB** located in the first row of the *Table* (see Figure 4–23).

The 0 (zero) identifies the Medical and Surgical section, D identifies the gastrointestinal system, and B identifies the operation as an excision. The fourth character of the code is **Q**, which identifies the anus. Only characters from the row that begins with **Q** may be used to complete the code.

REINFORCEMENT EXERCISES 4–10

Fill in the blank.

1. ICD-10-PCS was developed by 3M Health Information Systems under contract with _____.

2. ICD-10-PCS _____ are organized in sections that include procedure and treatment codes.

3. In the _____, *see* and *use* are cross-references for accurate code selection.

4. The first character of an ICD-10-PCS code refers to a specific ICD-10-PCS _____.

5. The first three characters of an ICD-10-PCS code are given in the _____ of a *Table*.

Match the ICD-10-PCS section in Column 1 with the root operations in Column 2.

ICD-10-PCS Section	Root Operation
1. _____ Medical and Surgical	**a.** Brachytherapy
2. _____ Obstetrics	**b.** Compression
3. _____ Placement	**c.** Delivery
4. _____ Administration	**d.** Fittings
5. _____ Osteopathic	**e.** Fluoroscopy
6. _____ Chiropractic	**f.** Irrigation
7. _____ Imaging	**g.** Manipulation
8. _____ Nuclear Medicine	**h.** Nonimaging Uptake
9. _____ Radiation Oncology Physical	**i.** Removal
10. _____ Rehabilitation and Diagnostic Audiology	**j.** Treatment

ICD-10-PCS Code Structure

All codes in ICD-10-PCS have seven alphanumeric characters. Each character is assigned a *value*, numbers 0–9 and alphabet letters with the exception of O and I. The character value represents an aspect of the procedure that identifies the following:

- Character 1 = ICD-10-PCS Section
- Character 2 = Body system
- Character 3 = Root operation
- Character 4 = Body part
- Character 5 = Approach
- Character 6 = Device
- Character 7 = Qualifier

The letters O and I are not used to avoid confusion with numbers 0 and 1. The seven characters are described individually.

Character 1: Section

The first character in any code *always* identifies an ICD-10-PCS section. Table 4–3 lists the value of character 1 for each section. The code for procedures that are included in Section 0, Medical and Surgical *always* begins with the character 0; obstetrics procedures *always* begin with the character 1; chiropractic procedures *always* begin with the character G; and so forth.

The remaining six characters of an ICD-10-PCS code have a standard value or meaning *within* a given section. Because the same characters are used in all 16 sections, the value of the characters may change depending on the section.

Character 2: Body System

The second character identifies the body system, the general physiological system or anatomical region involved in the procedure. Each section includes body systems for that specific section. Table 4–5 lists the "Medical and Surgical" section body systems and their values.

Each section has its own character 2, body system values. Figure 4–24 illustrates body system values for character 2 from the "Medical and Surgical," "Obstetrics," and "Placement" sections.

Character 3: Root Operation, Type, Modality

Character 3 identifies the root operation, which is a specific term that identifies the objective of the procedure. ICD-10-PCS has 31 root operations, each with a specific definition. These root operations apply to Section 0, Medical and Surgical. Table 4–6 lists the root operations, definitions, and examples.

Character 3 for sections one through nine (1–9) is also called the root procedure. The majority of the root procedures for these sections are unique to each section. For example, the root procedures for Section 2, Placement are called *compression, dressing, immobilization, packing, traction, change,* and *removal*; the root procedures for Section 4, Measurement and Monitoring are called *measurement* and *monitoring*; and the root procedure for Section 7, Osteopathic is called *treatment*.

TABLE 4–5

Character 2 Values: Medical and Surgical Body Systems

Character 2 Value	Body System	Character 2 Value	Body System
0	Central Nervous System	J	Subcutaneous Tissue and Fascia
1	Peripheral Nervous System	K	Muscles
2	Heart and Great Vessels	L	Tendons
3	Upper Arteries	M	Bursae and Ligaments
4	Lower Arteries	N	Head and Facial Bones
5	Upper Veins	P	Upper Bones
6	Lower Veins	Q	Lower Bones
7	Lymphatic and Hemic System	R	Upper Joints
8	Eye	S	Lower Joints
9	Ear, Nose, Sinus	T	Urinary System
B	Respiratory System	U	Female Reproductive System
C	Mouth and Throat	V	Male Reproductive System
D	Gastrointestinal System	W	Anatomical Regions, General
F	Hepatobiliary System and Pancreas	X	Anatomical Regions, Upper Extremities
G	Endocrine System	Y	Anatomical Regions, Lower Extremities
H	Skin and Breast		

"Medical and Surgical" Section (0) – Character 2 Values – Body Systems

0 = Central Nervous System
1 = Peripheral Nervous System…
8 = Eye…
T = Urinary System…

"Obstetrics" Section (1) – Character 2 Values – Body Systems

0 = Pregnancy

"Placement" Section (2) – Character 2 Values – Body Systems

W = Anatomic Regions
Y = Anatomic Orifices

Figure 4–24 ICD-10-PCS Character 2 Values—Body Systems

TABLE 4–6

Character 3 Root Operations, Definitions, and Examples		
Root Operation	**Definition**	**Example**
Alteration	Modifying the natural anatomic structure of a body part without affecting the function of the body part	Face lift, breast augmentation
Bypass	Altering the route of passage of the contents of a tubular body part	Coronary artery bypass, colostomy formation
Change	Taking out or off a device from a body part and putting back an identical or similar device in or on the same body part without cutting or puncturing the skin or a mucous membrane	Urinary catheter change, gastrostomy tube change
Control	Stopping or attempting to stop postprocedural bleeding	Control of post-prostatectomy hemorrhage, control of post-tonsillectomy hemorrhage
Creation	Making a new genital structure that does not take over the function of a body part Note: Used only for sex change operations	Creation of a vagina in a male, creation of a penis in a female
Destruction	Physical eradication of all or a portion of a body part by the direct use of energy, force, or a destructive agent	Fulguration of rectal polyp, cautery of skin lesion
Detachment	Cutting off all or part of the upper or lower extremities	Below the knee amputation, disarticulation of shoulder
Dilation	Expanding the orifice or the lumen of a tubular body part	Percutaneous transluminal angioplasty, pyloromyotomy
Division	Cutting into a body part without draining fluids and/or gases from the body part in order to separate or transect a body part	Spinal cordotomy, osteotomy
Drainage	Taking or letting out fluids and/or gases from a body part	Thoracentesis, incision and drainage
Excision	Cutting out or off, without replacement, a portion of a body part	Partial nephrectomy, liver biopsy
Extirpation	Taking or cutting out solid matter from a body part	Thrombectomy, choledocholithotomy
Extraction	Pulling or stripping out or off a portion of a body part by the use of force	Dilation and curettage, vein stripping
Fragmentation	Breaking solid matter in a body part into pieces	Extracorporeal shockwave lithotripsy, transurethral lithotripsy
Fusion	Joining together portions of an articular body part rendering the articular body part immobile	Spinal fusion, ankle arthrodesis

continued on the next page

continued from the previous page

Insertion	Putting in a nonbiological appliance that monitors, assists, performs, or prevents a physiological function but does not physically take the place of a body part	Insertion of a radioactive implant, insertion of central venous catheter
Inspection	Visually and/or manually exploring a body part	Diagnostic arthroscopy, exploratory laparotomy
Map	Locating the route of passage of electrical impulses and/or locating functional areas in a body part	Cardiac mapping, cortical mapping
Occlusion	Completely closing an orifice or the lumen of a tubular body part	Fallopian tube ligation, ligation of inferior vena cava
Reattachment	Putting back in or on, all or a portion of a separated body part to its normal location or other suitable location	Reattachment of hand, reattachment of avulsed kidney
Release	Freeing a body part from an abnormal physical constraint	Adhesiolysis, carpal tunnel release
Removal	Taking out or off a device from a body part	Drainage tube removal, cardiac pacemaker removal
Repair	Restoring, to the extent possible, a body part to its normal anatomic structure and function	Colostomy takedown, suture of laceration
Replacement	Putting in or on biological or synthetic material that physically takes the place and/or function of all or a portion of a body part	Total hip replacement, bone graft, free skin graft
Reposition	Moving to its normal location or other suitable location all or a portion of a body part	Reposition of undescended testicle, fracture reduction
Resection	Cutting out or off, without replacement, all of a body part	Total nephrectomy, total lobectomy of lung
Restriction	Partially closing an orifice or lumen of a tubular part	Esophagostric fundoplication, cervical cerclage
Revision	Correcting, to the extent possible, a portion of a malfunctioning device or the position of a displaced device	Adjustment of pacemaker lead, adjustment of hip prosthesis
Supplement	Putting in or on biological or synthetic material that physically reinforces and/or augments the function of a portion of a body part	Herniorrhaphy using mesh, free nerve graft, mitral valve ring annuloplasty
Transfer	Moving, without taking out, all or a portion of a body part to another location to take over the function of all or a portion of a body part	Tendon transfer, skin pedicle flap transfer
Transplantation	Putting in or on all or a portion of a living body part taken from another individual or animal to physically take the place and/or function of all or a portion of a similar body part	Kidney transplant, heart transplant

Section 0 Medical and Surgical

Section	**0** Medical and Surgical
Body System	**D** Gastrointestinal System
Operation	**B** Excision: Cutting out or off, without replacement, a portion of a body part

Section D Radiation Oncology

Section	**D** Radiation Oncology
Body System	**B** Respiratory System
Modality	**0** Beam Radiation

Section H Substance Abuse Treatment

Section	**H** Substance Abuse Treatment
Body System	**Z** None
Type	**4** Group Counseling: The application of psychological methods to treat two or more individuals with addictive behavior

Figure 4–25 ICD-10-PCS *Tables*, First Row

Character 3 for Section B, Imaging; Section C, Nuclear Medicine; Section F, Physical Rehabilitation and Diagnostic Audiology; Section G, Mental Health; and Section H, Substance Abuse Treatment is called type. Type indicates the treatment or service performed. For example, the types in Section B, Imaging include MRI (magnetic resonance imaging) and ultrasound; the types in Section C, Nuclear Medicine include tomographic imaging and PET (positron emission tomography); and the types in Section H, Substance Abuse Treatment include detoxification services and individual services.

Character 3 for Section D, Radiation Oncology is called modality, which identifies the mode by which the radiation is administered. The modalities include beam radiation, brachytherapy, stereotactic radiosurgery, and other radiation. Refer to Table 4–4 ICD-10-PCS sections for a complete list of the root operations, types, and modalities that represent character 3.

Characters 1 through 3 are always identified in the first row of the ICD-10-PCS *Tables*. Figure 4–25 illustrates the first row of three tables.

REINFORCEMENT EXERCISES 4–11

Write the designation for each ICD-10-PCS character.

1. Character 1 _____

2. Character 2 _____

3. Character 3 _____

continued on the next page

continued from the previous page

4. Character 4 _____

5. Character 5 _____

6. Character 6 _____

7. Character 7 _____

Match the root operation in Column 1 with the correct definition in Column 2.

Column 1

1. _____ alteration

2. _____ bypass

3. _____ detachment

4. _____ dilation

5. _____ extirpation

6. _____ excision

7. _____ occlusion

8. _____ replacement

9. _____ resection

10. _____ restriction

11. _____ revision

12. _____ transfer

Column 2

a. completely closing off the orifice or lumen of a tubular body part

b. cutting off or out all of a body part, without replacement

c. cutting off or out a portion of a body part, without replacement

d. modifying a body part structure without affecting its function

e. expanding the orifice or lumen of a tubular body part

f. correcting a portion or the position of a malfunctioning device

g. moving, without taking out, a body part to another location to take over the function of another body part

h. altering the route of the contents of a tubular body part

i. cutting off all or part of the upper or lower extremities

j. taking or cutting out solid matter from a body part

k. putting in or on biological or synthetic material that takes the place of or assumes the function of a body part

l. partially closing off the lumen or orifice of a tubular part

Character 4: Body Part, Body System/Region, Treatment Site, Qualifier

Depending on the ICD-10-PCS section, character 4 identifies the body part, body system/region, treatment site, or qualifier for the services performed. In ICD-10-PCS, qualifier is a general term that means *additional information*. The term qualifier is used in several ICD-10-PCS character designations. Table 4–7 lists character 4 designations and related ICD-10-PCS sections.

TABLE 4–7

ICD-10-PCS Character 4 Designations and Related ICD-10-PCS Sections	
Character 4 Designation	**ICD-10-PCS Section**
Body Part	**0** Medical and Surgical
	1 Obstetrics
	B Imaging
	C Nuclear Medicine
Body Region	**2** Placement
	7 Osteopathic
	8 Other Procedures
	9 Chiropractic
Body System	**4** Measurement and Monitoring
	5 Extracorporeal Assistance and Performance
	6 Extracorporeal Therapies
Body System/Region	**3** Administration
	F Physical Rehabilitation and Diagnostic Audiology
Treatment Site	**D** Radiation Oncology
Qualifier	**G** Mental Health
	H Substance Abuse Treatment

Values for character 4 are listed in the third row, first column of the *Tables*. Column titles are in the second row of the *Tables*. Figure 4–26 illustrates the location and column title for character 4.

Character 5: Approach, Duration, Contrast, Radionuclide, Modality Qualifier, Type Qualifier, and Qualifier

In eight ICD-10-PCS sections, character 5 defines the approach or technique used to reach the procedure site. The eight sections are: Section 0, Medical and Surgical; Section 1, Obstetrics; Section 2, Placement; Section 3, Administration; Section 4, Measurement and Monitoring; Section 7, Osteopathic; Section 8, Other Procedures; and Section 9, Chiropractic. Table 4–8 lists character 5 approaches, definitions, and examples for these sections.

The remaining ICD-10-PCS sections identify character 5 as *duration, contrast, radionuclide, modality qualifier, type qualifier,* and *qualifier*. Table 4–9 lists the sections associated with these character 5 designations.

Section 0 Medical and Surgical

Section	**0** Medical and Surgical
Body System	**D** Gastrointestinal System
Operation	**B** Excision: Cutting out or off, without replacement, a portion of a body part

Body Part	Approach	Device	Qualifier
1 Esophagus, Upper **2** Esophagus, Middle… **J** Appendix			

Section D Radiation Oncology

Section	**D** Radiation Oncology
Body System	**B** Respiratory System
Modality	**0** Beam Radiation

Treatment Site	Modality Qualifier	Isotope	Qualifier
0 Trachea **1** Bronchus **2** Lung			

Section H Substance Abuse Treatment

Section	**H** Substance Abuse Treatment
Body System	**Z** None
Type	**4** Group Counseling: The application of psychological methods to treat two or more individuals with addictive behavior

Qualifier	Qualifier	Qualifier	Qualifier
0 Cognitive **1** Behavioral **2** Cognitive-Behavioral **3** 12-step			

Figure 4–26 ICD-10-PCS *Tables*, Character 4

TABLE 4–8

Character 5 Approaches and Definitions with Examples	
Approach	**Definition with Example**
0 Open	Cutting through the skin or mucous membrane and as many body layers as necessary to expose the site of the procedure Example: abdominal hysterectomy
3 Percutaneous	Entry, by puncture or minor incision, of instrumentation through the skin or mucous membrane and any other body layers as necessary to reach the site of the procedure Example: needle biopsy of the liver

continued on the next page

continued from the previous page

Character 5 Approaches and Definitions with Examples	
Approach	**Definition with Example**
4 Percutaneous Endoscopic	Entry, by puncture or minor incision, of instrumentation through the skin or mucous membrane and any other body layers as necessary to reach and visualize the site of the procedure Example: arthroscopy
7 Via Natural or Artificial Opening	Entry of instrumentation through a natural or an artificial opening to reach the site of the procedure Example: endotracheal intubation
8 Via Natural or Artificial Opening, Endoscopic	Entry of instrumentation through a natural or artificial external opening to reach and visualize the site of the procedure Example: colonoscopy
F Via Natural or Artificial Opening Endoscopic with Percutaneous Endoscopic Assistance	Entry of instrumentation through a natural or artificial external opening *and* entry, by puncture or minor incision, of instrumentation through the skin or mucous membrane and any other body layers necessary to aid in the performance of the procedure Example: laparoscopic-assisted vaginal hysterectomy
X External	Procedures performed directly on the skin or mucous membrane and procedures performed indirectly by application of external force through the skin or mucous membrane Example: closed reduction, fracture

TABLE 4–9

ICD-10-PCS Sections with Character 5 Designations	
Section(s)	**Character 5 Designation with Definition**
5 Extracorporeal Assistance and Performance **6** Extracorporeal Therapies	*Duration* Duration specifies whether the procedure was a single or multiple occurrence, intermittent or continuous
B Imaging	*Contrast* Contrast is differentiated by the concentration of the contrast material used to enhance the image
C Nuclear Medicine	*Radionuclide* Radionuclide identifies the source of the radiation used to enhance the image
D Radiation Oncology	*Modality Qualifier* Modality Qualifier further specifies the type of radiation used during the procedure or treatment (e.g., photons, electrons)

continued on the next page

continued from the previous page

F Physical Rehabilitation and Diagnostic Audiology	*Type Qualifier* Type Qualifier identifies the precise test or method used during the service being performed (e.g., prosthesis fitting, therapeutic exercise treatment)
G Mental Health **H** Substance Abuse	*Qualifier* Qualifier indicates the need for an additional value to complete a seven-character code. For Sections **G** and **H**, character 5 has a value of "Z," which means None.

Values for character 5 are listed in the third row, second column of the *Tables*. Figure 4–27 illustrates the location and column title for character 5.

Character 6: Device, Equipment, Function, Isotope, Method, Substance, and Qualifier

In Section 0, Medical and Surgical; Section 1, Obstetrics; and Section 2, Placement, character 6 identifies a **device** that is left in place at the end of a procedure. Device values fall into four

Section 0 Medical and Surgical

Section	**0** Medical and Surgical		
Body System	**D** Gastrointestinal System		
Operation	**B** Excision: Cutting out or off, without replacement, a portion of a body part		

Body Part	Approach	Device	Qualifier
1 Esophagus, Upper **2** Esophagus, Middle… **J** Appendix	**0** Open **3** Percutaneous **4** Percutaneous Endoscopic…		

Section D Radiation Oncology

Section	**D** Radiation Oncology		
Body System	**B** Respiratory System		
Modality	**0** Beam Radiation		

Treatment Site	Modality Qualifier	Isotope	Qualifier
0 Trachea **1** Bronchus **2** Lung	**0** Photons <1 MeV **2** Photons 1–10 MeV **2** Photons >10 MeV		

Section H Substance Abuse Treatment

Section	**H** Substance Abuse Treatment		
Body System	**Z** None		
Type	**4** Group Counseling: The application of psychological methods to treat two or more individuals with addictive behavior		

Qualifier	Qualifier	Qualifier	Qualifier
0 Cognitive **1** Behavioral… **3** 12-step	**Z** None		

Figure 4–27 ICD-10-PCS *Tables*, Character 5

basic categories: grafts and prostheses, implants, simple or mechanical appliances, and electronic appliances. Other sections identify character 6 as *equipment, function, isotope, method, substance,* and *qualifier*. Table 4–10 lists the sections associated with character 6 designations. The value **Z** is used to represent *no device* or *none*.

TABLE 4–10

ICD-10-PCS Sections with Character 6 Designations	
Section(s)	**Character 6 Designation with Definition**
0 Medical and Surgical **1** Obstetrics **2** Placement	*Device* Device includes only devices that remain after the procedure is completed. Examples: skin graft, joint prostheses, urinary catheter, orthopedic pins, monitoring electrode
F Physical Rehabilitation and Diagnostic Audiology	*Equipment* General categories rather than specific types of equipment are listed. Examples: physical agents, assistive device, adaptive device, mechanical modalities
4 Measurement and Monitoring **5** Extracorporeal Assistance and Performance	*Function* Function identifies the physical or physiological function measured or monitored; or the physiological function assisted or performed. Examples: nerve conductivity, respiratory capacity, oxygenation, ventilation
D Radiation Oncology	*Isotope* Isotope identifies the isotope administered in oncology treatments Examples: Cesium 137, Iridium 192, other isotope
7 Osteopathic **8** Other Procedures **9** Chiropractic	*Method* Method identifies the way a treatment or service is performed or delivered. Examples: fascial release, general mobilization, acupuncture, therapeutic massage, non-manual, mechanically assisted, and other method
3 Administration	*Substance* Substance identifies agents or biological material that is administered or implanted during a procedure. Examples: nutritional substance, local anesthetic, fertilized ovum, pigment
B Imaging	*Qualifier* Qualifier identifies additional information about the imaging procedure. Examples: enhanced, unenhanced, laser
6 Extracorporeal Therapies **C** Nuclear Medicine **G** Mental Health **H** Substance Abuse Treatment	*Qualifier* Qualifier is used to indicate that a value for character 6 is needed to complete a seven-character code. For Sections **6**, **C**, **G**, and **H**, character 6 has a value of "Z," which means None.

Section 0 Medical and Surgical

Section	**0** Medical and Surgical
Body System	**D** Gastrointestinal System
Operation	**B** Excision: Cutting out or off, without replacement, a portion of a body part

Body Part	Approach	Device	Qualifier
1 Esophagus, Upper **2** Esophagus, Middle… **J** Appendix	**0** Open **3** Percutaneous **4** Percutaneous Endoscopic…	**Z** No Device	

Section D Radiation Oncology

Section	**D** Radiation Oncology
Body System	**B** Respiratory System
Modality	**0** Beam Radiation

Treatment Site	Modality Qualifier	Isotope	Qualifier
0 Trachea **1** Bronchus **2** Lung	**0** Photons <1 MeV **2** Photons 1–10 MeV **2** Photons >10 MeV	**Z** None	

Section H Substance Abuse Treatment

Section	**H** Substance Abuse Treatment
Body System	**Z** None
Type	**4** Group Counseling: The application of psychological methods to treat two or more individuals with addictive behavior

Qualifier	Qualifier	Qualifier	Qualifier
0 Cognitive **1** Behavioral… **3** 12-step	**Z** None	**Z** None	

Figure 4–28 ICD-10-PCS *Tables*, Character 6

Values for character 6 are listed in the third row, third column of the *Tables*. Figure 4–28 illustrates the location and column title for character 6.

Character 7: Qualifier

Character 7 values provide additional information about the treatment or procedure, if applicable. This character may have a narrow application to a specific root operation, body system, or body part. Each ICD-10-PCS section has its own values for character 7. When no value is available, "**Z**" which means none, is used to complete the seven-character code. Table 4–11 gives examples of character 7 designations.

Values for character 7 are listed in the third row, fourth column of the *Tables*. Figure 4–29 illustrates the location and column title for character 7.

TABLE 4–11

ICD-10-PCS Sections with Character 7 Designations	
Section(s)	**Character 7 Designation with Definition**
0 Medical and Surgical	*Qualifier* Examples: type of transplant, second site for a bypass, diagnostic excision (biopsy)
1 Obstetrics	*Qualifier* Examples: method of extraction, substance drained
2 Placement	*Qualifier* **Z** none
3 Administration	*Qualifier* Examples: may further specify a substance (e.g., high-dose interleukin-2, insulin)
4 Measurement and Monitoring	*Qualifier* Examples: may further specify anatomical location (e.g., right heart, left heart, pulmonary artery)
5 Extracorporeal Assistance and Performance	*Qualifier* Examples: may further specify equipment in the procedure (e.g., balloon pump)
6 Extracorporeal Therapies	*Qualifier* Examples: may further specify anatomic locations, fluids, substances (e.g., erythrocytes, peripheral vessels)
7 Osteopathic	*Qualifier* **Z** none
8 Other Procedures	*Qualifier* Examples: may further specify anatomic locations, fluids, specific services (e.g., blood, yoga therapy)
B Imaging	*Qualifier* Examples: may further specify elements of the imaging process (e.g., intraoperative, intravascular, transesophageal)
C Nuclear Medicine	*Qualifier* **Z** none
D Radiation Oncology	*Qualifier* Examples: intraoperative, none
F Physical Rehabilitation and Diagnostic Audiology	*Qualifier* **Z** none
G Mental Health **H** Substance Abuse Treatment	*Qualifier* **Z** none

Section 0 Medical and Surgical

Section	**0** Medical and Surgical
Body System	**D** Gastrointestinal System
Operation	**B** Excision: Cutting out or off, without replacement, a portion of a body part

Body Part	Approach	Device	Qualifier
1 Esophagus, Upper **2** Esophagus, Middle… **J** Appendix	**0** Open **3** Percutaneous **4** Percutaneous Endoscopic…	**Z** No Device	**X** Diagnostic **Z** No Qualifier

Section D Radiation Oncology

Section	**D** Radiation Oncology
Body System	**B** Respiratory System
Modality	**0** Beam Radiation

Treatment Site	Modality Qualifier	Isotope	Qualifier
0 Trachea **1** Bronchus **2** Lung	**0** Photons <1 MeV **2** Photons 1–10 MeV **2** Photons >10 MeV	**Z** None	**Z** None

Section H Substance Abuse Treatment

Section	**H** Substance Abuse Treatment
Body System	**Z** None
Type	**4** Group Counseling: The application of psychological methods to treat two or more individuals with addictive behavior

Qualifier	Qualifier	Qualifier	Qualifier
0 Cognitive **1** Behavioral… **3** 12-step	**Z** None	**Z** None	**Z** None

Figure 4–29 ICD-10-PCS *Tables*, Character 7

REINFORCEMENT EXERCISES 4–12

Briefly define the listed ICD-10-PCS character 5 designations.

1. open _____

2. percutaneous _____

3. external _____

4. duration _____

5. type qualifier _____

continued on the next page

continued from the previous page

Place an X next to the ICD-10-PCS sections that designate character 5 as an *approach*.

1. Section 0, Medical and Surgical _____

2. Section G, Mental Health _____

3. Section B, Imaging _____

4. Section 3, Administration _____

5. Section 4, Measurement and Monitoring _____

6. Section 2, Placement _____

7. Section D, Radiation Oncology _____

8. Section 1, Obstetrics _____

9. Section C, Nuclear Medicine _____

10. Section 9, Chiropractic _____

Write two (2) examples for each ICD-10-PCS character 6 designation.

1. device _____ _____

2. equipment _____ _____

3. function _____ _____

4. isotope _____ _____

5. method _____ _____

6. substance _____ _____

7. qualifier _____ _____

Match the ICD-10-PCS section in Column 1 with the character 7 descriptions in Column 2.

Column 1

1. _____ Section 0, Medical and Surgical

2. _____ Section 1, Obstetrics

3. _____ Section 2, Placement

4. _____ Section 3, Administration

5. _____ Section 4, Measurement and Monitoring

6. _____ Section 5, Extracorporeal Assistance and Performance

7. _____ Section 8, Other Procedures

Column 2

a. anatomical location

b. equipment (e.g., balloon pump)

c. method of extraction

d. none

e. specific services (e.g., Yoga therapy)

f. type of substance (e.g., insulin)

g. type of transplant; diagnostic excision

ICD-10-PCS Coding Guidelines

ICD-10-PCS coding guidelines provide additional direction for code assignment. Information in this chapter is based on the 2012 ICD-10-PCS *Official Guidelines*. Selected guidelines presented here include the following:

- General guidelines
- Body system guidelines
- Root operation guidelines
- Body part guidelines
- Approach guidelines
- Device guidelines

Complete ICD-10-PCS section guidelines are included in all commercial publications and encoders. The most current guidelines are available on the CMS website, http://www.cms.gov, using ICD-10-PCS guidelines as the search word.

General Guidelines

1. The first and most important guideline is that the assigned code *must* be justified by the documentation in the patient's record. Billing specialists and medical coders must not hesitate to query the physician or other provider when there is a question concerning the clarity of the procedure and services rendered.
2. Valid ICD-10-PCS codes must have seven characters. The characters must include a combination of choices in characters 4 through 7 selected within the same row of the table.

Body System Guidelines

1. Procedure codes should identify the specific body part *unless* the procedure is performed on an anatomical region, or when no information related to a specific body part is available.

   EXAMPLE
   Control of postoperative hemorrhage is coded to the root operation *Control* in the general anatomical regions body systems.
   In this example, controlling the hemorrhage applies to the body in general rather than a specific body part.

2. Body systems designated as upper or lower contain body parts located above or below the diaphragm.

   EXAMPLE
   Upper Veins body system includes veins above the diaphragm; and Lower Veins body system includes veins below the diaphragm.

Root Operation Guidelines

1. The full definition of the root operation, as given in the PCS *Tables*, must be used to determine the appropriate root operation character.
2. Components of a procedure specified in the root operation definition and explanation *are not* assigned separate codes. Procedural steps necessary to reach the operative site and close the operative site *are not* assigned separate codes.

EXAMPLE
Procedure: Liver biopsy, via laparotomy.
    In this procedure statement, laparotomy is the procedure used to reach the operative site and is *not* assigned a separate code. This procedure is coded as a percutaneous (through the skin) liver biopsy.

3. Multiple procedures completed during the same operative episode are assigned separate codes under the following conditions:
   a. The same root operation is performed on different body parts that have distinct PCS values. For example: Diagnostic excision of the liver and pancreas
   b. The same root operation is performed at different body sites that are included in the same body part value. For example: Excision of the sartorius muscle and excision of the gracilis muscle. Because the sartorius and gracilis muscles are distinct parts of the upper leg muscle, each procedure is coded separately.
   c. Multiple root operations with distinct objectives are performed on the same body part.
   d. The intended root operation is attempted using one approach, but is converted to a different approach. For example: Laparoscopic vaginal hysterectomy is converted to an abdominal (open) hysterectomy. In this example, the laparoscopic procedure is coded to *Inspection* and the abdominal hysterectomy is coded to *Excision*.

4. Discontinued procedures: When an intended procedure is discontinued, code the procedure to the root operation performed. For example: A planned open excision of the gallbladder is discontinued after the initial incision because the patient became medically unstable. The procedure is coded to an open inspection of the abdominal cavity.

5. Biopsy followed by a more definitive treatment or procedure: When a diagnostic biopsy is followed by a definitive procedure at the same site, assign codes to the diagnostic biopsy and definitive procedure. For example: A biopsy of a colon polyp followed by a partial resection of the colon requires a code for the biopsy and one for the resection.

6. Excision vs. resection: *Resection*, as a root operation, is defined as cutting out or off, without replacement, *all* of a body part. In ICD-10-PCS, anatomical subdivisions of a body part or an organ are identified as specific body parts (e.g., lobes of the liver or lung and segments of the intestine). For example: Excision of the right lobe of the liver is coded to *Resection*.

   Excision, as a root operation, is defined as cutting out or off, without replacement, a *portion* of a body part. For example: Partial nephrectomy, which means only a portion of the kidney was removed, is coded to *Excision*.

   Billing specialists and medical coders must give close attention to documentation like the operative or procedure report to accurately assign *resection* or *excision* codes.

7. Inspection procedures
   a. Inspection of a body part or parts performed in order to achieve the objective of a procedure is not coded separately. For example: A fiberoptic bronchoscopy performed for irrigation of the bronchus requires a code only for the irrigation of the bronchus. The fiberoptic bronchoscopy is not coded because it was performed to achieve bronchial irrigation.

b. When multiple tubular body parts are inspected, the most distal body part inspected is coded. For example: Cystoureteroscopy, inspection of the urinary bladder and ureters, is coded to the ureter body part value. Because the physician must pass the scope through the urinary bladder to inspect the ureters, the ureters are identified as the most distal body part.

8. Transplantation vs. administration: The root operation *transplantation* is used when a mature and functioning living body part taken from one individual or animal is placed in another individual. The root operation *administration* is used when autologous (from self) or nonautologous (from someone else) cells are placed into an individual. For example: A bone marrow transplant is coded to ICD-10-PCS *Administration* section, because bone marrow is categorized as a cellular body part. A heart transplant is coded to ICD-10-PCS *Transplantation* section, because a heart is a mature and functioning body part.

9. Body part guidelines
   a. When a procedure is performed on a portion of a body part that does not have a separate body part value code, select a value that corresponds with the whole body part. When the prefix "peri" is combine with a body part to identify the site of the procedure, the procedure is coded to the body part named.
   b. Bilateral (right and left) body part values are available for a limited number of body parts. When an identical procedure is performed on both sides of a body part, and a bilateral body part value exists, only one code is assigned. For example: *Insufflation of Fallopian tube, bilateral* is assigned one code. If no bilateral body part value exists, each procedure is coded separately. For example: *Repair of knee joints, bilateral* is coded as repair of knee joint, left; and repair of knee joint, right.

10. Approach guidelines
    a. When a procedure is performed via an open approach and the physician also uses percutaneous endoscopic assistance, the procedure is coded as an *open* approach.
    b. An *external* approach value is selected when:
       (1) The procedure is performed within an orifice (opening) on structures that are visible without the aid of any instrumentation (e.g., tonsillectomy). The tonsils, which are located at the back of the throat, are clearly visible.
       (2) The procedure is performed by indirect application of external force through the intervening body layers (e.g., closed reduction of a fracture). Closed reduction means external force is applied to the affected area in order to realign a fractured bone.

11. Device guidelines: A device value is selected *only* if a device remains after the procedure is completed. Materials such as sutures, ligatures, radiological markers, and temporary postoperative wound drains that are necessary for performing the procedure are not coded as devices. A separate procedure for the purpose of placing a drainage device is coded to the root operation "drainage" with device value "drainage device."

Root operations that apply to procedures performed on a device only, include Change, Irrigation, Removal, and Revision. Examples include irrigation of a feeding tube and changing a peritoneal dialysis port.

REINFORCEMENT EXERCISES 4–13

Write a short answer for each question or statement.

1. What is the first and most important coding guideline?

   _____

2. Where can the billing specialist find complete ICD-10-PCS guidelines?

   _____

3. Explain the difference between *excision* and *resection*.

   _____

4. Give two examples of assigning separate codes when multiple procedures are completed during the same operative episode.

   _____

   _____

5. When is it appropriate to select an *external* approach value.

   _____

Fill in the blank.

1. The _____ is the anatomical dividing point between upper and lower body systems.

2. The ICD-10-PCS _____ have the complete definitions of root operations.

3. The root operation _____ is used when a mature and functioning living body part is taken from one individual or animal and placed in another individual.

4. When cells are placed into an individual, _____ is the correct root operation.

5. A _____ value is assigned only when an item remains after the procedure is completed.

ASSIGNING ICD-10-PCS PROCEDURE CODES

Assigning ICD-10-PCS procedure codes requires the same attention to detail as ICD-10-CM diagnoses coding. Remember that ICD-10-PCS codes apply to procedures and treatments provided in hospitals and other inpatient settings. In these environments, medical coders are most often responsible for assigning procedure codes. However, billing specialists can benefit from an overall understanding of ICD-10-PCS coding practices. As with all coding, the documentation in the patient's record *must* support code assignment.

Identifying the principal procedure is the first step in ICD-10-PCS coding. The principal procedure is defined as the procedure performed for definitive treatment rather than for diagnostic or exploratory purposes; or the procedure performed to resolve a complication. If more than one procedure meets the definition of the principal procedure, the procedure most closely related to the principal diagnosis is selected as the principal procedure. The principal diagnosis is the condition that, after study, was chiefly responsible for the hospital admission.

> **EXAMPLE**
> Juanita, who was recently diagnosed with breast cancer, was admitted for a radical mastectomy, right breast. On the second postoperative day, she fell on the way to the bathroom and sustained a femoral neck (hip) fracture. The fracture was treated via open reduction with internal fixation.
>
> In this example, the principal diagnosis is breast cancer. Radical mastectomy is the procedure most related to the principal diagnosis, and it is coded as the principal procedure. The femoral neck fracture and open reduction with internal fixation are also coded.

The principal procedure must be listed first on the insurance claim.

Selecting the correct procedure code is the next step in ICD-10-PCS coding. The medical coder locates the procedure name in the *Alphabetic Index*. The *Index* directs the coder to the correct ICD-10-PCS *Table*. By following all instruction notes, and applying coding guidelines, the correct seven-character procedure code is identified and selected. Given the complexity of ICD-10-PCS codes, encoders are an invaluable tool for hospital and inpatient procedure coding.

 ABBREVIATIONS

Table 4–12 lists the abbreviations presented in this chapter.

TABLE 4–12

Abbreviations and Meanings	
Abbreviation	Meaning
AHA	American Hospital Association
AHIMA	American Health Information Management Association
CDC	Centers for Disease Control
CMS	Centers for Medicare and Medicaid Services
CPT	*Current Procedural Terminology*
ICD-10-CM	*International Classification of Diseases, Tenth Revision, Clinical Modification*
ICD-10-PCS	*International Classification of Diseases, Tenth Revision, Procedure Coding System*
MRI	magnetic resonance imaging
NCHS	National Center for Health Statistics
NEC	not elsewhere classified
NOS	not otherwise specified
PET	positron emission tomography
POA	present on admission
TURP	transurethral resection of the prostate
WHO	World Health Organization

SUMMARY

The *International Classification of Diseases, Tenth Revision, Clinical Modification* (ICD-10-CM) is used in all health care settings for coding and reporting diagnoses. The National Center for Health Statistics (NCHS), a division of the Centers for Disease Control (CDC), was responsible for developing ICD-10-CM. The classification system is updated annually by the Cooperating Parties, which include the American Hospital Association (AHA), the American Health Information Management Association (AHIMA), the Centers for Medicare and Medicaid Services (CMS), and the NCHS. In addition, the AHA publishes the quarterly *Coding Clinic*, the official publication for ICD-10-CM guidelines.

The ICD-10-CM has 21 chapters organized by body system and related conditions, diseases, and interactions with health care agencies. Codes consist of three to seven alphabetic and numeric characters. Coding conventions are part of the ICD-10-CM and provide billing specialists and medical coders direction for code assignment. The annual *ICD-10-CM Official Guidelines for Coding and Reporting* is available on the CDC website: http://www.cdc.gov/nchs/. These guidelines include information from the *Coding Clinic* and other updates from the Cooperating Parties.

The *International Classification of Diseases, Tenth Revision, Procedure Coding System* (ICD-10-PCS) is used for coding and reporting treatments provided in hospital and other inpatient settings. The ICD-10-PCS was developed by 3M Health Information Systems under contract with the CMS, which is responsible for updating ICD-10-PCS.

All ICD-10-PCS codes consist of seven characters and each character has a specific value or meaning within an ICD-10-PCS section. Coding conventions are part of the ICD-10-PCS and provide billing specialists and medical coders direction for code assignment. Current ICD-10-PCS guidelines are available on the CMS website.

The first, and most important, rule of accurate code assignment is that the documentation in the patient's record must clearly support every selected code. The billing specialist or medical coder must also understand and follow all coding conventions and guidelines.

 REVIEW EXERCISES

Multiple Choice

1. The *International Statistical Classification of Diseases and Related Health Problems* is published by

   a. NCHS.

   b. WHO.

   c. AMA.

   d. CMS.

2. The organization responsible for developing ICD-10-CM is the

   a. AMA.

   b. CMS.

   c. NCHS.

   d. WHO.

3. The objective of a procedure is known as a(n)

   a. approach.

   b. root operation.

   c. essential modifier.

   d. qualifier.

4. An ICD-10-CM code that represents a single disease or a group of closely related conditions is known as a

   a. three-character category code.

   b. classification code.

   c. four-character subcategory code.

   d. V code.

Short Answer

1. Explain the purpose of the point dash (.-).

   _____

   _____

   _____

2. Describe the purpose of the *Tables* that are included in ICD-10-PCS.

   _____

   _____

   _____

ICD-10-CM CODING PRACTICE SETS

The coding practice sets provide opportunities to become familiar with the ICD-10-CM system.

Assign the correct ICD-10-CM code for each diagnosis, condition, or encounter.

1. Aseptic meningitis. _____

2. Gastroenteritis due to salmonella. _____

3. Rotavirus enteritis. _____

4. Cystitis, acute, due to *Escherichia coli* (*E. coli*). _____

5. Viral hepatitis, type A. _____

6. Primary genital syphilis. _____

7. Anthrax pneumonia. _____

8. Type I diabetes with ketoacidosis. _____

9. Diabetic hypoglycemia. _____

10. Salmonellosis. _____

11. Acute follicular conjunctivitis. _____

12. Trigeminal neuralgia. _____

13. Unstable angina pectoris. _____

14. Bilateral thrombosis of carotid artery. _____

15. Hypertensive cardiovascular disease, malignant. _____

16. Ulcerative stomatitis. _____

17. Hay fever due to pollen. _____

18. Unilateral, vesicular emphysema. _____

19. Acute gastroenteritis. _____

20. Chronic maxillary sinusitis. _____

21. Diverticulosis of the large intestine. _____

22. Urinary tract infection. _____

23. Benign prostatic hypertrophy. _____

24. Nephrolithiasis. _____

25. Routine prenatal visit, first pregnancy. _____

26. Asian flu (influenza) shot (vaccination). _____

27. Chest pain, unspecified. _____

28. Pre-employment physical (examination). _____

29. Right lower quadrant abdominal pain, with nausea and vomiting. _____

30. Diarrhea. _____

Write the diagnosis(es) and assign the correct ICD-10-CM code.

1. This 10-year-old female is seen today for continued treatment of cystic fibrosis. She has gained three pounds and is in the 45th percentile for weight. Mom was advised to continue supplemental nutrition.

    Diagnosis(es): _____ Code(s): _____

2. This 3-year-old female is seen today rubbing and tugging at her right ear and in minimal distress. Inspection of the ear canals reveals acute suppurative otitis media on the right; the left is clear. Tympanic membranes are intact.

Diagnosis(es): _____ Code(s): _____

3. This 45-year-old male is seen for shortness of breath, low-grade fever, and general malaise. Examination revealed an acute upper respiratory infection with influenza.

Diagnosis(es): _____ Code(s): _____

4. During the patient's physical examination, heart sounds were consistent with mitral valve insufficiency.

Diagnosis(es): _____ Code(s): _____

5. Patient stepped on a broken bottle and sustained a 3 inch laceration, requiring seven sutures. He was instructed to return in 10 days for suture removal.

Diagnosis(es): _____ Code(s): _____

Write the main term and then assign the correct ICD-10-PCS code(s) for each procedure.

1. Cholecystectomy, open.

Main term: _____ Code(s): _____

2. Endoscopic removal of common bile duct calculi.

Main term: _____ Code(s): _____

3. Revision of ileostomy stoma.

Main term: _____ Code(s): _____

4. Bilateral total knee replacement of both knee joints.

Main term: _____ Code(s): _____

5. Bilateral breast reduction.

Main term: _____ Code(s): _____

Read the brief procedure/operative report. Write the procedure and assign the correct ICD-10-PCS code(s).

1. While playing in a championship basketball game, Margaret sustained a knee injury. She was admitted for an arthroscopic examination of her left knee. The procedure report included the following information:

PREOPERATIVE DIAGNOSIS: Tear of medial meniscus, left knee.

POSTOPERATIVE DIAGNOSIS: Tear of medial meniscus, left knee.

OPERATION PERFORMED: Arthroscopic examination of the left knee and arthroscopic partial medial meniscectomy.

Procedure: _____ ICD-10-PCS code(s): _____

2. Phillip was admitted to the hospital for repair of a deviated nasal septum and collapsed nasal cartilage. The operative report states, "Nasoseptal repair with cartilage graft to the nasal tip."

Procedure: _____ ICD-10-PCS code(s): _____

CODING CHALLENGE

Read the following medical reports and write the diagnoses and procedures in the space provided. Assign the correct ICD-10-CM and ICD-10-PCS codes.

1. DISCHARGE SUMMARY

PATIENT: Walker, Lamar
ADMISSION DATE: November 16, 20xx
DISCHARGE DATE: November 18, 20xx
ADMITTING DIAGNOSES: 1. Urinary retention secondary to benign prostatic hypertrophy. 2. Chronic obstructive pulmonary disease.
DISCHARGE DIAGNOSES: 1. Benign prostatic hypertrophy, secondary urinary retention. 2. Chronic obstructive pulmonary disease.
PROCEDURES: 1. Transurethral resection of the prostate. 2. Percutaneous suprapubic cystostomy.
HISTORY: The patient is a 72-year-old gentleman with a recent history of recurrent urinary retention. A cystoscopy performed in the office demonstrated a large obstructed prostate. Given his problems with recurrent urinary retention, the patient agreed to a transurethral resection of the prostate. Remainder of the patient's history is available in the admitting note.
HOSPITAL COURSE: Following admission, the patient was taken to the operating room and underwent a complicated transurethral resection of the prostate and a percutaneous suprapubic cystostomy. There was moderate hemorrhage, and the patient received one unit of packed red blood cells intraoperatively. His postoperative hemoglobin was stable at 10.3.

    During the postoperative period, he remained afebrile, and his urine gradually cleared. The Foley catheter was removed on the third postoperative day. At discharge, the patient was ambulating without assistance, able to void without difficulty, and tolerating a regular diet.
DISCHARGE INSTRUCTIONS: 1. Postoperative follow-up in my office in two weeks. 2. Normal activities, as tolerated. 3. Notify my office if clots appear in the urine.

PRINCIPAL DIAGNOSIS: _____

PRINCIPAL PROCEDURE: _____

OTHER DIAGNOSIS(ES): _____

OTHER PROCEDURE(S): _____

2. DISCHARGE SUMMARY

PATIENT: Mowafi, Ayeesha
ADMISSION DATE: December 10, 20xx
DISCHARGE DATE: December 13, 20xx
ADMITTING DIAGNOSES: 1. Ruptured left ectopic (tubal) pregnancy.
DISCHARGE DIAGNOSES: 1. Ruptured left ectopic (tubal) pregnancy. 2. Endometriosis.
PROCEDURES: 1. Laparoscopic left salpingectomy, partial.
HISTORY: The patient is a 30-year-old gravida I, para 0 female who presented in the emergency department with acute abdominal pain. A serum pregnancy test was positive. Pelvic ultrasound was negative for an intrauterine pregnancy. The patient had pelvic and left lower-quadrant tenderness. No pelvic mass was palpated. The patient has endometriosis.
HOSPITAL COURSE: The patient was admitted and taken to the operating room. Culdocentesis was positive. She underwent laparoscopic partial left salpingectomy. The patient tolerated the procedure well. She was discharged on the third postoperative day, tolerating a regular diet, ambulating without difficulty, and passing flatus.
DISCHARGE INSTRUCTIONS: 1. Postoperative follow-up in my office in two weeks. 2. Normal activities, as tolerated. 3. Return to the emergency department for swelling, elevated temperature, or pelvic pain.

PRINCIPAL DIAGNOSIS: _____

PRINCIPAL PROCEDURE: _____

OTHER DIAGNOSIS(ES): _____

OTHER PROCEDURE(S): _____

3. DISCHARGE SUMMARY

PATIENT: Mehrotra, Basu
ADMISSION DATE: May 20, 20xx
DISCHARGE DATE: May 26, 20xx
ADMITTING DIAGNOSES: 1. Right index finger infection.
DISCHARGE DIAGNOSES: 1. Suppurative tenosynovitis and osteomyelitis, right index finger. 2. Peripheral vascular disease.
PROCEDURES: 1. Incision and drainage of distal phalanx, open amputation of distal phalanx, and placement of flexor tendon sheath catheter for irrigation. 2. Debridement of bone and soft tissue.
HISTORY: The patient is a 48-year-old male who presented with a necrotic infection of the right index finger. See the admission history and physical for complete details.
HOSPITAL COURSE: The patient was admitted and started on intravenous antibiotics with poor results. He was taken to the operating room and underwent drainage and debridement of necrotic tissue, right index finger. The operative procedure revealed suppuration of the soft tissues and osteomyelitic involvement of the distal

continued on the next page

continued from the previous page

phalangeal remnant and distal portion of the middle phalanx. The distal phalanx was amputated. Purulent material was present in the distal portion of the flexor tendon sheath. A catheter was placed in the flexor tendon sheath for irrigation.

The patient's general condition remained stable. The acute infection in the right index finger resolved. On the fifth postoperative day, he returned to the operating room for further debridement of necrotic tissue. He tolerated this procedure well and was discharged on the next postoperative day.

DISCHARGE MEDICATIONS: Keflex 500 mg every six hours.

DISCHARGE INSTRUCTIONS: 1. Keep the index finger dressing intact until seen by me in follow-up in five days. 2. Diet and activities as tolerated. 3. Return to the emergency department for swelling, elevated temperature, or discharge from the site.

PRINCIPAL DIAGNOSIS: _____

PRINCIPAL PROCEDURE: _____

OTHER DIAGNOSIS(ES): _____

OTHER PROCEDURE(S): _____

OTHER DIAGNOSIS(ES): _____

 WEBSITES

American Health Information Management Association: http://www.ahima.org

American Hospital Association: http://www.aha.org

Centers for Disease Control: http://www.cdc.gov

Centers for Medicare and Medicaid Services: http://www.cms.org

National Center for Health Statistics: http://www.cdc.gov/nchs

CHAPTER 5

International Classification of Diseases, Ninth Revision, Clinical Modification (ICD-9-CM)

LEARNING OBJECTIVES

Upon successful completion of this chapter, the reader should have the knowledge to:

1. Identify the four Cooperating Parties responsible for maintaining and updating ICD-9-CM.
2. Describe the value of the American Hospital Association (AHA) publication *Coding Clinic for ICD-9-CM.*
3. Follow the ICD-9-CM coding conventions for assigning diagnostic and procedure codes.
4. Explain the features of the three ICD-9-CM volumes.
5. Define all cross-reference and coding instruction terms.
6. List diagnostic and procedure coding steps in the order of performance.
7. Explain the difference between a primary diagnosis and a principal diagnosis.
8. Discuss the significance of a principal procedure.
9. Accurately code diagnoses and procedures presented in this chapter.

KEY TERMS

American Health Information Management Association (AHIMA)

American Hospital Association (AHA)

Carryover line

Category

Centers for Medicare and Medicaid Services (CMS)

Closed biopsy

Code first [the] underlying condition

Code, if applicable, any causal condition first

Coding conventions

Concurrent condition

Congenital

Connecting words

Cooperating Parties

Current Procedural Terminology (CPT)

Due to

E codes

Encoders

Etiology

Excludes note

Failed procedure

First-listed diagnosis

General note

Histological

Hypertension Table

Includes note

International Classification of Diseases, Ninth Revision, Clinical Modification (ICD-9-CM)

International Classification of Diseases, Tenth Revision (ICD-10)

Late effect

Main term

More specific subterms

National Center for Health
    Statistics (NCHS)
Neoplasm Table
Nonessential modifier
Not elsewhere classified
    (NEC)
Not otherwise specified
    (NOS)
Omit code
Open biopsy

Open procedure
Perinatal period
Primary diagnosis
Principal diagnosis
Principal procedure
Puerperium
Residual
Secondary condition
Section
See

See also
See condition
Sequencing
Significant procedure
Subcategory
Subclassification
Subterm
Table of Drugs and Chemicals
Use additional code
V codes

OVERVIEW

As mentioned in Chapter 1, the two main coding systems associated with health insurance claims processing are the *International Classification of Diseases, Ninth Revision, Clinical Modification* (ICD-9-CM) for medical diagnoses and procedures and *Current Procedural Terminology* (CPT) for physician and other provider services and procedures. This chapter covers ICD-9-CM, which remains in effect until the *International Classification of Diseases, Tenth Revision* (ICD-10) is adopted.

Accurate coding is crucial to reimbursement and the avoidance of fraud and abuse charges. Insurance billing specialists need at least a basic understanding of medical coding. The purpose of this chapter is to provide the student with a foundation for ICD-9-CM coding. Topics presented include the following:

- Unique characteristics of *Volumes 1, 2,* and *3*
- Coding conventions, such as special instructional notes and the meaning of punctuation marks
- Sections of each volume that apply to physician office coding
- Coding guidelines from Sections II and IV of the ICD-9-CM *Official Guidelines for Coding and Reporting*

To gain the most from this chapter, have ICD-9-CM *Volumes 1, 2,* and *3* readily available as references. Some exercises provide opportunities to practice using the code books. This chapter also includes several figures and tables adapted from the 2013 official version of ICD-9-CM. The figures and tables allow the student to complete some of the review exercises if the code books are not available.

INTERNATIONAL CLASSIFICATION OF DISEASES, NINTH REVISION, CLINICAL MODIFICATION (ICD-9-CM)

The *International Classification of Diseases, Ninth Revision, Clinical Modification* (ICD-9-CM) is the medical coding and classification system used in the United States to gather information about diseases and injuries. ICD-9-CM is an adaptation of the *International Classification of Diseases, Ninth Revision* (ICD-9) developed by the World Health Organization (WHO) of the United Nations.

ICD-9-CM is a classification system that provides numeric codes for diagnoses, injuries, and procedures. The codes are contained in three volumes:

- *Volume 1* is a numeric tabular list of disease and injury codes.

- *Volume 2* is an alphabetic index of diseases and injuries.
- *Volume 3* is a combined tabular list and alphabetic index of procedure codes.

Volume 3 is used to code inpatient hospital procedures, whereas CPT is used to code physician office, ambulatory center, and hospital outpatient department procedures. CPT is published by the American Medical Association and is covered in Chapter 6 of this book. The official version of ICD-9-CM is available only on CD-ROM from the U.S. Government Printing Office in Washington, D.C. ICD-9-CM coding products are also available from commercial publishers. Electronic versions of the code books, called encoders, can be obtained from commercial sources. Although each publisher may offer special editorial features, the codes are the same as those published in the official version. The official version of ICD-9-CM is the reference of choice for this book.

The ICD-9-CM is updated every year, and changes are effective October 1 of that year. The Cooperating Parties, which consist of two professional associations and two governmental agencies, are responsible for maintaining and updating ICD-9-CM. The Cooperating Parties are:

- American Hospital Association (AHA)
- American Health Information Management Association (AHIMA)
- Centers for Medicare and Medicaid Services (CMS)
- National Center for Health Statistics (NCHS)

Table 5–1 describes the responsibilities of each party.

The ICD-9-CM Coordination Committee, which is composed of several federal ICD-9-CM users, is an advisory committee to the Cooperating Parties.

As shown in Table 5–1, the AHA publishes the *Coding Clinic for ICD-9-CM.* This valuable resource is released quarterly and is considered the official publication for ICD-9-CM coding guidelines. The information provided in the *Coding Clinic* is regarded as advice from the four Cooperating Parties. Billing specialists and medical coders in all settings, including physicians' offices, clinics, and hospitals, can rely on the *Coding Clinic* for up-to-date coding advice.

The *ICD-9-CM Official Guidelines for Coding and Reporting,* which became effective October 1, 2003, is published by the Department of Health and Human Services (HHS). These guidelines are updated annually and provide additional information for assigning ICD-9-CM codes.

The ICD-9-CM contains specific guidelines called coding conventions. Coding conventions include instructional notes, abbreviations, cross-reference notes, punctuation marks, and specific usage of the words "and," "with," and "due to." The conventions are a standard method for organizing ICD-9-CM entries and also provide mandatory rules for assigning medical codes.

TABLE 5–1

Responsibilities of the Cooperating Parties for ICD-9-CM	
NCHS	Maintains and updates the diagnosis portion of ICD-9-CM
CMS	Maintains and updates the procedure portion (*Volume 3*)
AHA	Maintains the Central Office on ICD-9-CM to answer questions from coders; publishes the *Coding Clinic for ICD-9-CM,* the *Official Guidelines* for ICD-9-CM usage
AHIMA	Provides training and certification for coding professionals

REINFORCEMENT EXERCISES 5–1

1. List and briefly define the ICD-9-CM volumes.

_____

_____

_____

2. What is the *Coding Clinic* for ICD-9-CM?

_____

_____

_____

3. Explain the phrase "Cooperating Parties."

_____

_____

_____

4. Name the groups that act as the Cooperating Parties.

_____

_____

_____

5. Briefly describe the phrase "coding conventions."

_____

_____

_____

ICD-9-CM COMPONENTS

As stated previously, ICD-9-CM has three volumes: the *Tabular List of Diseases and Injuries* (*Volume 1*), the *Alphabetic Index of Diseases and Injuries* (*Volume 2*), and the *Tabular List and Alphabetic Index of Procedures* (*Volume 3*). Historically, the volumes were published as three separate books. Publishers now offer a variety of options, such as a combination of *Volume 1* and *Volume 2*, with the alphabetic index placed before the tabular list.

Volume 1: Tabular List of Diseases and Injuries

Volume 1, the Tabular List of Diseases and Injuries, includes the following sections:

- Seventeen main chapters—listed in Table 5–2—that classify diseases and injuries by body system or etiology (cause).

TABLE 5–2

Tabular List Main Chapters

Chapter Number	Chapter Title	Code Categories
1	Infectious and Parasitic Diseases	001–139
2	Neoplasms	140–239
3	Endocrine, Nutritional, and Metabolic Diseases and Immunity Disorders	240–279
4	Diseases of Blood and Blood-Forming Organs	280–289
5	Mental Disorders	290–319
6	Diseases of the Nervous System and Sense Organs	320–389
7	Diseases of the Circulatory System	390–459
8	Diseases of the Respiratory System	460–519
9	Diseases of the Digestive System	520–579
10	Diseases of the Genitourinary System	580–629
11	Complications of Pregnancy, Childbirth, and the Puerperium	630–679
12	Diseases of Skin and Subcutaneous Tissue	680–709
13	Diseases of the Musculoskeletal System and Connective Tissue	710–739
14	Congenital Anomalies	740–759
15	Certain Conditions Originating in the Perinatal Period	760–779
16	Symptoms, Signs, and Ill-Defined Conditions	780–799
17	Injury and Poisoning	800–999

- Two supplementary classifications called "Classification of Factors Influencing Health Status and Contact with Health Services," commonly known as V codes, and "Classification of External Causes of Injury and Poisoning," commonly known as E codes.
- Four appendices that include codes for information about specific diseases and accidents.

Although most of the chapters in the *Tabular List* have self-explanatory titles, several chapters need a brief explanation.

Chapter 11: Complications of Pregnancy, Childbirth, and the Puerperium

Chapter 11 codes classify conditions that affect the management of pregnancy, childbirth, and the puerperium. The puerperium is the period of time that begins at the end of the third stage of labor and continues for six weeks. Codes from Chapter 11 are assigned only to conditions affecting the mother, not the newborn.

Chapter 14: Congenital Anomalies

Chapter 14 codes classify abnormal conditions that are congenital, which means "present at or since the time of birth." Although a congenital anomaly is present at birth, the condition may not manifest itself until later. Therefore, Chapter 14 codes may be assigned to patients of any age.

> **EXAMPLE: CONGENITAL CONDITION**
> Jenny, a 16-year-old high school sophomore, just received the results of her kidney scan. The physician tells Jenny that she has polycystic kidneys and explains that she was "born with" this condition. Even though Jenny is 16, the diagnosis of polycystic kidneys is coded as a congenital anomaly.

Chapter 15: Certain Conditions Originating in the Perinatal Period

Chapter 15 codes classify conditions specific to a newborn. The condition must be associated with the perinatal period, which begins before birth and lasts through the 28th day of life. Most perinatal conditions are resolved by time, treatment, or death. However, some conditions manifest themselves later in life.

> **EXAMPLE: CONDITION ORIGINATING IN THE PERINATAL PERIOD**
> Rachel is being treated for vaginal cancer. Rachel's health history reveals that her mother took the antinausea medication DES (diethylstilbestrol) during her pregnancy with Rachel. The physician explains to Rachel that her current condition could be a result of intrauterine exposure to DES.

In this case, the vaginal cancer is assigned the appropriate malignant neoplasm code. Intrauterine DES exposure is a significant factor in the development of vaginal cancer. Therefore, the code for vaginal cancer is selected, and the code for DES from Chapter 15 is also assigned.

Chapter 16: Symptoms, Signs, and Ill-Defined Conditions

Chapter 16 includes medical codes for symptoms, signs, abnormal test results, and ill-defined conditions that are not associated with a diagnosis that can be classified or coded in another ICD-9-CM chapter. Simply put, Chapter 16 codes classify conditions that are of questionable or unknown etiology. These codes should never be used when a more definitive diagnostic code is available. Symptoms and signs related to conditions associated with a specific body system are assigned codes from the appropriate ICD-9-CM chapter. Symptoms and signs associated with more than one disease or body system are coded to Chapter 16.

Chapter 17: Injury and Poisoning

Of all the chapters in ICD-9-CM, Chapter 17 has the least descriptive title. This chapter includes codes not only for injuries and poisoning but also for burns, adverse effects caused by external factors, complications of trauma, and complications of surgical and medical care or treatment. Chapter 17 can classify a simple fracture caused by falling off a skateboard as well as a complex injury, such as being stabbed in the eye with a wooden stick. Table 5–3 lists the sections in Chapter 17.

Tabular List Format

Each chapter in *Volume 1* is a numeric list of diseases and injuries organized by sections, categories, subcategories, and fifth-digit subclassifications. A section is a group of three-digit categories that represent a single disease or a group of closely related conditions.

TABLE 5-3

Sections of ICD-9-CM Chapter 17, Injury and Poisoning	
Section	Range of Codes
Fractures	800–829
Dislocation	830–839
Sprains and Strains of Joints and Adjacent Muscles	840–848
Intracranial Injury, Excluding Those with Skull Fracture	850–854
Internal Injury of the Thorax, Abdomen, and Pelvis	860–869
Open Wound of Head, Neck, and Trunk	870–879
Open Wound of Upper Limb	880–887
Open Wound of Lower Limb	890–897
Injury to Blood Vessels	900–904
Late Effects of Injuries, Poisonings, Toxic Effects, and Other External Causes	905–909
Superficial Injuries	910–919
Contusions with Intact Skin Surface	920–924
Crushing Injuries	925–929
Effects of Foreign Body Entering Through an Orifice	930–939
Burns	940–949
Injury to Nerves and Spinal Cord	950–957
Certain Traumatic Complications and Unspecified Injuries	958–959
Poisoning by Drugs, Medicinal and Biological Substances	960–979
Toxic Effects of Substances Chiefly Nonmedical as to Source	980–989
Other and Unspecified Effects of External Causes	990–995
Complications of Surgical and Medical Care Not Elsewhere Classified	996–999

© 2014 Cengage Learning, All Rights Reserved.

EXAMPLE
"Diseases of Esophagus, Stomach, and Duodenum" (530–539)

A category is a three-digit code that represents a single disease or a group of closely related conditions.

EXAMPLE
531, Gastric ulcer

Subcategories consist of four digits and provide more information about the disease, such as the site, cause, or other characteristics. A period or decimal point precedes the fourth digit.

EXAMPLE

531.0 represents an acute gastric ulcer with hemorrhage (.0)
531.1 is an acute gastric ulcer with perforation (.1)
531.2 is an acute gastric ulcer with hemorrhage and perforation (.2)
 The fourth digit identifies important information about the gastric ulcer.

Subclassifications are represented by a fifth digit and allow for even more specific information about the disease. Fifth-digit lists are found at the beginning of a chapter, section, category
code, and subcategory level. Fifth digits include as many numeric selections as necessary to complete the description of the disease.

EXAMPLE

The three-digit category code 531, gastric ulcer, has two fifth-digit choices: 0,
which means without mention of obstruction, and 1, which means with
obstruction.

 531.00 represents an acute gastric ulcer (531), with hemorrhage (.0),
 without mention of obstruction (0)
 531.01 represents an acute gastric ulcer (531), with hemorrhage (.0),
 with obstruction (1).

Figure 5–1 is an example of fifth-digit subclassifications at the chapter, category, and subcategory
levels.

 Billing specialists and medical coders must pay close attention to fourth-digit subcategories
and fifth-digit subclassifications. If the fourth and fifth digits are available, they *must* be included

LOCATION	DESCRIPTION
Chapter	Chapter 13. "Diseases of the Musculoskeletal System and Connective Tissue" (710–739)
	The following fifth-digit subclassification is used with categories 711–712, 715–716, 718–719, and 730:
	0 unspecified site; 1 shoulder region; 2 upper arm; 3 forearm; 4 hand; 5 pelvic region and thigh; 6 lower leg; 7 ankle and foot; 8 other specified sites; 9 multiple sites
Category	434 Occlusion of cerebral arteries The following fifth-digit subclassification is used with category 434:
	0 without mention of cerebral infarction; 1 with cerebral infarction
Subcategory	550.0 Inguinal hernia, with gangrene
	The following fifth-digit subclassifications apply to this subcategory:
	0 unilateral or unspecified (not specified as recurrent); 1 unilateral or unspecified, recurrent; 2 bilateral (not specified as recurrent); 3 bilateral, recurrent

Figure 5–1 Examples of Fifth-Digit Subclassifications

on the claim. Insurance carriers will deny payment for any claim that does not have the appropriate fourth or fifth digit.

Supplementary Classifications

The *Tabular List* has two supplementary classifications:

- "Supplementary Classification of Factors Influencing Health Status and Contact with Health Services" (V01–V91)—also called V codes.
- "Supplementary Classification of External Causes of Injury and Poisoning" (E800–E999)—also called E codes.

V codes provide a mechanism to classify interactions with health care providers when the individual is not sick. V codes also provide additional information about the individual's medical condition. As the name implies, the letter *V* precedes these codes. Figure 5–2 shows examples of V codes.

E codes describe the external cause of injury and poisoning, and they are often assigned with Chapter 17 codes. As the name implies, the letter *E* precedes these codes. Figure 5–3 shows examples of E codes.

Following this chapter's coverage of ICD-9-CM coding conventions, both V codes and E codes are discussed in depth.

Appendices

The *Tabular List* (*Volume 1*) includes four appendices:

- Appendix A: Morphology of Neoplasms
- Appendix C: Classification of Drugs by the American Hospital Formulary Service (AHFS) List Number and Their ICD-9-CM Equivalents
- Appendix D: Classification of Industrial Accidents According to Agency
- Appendix E: List of Three-Digit Categories

Effective with the October 1, 2004, update, Appendix B, "Glossary of Mental Disorders," was removed from the official government version of ICD-9-CM. The remaining appendices retained their original letter designations.

Appendix A: Morphology of Neoplasms

This appendix, which is also called the M codes, provides a list of optional codes for the histological (tissue) type and behavior of neoplasms. The codes consist of five digits preceded by the letter *M*. The first four digits identify the type of tissue, and the fifth digit describes the behavior of the neoplasm. Table 5–4 lists examples of the four-digit tissue codes.

The behavioral fifth digit of each M code is delineated by a slash followed by the number 1, 2, 3, 6, or 9. Fifth digits retain their meaning regardless of the histology code. Table 5–5 lists the M code fifth digits and their meanings. M codes are used primarily by cancer registries and are always accompanied by the appropriate neoplasm code from Chapter 2, Neoplasms of the main classification section.

> **EXAMPLE: MORPHOLOGY CODE**
> M8010/0 is the code for a benign epithelial tumor.

V codes

PERSONS WITHOUT REPORTED DIAGNOSIS ENCOUNTERED DURING EXAMINATION AND INVESTIGATION OF INDIVIDUALS AND POPULATIONS (V70-V82)

Note: Nonspecific abnormal findings disclosed at the time of these examinations are classifiable to categories 790-796.

V70 **General medical examinations**
Use additional code(s) to identify any special screening examination(s) performed (V73.0-V82.9)

V70.0 **Routine general medical examination at a health care facility**
Health checkup

EXCLUDES	*health checkup of infant or child over 28 days old (V20.2)*
	health supervision of newborn 8 to 28 days old (V20.32)
	health supervision of newborn under 8 days old (V20.31)
	pre-procedural general physical examination (V72.83)

V70.1 **General psychiatric examination, requested by the authority**

V70.2 **General psychiatric examination, other and unspecified**

V70.3 **Other medical examination for administrative purposes**
General medical examination for:
admission to old age home
adoption
camp
driving license
immigration and naturalization
insurance certification
marriage
prison
school admission
sports competition

| EXCLUDES | *attendance for issue of medical certificates (V68.0)* |
| | *pre-employment screening (V70.5)* |

Figure 5–2 V Code Examples

Appendix C: Classification of Drugs by American Hospital Formulary Service (AHFS) List This appendix lists the AHFS drug categories and the appropriate ICD-9-CM codes. The *American Hospital Formulary Service* is a publication that categorizes drugs into related groups. Each category or group has a specific ICD-9-CM code.

EXAMPLE

Penicillins – AHFS classification 8:12.16; ICD-9-CM 960.0

Anticoagulants – AHFS classification 20:12.04; ICD-9-CM 964.2

Insulins – AHFS classification 68:20.08; ICD-9-CM 962.3

E codes

DRUGS, MEDICINAL AND BIOLOGICAL SUBSTANCES CAUSING ADVERSE EFFECTS IN THERAPEUTIC USE (E930–E949)

Includes: correct drug properly administered in therapeutic or prophylactic dosage, as the cause of any adverse effect including allergic or hypersensitivity reactions

Excludes: *accidental overdose of drug and wrong drug given or taken in error (E850.0–E858.9)*
accidents in the technique or administration of drug or biological substance such as accidental puncture during injection, or contamination of drug (E870.0–E876.9)
administration with suicidal or homicidal intent or intent to harm, or in circumstances classifiable to E950.0–E950.5, E962.0, E980.0–E980.5

See Alphabetic Index for more complete list of specific drugs to be classified under the fourth-digit subdivisions. The American Hospital Formulary numbers can be used to classify new drugs listed by the American Hospital Formulary Service (AHFS). See Appendix C.

E930   Antibiotics

Excludes: *that used as eye, ear, nose, and throat [ENT], and local anti-infectives (E946.0–E946.9)*

E930.0   Penicillin

Natural	Semisynthetic, such as:
Synthetic	ampicillin
	cloxacillin
	nafcillin
	oxacillin

E930.1   Antifungal antibiotics

Amphotericin B	Hachimycin [trichomycin]
Griseofulvin	Nystatin

E930.2   Chloramphenicol group

Chloramphenicol	Thiamphenicol

Figure 5–3 E Codes

Appendix D: Classification of Industrial Accidents According to Agency This appendix classifies industrial accidents according to agency, which is the active force or substance that caused the disease or accident. Equipment, material, and the working environment are some of the "agencies" that may cause a disease or accident.

The classification, which was adopted on October 12, 1962, by the Tenth International Conference of Labor Statisticians, is used infrequently.

TABLE 5–4

Sample Four-Digit Tissue Codes	
Tissue Code	**Type of Neoplasm**
M8010–M8043	Epithelial neoplasms
M8090–M8110	Basal cell neoplasms
M8140–M8381	Adenomas; adenocarcinomas
M9180–M9200	Osteomas; osteosarcomas
M9820–M9825	Lymphoid leukemias

© 2014 Cengage Learning, All Rights Reserved.

TABLE 5–5

M Code Fifth Digits and Meanings	
Fifth Digit	**Meaning**
/0	Benign (noncancerous)
/1	Uncertain whether benign or malignant; borderline malignant
/2	Carcinoma in situ; intraepithelial, noninfiltrating, noninvasive
/3	Malignant (cancerous), primary site
/6	Malignant, metastatic site, secondary site
/9	Malignant, uncertain whether primary or metastatic site

© 2014 Cengage Learning, All Rights Reserved.

Appendix E: List of Three-Digit Categories This appendix lists the three-digit categories associated with each ICD-9-CM chapter.

Appendices A through E are part of the official version of ICD-9-CM published by the U.S. Government Printing Office. Commercial ICD-9-CM coding references may include these and other appendices.

REINFORCEMENT EXERCISES 5–2

1. Identify the two methods used to classify diseases and diagnoses listed in Chapter 1 through Chapter 17 of the *Tabular List*.

_____

_____

_____

continued on the next page

continued from the previous page

2. What is the difference between the puerperium and the perinatal period?

_____

_____

_____

3. List four additional categories of diseases or injuries found in Chapter 17, Injury and Poisoning.

_____

_____

_____

4. Provide a brief explanation of each term.

   a. Section

_____

_____

_____

   b. Category

_____

_____

_____

   c. Subcategory

_____

_____

_____

   d. Subclassification

_____

_____

_____

Volume 2: Alphabetic Index of Diseases and Injuries

Volume 2, Alphabetic Index of Diseases and Injuries, is referred to as the *Alphabetic Index* or simply the *Index.* As the name implies, this volume is organized alphabetically by disease or condition and is the key to finding codes in the *Tabular List (Volume 1).* Codes selected from the *Alphabetic Index* must be verified by reviewing the description of the code in the *Tabular List.*

The *Alphabetic Index* contains these sections:

- "Alphabetic Index to Diseases and Injuries"
- "Table of Drugs and Chemicals"
- "Alphabetic Index to External Causes of Injury and Poisoning" (E codes)

In addition to these sections, the *Alphabetic Index* has neoplasm and hypertension subterms arranged in tables. The table features of the *Alphabetic Index* are discussed later in this chapter.

The *Alphabetic Index* follows a unique format that includes indentation patterns and alphabetization rules.

Indentation Patterns

Diseases and conditions are generally classified as main terms, subterms, more specific subterms, and carryover lines. Each of these phrases has a specific and consistent indentation pattern.

Main terms are diseases, conditions, or injuries, such as appendicitis or a fracture. Main terms are set flush with the left margin, begin with a capital letter, and are printed in bold.

Subterms identify the site, type, or etiology for diseases, conditions, or injuries. Subterms are indented under a main term by one standard indentation, which is about two spaces. They begin with a lowercase letter and are printed in regular type.

More specific subterms are indented under a subterm by one standard indentation, farther to the right as needed. More specific subterms are listed in alphabetical order, provide additional information related to subterms, and are printed in regular type.

Carryover lines are used when a complete entry does not fit on one line. Carryover lines are indented two standard indentations to avoid being confused with subterms and more specific subterms. Figure 5–4 is an example of this organizational pattern.

The *Alphabetic Index* is carefully organized to conserve space. The structure of the *Index* is at times confusing and frustrating. However, billing specialists and coders must carefully follow the indentations to arrive at the correct code. When faced with literally pages of subterms, as with pneumonia codes, always begin with the main term and follow the subterms and more specific subterms until the correct description is located.

Although most conditions can be located by the name of the disease, condition, or injury as the main term, there are exceptions. Table 5–6 lists and provides examples of additional main terms.

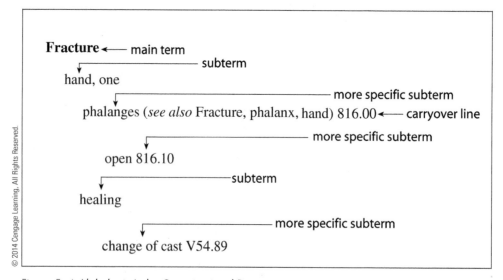

Figure 5–4 *Alphabetic Index* Organizational Pattern

TABLE 5–6

Additional Main Terms	
Main Term	**Description/Examples**
Anomaly	Congenital conditions, which are present at the time of birth, are listed alphabetically by anatomic site under the main term "Anomaly."
Delivery	Conditions identified as "delivery complicated by" are listed alphabetically under the main term "Delivery."
Labor	Conditions that complicate or affect the progress of labor are listed alphabetically under the main term "Labor."
Pregnancy	Conditions identified as "pregnancy complicated by" are listed alphabetically under the main term "Pregnancy."
Puerperal	Conditions originating in the puerperium—the time period between the end of third-stage labor and six weeks—are listed alphabetically under the main term "Puerperal."
Complications	Conditions originating as a complication of medical or surgical care are listed alphabetically under the main term "Complications."
Late, effect of	Conditions that originate as a result of treatment for an illness or injury are listed alphabetically under the main term "Late, effect of."

Alphabetization Rules

The *Alphabetic Index* follows a letter-by-letter alphabetization format, with the following exceptions:

- Ignore single spaces between words.
- Ignore single hyphens within words.
- Ignore the final "s" in possessive forms.
- Subterms for numerical characters and words indicating numbers are listed in *numerical order*.
- Subterms preceded by "with" or "without" are placed immediately after the main term.

Examples of these exceptions are provided in Figure 5–5.

In addition to "with" and "without," the *Alphabetic Index* makes special use of the words "due to" and "in." These words express a relationship between main terms and subterms as well as between subterms and more specific subterms. "Due to" and "in" are listed alphabetically in the *Index*. The main term "fracture" is a good example of a "due to" entry.

EXAMPLE: "DUE TO"

Fracture. . .
with
internal injuries in same region. . .
acetabulum. . .
acromion (process) (closed). . .
cuneiform. . .

EXCEPTION	EXAMPLE
Ignore:	
S in the possessive form	**Addison's** anemia
Single hyphens within words	**Addison-Biermer** anemia
Single spaces between words	**Addison-Gull** disease
	Addisonian crisis
Numerical Order:	
Numerical characters and words indicating numbers	**Paralysis, paralytic**
	nerve...
	Third or oculomotor
	Fourth or trochlear
	Sixth or abducens
	Accessory (congenital)
	Chromosome(s) NEC 758.5
	13–15...
	16–18...
	21 or 22...
With or **Without:**	
Immediately after the main term or related subterm	**Appendicitis** 541
	with
	perforation...540.0
	with peritoneal abscess 540.1
	peritoneal abscess 540.1
	acute...
	amebic...

Figure 5–5 Exceptions to Alphabetization Rules

due to
birth injury. . .
gunshot. . .
neoplasm. . .

In this example, the "due to" entries describe a causal relationship—i.e., fracture due to a birth injury, gunshot, or neoplasm.

REINFORCEMENT EXERCISES 5–3

Provide the correct term in each blank.

1. Diseases and conditions set flush left and printed in bold are called _____.

2. _____ identify the site, type, or etiology for diseases, conditions, or injuries.

3. When a complete entry does not fit on one line, a _____ is indented two standard indentations from the subterm.

continued on the next page

continued from the previous page

4. Congenital conditions are usually located under the main term _____.

5. _____ is the main term when the condition is the result of a surgical or medical complication.

6. How are numerical characters and words indicating numbers listed in the *Alphabetic Index?*

_____

7. Where would you look to find the subterm "with"?

_____

8. What are the main terms for conditions that complicate pregnancy, childbirth, or puerperium?

_____

Locate the main entry "Anomaly, anomalous (congenital) (unspecified type)" and give an example of an entry for each of the following anatomical sites; include the ICD-9-CM code.

1. Brain

   Entry:_____ Code:_____

2. Heart

   Entry:_____ Code:_____

3. Hip joint

   Entry:_____ Code:_____

4. Spinal cord

   Entry:_____ Code:_____

5. Ear

   Entry:_____ Code:_____

Tables

The *Alphabetical Index* has three tables that provide a systematic arrangement of codes for hypertension, neoplasms, and drugs and chemicals with associated E codes. Proper use of these tables gives the billing specialist access to more complex combinations of subterms and E codes. The format and alphabetization rules for these tables are consistent with the rest of the *Alphabetic Index*. Figure 5–6 through Figure 5–8 are examples of these tables. Refer to these figures as you read about the features of each table.

Hypertension, hypertensive			
	Malignant	Benign	Unspecified
Hypertension, hypertensive (arterial) (arteriolar) (crisis) (degeneration) (disease) (essential) (fluctuating) (idiopathic) (intermittent) (labile) (low renin) (orthostatic) (paroxysmal) (primary) (systemic) (uncontrolled) (vascular)	401.0	401.1	401.9
with			
chronic kidney disease			
stage I through stage IV, or unspecified	403.00	403.10	403.90
stage V or end stage renal disease	403.01	403.11	403.91
heart involvement (conditions classifiable to 429.0–429.3, 429.8, 429.9 due to hypertension) (*see also* Hypertension, heart)	402.00	402.10	402.90
with kidney involvement — *see* Hypertension, cardiorenal			
renal (kidney) involvement (only conditions classifiable to 585, 587) (excludes conditions classifiable to 584) (*see also* Hypertension, kidney)	403.00	403.10	403.90
with heart involvement — *see* Hypertension, cardiorenal			
failure (and sclerosis) (*see also* Hypertension, kidney)	403.01	403.11	403.91
sclerosis without failure (*see also* Hypertension, kidney)	403.00	403.10	403.90
accelerated (*see also* Hypertension, by type, malignant))	401.0	—	—
antepartum — *see* Hypertension, complicating pregnancy, childbirth, or the puerperium			
borderline	—	—	796.2
cardiorenal (disease)	404.00	404.10	404.90
with			
chronic kidney disease			
stage I through stage IV, or unspecified	404.00	404.10	404.90
and heart failure	404.01	404.11	404.91
stage V or end stage renal disease	404.02	404.12	404.92

Figure 5–6 Hypertension Table

Hypertension Table

The Hypertension Table has three main column headings, as shown in Figure 5–6. These headings are as follows:

- *Malignant:* A severe form of hypertension with vascular damage and a diastolic pressure of 130 mmHg or greater; the hypertension is out of control or there was a rapid change from a benign state.
- *Benign:* Hypertension is mild and in control.
- *Unspecified:* No documentation of benign or malignant status is stated in the diagnosis or patient's record.

Correct utilization of the Hypertension Table depends on careful observance of indentations and checking the *Tabular List* as directed.

After the main entry "Hypertension, hypertensive," several terms appear in parentheses. These terms are nonessential modifiers, which means they do not affect code selection. If no other diagnostic information is given, the billing specialist selects the code 401.9 from the Unspecified column. If the diagnostic statement specifies malignant or benign hypertension, the code comes from one of those columns. The billing specialist must verify the codes by reviewing the description in the *Tabular List*.

The indentation "with" indicates that another condition exists *with* the hypertension, but the relationship is not necessarily causal. The first indentation under "with" is "chronic kidney disease." Under chronic kidney disease, the first indentation is "stage I through stage IV or unspecified." The codes for this condition are 403.00, 403.10, and 403.90. To select one of these codes for hypertension with chronic kidney disease stage I through stage IV or unspecified, the diagnosis must include information about chronic kidney disease.

The second indentation under "chronic kidney disease" is "stage V or end-stage renal disease." To select a code from this entry, the diagnosis must identify the chronic kidney disease as stage V or as end-stage renal disease.

The second indentation under "with" is "heart involvement (conditions classifiable to 429.0–429.3, 429.8, 429.9 due to hypertension) (*see also* Hypertension, heart)." To select codes 402.00, 402.10, or 402.90, the diagnosis must include a heart condition that falls into one of the codes listed with this indentation. The instructional note "(*see also* Hypertension, heart)" gives the coder another subterm that may be helpful in selecting the correct code.

The first indentation under "heart involvement" is "with kidney involvement (*see* Hypertension, cardiorenal)." The coder must go to the subterm "cardiorenal" to continue coding. The entry "Hypertension, hypertensive, cardiorenal (disease)" lists codes for hypertension with both heart and kidney involvement.

Neoplasm Table

The Neoplasm Table is an extensive *Alphabetic Index* entry used to code neoplasms according to the behavior of the tumor. The term "neoplasm" literally means new growth, and not all neoplasms are malignant. A malignant neoplasm code can be assigned only when the pathology report confirms the presence of a malignancy. Never assign a malignant neoplasm code on the basis of a suspected or rule out diagnosis.

Correct utilization of the Neoplasm Table depends on careful attention to the diagnostic statement, reading and following all instructional notes, and careful use of the *Alphabetic Index*. Figure 5–7 is a sample of the Neoplasm Table. Refer to the figure as you read the explanation.

The Neoplasm Table provides codes for malignant, benign, uncertain behavior, and unspecified neoplasm. The table is arranged alphabetically by anatomical site. The codes listed with each site describe the behavior of the neoplasm.

Malignant neoplasms are cancerous and are coded as follows:

- *Primary:* The site where the neoplasm originated.
- *Secondary:* The site to which the neoplasm has spread.
- *In situ:* The malignant cells have not spread.

Benign neoplasms are not cancerous and do not spread or invade other sites. "Uncertain Behavior" describes a neoplasm that cannot be identified as benign or malignant. In these cases, the pathology or lab report is inconclusive and the pathologist is unable to make a definitive diagnosis. "Unspecified" is used when the documentation does not support a more specific code.

Although the Neoplasm Table is organized by anatomic site, neoplasm diagnoses are not. The diagnosis must first be located in the *Alphabetic Index*, which then directs the billing specialist to the Neoplasm Table.

EXAMPLE: ALPHABETIC INDEX NEOPLASM ENTRIES

To code the diagnosis cervical carcinoma, in situ, the billing specialist locates the main entry Carcinoma in the *Alphabetic Index*. The direction at the entry is "see also Neoplasm, by site, malignant." Under *Neoplasm, neoplastic, cervix (cervical) (uteri) (uterus)*, the billing specialist selects the code from the Malignant, Ca in situ column. He or she must verify the code by reviewing the description in the *Tabular List*.

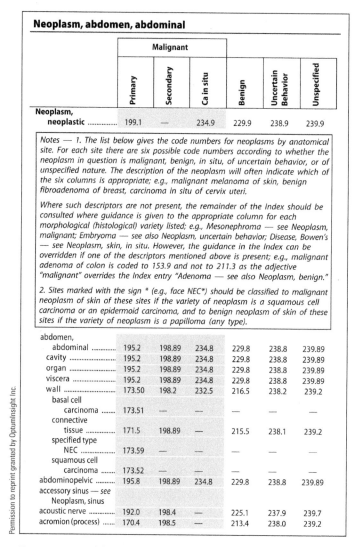

Figure 5–7 Neoplasm Table

Table of Drugs and Chemicals

The Table of Drugs and Chemicals is located after the last entry in the *Alphabetic Index*. Drugs and chemicals are listed in alphabetical order and include everything from antibiotics to zinc. This table enables the coder to select the appropriate poisoning code and associated E code. Figure 5–8 is a sample of the Table of Drugs and Chemicals. Refer to this figure as you read the explanation.

Poisoning is a condition caused by drugs, medicines, and biological substances when taken improperly or not in accordance with physician orders. Examples of poisoning are taking or receiving the wrong medication in error, taking or receiving the wrong dose of the right medication in error, overdose, prescription drugs taken with alcohol, and mixing prescription drugs and over-the-counter medications without physician advice or consent.

The Table of Drugs and Chemicals lists the names of the substances, the poisoning code for each substance, and five columns of E codes. The E code columns are labeled Accident, Therapeutic Use, Suicide Attempt, Assault, and Undetermined. Unless the patient record clearly states otherwise, the E code is selected from the Accident column. A poisoning code is never used in conjunction with an E code from the Therapeutic Use column. Diagnostic statements can include other problems caused by the poisoning.

1-propanol

	Poisoning	**External Cause (E-Code)**				
		Accident	Therapeutic Use	Suicide Attempt	Assault	Undeter-mined
1-propanol	980.3	E860.4	—	E950.9	E962.1	E980.9
2-propanol	980.2	E860.3	—	E950.9	E962.1	E980.9
2, 4-D (dichlorophenoxyacetic acid)	989.4	E863.5	—	E950.6	E962.1	E980.7
2, 4-toluene diiso-cyanate	983.0	E864.0	—	E950.7	E962.1	E980.6
2, 4, 5-T (trichlorophenoxy-acetic acid)	989.2	E863.5	—	E950.6	E962.1	E980.7
14-hydroxydihydromorphi-none	965.09	E850.2	E935.2	E950.0	E962.0	E980.0
ABOB	961.7	E857	E931.7	E950.4	E962.0	E980.4
Abrus (seed)	988.2	E865.3	—	E950.9	E962.1	E980.9
Absinthe	980.0	E860.1	—	E950.9	E962.1	E980.9
beverage	980.0	E860.0	—	E950.9	E962.1	E980.9
Acenocoumarin, aceno-coumarol	964.2	E858.2	E934.2	E950.4	E962.0	E980.4
Acepromazine	969.1	E853.0	E939.1	E950.3	E962.0	E980.3
Acetal	982.8	E862.4	—	E950.9	E962.1	E980.9
Acetaldehyde (vapor)	987.8	E869.8	—	E952.8	E962.2	E982.8
liquid	989.89	E866.8	—	E950.9	E962.1	E980.9
Acetaminophen	965.4	E850.4	E935.4	E950.0	E962.0	E980.0
Acetaminosalol	965.1	E850.3	E935.3	E950.0	E962.0	E980.0
Acetanilid(e)	965.4	E850.4	E935.4	E950.0	E962.0	E980.0
Acetarsol, acetarsone	961.1	E857	E931.1	E950.4	E962.0	E980.4
Acetazolamide	974.2	E858.5	E944.2	E950.4	E962.0	E980.4
Acetic						
acid	983.1	E864.1	—	E950.7	E962.1	E980.6
with sodium acetate (oint-ment)	976.3	E858.7	E946.3	E950.4	E962.0	E980.4
irrigating solution	974.5	E858.5	E944.5	E950.4	E962.0	E980.4
lotion	976.2	E858.7	E946.2	E950.4	E962.0	E980.4
anhydride	983.1	E864.1	—	E950.7	E962.1	E980.6
ether (vapor)	982.8	E862.4	—	E950.9	E962.1	E980.9

Permission to reprint granted by OptumInsight Inc.

Figure 5–8 Table of Drugs and Chemicals

EXAMPLE: DIAGNOSIS WITH POISONING PROBLEM

A child is treated for hives caused by ingesting her brother's psoriasis medication, triamcinolone. The billing specialist codes the hives as the reason for the visit and may also code the wrongful ingestion of triamcinolone as an accidental poisoning.

REINFORCEMENT EXERCISES 5–4

1. List the names of the three tables located in the *Alphabetic Index*.

_____

_____

_____

2. Write a brief definition for the following Hypertension Table main column headings.

a. Malignant

_____

_____

_____

continued on the next page

continued from the previous page

b. Benign

_____

_____

_____

c. Unspecified

_____

_____

_____

3. What is the purpose of the Neoplasm Table?

_____

_____

_____

4. Write a brief definition for each of the general categories listed in the Neoplasm Table.

a. Malignant

_____

_____

_____

b. Benign

_____

_____

_____

c. Uncertain Behavior

_____

_____

_____

d. Unspecified

_____

_____

_____

ICD-9-CM Coding Conventions

A thorough understanding of ICD-9-CM coding conventions is necessary to accurately assign diagnostic codes. Coding conventions fall into five categories:

- Cross-references
- Instructional notes
- Connecting words
- Abbreviations
- Punctuation

Cross-References

ICD-9-CM cross-references, which are usually found in the *Alphabetic Index,* include "see," "see also," and "see condition." The cross-references direct the billing specialist to look elsewhere in the code book(s) before assigning a code.

The see cross-reference is a mandatory direction, and the billing specialist or coder must refer to the term identified after the word "see."

> **EXAMPLE: MANDATORY "SEE" CROSS-REFERENCE**
> Under the entry Labor, with complications, the cross-reference note states "see Delivery, complicated." To ensure accurate coding, locate the Index entry Delivery, complicated, and continue from that entry.

See also directs the coder to another entry in the *Alphabetic Index* when the entry under consideration does not provide the needed code. Basically, "see also" means "if you cannot find the code you need here, check at this other location."

> **EXAMPLE: "SEE ALSO" CROSS-REFERENCE**
> Pneumonia, caseous code 011.6 is cross-referenced by "see also Tuberculosis." If code 011.6 does not accurately reflect the diagnosis in the patient's record, the billing specialist refers to the Tuberculosis entry for the correct code.

See condition directs the billing or coding specialist to use the condition, problem, or disease as the first search term (main entry).

> **EXAMPLE: "SEE CONDITION" CROSS-REFERENCE**
> The diagnosis is written as lobar pneumonia. The insurance biller uses lobar as a main term and finds the entry Lobe, lobar in the Alphabetic Index. The cross-reference states "see condition." In this case, pneumonia is the condition. The insurance biller locates Pneumonia, lobar in the Alphabetic Index in order to find the correct code.

Instructional Notes

Instructional notes provide additional guidance for accurate code selection. The types of instructional notes are:

- General notes
- Includes notes
- Excludes notes
- Use additional code, if desired

- Code first [the] underlying condition (disease)
- Code, if applicable, any causal condition first
- Omit code

General notes are found in all three ICD-9-CM volumes. In the *Alphabetic Index,* general notes are usually printed in italics and boxed. The most common application of general notes is to identify fifth-digit subclassifications in the *Tabular List* and *Alphabetic Index.* General notes are also used to clarify unique coding situations.

> **EXAMPLE: GENERAL NOTE**
> The main entry Fracture has general notes that describe open vs. closed fractures, and give directions for coding multiple fracture sites.

Includes notes are lists of conditions that are similar enough to be coded or classified by the same medical code. Includes notes are found at the beginning of a chapter and immediately following category, subcategory, and subclassification codes.

> **EXAMPLE: INCLUDES NOTE**
> Atherosclerosis, the narrowing of an arterial wall caused by deposits of fat and cholesterol, is coded to category 440. The inclusion note for the category lists several diagnoses, such as arteriosclerosis, arteriosclerotic vascular disease, and atheroma, which are covered by category 440.

Excludes notes are found immediately below the code to which the exclusion applies. A condition listed under the excludes note cannot be coded or classified by the medical code that has the excludes note. A code or range of codes for the excluded condition is part of the excludes note.

> **EXAMPLE: EXCLUDES NOTE**
> The 440.2 atherosclerosis code has an excludes note that reads "Excludes: atherosclerosis of bypass graft of the extremities (440.30–440.32)." Atherosclerosis of a bypass graft of the extremities cannot be coded to 440.2.

Use additional code means that more than one code may be necessary to provide a complete picture of the patient's problem.

> **EXAMPLE: USE ADDITIONAL CODE**
> The diagnosis of vaginitis, inflammation of the vagina, is supported by a lab test that reveals the presence of *E. coli* (*Escherichia coli*). Vaginitis is coded to 616.10. An instruction note for this code states "use additional code to identify [the] organism, such as *Escherichia coli* [*E. coli*] (041.41-041.49)."

Code first [the] underlying condition indicates that the patient's condition is a manifestation of an underlying disease. For inpatient billing, the code for the underlying disease must be listed on the insurance claim form before the manifestation code. In the physician office setting, the first code listed is the code that applies to the reason for the office visit.

> **EXAMPLE: INPATIENT – CODE FIRST [THE] UNDERLYING CONDITION**
> The diagnosis diabetic retinitis requires two codes: one for the diabetes and one for the retinitis. Diabetes is the underlying condition causing retinitis. Retinitis is a manifestation of diabetes. For inpatient insurance claims, the diabetes code is listed before the retinitis code.

EXAMPLE: OFFICE VISIT – CODE FIRST [THE] UNDERLYING CONDITION

For office visit insurance claims, the reason for the visit is listed first. If the patient is being treated for retinitis, retinitis is the reason for the office visit. The retinitis code is listed first.

Code, if applicable, any causal condition first means that the code with this instructional note may be sequenced or listed first as the principal diagnosis when the causal condition is unknown or not applicable. If the causal condition is known, then the code for the causal condition must be sequenced or listed first as the principal diagnosis.

EXAMPLE: CAUSAL CONDITION

In the *Tabular List*, Chapter 16, "Symptoms, Signs, and Ill-defined Conditions," code 788.3 urinary incontinence includes the instructional note "Code, if applicable, any causal condition first, such as: congenital ureterocele (753.23); genital prolapsed (618.00–618.9); and hyperplasia of prostate (600.00–600.9 with fifth-digit 1)." If the diagnosis includes any of the listed conditions as the cause of the urinary incontinence, then the code for the condition must be sequenced before the code for urinary incontinence.

Omit code means exactly what it says; no code is assigned when an *Index* entry contains this instruction.

REINFORCEMENT EXERCISES 5–5

Identify the coding convention described by each statement.

1. Lists the conditions or diagnoses covered by a particular code.

   _____

2. Lists the conditions or diagnoses not covered by a particular code.

   _____

3. Identifies the patient's condition as a manifestation of another disease or problem.

   _____

4. More than one code is used to describe the patient's condition.

   _____

5. Adjective was used as a main term.

   _____

6. Look further if necessary.

   _____

7. Mandatory cross-reference.

   _____

Connecting Words

Connecting words, which are subterms listed primarily in the *Alphabetic Index,* indicate a relationship between the main term and associated conditions or causes of disease. Commonly used connecting words include "associated with," "complicated (by)," "due to," "during," "following," "in," "of," "secondary to," "with," "with mention of," and "without." Except for "with" and "without," the connecting words are listed in alphabetic order under the main term. Figure 5–9 illustrates the use of connecting words "due to," "in," and "with." Narrative examples for each of these connecting words follow Figure 5–9.

The phrase **due to** indicates a causal relationship between two conditions.

> **EXAMPLE: CONNECTING WORDS "DUE TO"**
> The diagnosis pneumonia **due to** adenovirus means that the pneumonia is caused by an adenovirus organism. Because there is a cause-and-effect relationship between the virus and the pneumonia, the correct code is 480.0.

The connecting words "with," "associated with," and "in" identify codes that require two elements in the diagnostic statement.

> **EXAMPLE: CONNECTING WORDS "WITH" AND "IN"**
> The category for influenza is 487. A diagnosis of pneumonial influenza or influenza **with** pneumonia results in code 487.0, Influenza with pneumonia. Both conditions must be documented in order to use code 487.0.
>
> The diagnosis pneumonia **in** actinomycosis means that the patient has actinomycosis (a chronic systemic disease that often involves the lungs) and has developed pneumonia because of the disease. The correct code for pneumonia in actinomycosis is 039.1, Actinomycotic infections, pulmonary. Both the actinomycosis and the pneumonia must be documented in order to use code 039.1.

The word "and" means "and/or" when it appears in the title of a code.

> **EXAMPLE: CONNECTING WORD "AND"**
> Code 616.10, Vaginitis **and** *Vulvovaginitis,* unspecified, can be assigned to either condition.

Pneumonia...
    with influenza, flu, or grippe 487.0
    adenoviral 480.0...
    bacterial 482.9...
    due to
        adenovirus 480.0...
        Chlamydia, chlamydial 483.1...
    in
        actinomycosis 039.1
        anthrax 022.1*[484.5]*...

Figure 5–9 Connecting Words

Abbreviations

The abbreviations NEC (not elsewhere classified) and NOS (not otherwise specified) have the same meaning in all ICD-9-CM volumes. NEC and NOS are associated with the codes that include the fourth or fifth digits 8 and 9. These codes are known as residual subcategories.

NEC means that the diagnosis or condition, no matter how specific, does not have a separate code.

EXAMPLE: NEC DIAGNOSIS

Lumbar hernia, the protrusion of an abdominal organ into the loin, is a specific diagnosis that does not have a separate code. Lumbar hernia is one of several hernia diagnoses coded listed under code 553.8, Hernia of other specified sites. The usual fourth or fifth digit for NEC conditions is the number 8.

NOS means the same thing as "unspecified." This abbreviation is found only in the *Tabular List*. NOS codes should be used only when the diagnosis or the patient's medical record does not provide enough information for a more specific code.

EXAMPLE: NOS DIAGNOSIS

Regional enteritis, an inflammatory disease of the intestine, can affect the small intestine, large intestine, or both segments of the intestine. If the diagnosis is stated simply as *regional enteritis* and no additional information is available, the correct code is 555.9, Regional enteritis, unspecified site. The fourth or fifth digit for NOS codes is the number 9.

However, if the diagnosis is stated as *regional ileitis*, the correct code is 555.0, Regional enteritis, small intestine. The ileum is part of the small intestine, and therefore the term ileitis identifies the small intestine as the specific site of the regional enteritis.

Punctuation

Punctuation marks such as parentheses ( ), slanted square brackets *[ ]*, square brackets [ ], colons:, section marks §, braces }, and double braces { } are used to provide additional information for accurate coding. Some commercial ICD-9-CM publications do not use all punctuation marks.

Parentheses ( ) are used to enclose words that do *not* affect code selection and to enclose cross-references such as *see also*. Terms within the parentheses are nonessential modifiers and do not affect code assignment. Nonessential modifiers may or may not be included in the diagnostic statement.

EXAMPLE: NONESSENTIAL MODIFIERS

Category 440, Atherosclerosis, includes the diagnosis arteriosclerosis (obliterans) (senile). Obliterans and senile are nonessential modifiers, need not be present in the diagnostic statement, and do not affect code assignment. The correct code for senile arteriosclerosis is 440.9, Generalized and unspecified atherosclerosis.

Square brackets [ ] are used to enclose synonyms, alternate wordings, abbreviations, and phrases related to a section, category, subcategory, or subclassification. Information in square brackets is not a required part of the diagnostic statement.

EXAMPLE: SYNONYMS AND ABBREVIATIONS

Arteriosclerotic heart disease [ASHD] is included in the code 414.00, Coronary atherosclerosis, narrowing of the arteries of the heart. The abbreviation ASHD is included in square brackets because ASHD is synonymous with arteriosclerotic heart disease.

Square brackets are also used to note fifth digits associated with a specific code.

EXAMPLE: FIFTH DIGITS

The diagnosis Osteoarthrosis, generalized, is coded as 715.0, and the fifth digits 0, 4, and 9 are located under the code in square brackets [0,4,9]. An accurate code for Osteoarthrosis, generalized must include one of the three acceptable fifth digits. The 0 means site unspecified, 4 is the hand, and 9 is used when multiple sites are stated in the diagnosis.

Slanted square brackets [ ], found only in the *Alphabetic Index,* enclose the manifestation code associated with an underlying condition.

EXAMPLE: MANIFESTATION CODE

The alphabetic entry Anthrax, with pneumonia 022.1 *[484.5],* identifies the code for anthrax infection first and then the pneumonia code in slanted brackets. The pneumonia is a manifestation of the anthrax infection.

For inpatient insurance billing, the underlying condition must be listed before the manifestation code. For physician office billing, the reason for the office visit is listed first on the insurance claim form.

Colons : are used with includes notes and excludes notes and are placed after the included or excluded condition. Additional descriptions are indented and listed beneath the included or excluded condition. The diagnosis must contain at least one of the descriptions in order to apply the includes note or excludes note. Some commercial ICD-9-CM coding references no longer use colons. The word *includes* is boxed and printed in bold. The word *excludes* is boxed and printed in white. Diagnoses included in or excluded from a particular code are listed with the appropriate instruction.

Braces and double braces—{ and { }—serve the same purpose as colons. They connect a list or series of descriptions or diagnostic terms with a common stem or with a main term. Braces are used in the *Tabular List* to reduce repetitive wording by connecting a series of terms on the left with a statement on the right. Some ICD-9-CM coding references drop the use of braces.

Section marks § are used in the official Government Printing Office version of the ICD-9-CM. The section mark is placed at the left of any three- or four-digit code that requires a fifth digit. Other publishers use a variety of unique signals or marks, such as small flags or color-coded keys, to identify the fifth-digit requirement. Table 5–7 summarizes ICD-9-CM punctuation marks.

TABLE 5–7

ICD-9-CM Punctuation Marks	
Punctuation Mark	**Example**
Parentheses ( )	Enclose words that do not affect code assignment: Arteriosclerosis (obliterans) (senile)
Square brackets [ ]	Enclose information that does not affect code assignment: Arteriosclerotic heart disease [ASHD] Identify fifth digits associated with a specific code: 715.0 Osteoarthrosis, generalized [0,4,9]
Slanted square [ ] brackets	Enclose the manifestation code associated with an underlying condition: Anthrax, with pneumonia 022.1 *[484.5]* Pneumonia is the manifestation of the anthrax infection.

continued on the next page

continued from the previous page

Colons :	Identify required descriptions for exclusion and inclusion notes: 528.0 Stomatitis *Excludes: stomatitis:* *acute necrotizing ulcerative (101)* *aphthous (528.2)* *gangrenous (528.1)* *herpetic (054.2)* *Vincent's (101)*
Section mark(s) §	Identify code needing fifth digit: §662 Long Labor 662.0 Prolonged First Stage [0,1,3]
Braces {	Serve the same purpose as colons
Double braces { }	Serve the same purpose as colons

REINFORCEMENT EXERCISES 5–6

Identify the coding convention described in each statement.

1. Indicates that a specific diagnosis does not have a separate code.

_____

2. Means the same as "unspecified."

_____

3. Used to enclose or highlight fifth digits associated with a specific code.

_____

4. Causal relationship between two or more conditions.

_____

5. Identifies codes that require documentation of two conditions.

_____

6. Connect a list of descriptions with a main term.

_____

7. Encloses nonessential modifiers and cross-reference terms.

_____

continued on the next page

continued from the previous page

8. Enclose manifestation codes.

_____

9. Identifies the need for a fifth digit.

_____

Coding convention practice.

1. Locate the main entry "Pneumonia." Review this multicolumn entry and find an example for NEC, "due to," "with," "see also," and "see."

_____

_____

_____

_____

2. Locate the main entry "diabetes mellitus" and answer the following questions:

  a. Where is the word "mellitus" located? _____

  b. Is there a boxed instructional note? If yes, what is included? _____

  c. Write out the full entry for the first NEC code. _____

3. Locate the entry "diabetic cataract" and answer the following questions:

  a. What is the main term? _____

  b. What is the first code? _____

  c. What is the significance of the code in the slanted brackets? _____

  d. Find both codes for diabetic cataract in the *Tabular List.* _____ _____

ICD-9-CM OFFICIAL GUIDELINES FOR CODING AND REPORTING

The CMS and the NCHS develop and update guidelines for coding and reporting by using ICD-9-CM. The guidelines provide instructions in situations where ICD-9-CM does not provide instructions. The ICD-9-CM coding conventions take precedence over the guidelines. The Cooperating Parties—CMS, AHA, AHIMA, and NCHS—approve the guidelines. The guidelines are included in the official government version of the ICD-9-CM, in the *Coding Clinic for ICD-9-CM* published by the AHA and in commercial ICD-9-CM publications.

It is beyond the scope of this text to review the entire contents of the guidelines, which are available on the CMS website at http://www.cms.gov. Section IV, "Diagnostic Coding and Reporting Guidelines for Outpatient Services," and Section II, "Selection of Principal Diagnosis," are included in this chapter.

Section IV. Diagnostic Coding and Reporting Guidelines for Outpatient Services

The guidelines in Section IV of the ICD-9-CM *Official Guidelines for Coding and Reporting* are approved for hospital and provider-based outpatient services and office visits. This includes outpatient or ambulatory surgery, admission for observation, and physician office visits. Under the *Guidelines,* the terms "encounter" and "visit" are used interchangeably to describe outpatient service contacts. The reason for the encounter or visit is called the first-listed diagnosis, although some providers also use the term primary diagnosis. A summary of the guidelines is presented here and illustrated with examples as needed.

Guideline IV.A. Selection of First-Listed Condition (Diagnosis)

In determining the first-listed diagnosis, ICD-9-CM coding conventions as well as the general and disease-specific guidelines take precedence over the outpatient guidelines. Always begin the search for the correct code assignment through the *Alphabetic Index.* Never begin the initial search in the *Tabular List.*

1. Outpatient surgery: When a patient presents for outpatient surgery, code the reason for the surgery as the first-listed diagnosis (*reason for the encounter*), even if the surgery is not performed due to a contraindication.
2. Observation stay: When a patient is admitted for observation for a medical condition, assign a code for the medical condition as the first-listed diagnosis. When a patient presents for outpatient surgery and develops complications requiring admission for observation, code the reason for the surgery as the first-listed diagnosis, followed by codes for the complications as secondary diagnoses.

Guideline IV.B. Codes from 001.0 through V91.99

Appropriate ICD-9-CM codes, from 001.0 through V91.99, must be used to identify diagnoses, symptoms, problems, complaints, or other reasons for the encounter/visit.

Guideline IV.C. Accurate Reporting of ICD-9-CM Diagnosis Codes

For accurate reporting of ICD-9-CM diagnosis codes, the documentation should describe the patient's condition by using terminology that includes specific diagnoses as well as symptoms, problems, or reasons for the encounter. There are ICD-9-CM codes to describe all of these.

Guideline IV.D. Selection of Codes 001.0 through 999.9

Codes 001.0 through 999.9 are frequently used to describe the reason for the encounter. These codes are from the section of ICD-9-CM for the classification of diseases and injuries.

Guideline IV.E. Codes that Describe Symptoms and Signs

Codes that describe symptoms and signs, as opposed to diagnoses, are acceptable for reporting purposes when a diagnosis has not been established (confirmed) by the provider. ICD-9-CM *Volume 1,* Chapter 16, "Symptoms, Signs, and Ill-Defined Conditions" (780.0–799.9) contains many but not all codes for symptoms.

Guideline IV.F. Encounters for Circumstances Other Than Disease or Injury

ICD-9-CM V codes are used to report encounters for reasons other than disease or injury.

Guideline IV.G. Level of Detail in Coding

ICD-9-CM diagnosis codes are composed of three, four, or five digits that provide greater specificity. Use the full number of digits required for a code. A three-digit code is assigned only when further subdivisions (fourth or fifth digits) are not available. A code is invalid if it is not assigned to the highest level of specificity. The assigned code must be supported by the documentation in the patient's record.

> **EXAMPLE: HIGHEST LEVEL OF SPECIFICITY**
> Pansy is seen with a diagnosis of conductive hearing loss. The four-digit subcategory 389.0 Conductive hearing loss requires a fifth digit. Code 389.00, Conductive hearing loss, unspecified is the correct code.

Guideline IV.H. Code for the Diagnosis, Condition, Problem, or Other Reason for Encounter/Visit

List first the ICD-9-CM code for the diagnosis, condition, problem, or other reason for the encounter or visit shown in the medical record to be chiefly responsible for the services provided. List additional codes that describe any coexisting conditions. In some cases, the first-listed diagnosis may be a symptom when a diagnosis has not been established (confirmed) by the physician.

> **EXAMPLE: FIRST-LISTED DIAGNOSIS**
> Mark is seen in the physician's office for heart palpitations. He also has diabetes mellitus, type II, controlled. The first-listed diagnosis is palpitations, code 785.1. Diabetes mellitus, type II, controlled, code 250.00 is listed as an additional code for a coexisting condition.

Guideline IV.I. Uncertain Diagnosis

Do not code diagnoses documented as "probable," "suspected," "questionable," "rule out," "working diagnosis," or other similar terms indicating uncertainty. *Do* code the condition(s) to the highest degree of certainty for that encounter/visit, such as symptoms, signs, abnormal test results, or other reasons for the visit. This guideline does not apply to short-term care, acute care, psychiatric hospitals, or long-term care facilities.

> **EXAMPLE: UNCERTAIN DIAGNOSIS**
> Selina was seen in the physician's office with complaints of vertigo, nausea, and a headache. Rule out inner ear infection. In this case, if the inner ear infection is not confirmed, code the vertigo, nausea, and headache. The physician should indicate which symptom is primary.

Guideline IV.J. Chronic Diseases

Chronic diseases treated on an ongoing basis may be coded and reported as many times as the patient receives treatment and care for the condition(s).

Guideline IV.K. Code All Documented Conditions That Coexist

Code all documented conditions that coexist at the time of the encounter/visit and require patient care or affect treatment and management. *Do not* code conditions that were previously treated and no longer exist. However, history codes (V10–V19) may be used as secondary codes if the historical condition or family history has an impact on current care or influences treatment.

Guideline IV.L. Patients Receiving Diagnostic Services Only

When a patient receives only diagnostic services during an encounter/visit, sequence first the diagnosis, condition, problem, or other reason for the encounter/visit shown in the medical record to be chiefly responsible for the outpatient services provided during the encounter/visit. Codes for other diagnoses (e.g., chronic conditions) may be sequenced as additional diagnoses.

For encounters for routine laboratory/radiology testing in the absence of any symptoms, signs, or associated diagnoses, assign V72.5 and a code from subcategory V72.6. If routine testing is performed during the same encounter as a test to evaluate a symptom, sign, or diagnosis, it is appropriate to assign both the V code and the code describing the reason for the nonroutine test.

For outpatient encounters for diagnostic tests that have been interpreted by a physician and the final report available at the time of coding, code any confirmed or definitive diagnosis(es) documented in the interpretation. Do not code related symptoms and signs as additional diagnoses.

> **EXAMPLE: DIAGNOSTIC SERVICES WITH SYMPTOMS**
>
> Joel is seen for a colonoscopy because of frequent rectal bleeding, with a probable diagnosis of ulcerative colitis. In this case, the insurance billing specialist has two options:
>
> A. Submit the insurance claim before the results of the colonoscopy are available. The first-listed diagnosis in this option is rectal bleeding. Rectal bleeding is coded and sequenced first because that is the reason the colonoscopy was performed. The endoscopy is coded to the appropriate CPT category.
>
> B. Wait until the results of the colonoscopy are available and then submit the insurance claim. The diagnosis listed in the colonoscopy report is selected as the first-listed diagnosis, and coded and sequenced first. The endoscopy is coded to the appropriate CPT category.
>
> Because the results of the colonoscopy should provide a more specific diagnosis than rectal bleeding, option B is the best choice.

Guideline IV.M. Patients Receiving Therapeutic Services Only

For patients receiving only therapeutic services during the encounter/visit, sequence first the diagnosis, condition, problem, or other reason that is chiefly responsible for the encounter/visit. Codes for other conditions may be sequenced as additional diagnoses.

An exception to this guideline applies when the encounter is related to chemotherapy, radiation therapy, or rehabilitation. In these cases, the V code that identifies the treatment is listed first. The diagnosis or reason for the treatment is coded and listed after the V code.

Guideline IV.N. Patients Receiving Preoperative Evaluations Only

For patients receiving preoperative evaluations only, a code from category V72.8 "Other specified examinations" that describes the preoperative consultation is listed first. The reason for the surgery is coded and listed as an additional diagnosis. Also, code any findings related to the preoperative evaluation.

> **EXAMPLE: PREOPERATIVE EVALUATION**
>
> LaMar, whose medical treatment for an enlarged prostate has been unsuccessful, is seen for a preoperative evaluation prior to his scheduled TURP (transurethral resection of the prostate). The physician's note indicates that LaMar is diabetic and has hypertension.

In this case, the insurance billing specialist selects the V code that describes a preoperative evaluation. The V code is listed first, the code for enlarged prostate is second, and the codes for diabetes and hypertension are listed as additional diagnoses.

Guideline IV.O. Ambulatory Surgery

For ambulatory surgery, code the diagnosis for which the surgery was performed. If the postoperative diagnosis is known to be different from the preoperative diagnosis at the time the diagnosis was confirmed, code the postoperative diagnosis because it is the most definitive.

EXAMPLE: PREOPERATIVE VS. POSTOPERATIVE DIAGNOSIS
Because of the presence of several polyps, Maureen underwent a polypectomy of the descending colon. Familial polyposis was the preoperative diagnosis. The physician's postoperative note states that five polyps were removed—four benign and one malignant. Colorectal cancer is the postoperative diagnosis.
In this case, the postoperative diagnosis, colorectal cancer, is more definitive than familial polyposis. Colorectal cancer is coded and listed first. Do not code familial polyposis. The procedure is coded to the appropriate CPT category.

Guideline IV.P. Routine Outpatient Prenatal Visits

For routine outpatient prenatal visits when no complications are present, code V22.0, "Supervision of normal first pregnancy," and V22.1, "Supervision of other normal pregnancy," are the first-listed diagnosis codes. These codes should not be used in conjunction with codes from Chapter 11, "Complications of Pregnancy, Childbirth, and the Purperium."

Section II. Selection of Principal Diagnosis

The guidelines in Section II, "Selection of Principal Diagnosis," apply to services rendered in non-outpatient settings, such as hospitals, rehabilitation facilities, and nursing homes. In these settings, the principal diagnosis is the condition established after study to be chiefly responsible for the patient's admission for care. The code for the principal diagnosis is sequenced first on the insurance claim. A summary of guidelines A through J is included here. ICD-9-CM coding conventions take precedence over Section II guidelines. Additional information about inpatient coding and reporting is presented in Chapter 10, "Common UB-04 (CMS-1450) Completion Guidelines."

Guideline II.A. Codes for Symptoms, Signs, and Ill-Defined Conditions

Codes for symptoms, signs, and ill-defined conditions from ICD-9-CM Chapter 16 are not to be used as a principal diagnosis when a related definitive diagnosis has been established.

EXAMPLE: SYMPTOMS VS. DEFINITIVE DIAGNOSIS
Lekeitia is admitted to the hospital for severe nausea, vomiting, headache, and a stiff neck. The laboratory workup confirms the diagnosis of bacterial meningitis. Lekeitia is hospitalized for six days and is treated with intravenous antibiotics. In this example, bacterial meningitis is selected and coded as the principal diagnosis.

Guideline II.B. Two or More Interrelated Conditions, Each Potentially Meeting the Definition for Principal Diagnosis

When two or more interrelated conditions potentially meet the definition of principal diagnosis, either condition may be sequenced first, unless the circumstances of the admission, the therapy provided, the *Tabular List*, or the *Alphabetic Index* indicate otherwise.

EXAMPLE: INTERRELATED CONDITIONS OR DIAGNOSES

Following a car accident, Ramone was admitted with the diagnoses of closed fractures of the humerus and shaft of the ulna and radius. Both fractures were reduced without internal fixation. In this example, either fracture may be selected as the principal diagnosis.

Guideline II.C. Two or More Diagnoses That Equally Meet the Definition for Principal Diagnosis

In the unusual instance when two or more diagnoses equally meet the criteria for principal diagnosis as determined by the circumstance of admission, diagnostic workup, and/or therapy provided, and the *Tabular List*, *Alphabetic Index*, or other coding guidelines do not provide sequencing instructions, any one of the diagnoses may be sequenced first.

EXAMPLE: UNRELATED DIAGNOSES OR CONDITIONS

Wanda was admitted for elective surgery. A cystocele was repaired, and prolapsed internal hemorrhoids were removed. In this example, either the cystocele or prolapsed internal hemorrhoids may be selected as the principal diagnosis.

Guideline II.D. Two or More Comparative or Contrasting Conditions

In the rare instance when two or more contrasting or comparative diagnoses are documented as "either/or" (or similar terminology), the diagnoses are coded as if confirmed and sequenced according to the circumstances of the admission. If no further determination can be made as to which diagnosis is principal, either diagnosis may be sequenced first.

EXAMPLE: COMPARATIVE OR CONTRASTING DIAGNOSES

Liz's discharge diagnosis states "irritable bowel syndrome or spastic colon." Since neither irritable bowel syndrome nor spastic colitis is confirmed, either one of these diagnoses may be selected as the principal diagnosis and sequenced first.

Guideline II.E. A Symptom(s) Followed by Contrasting/Comparative Diagnoses

When a symptom(s) is followed by contrasting/comparative diagnoses, the symptom(s) code is sequenced first. All contrasting/comparative diagnoses should be coded as additional diagnoses.

EXAMPLE: SYMPTOMS WITH CONTRASTING/COMPARATIVE DIAGNOSES

Chen was admitted with symptoms of periodic vomiting with blood present in the vomitus, indigestion, and a low-grade fever over the past two weeks. Following workup, Dr. Samuelson dictated the following diagnostic statement: "Vomiting with frank blood due to either bleeding gastric ulcer or bleeding esophageal ulcer." In this example, the symptom "vomiting with frank blood" is selected as the principal diagnosis and sequenced first. "Bleeding gastric ulcer" and "bleeding esophageal ulcer" are coded as secondary diagnoses.

Guideline II.F. Original Treatment Plan Not Carried Out

Sequence as the principal diagnosis the condition that after study occasioned the admission to the hospital, even if treatment was not carried out because of unforeseen circumstances.

EXAMPLE: ORIGINAL TREATMENT PLAN NOT DONE

Travis was admitted for gastric bypass surgery. His diagnoses are morbid obesity and poorly controlled non–insulin-dependent diabetes mellitus, type II. Prior to the beginning of surgery, he exhibited an episode of hypotension and the surgery was canceled. In this example, morbid obesity is the principal diagnosis because it was the reason for the admission. Morbid obesity is coded and sequenced first. Non–insulin-dependent diabetes mellitus, type II, poorly controlled, is coded as a secondary or complicating diagnosis.

Guideline II.G. Complications of Surgery and Other Medical Care

When the admission is for treatment of a complication resulting from surgery or other medical care, the complication code is sequenced as the principal diagnosis. If the complication is classified to categories 996 through 999 and the code lacks the necessary specificity in describing the complication, an additional code for the specific complication should be assigned.

EXAMPLE: COMPLICATIONS

Oksana was treated for peritonitis following recent gastrointestinal surgery. The peritonitis was caused by the presence of nonabsorbable suture material accidentally left in her abdominal cavity. In this example, the complication code for a foreign body accidentally left during a procedure is coded as the principal diagnosis. An additional code for peritonitis is also assigned.

Guideline II.H. Uncertain Diagnosis

If the diagnosis documented at the time of discharge is qualified as "probable," "suspected," "likely," "questionable," "possible," "still to be ruled out," or other similar terms indicating uncertainty, code the condition as if it existed or was established. The bases for these guidelines are the diagnostic workup, arrangements for further workup or observation, and initial therapeutic approach that correspond most closely with the established diagnosis. This guideline applies only to inpatient admissions to short-term care, acute long-term care, and psychiatric hospitals.

EXAMPLE: UNCERTAIN DIAGNOSIS

Carla was admitted for acute onset of several episodes of explosive diarrhea and severe cramping within the past 24 hours. Patient described the stool as dark brown, "slimy," and foul-smelling. She was placed on a clear liquid diet and treated with intravenous hydrocortisone. Stool samples were taken for laboratory analysis. Colonoscopy was deferred pending resolution of acute symptoms. After three days, she was discharged on Prednisone. She is scheduled for a colonoscopy as an outpatient on Monday. Final diagnosis: probable ulcerative colitis.

Because the patient was admitted and treated for symptoms consistent with ulcerative colitis and an additional diagnostic procedure is scheduled, ulcerative colitis is the principal diagnosis and coded as if the condition existed.

Guideline II.I. Admission from Observation Unit

1. Admission following medical observation: When a patient is admitted to an observation unit for a medical condition, which either worsens or does not improve, and is subsequently admitted as an inpatient of the same hospital for the same medical condition, the principal diagnosis is the medical condition that led to the hospital admission.

2. Admission following postoperative observation: When a patient is admitted to an observation unit to monitor a condition (or complication) that develops following outpatient surgery and then is subsequently admitted as an inpatient of the same hospital, the principal diagnosis is the condition established after study to be chiefly responsible for the inpatient admission.

> **EXAMPLE: ADMISSION FOLLOWING POSTOPERATIVE OBSERVATION**
> Elmer underwent a transurethral resection of the prostate (TURP) as an outpatient procedure. Following the procedure, he exhibited a fever and hematuria (blood in the urine). He was admitted to an observation unit, and his condition did not improve. Elmer was then admitted as an inpatient for further treatment for fever and hematuria. In this case, the principal diagnosis is hematuria because it is the reason for the inpatient admission. Fever may also be coded as an additional problem.

Guideline II.J. Admission from Outpatient Surgery

When a patient receives surgery in the hospital's outpatient surgery department and is subsequently admitted for continuing inpatient care at the same hospital, the following guidelines should be followed in selecting the principal diagnosis for the inpatient admission:

- If the reason for the inpatient admission is a complication, assign the complication as the principal diagnosis.
- If no complication or other condition is documented as the reason for the inpatient admission, assign the reason for the outpatient surgery as the principal diagnosis.
- If the reason for the inpatient admission is another condition unrelated to the surgery, assign the unrelated condition as the principal diagnosis.

Diagnostic coding can be a challenge for any insurance billing specialist. There are several ICD-9-CM coding conventions to follow, and the coding guidelines described here are equally important. One final coding rule supersedes all others: Code only the conditions, problems, diagnoses, and procedures that are clearly documented in the patient's medical record.

REINFORCEMENT EXERCISES 5–7

Read each statement and mark it as True or False. Make the change(s) necessary to make the False statements True.

1. CMS and NCHS develop and update the *Official Guidelines for Coding and Reporting.*

---

2. The terms "encounter" and "visit" describe *hospital* inpatient services.

---

3. The first-listed diagnosis is the condition or disease responsible for the hospital admission.

---

continued on the next page

continued from the previous page

4. History codes may be used as secondary codes.

5. Routine outpatient prenatal visits are coded to ICD-9-CM Chapter 11, "Complications of Pregnancy, Childbirth, and the Purperium."

6. Symptoms, signs, and ill-defined conditions should not be used as a principal diagnosis.

7. A confirmed postoperative diagnosis is the first-listed diagnosis.

8. ICD-9-CM codes must be assigned to the highest level of specificity.

9. In a hospital setting, "probable" or "suspected" diagnoses may be coded as if the condition existed.

10. ICD-9-CM coding conventions take precedence over the *Official Guidelines for Coding and Reporting.*

ASSIGNING ICD-9-CM DIAGNOSTIC CODES

Accurate code assignment depends on three activities:

- Selecting diagnostic codes
- Sequencing diagnostic codes
- Following the official coding guidelines and all ICD-9-CM coding conventions

Only those diagnoses that are clearly documented in the patient's medical record are coded and submitted with the insurance claim.

Selecting the Diagnostic Codes

As with any task, there is a standard procedure for selecting ICD-9-CM diagnostic codes. The steps for code selection are enumerated and discussed here, and examples are provided.

1. Identify the main term(s) in the diagnostic statement. (In this example, the main term is in bold.)

> EXAMPLE
> Urinary tract **infection** due to *E. coli.*

2. Find the main term(s) in the *Alphabetic Index.*
3. Review the diagnostic statement for additional information concerning the main term.

> EXAMPLE
>
> "Urinary tract" identifies the anatomic location of the **infection.**

4. Review the subterms listed under the main term to determine if an entry matches the additional information in the diagnostic statement.

> EXAMPLE
>
> "Urinary (tract)" is a subterm listed under "Infection." There is no mention of "due to *E. coli.*"

5. Follow any cross-reference instructions such as "see" or "see also." If there are no cross-reference instructions, note the code listed with the subterm entry.

> EXAMPLE
>
> The code for "Infection, urinary (tract) NEC" is 599.0.

6. **Check the code listed in the *Alphabetic Index* with the description in the *Tabular List.***

> EXAMPLE
>
> Code 599.0 in the *Tabular List* is described as "Urinary tract infection, site not specified." Two synonymous terms, "bacteriuria" and "pyuria," are listed. The exclusion note identifies "candidiasis of urinary tract (112.2)." The coder is directed to use an additional code to identify the organism, such as "*Escherichia coli [E. coli]*" (041.41–041.49).

7. Read and follow all includes, excludes, and other instructional notes.

> EXAMPLE
>
> Use an additional code to identify the organism, such as "*Escherichia coli [E. coli]*" (041.41–041.49).

8. Assign the code(s) to the highest level of specificity:

 • Select a three-digit code only when no four-digit code is available.
 • Select a four-digit code only when no five-digit code is available.
 • Select a five-digit code when a fifth-digit subclassification is available.

> EXAMPLE
>
> Code 599.0 is the highest level of specificity for urinary tract **infection** due to *E. coli.* There is no fifth-digit subclassification.

9. Select and assign all codes that complete the diagnostic statement.

> EXAMPLE
>
> Urinary tract infection due to *E. coli* is coded 599.0, 041.49.

Step 6 is bolded for a very important reason. Because the *Tabular List* provides a complete description of conditions included and excluded under a particular code, a competent insurance billing specialist *never* codes directly from the *Alphabetic Index.*

Sequencing Diagnostic Codes

To ensure that the health care agency receives appropriate reimbursement for services, diagnostic codes must be accurately listed on the insurance claim (CMS-1500). Placing diagnostic codes in the correct order is called sequencing. Sequencing depends on the type of health care agency and on the definition of first-listed diagnosis and principal diagnosis.

The first-listed diagnosis is the condition noted as the reason for a specific encounter or visit. First-listed diagnosis criteria apply to outpatient settings, such as a physician's office.

> **EXAMPLE**
>
> A patient is seen in the office for strep throat. During the exam, the physician also reviews the current status of the patient's diabetes. The first-listed diagnosis in this case is strep throat (the reason for the visit) and is sequenced first on the insurance claim. Diabetes can be listed as a concurrent or secondary condition.

A concurrent condition is a problem that coexists with the first-listed diagnosis and complicates the treatment of the first-listed diagnosis. A secondary condition is a condition that coexists with the first-listed diagnosis but does not directly affect the outcome or treatment of the first-listed diagnosis.

The principal diagnosis is the diagnosis determined after study to be the reason for the patient's admission to a hospital. Principal diagnosis criteria apply to hospital or inpatient coding.

> **EXAMPLE**
>
> A patient is admitted to the hospital for rectal bleeding. After the appropriate tests, colorectal cancer is identified as the diagnosis. The principal diagnosis in this case is colorectal cancer, even though the initial reason for hospitalization was rectal bleeding.

Improper sequencing of diagnostic codes can lead to inadequate reimbursement for services rendered; denied or delayed reimbursement for services rendered; and, in a worst-case scenario, charges of fraud or abuse. Strict adherence to ICD-9-CM coding conventions, sequencing guidelines, and the *Official Guidelines for Coding and Reporting* prevents reimbursement problems.

REINFORCEMENT EXERCISES 5–8

Provide a short answer for each statement or question.

1. List three activities that lead to successful coding.

_____

_____

_____

2. What is the difference between the first-listed diagnosis and the principal diagnosis?

_____

_____

_____

continued on the next page

continued from the previous page

Rank each statement from 1 to 9. Place a 1 in front of the first step for selecting an ICD-9-CM diagnostic code and a 9 in front of the last step.

_____ Assign the code(s) to the highest level of specificity.

_____ Identify the main term(s) in the diagnostic statement.

_____ Follow any cross-reference instructions.

_____ Check the code listed in the *Alphabetic Index* with the description in the *Tabular List*.

_____ Find the main term(s) in the *Alphabetic Index*.

_____ Select and assign all codes that complete the diagnostic statement.

_____ Review the subterms listed under the main term in the *Alphabetic Index*.

_____ Read and follow all includes, excludes, and other instructional notes.

_____ Review the diagnostic statement for additional information concerning the main term.

Fill in the blank.

1. A condition that coexists with the first-listed diagnosis and complicates the treatment of the first-listed diagnosis is called a _____.

2. A condition that coexists with the first-listed diagnosis but does not directly affect the first-listed diagnosis outcome or treatment is called a _____.

3. Listing diagnostic codes in the correct order is known as _____.

4. Diagnostic codes must be selected to the highest level of _____.

5. Code only those conditions that are clearly _____ in the patient's medical record.

Write the main term and assign the correct ICD-9-CM code for each diagnosis.

1. Gastric influenza

   Main Term: _____ Code: _____

2. Laceration of the eyeball

   Main Term: _____ Code: _____

3. Acute pyogenic thyroiditis

   Main Term: _____ Code: _____

4. Malaria with hepatitis

   Main Term: _____ Code: _____

continued on the next page

continued from the previous page

5. Recurrent bleeding peptic ulcer

Main Term: _____ Code: _____

6. Hypoglycemia

Main Term: _____ Code: _____

7. Lymphangitis, acute

Main Term: _____ Code: _____

8. Ectopic pregnancy

Main Term: _____ Code: _____

9. Arthritis due to psoriasis

Main Term: _____ Code: _____

10. Appendicitis with perforation

Main Term: _____ Code: _____

SUPPLEMENTARY CLASSIFICATIONS

The supplementary classifications of ICD-9-CM are located in *Volume 1, Tabular List,* immediately following the 17 main chapters. These classifications are commonly called V codes and E codes. V codes are often used in physician office and ambulatory coding. E codes, which are for the most part optional, are used less often.

V Codes

V codes are found in the "Supplementary Classification of Factors Influencing Health Status and Contact with Health Services" section of the *Tabular List.* No wonder medical billers and coders refer to this section as the "V codes"! These codes apply to situations such as office visits for vaccinations, suture removal, and annual physical examinations. Table 5–8 lists the *Alphabetic Index* main terms that lead to V codes.

Although V codes are sometimes used in hospitals, they are more frequently assigned in health care settings, such as physician offices, clinics, and outpatient services. As with all coding activities, the billing specialist must be certain that the patient record supports the selected code and that the selected code is the most appropriate for the services rendered.

> **EXAMPLE: V CODE AS FIRST-LISTED DIAGNOSIS**
> Jolinda brings her 2-year-old son in for a well-child visit. During the physical exam, the physician notices that Miguel's throat is quite red and takes a throat culture. The results indicate that Miguel has strep throat. Jolinda leaves the office with a prescription for an antibiotic. In this case, the V code for a well-child visit is listed as the reason for the encounter. The appropriate codes for strep throat and throat culture are also submitted for reimbursement.

TABLE 5–8

Alphabetic Index Main Terms That Lead to V Codes		
Admission (encounter)	Dialysis	Outcome of delivery
Aftercare	Donor	Pregnancy
Attention to	Examination	Problem
Boarder	Exposure	Prophylactic
Care (of)	Fitting (of)	Replacement by
Carrier (suspected) of	Follow-up	Resistance, resistant
Checking	Health	Screening
Contact	Healthy	Status
Contraception, contraceptive	History (personal) of	Supervision (of)
Convalescence	Maintenance	Test(s)
Counseling	Maladjustment	Therapy
Dependence	Newborn	Transplant, transplanted
	Observation	Vaccination

There is no "magic list" of V codes that may be rejected by some or all third-party payers. Unacceptable V codes for Medicare and Medicaid patients are routinely updated. Fiscal intermediaries (insurance companies) may notify health care providers which V codes are unacceptable for reimbursement.

Table 5–9 lists the V code categories and titles. Information about each V code category is provided in the following discussion.

Categories V01–V06: Persons with Health Hazards Related to Communicable Diseases

Codes from categories V01 through V06 are assigned when the reason for the service includes vaccination and inoculation against a communicable disease. The patient may have been exposed to the disease or may fall into a high-risk category, as with flu shots for specific populations. *Alphabetic Index* terms such as "contact," "exposure," "prophylactic (preventive)," and "vaccination" lead to V01–V06 codes.

> **EXAMPLE: VACCINATION**
>
> Abby was seen by the pediatrician for a DPT vaccination (immunization). DPT is a combination immunization for diphtheria, pertussis, and tetanus. Because this is the reason for the visit, code V06.1, "Vaccination and inoculation against combinations of diseases, diphtheria-tetanus-pertussis, combined," is the appropriate ICD-9-CM code.

Categories V07–V09: Persons with Need for Isolation, Other Potential Health Hazards and Prophylactic Measures

Codes from categories V07 through V09 are usually assigned as an additional code when a condition is classified or coded elsewhere.

TABLE 5–9

V Code Categories and Titles	
Category	Title
V01–V06	Persons with Potential Health Hazards Related to Communicable Diseases
V07–V09	Persons with Need for Isolation, Other Potential Health Hazards, and Prophylactic Measures
V10–V19	Persons with Potential Health Hazards Related to Personal and Family History
V20–V29	Persons Encountering Health Services in Circumstances Related to Reproduction and Development
V30–V39	Liveborn Infants According to Type of Birth
V40–V49	Persons with a Condition Influencing Their Health Status
V50–V59	Persons Encountering Health Services for Specific Procedures and Aftercare
V60–V69	Persons Encountering Health Services in Other Circumstances
V70–V82	Persons without Reported Diagnosis Encountered during Examination and Investigation of Individuals and Populations
V83–V84	Genetics
V85	Body Mass Index
V86	Estrogen Receptor Status
V87	Other Specified Personal Exposures and History Presenting Hazards to Health
V88	Acquired Absence of Other Organs and Tissue
V89	Other Suspected Conditions Not Found
V90	Retained Foreign Body
V91	Multiple Gestation Placenta Status

EXAMPLE: ADDITIONAL CODE

Janelle was admitted to City Hospital and placed in isolation. Her diagnosis is necrotic septicemia due to vancomycin-resistant staphylococcus aureus (VRSA). The diagnosis code for necrotic septicemia is assigned as the principal diagnosis. V07.0 (Isolation) and V09.8 (VRSA) may be assigned as additional codes.

Categories V10–V19: Persons with Potential Health Hazards Related to Personal and Family History

Codes from categories V10 through V19 are assigned when there is a personal or family history of malignant neoplasms, mental health problems, allergies, or other diseases. Codes from these categories provide additional information about the patient and are rarely, if ever, submitted for reimbursement as the sole reason for the encounter.

EXAMPLE: HISTORY OF ALLERGY

The patient is seen for a sinus infection. During the exam, the patient states, "I'm allergic to penicillin." A sinus infection is the reason for the office visit. For billing purposes, the ICD-9-CM code for sinusitis is listed as the diagnostic code. The code V14.0, "Personal history of allergy to medicinal agents, penicillin," may be included as additional information, but it has no effect on reimbursement.

EXAMPLE: FAMILY HISTORY

A healthy 30-year-old woman is seen for an employment physical. She states that her mother and her dad's sister had breast cancer in their 30s. The physician completes the employment physical and orders a baseline mammography. In this case, the appropriate V code for an employment physical is selected as the first-listed diagnosis: V70.5, "General medical examination, pre-employment screening." If no other problems are identified, that is the code submitted with the insurance claim. If problems are found during the physical, the appropriate ICD-9-CM codes are submitted as additional diagnoses.

The reason for the mammography is a family history of breast cancer. If the patient's insurance covers this service, the radiologist's billing specialist submits V16.3, "Family history of malignant neoplasm, breast," as the first-listed diagnosis. If the mammogram reveals any problems, the appropriate ICD-9-CM codes are also submitted with the insurance claim.

Categories V20–V29: Persons Encountering Health Services in Circumstances Related to Reproduction and Development

Codes from categories V20 through V29 describe all stages of pregnancy, child development, and birth control. These categories are commonly used in the physician office setting. Table 5–10 lists the conditions associated with codes V20 through V29. Application examples are provided in the following discussion.

Codes from category V20 are assigned to routine health assessments of a healthy infant or child. Category V21 applies when the visit includes the identification of a specific developmental state.

EXAMPLE: ROUTINE HEALTH CHECK—CHILD

Martin is seen for a routine preschool hearing and vision screening. The physician notes that Martin has experienced a growth spurt that was greater than expected. Although there is no problem at this time, Martin's parents are advised to monitor his growth. Code V20.2, "Routine infant or child health check," is selected as the reason for the visit and submitted on the insurance claim. Code V21.0, "Period of rapid growth in childhood," may be included as an additional finding.

Codes from category V22 are assigned to supervision of a normal pregnancy. This category has three choices: "Supervision of a normal first pregnancy" is coded V22.0, and "Supervision of other [or subsequent] normal pregnancy" is coded V22.1. These codes are used in physician offices and clinics and can stand alone in those settings. Code V22.2, "Pregnant state, incidental," is assigned when the pregnancy is not the primary reason for the encounter.

TABLE 5–10

Pregnancy, Child Development, Birth Control V Codes	
Condition	**V Codes**
Pregnancy, postpartum, procreative management	V22 Normal pregnancy
	V23 Supervision of high-risk pregnancy
	V24 Postpartum care and examination
	V26 Procreative management
	V27 Outcome of delivery
	V28 Encounter for antenatal screening of mother
Child development	V20 Health supervision of infant or child
	V21 Constitutional states in development
	V29 Observation and evaluation of newborns and infants for suspected condition not found
Birth control	V25 Encounter for contraceptive management

EXAMPLE: PREGNANCY STATE, INCIDENTAL

Jolinda is seen for follow-up treatment and evaluation of psoriasis. She is six months pregnant and states she feels fine. In this example, the reason for the visit is related to psoriasis. The appropriate ICD-9-CM diagnosis code for psoriasis is submitted with the insurance claim. Code V22.2, "Pregnant state, incidental," is optional, as long as follow-up for psoriasis is unrelated to the pregnancy and does not affect the management of the pregnancy.

EXAMPLE: ROUTINE PRENATAL VISIT

Roberta, who is three months pregnant, is seen for a routine prenatal visit. Roberta has gained 8 pounds and is pleased that she is doing better with her weight this time. During her last pregnancy, she gained 15 pounds in the first trimester. In this example, code V22.1, "Supervision of other normal pregnancy," accurately describes the reason for this visit. In the absence of any other diagnostic statement, this code stands on its own.

Codes from category V23 are assigned when a condition is present that may add risk to the pregnancy. These codes are listed in the *Alphabetical Index* under "Pregnancy, supervision (of) (for)" or "Pregnancy, management affected by." The condition must be clearly identified in the patient's record and includes statements such as "pregnant with a history of neonatal death."

EXAMPLE: SUPERVISION OF HIGH-RISK PREGNANCY

Given her history of two stillbirths in three pregnancies, Miranda was relieved when she heard strong fetal heart sounds. She is advised to continue with her current activity level and dietary program. Her next prenatal visit is scheduled in one month. In this example, the patient has a history of stillbirths. This justifies the code V23.5, "Supervision of high-risk pregnancy, pregnancy with other poor reproductive history (stillbirth or neonatal death)." In the absence of any other diagnostic statement, this code stands alone.

Codes from category V24 are assigned for uncomplicated and routine postpartum care and examination. The postpartum period is the six weeks following delivery. If a postpartum complication is identified during the visit, the code for the complication is selected as the first-listed diagnosis.

EXAMPLE: ROUTINE POSTPARTUM VISIT

Martina is seen for a six-week appointment following delivery of a healthy baby girl. She offers no complaints, and no complications are noted. This is an example of a routine postpartum visit. Code V24.2, "Routine postpartum follow-up," is the correct code, and it stands alone.

EXAMPLE: POSTPARTUM CONDITION

Sara is seen three weeks following delivery of a healthy baby boy. Examination today reveals a swollen red area surrounding the episiotomy site. There is no exudate from the wound. Sara states there is "itching and burning" in the area. A topical antibiotic cream is prescribed. In this case, an infection developed within the postpartum period and involves the episiotomy site. The billing specialist selects the correct ICD-9-CM diagnostic code for a postpartum infection of the episiotomy site. Code 674.34, "Other complications of obstetrical surgical wounds, postpartum," includes this infection. A code from category V24 is not assigned.

Codes from category V25 are assigned when the purpose of the office visit is related to contraceptive management, commonly called birth control. Many insurance companies do not cover health care encounters associated with birth control.

EXAMPLE: VOLUNTARY STERILIZATION

Darryl is seen for voluntary vasectomy for purposes of birth control. Darryl must return for a postvasectomy sperm count. Code V25.2, "Sterilization, interruption of the vas deferens," is submitted with the insurance claim, provided the patient's insurance covers office visits related to voluntary sterilization.

Codes from category V26 apply to artificial insemination, repair of fallopian tubes or vas deferens following sterilization, genetic counseling, and other procreative treatments. Many of these treatments or procedures are classified as experimental and must be paid for by the patient. Fertility specialists may use these codes for statistical purposes.

Codes from category V27 are intended to code the outcome of delivery in the mother's medical record. These codes are for statistical purposes only and are not used for reimbursement.

Codes from category V28 are assigned to screening activities that involve amniocentesis and ultrasound. Ultrasound has become a fairly common prenatal screening tool, but its use must be clinically justified.

EXAMPLE: FETAL ULTRASOUND

Denise, who began her pregnancy at a normal weight, is estimated at 30 weeks gestation and has gained only 5 pounds. Her obstetrician is concerned about fetal size compared with the estimated gestational age. An ultrasound is performed to evaluate fetal growth and development. No abnormalities are found. In this case, code V28.4, "Antenatal screening, screening for fetal growth retardation using ultrasonics," is the correct diagnostic code. If the screening identifies an abnormal finding, then the abnormal condition is coded as the diagnostic statement.

Codes from category V29 are assigned to situations in which a newborn is suspected of having a particular condition that is ruled out after examination and observation. A newborn is an infant in the first 28 days of life (also called the neonatal period).

EXAMPLE: NEONATAL SCREENING

During her last trimester, Maureen developed a vaginal yeast infection. Conservative medical management controlled the symptoms. The normal vaginal delivery resulted in the birth of a healthy baby girl. Candidiasis is the organism that causes vaginal yeast infections and thrush. Maureen's family physician scheduled weekly appointments to monitor the newborn for thrush.

In this case, code V29.0, "Observation for suspected infectious condition," is the appropriate diagnostic code and is submitted with the insurance claim. If at any time during the observation period a diagnosis is identified, then the V29 code would no longer be appropriate.

REINFORCEMENT EXERCISES 5–9

Match the V code titles in Column A with the V code categories in Column B.

Column A		Column B
1. Encounter for antenatal screening of mother	_____	V20
2. Constitutional states in development	_____	V21
3. Contraceptive management	_____	V22
4. Health supervision, infant or child	_____	V23
5. Normal pregnancy	_____	V24
6. Observation and evaluation of newborns and infants	_____	V25
7. Outcome of delivery	_____	V26
8. Postpartum care and evaluation	_____	V27
9. Procreative management	_____	V28
10. Supervision of high-risk pregnancy	_____	V29

continued on the next page

continued from the previous page

Provide a short answer for each statement or question.

1. Name the V code categories that are used to identify liveborn infants in the hospital setting.

   _____

   _____

   _____

2. List the V codes and their descriptions that are included in the supervision of a normal pregnancy category.

   _____

   _____

   _____

3. When would the coder/biller assign V22.2, "Pregnancy state, incidental"?

   _____

   _____

   _____

4. What is the purpose of codes from category V27, "Outcome of delivery"?

   _____

   _____

   _____

5. Give an example of a condition that would justify selecting a code from category V23, "Supervision of high-risk pregnancy."

   _____

   _____

   _____

Categories V30–V39: Liveborn Infants according to Type of Birth

Codes in categories V30–V39 are assigned to liveborn infants who are occupying a hospital crib or bassinet. Three-digit categories identify single, twin, or multiple births, and the status of the twin or multiple mates. Four-digit subcategories identify whether or not the infant(s) was born in the hospital. Fifth-digit subcategories identify delivery with or without mention of cesarean section.

EXAMPLE: CESAREAN DELIVERY

Mrs. Cho gave birth to healthy twin girls by cesarean delivery. The mother's admission is coded as a live birth, cesarean delivery, twins. Each infant admission is assigned code V31.01, twin, mate born live, in the hospital by cesarean delivery.

Categories V40–V49: Persons with a Condition Influencing Their Health Status

Codes in categories V40 through V49 are used under the following circumstances:

- Nonspecific diagnoses that usually begin with the words "problem with"
- Postsurgical conditions involving organ transplants, artificial openings, and implanted devices
- Dependence on machines
- Problems with internal organs, head, neck, trunk, and limbs

These codes are typically assigned as additional diagnostic codes and can often explain or justify services that are rendered. Diagnostic statements for V codes 40–49 usually begin with "status post" or "dependence on."

EXAMPLE: STATUS POST

Patient is seen with a diagnosis of umbilical hernia. Status post ileostomy. The umbilical hernia, 553.1, is coded as the reason for the visit with V44.2, "Artificial opening status post, ileostomy," as an additional code.

Categories V50–V59: Persons Encountering Health Services for Specific Procedures and Aftercare

Codes from categories V50–V59 can be assigned as the primary diagnosis in the physician office and clinic settings. These codes are selected in the following circumstances:

- To indicate a reason for care in patients who have already been treated for some disease or injury not now present or who are receiving care to consolidate treatment
- To deal with residual states
- To prevent recurrence

EXAMPLE: ATTENTION TO ARTIFICIAL OPENINGS

As a result of severe ulcerative colitis, a patient has a total proctocolectomy—removal of the rectum and entire large intestine—with construction of an ileostomy. The ulcerative colitis is now "cured." However, the patient may need treatment or services related to the ileostomy. Codes listed under V55, "Attention to artificial openings," apply to services related to an ileostomy.

Codes from category V50 are assigned to a wide variety of situations, such as hair transplant, circumcision, ear piercing, and prophylactic organ removal.

Codes from category V51 apply to aftercare involving the use of plastic surgery. Cosmetic plastic surgery and plastic surgery as a treatment for a current condition are excluded from category V51.

Codes from category V52 are assigned to services related to artificial limbs, eyes, dental devices, and breast prosthetics and implants.

EXAMPLE: ARTIFICIAL LIMB

After losing 50 pounds, a patient is measured and fitted with a new artificial leg. Code V52.1, "Fitting and adjustment of . . . [an] artificial leg," is the diagnostic code for the office visit.

Codes from category V53 cover nervous system and special sense devices; cardiac pacemakers and defibrillators; intestinal, urinary, and orthopedic devices; wheelchairs; and other unspecified devices.

Codes in category V54 cover orthopedic aftercare involving internal fixation devices, healing traumatic and pathologic fractures, and cast removal.

EXAMPLE: REMOVAL OF INTERNAL FIXATION DEVICE

Eight weeks after a motor vehicle accident, the patient was seen in the office. The foot and leg cast was taken off, and the heel pin was removed. Codes V54.01, "Removal of . . . internal fixation device (pins)," and V54.89, "Removal of . . . cast," are the diagnostic codes for the office visit. These codes are submitted with the insurance claim.

Codes in category V55 are assigned to services related to artificial openings such as catheter care, closure of the opening, and passage of sounds or bougies. Problems with an external stoma are not covered in category V55.

EXAMPLE: CYSTOSTOMY TUBE

The patient is seen for replacement of the cystostomy tube. Code V55.5, "Attention to artificial openings, cystostomy," is the diagnostic code for this office visit.

Codes in category V56 include services related to dialysis and dialysis catheter care. An additional code to identify the associated condition is required.

EXAMPLE: DIALYSIS

Victoria completed her peritoneal dialysis and returned home with a new supply of dialysis solution. She was diagnosed with renal failure in May of last year. Codes V56.8, "Encounter for . . . peritoneal dialysis," and 586, "Renal failure, unspecified," are the diagnostic codes for this visit.

Codes in category V57 are assigned when the service provided includes physical, occupational, vocational, and speech therapy. As with the dialysis V codes, this category requires an additional code to identify the underlying condition.

EXAMPLE: PHYSICAL THERAPY

Melissa is seen for physical therapy for hemiplegia. Codes 342.90, "Hemiplegia, unspecified, affecting unspecified side," and V57.1, "Care involving . . . other physical therapy," are the diagnostic codes for the office visit.

Categories V60–V69: Persons Encountering Health Services in Other Circumstances

Codes from categories V60–V69 can be assigned as the primary diagnosis in the physician office and clinic settings. These codes cover a variety of circumstances, from homelessness (V60.0, "Lack of housing") to problems related to lifestyles (V69.3, "Gambling and betting").

Category V65 includes circumstances such as counseling sessions for dietary surveillance, HIV and other sexually transmitted diseases, exercise, and health education or instruction.

Category V66 often applies to long-term and hospice care following surgery, radiotherapy, or chemotherapy.

Category V67 is used for surveillance only following completed treatment. These codes are located in the *Alphabetic Index* under the phrases "Follow-up," "Encounter, for, follow-up," and "Admission, for, follow-up."

> EXAMPLE: FOLLOW-UP EXAMINATION
>
> Rhonda is seen for an examination following successful treatment of pyoderma gangrenosum (purulent skin disease associated with ulcerative colitis) with Dapsone. Because Dapsone can cause liver damage, code V67.51, "Follow-up examination . . . following completed treatment with high-risk medication," is assigned as the reason for the follow-up visit.

Category V68 includes situations such as issuing a medical certificate, repeat prescriptions, and request for expert advice.

Category V69 covers lack of physical exercise, high-risk sexual behavior, gambling, and problems related to lifestyle.

REINFORCEMENT EXERCISES 5–10

Match the V codes in Column A with the titles in Column B.

Column A

Column B

1. V40–V49 _____

2. V50–V59 _____

3. V50 _____

4. V60–V69 _____

5. V52 _____

6. V55 _____

7. V56 _____

8. V57 _____

9. V67 _____

10. V68 _____

a. Administrative purposes

b. Attention to artificial openings

c. Conditions influencing health status

d. Dialysis and catheter care

e. Elective surgery

f. Encountering health services, other circumstances

g. Encountering health services, specific procedures and aftercare

h. Fitting and adjustment of prosthetic device and implant

i. Follow-up examinations

j. Rehabilitation procedures

Categories V70–V82: Persons Without Reported Diagnosis Encountered During Examination and Investigation of Individuals and Populations

Codes from categories V70–V82 include the following:

- All types of routine medical examinations
- Observation and evaluation for suspected conditions not found, such as mental illness, malignant neoplasms, rape, and other specified suspected conditions
- Special screening for sexually transmitted, bacterial, infectious, endocrine, nutritional, metabolic, viral, neurological, and immunity disorders and other body system diseases and malignant neoplasms

Most of the categories in this section are appropriate as stand-alone codes for the physician office or clinic setting. Abnormal findings disclosed at the time of these examinations must be coded to the appropriate ICD-9-CM chapter.

Category V70 includes codes that apply to routine visits and to preventive care when no complaints are present. Category V70 codes are located under the alphabetic entries "examination and examination, medical (for) (of)." When a specific condition, sign, or diagnosis is being evaluated, the code for the condition must be included on the insurance claim. Table 5–11 lists the general medical examination categories, titles, and examples.

EXAMPLE: SPORTS PHYSICAL

Lance, an accomplished swimmer, is seen for completion of the required sports physical. No abnormalities are found, and no restrictions for participation are documented. Code V70.3, "Other medical examination for administrative purposes, . . . sports competition," is assigned as the reason for the encounter.

TABLE 5–11

V70 General Medical Examinations	
V Code	Title/Example
V70.0	Routine general medical examination at a health care facility; excludes infant or child
V70.1	General psychiatric examination, requested by the authority
V70.2	General psychiatric examination, other and unspecified
V70.3	Other medical examination for administrative purposes; sports competition, driving license, adoption, marriage, etc.; excludes attendance for issuance of medical certificates, pre-employment screening
V70.4	Examination for medicolegal reasons; blood-alcohol tests, blood-drug testing, paternity testing; excludes accidents, assault, rape
V70.5	Health examination of defined subpopulations; armed forces personnel, occupational health, pre-employment screening, preschool children, etc.
V70.6	Health examinations in population surveys
V70.7	Examination of participant in clinical trial
V70.8	Other specified general medical examinations
V70.9	Unspecified general medical examination

Codes from category V71 are assigned when a person without a diagnosis is suspected of having an abnormal condition that requires examination and observation even if no symptoms or signs of the condition are present. Conditions in this category include examination of the victim or culprit following alleged rape or seduction (V71.5), observation for suspected tuberculosis (V71.2), and observation and evaluation of abuse and neglect (V71.81). If the suspected condition is not found, category V71 codes are assigned as the reason for the examination or observation.

Codes from category V72 include routine examination of specific systems, such as eyes and vision and ears and hearing as well as dental exams, annual or routine gynecological exams, and routine preoperative examinations. Diagnostic activities such as radiology, laboratory tests, and skin tests for allergies are coded to this category.

Categories V73 through V82 include codes to identify screening examinations for specific conditions and disorders that may or may not be found. These codes are located in the *Alphabetic Index* under the entry "Screening (for)." The conditions covered in these categories range from anemia to suspected maternal and fetal conditions. Table 5–12 lists categories V73 through V82, with examples.

Categories V83, Genetics through V91, Multiple Gestation Placenta Status cover specific conditions. Table 5–13 lists these categories and examples.

TABLE 5–12

Categories V73 Through V82 with Examples		
Code	**Category Name**	**Examples**
V73	Special screening examination for viral and chlamydial diseases	V73.0 Poliomyelitis V73.1 Smallpox V73.88 Other specified chlamydial diseases
V74	Special screening examination for bacterial and spirochetal diseases	V74.0 Cholera V74.1 Pulmonary tuberculosis V74.2 Leprosy (Hansen's disease)
V75	Special screening examination for other infectious diseases	V75.0 Rickettsial diseases V75.1 Malaria V75.2 Leishmaniasis
V76	Special screening for malignant neoplasms	V76.0 Respiratory organs V76.10 Breast screening, unspecified
V77	Special screening for endocrine, nutritional, metabolic, and immunity disorders	V77.0 Thyroid disorders V77.1 Diabetes mellitus V77.2 Malnutrition

continued on the next page

continued from the previous page

V78	Special screening for disorders of blood and blood-forming organs	V78.0 Iron deficiency anemia V78.1 Other and unspecified deficiency anemia V78.2 Sickle cell disease or trait
V79	Special screening for mental disorders and developmental handicaps	V79.0 Depression V79.1 Alcoholism V79.2 Mental retardation
V80	Special screening for neurological, eye, and ear diseases	V80.0 Neurological conditions V80.1 Glaucoma V80.2 Other eye conditions
V81	Special screening for cardio-vascular, respiratory, and genitourinary diseases	V81.0 Ischemic heart V81.1 Hypertension V81.2 Other and unspecified cardiovascular conditions
V82	Special screening for other conditions	V82.0 Skin conditions V82.1 Rheumatoid arthritis

TABLE 5–13

Categories V83 Through V91 with Examples	
Category	**Example**
V83–V84 Genetics	Hemophilia A carrier; susceptibility to malignant neoplasm; cystic fibrosis gene carrier
V85 Body Mass Index	Body mass index value by age, pediatric to adults 70 and over
V86 Estrogen Receptor Status	Positive or negative estrogen receptor status associated with malignant neoplasm of the breast
V87 Other Specified Personal Exposures and History Presenting Hazards to Health	Exposure or contact with hazardous metal, chemicals, and mold
V88 Acquired Absence of Other Organs and Tissue	Absence of various organs or body parts as a result of treatment or surgery
V89 Other Suspected Conditions Not Found	Applies to suspected conditions related to fetal growth and development when the conditions are not found
V90 Retained Foreign Body	Applies to foreign substances that remain in a body part or cavity not related to treatment or surgery; retained animal tooth, wood, or metal
V91 Multiple Gestation Placenta Status	Applies to the status of the placenta when multiple fetuses are present

REINFORCEMENT EXERCISES 5–11

Match the V codes in Column A with the statements in Column B.

Column A

1. V70   _____

2. V72   _____

3. V75   _____

4. V76   _____

5. V77   _____

Column B

a. dental examinations

b. general medical examinations

c. screening, endocrine disorders

d. screening, infectious diseases

e. screening, malignant neoplasms

Write the exclusions for the listed V code categories.

1. V70.0, "General medical examination at a health care facility"

_____

2. V70.3, "Other medical examination for administrative purposes"

_____

3. V70.4, "Examination for medicolegal reasons"

_____

4. V70.6, "Health examination in population surveys"

_____

5. V76.2, "Special screening for malignant neoplasms"

_____

6. V80.2, "Special screening for . . . eye . . . diseases, Other eye conditions"

_____

7. V81.4, "Special screening for respiratory conditions"

_____

8. V82.4, "Postnatal screening for chromosomal anomalies"

_____

9. V87.0, "Contact with and (suspected) exposure to hazardous metals"

_____

10. V87.4, "Personal history of drug therapy"

_____

E Codes

E codes are listed in the "Supplementary Classification of External Causes of Injury and Other Adverse Effects." As with V codes, health care professionals refer to this section simply as "E codes." E codes provide an avenue to classify environmental events, circumstances, and conditions that cause injury, poisoning, adverse effects, and other abnormal conditions.

E codes are intended to provide data for injury research and prevention. The codes capture information about the following:

- Cause: How the injury or poisoning occurred (fall, flood, explosion)
- Intent: Why the injury or poisoning occurred (accident, assault, suicide attempt)
- Place: Where the injury or poisoning occurred (home, public building, workplace)

The use of E codes in many health care settings is optional, except for categories E930 through E949. This section is titled "Drugs, Medicinal and Biological Substances Causing Adverse Effects in Therapeutic Use." A portion of this section is shown in Figure 5–10. Review the figure, and pay close attention to the includes and excludes notes.

Some state laws require the use of E codes, as in cases of firearms accidents, mass transport accidents, and other incidents related to public health and safety. E codes cannot be assigned as

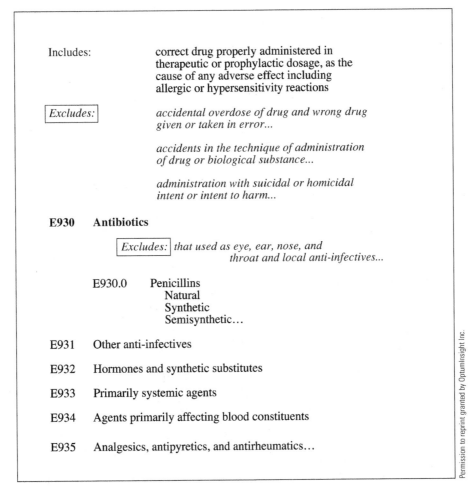

Figure 5–10 Drugs, Medicinal and Biological Substances Causing Adverse Effects in Therapeutic Use (E930–E949)

the only diagnostic code for a particular case. In most coding references, the alphabetic index for E codes, "Index to External Causes," follows the "Table of Drugs and Chemicals Index."

MISCELLANEOUS CODING GUIDELINES

Late effects, burns, and HIV/AIDS have coding guidelines unique to each condition. The guidelines are discussed individually.

Late Effects

A variety of illnesses and injuries once treated may result in a temporary or permanent medical problem or condition. This condition is called a residual.

> **EXAMPLE**
> A severe burn may result in a scar as a residual; a stroke may result in aphasia.

A late effect is the residual condition that remains after the acute phase of an illness or injury has been resolved. There is no definitive timetable for late effects. Documentation of late effects may include wording such as "residual of," "old," "sequela of," "late," and "due to" or "following" a previous illness or injury.

Late effects often require two codes: one for the residual condition that is currently affecting the patient and another code to describe the original injury or illness. The residual condition code is sequenced first. In some cases, there is a combination code that includes the residual condition and the underlying cause.

> **EXAMPLE: CODING LATE EFFECTS**
> Keloid formation of the right forearm due to previous laceration. In this example, keloid is the residual late effect and is coded 701.4, "Keloid scar." The cause of the keloid, previous laceration, is coded 906.1, "Late effect of open wound of extremities without mention of tendon injury."

> **EXAMPLE: COMBINATION LATE EFFECT CODE**
> Hemiplegia due to old cerebrovascular accident (CVA). Code 438.20, "Late effects of cerebrovascular disease, hemiplegia affecting unspecified side," includes both the late effect and its cause.

When the diagnostic statement does not include the residual condition, code only the cause of the late effect. Late effect codes are located in the *Alphabetic Index* under the main term "Late" and the subterm "effect(s) (of)."

Burns

Codes from ICD-9-CM categories 940 through 949 apply to current unhealed burns with the exception of sunburn and friction burns. Sunburns are classified as dermatitis, and friction burns are classified as superficial injuries. Scars and contractures that remain when the burn has healed are coded as late effects.

> **EXAMPLE: DERMATITIS LATE EFFECT**
> Elizabeth is seen for treatment of sunburn. Code 692.71, "Contact dermatitis and other eczema, Due to solar radiation, Sunburn," is the correct diagnostic code.

EXAMPLE: SUPERFICIAL INJURY

Ronald is seen for an abrasion of the left leg due to skidding across the basketball court. Code 916.0, "Superficial injury of . . . leg . . ., Abrasion without mention of infection," is the correct diagnostic code.

EXAMPLE: CONTRACTURE

Brett is seen for the assessment of contracture of three fingers on his left hand. Sequela of a previous grease burn. Codes 709.2, "Scar conditions and fibrosis of skin," and 906.6, "Late effect of burn, wrist or hand," are the correct diagnostic codes. The contracture code, 709.2, is sequenced first.

Burn diagnoses require at least two codes: one for the site and degree of the burn and another for the percentage of body surface affected. Category 948, "Burns classified according to extent of body surface involved," provides codes ranging from less than 10% of body surface (948.00) to 90% or more of the body surface (948.99). Body surface involvement is estimated based on the "rule of nines," which assigns a body surface burn percentage. Figure 5–11 illustrates the rule of nines.

The percentages are adjusted for infants, children, and adults with large buttocks, abdomens, or thighs. It is the physician or health care provider's responsibility to calculate the extent of the burn.

HIV/AIDS

Because of the prejudicial nature of HIV- and AIDS-related diagnoses, the patient must sign an Authorization for Release of HIV Status so these codes can be included on an insurance claim.

Category 042 is used to code acquired immunodeficiency syndrome (AIDS), AIDS-like syndrome, AIDS-related complex (ARC), and symptomatic HIV infection. Specific conditions, such as Kaposi's sarcoma, should also be coded.

Several V codes apply to HIV/AIDS conditions. Code V08, "Asymptomatic human immunodeficiency virus infection," is used when the patient has tested positive for HIV and displays no symptoms. Code V72.69, "Other Laboratory examination," is selected when the visit includes a lab test to rule out HIV infection. Code V73.89, "Other specified viral diseases," is selected when patient exposure to HIV is unknown. Code V01.79, "Contact with or exposure to . . . other viral diseases," is selected when the patient has been exposed to the AIDS virus.

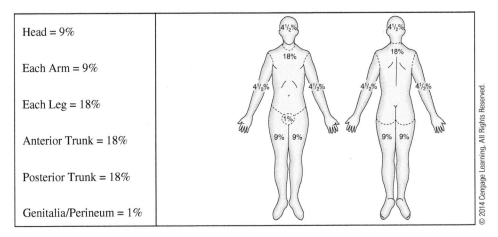

Figure 5–11 **Rule of Nines**

There are two coding guidelines for reporting services rendered to HIV-infected and AIDS patients:

1. When treating or evaluating an HIV-related illness, the first-listed diagnosis code is 042. Codes related to other conditions or manifestations, such as Kaposi's sarcoma, are listed as secondary conditions.
2. When treating or evaluating a condition unrelated to HIV-related illnesses, the reason for the visit is coded and is the first-listed diagnosis. The HIV disease and related manifestations are sequenced as secondary diagnoses.

Do not assign an HIV or AIDS code to cases documented as "probable," "possible," or "questionable." Use V08 or 795.71, "nonspecific serological evidence of human immunodeficiency virus."

Volume 3: Tabular List and Alphabetic Index of Procedures

Volume 3, the *Tabular List and Alphabetic Index of Procedures,* is often referred to as the "Procedure Codes." The procedure codes in *Volume 3* are used to code and report services rendered during an inpatient or hospital episode of care. The organizational patterns, format, and conventions in *Volume 3* are nearly identical to those in *Volume 1* and *Volume 2*. The few differences are presented after the overview of the components of *Volume 3*.

Volume 3 includes two main sections: the *Alphabetic Index to the Tabular List* of procedure codes and 18 chapters in the *Tabular List* of procedure codes. The specific characteristics of each section are described individually.

Alphabetic Index

The *Alphabetic Index* is a listing of procedures, tests, operations, surgeries, and other therapies. The organization of the *Alphabetic Index* to procedures is very similar to the format of the *Alphabetic Index of Diseases and Injuries* (*Volume 2*). Main terms are bolded and flush left. Main terms for the *Alphabetic Index* to procedures include the following:

- Eponyms, such as "Billroth II operation" (partial gastrectomy with gastrojejunostomy)
- Nouns, such as "examination," "bypass," "operation"
- Operations, such as diverticulectomy, gastrectomy, proctocolectomy
- Procedures or tests, such as amniocentesis, colonoscopy, scan
- Verbs, such as "closure," "excision," "repair"

Subterms associated with main terms and other subterms are indented and listed in alphabetic order—*except for* subterms that begin with the words "as," "by," and "with." These words are known as "connecting words" and immediately follow a main term or subterm entry as appropriate. Figure 5–12 is an example of an entry from the *Volume 3 Alphabetic Index*.

The entries in the *Alphabetic Index* are fairly comprehensive. A specific entry in the *Alphabetic Index* may in fact be coded to a less specific category in the *Tabular List* of procedures.

EXAMPLE: SPECIFIC ALPHABETIC INDEX ENTRY

Following a motor vehicle accident, Caleb was admitted for a cervical spine injury and placed in a Thomas collar.

In this example, the *Alphabetic Index* lists "Thomas collar" as a subterm under the main term "Application." The code noted in the *Index* is 93.52.

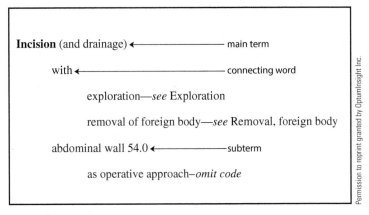

Figure 5–12 *Volume 3 Alphabetic Index* Entry

In the *Tabular List*, code 93.52 is "Application of neck support." Even though "Thomas collar" is not included in the list of neck supports noted under the code, the billing specialist or medical coder relies on the accuracy of the *Tabular List* and assigns 93.52 as the code for the application of a Thomas collar.

Tabular List

The *Tabular List* in *Volume 3* contains 18 chapters. With the exception of Chapter 1, "Procedures and Interventions Not Elsewhere Classified," Chapter 13, "Obstetrical Procedures," and Chapter 16, "Miscellaneous Diagnostic and Therapeutic Procedures," the chapters are organized by body systems and organs. Table 5–14 lists the *Tabular List* chapters and code categories.

Procedure codes in the *Tabular List* consist of three or four digits. Two digits precede a decimal point, and one or two digits follow the decimal point. As with disease and condition codes, a three-digit code cannot be used if a four-digit code is available. The third and fourth digits provide additional information about the procedure. The *Tabular List* includes important inclusion and exclusion notes. Figure 5–13 is an example of a *Tabular List* entry.

Volume 3 Coding Conventions

Most of the coding conventions discussed for *Volume 1* and *Volume 2* also apply to *Volume 3*. The exceptions are "code also," "omit code," and slanted square brackets [ ]. These conventions are discussed and examples are given here.

"Code also" means that additional procedures and use of special equipment must be coded and submitted with the insurance claim. "Code also" instructions provide a list of codes that are acceptable additional codes.

EXAMPLE

Pedro was admitted for a permanent colostomy. Colostomy is coded to subcategory 46.13, which includes the instruction to "code also any synchronous resection (45.49, 45.71–45.79, 45.8)." The permanent colostomy is coded as 46.13. The operative report is reviewed to discover how much of the large intestine was removed (resected) during the colostomy procedure. The appropriate code from the "code also" list is assigned to the resection.

TABLE 5–14

Volume 3 Tabular List Chapters and Categories		
Chapter Number	Chapter Titles	Categories
0	Procedures and Interventions, Not Elsewhere Classified	00–00.9
1	Operations on the Nervous System	01–05
2	Operations on the Endocrine System	06–07
3	Operations on the Eye	08–16
3A	Other Miscellaneous Diagnostic and Therapeutic Procedures	17
4	Operations on the Ear	18–20
5	Operations on the Nose, Mouth, and Pharynx	21–29
6	Operations on the Respiratory System	30–34
7	Operations on the Cardiovascular System	35–39
8	Operations on the Hemic and Lymphatic System	40–41
9	Operations on the Digestive System	42–54
10	Operations on the Urinary System	55–59
11	Operations on the Male Genital Organs	60–64
12	Operations on the Female Genital Organs	65–71
13	Obstetrical Procedures	72–75
14	Operations on the Musculoskeletal System	76–84
15	Operations on the Integumentary System	85–86
16	Miscellaneous Diagnostic and Therapeutic Procedures	87–99

The "omit code" is found in both the *Tabular List* and *Alphabetic Index* of *Volume 3*. As the phrase implies, the instruction tells the billing specialist or medical coder not to assign a procedure code. The "omit code" usually applies to procedures that are:

- Closures of given procedures
- Exploratory and incidental to another procedure that is carried out
- Lysis of adhesions by blunt, digital, manual, or mechanical methods
- Usual surgical approaches of a given procedure

Slanted square brackets [ ] are found in the *Alphabetic Index* of *Volume 3*. Slanted square brackets alert the billing specialist or medical coder that closely related procedures require two codes.

EXAMPLE: CLOSELY RELATED PROCEDURES
Becky was admitted for anastomosis of the bladder to the ileum.
In this example, the entry in the *Alphabetic Index* is "**Anastomosis**, bladder to ileum 57.87 *[45.51]*." Because code 45.51 is in slanted brackets, the billing specialist or medical coder knows that two codes must be assigned for this procedure.

---

7. OPERATIONS ON THE CARDIOVASCULAR SYSTEM (35–39)

35   Operations on valves and septa of heart

Includes: sternotomy (median)

(transverse)

thoracotomy

Code also cardiopulmonary bypass [extracorporeal

circulation] [heart-lung machine] (39.61)

35.0   Closed heart valvotomy

Excludes: *percutaneous (balloon) valvuloplasty*
            (35.96)

35.00   Closed heart valvotomy, unspecified valve

35.01   Closed heart valvotomy, aortic valve

35.02   Closed heart valvotomy, mitral valve

35.03   Closed heart valvotomy, pulmonary valve

35.04   Closed heart valvotomy, tricuspid valve

Figure 5–13 *Volume 3 Tabular List* Entry

In the *Tabular List* of *Volume 3*, code 57.87, "Reconstruction of urinary bladder," includes the notation to "code also resection of intestine (45.50–45.52)." Code 45.51, the slanted bracket code, falls in the range of the "code also" instruction.

The anastomosis is coded to 57.87 and sequenced first. Code 45.51, "Isolation of segment of small intestine," is also selected and included on the health insurance claim.

ASSIGNING ICD-9-CM PROCEDURE CODES

Accurate procedure code assignment depends on three activities:

- Identifying the principal procedure
- Selecting and sequencing procedure codes
- Following applicable ICD-9-CM coding conventions and all instructions noted in ICD-9-CM *Volume 3*

As stated previously, ICD-9-CM procedure codes are used for coding and reporting inpatient or hospital episodes of care. Documentation in the patient's record must support all procedure codes submitted for reimbursement.

Identifying the Principal Procedure

The principal procedure is the procedure performed for definitive treatment rather than for diagnostic or exploratory purposes or the procedure performed to resolve a complication. If more than one procedure meets the definition of the principal procedure, the procedure most closely related to the principal diagnosis(es) is selected as the principal procedure.

> **EXAMPLE**
>
> Juanita, who was recently diagnosed with breast cancer, was admitted for a radical mastectomy, right breast. On the second postoperative day, she fell on the way to the bathroom and sustained a femoral neck (hip) fracture. The fracture was treated via open reduction with internal fixation.
>
> In this case, the principal diagnosis is breast cancer. Radical mastectomy is the procedure most related to the principal diagnosis, and it is coded and sequenced first as the principal procedure. The femoral neck fracture is coded and sequenced after the principal diagnosis; the closed reduction with internal fixation is coded and sequenced after the principal procedure.

Selecting and Sequencing Procedure Codes

Codes assigned to the principal procedure are always sequenced first. In addition to the principal procedure, other significant procedures are coded. A significant procedure is surgical in nature, carries a procedural and/or anesthetic risk, and requires specialized training. Codes for significant procedures are sequenced *after* the principal procedure code.

The steps for selecting procedure codes are enumerated and discussed here. Examples are provided as needed. Refer to Figure 5–14 as you study the procedure coding steps.

1. Identify the main term in the procedure statement. (In this example, the main term is in bold.)

   > **EXAMPLE: MAIN TERM**
   > Carotid **endarterectomy**

2. Locate the main term in the *Volume 3 Alphabetic Index.*

   > **EXAMPLE: MAIN TERM** *INDEX* **ENTRY**
   > Locate **endarterectomy** in the *Index*.

3. Review the procedure statement for additional information about the main term.

   > **EXAMPLE: ADDITIONAL INFORMATION**
   > Carotid refers to the carotid artery and identifies the anatomic location of the **endarterectomy.**

4. Review the subterms listed under the main term to determine if any entry matches the additional information in the procedure statement.

   > **EXAMPLE: SUBTERM** *INDEX* **ENTRY**
   > In this example, "carotid" is not listed as a subterm under the main term. Because the carotid artery is located in the neck, the subterms "head" and "neck" apply.

5. Follow any cross-reference instructions, such as "code also." If there are no cross-reference instructions, note the code listed with the applicable subterm entry.

PROCEDURE: Carotid Endarterectomy	
ALPHABETIC INDEX	TABULAR LIST
Endarterectomy (gas) (with patch graft) 38.10	**38 Incision, excision, and occlusion of vessels...**
abdominal 38.16	The following fourth-digit subclassification is for
aortic (arch) (ascending) (descending) 38.14	use with appropriate categories in sections 38.0,
coronary artery—*see* category 36.0	38.1, 38.3, 38.5, 38.6, and 38.8 according to site...
open chest approach 36.03	**0 unspecified site**
head and neck (open) NEC 38.12	**1 intracranial vessels**
percutaneous approach, intracranial	Cerebral (anterior) (middle)
vessel(s) 00.62	Circle of Willis
percutaneous approach, precerebral	Posterior communicating artery
(extracranial) vessels(s) 00.61	**2 other vessels of head and neck**
intracranial (open) NEC 38.11	Carotid artery (common) (external) (internal)
percutaneous approach, intracranial	Jugular vein (external) (internal)...
vessel(s) 00.62	**38.1 Endarterectomy**
percutaneous approach, precerebral	Endarterectomy with:
(extracranial) vessel(s) 00.61	embolectomy
lower limb 38.18	patch graft
thoracic NEC 38.15	temporary bypass during procedure
upper limb 38.13	thrombectomy

Figure 5–14 Selecting Procedure Codes

EXAMPLE: CROSS-REFERENCE
In this example, there are no cross-reference instructions. The code for "endarterectomy, head and neck (open) NEC" is 38.12.

6. **Check the code listed in the *Alphabetic Index* with the description in the *Tabular List*.**

EXAMPLE: TABULAR LIST ENTRY
Section 38.1 in the *Tabular List* is "Endarterectomy."

7. Read and follow all includes, excludes, and other instructional notes.

EXAMPLE: INSTRUCTIONAL NOTES
The instruction note for category 38 states that a fourth digit is required in sections 38.0, 38.1, and 38.3. "Endarterectomy" is in section 38.1, and a fourth digit is required to complete the code.

8. Assign the code(s) to the highest level of specificity by selecting a three-digit code only when no four-digit code is available.

> **EXAMPLE: FOURTH DIGIT REQUIRED**
> A fourth digit is needed to complete the code. The fourth digit 2 indicates that the carotid artery is the site of the endarterectomy. The *Tabular List* confirms that the correct code for carotid endarterectomy is 38.12.

Step 6 is bolded here for the same reason it was bolded under diagnostic coding: A competent insurance billing specialist or medical coder *never* codes directly from the *Alphabetic Index*.

MISCELLANEOUS CODING GUIDELINES FOR PROCEDURES AND BIOPSIES

Additional coding guidelines cover the following situations: bilateral procedures; canceled, incomplete, or failed surgeries or procedures; and biopsies.

Bilateral Procedures

When a single code is available to describe a procedure as bilateral, the code is selected and listed once on the insurance claim.

> **EXAMPLE: SINGLE CODE – BILATERAL PROCEDURE**
> Belinda was admitted for a bilateral oophorectomy, which is the removal of both ovaries. The surgeon completed the surgery, and Belinda was discharged in good condition. In this example, code 65.51, "bilateral oophorectomy,. . . Removal of both ovaries at same operative episode," accurately describes the procedure.

When a bilateral procedure code is not available and the same procedure is done bilaterally at the same time, the procedure code is selected and listed twice on the insurance claim.

> **EXAMPLE: TWO CODES – BILATERAL PROCEDURE**
> Roland was admitted for bilateral orchiopexy, which is the surgical fixation of undescended testes into the scrotum. In this example, there is no code for bilateral orchiopexy. Code 62.5, "Orchiopexy," is selected and listed twice on the insurance claim.

Canceled, Incomplete, and Failed Procedures

When a scheduled surgery or procedure is not completed or is considered to have failed, codes are assigned to the level of service that was actually performed or completed. In these situations, the following general guidelines apply:

1. An endoscopic operative approach is coded as an exploratory endoscopy of the anatomic site.
2. An open procedure, defined as opening or entering a body cavity or space, is coded as an exploration of the anatomic site.
3. When only an incision is made, code the incision of the anatomic site.

4. A failed procedure, which is a procedure that did not achieve the desired result, is coded as a performed procedure.
5. V codes related to the reason for the incomplete or canceled procedure may also be assigned.
6. A surgery or procedure that is canceled before it begins is coded only to the appropriate V code related to the reason for canceling the surgery or procedure.

A careful review of the operative or procedure report provides information for accurate coding. Examples for these guidelines are given here.

EXAMPLE OF GUIDELINE 1

Maria was admitted for a laparoscopic, bilateral tubal ligation. After placement of the laparoscope, she developed tachycardia, and the procedure was canceled.

In this example, the endoscopic operative approach is coded as an exploratory laparoscopy. Code 54.21, "diagnostic procedures of abdominal region, Laparoscopy," appropriately describes the level of service rendered and is coded as the principal procedure. The appropriate V code for the canceled procedure is also assigned.

EXAMPLE OF GUIDELINE 2

Takeesha was admitted for a total abdominal hysterectomy due to persistent menorrhagia. After the pelvic cavity was opened and entered, the patient exhibited a drop in blood pressure and respiratory rate. The procedure was stopped, and the operative site was closed.

In this example, code 54.11, "Exploratory laparotomy," is assigned as the principal procedure code. The appropriate V code for the canceled procedure is also assigned.

EXAMPLE FOR GUIDELINE 3

Takeesha was admitted for a total abdominal hysterectomy due to persistent menorrhagia. Shortly after the incision was made, she developed tachycardia. The procedure was stopped, and the incision was closed.

In this example, code 54.0, "Incision of abdominal wall," is assigned as the principal procedure code.

EXAMPLE FOR GUIDELINE 4

Gera was admitted for percutaneous transluminal angioplasty of the carotid artery. Immediately after the procedure, the artery again occluded.

In this case, the procedure was performed, but the desired result was not obtained. Code 00.61, "Percutaneous angioplasty or atherectomy of precerebral (extracranial) vessel(s)," is assigned as the principal procedure code.

EXAMPLE FOR GUIDELINE 5

Maria was admitted for a laparoscopic, bilateral tubal ligation. After placement of the laparoscope, she developed tachycardia, and the procedure was canceled. The operative approach is coded as an exploratory laparoscopy and is the principal procedure. Code V64.1, "procedure not carried out because of contraindication," is also assigned.

EXAMPLE FOR GUIDELINE 6

Takeesha was admitted for a total abdominal hysterectomy due to persistent menorrhagia. Prior to surgery, she developed a low-grade fever, and the surgery was canceled.

In this example, no procedure code is assigned. Menorrhagia is coded as the principal diagnosis, and V64.1 is assigned to identify that the procedure was not performed.

Biopsy Coding

When a biopsy is performed during an inpatient or hospital episode of care, codes from ICD-9-CM *Volume 3* are assigned. Biopsies are categorized as open or closed. An open biopsy is performed via an incision into the appropriate anatomic site or space, and tissue is taken for microscopic examination. A closed biopsy is performed without an incision. Tissue is taken percutaneously, endoscopically, by needle (often called "needle aspiration biopsy"), or by a bristle-type instrument called a brush (often called a "brush biopsy"). Figure 5–15 illustrates a biopsy entry in the *Tabular List* of *Volume 3*.

General guidelines for coding biopsies include the following:

1. Endoscopic biopsies may be assigned to codes that identify both the endoscopic procedure and the biopsy.
2. Endoscopic biopsies that cannot be assigned to codes that identify both the endoscopic procedure and the biopsy are assigned separate codes for the endoscopy and the biopsy. The endoscopy is the principal procedure and is coded and sequenced first. The biopsy is coded and sequenced after the principal procedure.
3. When a biopsy is performed and immediately followed by a more extensive surgical procedure, the surgical procedure is the principal procedure and is coded and sequenced first. The biopsy is coded and sequenced after the principal procedure.

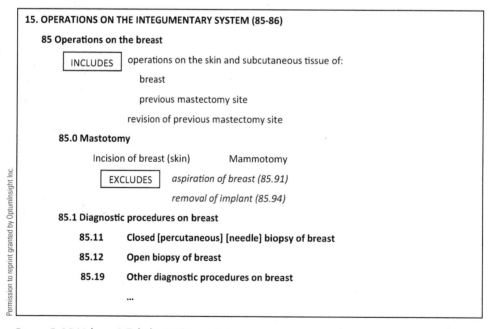

Figure 5–15 *Volume 3 Tabular List* Biopsy Entry

4. An open biopsy is coded as such. Because an incision is implicit in an open biopsy, do not assign a separate code for the incision.

A careful review of the procedure report provides information for accurate biopsy coding. Examples for these guidelines are given here.

EXAMPLE FOR GUIDELINE 1
During Pedro's recent hospitalization, he underwent a transbronchial lung biopsy. The pathology report was negative for malignant cells.

   In this example, the transbronchial lung biopsy is assigned code 33.27, "Closed endoscopic biopsy of lung." This code identifies both the endoscopic procedure and the biopsy.

EXAMPLE FOR GUIDELINE 2
During Katerina's recent hospitalization, a mediastinoscopy with lymph tissue biopsy was performed. The pathology report was positive for cellular dysplasia.

   In this example, there is no code that covers both the mediastinoscopy and the biopsy. Two codes are assigned. Code 34.22, "Mediastinoscopy," is sequenced before the biopsy code. The instruction note states, "Code also any lymph node biopsy, if performed." The biopsy is coded to 40.11, "Biopsy of lymphatic structure."

EXAMPLE FOR GUIDELINE 3
Pedro was hospitalized for an open lung biopsy with frozen section and possible pneumonectomy. The pathology report was positive for lung cancer, and the surgeon removed Pedro's right lung. The procedure statement was "open biopsy of the lung with frozen section and pneumonectomy, right lung."

   In this case, the pneumonectomy is assigned code 32.59, "Other and unspecified pneumonectomy," and sequenced first. The open biopsy is coded to 33.28, "Open biopsy of lung."

EXAMPLE FOR GUIDELINE 4
Hazel was hospitalized for a wedge biopsy of the liver via laparotomy and for possible removal of the liver. The pathology report was negative.

   In this case, laparotomy indicates that a wedge biopsy is an open biopsy. The laparotomy is the incision and is not coded. The wedge biopsy is coded to 50.12, "Open biopsy of liver."

REINFORCEMENT EXERCISES 5–12

Fill in the blank.

1. ICD-9-CM *Volume 3* is commonly called the _____.

2. The _____ is a listing of procedures, tests, operations, surgeries, and therapies.

3. The subterms "as," "by," and "with" are known as _____.

continued on the next page

continued from the previous page

4. The _____ in ICD-9-CM *Volume 3* has 18 chapters.

5. ICD-9-CM procedure codes consist of _____ or _____ digits.

6. _____ means that the use of special equipment must be coded.

7. _____ indicate that closely related procedures require two codes.

8. The _____ convention applies to the usual surgical approach of a given procedure.

9. In *Volume 3*, _____ are bolded and flush left.

10. The *Tabular List* is predominantly organized by _____ and _____.

Rank each statement from 1 to 8. Place a 1 in front of the first step for selecting an ICD-9-CM procedure code and an 8 in front of the last step.

_____ Assign codes to the highest level of specificity.

_____ Check the code listed in the *Alphabetic Index* with the description in the *Tabular List*.

_____ Follow any cross-reference instructions, such as "code also."

_____ Identify the main term in the procedure statement.

_____ Locate the main term in the *Alphabetic Index*.

_____ Read and follow all includes, excludes, and other instruction notes.

_____ Review the procedure statement for additional information about the main term.

_____ Review the subterms listed under the main term.

Mark each statement as True (T) or False (F).

1. _____ Bilateral procedure codes are available for all surgeries.

2. _____ Biopsy codes must be sequenced first.

3. _____ Closed biopsies are often accomplished via endoscopy.

4. _____ Incisions related to open biopsies are assigned a separate code.

5. _____ Two codes may be necessary for bilateral procedures.

6. _____ V codes are assigned to failed procedures.

7. _____ V codes may be assigned when a procedure is canceled before it begins.

ABBREVIATIONS

Table 5–15 lists the abbreviations presented in this chapter.

TABLE 5–15

Abbreviations and Meanings	
Abbreviation	**Meaning**
AHA	American Hospital Association
AHFS	American Hospital Formulary Service
AHIMA	American Health Information Management Association
AIDS	acquired immunodeficiency syndrome
ARC	AIDS-related complex
CMS	Centers for Medicare and Medicaid Services
CPT	*Current Procedural Terminology*
CVA	cerebrovascular accident
DES	diethylstilbestrol
DPT	diphtheria, pertussis, and tetanus
HHS	Health and Human Services (U.S. Department of)
HIV	human immunodeficiency virus
ICD-9-CM	*International Classification of Diseases, Ninth Revision, Clinical Modification*
ICD-10	*International Classification of Diseases, Tenth Revision*
NCHS	National Center for Health Statistics
NEC	not elsewhere classified
NOS	not otherwise specified
TURP	transurethral resection of the prostate
VRSA	vancomycin-resistant staphylococcus aureus
WHO	World Health Organization

 SUMMARY

This chapter included a review of ICD-9-CM diagnostic and procedure coding. The history of ICD-9-CM and the unique features of *Volume 1* (the *Tabular List of Diseases and Injuries*), *Volume 2* (the *Alphabetic Index of Diseases and Injuries*), and *Volume 3* (the *Tabular List and Alphabetic Index of Procedures*) were presented. Coding conventions were discussed, and examples of the conventions were given. Accurate coding has a direct effect on the financial health of all health care agencies. Inappropriate coding can result in rejected claims, inadequate reimbursement, and, in the worst case, charges of fraud or abuse.

REVIEW EXERCISES

Short Answer

Write a short answer for each statement.

1. A temporary or permanent medical problem or condition resulting from an illness or injury.

2. Residual condition that remains after the illness or injury has been resolved.

3. Used to calculate the extent of a burn injury.

4. Short name for ICD-9-CM *Volume 1*.

5. Short name for ICD-9-CM *Volume 2*.

6. Diseases, conditions, or injuries printed in bold and flush left in the *Alphabetic Index*.

7. Precedes subterms and is placed immediately after the main term.

8. How codes in the Neoplasm Table are arranged.

9. Direct the billing specialist or medical coder to look elsewhere.

10. Lists of conditions that are coded to the same ICD-9-CM code.

11. Lists of conditions not covered by a specific ICD-9-CM code.

12. Placing diagnostic codes in the correct order.

13. Supplementary classifications or codes that are frequently assigned in a clinic, office, and outpatient setting.

14. Directions and guidelines that assist in accurate code assignment.

_____

15. Mandatory cross-reference term.

_____

16. Enclose nonessential modifiers.

_____

17. Abbreviation that means the same thing as "unspecified."

_____

18. Abbreviation indicating that a specific diagnosis does not have a separate code.

_____

19. Connect a list or series of descriptions or diagnoses to a common main term or code.

_____

20. Enclose a manifestation code.

_____

21. A(n) _____ procedure indicates that an incision is necessary to enter a body cavity or space.

22. A(n) _____ procedure indicates that the procedure was done and the desired result was not achieved.

23. Tissue taken by a bristle-type instrument is called a(n) _____ biopsy.

24. In *Volume 3*, the phrase _____ applies to the usual surgical approach of a given procedure.

25. The _____ procedure is performed for definitive treatment rather than for diagnostic or exploratory purposes.

ICD-9-CM CODING PRACTICE SETS

The best way to learn how to code is to practice coding. The ICD-9-CM coding practice sets are organized by *Tabular List* chapters. The practice sets are *not* all-inclusive, nor do they cover all coding situations. The goal of this section is to present a variety of diagnostic statements for coding.

Write the main term and then assign the correct ICD-9-CM code(s) for each diagnostic statement. Include E codes where applicable.

General

1. Asian flu (influenza) shot (vaccination).

   Main Term: _____ Code: _____

2. Viral hepatitis inoculation.

   Main Term: _____ Code: _____

3. Pre-employment physical (examination).

   Main Term: _____ Code: _____

4. Sports physical.

   Main Term: _____ Code: _____

5. Routine prenatal visit, first pregnancy.

   Main Term: _____ Code: _____

6. Removal of leg cast.

   Main Term: _____ Code: _____

7. Screening for diabetes mellitus.

   Main Term: _____ Code: _____

8. Exposure to HIV.

   Main Term: _____ Code: _____

9. Patient stepped on a broken bottle and sustained a three-inch laceration, requiring seven sutures. Instructed to return in 10 days for suture removal.

   Main Term: _____ Code: _____

10. This 4-year-old patient is being evaluated for delayed development due to the toxic effect of lead paint ingested over the past two years.

    Main Term: _____ Code: _____

Symptoms, Signs, and Ill-Defined Conditions

1. Abdominal pain.

   Main Term: _____ Code: _____

2. Anorexia.

   Main Term: _____ Code: _____

3. Chest pain, unspecified.

   Main Term: _____ Code: _____

4. Diarrhea.

   Main Term: _____ Code: _____

5. Labile hypertension.

   Main Term: _____ Code: _____

6. Syncope.

   Main Term: _____ Code: _____

7. Cardiogenic shock.

   Main Term: _____ Code: _____

8. Functional heart murmur.

   Main Term: _____ Code: _____

9. Abnormal mammogram.

   Main Term: _____ Code: _____

10. Right lower quadrant abdominal pain, with nausea and vomiting.

   Main Term: _____ Code: _____

Infectious and Parasitic Diseases

1. Aseptic meningitis.

   Main Term: _____ Code: _____

2. Gastroenteritis due to salmonella.

   Main Term: _____ Code: _____

3. Rotavirus enteritis.

   Main Term: _____ Code: _____

4. Cystitis, acute, due to Escherichia coli (E. coli).

   Main Term: _____ Code: _____

5. Viral hepatitis, type A.

   Main Term: _____ Code: _____

6. Primary genital syphilis.

   Main Term: _____ Code: _____

7. Anthrax pneumonia.

   Main Term: _____ Code: _____

Endocrine, Nutritional and Metabolic Diseases, and Immunity Diseases

1. Type I diabetes with ketoacidosis.

   Main Term: _____ Code: _____

2. Gouty arthritis.

   Main Term: _____ Code: _____

3. Diabetic hypoglycemia.

   Main Term: _____ Code: _____

4. Cushing's syndrome.

   Main Term: _____ Code: _____

5. Familial hypercholesterolemia.

   Main Term: _____ Code: _____

6. AIDS-related complex.

   Main Term: _____ Code: _____

7. Salmonellosis.

   Main Term: _____ Code: _____

8. Hyperthyroidism.

   Main Term: _____ Code: _____

9. This 10-year-old female is seen today for continued treatment of cystic fibrosis. She has gained 3 pounds and is in the 45th percentile for weight. Mom was advised to continue supplemental nutrition.

   Main Term: _____ Code: _____

10. This 35-year-old male is seen today for exogenous obesity. Weight loss this visit was 3 pounds. Total weight loss is 45 pounds. Patient was advised to continue with his weight reduction program.

    Main Term: _____ Code: _____

Nervous System and Sense Organs

1. Rheumatoid arthritis.

   Main Term: _____ Code: _____

2. Acute follicular conjunctivitis.

   Main Term: _____ Code: _____

3. Classical migraine.

   Main Term: _____ Code: _____

4. Bacterial meningitis.

   Main Term: _____ Code: _____

5. Trigeminal neuralgia.

   Main Term: _____ Code: _____

6. Senile macular degeneration.

    Main Term: _____ Code: _____

7. This 3-year-old female is seen today rubbing and tugging at her right ear and in minimal distress. Inspection of the ear canals reveals acute suppurative otitis media on the right; the left is clear. Tympanic membranes are intact.

    Main Term: _____ Code: _____

8. Routine eye examination revealed a partial retinal detachment, with a single defect noted.

    Main Term: _____ Code: _____

Circulatory System

1. Unstable angina pectoris.

    Main Term: _____ Code: _____

2. Arteriosclerotic heart disease.

    Main Term: _____ Code: _____

3. Thrombophlebitis of deep femoral vein.

    Main Term: _____ Code: _____

4. Hemorrhoids.

    Main Term: _____ Code: _____

5. Orthostatic hypotension.

    Main Term: _____ Code: _____

6. Hypertensive cardiovascular disease, malignant.

    Main Term: _____ Code: _____

7. Bilateral thrombosis of carotid artery.

    Main Term: _____ Code: _____

8. Atrial fibrillation.

    Main Term: _____ Code: _____

9. This 55-year-old female is seen with complaints of nocturnal angina pectoris that is relieved with nitroglycerin tablets, sublingual.

    Main Term: _____ Code: _____

10. During the patient's physical examination, heart sounds were consistent with mitral valve insufficiency.

    Main Term: _____ Code: _____

Respiratory System

1. Obstructive chronic bronchitis.

   Main Term: _____ Code: _____

2. Chronic maxillary sinusitis.

   Main Term: _____ Code: _____

3. Hay fever due to pollen.

   Main Term: _____ Code: _____

4. Chronic obstructive pulmonary disease.

   Main Term: _____ Code: _____

5. Pneumonia due to SARS-associated coronavirus.

   Main Term: _____ Code: _____

6. Hypertrophy of tonsils and adenoids.

   Main Term: _____ Code: _____

7. Purulent bronchitis.

   Main Term: _____ Code: _____

8. Unilateral, vesicular emphysema

   Main Term: _____ Code: _____

9. This 45-year-old male is seen for shortness of breath, low-grade fever, and general malaise. Examination revealed an acute upper respiratory infection with influenza.

   Main Term: _____ Code: _____

Digestive System

1. Ulcerative stomatitis.

   Main Term: _____ Code: _____

2. Bleeding gastric ulcer.

   Main Term: _____ Code: _____

3. Reflux esophagitis.

   Main Term: _____ Code: _____

4. Hiatal hernia.

   Main Term: _____ Code: _____

5. Acute gastroenteritis.

   Main Term: _____ Code: _____

6. Acute cholecystitis with choledocholithiasis.

   Main Term: _____ Code: _____

7. Diverticulosis of the large intestine.

   Main Term: _____ Code: _____

8. Alcoholic cirrhosis of the liver.

   Main Term: _____ Code: _____

9. Recurrent left inguinal hernia.

   Main Term: _____ Code: _____

10. This 36-year-old female has been seen for repeated episodes of explosive diarrhea, severe cramping, and lack of bowel control. Colonoscopy today reveals moderate ulcerative colitis of the sigmoid colon and rectum.

    Main Term: _____ Code: _____

Genitourinary System

1. Hematuria.

   Main Term: _____ Code: _____

2. Urinary tract infection.

   Main Term: _____ Code: _____

3. Benign prostatic hypertrophy.

   Main Term: _____ Code: _____

4. Vaginitis.

   Main Term: _____ Code: _____

5. Urethritis.

   Main Term: _____ Code: _____

6. Spermatocele.

   Main Term: _____ Code: _____

7. Premenstrual syndrome.

   Main Term: _____ Code: _____

8. Nephrolithiasis.

   Main Term: _____ Code: _____

9. Endometriosis of the ovary.

   Main Term: _____ Code: _____

10. This 30-year-old female patient is seen today to discuss the results of her recent Pap test, which revealed dysplasia of the cervix (uteri).

   Main Term: _____ Code: _____

Write the main term and then assign the correct ICD-9-CM code(s) for each procedure.

1. Coronary artery bypass graft of three vessels.

   Main term: _____ Code(s): _____

2. Cholecystectomy, open.

   Main Term: _____ Code: _____

3. Total proctocolectomy with permanent exterior ileostomy.

   Main term: _____ Code(s): _____

4. Endoscopic removal of common bile duct calculi.

   Main term: _____ Code(s): _____

5. Temporary tracheostomy and insertion of tracheal tube.

   Main term: _____ Code(s):_____

6. Revision of ileostomy stoma.

   Main term: _____ Code(s): _____

7. Radical nephrectomy of right kidney due to polycystic kidney disease.

   Main term: _____ Code(s): _____

8. Bilateral breast reduction.

   Main term: _____ Code(s): _____

9. Bilateral total knee replacement of both knee joints.

   Main term: _____ Code(s): _____

10. Bilateral myringtomy, placement of tympanostomy tubes, general anesthesia.

   Main term: _____ Code(s): _____

11. Phillip was admitted to the hospital for repair of a deviated nasal septum and collapsed nasal cartilage. The operative report states, "Nasoseptal repair with cartilage graft to the nasal tip."

   Main term: _____ Code(s): _____

12. While playing in a championship basketball game, Margaret sustained a knee injury. She was admitted for an arthroscopic examination of her left knee. The procedure report included the following information:

PREOPERATIVE DIAGNOSIS: Tear of medial meniscus, left knee.

POSTOPERATIVE DIAGNOSIS: Tear of medial meniscus, left knee.

OPERATION PERFORMED: Arthroscopic examination of the left knee and arthroscopic partial medial meniscectomy.

Main term: _____ Code(s): _____

CODING CHALLENGE

Read the following medical reports and write the diagnoses and procedures in the space provided. Assign the correct ICD-9-CM diagnosis and procedure codes. Sequence the codes according to principal diagnosis and principal procedure guidelines. These cases relate to inpatient episodes of care.

1. DISCHARGE SUMMARY

PATIENT: Walker, Lamar
ADMISSION DATE: November 16, 20xx
DISCHARGE DATE: November 18, 20xx
ADMITTING DIAGNOSES: 1. Urinary retention secondary to benign prostatic hypertrophy. 2. Chronic obstructive pulmonary disease.
DISCHARGE DIAGNOSES: 1. Benign prostatic hypertrophy, secondary urinary retention. 2. Chronic obstructive pulmonary disease.
PROCEDURES: 1. Transurethral resection of the prostate. 2. Percutaneous suprapubic cystostomy.
HISTORY: The patient is a 72-year-old gentleman with a recent history of recurrent urinary retention. A cystoscopy performed in the office demonstrated a large obstructed prostate. Given his problems with recurrent urinary retention, the patient agreed to a transurethral resection of the prostate. Remainder of the patient's history is available in the admitting note.
HOSPITAL COURSE: Following admission, the patient was taken to the operating room and underwent a complicated transurethral resection of the prostate and a percutaneous suprapubic cystostomy. There was moderate hemorrhage, and the patient received one unit of packed red blood cells intraoperatively. His postoperative hemoglobin was stable at 10.3.

   During the postoperative period, he remained afebrile, and his urine gradually cleared. The Foley catheter was removed on the third postoperative day. At discharge, the patient was ambulating without assistance, able to void without difficulty, and tolerating a regular diet.
DISCHARGE INSTRUCTIONS: 1. Postoperative follow-up in my office in two weeks. 2. Normal activities, as tolerated. 3. Notify my office if clots appear in the urine.

PRINCIPAL DIAGNOSIS: _____

PRINCIPAL PROCEDURE: _____

OTHER DIAGNOSIS(ES): _____

OTHER PROCEDURE(S): _____

2. DISCHARGE SUMMARY

PATIENT: Mowafi, Ayeesha
ADMISSION DATE: December 10, 20xx
DISCHARGE DATE: December 13, 20xx
ADMITTING DIAGNOSES: 1. Ruptured left ectopic (tubal) pregnancy.
DISCHARGE DIAGNOSES: 1. Ruptured left ectopic (tubal) pregnancy.
    2. Endometriosis.
PROCEDURES: 1. Laparoscopic left salpingectomy, partial.
HISTORY: The patient is a 30-year-old gravida I, para 0 female who presented in the
    emergency department with acute abdominal pain. A serum pregnancy test was
    positive. Pelvic ultrasound was negative for an intrauterine pregnancy. The patient
    had pelvic and left lower-quadrant tenderness. No pelvic mass was palpated. The
    patient has endometriosis.
HOSPITAL COURSE: The patient was admitted and taken to the operating room.
    Culdocentesis was positive. She underwent laparoscopic partial left salpingectomy.
    The patient tolerated the procedure well. She was discharged on the third postopera-
    tive day, tolerating a regular diet, ambulating without difficulty, and passing flatus.
DISCHARGE INSTRUCTIONS: 1. Postoperative follow-up in my office in two weeks.
    2. Normal activities, as tolerated. 3. Return to the emergency department for swell-
    ing, elevated temperature, or pelvic pain.

PRINCIPAL DIAGNOSIS: _____

PRINCIPAL PROCEDURE: _____

OTHER DIAGNOSIS(ES): _____

OTHER PROCEDURE(S): _____

3. DISCHARGE SUMMARY

PATIENT: Mehrotra, Basu
ADMISSION DATE: May 20, 20xx
DISCHARGE DATE: May 26, 20xx
ADMITTING DIAGNOSES: 1. Right index finger infection.
DISCHARGE DIAGNOSES: 1. Suppurative tenosynovitis and osteomyelitis, right
    index finger. 2. Peripheral vascular disease.
PROCEDURES: 1. Incision and drainage of distal phalanx, open amputation of distal
    phalanx, and placement of flexor tendon sheath catheter for irrigation. 2. Debride-
    ment of bone and soft tissue.
HISTORY: The patient is a 48-year-old male who presented with a necrotic infection of
    the right index finger. See the admission history and physical for complete details.
HOSPITAL COURSE: The patient was admitted and started on intravenous antibiotics
    with poor results. He was taken to the operating room and underwent drainage and
    debridement of necrotic tissue, right index finger. The operative procedure revealed
    suppuration of the soft tissues and osteomyelitic involvement of the distal phalangeal

remnant and distal portion of the middle phalanx. The distal phalanx was amputated. Purulent material was present in the distal portion of the flexor tendon sheath. A catheter was placed in the flexor tendon sheath for irrigation.

The patient's general condition remained stable. The acute infection in the right index finger resolved. On the fifth postoperative day, he returned to the operating room for further debridement of necrotic tissue. He tolerated this procedure well and was discharged on the next postoperative day.

DISCHARGE MEDICATIONS: Keflex 500 mg every six hours.

DISCHARGE INSTRUCTIONS: 1. Keep the index finger dressing intact until seen by me in follow-up in five days. 2. Diet and activities as tolerated. 3. Return to the emergency department for swelling, elevated temperature, or discharge from the site.

PRINCIPAL DIAGNOSIS: _____

PRINCIPAL PROCEDURE: _____

OTHER DIAGNOSIS(ES): _____

OTHER PROCEDURE(S): _____

4. DISCHARGE SUMMARY

PATIENT: Wellington, Martha

ADMISSION DATE: June 10, 20xx

DISCHARGE DATE: June 18, 20xx

ADMITTING DIAGNOSES: Possible pulmonary abscess due to pneumonia.

DISCHARGE DIAGNOSES: Pulmonary abscess, right lower lobe, due to pneumonia.

PROCEDURES: 1. Right thoracotomy. 2. Decortication and wedge resection, right lower lobe of the lung.

HISTORY: The patient is a 43-year-old female with complaints of increasing right chest pain and shortness of breath for several days prior to admission. Initially, the patient had been diagnosed with left pleurisy that had resolved. About one month ago, the patient had complaints of shortness of breath, green and blood-tinged sputum, 102-degree fever, and night sweats. She denies any tuberculosis exposure.

HOSPITAL COURSE: The patient was admitted and treated on the medical unit with intravenous fluid and intravenous antibiotics, including Timentin and Flagy. Her condition did not appreciably improve, and she was transferred to the surgical unit. She subsequently underwent a right thoracotomy, decortication, and wedge resection of the right lower lobe of the lung. Two chest tubes were placed. The anterior tube was removed on the second postoperative day. The posterior tube was removed on the day prior to discharge. The patient's condition improved, and chest x-rays taken just prior to discharge revealed a small amount of right-sided pleural effusion. The left lung was clear. No pneumothorax was seen. The lungs were free of active infiltrate. The cardiac size was within normal limits. The patient continued on antibiotics until the day before discharge. She was discharged on the sixth postoperative day in good condition.

DISCHARGE MEDICATIONS: Tylenol #3, one to two tablets every four hours as needed.

DISCHARGE INSTRUCTIONS: 1. No heavy lifting for six weeks. 2. Sponge baths. 3. See me in my office in two days for staple removal and wound check. 4. Return to the emergency department for shortness of breath, elevated temperature, or discharge from the site.

PRINCIPAL DIAGNOSIS: _____

PRINCIPAL PROCEDURE: _____

OTHER DIAGNOSIS(ES): _____

OTHER PROCEDURE(S): _____

5. OPERATIVE REPORT

PATIENT: Kempanin, Salmi
DATE OF OPERATION: July 10, 20xx
PREOPERATIVE DIAGNOSIS: Possible intermittent left testicular torsion.
POSTOPERATIVE DIAGNOSES: 1. Torsion and necrosis of left appendix testis. 2. Hydrocele.
OPERATION PERFORMED: 1. Excision of left appendix testis. 2. Left hydrocelectomy. 3. Bilateral orchiopexy.
DESCRIPTION: The patient was brought to the operating room, placed in the supine position, and general anesthesia was administered. The genital area was prepped and draped in the usual sterile manner. A midline scrotal incision was made through the dartos layers, revealing a necrotic appendix testis that was subsequently resected. A 3-0 Prolene suture was taken through the dependent portion of the testicle to the dartos layer to prevent subsequent torsion. Fluid was drained from the hydrocele, and the hydrocele sac was removed completely. Through the same incision, a 3-0 Prolene suture was used to fix the right testicle in position to prevent torsion on that side. The wound was closed in two layers of running 4-0 Dexon, and a modified pressure dressing was applied. The patient was returned to the recovery room in satisfactory condition. Blood loss was negligible. Sponge and needle counts were correct × 2.

PRINCIPAL DIAGNOSIS: _____

PRINCIPAL PROCEDURE: _____

OTHER DIAGNOSIS(ES): _____

OTHER PROCEDURE(S): _____

WEBSITES

American Health Information Management Association: http://www.ahima.org
American Hospital Association: http://www.aha.org
American Medical Association: http://www.ama-assn.org
Centers for Medicare and Medicaid Services: http://www.cms.hhs.gov
National Center for Health Statistics: http://www.cdc.gov/nchs

Current Procedural Terminology (CPT) and Healthcare Common Procedure Coding System (HCPCS)

LEARNING OBJECTIVES

Upon successful completion of this chapter, the reader should have the knowledge to:

1. Identify the two organizations responsible for maintaining and updating the CPT and HCPCS coding systems.
2. Describe the contents of the six sections of the *Current Procedural Terminology* coding reference.
3. Define the two levels of HCPCS codes.
4. Explain the difference between the ICD-9-CM, CPT, and HCPCS coding systems.
5. Interpret the meaning of symbols used in CPT coding.
6. Illustrate the use of CPT modifiers.
7. Define the cross-reference terms used in CPT coding.
8. Accurately assign CPT and HCPCS codes.

KEY TERMS

Add-on code
Ambulatory surgery center (ASC)
American Medical Association (AMA)
Bullet (•)
Category/subsection
Centers for Medicare and Medicaid Services (CMS)
Circle (○)
Circled bullet (⊙)
Complex chronic care coordination (CCCC)
Current Procedural Terminology (CPT)

Department of Health and Human Services (HHS)
Downcoding
Durable medical equipment (DME)
Durable medical equipment, prosthetics, orthotics, and supplies (DMEPOS)
Evaluation and Management (E/M)
Examination
Facing triangles (►◄)
Flash symbol (✗)
Global surgery concept
Health Insurance Portability and Accountability Act (HIPAA)

Healthcare Common Procedure Coding System (HCPCS)
History
Instructional note
Key components
Level II codes
Main term
Medical decision making
Moderate (conscious) sedation
Modifier
Modifier -51
Modifying term
National codes
Null zero (Ø)
Number symbol (#)

Physical status modifier	See	Transitional care
Plus sign (+)	See also	management (TCM)
Procedure/service	Semicolon (;)	Triangle (▲)
Professional component	Separate procedure	Unbundling
Qualifying circumstances	Subcategory	Upcoding
Section	Surgical package	Universal no code (∅)
Section guideline	Technical component	

OVERVIEW

Current Procedural Terminology (CPT) and the *Healthcare Common Procedure Coding System* (HCPCS) are used to code the treatment a patient receives at a physician or provider's office, at an ambulatory surgery center (ASC), or as a hospital outpatient. CPT is updated and published by the American Medical Association (AMA). HCPCS was developed by the Centers for Medicare and Medicaid Services (CMS) to complement the CPT coding system. CPT codes are also called HCPCS level I codes. The alphanumeric HCPCS codes are also called HCPCS level II codes. CMS is a division of the Department of Health and Human Services (HHS).

CPT and HCPCS codes are used in conjunction with ICD-9-CM (ICD-10-CM when adopted) diagnosis codes to communicate patient services to insurance carriers (also called fiscal intermediaries) and to government and regulatory agencies. Both diagnoses and procedure codes are used to determine provider reimbursement. The documentation in the patient's medical record must clearly support *all* codes.

Inaccurate coding results in delayed or denied reimbursement. Intentional coding errors can lead to charges of insurance fraud, whereas unintentional coding errors can lead to charges of insurance abuse. Both fraud and abuse can result in civil and criminal penalties. Because reimbursement is based on the codes submitted, all health insurance companies and CMS have increased monitoring and auditing activities related to coding.

This chapter is an introduction to CPT and HCPCS coding conventions and applications and is not intended to be a comprehensive presentation of either system.

CURRENT PROCEDURAL TERMINOLOGY

The AMA developed CPT to provide a uniform language to accurately describe physician and provider services. The first edition was published in 1966 and consisted primarily of codes for surgical procedures and limited codes for other services, such as radiology, laboratory, and pathology. Over the years, CPT has been revised and expanded, and it is now the accepted coding system for nearly all provider services in ambulatory or outpatient settings and for some provider services related to hospital and long-term care.

CPT is updated annually by the CPT editorial panel. An advisory committee, which includes physicians and other health care professionals, assists the editorial panel with the annual revision. The annual revision is released late in the fall of each year, and the codes become effective on January 1. CPT codes answer this question: What did the provider do for the patient's problems? Billing specialists and medical coders need the most current edition of CPT to ensure accurate code assignment. Many physicians' offices have CPT codes printed on the encounter form (or route slip). The codes on the encounter form must be updated.

TABLE 6–1

CPT Components and Description	
Component	**Description**
Introduction	Instructions for using the CPT manual, definitions of terms, and roots, prefixes, and suffixes for medical terms. Some CPT editions also include anatomical illustrations and procedural illustrations.
Main Sections	Guidelines for each section, the range of codes for the section, definitions of terms, and, in some editions, illustrations of selected services.
Appendices	A quick reference for modifier descriptions; clinical examples of evaluation and management (E/M) codes; summaries of CPT code changes, deletions, and additions; CPT add-on codes; CPT codes exempt from modifier -51; CPT codes exempt from modifier -63; CPT codes that include moderate (conscious) sedation; genetic testing code modifiers; electrodiagnostic medicine codes; products pending Food and Drug Administration (FDA) approval codes; vascular families; a crosswalk to deleted CPT codes; and a summary of resequenced CPT codes.
Category II Codes	Supplemental tracking codes that can be used for performance measurement. These codes are intended to facilitate data collection related to quality of care. The use of these codes is optional.
Category III Codes	Temporary codes for emerging technology, services, and procedures that have not yet been assigned a Category I CPT code. If a Category III code is available for a specific technology, service, or procedure, it must be used instead of a Category I unlisted code. Category III codes consist of four numeric characters and one alpha character as the fifth character.
Alphabetic Index	The key to locating codes in the main sections. The index is organized by main terms that include the type of procedure or service; by the organ or anatomical site; by the condition, such as "fracture"; or by synonyms, eponyms, and abbreviations, such as EEG and Pomeroy's operation.

CPT Components

The CPT code book has an Introduction, six main sections, 15 appendices, a list of CPT category II codes, a list of CPT category III codes, and an alphabetic index. Table 6–1 lists the CPT components with a brief description.

CPT Main Sections

Each CPT main section is preceded by guidelines that explain the unique coding conventions for the section. A specific range of codes relates to each of the six main sections. CPT codes—each of which is a five-digit number—represent a specific service. The six main sections and their range of codes are:

- "Evaluation and Management (E/M)": 99201 through 99499
- "Anesthesia": 00100 through 01999
- "Surgery": 10021 through 69990
- "Radiology": 70010 through 79999

TABLE 6–2

CPT Section, Category/Subsection, Subcategory, Procedure/Service			
Section	Category/Subsection	Subcategory	Procedure/Service
Evaluation/ Management	Office or Other Outpatient Services	New Patient	99201: New patient office visit; presenting problem is self-limited or minor
Surgery	Urinary System	Kidney	50205: Renal biopsy; by surgical exposure of kidney
Medicine	Cardiovascular	Cardiography	93040: Rhythm ECG, 1–3 leads; interpretation and report

© 2014 Cengage Learning, All Rights Reserved.

- "Pathology and Laboratory": 80047 through 89398
- "Medicine": 90281 through 99199 and 99500 through 99607

The main sections are divided into categories or subsections, subcategories, and procedures or services. The section divisions are used to identify services, procedures or therapies, examinations or tests, body systems, or anatomic sites. Table 6–2 provides an example of the divisions of CPT main sections.

CPT Appendices

The CPT appendices include:

- **Appendix A:** "Modifiers"—A list of modifiers that may be added to a five-digit code to further explain the service provided
- **Appendix B:** "Summary of Additions, Deletions, and Revisions"—A summarization of CPT codes that have been added, deleted, and revised
- **Appendix C:** "Clinical Examples"—Clinical examples of services that represent "Evaluation and Management" CPT codes
- **Appendix D:** "Summary of CPT Add-on Codes"—A list of add-on codes, which are CPT codes that are used in conjunction with another CPT code
- **Appendix E:** "Summary of CPT Codes Exempt from Modifier 51"—A list of codes that may not be used with modifier -51
- **Appendix F:** "Summary of CPT Codes Exempt from Modifier 63"—A list of codes that may not be used with modifier -63
- **Appendix G:** "Summary of CPT Codes that Include Moderate (Conscious) Sedation"—A list of CPT procedure codes that include moderate (conscious) sedation as a part of the procedure
- **Appendix I:** "Genetic Testing Code Modifiers"—A list of modifiers that apply to molecular laboratory procedures related to genetic testing
- **Appendix J:** "Electrodiagnostic Medicine Listing of Sensory, Motor, and Mixed Nerves"— A list of codes that apply to each sensory, motor, and mixed nerve. Each nerve constitutes one unit of service. These codes are used to enhance codes 95900, 95903, and 95904.
- **Appendix K:** "Product Pending FDA Approval"—A list of codes for some vaccine products that are pending FDA approval

- **Appendix L:** "Vascular Families"—A summary of the branches of vascular families when the starting point of intravascular catheterization is the aorta
- **Appendix M:** "Deleted CPT Codes"—A summary of deleted CPT codes that can be crosswalked to new or revised codes
- **Appendix N:** "Summary of Resequenced CPT Codes"—A summary of CPT codes that do not appear in numeric sequence in the listing of CPT codes; allows existing codes to be relocated without renumbering the code; the # symbol alerts medical coders to the location of the resequenced code
- **Appendix H:** "Alphabetical Clinical Topics Listing" has been removed from the CPT codebook. This appendix is available solely on the AMA website at http://www.ama-assn.org/go/cpt.
- **Appendix O:** "Multianalyte Assays with Algorithmic Analyses" (MAAA) procedures that by their nature are typically unique to a single clinical laboratory or manufacturer

The appendices provide the billing specialist with a quick reference to CPT code changes and updates.

CPT Alphabetic Index

The CPT alphabetic index is organized by main terms, also called main entries. Main terms are printed in bold. There are four (4) types of main terms:

- Procedure or service: Laparoscopy, repair, cast
- Organ or anatomic site: Heart, skin, thyroid gland
- Condition: Fracture, ectopic pregnancy, pressure ulcer (decubitus)
- Synonyms, eponyms, and abbreviations: EEG, Caldwell-Luc procedure, Pomeroy's operation

Main terms may be followed by a series of indented modifying terms that apply to the main term and affect code selection.

In Figure 6–1, note that the main term "fracture" has several modifying terms. The billing specialist compares the procedure statement with the main term and then reviews the modifying

Fracture	
Ankle	
Bimalleolar	27808–27814
Closed	27816–27818
Lateral	27786–27814, 27792
Intertrochanteric	
Closed treatment	27238
Intramedullary implant	27245
Plate/Screw implant	27244
Treatment with implant	27244–27245

Figure 6–1 Modifying Terms for Fracture

terms to locate the code that best matches the procedure's description. For "intertrochanteric fracture of the femur, with intramedullary implant," the billing specialist selects code 27245 and verifies the code with the full description found in the "Musculoskeletal" chapter.

The instructions for using the CPT index include a description of code ranges and modifying terms. The billing specialist and medical coder are clearly instructed *not* to assign codes from the index. *Always* refer to the main sections to ensure coding accuracy.

REINFORCEMENT EXERCISES 6–1

Spell out the abbreviations.

1. CPT

2. HCPCS

3. ASC

4. HHS

5. AHA

Provide a short answer for each item.

1. How often is CPT updated?

2. What agency requires the use of HCPCS codes?

3. Identify and define three CPT appendices.

continued on the next page

continued from the previous page

4. Identify the effective date of revised CPT codes.

_____

_____

_____

5. List the six main sections of the CPT code book.

_____

_____

_____

_____

_____

_____

CPT Coding Conventions

CPT coding conventions include symbols and cross-references. The symbols are semicolons (;), bullets (•) and triangles (▲), facing triangles (▶◀), plus signs (+), circles (○), circled bullets (⊙), null zero or universal no code (∅), the flash symbol (ⵗ), and the number symbol (#). The cross-references are "see" and "see also."

Semicolon

The semicolon (;) is used to identify the common part or main entry for indented modifying terms or descriptions. When several codes and descriptions refer to a specific procedure or have a shared beginning description, a semicolon follows the shared portion. Figure 6–2 is an example of CPT semicolon use.

In the figure the procedure is colonoscopy, and several descriptions and codes apply to variations of that procedure. "Colonoscopy, flexible, proximal to splenic flexure" is the common description shared by codes 45378 through 45382. Therefore, the full description for CPT code

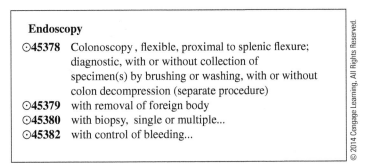

Figure 6–2 Semicolon Use

45380 is "Colonoscopy, flexible, proximal to splenic flexure; with biopsy, single or multiple." Note that the full description for CPT code 45378 is "Colonoscopy, flexible, proximal to splenic flexure; diagnostic, with or without collection of specimen(s) by brushing or washing, with or without colon decompression (separate procedure)." The description following the semicolon applies only to code 45378.

The billing specialist carefully reviews the patient's record to ensure that the correct code is selected.

> EXAMPLE
>
> Dr. Johnson circled "colonoscopy" on the route slip. The billing specialist reviewed the patient's record and discovered that the procedure note states, "Bleeding was controlled by cauterization." Colonoscopy with no mention of bleeding or specimen collection is coded as 45378. Based on the information in the procedure note, the correct code is 45381 "colonoscopy ... *with control of bleeding...."*

Because the reimbursement for colonoscopy with control of bleeding is more than the reimbursement for colonoscopy with no mention of bleeding, the record review in this case helped ensure appropriate payment for the service provided.

The indented statements following the semicolon may provide additional diagnostic information, additional or other anatomic sites, additional or other procedures, or additional codes for extensive procedures. These semicolon applications are shown in examples A through D.

> EXAMPLE
>
> A. *Additional Diagnostic Information*
>   49585 Repair umbilical hernia, age 5 years or over; reducible
>   49587 incarcerated or strangulated
> Code 49587 is used when the diagnostic statement includes additional information about the hernia.
>
> B. *Additional or Other Anatomic Sites*
>   27050 Arthrotomy, with biopsy; sacroiliac joint
>   27052 hip joint
> Code 27052 is used when the arthrotomy, with biopsy is performed on a hip joint.
>
> C. *Additional Procedures*
>   44155 Colectomy, total, abdominal, with proctectomy; with ileostomy
>   44156 with continent ileostomy
> Code 44156 is used when the total abdominal colectomy and proctectomy includes a continent ileostomy.
>
>   *Additional Codes for Extensive Procedures*
> 11042 Debridement, subcutaneous tissue (includes epidermis and dermis, if performed); first 20 sq cm or less
> #+ 11045 each additional 20 sq cm, or part thereof (List separately in addition to code for primary procedure)
> Codes 11042 and 11045 are used when the debridement includes the amount of tissue mentioned with each code.

Bullets and Triangles

A bullet (•) placed before a CPT code identifies the code as a new addition or new code. A triangle (▲) placed before a code identifies a revision in the narrative description of the code. Examples A and B illustrate these conventions.

> **EXAMPLE**
> A. *New Code*
> • 29582 Application of multi-layer compression system; thigh and leg, including ankle and foot, when performed
>
> B. *Revised Code*
> ▲ 29581 Application of multi-layer compression system; leg (below the knee), including ankle and foot

Appendix B of the CPT manual is a numerical list of additions, revisions, and deletions.

Facing Triangles

Facing triangles (▶◀) are used to set off new or revised information in the CPT guidelines, the beginning of each main section, and throughout the CPT manual wherever descriptions have been changed.

> **EXAMPLE**
> Surgery/Integumentary System/Breast Repair and/or Reconstruction
> ▶ *(For biologic implant for soft tissue reinforcement, use 15777 in conjunction with primary procedure)* ◀

Plus Sign

The plus sign (+), which is placed in front of a five-digit CPT code, identifies an add-on code. Add-on codes are CPT codes that must be used with a related procedure code. In addition to the plus sign, the narrative description of add-on codes includes instructional notes as reminders that the codes must be used with another code. The following example illustrates how to apply add-on codes.

> **EXAMPLE**
> Surgery/Integumentary System
> Debridement
> 11000   Debridement of extensive eczematous or infected skin; up to 10% of body surface
> +11001   each additional 10% of the body surface, or part thereof (List separately in addition to code for primary procedure)
> (Use 11001 in conjunction with code 11000)
> Dr. Romero debrides the eczema from 30% of Loretta's body surface, which includes her trunk and legs. Code 11000 is selected to indicate that 10% of [the] body surface was debrided. Code 11001 is selected twice to indicate that an additional 20% of [the] body surface was also debrided. Three codes, 11000, 11001, and 11001, are used to accurately describe what Dr. Romero did for this patient.

Circle

A circle (○) is placed before a CPT code to indicate that the code has been reinstated or recycled.

Circled Bullets

A circled bullet (⊙) is placed before a CPT code to indicate that the service or procedure includes the use of moderate (conscious) sedation. Moderate sedation is the use of sedatives or pain relievers to minimize pain and discomfort without causing complete unconsciousness. Patients under moderate sedation are usually able to respond to verbal cues and communicate discomfort during the procedure. According to CPT coding guidelines, the physician who performs a procedure that includes moderate sedation should not submit a separate claim for the moderate sedation. When anesthesia services—moderate sedation or otherwise—are performed by someone other than the physician performing the procedure, the anesthesia code should be reported.

Null Zero or Universal No Code

The null zero or universal no code (Ø) identifies CPT codes that may not be used with modifier -51. Modifier -51 is used when multiple procedures are performed by the same provider during a single encounter.

A CPT modifier is a two-digit number that is added to the five-digit CPT code or a five-digit number that is reported in addition to the CPT code. The modifier provides additional information about the procedure. Modifiers and their descriptions are presented with Surgery section codes.

Flash Symbol

The flash symbol (⁄) identifies CPT codes that classify products pending FDA approval.

Number Symbol

The number symbol (#) identifies CPT codes that are listed out of numeric order.

> **EXAMPLE**
>
> | 27618 | Excision, tumor, soft tissue of leg or ankle area, subcutaneous; less than 3 cm |
> |---|---|
> | # 27632 | 3 cm or greater |
> | 27619 | Excision, tumor, soft tissue of leg or ankle area, subfascial (e.g., intramuscular); less than 5 cm |
> | # 27634 | 5 cm or greater |

See and See Also

The cross-references see and see also are found in CPT's main sections and alphabetic index. These references tell the billing specialist or medical coder to look at other CPT codes or sections. Accurate CPT code assignment depends on compliance with the "see" and "see also" instructions. Figure 6–3 shows examples of these instructions.

A. "See"

ALPHABETIC INDEX

Abbe-Eslander Procedure

See Reconstruction; Repair, Cleft Lip

B. "See Also"

MAIN SECTION

Anus/Incision

46050 Incision and drainage, perianal abscess, superficial

  (*See also* 45020, 46060)

Figure 6–3 "See" and "See Also" Instructional Notes

Instructional Notes

In addition to symbols and cross-references used as coding conventions, CPT has extensive instructional notes and section guidelines. Instructional notes, which provide the billing specialist or coder with details about code selection, are located at the beginning of a heading, in parentheses before or after a code, or in parentheses as part of the code's description. Section guidelines are located at the beginning of each CPT section.

Heading Notes

Instructional notes located at the beginning of a CPT heading provide information about the following:

- Components of a service or procedure
- Definitions of terms and codes
- Directions for additional code assignment

Figure 6–4 lists an example of each heading instructional note.

Notes Before/After CPT Codes

Instructional notes placed before or after the CPT code primarily consist of additional, alternate, or deleted codes as well as other general information. Table 6–3 gives examples of before and after instructional notes.

Section Guidelines

The section guidelines precede each of the six main CPT sections and are clearly labeled. The guidelines provide the billing specialist and medical coder with information that increases coding accuracy. Guidelines are discussed with each main section.

COMPONENTS OF A SERVICE OR PROCEDURE

Digestive System Surgery: Esophagus

Endoscopy

For endoscopic procedures, code appropriate endoscopy for each anatomic site examined. Surgical endoscopy always includes diagnostic endoscopy.

DEFINITIONS OF TERMS AND CODES

Digestive System Surgery: Vestibule of the Mouth

The vestibule of the mouth is the part of the oral cavity outside the dentoalveolar structures; it includes the mucosal and submucosal tissue of the lips and cheeks.

ADDITIONAL CODE ASSIGNMENT

The instructional notes under *Repair*, *Hernioplasty*, *Herniorrhaphy*, *Herniotomy* in the digestive surgery codes direct the billing specialist or coder to use an additional code for the repair of strangulated organs or structures.

Figure 6–4 CPT Heading Instructional Notes

TABLE 6–3

Instructional Notes before and after CPT Codes
Alternative Codes
10081 Incision and drainage of pilonidal cyst; complicated
(For excision of pilonidal cyst, see 11770-11772)
The note in parentheses indentifies the code range for an excision of the cyst.
Additional Codes
+ 11201 Removal of skin tags…each additional 10 lesions…
(Use 11201 in conjunction with 11200)
The note in parentheses identifies code 11201 as an additional code used with code 11200. The plus sign also identifies 11201 as an add-on code.
Deleted Codes
The note ▶ (11975 has been deleted. To report insertion of non-biodegradable drug delivery implant for contraception, use 11981) ◀ identifies a deleted code. Procedures previously coded to 11975 are coded to 11981. The facing triangles highlight this note as new information.

REINFORCEMENT EXERCISES 6–2

Fill in the blank.

1. A(n) _____ is used to identify the main entry for indented modifying terms or descriptions.

continued on the next page

continued from the previous page

2. A new CPT code is identified by a(n) _____ placed in front of the code.

3. Revised CPT code descriptions have a(n) _____ placed in front of the code.

4. _____ are used to set off new or revised information in CPT guidelines and main sections.

5. Add-on CPT codes are identified by a(n) _____ placed in front of the code.

6. A(n) _____ placed before a CPT code means that moderate sedation is included in the procedure.

7. The _____ identifies CPT codes that may not be used with modifier -51.

8. A _____ is a two-digit number that is added to the CPT code.

9. A reinstated or recycled CPT code is preceded by a(n) _____.

10. A _____ symbol indicates a product that is pending FDA approval.

11. The _____ symbol identifies a resequenced CPT code.

Evaluation and Management Section (99201–99499)

CPT Evaluation and Management (E/M) section codes identify medical services, as opposed to surgical services. E/M codes are used to report physician or provider activities associated with evaluating an individual's health status and managing or implementing a plan of care related to that status. E/M services range from a routine sports physical to planning and implementing care for critically ill or injured individuals. Services can be provided in the physician's office, a hospital, nursing home, assisted living facility, or in the patient's home. Figure 6–5 illustrates a physician examining a patient.

There are several pages of "Evaluation and Management Services Guidelines." This chapter includes a brief discussion of E/M terms and a detailed discussion of the instructions for selecting E/M CPT codes. Refer to the CPT manual for a complete review of the E/M guidelines.

Commonly Used Terms

Certain keywords and phrases are used throughout the E/M section. The "Evaluation and Management Service Guidelines" provide a definition or description of the commonly used terms and phrases. Table 6–4 summarizes the definitions for CPT key terms and phrases.

E/M Categories

There are 21 categories of E/M codes, which range from office visits to work-related and medical disability evaluation services. Each category has specific guidelines that describe the type of services that fall into the category. Table 6–5 lists the E/M categories, and Table 6–6 summarizes the guidelines for each category. The complete guidelines and instructions are found in the CPT manual.

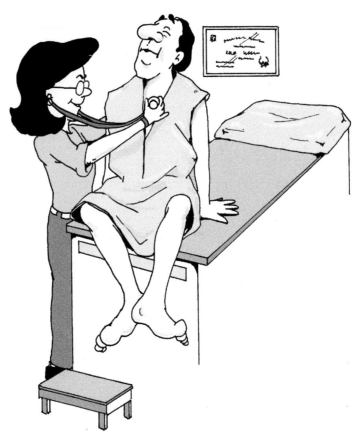

Figure 6–5 Take a Deep Breath

TABLE 6–4

Evaluation and Management Definitions	
Term	**Definition**
Chief complaint	A description of the problem that caused the patient to seek treatment, usually stated in the patient's words
Clinical examples	Examples of the clinical situations associated with various E/M services that are listed in Appendix C
Concurrent care	The provision of similar services to the same patient on the same day by more than one physician or provider
Counseling	A discussion with the patient or family about one or more of the following: diagnostic results, impressions, and recommendations; prognosis; risks and benefits of treatment options; treatment or follow-up instructions; importance of compliance with treatment options; reducing risk factors; and patient and family education.

continued on the next page

continued from the previous page

Established patient	A person who has received professional services within the past three years from physicians of the exact same specialty and subspecialty who belong to the same group practice
Face-to-face time	The time a physician spends face-to-face with the patient or family; a component of E/M codes
Family history	A review of medical events in the patient's family that includes significant information about the health status or cause of death of parents, siblings, and children and about diseases that may be hereditary or place the patient at risk
History of present illness	A chronological description of the patient's current problem, from the first sign or symptom to the time the patient seeks treatment
New patient	A person who has not received any professional services within the past three years from physicians of the exact same specialty and subspecialty who belong to the same group practice
Non–face-to-face time	The time spent doing work before and after seeing the patient or family; not a component of E/M codes
Past history	A narrative of the patient's past illnesses, injuries, treatments, operations, hospitalizations, allergies, and other age-appropriate information
Professional services	Face-to-face services rendered by a physician and reported by one or more specific CPT codes. This definition of professional services is used only to distinguish between new and established patients
Social history	An age-appropriate review of marital status, employment history, substance use and abuse, sexual history, and level of education
Special report	Documentation that supports the necessity for providing services that are unusual or not listed in the CPT manual
System review (review of systems; ROS)	An inventory of body systems through a series of questions to help define the problem, clarify the differential diagnosis, identify needed testing, or provide baseline patient data
Transfer of care	A physician who is providing management for some or all of the patient's problems relinquishes this responsibility to another physician who explicitly agrees to accept this responsibility.
Unit/floor time	The time the physician is present on the patient's hospital unit and at the bedside for the purpose of rendering service to the patient that is a component of E/M codes. Unit/floor time applies to hospital observation services, inpatient hospital care, initial and follow-up hospital consultations, and nursing facility visits.
Unlisted service	An evaluation or management service provided to the patient that is not listed in the E/M CPT codebook. These services are coded as: 99429, Unlisted preventive medicine service; and 99499 Unlisted E/M service.

TABLE 6–5

Evaluation and Management Categories	
Category	**Range of Codes**
Office/Other Outpatient Services	99201–99215
Hospital Observation Services	99217–99226
Hospital Inpatient Services	99221–99239
Consultations	99241–99255
Emergency Department Services	99281–99288
Critical Care Services	99291, 99292
Nursing Facility Services	99304–99318
Domiciliary, Rest Home (e.g., Boarding Home), or Custodial Care Services	99324–99337
Domiciliary, Rest Home (e.g., Assisted-Living Facility), or Home Care Plan Oversight Services	99339, 99340
Home Services	99341–99350
Prolonged Services	99354–99359
Physician Standby Services	99360
Case Management Services	99363–99368
Care Plan Oversight Services	99374–99380
Preventive Medicine Services	99381–99397
Counseling Risk Factor Reduction and Behavior Change Intervention	99401–99429
Non–Face-to-Face Physician Services	99441–99444
Special E/M Services (Basic Life and/or Disability Evaluation Services and Work-Related or Medical Disability Evaluation Services)	99450–99456
Newborn Care Services	99460–99465
Inpatient Neonatal Intensive Care Services and Pediatric and Neonatal Critical Services	99466–99480
Complex Chronic Care Coordination (CCCC) Services	99487, 99488, 99489
Transitional Care Management (TCM) Services	99495, 99496
Other Evaluation and Management Services (unlisted evaluation and management services)	99499

Levels of Service

Most E/M categories and subcategories have several codes that represent different levels of service. Levels of service are related to the nature of the patient's problem(s) and the complexity of the provider's evaluation. The following example lists five office visit codes, identifies the level of each code, and provides a brief description of the severity of the patient's problems.

TABLE 6-6

E/M Category Guidelines

Office or Other Outpatient Services (99201–99215)

CPT codes from this category are used to report E/M services provided in the physician or provider's office or in an outpatient or other ambulatory facility. The patient is an outpatient until admission to an inpatient facility occurs. Codes are divided between new and established patient services, and code selection depends on the complexity of the service provided.

Hospital Observation Services (99217–99220)

CPT codes from this category are used to report E/M services provided to individuals who are admitted to an inpatient facility as "observation status." Initial observation care, subsequent observation care, and discharge services are included in this category. The codes for new and established patients are the same, and code selection depends on the complexity of the service provided.

Hospital Inpatient Services (99221–99239)

CPT codes from this category are used to report E/M services provided to hospital inpatients. Initial hospital care, subsequent hospital care, same-day admission and discharge, and hospital discharge services are included in this category. The codes for new and established patients are the same, and code selection depends on the complexity of the service provided.

Consultations (99241–99255)

CPT codes from this category are used to report office or other outpatient consultations and inpatient consultations. The codes for new or established patients are the same, and code selection depends on the complexity of the service provided.

Emergency Department Services (99281–99288)

CPT codes from this category are used to report E/M services to individuals who seek treatment at an emergency room or department. An emergency department is an organized hospital-based facility that is available 24 hours a day for the provision of unscheduled health care services to patients who need immediate medical attention. Codes for new or established patients are the same, and code selection depends on the complexity of the service provided.

Critical Care Services (99291, 99292)

CPT codes for critical care services depend on the total amount of time the physician devoted solely to providing services directly to the critically ill patient. The physician cannot provide services to any other patient during this time. The first 74 minutes of critical care services are covered by code 99291, and code +99292 (an add-on code) is used to report each additional 30 minutes of critical care services. The guidelines for this category are extensive and fully explained in the CPT manual.

Nursing Facility Services (99304–99318)

CPT codes from this category are used to report E/M services provided to patients in nursing facilities, intermediate care facilities, or long-term care facilities. Comprehensive nursing facility assessments, subsequent nursing facility care, and nursing facility discharge services are included in this category. Codes for new or established patients are the same, and code selection depends on the complexity of the service provided.

Domiciliary, Rest Home (e.g., Boarding Home), or Custodial Care Services (99324–99337)

CPT codes from this category are used to report E/M services rendered to individuals who live in a facility that provides room, board, and other personal assistance. There are separate codes for new and established patients, and code selection depends on the complexity of the E/M services.

continued on the next page

continued from the previous page

E/M Category Guidelines

Domiciliary, Rest Home (e.g., Assisted-Living Facility), or Home Care Plan Oversight Services (99339–99340)

CPT codes from this category are used to report physician services related to overseeing an individual's plan of care.

Home Services (99341–99350)

CPT codes from this category are used to report E/M services provided to individuals in their homes or other private residences. There are separate codes for new and established patients, and code selection depends on the complexity of the E/M services.

Prolonged Services (99354–99359)

CPT codes from this category are reported as add-on codes in conjunction with other E/M codes. Prolonged services can be provided with or without direct patient contact, must be more than 30 minutes, and are reported at 30-minute intervals after the first 74 minutes.

Physician Standby Services (99360)

This CPT code is used to report physician standby services when the standby is requested by another physician. The standby physician may not treat other patients during this time, and services are reported at every full 30 minute interval *after* the first 30 minutes. Standby service of less than 30 minutes on a given date is not reported separately.

Case Management Services (99363–99368)

CPT codes for anticoagulant management and medical team conferences are included in this section. Team conferences are usually related to physician participation on an interdisciplinary health care team that plans and coordinates patient care services.

Care Plan Oversight Services (99374–99380)

These services usually include a review of clinical information and communication with other professionals involved in the patient's care; no more than one service within a calendar month; and only one physician may report services for the given time frame.

Preventive Medicine Services (99381–99397)

CPT codes from this category are used to report services provided to individuals to promote health and prevent illness or injury. These services may not be a part of other E/M services. There are separate codes for preventive medicine services for new and established patients.

Counseling Risk Factor Reduction and Behavior Change Intervention (99401–99429)

CPT codes from this section are used to report services related to health promotion and illness or injury prevention. These codes apply to both new and established patients.

Non–Face-to-Face Physician Services (99441–99444)

CPT codes in this category include telephone services and online medical evaluation.

Special Evaluation and Management Services (Basic Life and/or Disability Evaluation Services and Work-Related or Medical Disability Evaluation Services) (99450–99456)

CPT codes in this section are used to report evaluations performed when the patient or individual is applying for life or disability insurance. Under these codes, there is no active management of the problem or problems identified.

Newborn Care Services (99460–99465)

CPT codes from this section are used to report services provided to newborns in several different settings. Most codes relate to services rendered to a normal newborn.

continued on the next page

continued from the previous page

Inpatient Neonatal Intensive Care Services and Pediatric and Neonatal Critical Services (99466–99480)
CPT codes in this category are used to report services provided to individuals from less than 28 days of age through 5 years of age. The CPT manual provides extensive instructions for these codes.
Complex Chronic Care Coordination Services (99487–99489)
CPT codes from this section are used to report patient centered management and support services provided to individuals in a home, domiciliary, rest home, or assisted living facility. Services commonly require coordination of a number of specialties and services.
Transitional Care Management (99495, 99496)
CPT codes from this category are used to report patient centered care management when the transition in care is from a hospital setting or skilled nursing/nursing facility to the patient's community setting (home, domiciliary, rest home, or assisted living). The codes apply to established patients with problems that require moderate or high complexity medical decision making during transitions in care.
Other Evaluation and Management Services (99499)
This CPT code is used to report E/M services not covered elsewhere. Selection of this code usually requires the physician to provide a written report explaining the service and the reason for it.

© 2014 Cengage Learning, All Rights Reserved.

REINFORCEMENT EXERCISES 6–3

Provide a short answer for each item.

1. List five categories of CPT E/M services.

   _____

   _____

   _____

   _____

   _____

2. Describe the purpose of E/M codes.

   _____

   _____

   _____

Fill in the blank.

1. A(n) _____ is a person who has not received professional services within the past three years.

2. A(n) _____ is a person who has received professional services within the last three years.

3. The _____ is a description of the problem that caused the patient to seek treatment.

continued on the next page

continued from the previous page

4. _____ is the time the physician is present on the patient's hospital unit and at the bedside.

5. A service provided to the patient that does not have an associated CPT code is called a(n) _____.

6. Services provided to promote health and prevent illness are called _____.

7. The _____ is a chronological description of the patient's current problem.

8. Team conferences and telephone consultations are included in the _____ services E/M codes.

EXAMPLE

OFFICE/OTHER OUTPATIENT VISITS: 99201 through 99205

Code	Level	Description
99201	I	Self-limited or minor problem(s)
99202	II	Low to moderately severe problem(s)
99203	III	Moderately severe problem(s)
99204	IV	Moderate to severe problem(s)
99205	V	Moderate to severe problem(s) with high complexity

This example shows the relationship between the E/M code and the level of service.

Seven factors contribute to E/M levels of service and affect E/M code selection. The CPT manual calls these factors "components." Table 6–7 lists the components with a brief description. The CPT manual has a complete discussion of the seven components.

All seven components are not a part of every E/M code. E/M guidelines identify three key components—history, examination, and medical decision making—that are required for most E/M codes. Because the three key components affect many E/M codes, they are described in detail.

History

The extent of the history depends on the clinical judgment of the provider and the nature of the presenting problems. The history includes information about the patient's previous health care encounters, family health, and lifestyle. In general, a history includes a chief complaint (CC); history of present illness (HPI); review of systems (ROS); and past, family, and social history. CPT describes four types of history that are defined as follows:

- *Problem-focused history:* Consists of a CC and a brief history of the present illness or problem
- *Expanded problem-focused history:* Consists of a CC, brief history of the present illness, and a review of the systems that relate to the patient's problem

TABLE 6-7

Description of E/M Code Components

Component	Description
History	A chronological review of the individual's past medical and surgical history, family history, and social history as well as a review of one or more body systems. E/M codes that reflect a higher level of service require a more comprehensive history.
Examination	A physical examination of the individual that includes an assessment of one or more body systems or organ function. E/M codes that reflect a higher level of service require an examination of more body systems.
Medical decision making	The complexity of establishing a diagnosis or selecting a management option based on the number of possible diagnoses; the amount of medical information obtained, reviewed, and analyzed; and the risk of complications or death. E/M codes that reflect a higher level of service require an increased complexity of medical decision making.
Counseling	A discussion with the individual about diagnoses, treatment options, risks and benefits, follow-up, risk factor reduction, and compliance with treatment plans.
Coordination of care	Activities related to ordering, referring, and discussing the patient's treatment with other providers, agencies, and the patient.
Nature of presenting problem	The level of severity or complexity of the individual's problem, disease, condition, illness, injury, symptom, or complaint; ranges from minimal severity to high severity.
Time	The number of minutes a provider spends with the individual; the number of minutes the provider spends reviewing tests, records, and other patient-related information.

© 2014 Cengage Learning, All Rights Reserved.

- *Detailed history:* Consists of a CC; extended history of present illness; a review of the systems that relate to the patient's problem as well as a review of a limited number of additional systems; and pertinent past, family, and social history directly related to the patient's problems
- *Comprehensive history:* Consists of a CC; extended history of present illness; review of all body systems; and a complete past, family, and social history.

Note: A comprehensive history associated with preventive medicine E/M services is not problem-oriented and does not involve a CC or present illness. A preventive medicine history does include a comprehensive system review; a comprehensive or interval past, family, and social history; and a comprehensive assessment or history of pertinent risk factors.

Figure 6-6 illustrates each type of history.

Examination

This is the physical examination of the patient. There are four types of examination:

- *Problem-focused examination:* A limited examination of the affected body area or organ

Figure 6-6 Types of History

- *Expanded problem-focused examination:* A limited examination of the affected body area or organ system and other symptomatic or related organ system(s)
- *Detailed examination:* An extended examination of the affected body area(s) and other symptomatic or related organ system(s)
- *Comprehensive examination:* A general multisystem examination or a complete examination of a single organ system

Medical Decision Making

Medical decision making is the complex process of establishing a diagnosis and selecting a management or treatment option. Medical decision making is affected by these factors:

- The number of possible diagnoses or the number of management options that must be considered
- The amount or complexity of medical records, diagnostic tests, and other information that must be obtained, reviewed, and analyzed
- The risk of significant complications, morbidity, or mortality as well as comorbidities associated with the patient's presenting problem(s), the diagnostic procedure(s), or the possible management options

In order to qualify for a specific type of medical decision making, two of the three factors must be present. There are four types of medical decision making:

- *Straightforward:* Indicating a minimal number of diagnoses; a minimal amount of information to be reviewed; and a minimal risk of complication, morbidity, or mortality; basically, an uncomplicated presenting problem.

TABLE 6-8

Types of Medical Decision Making

Type of Medical Decision Making	Number of Diagnoses or Management Options	Amount or Complexity of Information to Be Reviewed	Risk of Complications, Morbidity, or Mortality
Straightforward	Minimal	Minimal or none	Minimal
Low Complexity	Limited	Limited	Low
Moderate Complexity	Multiple	Moderate	Moderate
High Complexity	Extensive	Extensive	High

- *Low complexity:* Indicating a limited number of diagnoses; a limited amount of information to be reviewed; and a low risk of complication, morbidity, or mortality; includes a controlled chronic disease.
- *Moderate complexity:* Indicating multiple diagnoses; a moderate amount of information to be reviewed or analyzed; and a moderate risk of complication, morbidity, or mortality; a multiple or in-depth system review is associated with this level of complexity.
- *High complexity:* Indicating extensive diagnoses; extensive amounts of information to be reviewed or analyzed; and a high risk of complications, morbidity, or mortality; complicated, multisystem problems are associated with this level of complexity.

Table 6-8 summarizes the factors that contribute to each type of medical decision making. Two of the three factors must be *documented* in the patient's medical record to demonstrate the level of medical decision making. Example A through Example D illustrate each type of medical decision making.

EXAMPLES

A. *Straightforward Medical Decision Making*

Mrs. Pelletier is seen today with a rash and itching. She had contact within the last 48 hours with poison ivy. Diagnosis: Contact dermatitis.

B. *Low-Complexity Medical Decision Making*

Mr. Victor is seen today with mild irritation of the eyes, tearing, light sensitivity, and blurred vision. After slit-lamp examination and vision testing, opacity in both corneas was noted. Fluorescein strip staining of the eyes revealed chronic dendritic keratitis requiring long-term topical treatment. Diagnosis: Chronic dendritic keratitis.

C. *Moderate-Complexity Medical Decision Making*

Mr. Weller, a 77-year-old-male, presents today in mild distress. He relates a three-month history of substernal chest pain, episodic in nature. His hypertension has been fairly well controlled with his current medication. Mr. Weller states that the pain seems to be brought on by exertion. Diagnosis: No clear-cut diagnosis; several tests must be done to determine the cause of the substernal chest pain.

D. High-Complexity Medical Decision Making

Ms. Yoha is a 70-year-old woman with diabetes mellitus and hypertension. She is accompanied by her sister, who explains that for the past two months, "my sister has been experiencing agitation, confusion, and short-term memory loss." Glucose monitoring at home indicates sporadic control of the diabetes, and Ms. Yoha's blood pressure today is 190/110. Diagnoses: Diabetes mellitus and hypertension, poorly controlled. Several diagnostic tests, including a CT scan, are ordered to *rule out* transient ischemic attacks, cerebrovascular accident, or basal artery insufficiency.

Some E/M codes require documentation of all three key components: history, examination, and medical decision making. Others require two of the three key components. Table 6–9 lists E/M subcategories that require two or three of the key components.

TABLE 6–9

E/M Categories and Number of Key Components		
Category	**E/M Codes**	**Key Components**
Office or Other Outpatient Services—*New Patient*	99201–99205	3
Office or Other Outpatient Services—*Established Patient*	99212–99215	2
Initial Hospital Observation Care—*New/Established Patient*	99218–99220	3
Subsequent Observation Care	99224–99226	2
Initial Hospital Care—*New or Established Patient*	99221–99223	3
Subsequent Hospital Care	99231–99233	2
Observation or Inpatient Care Services—*Patients admitted and discharged on the same day*	99234–99236	3
Office or Other Outpatient Consultations—*New/Established Patients*	99241–99245	3
Initial Inpatient Consultation—*New/Established Patient*	99251–99255	3
Emergency Department Services—*New or Established Patient*	99281–99285	3
Initial Nursing Facility Care—*New or Established Patient*	99304–99306	3
Subsequent Nursing Facility Care—*New/Established Patient*	99307–99310	2
Nursing Facility Discharge Services	99318	3
Domiciliary, Rest Home (e.g., Boarding Home), or Custodial Care Services—*New Patient*	99324–99328	3
Domiciliary, Rest Home (e.g., Boarding Home), or Custodial Care Services—*Established Patient*	99334–99337	2
Home Services—*New Patient*	99341–99345	3
Home Services—*Established Patient*	99347–99350	2

ELIZABETH FOY, MD CHARLES FRENCH, MD ROBERT HOWARD, MD DENZEL HAMILTON, MD ROBERTA PHARYNGEAL, MD HENRY ROMERO, MD				**SUPERIORLAND CLINIC** 714 HENNEPIN AVENUE BLUEBERRY, ME 49855 PHONE: (906) 336-4600 FAX: (906) 336-4020					
NEW PATIENT	**CODE**	**FEE**	**LAB TEST**	**CODE**	**FEE**	**LAB TEST**	**CODE**	**FEE**
Level I	99201		AST	84450		LDH	83615	
Level II	99202		Albumin/Serum	82040		Lipid Panel	80061	
Level III	99203		Alk Phos	84075		Metabolic Panel Comp	80053	
Level IV	99204		BUN	84520		Obstetric Panel	80055	
Level V	99205		CBC/Automated	85027		Occult Blood	82270	
ESTABLISHED PATIENT			CBC/diff/Automated	85025		PAP Smear/Automated	88147	
Level I	99211		CK/CPK/Isoenzymes	82552		PPD Skin Test	86580	
Level II	99212		Drug Screen	80100		Prothrombin Time	85610	
Level III	99213		Electrolyte Panel	80051		PSA	84152	
Level IV	99214		Estrogen	82671		Rapid Strep Screen	87880	
Level V	99215		Glucose/Blood	82947		Sed Rate/Automated	85652	
OFFICE CONSULTATION			GTT	82951		TSH	84443	
Level I	99241		HgbA1C	83036		Urinalysis/Automated/Micro	81001	
Level II	99242		Hepatitis Panel	80074				
Level III	99243		HIV-1/HIV-2/Single Result	86703				
Level IV	99244							
Level V	99245							

Figure 6–7 Encounter Form

Documentation Requirements

Selecting the appropriate E/M CPT code is a complex clinical decision that is the responsibility of the physician or provider. Many providers document the E/M code by circling or checking one of the E/M codes preprinted on the encounter form or route slip. Figure 6–7 is a sample encounter form with the E/M and diagnosis codes circled.

The encounter form is routed to the billing office, and the billing specialist submits an insurance claim by using the codes noted on the form. However, with the passage of the 1996 Health Insurance Portability and Accountability Act (HIPAA), insurance carriers are closely monitoring E/M codes. The documentation in the patient's record must clearly support E/M codes as well as the diagnoses codes.

In today's health care environment, billing specialists and medical coders are often expected to review the patient's record for documentation and additional information that may affect coding accuracy. In some practices, the billing specialist or medical coder codes "from the record" and compares the results with the encounter form codes. The following example illustrates this activity.

EXAMPLE

Brenda, the billing specialist in Dr. Hamilton's office, is preparing an insurance claim for Jenny Lind. On Ms. Lind's encounter form, Dr. Hamilton selected 99213 as the E/M code and urinary tract infection as the diagnosis.

Brenda checks the key components for 99213 and notes that this code requires two of the three key components: an expanded problem-focused history, an expanded problem-focused exam, and low-complexity medical decision making. The only documentation related to this visit is a progress note that states: "Patient seen today for pain on urination. Urinalysis ordered. Pending results, will start the patient on amoxicillin."

Based on the progress note in this example, the billing specialist alerts the provider that code 99213 requires documentation of either a history or exam related to the problem. In addition, the billing specialist also checks the patient's record for the urinalysis lab slip. If it is in the record, urinalysis should be checked on the encounter form, and the insurance claim should include a charge for that service.

The billing specialist and medical coder do not challenge the clinical judgment of the physician. The record review ensures that the documentation in the patient record supports the physician- or provider-selected code.

Approaching the provider about the accuracy of a selected code may be difficult. However, it is better to clarify the code before submitting the insurance claim. Insurance carriers and regulatory agencies monitor E/M codes for upcoding and downcoding. Upcoding is selecting codes at a higher level than the level substantiated by the patient's record. Downcoding is selecting codes at a lower level than the service requires. Upcoding results in overpayment for services rendered. Some providers downcode under the mistaken assumption that this prevents insurance carrier or regulatory agency audits. In fact, both upcoding and downcoding can be categorized as insurance fraud or abuse.

Documentation guidelines for E/M codes are covered in the CPT manual. In addition to those guidelines, the CMS and the AMA have developed an extensive set of guidelines for E/M codes. The guidelines are available from the CMS website and several commercial vendors.

The CMS/AMA guidelines are substantial. It is beyond the scope of this text to cover or reproduce these guidelines in their entirety. Table 6–10 through Table 6–12 summarize the documentation requirements for each of the key components of E/M codes.

TABLE 6–10

History Documentation Requirements

Type of History	Chief Complaint	History of Present Illness	Review of Systems	Past, Family, and Social History
Problem-Focused	Required	*Brief	Not required	Not required
Expanded Problem-Focused	Required	*Brief	Problem pertinent; all systems that pertain to the problem	Not required
Detailed	Required	**Extended	Extended; all systems directly related to the problem and a limited number of additional systems; review of two to nine body systems is documented	Pertinent; at least one of the following is documented: past history, family history, or social history
Comprehensive	Required	**Extended	Complete; all systems related to the problem and all additional body systems; review of 10 organ systems is documented	Complete; two or three of the following are documented: past history, family history, and social history

*Includes one to three of the following: location, severity, quality, duration, timing, context, modifying factors, and associated signs and symptoms that relate to the patient's present problem or illness.

**Includes at least four of the following: location, severity, quality, duration, timing, context, modifying factors, and associated signs and symptoms that relate to the patient's present problem or illness; or the status of at least three chronic or inactive conditions.

TABLE 6–11

Examination Documentation Requirements	
Type of Examination	**Documentation Requirements**
Problem-Focused Exam	A limited examination of the affected body area* or organ system that includes documentation of the results of assessing one to five structures or functions of the affected area or organ system**
Expanded Problem-Focused Exam	A limited examination of the affected body area or organ system and other symptomatic or related systems that includes documentation of the results of assessing at least six structures or functions of one or more body areas or systems
Detailed Exam	An extended examination of the affected body areas and other symptomatic or related organ systems that includes documentation of the results of assessing at least 2 structures or functions in six organ systems or the results of assessing at least 12 structures or functions in two or more organ systems
Comprehensive Exam	A general multisystem exam that includes documentation of the results of assessing at least two structures or functions in nine organ systems or the results of assessing all structures and functions in the affected organ system and at least one structure or function of the remaining organ systems

*CPT body areas include head and face; neck; chest, breast, and axilla; abdomen; genitalia, groin, and buttocks; back; and each extremity.

**CPT organ systems include eyes; ears, nose, mouth, and throat; cardiovascular; respiratory; gastrointestinal; genitourinary; musculoskeletal; skin; neurologic; psychiatric; and hematologic, lymphatic, and immunologic systems.

Table 6–10 summarizes the history documentation requirements. Table 6–11 summarizes the examination documentation requirements. Table 6–12 summarizes the medical decision-making documentation requirements.

After reviewing the documentation requirement tables, it is obvious that E/M coding is a complex clinical process. To receive appropriate reimbursement, the provider must be sure that

TABLE 6–12

Medical Decision Making Documentation Requirements	
Type of Medical Decision Making	**Documentation Requirements**
Straightforward	Documentation of a self-limited problem or diagnosis that presents a minimal risk for complications, development of additional problems, loss of organ structure or function, or death; review of a *minimal amount* of clinical data (e.g., previous medical records, routine lab tests, and x-ray results)
Low Complexity	Documentation of two or more self-limited problems, a stable chronic condition, or an acute, uncomplicated illness or injury that presents a low risk for complications, development of additional problems, loss of organ structure or function, or death; review of a limited amount of clinical data (e.g., previous medical records, lab tests, superficial needle biopsies)

continued on the next page

continued from the previous page

Medical Decision Making Documentation Requirements	
Type of Medical Decision Making	**Documentation Requirements**
Moderate Complexity	Documentation of multiple problems or diagnoses, chronic illnesses with mild increase in progression, uncertain new diagnoses requiring additional tests, or acute illness that affects several body systems that present a moderate risk for complications, development of additional problems, loss of organ structure or function, or death; review of a moderate amount of clinical data (e.g., stress tests or invasive diagnostic procedures, such as endoscopies, cardiac catheterization, lumbar puncture)
High Complexity	Documentation of extensive problems or diagnoses, chronic illness with a severe increase in progression, acute or chronic illness or injuries that threaten the patient's life or body function that present a high risk for complications, development of additional problems, loss of organ structure or function, or death; review of extensive amounts of clinical data that results in major elective or emergency surgery, poor prognosis, or other management options associated with high-risk illness, injury, or disease

the requirements for each E/M code or level of service are clearly noted in the patient's record. The familiar saying "If it isn't documented, it hasn't been done" applies more than ever. Given the increased focus on reducing health care costs, the increased focus on insurance billing fraud or abuse, and the increased availability of electronic monitoring by CMS and insurance carriers, providers should welcome the billing specialist's or medical coder's efforts related to reviewing patient records for documentation and coding purposes.

REINFORCEMENT EXERCISES 6–4

Write a short answer for each item.

1. Identify the three key components that are required for many E/M codes.

_____

_____

_____

2. Identify the four types of history and examination.

_____

_____

_____

_____

continued on the next page

continued from the previous page

3. What are the required elements of a problem-focused history?

_____

_____

_____

4. Identify the elements of a comprehensive history.

_____

_____

_____

5. List the three conditions that affect medical decision making.

_____

_____

_____

6. List the four types of medical decision making.

_____

_____

_____

_____

7. Identify two requirements for high-complexity medical decision making.

_____

_____

8. What are two of the three requirements for moderate-complexity medical decision making?

_____

_____

9. Briefly define upcoding.

_____

_____

_____

continued on the next page

continued from the previous page

10. Briefly define downcoding.

_____

_____

_____

Fill in the blank.

1. The complexity of establishing diagnoses and selecting treatment options is called _____.

2. A(n) _____ exam is limited to the affected body area or organ.

3. A(n) _____ examination consists of a limited examination of the affected body area or organ system and other symptomatic or related organ systems.

4. An extended examination of the affected body area(s) and other symptomatic or related organ system(s) is called a(n) _____ examination.

5. A(n) _____ examination consists of a general multisystem examination or a complete examination of a single organ system.

Selecting Evaluation and Management Codes

E/M codes are listed in the CPT alphabetic index by type of service. For example, office visit codes are listed under "Office and/or Other Outpatient Services"; consultations under "Consultation"; hospital visits under "Hospital Services"; and so forth.

When services are provided in the physician's or provider's office, the CPT code is usually preprinted on the encounter form or route slip. The physician selects the CPT code, and the billing specialist uses that code for insurance billing.

Even though CPT code assignment is the provider's responsibility, the billing specialist or medical coder reviews the encounter form and patient record to determine if the E/M CPT code accurately describes the diagnosis or service rendered.

> **EXAMPLE**
> The billing specialist receives the encounter form/route slip for a new patient recently treated for acute sinusitis. The provider selected code 99203, "Office or other outpatient visit," which requires the three key components of a detailed history, a detailed examination, and medical decision making of low complexity. The billing specialist knows that this type of service has often been coded as 99202 and takes the following steps:
>
> • Reviews the patient's medical record for additional information
> • Reviews the clinical examples for codes 99202 and 99203 in Appendix C of the CPT manual for a similar situation

In this case, the CPT manual has an example for acute maxillary sinusitis, which is assigned to code 99202. If the patient's record does not furnish additional information, the billing specialist asks the provider for clarification.

In some situations a higher-level E/M code should have been selected, and the billing specialist takes the same steps to verify the accuracy of the selected code. Appendix C, "Clinical Examples," of the CPT manual is a valuable reference because it provides the billing specialist with examples of clinical documentation for the following E/M codes:

- Office or Other Outpatient Services: 99201–99215
- Hospital Inpatient Services: 99221–99233
- Consultations—Office or Other Outpatient Consultations: 99241–99245
- Inpatient Consultations: 99251–99255
- Emergency Department Services: 99281–99285
- Critical Care Services: 99291
- Prolonged Services: 99354, 99355, 99356, 99358, 99359
- Physician Standby Services: 99360
- Care Plan Oversight Services: 99375

The introduction to Appendix C clearly states that the clinical examples are just that—examples—and the required number of key components must be documented in the patient's medical record to select or report a particular E/M code.

When services are provided outside the provider's office, as with hospital services, the provider notes the service and brings the information to the billing specialist or medical coder. In this situation, the billing specialist may be expected to select the appropriate code for insurance billing. Review the following examples and follow the coding steps using a CPT reference, if you have one available.

EXAMPLES

Dr. Rodriguez arrives at the office after making hospital rounds and gives the billing specialist the following list of hospital visits:

A. John Wu—initial inpatient evaluation, detailed H&P, low complexity.
B. Elizabeth Brooks—discharged, 30 minutes.
C. Erik Gervais—hospital visit, second day, detailed exam, high complexity.

A. The billing specialist or medical coder locates Hospital Services in the CPT index. The first entry is "Inpatient Services," which is further indented with descriptions of hospital inpatient services. The range of codes for "Initial Care, new or established patient" is 99221–99233. For John Wu, the billing specialist refers to that range of codes in the "Evaluation and Management" section and selects 99221, "Initial hospital care: detailed or comprehensive history and examination; medical decision making, straightforward or low complexity." All three components are required.

B. The range of codes for "Discharge Services" is 99238–99239. For Elizabeth Brooks, the billing specialist refers to that range of codes in the "Evaluation and Management" section and selects 99238, "Hospital discharge day management; 30 minutes or less."

C.   The range of codes for "Subsequent Hospital Care" is 99231–99233. For Erik Gervais, the billing specialist refers to that range of codes in the "Evaluation and Management" section and selects 99233, "Subsequent hospital care; detailed interval history; detailed examination; medical decision making, high complexity." Two of the three components are required.

Selecting and verifying the accuracy of E/M codes has a positive effect on the financial health of the provider's practice. Accurate codes ensure timely and appropriate reimbursement for services rendered. Inaccurate coding results in payment delays or denials and may even lead to an investigation for fraud or abuse.

Evaluation and Management Modifiers

Although most modifiers apply to surgery or procedure codes, three modifiers are used with E/M codes. Each modifier is listed and described. An example follows each description.

Modifier -24: Unrelated Evaluation and Management Service by the Same Physician [Provider] during a Postoperative Period Modifier -24 identifies that an E/M service unrelated to the original procedure was performed during the procedure's postoperative period.

EXAMPLE

Roger Dodger sees Dr. Pharyngeal for a routine postoperative office visit and suture removal for his recent carpal tunnel surgery. During the visit, Roger tells Dr. Pharyngeal that he has noticed bright red blood in his stools. Dr. Pharyngeal does a rectal exam and notes that Roger has external hemorrhoids. She prescribes a topical medication.

In this example, the correct E/M code is 99212 with modifier -24 to indicate that the physician provided a service unrelated to the suture removal. The billing specialist submits the insurance claim and lists the diagnosis code for hemorrhoids as the first diagnosis and 99212-24 as the first CPT code.

Modifier -25: Significant, Separately Identifiable Evaluation and Management Service by the Same Physician on the Same Day of the Procedure or Other Service Modifier -25 identifies that an E/M service was performed on the same day of a procedure and that the E/M service was above and beyond the usual preoperative or postoperative care. The E/M service may be prompted by the condition that necessitated the procedure.

EXAMPLE

Mr. Wattson was hospitalized for a total hip replacement. Upon returning to his room after surgery, he attempted to get out of bed and fell. Dr. Romero, the surgeon who performed the surgery, was making rounds and assessed Mr. Wattson's injuries and the operative site. Fortunately, Mr. Wattson only suffered a minor bruise on the nonsurgical buttock.

In this example, the correct E/M code is 99232 with modifier -25 to indicate that the assessment of the fall was separate and distinct from the operative service. The physician provides the billing specialist with documentation of the assessment, including a diagnosis. The billing specialist submits an insurance claim with hematoma as the diagnosis and code 99232-25 as the E/M code.

Modifier -57: Decision for Surgery Modifier -57 identifies that an E/M service resulted in the initial decision to perform surgery.

EXAMPLE

Jacqueline Beckwith, a 7-year-old girl, is seen for a sore throat. Rapid strep culture results indicate that Jacqueline has strep throat. This is her fourth episode in six months. Dr. French is concerned that Jacqueline is developing a high tolerance for antibiotic therapy and recommends a tonsillectomy. The parents agree, the surgery is scheduled for the next day, and the doctor completes a preoperative assessment. The Beckwiths' insurance plan includes preoperative services the day before surgery as part of the reimbursement for the surgery.

In this example, the correct E/M code is 99212 with modifier -57 to indicate that the office visit resulted in the initial decision for surgery. The billing specialist submits an insurance claim with the diagnosis code for strep throat and CPT code 99212-57 as the office visit code.

REINFORCEMENT EXERCISES 6–5

Select the correct CPT E/M code for the following services.

1. Office consultation, established patient, with a detailed history and examination, and medical decision making of low complexity. _____

2. New patient office visit, with a problem-focused history and examination, and straightforward medical decision making. _____

3. Initial neonatal intensive care for a critically ill infant. _____

4. New patient home visit with a problem-focused history and examination and straight-forward medical decision making. _____

5. Office visit for a 65-year-old female, established patient, seen for her B-12 injection by the nurse. _____

6. Emergency department visit for a 16-year-old male, who was thrown from his bike, suffered a brief loss of consciousness, and presents with a 4-inch separation of his lower lip and skin from gingival tissue. _____

7. Follow-up consultation for 45-year-old female, status post total proctocolectomy this admission, with terminal ileus requiring revision of stoma, excessive blood loss during second surgery, transfused 5 units of whole blood; recent history of femoral artery blood clot treated with Coumadin. _____

Anesthesia Section (00100–01999)

Anesthesia is the pharmacological suppression of nerve function that is administered by general, regional, or local method. The CPT codes for anesthesia are used to report the administration of anesthesia by an anesthesiologist or nurse anesthetist under the responsible supervision of an anesthesiologist. Anesthesia codes include the following services:

- General, regional, and local anesthesia
- Other support services deemed necessary by the anesthesiologist during the procedure
- Preoperative and postoperative visits by the anesthesiologist
- Care during the procedure
- Monitoring of vital signs
- Administration of blood or any other fluid

Unusual forms of monitoring, such as intra-arterial, central venous, and Swan-Ganz, are not included in the anesthesia codes and should be reported separately.

Moderate (conscious) sedation, with or without analgesia, is reported by using codes 99143–99150 in CPT's "Medicine" section. Codes 99143–99145 apply when the physician performing the procedure also provides the moderate sedation. Codes 99148–99150 apply when the moderate sedation is provided by a physician *other* than the health care professional performing the diagnostic or therapeutic service requiring the sedation. CPT procedure codes that include moderate (conscious) sedation as a part of providing the procedure are summarized in CPT's Appendix G. For these procedures, the physician providing the service *does not* report or submit an insurance claim for the procedure and the sedation.

Anesthesia codes are primarily organized by anatomic site. Table 6–13 lists the anesthesia code categories.

Radiological procedure codes (01916–01936) are used to report anesthesia services related to radiography procedures, such as diagnostic arteriography and cardiac catheterization.

Other procedure codes (01990–01999) are used to report anesthesia for maintaining organ health when harvesting organs from a brain-dead patient, for diagnostic and therapeutic nerve blocks and injections, and for daily management of epidural or subarachnoid continuous drug administration.

Anesthesia Modifiers

Anesthesia services are reported with a five-digit CPT code plus the addition of a physical status modifier that addresses the overall health status of the patient. Table 6–14 lists the modifiers and their meanings. In addition to the physical status modifiers, other CPT modifiers apply to anesthesia codes. Examples follow the modifier descriptions.

Modifier -23: Unusual Anesthesia   Modifier -23 is used to identify situations in which general anesthesia is administered during a procedure that is usually done with no anesthesia or with local anesthesia.

> EXAMPLE
>
> Mrs. Coder's 6-year-old daughter, Melanie, is seen in the emergency department because she pushed a pebble into her left nostril. Although the object can be reached with a snare, Melanie is very agitated and will not allow the physician to remove the pebble. The nurse anesthetist administers a general anesthetic, and the pebble is removed.
>
> In this example, the correct anesthesia code is 00160-23, "Anesthesia for procedures on nose...," with modifier -23 to indicate that the procedure does

TABLE 6–13

Anesthesia Code Categories	
Category	CPT Code Range
Head	00100–00222
Neck	00300–00352
Thorax (Chest Wall and Shoulder Girdle)	00400–00474
Intrathoracic	00500–00580
Spine and Spinal Cord	00600–00670
Upper Abdomen	00700–00797
Lower Abdomen	00800–00882
Perineum	00902–00952
Pelvis (Except Hip)	01112–01190
Upper Leg (Except Knee)	01200–01274
Knee and Popliteal Area	01320–01444
Lower Leg (Below Knee, Ankle, and Foot)	01462–01522
Shoulder and Axilla	01610–01682
Upper Arm and Elbow	01710–01782
Forearm, Wrist, and Hand	01810–01860
Radiological Procedures	01916–01936
Burn Excisions or Debridement	01951–01953
Obstetrics	01958–01969
Other Procedures	01990–01999

© 2014 Cengage Learning, All Rights Reserved.

TABLE 6–14

Anesthesia Physical Status Modifiers	
Modifier	Description
P1	Normal healthy patient
P2	Patient with mild systemic disease
P3	Patient with severe systemic disease
P4	Patient with severe systemic disease that is a constant threat to life
P5	A moribund patient who is not expected to survive without the operation
P6	A declared brain-dead patient whose organs are being removed for donor purposes

© 2014 Cengage Learning, All Rights Reserved.

not usually require anesthesia and this is an unusual case. The anesthesiologist's billing specialist submits an insurance claim with the diagnosis code for presence of a foreign object and the CPT code 00160 with modifier -23 to identify that the anesthesia services were provided under unusual circumstances.

The physician's billing specialist submits an insurance claim with the diagnosis code for presence of a foreign object and the CPT code 30310 for removal of a foreign body, intranasal requiring general anesthesia. Modifier -23 may be added to the CPT code.

Modifier -51 Multiple Procedures   Modifier -51 is used to identify situations in which multiple anesthesia services were provided on the same day or during the same operative episode.

EXAMPLE

Victoria Gervais, a 67-year-old female, was hospitalized for a total hip replacement. Within 12 hours of surgery, she developed "trash foot" syndrome, and it was determined that she had an embolus in her external iliac artery. She was returned to the OR for a direct embolectomy.

In this example, the correct anesthesia code is 01502-51, "Anesthesia... embolectomy direct...," with modifier -51 to identify that this anesthesia service was provided on the same day as another anesthesia service. The billing specialist submits the insurance claim with the diagnosis and anesthesia codes for the total hip replacement listed first and the diagnosis and anesthesia codes for the embolectomy listed next.

Modifier -53: Discontinued Procedure   Modifier -53 is used to identify situations in which the physician elects to terminate or discontinue a procedure because of risk to the patient's health. Do not use this modifier when the procedure is canceled before the patient is prepped for the procedure or anesthesia is started.

EXAMPLE

Ron Lawrence is scheduled for a unilateral radical abdominal orchiectomy for testicular cancer. During the first 10 minutes of the procedure, Mr. Lawrence's blood pressure "bottoms out," and the surgeon decides to close immediately and reschedule the surgery.

In this example, the correct anesthesia code is 00928-53, "Anesthesia... radical orchiectomy abdominal," with modifier -53 to identify that the procedure was discontinued after the induction of the anesthetic agent. The billing specialist submits an insurance claim with the diagnosis code for testicular cancer and the anesthesia code 00928-53.

Anesthesia Add-On Codes

Anesthesia add-on codes are used to describe very difficult circumstances that significantly affect the anesthesia service. The "Anesthesia" guidelines explain these situations, called qualifying circumstances. The qualifying circumstances include extraordinary condition of the patient, notable operative conditions, and unusual risk factors. Add-on codes are not reported alone but in addition to the selected anesthesia CPT code. For purposes of the anesthesia qualifying circumstances

TABLE 6–15

Anesthesia Qualifying Circumstances Add-on Codes	
Add-on Code	**Description**
+99100	Anesthesia for patients of extreme age, younger than 1 year and older than 70
	(For procedures performed on infants younger than 1 year of age at the time of surgery, see 00326, 00561, 00834, 00836.)
+99116	Anesthesia complicated by utilization of total body hypothermia
+99135	Anesthesia complicated by utilization of controlled hypotension
+99140	Anesthesia complicated by emergency conditions; specify the emergency conditions

© 2014 Cengage Learning, All Rights Reserved.

add-on codes, an emergency exists when a delay in treatment would lead to a significant increase in the threat to the patient's life or body part. Table 6-15 lists the qualifying circumstances codes with their meanings.

Anesthesia Code Selection and Reporting

CPT codes from the "Anesthesia" section must be reported on all Medicare insurance claims. Some insurance carriers require anesthesia services to be reported with the applicable surgery code. The billing specialist follows the insurance carrier's guidelines in determining which CPT codes are appropriate for reporting anesthesia services.

> **EXAMPLE**
> Procedure: Thromboendarterectomy of the right carotid artery. Patient is otherwise normal and healthy.
> *Medicare Claim:* CPT code 00350-P1, "anesthesia for procedures on major vessels of [the] neck; not otherwise specified, normal health patient (P1)," is reported on the insurance claim filed for the anesthesiologist and surgeon. The surgeon does not charge for the anesthesia services.
>
> *Non-Medicare Claim:* CPT code 35301, "thromboendarterectomy, including patch graft, if performed; carotid, vertebral, subclavian [arteries], by neck incision," is reported on the surgeon's insurance claim. Depending on the insurance carrier's guidelines, the anesthesia code may or may not be reported with the surgeon's claim.
>
> The anesthesiologist's insurance claim includes the CPT anesthesia code, and may or may not include the CPT procedure code.

When a physician provides anesthesia for surgery that she performs, the appropriate codes from the "Surgery" section are reported with the addition of modifier -47, "Anesthesia by surgeon." Physicians who provide services with moderate sedation, which is sedation with or without analgesia, report the sedation services by using codes 99143–99150, located in the CPT "Medicine" section.

REINFORCEMENT EXERCISES 6–6

Provide a short answer for each item.

1. When is it appropriate to use moderate (conscious) sedation codes from the "Medicine" section?

_____

_____

_____

2. What is the purpose of anesthesia modifiers that begin with the letter P?

_____

_____

_____

3. Write brief definitions for anesthesia modifiers -23, -51, and -53.

_____

_____

_____

4. Briefly describe when it is appropriate to use anesthesia add-on codes.

_____

_____

_____

Surgery Section (10021–69990)

The CPT "Surgery" section includes codes for procedures performed by physicians of any specialty, such as general surgeons, ophthalmologists, dermatologists, and gynecologists. CPT defines surgical procedures in the broadest possible sense of the term, from heart transplant to cystoscopy. The "Surgery" section is organized by body system. Table 6–16 lists the surgery categories and code ranges.

Nearly all surgical categories have several subcategories organized by specific organ, anatomical site, and type of procedure. Accurate code selection depends on a careful review and application of category and subcategory instructions. The patient's medical record must clearly support the selected procedure or surgical CPT code. The physician's notes and operative or procedure report are source documents for identifying the service rendered.

Surgical and procedure codes are listed in the CPT alphabetic index by the specific name of the procedure (e.g., cystoscopy); the type of procedure (e.g., incision, excision,

TABLE 6–16

Surgery Categories and Codes	
Category	**Code Range**
General	10021–10022
Integumentary System	10040–19499
Musculoskeletal System	20005–29999
Respiratory System	30000–32999
Cardiovascular System	33010–37799
Hemic and Lymphatic Systems	38100–38999
Mediastinum and Diaphragm	39000–39599
Digestive System	40490–49999
Urinary System	50010–53899
Male Genital System	54000–55899
Reproductive System Procedures	55920
Intersex Surgery (male to female; female to male)	55970, 55980
Female Genital System	56405–58999
Maternity Care and Delivery	59000–59899
Endocrine System	60000–60699
Nervous System	61000–64999
Eye and Ocular Adnexa.	65091–68899
Auditory System	69000–69979
Operating Microscope	69990

repair, removal); or anatomic site. The billing specialist or medical coder finds surgery or procedure code or code ranges in the alphabetic index. The code or range of codes in the category or subcategory is compared to the documentation in the patient's record and the correct code is selected.

Surgical Package

A surgical package, called a global surgery concept by Medicare, is the range of services included in a surgical procedure. According to CPT guidelines, a surgical package includes:

- Administration of local infiltration, metacarpal/metatarsal/digital block, or topical anesthesia

- Following the decision for surgery, one related E/M encounter on the date of surgery or the day immediately before surgery
- Immediate postoperative care, such as dictating operative notes or talking with the family and other physicians
- Writing orders
- Evaluating the patient in the postanesthesia recovery area
- Typical postoperative follow-up care

For reimbursement purposes, a surgical package is reported under the appropriate surgery or procedure code. For documentation or administrative purposes, the postoperative follow-up office visit is coded and reported with no charge.

EXAMPLE

Following a motor vehicle accident, Marilyn underwent an open reduction, internal fixation for a fractured calcaneus, code 28415. She is seen today for cast removal.

In this example, there is no charge for the cast removal because the service is included in the normal, uncomplicated follow-up care for the open reduction and internal fixation of the fracture. Figure 6–8 illustrates no charge for cast removal.

Figure 6–8 No Charge for Cast Removal

When the postoperative follow-up visits require treatment for surgical complications, the appropriate E/M code is reported for reimbursement for services related to the complication. The diagnosis code for the complication is submitted with the insurance claim.

EXAMPLE

Following a motor vehicle accident, Marilyn underwent an open reduction, internal fixation for a fractured calcaneus, code 28415. She is seen today and states that her foot feels hot. The physician removes a portion of the cast and notes that the surgical site is red and warm to the touch, and he prescribes an antibiotic for a suspected postoperative infection.

If the third-party payer allows payment for services related to postoperative complications, the billing specialist submits an insurance claim for this office visit.

Third-party payers may have a different definition of the surgical package. For patients covered by Medicare, the surgical package is called a global surgery concept. For major surgeries, the Medicare global surgery definition includes the following:

- Preoperative services provided one day prior to surgery or the day of surgery, except when the preoperative service resulted in the initial decision to perform the surgery or when the service provided by the same physician during a postoperative period is unrelated to the original procedure
- The actual surgical procedure
- Postoperative services provided within 90 days of the surgical procedure, except when the service is unrelated to the surgical procedure
- Postoperative services that do not require a return to the operating room, such as dressing changes and care of the operative incision site; removal of sutures, staples, wires, lines, tubes, drains, casts, and splints; urinary catheter care; and care of other postoperative tubes and intravenous lines

For minor and endoscopic procedures, the Medicare global surgery definition includes:

- Preoperative services provided one day prior to surgery or the day of surgery, except when the preoperative service resulted in the initial decision to perform the surgery or when the service provided by the same physician during a postoperative period is unrelated to the original procedure
- The actual procedure
- Postoperative services provided within 10 days of the surgical procedure, except when the service is unrelated to the surgical procedure

Services that are part of a surgical package or global surgery concept cannot be billed individually. This practice is called unbundling and constitutes fraud. Unbundling results in additional reimbursement to the provider for services that are covered by one fee. The billing specialist never unbundles services that are included in a surgical package.

REINFORCEMENT EXERCISES 6–7

Write a short answer for each item.

1. List three ways surgical and procedure codes can be located in the CPT manual alphabetic index.

_____

_____

_____

2. Identify the services included in the CPT definition of a surgical package.

_____

_____

_____

3. What is included in the Medicare global surgery concept?

_____

_____

_____

4. Briefly define unbundling.

_____

_____

_____

Separate Procedures

CPT codes designated as separate procedures are usually carried out as a component of another more comprehensive procedure and under that circumstance cannot be billed separately. In fact, it is fraudulent to attempt to secure reimbursement for a separate procedure when it is part of a more comprehensive procedure or service.

> **EXAMPLE**
> Maria Delgado is hospitalized for a total abdominal hysterectomy, which is to include removal of the ovaries and fallopian tubes.
>   The billing specialist submits an insurance claim for this procedure. Only one procedure code—58150, "Total abdominal hysterectomy (corpus and cervix) with or without removal of tube(s), with or without removal of ovary or ovaries"—is entered on the claim form.

The billing specialist must not code the removal of each organ as a separate procedure (i.e., removal of the cervix, removal of the ovaries, and removal of the fallopian tubes). However, if the separate procedure is actually performed independently, not as a component of another procedure, it may be coded and billed as such.

EXAMPLE

Maria Delgado is hospitalized for removal of ovaries and fallopian tubes. Her uterus and cervix are left intact.

The billing specialist submits an insurance claim for this procedure. The procedure is coded as 58720, "Salpingo-oophorectomy, complete or partial, unilateral or bilateral (separate procedure)." "Modifier -59, distinct service," may be added to the code to explain that the procedure was not performed as a component of a larger procedure.

Modifiers

Modifiers provide additional information about a service or procedure. Surgical modifiers identify the following information:

- A service or procedure has both a professional and a technical component.
- A service or procedure was performed by more than one physician or in more than one location.
- A service or procedure has been increased or reduced.
- Only part of a service was performed.
- An adjunctive service was performed.
- A bilateral procedure was performed.
- A service or procedure was provided more than once.
- Unusual events occurred.

Modifiers are expressed as either a two-digit or a five-digit number, depending on the preference of the third-party payer. A five-digit modifier always begins with 099, and it is the last two digits that distinguish one modifier from another. A hyphen precedes a two-digit modifier. Therefore, modifier -47 and 09947, "Anesthesia by Surgeon," indicates that the surgeon provided regional or general anesthesia for a surgical procedure. Table 6–17 lists the modifiers that can be used with surgery codes. A complete list of all CPT modifiers, with complete descriptions and examples, is located in Appendix A of the CPT manual. Selected examples follow.

EXAMPLE: MODIFIER -47 ANESTHESIA BY SURGEON

Geralyn Adamski, who is in the hospital for delivery of her second child, develops complications that require an emergency cesarean section. The obstetrician administers a saddle block, a regional anesthesia that acts on the perineum and buttocks, and performs the c-section.

In this example, the correct codes are 59514 with modifier -47 to indicate that the obstetrician performed the cesarean section and administered the regional anesthesia and 62311, "Injection...(including anesthetic)... lumbar...," which applies to the saddle block.

EXAMPLE: MODIFIER -50 BILATERAL

Procedure Durwin Rogers, who has experienced recurrent reducible inguinal hernias for the past year, is seen as an outpatient for bilateral hernia repair. The procedure is successful, and Durwin is discharged home within 18 hours.

TABLE 6–17

Surgery Modifiers	
Modifier	**Description**
-22: Increased Procedural Services	The service provided is greater than the service usually associated with a specific procedure.
-26: Professional Component	The physician or other qualified health care professional service is reported separately.
-32: Mandated Service	The service is provided because a third party(e.g., insurance carrier, regulatory agency) requires it.
-47: Anesthesia by Surgeon	The surgeon provided the regional or general (not local) anesthesia for a surgical procedure. Note: Modifier -47 is not used with anesthesia codes.
-50: Bilateral Procedure	Bilateral procedures are performed during the same operative episode; with the exception of procedures that are specified as bilateral.
-51: Multiple Procedures	Multiple procedures are performed on the same day or during the same operative episode; list the primary procedure first; secondary procedures with modifier -51.
-52: Reduced Services	Part of the procedure or service is reduced or eliminated at the discretion of the physician or other qualified health care professional; applies to inpatient procedures or services.
-53: Discontinued Procedure	The procedure is discontinued because of a risk to the patient's well-being; not to be used if an elective procedure is canceled prior to surgical preparation or induction of anesthesia; applies to inpatient procedures or services.
-54: Surgical Care Only	One physician or qualified health care professional performs the surgical procedure and another physician or qualified health care professional provides the preoperative and postoperative care.
-55: Postoperative Management Only	The physician or other qualified health care professional provides postoperative services only.
-56: Preoperative Management Only	The physician or other qualified health care professional provides preoperative services only.
-57: Decision for Surgery	The evaluation and management service results in the initial decision to perform surgery. Note: This modifier applies to evaluation and management codes.
-58: Staged or Related Procedure or Service by the Same Physician or Other Qualified Health Care Professional during the Postoperative Period	An additional procedure related to the original procedure is performed during the postoperative period of the original procedure; the same physician must provide the additional procedure.
-59: Distinct Procedural Service	A procedure or service that is distinct from the original services is provided on the same day as the original services; usually requires a different operative site or organ, a separate incision or excision, or a separate lesion or injury; do not use this modifier if another modifier is more applicable to the situation.

continued on the next page

continued from the previous page

-62: Two Surgeons	Two surgeons are required to perform the procedure; both surgeons must report the service with modifier -62; does not apply to assistant surgeon(s) (see modifier -80).
-63: Procedure Performed on Infants Less than 4 Kilograms	This applies to procedures performed on neonates and infants up to a present body weight of 4 kilograms.
-66: Surgical Team	Procedure is performed by a surgical team; applies to very complex procedures (e.g., organ transplants).
-76: Repeat Procedure or Service by Same Physician or Other Qualified Health Care Professional	A procedure is repeated by the same physician or other qualified health care professional who performed the original procedure.
-77: Repeat Procedure by Another Physician or Other Qualified Health Care Professional	The procedure is repeated by a physician or other qualified health care professional different from the one who performed the original procedure.
-78: Unplanned Return to the Operating/Procedure Room by the Same Physician or Other Qualified Health Care Professional Following Initial Procedure for a Related Procedure during the Postoperative Period	A procedure related to the original procedure is performed during the original procedure's postoperative period (e.g., return to the operating room for malunion of a compound fracture that required surgery). For repeat procedures on the same day, see modifier -76.
-79: Unrelated Procedure or Service by the Same Physician or Other Qualified Health Care Professional during the Postoperative Period	A procedure or service that is unrelated to the original procedure is performed during the original procedure's postoperative period. For repeat procedures on the same day, see modifier -76.
-80: Assistant Surgeon	The physician who assists a surgeon during a particular procedure reports the procedure with modifier -80; the operating surgeon does not use modifier -80.
-81: Minimum Assistant Surgeon	The physician who provided minimal assistance to the operating surgeon reports the procedure with modifier -81; the operating surgeon does not use modifier -81.
-82: Assistant Surgeon (when a qualified resident surgeon is not available)	This applies primarily to teaching hospitals, where surgical residents are often the assistant surgeon; when a surgical resident is not available, another physician may assist the operating surgeon; the operating surgeon does not use modifier -82.
-90: Reference (Outside) Laboratory	This signifies that laboratory procedures/tests were performed by a lab outside the control of the reporting physician or other qualified health care professional.
-91: Repeat Clinical Diagnostic Laboratory Test	This signifies the need to repeat a lab test on the same day that the original test is done; used when multiple test results are necessary to establish a diagnosis; do not use modifier -91 when a test is repeated because of specimen or equipment problems or when the test itself requires multiple results.
-92: Alternative Laboratory Platform Testing	Indicates that the laboratory test is performed using a kit or transportable instrument that is wholly or in part a single use, disposable analytical chamber.
-99: Multiple Modifiers	Alerts insurance carriers that more than one modifier is being submitted on a claim; many insurance carriers limit the number of modifiers that may be reported.

Current Procedural Terminology © 2013 American Medical Association. All Rights Reserved.

In this example, the correct code is 49520 with modifier -50 to signify that two hernia repairs were done during the same procedure. The billing specialist submits an insurance claim that includes the diagnosis code for the bilateral recurrent inguinal hernias and CPT code 49520-50.

EXAMPLE: MODIFIER -51 MULTIPLE PROCEDURES

René Jean was seen for wide excision of basal cell carcinoma, left cheek, and full-thickness skin graft, 15 sq cm, from the right thigh. The skin graft was removed from the patient and the wound closed. The basal cell carcinoma was excised, and the lesion measured 3.0 cm. The wound was covered with the full-thickness graft. All sites were secured with 5-0 Prolene sutures.

In this example, the correct CPT codes are 11643-51 and 15220. Code 11643-51 identifies the excision of carcinoma and another procedure done at the same time. Code 15220 identifies the skin graft as the other procedure.

EXAMPLE: MODIFIER -80 ASSISTANT SURGEON

Dr. Heubert performs a suboccipital craniectomy with cervical laminectomy for decompression of the medulla and spinal cord, with a dural graft. The purpose of the surgery is to correct a malformation of the spine. Dr. Crush assists with the surgery.

In this example, the correct CPT code for reporting Dr. Heubert's service is 61343, "Craniectomy, suboccipital with cervical laminectomy...with or without dural graft...." No modifier is used with Dr. Heubert's bill. The correct CPT code for reporting Dr. Crush's service is 61343-80 to identify Dr. Crush as the assistant surgeon. Both insurance claims must include the diagnosis code that justifies the procedure.

Ambulatory Surgery Center Modifiers

Several CPT modifiers are approved for use with procedures provided in ambulatory surgery centers (ASC) and hospital outpatient departments. CPT modifiers that apply to ASC and hospital outpatient departments include the following:

-**25:** Significant, Separately Identifiable Evaluation and Management Service by the Same Physician or Other Qualified Health Care Professional on the Same Day of the Procedure or Other Service

-**27:** Multiple Outpatient Hospital E/M Encounters on the Same Date

-**50:** Bilateral Procedure

-**52:** Reduced Services

-**58:** Staged or Related Procedure or Service by the Same Physician or Other Qualified Health Care Professional during the Postoperative Period

-**59:** Distinct Procedural Service

-**73:** Discontinued Outpatient Hospital/Ambulatory Surgery Center Procedure Prior to Administration of Anesthesia

-**74:** Discontinued Outpatient Hospital/Ambulatory Surgery Center Procedure after Administration of Anesthesia

-**76:** Repeat Procedure by Same Physician or Other Qualified Health Care Professional

-**77:** Repeat Procedure by Another Physician or Other Qualified Health Care Professional

-78: Unplanned Return to the Operating/Procedure Room by the Same Physician or Other Qualified Health Care Professional Following Initial Procedure for a Related Procedure during the Postoperative Period

-79: Unrelated Procedure or Service by the Same Physician or Other Qualified Health Care Professional during the Postoperative Period

-91: Repeat Clinical Diagnostic Laboratory Test

Except for modifier -27, the description and examples for modifiers that apply to ASC are found on the previous pages and in Table 6–17. For hospital outpatient reporting purposes, modifier -27 may be used to report separate and distinct E/M encounters or services performed in multiple outpatient hospital settings on the same day. Modifier -27 is *not* to be used for services provided by the same physician on the same date in multiple outpatient settings.

REINFORCEMENT EXERCISES 6–8

Fill in the blank.

1. CPT codes designated as _____ are usually part of a more comprehensive procedure.

2. Modifiers are written as a(n) _____ or _____ number.

3. A five-digit modifier always begins with _____.

4. A(n) _____ precedes a two-digit modifier.

Supply the correct CPT code for each procedure.

1. Incisional biopsy of the breast. _____

2. Flexible sigmoidoscopy. _____

3. Repair of bilateral inguinal hernia for a 40-year-old patient. _____

4. Total abdominal proctocolectomy with ileostomy. _____

5. Removal of four benign skin lesions from the back, laser procedure. _____

6. Closed reduction of proximal humerus fracture. _____

7. After falling down a short flight of stairs, Reggie underwent a limited arthroscopic synovectomy of the left knee. The procedure went well, and Reggie is scheduled for discharge this afternoon. _____

8. Myra, a 4-year-old female, has had recurrent episodes of otitis media, difficult to treat with antibiotic therapy. Based on her pediatrician's recommendation, Myra's parents authorized a bilateral myringotomy with placement of tympanostomy tubes. The procedure was done under general anesthetic. _____

9. Willa's abdominal ultrasound revealed the presence of an abdominal aortic aneurysm. Surgical intervention was required, and Willa successfully underwent a repair of the aneurysm. Her prognosis is good. _____

10. Because of failure to pass the kidney stones under medical management, Hank agreed to an ESWL (extracorporeal shock wave lithotripsy). _____

TABLE 6–18

Radiology Categories and Codes	
Category	Code Range
Diagnostic Radiology (Diagnostic Imaging)	70010–76499
Diagnostic Ultrasound	76506–76999
Radiologic Guidance	77001–77032
Breast Mammography	77051–77059
Bone/Joint Studies	77071–77084
Radiation Oncology	77261–77799
Nuclear Medicine	78012–78999

© 2014 Cengage Learning, All Rights Reserved.

Radiology Section (70010–79999)

Radiology procedures are also known as diagnostic imaging procedures. Radiologists and radiology technicians provide radiology services. The radiologist's services are called the professional component, and the radiology technician's services are known as the technical component. The professional component includes supervising the service, reading and interpreting the results, and documenting the interpretation in a report. The technical component includes activities associated with actually doing the diagnostic imaging and the expenses for supplies and equipment. A radiologist may perform both the professional and technical components.

"Radiology" section codes are organized by type of imaging and anatomic site. "Radiology" subsections include instructional notes to assure coding accuracy. The billing specialist or medical coder must pay close attention to these instructional notes. Table 6–18 lists the categories of radiology services and code ranges.

Radiology codes are listed in the alphabetic index by type of exam and anatomic site. For example, brachial angiography is indexed under "Angiography, brachial" and "Artery, brachial angiography."

Radiological Supervision and Interpretation

Many codes in the "Radiology" section include the phrase "radiological supervision and interpretation." When a physician performs the procedure and also provides the supervision and interpretation, two codes are needed. One code relates to the actual radiology service, and the other relates to the injection or introduction of a contrast medium with a needle or catheter.

> **EXAMPLE**
> Bill Hobbs, a local high school football player, is seen for an arthrography of the knee with contrast. Dr. Pierce, an orthopedic physician, injects the contrast medium, completes the arthrography, reviews the film, and documents the findings.
>
> Two CPT codes are needed to fully describe the physician's services. Code 73580 identifies the supervision, interpretation, and documentation of the

findings. Code 27370 identifies the injection of the contrast medium. The instruction note for code 27370 tells the billing specialist to use 75380 to report radiological supervision and interpretation. The billing specialist submits an insurance claim with the diagnosis code and CPT codes 73580 and 27370.

When the radiologist interprets and documents the results of a radiographic procedure, modifier -26, "Professional component," is used to identify the service.

> **EXAMPLE**
>
> Rita Hobbs had a mammogram as part of her annual physical. The radiology technician did a bilateral mammography with two views of each breast. Dr. Watts, a radiologist, reviewed and interpreted the films and documented that there were no changes from the previous films. Dr. Watts sent a copy of the report to Rita's family physician.
>
> The correct radiology code is 77057, "Screen mammography, bilateral, two views of each breast," with modifier -26 to identify that the radiologist completed the professional component of the mammography. The radiologist's billing specialist submits an insurance claim with the diagnosis code and CPT radiology code 77057-26.

Pathology and Laboratory Section (80047–89398)

The CPT "Pathology and Laboratory" section includes services by a physician or by technicians under the responsible supervision of a physician. This section includes codes for services and procedures that range from a straightforward urinalysis to the more complex cytogenetic studies. Table 6–19 lists the categories of pathology and laboratory services and code ranges.

Pathology and laboratory codes are listed in the CPT alphabetic index by the specific name of the test; specific substance, specimen, or sample being tested; and the method used to gather the sample or conduct the test.

> **EXAMPLE**
>
> Complete blood count is indexed under "complete blood count"; bone marrow biopsy is indexed under "bone marrow" and "biopsy, bone marrow"; and fine needle aspiration of thyroid tissue is indexed under "fine needle aspiration."

There is one CPT modifier that is unique to this section. Modifier -90, "Reference (Outside) Laboratory," is used to indicate that a party other than the reporting physician performed the actual laboratory procedure.

Providers who operate a clinical lab within the office practice include frequently ordered lab tests and related CPT codes on the preprinted encounter form. The insurance billing specialist or medical coder must make certain that these codes are updated annually.

Medicine Section (90281–99607)

The "Medicine" section includes a wide range of medical services and procedures, from routine childhood vaccinations to renal dialysis. Table 6–20 lists and briefly describes the categories of medical services and procedures.

Medicine codes are listed in the CPT alphabetic index by type of service and anatomic site. For example, heart catheterization is indexed under "Catheterization, cardiac, left heart, right heart," and "Heart, catheterization."

TABLE 6–19

Pathology and Laboratory Categories and Codes	
Category	Code Range
Organ- or Disease-Oriented Panels	80047–80076
Drug Screening Testing	80100–80104
Therapeutic Drug Assays	80150–80299
Evocative/Suppression Testing	80400–80440
Consultations (Clinical Pathology)	80500–80502
Urinalysis	81000–81099
Molecular Pathology	81200–81479
Multianalyte Assays with Algorithmic Analyses	81500–81599
Chemistry	82000–84999
Hematology and Coagulation	85002–85999
Immunology	86000–86849
Transfusion Medicine	86850–86999
Microbiology	87001–87999
Anatomic Pathology	88000–88099
Cytopathology	88104–88199
Cytogenetic Studies	88230–88299
Surgical Pathology	88300–88399
In Vivo (e.g., Transcutaneous) Laboratory Procedures	88720–88749
Other Procedures	89049–89240
Reproductive Medicine Procedures	89250–89398

TABLE 6–20

Medicine Categories and Descriptions	
Category	Description
Immune Globulins (90281–90399)	Codes identify serum globulin products; report with the CPT administration code.
Immunization Administration for Vaccines/ Toxoids (90460–90474)	Codes apply to administration only; report with the correct vaccine or toxoid code.
Vaccines, Toxoids (90476–90749)	Codes apply to vaccine or toxoid products only.
Psychiatry (90785–90899)	Includes a variety of psychotherapy modalities in various health care settings.

continued on the next page

continued from the previous page

Biofeedback (90901, 90911)	Codes apply to biofeedback methods for retraining sphincter muscles.
Dialysis (90935–90999)	Codes for end-stage renal disease services, hemodialysis, and miscellaneous dialysis procedures.
Gastroenterology (91010–91299)	Codes for various tests related to esophageal, gastric motility, and gastric secretions.
Ophthalmology (92002–92499)	Codes related to ophthalmology services, including supplies.
Special Otorhinolaryngologic Services (92502–92700)	Codes for services related to hearing, vision, and laryngeal functioning.
Cardiovascular (92920–93799)	Codes for therapeutic and diagnostic tests related to the heart and its vessels.
Noninvasive Vascular Diagnostic Studies (93880–93998)	Codes for diagnostic tests related to the function of arteries and veins.
Pulmonary (94002–94799)	Codes for a variety of pulmonary and respiratory function tests.
Allergy and Clinical Immunology (95004–95199)	Codes for a variety of allergy tests and allergy immunotherapy.
Endocrinology (95250, 95251)	Codes for 72-hour glucose monitoring.
Neurology and Neuromuscular Procedures (95782–96020)	Codes for a variety of nerve and muscle function tests (e.g., sleep testing, electromyography, and seizure studies).
Medical Genetics and Genetic Counseling Services (96040)	This code applies to genetic counseling services for each 30 minutes of face-to-face time with the patient or family.
Central Nervous System Assessments/Tests (96101–96125)	Codes apply to services related to CNS function tests (e.g., MMPI, Developmental Screening Test II, and Early Language Milestone Screen).
Health and Behavior Assessment/Intervention (96150–96155)	Codes for assessments related to biopsychosocial factors of physical health problems.
Hydration, Therapeutic, Prophylactic, Diagnostic Injections and Infusions, and Chemotherapy and Other Highly Complex Drug or Highly Complex Biologic Agent Administration (96360–96549)	Codes apply to administration of chemotherapeutic agents by several methods.
Photodynamic Therapy (96567–96571)	Codes for the application of light to destroy lesions.
Special Dermatological Procedures (96900–96999)	Codes apply to dermatology services not covered elsewhere.

continued on the next page

continued from the previous page

Medicine Categories and Descriptions

Category	Description
Physical Medicine and Rehabilitation (97001–97799)	Codes apply to various services related to physical therapy, occupational therapy, tests and measurements, and other services related to rehabilitation medicine.
Medical Nutrition Therapy (97802–97804)	Codes apply to assessment and intervention related to nutrition.
Acupuncture (97810–97814)	Codes apply to acupuncture with or without electrical stimulation.
Osteopathic Manipulative Treatment (98925–98929)	Codes apply to services provided by an osteopathic physician.
Chiropractic Manipulative Treatment (98940–98943)	Codes apply to services provided by a chiropractor.
Education and Training for Patient Self-Management (98960–98962)	Codes apply to patient education services prescribed by a physician and provided by a qualified nonphysician health care provider using a standardized curriculum.
Non-Face-to-Face Nonphysician Services (98966–98969)	Codes apply to telephone and online medical services provided by a nonphysician health care professional.
Special Services, Procedures, and Reports (99000–99091)	Codes apply to a variety of services not covered elsewhere.
Qualifying Circumstances for Anesthesia (99100–99140)	Codes related to complicated anesthesia situations.
Moderate (Conscious) Sedation (99143–99150)	Codes apply to cases when the patient must be able to respond to stimulation or verbal commands during a procedure; a trained observer must be present to assist the physician in monitoring the patient's level of consciousness.
Other Services and Procedures (99170–99199)	Various codes for services not covered elsewhere.
Home Health Procedures/Services (99500–99602)	Codes apply to nonphysician health care professionals providing services in the patient's home.
Medication Therapy Management Services (99605–99607)	Codes apply to a face-to-face assessment between a pharmacist and a patient that is related to the patient's medication regiment.

When a physician or provider renders more than one service on the same day or during the same office or other outpatient visit, each service is coded and submitted for reimbursement.

> **EXAMPLE**
>
> Scott Williamson, a 45-year-old male, is seen for follow-up of the effectiveness of a new hypertension medication and receives a hepatitis B vaccination.

The office visit, established patient, is coded as 99212. The hepatitis B vaccination requires two codes, one for the vaccine and one for the administration of the vaccine: 90746, "Hepatitis B vaccine, adult dosage, for intramuscular use" and 90471, "Immunization administration...one vaccine."

The billing specialist submits an insurance claim for the office visit and vaccination that includes all three codes. As with all insurance billing activities, the patient's record must have sufficient documentation to support all reported services.

REINFORCEMENT EXERCISES 6–9

Fill in the blank.

1. The _____ component of radiology services includes expenses for supplies and equipment.

2. Reading and interpreting the results of a radiology film are part of the _____ component of the service.

3. Modifier _____ identifies the professional component of a radiology service.

4. Modifier _____ is unique to the "Pathology and Laboratory" section of the CPT manual.

Assign the correct CPT codes.

1. A/P and lateral view of the chest. _____

2. Barium enema. _____

3. Follow-up ultrasound, pregnant uterus. _____

4. Blood glucose tolerance test to confirm diabetes mellitus. Three specimens are drawn. _____

5. Gross and microscopic autopsy, without the brain and spinal cord. _____

6. Gross and microscopic examination of prostate tissue following transurethral resection of the prostate. _____

7. Based on Lyle's symptoms, Dr. Howard ordered a blood test to confirm the presence of Epstein-Barr virus or related antibodies. _____

8. Prior to employment, Ellen was vaccinated for hepatitis B. _____

9. Following a stroke, Marty Jones was seen for physical and occupational therapy evaluations. _____

10. Mrs. Shaski, who is diagnosed with end-stage renal disease, and her daughter completed training for peritoneal dialysis with an automated cycler. _____

HEALTHCARE COMMON PROCEDURE CODING SYSTEM (HCPCS)

The information presented here is a brief introduction to the *Healthcare Common Procedure Coding System* (HCPCS). Two levels of codes are associated with HCPCS. HCPCS level I codes are the *Current Procedural Terminology* (CPT) codes. HCPCS level II codes, also called HCPCS national codes, were developed by the CMS. HCPCS level II codes are required by Medicare insurance carriers as well as other health insurance companies. Bulletins provided by Medicare and private insurance carriers alert the agency to the mandated HCPCS codes.

HCPCS level II codes (or HCPCS national codes) are used to report physician and nonphysician services, such as ambulance services, chiropractic services, dental procedures, drugs and medications, and durable medical equipment (DME) companies. Durable medical equipment companies are called durable medical equipment, prosthetics, orthotics, and supplies (DMEPOS) dealers. Medicare guidelines describe DME as equipment that can withstand repeated use, is primarily used to service a medical purpose, is used in the patient's home, and would not be used in the absence of illness or injury. DMEPOS include artificial limbs, braces, medications, surgical dressings, and wheelchairs.

Complete listings of HCPCS codes may be purchased from the U.S. Government Printing office, the local Medicare insurance carrier, or commercial publishers. A read-only spreadsheet with HCPCS codes can be viewed on the CMS website, http://www.cms.gov, using *alpha-numeric HCPCS* as the search phrase. The American Dental Association has copyrighted the D codes, which apply to dental services. A list of D codes must be purchased from that association.

HCPCS Level II: National Codes

Level II HCPCS codes consist of five-digit alphanumeric characters, beginning with a letter and ending with four numbers. Table 6–21 lists the HCPCS sections.

HCPCS Level II: Modifiers

In addition to the alphanumeric codes, HCPCS uses modifiers that provide further information about services provided to the patient. For Medicare claims, HCPCS level II modifiers may be used with either HCPCS or CPT codes. Private insurance carriers may also allow level II modifiers to be combined with CPT codes. Modifiers do not change the basic definition of the service or procedure and are used to describe the following types of information:

- The service was provided by an anesthesiologist.
- The service was performed by a nonphysician health care professional (clinical psychologist, nurse practitioner, physician assistant).
- The service was provided as part of a specific government program.
- Equipment was purchased or rented.
- Single or multiple patients were seen during nursing home visits.

There are literally hundreds of modifiers, and they are updated as needed. Table 6–22 and Table 6–23 list some of the more commonly used modifiers. Table 6–22 includes modifiers associated with services and procedures. Table 6–23 includes modifiers associated with transportation or ambulance services that identify the point of origin and the point of destination of the ambulance.

TABLE 6–21

HCPCS Level II Sections	
Section	**Description**
A codes	Transportation Services, Including Ambulance, Medical and Surgical Supplies, Administrative, Miscellaneous, and Investigational Services
B codes	Enteral and Parenteral Therapy
C codes	Outpatient Prospective Payment System
D codes	Dental Procedures
E codes	Durable Medical Equipment (DME) (e.g., wheelchair)
G codes	Procedures/Professional Services (Temporary)
H codes	Alcohol and Drug Abuse Treatment Services
J codes	Drugs Administered Other Than Oral Method
K codes	Temporary Codes (Durable Medical Equipment codes established by Medicare Administrative Contractors)
L codes	Orthotic Procedures and Devices
M codes	Medical Services
P codes	Pathology and Laboratory Services
Q codes	Miscellaneous Services (Temporary Codes)
R codes	Diagnostic Radiology Services
S codes	Temporary National Codes (Non-Medicare)
T codes	National T Codes Established for State Medicaid Agencies
V codes	Vision Services

TABLE 6–22

HCPCS Modifiers for Services/Treatment	
Modifier	**Description**
-AA	Anesthesia services furnished by anesthesiologist
-AH	Clinical psychologist
-AJ	Clinical social worker
-AS	Physician assistant, nurse practitioner, or clinical nurse specialist for assistant at surgery
-E1	Eyelid, upper left
-F1	Left hand, second digit

continued on the next page

continued from the previous page

HCPCS Modifiers for Services/Treatment

Modifier	Description
-F5	Right hand, thumb
-LC	Left circumflex coronary artery (Hospitals use with codes 92980–92984, 92995, 92996)
-LT	Left side
-NU	New equipment
-RC	Right coronary artery (Hospitals use with codes 92980–92984, 92995, 92996)
-RT	Right side
-TD	Registered nurse
-T1	Left foot, second digit
-T5	Right foot, great toe

© 2014 Cengage Learning, All Rights Reserved.

TABLE 6–23

HCPCS Transportation Modifiers

Modifier	Description
D	Diagnostic or therapeutic site other than P or H when these are used as origin codes
E	Residential, domiciliary, custodial facility (except skilled nursing facility)
G	Hospital-based End-Stage Renal Disease (ESRD) facility
H	Hospital
I	Site of transfer (e.g., airport or helicopter pad) between modes of ambulance transport
J	Free-Standing ESRD facility
N	Skilled nursing facility (SNF)
P	Physician's office
R	Residence (e.g., patient's home)
S	Scene of accident or acute event
X	Destination code only; intermediate stop at physician's office (includes nonhospital facility or clinic) en route to the hospital

© 2014 Cengage Learning, All Rights Reserved.

EXAMPLE: HCPCS MODIFIER FOR PROCEDURES/SERVICES

Marissa was recently diagnosed with obsessive-compulsive disorder (OCD). She meets with a clinical psychologist for a 30-minute individual counseling session.

The billing specialist submits the insurance claim with the code 90832-AH. CPT code 90804 means the patient received up to 30 minutes of face-to-face counseling, and the modifier -AH means the service was provided by a clinical psychologist.

Rebecca Stone, a 70-year-old Medicare patient, underwent excision of tendons, right palm and left middle finger.

The correct CPT codes are 26180, *excision of tendon, finger, flexor, each tendon*; and 26170, *excision of tendon, palm, flexor, single, each [tendon]*.

Since these codes are noted as "separate procedures," CPT modifier -59 is needed to indicate that the procedures were distinct and unrelated.

HCPCS modifiers -F2, *third digit, left hand* and -RT, *right side,* are needed to clarify the location of each procedure.

The billing specialist submits an insurance claim with the following codes:

    26180-F2, *excision of tendon, finger, flexor…, each tendon, third digit, left hand.*

    26170-59-RT, *excision of tendon, palm flexor, single…, each, distinct procedural service, right side.*

Figure 6–9 CPT/HCPCS Modifiers

EXAMPLE: HCPCS TRANSPORTATION MODIFIER

Vicki Gervais went into insulin shock and was transported by ambulance from her home to the local hospital.

    The appropriate HCPCS code for ambulance service is modified with the letters RH. The letter *R* identifies the point of origin as the patient's home (residence), and the letter *H* identifies the destination as a hospital. For transportation modifiers, the point of origin character is first and the destination character is second.

Figure 6–9 gives examples of CPT codes that include HCPCS modifiers.

Selecting HCPCS Level II Codes

Depending on payer guidelines, some services must be reported with both the CPT and HCPCS codes. The administration of an injection is a good example of assigning a CPT and HCPCS code. The CPT code is assigned to the service, administrating the injection, and the HCPCS code identifies the medication.

Most nongovernment insurance carriers require CPT codes. However, if a CPT code does not provide specific enough information to ensure correct payment, the HCPCS level II code may provide enough detail for reimbursement.

When a service can be identified by both a CPT and HCPCS code, Medicare guidelines give priority to the HCPCS code *when the CPT code is less specific than the HCPCS code.*

ABBREVIATIONS

Table 6–24 lists the abbreviations presented in this chapter.

TABLE 6–24

Abbreviations and Meanings	
Abbreviation	**Meaning**
AMA	American Medical Association
ASC	ambulatory surgery center
CC	chief complaint
CCCC	complex chronic care coordination
CMS	Centers for Medicare and Medicaid Services
CPT	*Current Procedural Terminology*
CT	computerized tomography (scan)
DME	durable medical equipment
DEMPOS	durable medical equipment, prosthetics, orthotics, and supplies
ECG	electrocardiogram
EEG	electroencephalogram
E/M	Evaluation and Management
ESWL	extracorporeal shock wave lithotripsy
FDA	Food and Drug Administration
FH	family history
HCPCS	*Healthcare Common Procedure Coding System*
HHS	Department of Health and Human Services
HIPAA	Health Insurance Portability and Accountability Act
HPI	history of present illness
OCD	obsessive-compulsive disorder
ROS	review of systems
SH	social history
SNF	skilled nursing facility
TCM	transitional care management

 SUMMARY

Current Procedural Terminology (CPT) is the accepted coding system for nearly all provider services in ambulatory or outpatient settings and some provider services associated with hospital and long-term care. CPT is maintained and published by the American Medical Association (AMA).

The CPT manual and codes are updated annually. Billing specialists and medical coders must use the most current version so accurate codes are assigned. Extensive instructions throughout the CPT manual provide guidelines for code assignment. CPT's six main sections are "Evaluation and Management," "Anesthesia," "Surgery," "Radiology," "Pathology and Laboratory," and "Medicine." Each section has additional instructions that are unique to the section.

Coding conventions for CPT include semicolons, bullets, triangles, facing triangles, plus signs, circled bullets, null zero or the universal no code symbol, the number symbol, and the cross-reference terms "see" and "see also." The conventions provide information about a specific code. Modifiers, which are expressed as a two-digit number preceded by a hyphen, are reported with the main CPT code and indicate that special circumstances affected the provided service.

Healthcare Common Procedure Coding System (HCPCS), a common procedure coding system, is maintained and published by the Centers for Medicare and Medicaid Services (CMS). HCPCS includes level I, CPT codes, and level II, national codes. Level II codes are used to report services such as drugs, chiropractic services, dental procedures, and durable medical equipment. Level II codes are a five-digit alphanumeric number. Modifiers are used to identify special circumstances related to the level II codes.

All insurance carriers closely monitor CPT and HCPCS codes for accuracy. Medicare insurance carriers are bound by law to report any suspected fraudulent or abusive billing practices, which are often associated with inaccurate coding. Upcoding, downcoding, and unbundling are three examples of fraudulent activities associated with coding. The billing specialist and medical coder play an important role in ensuring coding accuracy by reviewing the patient's record for documentation that supports the provider-selected code.

REVIEW EXERCISES

CPT Coding Exercises

Assign the correct CPT code to each statement or case. Use modifiers as necessary.

1. Laparoscopic cholecystectomy with cholangiography. _____

2. Diagnostic arthroscopy followed by removal of the medial meniscus by arthrotomy. _____

3. Cardiac catheterization, right side only, with conscious sedation, IV. _____

4. Influenza vaccine, intramuscular, 65-year-old patient. _____

5. GI series x-ray, with small bowel and air studies, without KUB (kidneys, ureters, and bladder). _____

6. Retrograde pyelography with KUB. _____

7. Stool for occult blood. _____

8. Throat culture, bacterial. _____

9. Home visit, problem-focused, established. _____

10. Initial hospital visit, new patient, high complexity. _____

11. Office consultation for an established patient, high complexity with surgery scheduled for tomorrow. _____

12. Assistant surgeon, cesarean section, delivery only. _____

13. Abdominal hysterectomy, surgery only. _____

14. Postoperative management of vaginal hysterectomy. _____

15. Mrs. Rogers, a new patient, is seen for a complete physical examination. She has osteoarthritis, hypertension, and insulin-dependent diabetes mellitus. A detailed history and exam was performed with medical decision making of low complexity. _____

16. Normal newborn history and physical examination. _____

17. Routine well-baby care for 6-month-old infant, previously seen at six-week checkup. _____

18. Cardiovascular stress test on a 56-year-old male with recent EKG changes, physician supervision only. _____

19. Dr. Chen performed an ultrasound on a pregnant woman, 16 weeks gestation, for complete fetal and maternal evaluation (first pregnancy). _____

20. Endometrial biopsy for postmenopausal bleeding on a new patient. _____

21. Syphilis test qualitative. _____

22. MaryAnn Parrish is seen in the office today for a blood pressure check, which is performed by the nurse under the physician's supervision. _____

23. Tonia Zeebart, a 45-year-old female, is seen in the office today for an annual physical. She is in good health and has no complaints. Dr. Roy performs a comprehensive history and physical and counsels Tonia on proper diet and exercise. Tonia is a new patient. _____

24. Left nasal endoscopy for control of epistaxis. _____

25. Flexible fiber-optic laryngoscopy performed for removal of a dime that was stuck in the patient's larynx. _____

26. Active immunization with live measles, mumps, and rubella virus vaccine during an annual preventive medicine visit on a 5-year-old, established patient. _____

27. Bonita Matilda arrives at the emergency department by ambulance. She was involved in a motor vehicle accident. The ED (emergency department) physician performs a comprehensive physical examination and notes swelling of the left foot at the medial and lateral malleolus with ecchymosis on the dorsal surface of the foot. There is tenderness at both malleoli and on the heel portion of the foot. The extensor tendon sheaths appear swollen. X-ray of the left foot and thigh show a lateral malleolus avulsion and a lateral calcaneus comminuted fracture. Dr. Footloose is called for a surgical consultation. He examines Bonita and admits her to the operating room for an open reduction, pin fixation of the fractured calcaneus. _____

28. Rashael Kroll, a 10-year-old female, was chasing her younger sister Chelsea and fell through a sliding glass door. Rashael sustained two lacerations: Left knee, 5.5 cm laceration involving deep subcutaneous tissue and fascia, repaired with layered closure using 1% lidocaine local anesthesia; left hand, 2.5 cm laceration of the dermis, repaired with simple closure under local anesthesia. Follow-up in 10 days for suture removal. _____

CODING CHALLENGE

Read the following procedure reports and write the diagnosis and procedures in the space provided. Assign the diagnosis codes and CPT procedure codes. These cases relate to outpatient or ambulatory episodes of care.

1. PROCEDURE REPORT

> PATIENT NAME: Loonsfoot, Peter
> DATE OF PROCEDURE: January 11, 20xx
> PROCEDURE: Sigmoidoscopy and hemorrhoidectomy.
> INDICATIONS: Mr. Loonsfoot developed perianal discomfort, itching, and a palpable
> perianal mass. There was no history of blood loss.
> DESCRIPTION: The patient was brought to the operating room, placed in the recumbent position, and general anesthesia was induced. He was then placed in the lithotomy position. Proctosigmoidoscopy was carried out with a rigid scope and inserted to approximately 25 centimeters. No mucosal lesions were seen. One prolapsed and thrombosed hemorrhoid was revealed. The scope was withdrawn and the perianal area prepped and draped in the usual manner. The hemorrhoid was grasped with a clamp and placed in traction. An elliptical incision was made and the hemorrhoid was resected without difficulty. Several bleeders were electrocoagulated, but no significant bleeding occurred. The area was prepped and a Nupercainal impregnated sponge was placed in the anal canal. Sterile dressings were applied. The patient was taken to recover in good condition.
> FINDINGS: Internal hemorrhoid with prolapse and partial thrombosis.

DIAGNOSIS(ES): _____

PROCEDURE(S): _____

2. PROCEDURE REPORT

> PATIENT NAME: Estrada, Justin
> DATE OF PROCEDURE: February 20, 20xx
> DIAGNOSIS: Family medical history of colon cancer, 1st degree relative.
> PROCEDURE: Colonoscopy with polypectomy.
> INDICATIONS: Mr. Estrada is a 60-year-old male with a family history of colon cancer. His father died at age 68 from colon cancer.
> DESCRIPTION: The patient was brought to the procedure room and was put into conscious sedation. He was placed in the left lateral decubitus position, and the colonoscope was introduced through the anus and advanced to the cecum. The quality of the prep was good, and the colon was clean. The colonoscope was slowly withdrawn, and visual inspection revealed a 2 mm sessile polyp in the ascending colon. No bleeding was present. Polypectomy was performed with hot forceps. Resection was complete and all tissue retrieved. Examination of the sigmoid colon revealed the presence of a few diverticula.
> FINDINGS: 1. Single polyp, all tissue removed. 2. Diverticulosis.

> OUTCOME/INSTRUCTIONS: The patient tolerated the procedure well. There were no complications, and he was discharged to his wife. The patient was advised not to drive or operate any equipment or machinery for 24 hours. He should immediately report any bloating, rectal bleeding, or fever.

DIAGNOSIS(ES): _____

PROCEDURE(S): _____

3. PROCEDURE REPORT

> PATIENT NAME: Fishbone, Wanda
> DATE OF PROCEDURE: March 20, 20xx
> DIAGNOSIS: Nuclear cataract with cortical spoking, right eye.
> PROCEDURE: Extracapsular cataract extraction (ECCE) with a posterior chamber intraocular lens implant, right eye.
> DESCRIPTION: The patient was brought to the procedure room and placed in the supine position. Periorbital akinesia and anesthesia were achieved with a 50/50 mixture of 2% Xylocaine and 0.75% Marcain given in a retrobulbar fashion. A total of 3 cc of solution was used. The patient's periorbital areas were prepped and the right eye was draped in the usual fashion. The lids of the right eye were retracted, and an 8-0 black silk bridle suture was passed under the superior rectus tendon, and the globe was retracted downward. A conjunctival peritomy was then performed for 180 degrees. Hemostasis was obtained with wet-field cautery. A corneoscleral groove was then formed approximately 2 mm posterior to the surgical limbus and beveled anteriorly. The anterior chamber was entered with a razor blade incision and filled with Healon. The anterior capsulotomy was then performed using a can-opener technique. The wound was opened to its full extent with scissors. The nucleus was expressed without difficulty. A model 6741-B, 23 diopter, posterior chamber lens was irrigated and inserted into the capsular bag without difficulty. The surgical site was closed in the usual manner.
>
> The patient tolerated the procedure well and was transferred to the recovery area in excellent condition. Barring any difficulties, she will be discharged home early this evening.

DIAGNOSIS(ES): _____
PROCEDURE(S): _____

4. PROCEDURE REPORT

> PATIENT NAME: Applewood, Cedric
> DATE OF PROCEDURE: March 20, 20xx
> PROCEDURE: Catheterization of the left heart with left ventricular angiography.
> INDICATIONS: Mr. Applewood presented in the ER with unstable angina pectoris, symptomatically.

> DESCRIPTION: The patient was brought to the catheterization laboratory, and the right groin was prepped, draped, and anesthetized. The right femoral artery was accessed. A #7 French sheath was introduced and a #7 French JL4 catheter was advanced to the left coronary artery and was visualized. This was then exchanged for an Amplatz R1 catheter, and the right coronary artery was visualized in different views. This was then exchanged for a #7 French pigtail, and left ventricular angiograms were obtained. The patient tolerated the procedure well, and the sheaths were left in place.
>
> FINDINGS: 1. Mild coronary artery disease with 30% occlusion of the left circumflex artery, native. 2. A 20% occlusion of the right coronary artery, native, and a 30% stenosis of the left anterior descending artery, native. 3. Left ventricular angiography revealed a normal size left ventricle and no mitral regurgitation.

DIAGNOSIS(ES): _____

PROCEDURE(S): _____

5. PROCEDURE REPORT

> PATIENT NAME: Brindley, Sandra
> DATE OF PROCEDURE: April 15, 20xx
> INDICATIONS: Recurrent epigastric distress.
> PROCEDURE PERFORMED: Esophagogastroduodenoscopy (EGD) with removal of foreign bodies (bezoar), biopsy of the duodenum and stomach.
> DESCRIPTION: Under sedation, the patient's throat was anesthetized with Cetacaine spray, and the Olympus video endoscope was introduced. The gastroesophageal junction was encountered, and the stomach was entered, insufflated, and examined. The bezoar was immediately noted. The bezoar was plucked with biopsy forceps and flushed. It was suctioned and gently irrigated in the distal duodenum. The duodenal bulb was examined. The scope was withdrawn into the stomach, and remaining bezoar material was identified and removed. The scope was then reintroduced into the pylorus, and duodenal and bulbar biopsies were obtained. Mild bleeding was noted and hemostasis achieved. The patient tolerated the procedure well and was taken to the recovery room in excellent condition.
> FINDINGS: At the gastroesophageal junction, there was minimal erythema, consistent with grade I gastroesophageal reflux disease. Underlying diffuse gastritis was present. Pyloric and duodenal bulb ulcerations were present. Biopsies of the duodenal bulb, gastric pylorus, and gastric antrum were obtained after removal of the bezoar.

DIAGNOSIS(ES): _____

PROCEDURE(S): _____

CHALLENGE EXERCISE

1. Obtain copies of various physician office encounter forms. Review the forms for CPT codes and check the codes against the current CPT manual. Are any codes on the encounter form outdated? Are there typographical errors in the code section? As the billing specialist, how would you approach the manager or provider in order to solve these problems?

WEBSITES

American Medical Association: http://www.ama-assn.org
Centers for Medicare and Medicaid Services: http://www.cms.gov/hcpcs

CHAPTER 7

Developing and Processing an Insurance Claim

LEARNING OBJECTIVES

Upon successful completion of this chapter, the reader should have the knowledge to:

1. Describe the activities associated with developing and processing an insurance claim.
2. Define all key terms presented in the chapter.
3. Differentiate between primary and secondary insurance.
4. Describe three source documents for completing the CMS-1500.
5. Discuss the purpose of an explanation of benefits and health care claim summary.

KEY TERMS

Adult primary policy
Adult secondary policy
Allowed charge
Birthday rule
Charge slip
Clean claim
CMS-1500
Co-insurance
Co-insurance payment
Co-pay
Co-payment
Custodial parent
Daily accounts receivable journal

Daily transaction journal
Day sheet
Delinquent claim
Dirty claim
Electronic health (medical) record (EHR; EMR)
Encounter form
Explanation of benefits (EOB)
Fair Debt Collection Practices Act (FDCPA)
Final notice
Health care claim summary

Health Insurance Portability and Accountability Act (HIPAA)
New patient
Noncustodial parent
Patient account ledger
Pending claim
Primary insurance
Reimbursement
Remittance advice (RA)
Routing form
Secondary insurance
Superbill
Transaction journal

OVERVIEW

The health care industry exists primarily to provide health and medical services to patients. From the largest university-based hospital to the solo physician practice, members of a health care team take pride in their ability to provide quality patient care. All health care agencies must receive payment for services rendered. If the hospital, physician office, or clinic cannot remain solvent, everybody loses. Patients lose services, employees lose jobs, and the community loses the services of the agency and the benefits of the revenue generated by the agency.

Reimbursement, which means receiving payment for services rendered, is everybody's business. From the moment the patient enters the office until the insurance claim is submitted and paid, complete and accurate information must be captured. Many health care providers and agencies process or submit insurance claims for their patients. The patient must give complete and accurate information in order to take advantage of this service. Office staff must accurately record patient demographic and insurance information; clinical staff must accurately record services rendered to the patient, and the reasons for the services; medical coders must accurately assign diagnosis and treatment codes; and insurance billing specialists must accurately report the required information to the insurance carrier.

This chapter covers the activities associated with developing and processing an insurance claim. Developing an insurance claim includes patient registration, clinical assessment and treatment, and patient departure procedures. Insurance claims processing includes generating and submitting an insurance claim, claims follow-up, and credit and collections. Patient registration and insurance billing are often the first steps taken to implement an electronic health (medical) record (EHR; EMR).

> EXAMPLE
>
> Patient registration is accomplished by entering the patient's name and demographics into a database. The database is updated as necessary. Charges for the visit are entered, and software programs generate various forms such as a route slip, current account statement, and the insurance billing document.

Whether the office uses a manual or computer system, the process remains the same. In fact, the agency must have a well-organized manual system prior to adopting an electronic health record. If the manual system is faulty, the problems will carry over to the electronic system. The old saying "garbage in, garbage out" remains true today!

 ## DEVELOPING AN INSURANCE CLAIM

Developing an insurance claim begins when an individual calls to schedule an appointment. If the individual is a new patient, preliminary information is taken to be sure the physician can provide the appropriate services. If the individual is an established patient, the appointment is scheduled.

Health Insurance Portability and Accountability Act (HIPAA) privacy and security rules have a direct impact on patient registration procedures. Most offices have installed "privacy" windows in the registration area to prevent patients who are waiting to be seen from overhearing staff conversations and phone calls. Patient sign-in sheets are modified so that only a blank line is available. This prevents patients from seeing the names of individuals who were seen throughout the day. Computer monitors are fitted with privacy shields so that information on a computer screen is visible only to the individual using the computer. HIPAA privacy and security rules are discussed in Chapter 2.

New Patient Procedures

A new patient is defined as a person who is being seen by a physician for the first time or a person who has not received services within the past three years. In a multispecialty clinic, a new patient is a person who is being seen for the first time or who has not received services from any physician or provider of the same specialty within the past three years.

When a new patient calls for an appointment, the receptionist asks for the following information:

- Patient's name, address, phone number, and birth date; if the patient is a minor, the name and phone number of the parent or guardian
- The reason for the appointment
- Name of the insurance company, identification numbers, insured's name, and the employer's name (if the insurance is provided through the employer)

When the insurance plan is unfamiliar to the office staff or when there is a question about which physician the patient should see, offer to return the patient's call within a specific time frame. This gives the insurance billing specialist time to verify insurance eligibility and benefit coverage. Clinical staff can use this time to determine whether the patient should be seen and to identify the health care professional who can best provide the service.

> **EXAMPLE**
>
> Yolanda calls and asks for an appointment with Dr. Small. Yolanda is new to the area, and a neighbor has recommended this physician. Yolanda has diabetes and has ABC insurance through her employer. Dr. Small, an internist, usually does not see people with diabetes. Another physician, Dr. Large, takes those cases. In addition, the practice has no experience with ABC insurance.
>
> The receptionist offers to return the call and explains that Dr. Large usually takes new patients with a diabetes diagnosis. The receptionist then discusses the new patient request with the physician and routes the insurance information to the billing specialist. The billing specialist communicates with the insurance carrier and inquires about deductibles, co-payments, and benefit coverage.

Once the physician has agreed to take the new patient and insurance information is verified, the receptionist calls the individual and schedules an appointment. At this time, the receptionist should:

1. Ask the patient about previous medical treatment. The patient should arrange to supply medical records before the initial appointment. If this is not possible, the patient must sign an authorization to release information when he or she registers as a new patient.
2. Remind the patient to bring insurance verification, which is usually an insurance identification card.
3. Discuss the provider's payment policy.

Some providers collect the co-pay or co-insurance on the day of the appointment. Many practices expect payment if the charges are less than a certain amount, regardless of insurance coverage. If the physician is a nonparticipating or out-of-network provider, the patient will likely be responsible for a greater percentage, if not all, of the bill.

Individuals enrolled in a managed care plan and who expect the managed care plan to pay for services must have preauthorization from the primary care physician in order to see a specialist. Preauthorization can be a referral form or letter from the primary care physician or a phone call from a case manager who provides verbal authorization. The referral can be faxed to the specialist's office or hand-carried by the patient. Individuals enrolled in a managed care plan may see a specialist at their own expense without preauthorization.

Patient Registration Form and Authorizations: New Patient

Many offices ask new patients to come in a few minutes before the scheduled appointment. When the patient arrives, the receptionist provides a copy of the patient registration form and makes a copy, front and back, of the insurance card. Figure 7–1 is a sample patient registration form.

When the registration form is completed, the receptionist checks for any unanswered questions; obtains the patient's authorization to release information to the insurance company; reviews the payment policy; and gives the patient a copy of the office's privacy policy. If previous medical records are needed, the patient signs an authorization to release information for each office or hospital that has the medical information. A sample release of information form for medical records is shown in Chapter 2. Figure 7–2 is a sample authorization for insurance billing.

The receptionist prints an encounter form, which is also called a charge slip, routing form, or superbill. The encounter form is one of the source documents for financial, diagnostic, and treatment information related to the office visit or episode of care. Figure 7–3 is a sample encounter form.

The encounter form includes the following sections:

Heading: physician names; office or clinic information
Examination and Treatment Section: type of visit; lab tests; treatments; diagnoses; referrals/comments; diagnosis and treatment codes. The charges for the visit, lab tests, and treatments are entered in the Fee columns.
Billing Information: date of service; patient name and DOB; charges; payment; balance; assignment of benefits; patient signature with date

The receptionist circles the name of the physician who will see the patient and attaches the encounter form to the medical record. The rest of the encounter form is completed by the physician and billing clerk or billing specialist.

In an electronic environment, the receptionist enters patient registration information into the database by using the registration form as a source document, or asking the patient for the information. Figure 7–4 through Figure 7–7 illustrate patient registration information.

Figure 7–4 shows the patient's demographic information. Note that the patient's account number, name, and physician are at the top of the screen. Field 21 at the bottom, right corner of the screen identifies the responsible party for paying the bill. When *self* is checked, the patient has insurance; when *guarantor* is checked, the patient is covered by someone else's insurance.

Figure 7–5 shows the name of the patient's spouse, parent, or legal guardian. When the patient is covered by the spouse's, parent's, or legal guardian's insurance, *yes* is selected in Field 2, *Guarantor.*

Figure 7–6 shows information related to the primary insurance, the insurance company that is billed first. In this figure, Deanna Hartsfeld has Medicare as her primary insurance.

SUPERIORLAND CLINIC
714 Hennepin Avenue
Blueberry, ME 49855

PATIENT REGISTRATION

DATE: 06/05/20xx

PATIENT INFORMATION

PATIENT'S LAST NAME:	FIRST NAME:	MIDDLE INITIAL:	DOB:	SSN:
HELLMAN	ABIGAIL	M	10/30/1960	555-50-5555

PATIENT'S ADDRESS:	PHONE: Home: (906) 555-2345
714 HENNEPIN ANYTOWN ME 49855	Work: (906) 555-3456

SINGLE: MARRIED: X WIDOWED:	MALE: FEMALE: X

OCCUPATION:	EMPLOYER/ADDRESS:	EMPLOYER PHONE:
TEACHER	ANYTOWN ELEMENTARY SCHOOL 301 W SPRUCE ANYTOWN ME 49855	(906) 555-3456

EMERGENCY CONTACT:	RELATIONSHIP TO PATIENT:	PHONE: Home: (906) 555-2345
PAUL HELLMAN	HUSBAND	Work: (906) 555-6066

REASON FOR TODAY'S VISIT:
SORE THROAT

WORK RELATED INJURY/ILLNESS?	AUTO ACCIDENT?	OTHER ACCIDENT?
YES: NO: X DATE:	YES: NO: X DATE:	YES: NO: X DATE:

INSURANCE INFORMATION

INSURANCE CO.	GROUP NO:	INSURED'S ID NO:
AETNA	87000	503529750

INSURED'S NAME:	INSURED'S DOB:	RELATIONSHIP TO INSURED:
ABIGAIL HELLMAN	10/30/1960	SELF: X SPOUSE: CHILD: OTHER:

INSURED'S ADDRESS:	INSURED'S PHONE:	INSURED'S EMPLOYER:
SAME	SAME	SEE ABOVE

OTHER INSURANCE

SECONDARY INSURANCE:	GROUP NO:	ID NUMBER:	EMPLOYER:
CIGNA	89000	614630861	QUALITY CONTRACTORS

OTHER INSURED'S NAME:	OTHER INSURED'S DOB:	RELATIONSHIP TO PATIENT:
PAUL HELLMAN	11/12/1959	SPOUSE

OTHER INSURED'S ADDRESS:	OTHER INSURED'S PHONE:
SAME	SAME

AUTHORIZATION

I hereby authorize my insurance company benefits to be paid directly to the physician. I realize that I am responsible to pay for any non-covered services. I hereby authorize the release of pertinent medical information to the insurance company.

Patient/Legal Representative Signature: *Abigail Hellman*   Date: 06/05/20xx

Figure 7–1 Patient Registration Form

(Practice Letterhead Here)

*Authorization for Release of Medical Information to the Insurance Carrier
and Assignment of Benefits to Physician*

COMMERCIAL INSURANCE

I hereby authorize release of medical information necessary to file a claim with my insurance company and ASSIGN BENEFITS OTHERWISE PAYABLE TO ME TO _____(fill in physician's name)_____ MD, PA.

I understand that I am financially responsible for any balance not covered by my insurance carrier. A copy of this signature is as valid as the original.

Signature of patient or guardian_____   Date _____

MEDICARE INSURANCE

BENEFICIARY _____   MEDICARE NUMBER_____

I request that payment of authorized Medicare benefits be made either to me or on my behalf to ____(fill in physician's name)____ for any services furnished to me by that physician. I authorize any holder of medical information about me to release to the Centers for Medicare and Medicaid Services and its agents any information needed to determine these benefits or the benefits payable for related services.

Beneficiary Signature _____   Date _____

MEDICARE SUPPLEMENTAL INSURANCE

BENEFICIARY _____   Medicare Number _____

                                                                                 Medigap ID Number _____

I hereby give (name of physician or practice) permission to ask for Medicare Supplemental Insurance payments for my medical care.

I understand that (name of Medicare supplemental insurance carrier) needs information about me and my medical condition to make a decision about these payments. I give permission for that information to go to (name of Medicare supplemental insurance company).

I request that payment of authorized Medicare supplemental benefits be made either to me or on my behalf to (name of physician or practice) for any services furnished me by that physician. I authorize any holder of medical information about me to release to (name of Medicare supplemental insurance company) any information required to determine and pay these benefits.

Beneficiary Signature _____   Date _____

Figure 7–2 Authorization for Insurance Billing

Figure 7–7 displays information related to the secondary insurance, the insurance company that is billed after payment is received from the primary insurance. In this figure, Simon Hartsfeld is Deanna's spouse, and he also has insurance through his employer.

In an electronic environment, the patient's insurance card may be scanned into the database. Some health care providers also require some form of identification, such as a driver's license, which is also scanned into the database. Patient registration information and scanned items like the insurance card and driver's license establish the patient's electronic medical (health) record (EMR).

ELIZABETH FOY, MD CHARLES FRENCH, MD ROBERT HOWARD, MD DENZEL HAMILTON, MD ROBERTA PHARYNGEAL, MD HENRY ROMERO, MD						**SUPERIORLAND CLINIC** 714 HENNEPIN AVENUE BLUEBERRY, ME 49855 PHONE: (906) 336-4600 FAX: (906) 336-4020			
NEW PATIENT	**CODE**	**FEE**	**LAB TEST**	**CODE**	**FEE**	**LAB TEST**		**CODE**	**FEE**
Level I	99201		AST	84450		LDH		83615	
Level II	99202		Albumin/Serum	82040		Lipid Panel		80061	
Level III	99203		Alk Phos	84075		Metabolic Panel/Comp		80053	
Level IV	99204		BUN	84520		Obstetric Panel		80055	
Level V	99205		CBC/Automated	85027		Occult Blood		82270	
ESTABLISHED PATIENT			CBC/Diff/Automated	85025		PAP Smear/Automated		88147	
Level I	99211		CK/CPK/Isoenzymes	82552		PPD Skin Test		86580	
Level II	99212		Drug Screen	80100		Prothrombin Time		85610	
Level III	99213		Electrolyte Panel	80051		PSA		84152	
Level IV	99214		Estrogen	82671		Rapid Strep Screen		87880	
Level V	99215		Glucose/Blood	82947		Sed Rate/automated		85652	
OFFICE CONSULTATION			GTT	82951		TSH		84443	
Level I	99241		HgbA1C	83036		Urinalysis/automated/ micro		81001	
Level II	99242		Hepatitis Panel	80074					
Level III	99243		HIV-1/HIV-2/Single Result	86703					
Level IV	99244								
Level V	99245		**OTHER TESTS**			**OTHER TESTS**			
HOSPITAL INPATIENT			A/P Chest X-ray			Holter/24 hr			
Initial/Complex	99223		DXA Scan	77080		Sigmoidoscopy		45330	
Subsequent	99231		EKG Int/Report	93000		Stress Test		93015	
EMERGENCY DEPARTMENT SERV.			Rhythm EKG	93040					
Level I	99281								
Level II	99282								
Level III	99283		**TREATMENTS**	**CODE**	**FEE**	**TREATMENTS**		**CODE**	**FEE**
Level IV	99284		Flu Shot	90658					
Level V	99285								

DIAGNOSIS						
Abdominal Pain	789.00	Gastritis	535.50	OTHER DIAGNOSIS		CODE
Angina Pectoris, Unspec.	413.9	Hemorrhoids, NOS	455.6			
Asthma, Unspecified	493.90	Hiatal Hernia	553.3			
Bronchitis, Acute	466.0	Hyperlipidemia, NOS	272.4			
Bursitis	727.3	Hypertension, Unspec.	401.9			
CHF	428.0	Hyperthyroidism	242.90	REFERRAL/COMMENTS		
Colon Polyp	211.3	Hypothyroidism	244.9			
Conjunctivitis, Unspec.	372.00	Osteoarthritis, Unspec	715.90			
Diabetes Mellitus, Type I	250. 01	Osteoporosis, Postmen.	733.01			
Diabetes Mellitus, Type II	250.00	Pleurisy	511.0			
Diverticulosis, Colon	562.10	Serious Otitis Media, Acute	381.01			
Emphysema	492.8	UTI	599.0			

DATE	PATIENT NAME		DOB	CHARGES	PAYMENT	BALANCE

I authorize my insurance benefits to be paid directly to the above named physician. I understand that I am obligated to pay deductibles, copayments, and charges for non-covered services. I authorize release of my medical information for billing purposes.

PATIENT SIGNATURE: **DATE:**

Figure 7–3 Encounter Form

Established Patient Procedures

When an established patient requests an appointment, the appointment is scheduled, and the receptionist may update the patient's database at that time. The patient is instructed to bring his or her insurance card, especially if the patient has a new or different insurance plan. At the time of the appointment, demographic and insurance information is updated or verified as necessary.

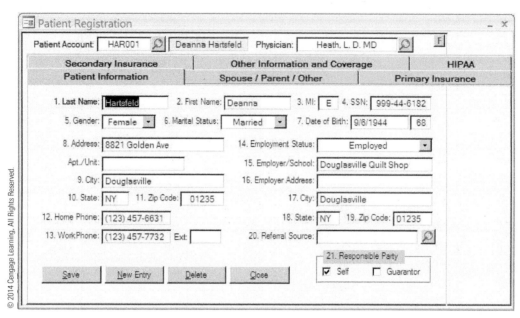

Figure 7–4 Patient Demographic Information

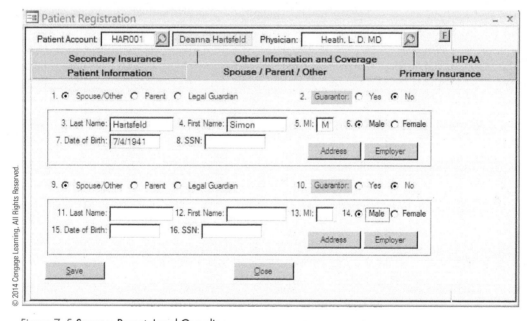

Figure 7–5 Spouse, Parent, Legal Guardian

If the insurance plan has changed, the new insurance card is either copied (front and back) or scanned into the database. The patient must also sign an authorization to release information to the new insurance company. An established patient has the option to accept a copy of the privacy policy, or sign a waiver refusing the copy.

Primary and Secondary Insurance Policies

Patients may have more than one health insurance policy. The insurance billing specialist identifies the primary payer, the insurance company that is billed first. Once the primary payer has

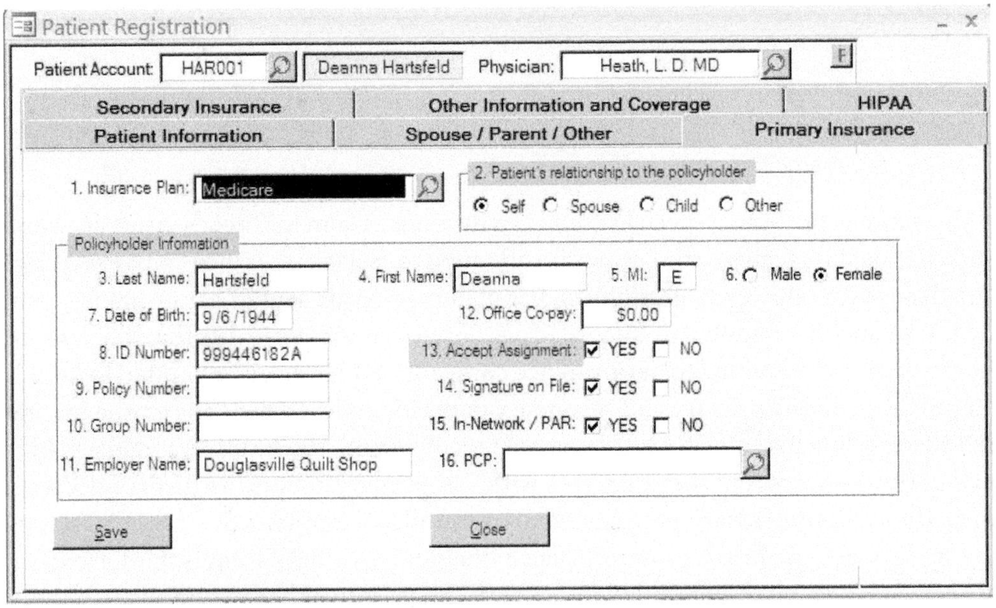

Figure 7–6 Primary Insurance

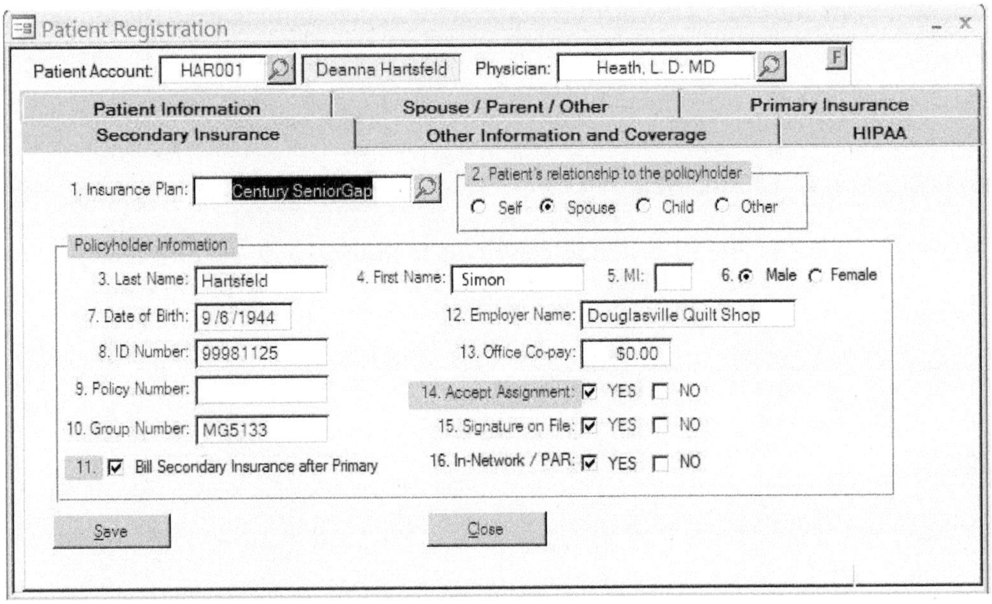

Figure 7–7 Secondary Insurance

fulfilled its responsibility, the claim is submitted to the secondary payer. Insurance benefits must be coordinated so the total amount paid does not exceed 100% of the charges.

Determining primary and secondary payer status depends on whether the patient is an adult or a child. When the patient is an adult, the adult primary policy is the insurance policy that lists the patient as the subscriber, insured, or dependent on the primary insurance plan. The adult secondary policy is the insurance policy that lists the patient as the subscriber, insured, or dependent on the secondary insurance plan.

EXAMPLE

Roger is employed at Penelope Paints. His employer provides health insurance. Roger is identified as the subscriber on his company insurance policy. Roger's wife, Helen, who is employed by Rhoda Rooter, Inc., lists Roger as a dependent on her company insurance policy.

In this example, the billing specialist sends an insurance claim to Roger's insurance company first. Once payment is received, the balance is submitted to Helen's insurance company. If Helen is listed as a dependent on Roger's health plan, her medical bills are sent to her insurance company first, and the balance is submitted to Roger's. If neither Roger nor Helen lists the other as a dependent, Roger's claim is submitted to his insurance company and Helen's is submitted to hers.

Determination of the primary and secondary payer for children depends on the marital and custodial status of the parents. When the parents are divorced, the health insurance plan of the custodial parent—the parent the child lives with—is primary, unless the divorce decree states otherwise. If the parents remarry, the custodial parent plan is primary, the custodial stepparent plan is secondary, and the health insurance plan of the noncustodial parent is third. However, the divorce decree may assign responsibility for medical expenses to either parent.

For children living with both parents—and if both parents have insurance coverage—primary and secondary payer status is determined by the birthday rule. Under the birthday rule, the primary payer is the insurance policy of the parent whose birth month and day come earlier in the calendar year. The year of the birth is not a factor in determining primary and secondary payer status.

REINFORCEMENT EXERCISES 7–1

Briefly describe how the listed individuals contribute to insurance claims processing.

1. Patient

_____

_____

2. Receptionist

_____

_____

3. Clinical staff

_____

_____

4. Insurance billing specialist

_____

_____

continued on the next page

continued from the previous page

5. Medical coder

_____

_____

Provide a brief definition for each term or a short answer for each question.

1. New patient

_____

_____

_____

2. Patient registration form

_____

_____

_____

3. List the three instructions the receptionist should give to a new patient when an appointment is scheduled.

_____

_____

_____

4. Name two forms that a new patient completes during the first encounter.

_____

_____

_____

Fill in the blank with the correct term or phrase.

1. The insurance company billed first is called the _____ .

2. The insurance company billed second is called the _____ .

3. For children, the health insurance plan of the _____ is billed first when parents are divorced, unless the divorce decree states otherwise.

4. The _____ is the insurance policy that lists the patient as the subscriber or policyholder.

5. The patient's _____ is verification of insurance coverage.

CLINICAL ASSESSMENT AND TREATMENT

Once registration is completed, the patient is ready to be seen by the health care provider. The patient's concerns and reason for the appointment are assessed. The assessment can be a brief medication review or a comprehensive physical examination. Diagnostic and laboratory tests may be ordered and completed during the visit. The health care provider is responsible for documenting all aspects of patient care and treatment. The health care provider enters sufficient information in the patient's medical record to justify the services provided and the charges billed. Written clinical justification is required for every diagnostic test and treatment.

The health care provider also completes the clinical sections of the encounter form, which include examinations, laboratory tests, and diagnosis. The encounter form (Figure 7–3) lists five different codes for *new patient, established patient, office consultation,* and *emergency department services*; and two different codes for *hospital inpatient*. The physician checks the level and code that best describes the services rendered. If the office has its own clinical laboratory, the physician checks the lab tests that the patient needs. When lab or diagnostic tests are done outside of the office, the patient receives an order for those tests.

The physician or provider makes note of referrals, the time frame for follow-up appointments, or other comments in the space labeled "Referral/Comments." The authorization statement to pay the physician directly and to release medical information to insurance carriers is signed by the patient.

In an electronic environment, the physician enters information into the patient's electronic medical record. Laptops and other portable data entry devices are becoming common place in the physician's office. The physician and other health care providers access assessment and clinical screens. Documentation is captured by clicking on preset information such as the level of service and diagnoses; or by keying text, such as symptoms and signs. At the conclusion of the visit, the patient is instructed to take the encounter form to the reception area.

PATIENT DEPARTURE PROCEDURES: NEW AND ESTABLISHED PATIENTS

Patient departure procedures include scheduling another appointment if necessary; computing the charges for current services; posting charges and payments; and assigning numeric codes to all procedures and diagnoses. Once all of the information is collected, the billing specialist generates and submits the insurance claim form.

Scheduling and Billing

After seeing the health care provider, the patient is directed to the reception area, and if necessary, another appointment is scheduled. The receptionist may also enter today's charges on the encounter form and ask the patient if he or she intends to make a payment. The patient signs the authorization statement on the encounter form. In many offices, once the receptionist has taken care of appointments or referrals, the patient is directed to the billing clerk. The billing clerk enters the current charges and inquires about a payment.

Patients without insurance are responsible for the entire charge. The agency may require full payment for charges under a specific dollar amount. This information should be clearly posted or communicated to the patient when the appointment is scheduled. Charges that exceed the full-payment threshold are billed to the patient. Some agencies have a payment schedule that includes a monthly finance charge for the unpaid balance.

Patients with health insurance may be required to pay a portion of the charge. Most insurance policies stipulate a co-payment, also called co-pay, or a co-insurance payment, also called co-insurance. A co-payment is a specific dollar amount that the patient must pay the provider for each encounter. A co-insurance payment is a specific percentage of the charge that the patient must pay. Example A illustrates co-payment, and example B illustrates co-insurance.

EXAMPLE A
ABC Insurance Company requires a $20 co-payment for each encounter. The patient is responsible for $20, and the remainder is submitted to the insurance company. In this example, the co-payment should be collected during the departure procedures.

EXAMPLE B
ABC Insurance Company pays 80% of all charges, and the patient is responsible for the remaining 20% as a co-insurance payment. In this example, the billing specialist has two options: (1) compute the patient's share of the charge and collect all or a portion of that amount or (2) inform the patient that once the insurance payment is received, the patient will receive a bill for the balance.

When a payment is made, the balance due is entered in the appropriate space of the encounter form. The patient receives a receipt for the payment, and a copy of the encounter form. In an electronic environment, charges are posted to the patient's account. The patient may sign an electronic signature pad to authorize release of information for billing purposes, and to allow the insurance company to send the payment directly to the physician. The billing clerk prints a copy of the receipt and encounter form for the patient.

Posting Charges and Payments

The billing department is responsible for posting (entering) all charges and payments to the patient's account. Encounter forms are the source documents for charges. Checks, receipts, and insurance statements are the source documents for payments. Charges and payments are posted to the patient account ledger, which is a permanent record of financial transactions between the patient and the agency, and to the daily accounts receivable journal, which is also called a day sheet or daily transaction journal. The transaction journal is a summary of charges, payments, and current balance for a given day.

Most health care agencies use a computerized billing system. The billing system may be an application of the electronic health record software or a separate software program. In the electronic environment, charges, payments, and other billing information are entered into the patient's database. Each patient is assigned an identification number that allows any information to be entered or retrieved by that number. Once the billing information is entered, the software simultaneously updates patient accounts and other financial records. The billing specialist can generate statements, receipts, insurance claim forms, patient account ledgers, accounts receivable journals, and other financial reports as needed. Figure 7–8 is a sample of an electronic patient account ledger. Refer to the figure as you read the description of each field.

The top of the screen displays the patient's account number and name.

- Field 1, Ref Number, captures the name or identification number of a referring physician.
- Field 2 is the name of the physician or provider who saw the patient.
- Field 3, POS, is the point of service, which is the location where the service was provided. The number 11 is the code for "physician office."

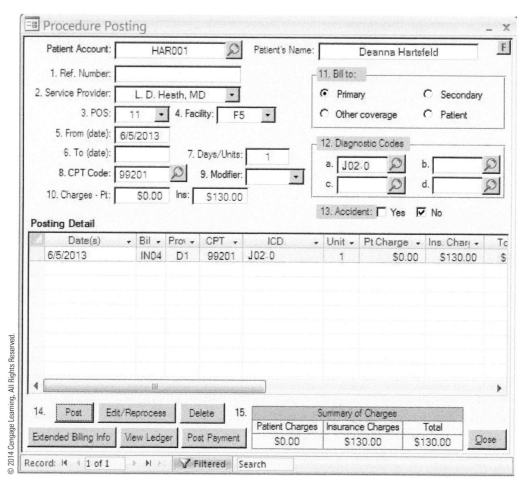

Figure 7-8 Patient Account Ledger

- Field 4, Facility, captures the code for the name of the facility that provided the service.
- Field 5, From (date), and Field 6, To (date), capture the dates of service. When services are provided on one day, only Field 5 is completed.
- Field 7, Days/Units, indicates the number of services rendered. In Figure 7–8, only one service—the office visit—is posted. The number 1 is entered in Field 7.
- Field 8, CPT code, and Field 9, Modifier, capture the CPT code and any modifier code that apply to the service.
- Field 10, Charges Pt./Ins:, is used to enter charges the patient is responsible for, such as co-pays, and charges that will be submitted to the insurance company.
- Field 11, Bill to:, indicates if the claim is submitted to the primary, secondary, other insurance, or directly to the patient.
- Field 12, Diagnostic Codes, captures the diagnoses codes that justify the services identified in Field 8. Note: Field 12 is an ICD-10-CM diagnosis code.
- Field 13, Accident, identifies if the patient's problems are the result of an accident. Injuries due to work-related or other accidents may be covered by worker's compensation insurance, or other home, auto, or business insurance.

In Figure 7–8, the "Posting Detail" fields are automatically filled in when the billing specialist clicks on "Post" in Field 14. Field 15, Summary of Charges, is also automatically filled-in.

SUPERIORLAND CLINIC		TRANSACTIONS JOURNAL			06/25/20XX	
PATIENT ID	PATIENT	DESCRIPTION	PREV BAL	CHARGE	PAYMENT	NEW BAL
121548	HELLMAN A	99213 OV	450.00	45.00	50.00	445.00
121548	HELLMAN A	BCBS PAYMENT	445.00		45.00	405.00
121550	BURLESON T	AETNA PAYMENT	100.00		50.00	50.00
121551	SMART I	PT CHCK 3234	50.00		50.00	0.00
121552	LIGHTFOOT C	99205 OV	0.00	75.00		75.00
121552	LIGHTFOOT C	LAB TESTS	75.00	200.00		275.00
121552	LIGHTFOOT C	PT CHCK 501	275.00		60.00	215.00
TOTAL			1395.00	320.00	255.00	1460.00

Figure 7–9 Sample Transaction Journal

The Posting Detail summarizes the information from Fields 1 through 12. The headings for the Posting Detail are:

Date(s): the date of service
Bil: the identification code assigned to the insurance company
Prov.: the identification code assigned to the physician or provider
CPT: the CPT code for the service rendered
ICD: the current ICD code for the diagnosis
Unit: the number of services provided
Pt Charge: the amount charged to the patient
Ins. Charge: the amount billed to the insurance carrier

The billing specialist enters information for each service that was provided on a given date of service.

After all charges and payments are entered into the system, the billing specialist can generate a daily transaction journal (day sheet). The transaction journal summarizes the charges, payments, and current balance for each patient treated on a specific day. Figure 7–9 is an example of a transaction journal.

ASSIGNING NUMERIC CODES

Accurate treatment, procedure, and diagnosis codes are needed for reimbursement. The provider is responsible for circling all applicable preprinted codes on the encounter form. When the encounter form is the source document for entering codes, the billing specialist uses the circled codes for insurance claims. In an electronic environment, when the physician selects the diagnoses, lab tests, and other treatments from preset lists, the CPT and ICD codes are automatically entered in the patient's EMR.

If the physician or provider documents diagnoses, lab tests, and treatments that are not printed on the encounter form, or are not part of the EMR database, the diagnoses, lab tests, and treatments must be coded. Medical coders may be responsible for assigning these codes and entering them into the patient's EMR. Every lab test and treatment must be related to a diagnosis or problem that was addressed during the office visit. Variations between diagnoses and tests can result in delayed or denied claims. In a worst case scenario, variations between diagnoses and lab tests or treatments can lead to allegations of fraud.

EXAMPLE

Marilyn is seen for an infected insect bite. The physician examines the area and writes a prescription for a topical antibiotic. Marilyn has diabetes and is concerned about the accuracy of her glucometer. The physician orders a blood glucose lab test. "Infected insect bite" is written on the encounter form, and the glucose lab test and related code are circled.

If the billing specialist submits the insurance claim with the codes for an infected insect bite diagnosis and a blood glucose lab test, there is a good chance the claim will be denied. A blood glucose test is not related to an infected insect bite. To receive payment for the blood test, the appropriate diabetes code must be included on the insurance claim.

REINFORCEMENT EXERCISES 7–2

Provide a brief definition for each term or a short answer for each question.

1. What is the difference between co-payment and co-insurance?

_____

_____

_____

2. Patient account ledger

_____

_____

_____

3. Transaction journal

_____

_____

_____

4. What is the purpose of assigning numeric codes to patient services?

_____

_____

_____

continued on the next page

continued from the previous page

5. List and describe three activities associated with patient departure procedures.

 INSURANCE CLAIMS PROCESSING

Insurance claims processing includes submitting the insurance claim, posting payments, and resolving problem claims. Once charges are posted and diagnoses and procedures are coded, the billing specialist submits either a paper or electronic insurance claim. A paper claim is submitted on the CMS-1500, which is the most commonly used insurance claim form. The patient's insurance identification, registration form, encounter form, and medical and account records are source documents for CMS-1500 completion. The CMS-1500, developed by the Centers for Medicare and Medicaid Services (CMS) and approved by the American Medical Association (AMA), has been in use for many years. A detailed discussion of CMS-1500 completion guidelines is presented in Chapter 8. In today's health insurance environment, most claims are submitted electronically. A detailed discussion of electronic claims submission is covered in Chapter 9. Claims are usually submitted in batches that cover a specific time frame, either daily or weekly.

Insurance Carrier Procedures

Once the insurance carrier receives a claim, it is reviewed for errors and omissions. Standard error edits, which are part of the insurance company's computer program, search for the following:

- Patient and policy identification to validate that the patient is covered by the policy
- CPT codes to determine if the services are covered by the policy
- ICD codes to confirm the medical necessity of the services and treatment

Insurance carriers may have other standard edits unique to a specific insurance policy. For example, if the patient is a full-time student between the ages of 19 and 23, an edit function could request verification of enrollment. Discrepancies between gender and condition may be reviewed. For example, a claim for a patient coded as "male" with a "postmenopausal syndrome" diagnosis would trigger an error/edit flag. Payment for the claim is put on hold until the discrepancy is resolved.

If the claim is accepted, the insurance carrier computes the payment due to the provider or patient. Payment is sent to the provider when the patient assigns the benefit to the provider. Otherwise, the payment is sent to the patient. Payment depends on the deductible, co-payment, co-insurance, and the allowed charge. The allowed charge is the maximum amount paid for a specific service. Allowed charges are based on a variety of factors, which may include the following:

- The average or usual and customary fee in a geographic area for a specific service
- The average or usual and customary fee by provider type for a specific service
- A percentage of the average or usual and customary fee
- The amount negotiated by the policyholder, employer, or provider with the insurance company
- An arbitrary amount set by the insurance policy or carrier

Allowed charges are usually less than the provider fee. Allowed charges are *never* more than the provider fee.

The insurance company generates an explanation of benefits (EOB), which explains how the reimbursement is determined. An EOB is always sent to the patient and the provider. The provider's EOB, also called remittance advice (RA), is a summary of all benefits paid to the provider, within a certain time frame, for all patients covered by a specific insurance policy. Figure 7–10 is an example of a generic provider EOB. Note that more than one patient is listed on the EOB.

In Figure 7–10, each entry includes the patient's name, procedure code, date of service, charges, approved amounts, amount the patient (subscriber) may owe the provider, and the amount that the insurance policy paid toward the bill. Few, if any, insurance plans pay 100% of the original charges. The difference between the amount charged and the amount paid may be billed to the patient. However, several government-sponsored health insurance programs do not allow the physician to bill the balance to the patient.

The patient receives an EOB, also called a health care claim summary. The EOB summarizes how the insurance company determined the reimbursement for the services the patient received. The reverse side of an EOB often has answers to commonly asked questions about the EOB, an antifraud hotline number, and definitions for terms used in the EOB. Figure 7–11 is a sample patient EOB. In this example the provider participates in the insurance carrier's reimbursement program and agrees to accept the insurance benefit as payment in full. Note that the form is clearly marked with the statement "This Is Not a Bill."

Review the EOB in Figure 7–11 and note the following:

- The name of the provider for each service is listed.
- Provider charges are itemized.
- The insurance payment is subtracted from the total charge.
- The balance of the charge not covered in the payment is highlighted (boxed).
- The explanation statement tells the patient why a certain amount was not paid.

The EOB provides a toll-free number and an address for patient inquiries.

Posting Insurance Payments

Once the insurance carrier sends the EOB with a payment, the billing specialist enters or posts the payments to the appropriate patient account. Figure 7–12 illustrates the information captured for a payment posting:

- Top of Screen. Patient account number; patient name
- Field 1. Procedure Charge History: list of charges
- Field 2. Payer: insurance company identification number and name
- Field 3. Date: posting date
- Field 4. P'mnt Type (Insurance Payment): PAYINS means insurance payment
- Field 5. Reference #: payment identification number, such as a check number
- Field 6. Amount Paid: self-explanatory
- Field 7. P'mnt Type (Patient Payment): patient cash; patient check; other (credit card)
- Field 8. Reference #: patient check number; credit card number
- Field 9. Amount Paid: self-explanatory
- Field 10. Adjust: code for the reason a charge was adjusted
- Field 11. Adj. Amt: dollar amount of the adjustment

Any Insurance Company, USA		EXPLANATION OF BENEFITS Check Voucher				Check # 88099 Provider: 007
PATIENT NAME	PROCEDURE CODE	SERVICE DATE	ORIGINAL CHARGES	APPROVED AMOUNT	SUBSCRIBER MAY OWE	ANY INSURANCE PAID
APPLE A1230	99215	06-28-xxxx	193.99	161.09	16.10	144.99 sub total: 144.99
BELL B4560	85023 83718 81000 36415 80016	06-24-xxxx 06-24-xxxx 06-24-xxxx 06-24-xxxx 06-24-xxxx	36.75 59.06 21.00 6.04 51.45	28.96 10.27 16.05 5.37 36.85	.00 .00 .00 .00 .00	28.96 10.27 16.05 5.37 36.85 sub total: 97.50
CHAMP C7890	85023 83718 81000 36415 80016	06-25-xxxx 06-25-xxxx 06-25-xxxx 06-25-xxxx 06-25-xxxx	36.75 59.06 21.00 6.04 51.45	28.96 10.27 16.05 5.37 36.85	.00 .00 .00 .00 .00	28.96 10.27 16.05 5.37 36.85 sub total: 97.50
DELL D0120	99215 85641 81000 36415	06-29-xxxx 06-29-xxxx 06-29-xxxx 06-29-xxxx	193.99 25.20 21.00 6.04	161.09 17.12 16.05 5.37	16.10 .00 .00 .00	144.99 17.12 16.05 5.37 sub total: 183.53
ECHO E0340	45330	06-22-xxxx	241.24	217.96	.00	217.96 sub total: 217.96
FRANK F0560	85023 80002	06-29-xxxx 06-29-xxxx	36.75 40.52	28.96 30.54	.00 .00	28.96 30.54 sub total: 59.50
GRAY G0780	36415	06-24-xxxx	6.04	5.37	1.07	4.30 sub total: 4.30
HEATH H0900	76075 36415	06-28-xxxx 06-28-xxxx	253.05 6.04	185.15 5.37	.00 .00	185.15 5.37 sub total: 190.52
INCH	81000	06-22-xxxx	21.00	16.05	1.60	14.45 sub total: 14.45
JAVA	82270	06-22-xxxx	28.35	8.95	1.79	7.16 sub total: 7.16
KELLY	82270	06-28-xxxx	28.35	8.95	.00	8.95 sub total: 8.95
Check Date: 07-07-xxxx		Provider Code: 0 F3 7149			Page Total	1026.36

FOR INQUIRIES PLEASE USE YOUR ANY INSURANCE COMPANY TOLL FREE SERVICE NUMBER

Figure 7–10 Provider Explanation of Benefits

- Field 12: Deductible: self-explanatory
- Field 13: Balance Due: amount the patient owes, including any unpaid deductible

Once the payment is posted, the patient account ledger is updated. Figure 7–13 is a sample patient ledger. Field 8 displays a summary of the posting and the balance due.

| ID NO | 406-76-1759 | DATE | JUN 08, 20xx |

HEALTH CARE CLAIM SUMMARY

This summary shows claims processed for the insured of   Baril, Viola   ID NUMBER   406-7

Any payments shown were made during the period of   JUN 01, 20xx   through   JUN 08, 20xx

| TOTAL CHARGES PROCESSED | $400.00 |

| TOTAL PAID TO YOU | $.00 | TOTAL PAID TO PROVIDER | $360.00 |

| TOTAL AMOUNT NOT PAID | $40.00 |

This amount is the sum of the LESS DEDUCTIBLE column plus the AMOUNT NOT PAID column

PLEASE REFER TO THE CODES IN THE EXPL COLUMN AND THEIR EXPLANATIONS.

CLAIM NUMBER	PATIENT	PROVIDER (PROV)	TYPE OF SERVICE	SERVICE DATES FROM	TO	TOTAL CHARGES	BASIC PAYS YOU OR PROVIDER	ELIGIBLE CHARGES	MAJOR MEDICAL LESS DEDUCT-IBLE	PAYS YOU OR PROVIDER	AMOUNT NOT PAID
8138064538	BARIL	H. Sleeper	ANESTHESIA	040300	040300	400.00		400.00		360.00PROV	40.00
						400.00	.00PROV	400.00	.00	360.00PROV	40.00

IF YOUR BENEFIT SUMMARY INCLUDES CHARGES YOU DON'T RECOGNIZE, IT COULD BE THE RESULT OF A MISHANDLED OR FRAUDULENT CLAIM. PLEASE NOTIFY YOUR CUSTOMER SERVICE REPRESENTATIVE.

EXPLANATION:

872 THIS AMOUNT IS THE COINSURANCE (SHARE) THAT IS YOUR RESPONSIBILITY UNDER YOUR POLICY

THIS IS NOT A BILL

FOR CUSTOMER ASSISTANCE CALL TOLL FREE 1-800-553-2084

SEND WRITTEN INQUIRIES TO: ANTHEM INSURANCE COMPANIES, INC, PO BOX 590, GREENWOOD IN 46142-0590

DEAR INSURED: This summary of claims received on behalf of you and any other persons covered under your policy. We are providing it to you to help you better understand how your coverage is working to protect you.

CONTACT US AT THE PHONE OR ADDRESS SHOWN ABOVE:

IF YOU HAVE MOVED; we will correct your address.

IF YOUR IDENTIFICATION CARD HAS BEEN LOST OR STOLEN; we will replace it.

IF YOU HAVE ANY QUESTIONS ABOUT THIS CLAIM SUMMARY OR YOUR COVERAGE; we will be glad to answer them.

ADDITIONAL REMINDERS:

- WE CANNOT RETURN ANY PAPERS YOU SEND US. If you need to send us this summary or any other papers, please make photocopies beforehand. You may need them for income tax purposes.
- YOU HAVE THE RIGHT TO APPEAL ANY CLAIM WE DON'T PAY OR PAY ONLY IN PART. Mail us a request to review your claim within sixty (60) days of the date you received this summary.   32N-0233 r3(09-90) D

Figure 7–11 Patient Explanation of Benefits

Insurance Claim Follow-Up

Claims that are paid on the first submission are often called clean claims. Unfortunately, all insurance claims do not fall into this category. The billing specialist works with a variety of problem claims. Problem claims include denied and delinquent claims. Claims that are denied, delayed, or

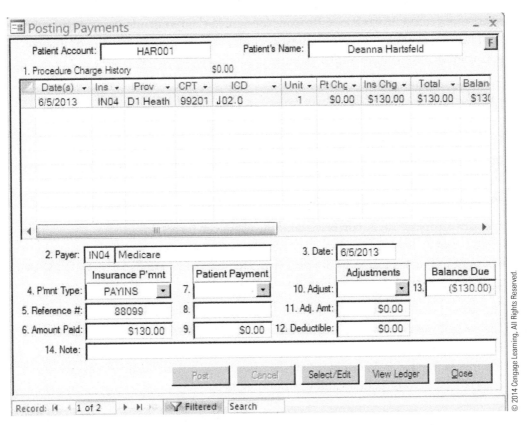

Figure 7–12 **Posting Payments**

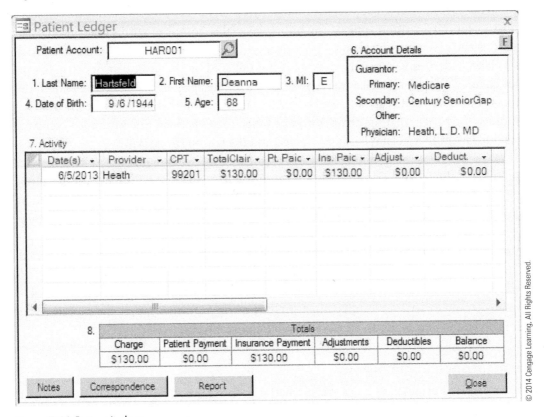

Figure 7–13 **Patient Ledger**

rejected are often called dirty claims. Reasons for denied claims fall into two categories: technical errors and insurance policy coverage issues. Technical errors include missing or incorrect information. Common errors or omissions include:

- Transposed numbers
- Incorrect patient insurance identification number
- Incorrect or incomplete diagnosis or procedure codes
- Incorrect or inconsistent dates of service
- Incorrect year of service
- Missing information such as place of service, provider address, or identification
- Mathematical errors

These types of errors are easily corrected, and the claim can be resubmitted.

Denials based on insurance policy coverage issues are more complex and often require involving the patient in the resolution of the problem. Denied claims are usually related to insurance coverage issues, which may include the following:

- The service rendered is not covered by the policy.
- The patient was not covered by the policy at the time the service was rendered.
- The service was related to a pre-existing condition not covered by the policy.
- The insurance carrier determines that the service was not medically necessary.
- Precertification was required and was not obtained.

When a claim is denied, the billing specialist contacts the insurance carrier to find out if additional steps must be taken in order for the claim to be paid. The insurance carrier may request additional documentation to support the medical necessity of the service or may direct the billing specialist to submit a written appeal. The billing specialist complies with the insurance carrier's instructions and resubmits the claim.

If a claim is denied because the service is not covered by the policy or because the patient was not covered when the service was rendered, the billing specialist notifies the patient that the claim was denied. A phone call, followed by written notification that includes a copy of the claims denial, alerts the patient that the charges may be billed to the patient. The insurance company also notifies the patient that a claim has been denied and the reason for denial.

Delinquent claims, also called pending claims, are those claims that are neither rejected nor denied but for which payment is overdue. The most common reason for a pending claim is that the claim is lost or misplaced. Paper claims can be lost in the mail. Electronic claims can be lost because of transmission problems, computer hardware and software problems, or electrical power outages. The claim can even be lost once it has reached the insurance carrier.

When the billing specialist identifies a delinquent claim, the insurance company is queried as to the status of the claim. The inquiry is made by phone, electronically (e-mail), or in writing. Written inquiries may be submitted by using an insurance claim tracer form, as shown in Figure 7–14.

An electronic or written inquiry must include a copy of the original claim. The insurance carrier is obligated to respond to inquiries about delinquent claims.

State Insurance Commission

Insurance carrier business practices are subject to both state and federal laws. These laws range from compliance with fair employment practices to paying benefits in a timely fashion. Each state has a department or agency, often called the State Insurance Commission, responsible for

INSURANCE COMPANY_____ DATE _____

ADDRESS:_____

PATIENT NAME_____ NAME OF INSURED_____

IDENTIFICATION NUMBER_____

EMPLOYER NAME & ADDRESS_____

DATE CLAIM FILED_____ CLAIM AMOUNT_____

Attached is a copy of the original claim submitted to you on _____. We have not yet received a request for additional information and still await payment of this claim. Please review the attached duplicate and process it for payment.

If there are any questions regarding this claim, please answer the following and return this letter to our office.

IF CLAIM HAS BEEN PAID:

          Date of payment: _____

          Amount of payment: _____

          Payment made to: _____

IF CLAIM HAS BEEN DENIED:

          Reason for denial: _____

                                  _____

          Has the patient been notified?   ☐ Yes   ☐ No

IF CLAIM IS STILL PENDING:

          Please state reason why.

                        _____

                        _____

Sincerely,

Judy Jolly, CMA
Insurance Specialist

Figure 7–14 Insurance Claims Tracer

monitoring insurance company activities. Responsibilities of the State Insurance Commission include the following:

- Monitoring the financial strength of insurance companies
- Protecting the interests of the insured and policyholders
- Verifying that insurance contracts are executed in good faith
- Releasing information about the number of complaints filed against a specific insurance company in a year
- Resolving insurance conflicts

The head of the agency is usually called the state insurance commissioner.

The insurance billing specialist has an interest in the role of the state insurance commissioner as related to benefit payments. If a provider consistently has problems obtaining reimbursement from a particular insurance carrier and all direct attempts to resolve the problem fail, the billing specialist may file a formal complaint with the State Insurance Commission. Types of problems that should be referred to the State Insurance Commission are:

- The improper denial, delay, or reduction of payment for services
- The inability of two insurance carriers to reach an agreement about primary payer status

The provider or the patient may submit a written request or complaint to the insurance commissioner. In some states, the request or complaint must come from the insured or patient. The billing specialist may assist the insured or patient in this process. The request should include the following information:

- The name, address, and telephone number of the person submitting the request or complaint
- The name, address, and telephone number of the insured and the patient
- The name and address of the insurance company
- The name, address, and telephone number of the insurance agent, if known
- The dates the insurance coverage was in effect
- A copy of the policy, if possible
- A narrative description of the problem, including the date the claim was submitted
- Copies of related correspondence

If the billing specialist assists the patient in preparing the complaint, the patient or the insured should sign the cover letter.

Insurance companies are highly motivated to avoid insurance commission complaints and usually work directly with the provider, patient, or insured to resolve delinquent claim problems. A high number of complaints or requests for review will negatively affect an insurance company's ability to do business in a given state. Most insurance billing specialists can work their entire careers without ever becoming involved with the insurance commission complaint process.

CREDIT AND COLLECTIONS

Regardless of insurance coverage, the patient is ultimately responsible for paying the bill for services rendered. It is becoming common practice for providers to collect co-pays at the time of service. Once an insurance payment is received, the patient is billed for the balance. The insurance company's EOB also alerts the patient that a balance may be due to the provider. The balance due may be part of the unmet insurance deductible, or the difference between the allowed charge paid by the insurance company and the amount charged by the provider. Figure 7–15 is a sample patient statement.

The statement includes the date of service, CPT procedure code (99201), and a note to the patient. The patient may send a check for the payment, use a credit card to pay the bill, or call the billing department to set up a payment schedule. Many offices accept credit card payments for services rendered.

Most offices continue to send statements to the patient that show the age of the balance due. At some point, usually when an account is more than 120 days old, the statements include a strongly worded notice or collection letter. If the patient does not respond to collection letters, the billing specialist can send a final notice. The final notice informs the patient that the account

Douglasville Medicine Associates
5076 Brand Blvd., Suite 401
Douglasville, NY 01234
Ph: (123) 456-7890
Fax: (123) 456-7891
Email: admin@dfma.com
Website: www.dfma.com

STATEMENT

DEANNA HARTSFELD   Date: 7/5/2013
8821 GOLDEN AVENUE   Account no: 263336
DOUGLASVILLE, NY 01235

Date	Patient	Procedure	Total Charges	Patient Co-Pay	Insurance Payment	Adjust-ments	Deduct-ibles	Current Balance
05-Jun-13	DEANNA HARTSFELD	99201	$130.00	$0.00	$0.00	$0.00	$0	$130.00
		Totals:	$130.00	$0.00	$0.00	$0.00	$0	$130.00

Please make checks payable to:
Douglasville Medicine Associates

BALANCE DUE   **$130.00**

Important Note:
No payment from your insurance carrier was received for this service. The balance is due upon receipt of this statement.

Figure 7–15 Patient Statement

will be turned over to a collection agency within a specific time frame. Figure 7–16 illustrates a sample final notice letter.

Once a collection agency is involved in securing payment, the provider receives a percentage of the amount collected. The following example illustrates the relationship between a collection agency and the provider.

Douglasville Medicine Associates
5076 Brand Blvd., Suite 401
Douglasville, NY 01234
Ph: (123) 456-7890
Fax: (123) 456-7891
Email: admin@dfma.com
Website: www.dfma.com

MEGAN CALDWELL
83 Crestview Drive
Douglasville, NY 01234

Date: 7/9/2013
Account no: CAL001

FINAL NOTICE

Dear Ms. Caldwell:

According to our records, the balance on your account remains unpaid. We have requested payment by letter and telephone on several occasions.

If we do not receive a response from you by July 23, 2013, your account will be turned over to a collection agency. A statement of your account is enclosed.

Barbara Biller, Account Manager

Encl

Figure 7–16 Final Notice Letter

EXAMPLE

XYZ Physician Group contracts with ABC Collection Company to recover payment for delinquent accounts. The physician group will receive 20% of the total amount collected. ABC collects $100,000 on $250,000 worth of delinquent accounts.

XYZ Physician Group receives $20,000 and ABC Collection Company keeps the remaining $80,000.

Collections agencies are regulated by federal laws such as the Fair Debt Collection Practices Act (FDCPA), which specifies what a collection agency may or may not do when pursuing payment of past-due accounts.

REINFORCEMENT EXERCISES 7–3

Provide a short answer for each item.

1. What is the CMS-1500?

_____

_____

_____

continued on the next page

continued from the previous page

2. Briefly describe the phrase "allowed charge."

_____

_____

_____

3. What is the purpose of an EOB?

_____

_____

_____

4. List three reasons an insurance claim may be denied.

_____

_____

_____

5. Discuss the purpose of a final notice letter.

_____

_____

_____

6. Briefly describe the role of the State Insurance Commission.

_____

_____

_____

Fill in the blank with the correct term or phrase.

1. Claims that are paid on the first submission are called _____.

2. Claims that are denied or rejected are called _____.

3. Claims that have no action taken are called _____.

4. Regardless of insurance coverage, the _____ is responsible for paying the bill for services rendered.

5. An _____ diagnosis code confirms the medical necessity of a laboratory test or treatment.

6. The _____ specifies what a collection agency may or may not do when pursing payment of past-due accounts.

ABBREVIATIONS

Table 7–1 lists the abbreviations presented in this chapter.

TABLE 7–1

Abbreviations and Meanings	
Abbreviation	**Meaning**
AMA	American Medical Association
CMS	Centers for Medicare and Medicaid Services
EHR	electronic health record
EMR	electronic medical record
EOB	explanation of benefits
FDCPA	Fair Debt Collection Practices Act
HIPAA	Health Insurance Portability and Accountability Act
POS	point of service
RA	remittance advice

SUMMARY

Although the health care industry exists primarily to provide health and medical services to patients, the industry must remain solvent. Activities associated with developing an insurance claim are patient registration, clinical assessment and treatment, and patient departure procedures. Activities associated with processing an insurance claim include posting charges, submitting the claim, and insurance claim follow-up. The patient's medical and financial records, registration form, and encounter form are the source documents for insurance claim processing.

Once a claim has been received and accepted, the insurance carrier generates an explanation of benefits (EOB). Both the patient and the provider receive an EOB, which explains how the insurance carrier determined the amount paid for the services rendered. The insurance billing specialist maintains an insurance claim register, which is used to keep track of the payment status of insurance claims. Problem claims include denied, delayed, and pending claims. The billing specialist is often responsible for resolving the problem.

Credit and collections are handled by the billing department. The billing specialist maintains patient accounts, sends statements to the patient when a balance is due, and may interact with collection agencies.

REVIEW EXERCISES

Write a brief definition for each term or answer the question.

1. Co-payment

   _____

   _____

   _____

2. Transaction journal

   _____

   _____

   _____

3. Encounter form

   _____

   _____

   _____

4. New patient

   _____

   _____

   _____

5. Patient account ledger

   _____

   _____

   _____

6. Patient registration form

   _____

   _____

   _____

7. Pending or delinquent claims

   _____

   _____

   _____

8. List three reasons a claim may be rejected.

_____

_____

_____

9. Describe the insurance coverage issues that may result in denied claims.

_____

_____

_____

10. List three alternative names for an encounter form.

_____

_____

_____

Identify each statement as either a patient registration (PR) or a patient departure (PD) activity.

1. Assign numeric codes to procedures and diagnoses. _____

2. Check the registration form for unanswered questions. _____

3. Collect the payment from the patient. _____

4. Copy the front and back of the insurance card. _____

5. Enter the total charges on the encounter form. _____

6. Generate the insurance claim form. _____

7. Obtain authorization to bill the insurance company. _____

8. Patient fills out the registration form. _____

9. Patient signs authorization to obtain previous medical records. _____

10. Post charges and payments to the patient's account ledger. _____

11. Review the payment policy. _____

12. Schedule another appointment if necessary. _____

13. Submit the claim form to the insurance company. _____

Fill in the blank with the appropriate term.

1. The _____ is a standardized insurance claim form.

2. An insurance company document that describes the amount paid for services rendered is called a(n) _____.

3. The _____ is the maximum amount the insurance carrier pays for a service.

4. Another term for the provider's EOB is _____.

5. A _____ is a specific amount a patient with health insurance must pay for a service.

6. _____ means receiving payment for services rendered.

7. The _____ is used to determine the primary insurance for a child when both parents have insurance.

8. Every lab test and treatment must be justified by a corresponding _____ or _____ that was treated during the office visit.

9. The _____ is responsible for selecting the level of service code.

10. The POS identifies the _____ where a service is provided.

CHALLENGE EXERCISES

1. Develop a telephone procedure that includes the types of questions the receptionist should ask a new patient.
2. Review an explanation of benefits that has been sent to you or a family member. Is the EOB easy to read and understand? Is it clearly marked "This Is Not a Bill"? How would you improve the EOB?

WEBSITE

Centers for Medicare and Medicaid Services: http://www.cms.hhs.gov/CMSForms

CHAPTER 8

CMS-1500 Completion Guidelines: Private and Commercial Insurance Claims

LEARNING OBJECTIVES

Upon successful completion of this chapter, the reader should have the knowledge to:

1. Describe the two main sections of the CMS-1500.
2. Accurately complete the CMS-1500 data fields.
3. List 10 guidelines for submitting optically scanned CMS-1500 claim forms.
4. Describe seven common errors that are made when completing the CMS-1500.
5. Abstract information from a case study to complete the CMS-1500 form.

KEY TERMS

CMS-1500
Employer identification
  number (EIN)
Federal Employees'
  Compensation Act
  (FECA)

Last menstrual period
  (LMP)
National provider identifier
  (NPI)
National Uniform Claim
  Committee (NUCC)

Place of service (POS)
Physician/provider
  identification number
  (PIN)
Signature on file (SOF)
Social Security number (SSN)

OVERVIEW

The CMS-1500 is an insurance billing form that is used by physicians, other health care providers, and medical suppliers to submit claims for services or items provided to patients who are not hospitalized. The CMS-1500, which was developed by the Centers for Medicare and Medicaid Services (CMS) and approved by the American Medical Association (AMA), has been in use for many years. The CMS-1500 is accepted by Medicare, Medicaid, TRICARE/CHAMPUS (Office of Civilian Health and Medical Program of the Uniformed Services), CHAMPVA (Civilian Health and Medical Program of the Department of Veterans Affairs), FECA (Federal Employees' Compensation Act), and most private insurance companies. Although most insurance claims are filed electronically, billing specialists must be familiar with the CMS-1500. When needed, paper claims are filed via the CMS-1500. Figure 8–1 is an example of the CMS-1500.

(1500)

HEALTH INSURANCE CLAIM FORM

APPROVED BY NATIONAL UNIFORM CLAIM COMMITTEE 08/05

| | PICA | | | | | | | PICA | |

1. MEDICARE   MEDICAID   TRICARE   CHAMPVA   GROUP HEALTH PLAN   FECA BLK LUNG   OTHER
   (Medicare #)   (Medicaid #)   CHAMPUS (Sponsor's SSN)   (Member ID #)   (SSN or ID)   (SSN)   (ID)

1a. INSURED'S I.D. NUMBER   (For Program in Item 1)

2. PATIENT'S NAME (Last Name, First Name, Middle Initial)

3. PATIENT'S BIRTH DATE   MM   DD   YY   SEX   M   F

4. INSURED'S NAME (Last Name, First Name, Middle Initial)

5. PATIENT'S ADDRESS (No., Street)

6. PATIENT RELATIONSHIP TO INSURED   Self   Spouse   Child   Other

7. INSURED'S ADDRESS (No., Street)

CITY   STATE

8. PATIENT STATUS   Single   Married   Other

CITY   STATE

ZIP CODE   TELEPHONE (Include Area Code) (   )

Employed   Full-Time Student   Part-Time Student

ZIP CODE   TELEPHONE (Include Area Code) (   )

9. OTHER INSURED'S NAME (Last Name, First Name, Middle Initial)

10. IS PATIENT'S CONDITION RELATED TO:

11. INSURED'S POLICY GROUP OR FECA NUMBER

a. OTHER INSURED'S POLICY OR GROUP NUMBER

a. EMPLOYMENT? (Current or Previous)   YES   NO

a. INSURED'S DATE OF BIRTH   MM   DD   YY   SEX   M   F

b. OTHER INSURED'S DATE OF BIRTH   MM   DD   YY   SEX   M   F

b. AUTO ACCIDENT?   PLACE (State)   YES   NO

b. EMPLOYER'S NAME OR SCHOOL NAME

c. EMPLOYER'S NAME OR SCHOOL NAME

c. OTHER ACCIDENT?   YES   NO

c. INSURANCE PLAN NAME OR PROGRAM NAME

d. INSURANCE PLAN NAME OR PROGRAM NAME

10d. RESERVED FOR LOCAL USE

d. IS THERE ANOTHER HEALTH BENEFIT PLAN?   YES   NO   *If yes*, return to and complete item 9 a-d.

READ BACK OF FORM BEFORE COMPLETING & SIGNING THIS FORM

12. PATIENT'S OR AUTHORIZED PERSON'S SIGNATURE I authorize the release of any medical or other information necessary to process this claim. I also request payment of government benefits either to myself or to the party who accepts assignment below.

SIGNED _____   DATE _____

13. INSURED'S OR AUTHORIZED PERSON'S SIGNATURE I authorize payment of medical benefits to the undersigned physician or supplier for services described below.

SIGNED _____

14. DATE OF CURRENT: MM   DD   YY   ILLNESS (First symptom) OR INJURY (Accident) OR PREGNANCY (LMP)

15. IF PATIENT HAS HAD SAME OR SIMILAR ILLNESS, GIVE FIRST DATE   MM   DD   YY

16. DATES PATIENT UNABLE TO WORK IN CURRENT OCCUPATION   FROM   MM   DD   YY   TO   MM   DD   YY

17. NAME OF REFERRING PROVIDER OR OTHER SOURCE   17a.   17b. NPI

18. HOSPITALIZATION DATES RELATED TO CURRENT SERVICES   FROM   MM   DD   YY   TO   MM   DD   YY

19. RESERVED FOR LOCAL USE

20. OUTSIDE LAB?   YES   NO $ CHARGES

21. DIAGNOSIS OR NATURE OF ILLNESS OR INJURY (Relate Items 1, 2, 3, or 4 to Item 24E by Line)
   1. ___ . ___   3. ___ . ___
   2. ___ . ___   4. ___ . ___

22. MEDICAID RESUBMISSION   CODE   ORIGINAL REF. NO.

23. PRIOR AUTHORIZATION NUMBER

24. A. DATE(S) OF SERVICE From MM DD YY To MM DD YY	B. PLACE OF SERVICE	C. EMG	D. PROCEDURES, SERVICES, OR SUPPLIES (Explain Unusual Circumstances) CPT/HCPCS	MODIFIER	E. DIAGNOSIS POINTER	F. $ CHARGES	G. DAYS OR UNITS	H. EPSDT Family Plan	I. ID. QUAL	J. RENDERING PROVIDER ID. #
1										NPI
2										NPI
3										NPI
4										NPI
5										NPI
6										NPI

25. FEDERAL TAX I.D. NUMBER   SSN   EIN

26. PATIENT'S ACCOUNT NO.

27. ACCEPT ASSIGNMENT? (For govt. claims, see back)   YES   NO

28. TOTAL CHARGE $

29. AMOUNT PAID $

30. BALANCE DUE $

31. SIGNATURE OF PHYSICIAN OR SUPPLIER INCLUDING DEGREES OR CREDENTIALS (I certify that the statements on the reverse apply to this bill and are made a part thereof.)

SIGNED _____   DATE _____

32. SERVICE FACILITY LOCATION INFORMATION

a.   b.

33. BILLING PROVIDER INFO & PH # (   )

a.   b.

NUCC Instruction Manual available at: www.nucc.org

APPROVED OMB-0938-0999 FORM CMS-1500 (08-05)

CARRIER

PATIENT AND INSURED INFORMATION

PHYSICIAN OR SUPPLIER INFORMATION

For instructional use only. Courtesy of the Centers for Medicare and Medicaid Services, www.cms.hhs.gov.

Figure 8–1 Sample CMS-1500

This chapter presents detailed guidelines for completing the CMS-1500. These guidelines are common to most commercial health insurance companies, such as Aetna, United Health Care, Prudential, Cigna, and others. Instructions for government insurance programs, Blue Cross/BlueShield, and workers' compensation guidelines are presented in separate chapters.

The National Uniform Claim Committee (NUCC) is a voluntary organization created to develop a standardized data set to transmit information to all third-party payers. Committee members come from a broad spectrum of the health care industry, including the AMA, the CMS, and the Veterans Health Administration (VA). The guidelines in this chapter are based on the NUCC's CMS-1500 instruction manual in effect at the time of publication. The most current instruction manual is available at the NUCC website, http://www.nucc.org/. The NUCC instruction manual clearly states that "the instructions in this manual are not specific to any…payer. Refer to specific instructions issued by your payer, clearinghouse, and/or vendor for further clarification of reporting guidelines." Therefore, billing specialists *must* have access to claims submission guidelines for all payers associated with their employer.

OPTICAL SCANNING GUIDELINES

The CMS-1500 is printed in red to allow for optical scanning. For insurance carriers to process the scannable CMS-1500, data must be entered according to the following guidelines:

- All data must be entered within the borders of each field (box).
- Data is keyed (typed). For paper claims submission, provider and patient signatures are acceptable.
- Enter all alphabetic characters in uppercase letters.
- Enter a space for the following, which are preprinted on the form:
  - Dollar sign or decimal in all charges or totals
  - Decimal point in a diagnosis code number
  - Parentheses surrounding the area code in a telephone number
- Enter commas between the patient or policyholder's last name, first name, and middle initial. This guideline applies to optical scanning. Most electronic claims software does not require commas.
- Enter two zeros in the cents column of monetary fields when the fee or charge is in whole dollars.
- Enter birth dates as an eight-digit number with spaces between the digits for the month, date, and year; two digits are used for the month and date, and four digits are used for the year (MM DD YYYY). Entering a space between the sets of digits keeps the numbers within the designated block or field. This guideline applies to optical scanning. Most electronic claims software does not require spaces between digits.
- Enter other dates as six- or eight-digit numbers as directed by the insurance carrier. Six-digit dates are entered as MMDDYY (two-digit month, two-digit date, and two-digit year). Eight-digit dates are entered as MMDDYYYY (two-digit month, two-digit date, and four-digit year). Spaces between sets of numbers may or may not be required.
- Do not key the letter O for the number zero.
- Do not enter a hyphen between CPT and HCPCS code and a modifier. Enter a space between the code and modifier. If multiple modifiers are used, enter a space between modifiers.
- Do not enter hyphens or spaces in a Social Security number (SSN) or in an employer identification number (EIN).
- Do not use punctuation in the names entered on the form, except for a hyphenated last name, which is known as a compound name. Do not use designations of birth order (e.g., Jr., III) unless such designations are on the patient's insurance ID card.

CMS-1500 GUIDELINES

Instructions for completing the CMS-1500 are divided into two major categories: (1) patient information and (2) treatment and provider information. A sample of each section of the CMS-1500 is shown in a figure that corresponds to the discussion of the section. Refer to the figures as you read the explanation.

CMS-1500 PATIENT INFORMATION

The first 13 CMS-1500 blocks or fields capture information about the patient and the patient's health insurance policy. Figure 8–2 shows the top of the form that includes blocks 1 and 1a.

Block 1: Insurance Plan

Enter an X in the box that describes the type of insurance plan. Group Health Plan and Other are used to identify most private and commercial insurance programs. Medicare, Medicaid, TRICARE/CHAMPUS, CHAMPVA, and FECA/Black Lung are government-sponsored programs.

Block 1a: Insured's I.D. Number

Enter the health insurance identification number as it appears on the patient's insurance card. Do not enter hyphens or spaces in the number.

Blocks 2 through 8 capture patient and insured identification information. The patient and the insured may or may not be the same individual. When the patient is a dependent child, the insured is the name of the individual who has the insurance policy that covers the child. A wife covered by her husband's health plan is listed as the patient, and the insured is her husband. When the patient is the individual who has the insurance policy, then the patient and the insured are the same. Figure 8–3 highlights blocks 2 through 8.

Block 2: Patient's Name

Enter the patient's last name, first name, and middle initial in uppercase letters. Do not include titles or birth designations such as Sr. or Jr. unless the patient's insurance ID has that information.

Figure 8–2 Blocks 1 and 1a CMS-1500

For instructional use only. Courtesy of the Centers for Medicare and Medicaid Services, www.cms.hhs.gov.

Figure 8–3 CMS-1500 Blocks 2–8

For instructional use only. Courtesy of the Centers for Medicare and Medicaid Services, www.cms.hhs.gov.

Block 3: Patient's Birth Date and Sex (Gender)

Enter the patient's eight-digit birth date as MMDDYYYY. Enter an X in the appropriate box to indicate male or female. If the patient's gender is unknown, leave blank.

Block 4: Insured's Name

Enter the insured's (policyholder's) last name, first name, and middle initial. Some insurance companies allow you to enter SAME in block 4 when the patient and the insured are the same person.

Block 5: Patient's Address

Enter the patient's mailing address and ZIP code. Enter a hyphen to separate the first five and last four numbers of a nine-digit ZIP code. Enter the patient's telephone number. Do not put parentheses around the area code. The area code may automatically fill the preprinted parentheses.

Block 6: Patient Relationship to Insured

Enter an X in the appropriate box to indicate the patient's relationship to the insured: Self when the patient and insured are the same person; Spouse when the patient is married to the insured; Child when the patient is the child or stepchild of the insured; and Other if the patient is the insured's unmarried domestic partner.

Block 7: Insured's Address

Enter the insured's (policyholder's) full address. Some commercial insurance companies allow you to enter SAME in block 7 when the patient's and insured's address are the same.

Block 8: Patient Status

Because *Patient Status* may not be required for electronic claims submission, the NUCC recommends that this block not be used.

If a specific payer requires this information, enter an X in the box that indicates the patient's marital status. If the patient is an unmarried domestic partner, enter an X in Other. Enter an X in Employed if the patient has a job. Enter an X in the appropriate box to indicate the patient's status as a student. Student status, full- or part-time, applies to patients between the ages of 19 and 23 who are the insured's dependents. Some insurance policies cover only full-time students. The insurance company may require written acknowledgment of the student's status from the school, college, or university. If the patient is unemployed and/or not a full- or part-time student, leave blank.

Blocks 9–11: Other Insured's Name; Is Patient Condition Related To; Insured's Policy Group or FECA Number

Block 9 is completed when the patient is covered by more than one health insurance plan. Blocks 10 and 11 are completed for all patients. Figure 8–4 shows blocks 9 through 11.

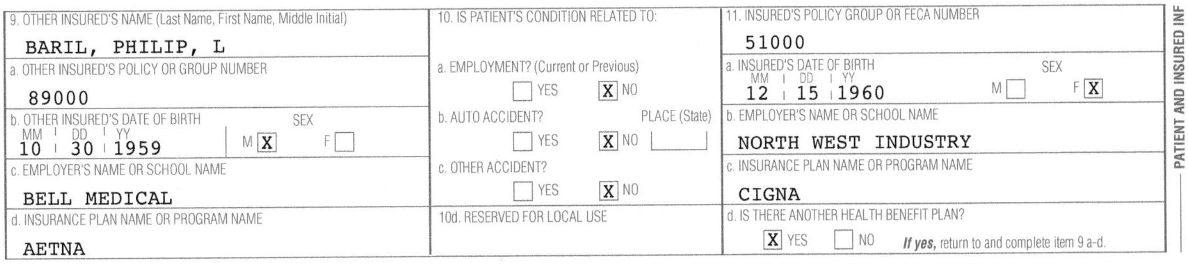

Figure 8–4 CMS-1500 Blocks 9–11

Blocks 9–9d: Other Insured's Name; Policy Number; Date of Birth; Employer's or School Name; Insurance Plan Name or Program Name

Blocks 9–9d are completed when the patient is covered by more than one health insurance policy. The secondary (or supplemental) insurance policy information is entered in blocks 9–9d. If there is no secondary or supplemental insurance policy, leave blocks 9–9d blank.

Block 9: Other Insured's Name

Enter the insured's (policyholder's) last name, first name, and middle initial.

Block 9a: Other Insured's Policy or Group Number

Enter the policy or group number of the individual named in block 9.

Block 9b: Other Insured's Birth Date

The *Other Insured's Policy or Group Number* and *Sex* may not be required for electronic claims submission. The NUCC recommends that block 9b not be used.

If a specific payer requires this information, enter the eight-digit birth date and sex of the individual named in block 9. If the gender is unknown, leave that field blank.

Block 9c: Employer's Name or School Name

The *Employer's Name or School Name* may not be required for electronic claims submission. The NUCC recommends that block 9c not be used.

If a specific payer requires this information, enter the name of the employer or school attended for the person named in block 9.

Block 9d: Insurance Plan Name or Program Name

Enter the name of the insurance plan or program for the person identified in block 9.

Blocks 10–10d: Is Patient's Condition Related To

Enter an X in the appropriate box to indicate if the patient's condition is related to work, an auto accident, or other accident.

Block 10a: Employment? (Current or Previous)

Enter an X in YES if the condition is work-related; otherwise, enter an X in NO. A work-related injury falls under workers' compensation insurance.

Block 10b: Auto Accident? Place (State)

Enter an X in YES if the condition is the result of an automobile accident; otherwise, enter an X in NO. If yes, enter the two-character abbreviation for the state of the patient's residence. Treatment of injuries sustained during an auto accident may be billed to the automobile insurance company.

Block 10c: Other Accident

Enter an X in YES if the condition is a result of an accident not related to employment or automobile; otherwise, enter an X in NO. Payment for treating injuries sustained on private or business properties may be the responsibility of a homeowner's or business insurance policy.

EXAMPLE: HOMEOWNERS INSURANCE
At a neighborhood picnic, Janelle's 3-year-old son falls off the neighbor's jungle gym and sustains a broken arm. The neighbor's homeowner's insurance may be liable for medical expenses related to the child's injury.

EXAMPLE: BUSINESS INSURANCE
Mr. Howard slips on the ice in front of the local department store and sustains a sprained ankle. The store's liability insurance may be responsible for medical expenses related to treating Mr. Howard's injury.

Block 10d: Reserved For Local Use

Leave this blank.

Blocks 11–11d: Insured's Policy Group Number or FECA Number; Insured's Date of Birth; Employer's Name or School Name; Insurance Plan Name or Program; Is There Another Health Benefit Plan?

Blocks 11–11c are used to gather additional information about the health insurance policy for the individual named in block 4 (*Insured's Name*). Block 11d identifies whether or not the patient is covered by another insurance plan.

Block 11: Insured's Policy Group or FECA Number

Enter the insurance policy number or group number for the individual named in block 4 (*Insured's Name*). Do not enter hyphens or spaces in the policy or group number.

Enter the FECA number, if applicable. The FECA number is assigned to a patient who is covered by the workers' compensation program for individuals employed by the federal government.

EXAMPLE
Coal miners with black lung disease and the federal workers injured in the 1995 Oklahoma City bombing tragedy are covered by FECA.

Block 11a: Insured's Date of Birth

Enter the insured's (named in block 4) eight-digit birth date as MM DD YYYY. Enter an X in the appropriate box to indicate the insured's gender. If the gender is unknown, leave this blank.

Block 11b: Employer Name or School Name

The *Employer's Name or School Name* may not be required for electronic claims submission. The NUCC recommends that block 9c not be used.

If a specific payer requires this information, enter the name of the insured's (named in block 4) employer, if employed. Enter the name of the school if the insured is unemployed and considered to be a full- or part-time student. Otherwise, leave this blank.

Block 11c: Insurance Plan Name or Program

Enter the name of the insured's (named in block 4) health insurance plan or program.

Block 11d: Is There Another Health Benefit Plan?

Enter an X in NO when the patient is covered by only one insurance plan. Enter an X in YES when the patient is covered by a secondary or supplemental health insurance plan. If YES is marked, blocks 9–9d must be completed.

12. PATIENT'S OR AUTHORIZED PERSON'S SIGNATURE I authorize the release of any medical or other information necessary to process this claim. I also request payment of government benefits either to myself or to the party who accepts assignment below.	13. INSURED'S OR AUTHORIZED PERSON'S SIGNATURE I authorize payment of medical benefits to the undersigned physician or supplier for services described below.
SIGNED **SIGNATURE ON FILE** DATE _____	SIGNED **SIGNATURE ON FILE**

READ BACK OF FORM BEFORE COMPLETING & SIGNING THIS FORM.

Figure 8–5 CMS-1500 Blocks 12 and 13

For instructional use only. Courtesy of the Centers for Medicare and Medicaid Services, www.cms.hhs.gov.

Blocks 12 and 13: Patient Authorization

Blocks 12 and 13 document the patient's authorization to release information and assign insurance benefits to the provider. These blocks are shown in Figure 8–5.

Block 12: Patient's or Authorized Person's Signature

The patient or authorized person's signature, or the phrase "signature on file," must be entered to allow the release of medical information necessary for claims processing. Signature on file (SOF) means that the patient has signed an authorization form, which is kept on file. When the patient's signature is *on file* the date may be left blank.

Block 13: Insured's or Authorized Person's Signature

The insured's or authorized person's signature or the phrase SIGNATURE ON FILE must be entered to allow the insurance company to send payment directly to the provider.

REINFORCEMENT EXERCISES 8-1

Complete blocks 1–13 of the CMS-1500 form (Figure 8–6) by using the information on the patient registration form (Figure 8–7).

Figure 8–6 CMS-1500 Blocks 1–13

FAMILY MD

800 Medical Drive
Anytown, ME 49855

PATIENT REGISTRATION

DATE: 06/04/20xx

PATIENT INFORMATION

PATIENT'S LAST NAME:	FIRST NAME:	MIDDLE INITIAL:	DOB:
HELLMAN	ABIGAIL	M.	10/30/19xx

PATIENT'S ADDRESS:	PHONE:
724 HENNEPIN ANYTOWN ME 49855	Home: (906) 555-2345 Work: (906) 555-3456

SINGLE: MARRIED: X WIDOWED:	MALE:	FEMALE: X

OCCUPATION:	EMPLOYER/ADDRESS:	EMPLOYER PHONE:
TEACHER	ANYTOWN ELEMENTARY SCHOOL 301 W. SPRUCE ANYTOWN, ME 49855	(906) 555-3456

EMERGENCY CONTACT:	RELATIONSHIP TO PATIENT:	PHONE:
PAUL HELLMAN	SPOUSE	(906) 555-2345 (906) 250-6066

REASON FOR TODAY'S VISIT:

SORE THROAT

WORK RELATED INJURY/ILLNESS? YES: NO: X DATE:	AUTO ACCIDENT? YES: NO: X DATE:	OTHER ACCIDENT? YES: NO: X DATE:

INSURANCE INFORMATION

INSURANCE CO.	GROUP NO:
AETNA	87000

INSURED'S NAME:	INSURED'S ID NO:	RELATIONSHIP TO INSURED:
ABIGAIL M. HELLMAN	**503529750**	SELF: X SPOUSE: CHILD: OTHER:

INSURED'S ADDRESS:	INSURED'S PHONE:
SAME	SAME

OTHER INSURANCE

SECONDARY INSURANCE:	GROUP NO:	ID NUMBER:	EMPLOYER:
CIGNA	89000	614630861	QUALITY CONTRACTORS

OTHER INSURED'S NAME:	OTHER INSURED'S DOB:	RELATIONSHIP TO PATIENT:
PAUL HELLMAN	11/12/19xx	SPOUSE

OTHER INSURED'S ADDRESS:	OTHER INSURED'S PHONE:
SAME	(H) (906) 555-2345 (W) (906) 250-6066

AUTHORIZATION

I hereby authorize my insurance company benefits to be paid directly to the physician. I realize that I am responsible to pay for any non-covered services. I hereby authorize the release of pertinent medical information to the insurance company.

Patient/Legal Representative Signature: **Date:**

Figure 8–7 Patient Registration Form

CMS-1500 TREATMENT AND PROVIDER INFORMATION

Treatment and provider information begins with block 14, Date of Current Illness, and continues through block 33, Billing Provider Info & PH #. Diagnostic and treatment information must be supported by documentation in the patient's medical record. Insurance carriers closely monitor diagnosis and treatment codes. Inconsistencies, errors, or questionable codes result in delayed claims processing or denied payment. In the worst-case scenario, coding errors may lead to fraud or abuse investigations.

Blocks 14, 15, 16, and 18 refer to dates related to the onset of illness, hospitalization, and the estimated time a patient is unable to work. Figure 8–8 shows blocks 14 through 18.

Block 14: Date of Current: Illness (First symptom) OR Injury (Accident) OR Pregnancy (LMP)

Block 14 is used in four different ways: (1) Date of Current Illness—enter the date of the current episode of care or service; (2) First Symptom—enter the date that the symptoms of the current illness/problem first appeared; (3) Injury—for workers' compensation and other problems that resulted from an accident, enter the date that the injury first occurred; (4) Pregnancy (LMP)—enter the date of the patient's last menstrual period (LMP). The patient's medical record is the source document for dates related to first symptom, injury, or pregnancy. The date is entered as an eight-digit (MMDDYYYY) or six-digit (MMDDYY) number, depending on insurance carrier preference.

> **EXAMPLE**
>
> *Current Illness:* When the current episode of care is not related to a first symptom, injury, or pregnancy, enter the date of the office visit.
>
> *First Symptom:* A note dated 3/8/20YY states that the patient exhibited symptoms two months ago. The date of current illness (first symptom) is 010820YY (January 8, 20YY).
>
> *Injury First Occurred:* A note dated 6/19/20YY states "the patient is seen for follow-up of a sprained wrist sustained after falling off a jungle gym two weeks ago." The date that the injury first occurred is 060520YY (June 5, 20YY).
>
> *Pregnancy (LMP):* A note dated 7/20/20YY states "the patient is seen to confirm pregnancy." LMP was 5/20/20YY. The date of the LMP is 052020YY.

Block 15: If Patient Has Had Same or Similar Illness, Give First Date

If Patient Has Had Same or Similar Illness, Give First Date may not be required for electronic claims submission. The NUCC recommends that block 15 not be used.

If a specific payer requires the information, enter the date, either six or eight digits, when the patient had the same or similar illness and the previous illness is documented in the patient's record. Otherwise, leave this blank. Previous pregnancies are not a similar illness.

Block 16: Dates Patient Unable to Work in Current Occupation

Enter the six or eight digit dates that the patient is/was unable to work in his or her current occupation. Otherwise, leave this blank. Block 16 is especially significant for short- or long-term disability claims.

14. DATE OF CURRENT: ILLNESS (First symptom) OR INJURY (Accident) OR PREGNANCY (LMP) MM DD YY 06 12 20YY	15. IF PATIENT HAS HAD SAME OR SIMILAR ILLNESS, GIVE FIRST DATE MM DD YY	16. DATES PATIENT UNABLE TO WORK IN CURRENT OCCUPATION MM DD YY MM DD YY FROM TO
17. NAME OF REFERRING PROVIDER OR OTHER SOURCE	17a. 17b. NPI	18. HOSPITALIZATION DATES RELATED TO CURRENT SERVICES MM DD YY MM DD YY FROM TO

Figure 8–8 CMS-1500 Blocks 14, 15, 16, and 18

For instructional use only. Courtesy of the Centers for Medicare and Medicaid Services, www.cms.hhs.gov.

17. NAME OF REFERRING PROVIDER OR OTHER SOURCE	17a.		18. HOSPITALIZATION DATES RELATED TO CURRENT SERVICES
ROBERT CIMA MD	17b. NPI	1234567890	MM DD YY MM DD YY FROM TO
19. RESERVED FOR LOCAL USE			20. OUTSIDE LAB? $ CHARGES [X] YES [ ] NO 300 00

Figure 8–9 CMS-1500 Blocks 17, 19, and 20

For instructional use only. Courtesy of the Centers for Medicare and Medicaid Services, www.cms.hhs.gov.

Block 18: Hospitalization Dates Related to Current Services

Enter the hospital admission (FROM) and discharge (TO) dates, either six or eight digits, if the patient received inpatient services (e.g., hospital, skilled nursing facility). If the patient has not been discharged at the time the claim is submitted, leave the discharge date (TO) blank. If there is no hospitalization related to the current services, leave this blank.

Blocks 17, 19, and 20

Blocks 17, 19, and 20 are used to record information about a referring provider, specific local or insurance carrier data, and outside laboratory services. Figure 8–9 shows these blocks.

Block 17: Name of Referring Provider or Other Source

Enter the first name, middle initial (if known), last name, and credentials of the professional who referred or ordered health care services or supplies reported on the claim. Do not use punctuation. If there is no referring provider, leave this blank.

Block 17a (no title, shaded):

This block is used when the insurance carrier or other entity assigns a unique identifier to provider. Enter the unique identifier for the provider entered in block 17. In many cases, block 17a is left blank. A unique identifier may be an EIN or a physician/provider identification number (PIN) assigned by the insurance company.

Block 17b: NPI (unshaded)

Enter the 10-digit national provider identifier (NPI) of the provider entered in block 17. Otherwise, leave this blank. CMS developed national provider identification (NPI) numbers for all providers who submit claims to government-sponsored health insurance programs. Nongovernment health insurance carriers may also require the NPI.

Block 19: Reserved for Local Use

Block 19 is often left blank.

Block 20: Outside Lab?

Enter an X in the NO box if all laboratory procedures reported on the claim were performed in the provider's office. Enter an X in the YES box if the laboratory procedures reported on the claim were performed by an outside laboratory and billed to the provider.

When YES is checked, enter the total amount charged by the outside laboratory in $ CHARGES. Enter the outside laboratory's name, mailing address, and NPI in blocks 32 and 32a, respectively. If the outside laboratory has an identification number other than the NPI, enter that number in block 32b.

Block 21: Diagnosis or Nature of Illness or Injury (Relate Items 1, 2, 3, or 4 to Item 24E by Line)

Block 21 is used to record ICD diagnosis codes. Figure 8–10 illustrates block 21.

21. DIAGNOSIS OR NATURE OF ILLNESS OR INJURY (Relate Items 1, 2, 3, or 4 to Item 24E by Line)		22. MEDICAID RESUBMISSION CODE	ORIGINAL REF. NO.
1. 491 21	3. 485	23. PRIOR AUTHORIZATION NUMBER	
2. 788 1	4.		

Figure 8–10 CMS-1500 Blocks 21, 22, and 23

For instructional use only. Courtesy of the Centers for Medicare and Medicaid Services, www.cms.hhs.gov.

Enter current ICD diagnosis codes as follows: 1. First-listed (primary) diagnosis code; and other diagnoses codes in items 2 through 4. All codes are entered to the highest degree of specificity. Enter the fourth, fifth, and sixth digits, when applicable, to the right of the preprinted period in items 1 through 4. Each service/treatment code entered in block 24D must be related to at least one of the diagnosis codes in block 21.

Block 22: Medicaid Resubmission Code

Block 22 is used when resubmitting a Medicaid claim. Otherwise, leave blank. See Figure 8–10.

Block 23: Prior Authorization Number

The "Prior Authorization Number" refers to a number assigned by the payer (insurance program) that indicates the service is authorized. This block is used when the patient must obtain preauthorization in order for the insurance carrier to pay the claim. Enter the prior authorization number or leave this blank. See Figure 8–10.

REINFORCEMENT EXERCISES 8–2

Read the following progress note and complete blocks 14–23 of the CMS-1500 (Figure 8–11). Use June 12, 20YY, as the date of service.

PROGRESS NOTE: Viola is seen today for a sore throat that first presented three days ago. The patient has a low-grade fever of 100.2°F. Physical examination was essentially normal with the exception of an inflamed throat. Swab culture was taken and confirmed the presence of streptococcus for a diagnosis of streptococcal pharyngitis. Erythromycin was prescribed. The patient is to return in 10 days for follow-up. Office visit code is 99212. Signed by: Roberta Pharyngeal, MD.

DIAGNOSIS CODE: Streptococcal pharyngitis, 034.0 (ICD-10-CM J02.0)

CPT CODE: Throat culture, 87081

---

14. DATE OF CURRENT: MM DD YY ILLNESS (First symptom) OR INJURY (Accident) OR PREGNANCY (LMP)	15. IF PATIENT HAS HAD SAME OR SIMILAR ILLNESS, GIVE FIRST DATE MM DD YY	16. DATES PATIENT UNABLE TO WORK IN CURRENT OCCUPATION MM DD YY MM DD YY FROM TO
17. NAME OF REFERRING PROVIDER OR OTHER SOURCE	17a. 17b. NPI	18. HOSPITALIZATION DATES RELATED TO CURRENT SERVICES MM DD YY MM DD YY FROM TO
19. RESERVED FOR LOCAL USE		20. OUTSIDE LAB? ☐ YES ☐ NO $ CHARGES
21. DIAGNOSIS OR NATURE OF ILLNESS OR INJURY (Relate Items 1, 2, 3, or 4 to Item 24E by Line) 1. 3.		22. MEDICAID RESUBMISSION CODE ORIGINAL REF. NO.
2. 4.		23. PRIOR AUTHORIZATION NUMBER

Figure 8–11 CMS-1500 Blocks 14–23

For instructional use only. Courtesy of the Centers for Medicare and Medicaid Services, www.cms.hhs.gov.

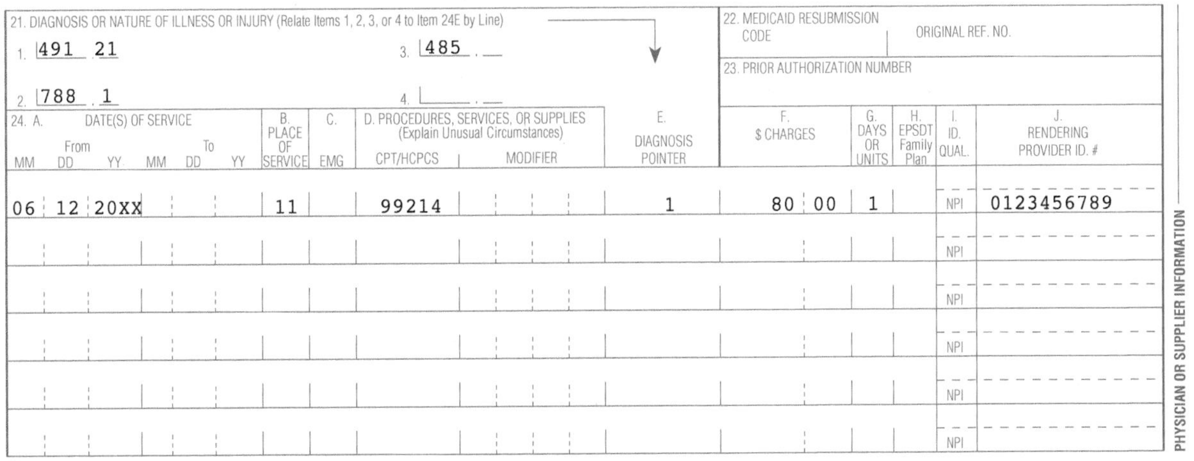

Figure 8–12 CMS-1500 Block 24A–J

For instructional use only. Courtesy of the Centers for Medicare and Medicaid Services, www.cms.hhs.gov.

Blocks 24A–J: Dates of Service; Procedures; Charges; Miscellaneous

Blocks 24A–J is a multi-item block used to record the date, place, charge, and treatment codes for services rendered to the patient. Only six services can be submitted on one claim form. Complete each horizontal line (A–J) before entering data into the next line. Required fields in this block may vary by insurance carrier. Figure 8–12 illustrates one line of blocks 24A–J.

Block 24A: Dates of Service

Enter the date the procedure or service was performed in the From column. A six-digit date is entered as MMDDYY; an eight-digit date is entered as MMDDYYYY without spaces. When a specific service is provided on one date, insurance carriers may require the date to be entered in the From and To fields or only in the From field. When the same service is performed on consecutive days, insurance carriers usually require the range of dates to be entered in the From and To fields.

Block 24B: Place of Service

Enter the appropriate two-digit place of service (POS) code to identify where the patient received the service (e.g., a physician's office). Table 8–1 lists POS codes.

Block 24C: EMG

Enter a Y (for yes) in this block when the patient receives emergency treatment. An emergency is usually defined as a condition or injury that without immediate treatment is likely to result in loss of life or serious impairment of organ structure or function. Otherwise, leave this blank. Receiving treatment in an emergency department does *not* in itself constitute an emergency.

Block 24D: Procedures, Services, or Supplies

Enter the CPT or HCPCS level II code, plus required modifiers as applicable, for the services or procedures performed on the date(s) included in block 24A. Four modifiers can be entered for each CPT/HCPCS code. Note the separate fields for CPT/HCPCS codes and four modifiers.

Block 24E: Diagnosis Code

Enter the diagnosis pointer number (1 through 4) from block 21 for the diagnosis that best justifies the medical necessity for the service listed in block 24D.

TABLE 8–1

CMS-1500 Place of Service Codes	
Place of Service	**Code**
Pharmacy	01
School	03
Homeless Shelter	04
Indian Health Service Free-Standing Facility	05
Indian Health Service Provider-Based Facility	06
Tribal 638 Free-Standing Facility	07
Tribal 638 Provider-Based Facility	08
Prison Correctional Facility	09
Provider's Office	11
Patient's Home	12
Assisted Living Facility	13
Group Home	14
Mobile Home	15
Urgent Care Facility	20
Inpatient Hospital	21
Outpatient Hospital	22
Emergency Room Hospital	23
Ambulatory Surgery Center	24
Birthing Center	25
Military Treatment Facility or Uniformed Service Treatment Facility	26
Skilled Nursing Facility	31
Nursing Facility	32
Custodial Care Facility	33
Hospice	34
Ambulance–Land	41
Ambulance–Air or Water	42
Independent Clinic	49
Federally Qualified Health Center	50
Inpatient Psychiatric Facility	51
Psychiatric Facility–Partial Hospitalization	52

continued on the next page

continued from the previous page

Community Mental Health Center	53
Intermediate Care Facility/Mentally Retarded	54
Residential Substance Abuse Treatment Center	55
Psychiatric Residential Treatment Center	56
Nonresidential Substance Abuse Treatment Facility	57
Mass Immunization Facility	60
Comprehensive Inpatient Rehabilitation Facility	61
Comprehensive Outpatient Rehabilitation Facility	62
End-Stage Renal Disease Treatment Facility	65
Public Health Clinic	71
Rural Health Clinic	72
Independent Laboratory	81
Other Places of Service	99

Block 24F: Charges

Enter the fee charged for each reported procedure or service. See Figure 8–12. When the same procedure is performed on consecutive days and reported on one line or when the same procedure is performed more than once during a single encounter, enter the total charges in block 24F. Do not enter commas, periods, or dollar signs. Do not enter negative amounts. Enter 00 in the cents area if the amount is a whole number.

EXAMPLE

Mrs. Britley is seen on three consecutive days for a brief office visit and receives a series of injections. The fee for each visit is $50. If these encounters are reported on one line of block 24, then the total charge of 150 00 is entered in block 24F.

EXAMPLE

Mr. Rodriguez provides three separate urine samples for three separate urinalysis tests over a period of 12 hours. The fee for each urinalysis is $25. The total charge of 75 00 is entered in block 24F.

Block 24G: Days or Units

Enter the number of days or units for procedures or services reported in block 24D. If just one procedure or service is reported in block 24D, enter a 1 in block 24G. Other guidelines for completing block 24G include the following:

- Anesthesia services are reported as the number of minutes the patient received anesthesia. Therefore, two hours of anesthesia services are reported as 120 minutes in block 24G.
- Bilateral and multiple procedures are listed as individual procedures in block 24D and reported as one unit each in block 24G.

- Inclusive dates for the same service or procedure are reported in block 24G as the number of days identified in block 24A—Dates of Service, From and To. Therefore, brief office visits from January 1 to January 5 are reported as five units in block 24G.
- Identical radiology studies performed more than once during the same day are counted as individual units. Therefore, three chest x-rays taken on the same day are reported as three units in block 24G. Do not report the number of x-ray views taken for a specific radiology study. For example, a posteroanterior and lateral view of the chest, which is one chest x-ray with two views, is reported as one unit in block 24G.

Block 24H: EPSDT Family Plan (Early and Periodic Screening for Diagnosis and Treatment)

Leave this blank. This block is used to identify services provided under the Medicaid EPSDT program.

Block 24I: ID. QUAL. (shaded area)

Enter the provider's type of identification number as assigned by the insurance carrier. This may be a PIN, EIN, or another unique identification number. Otherwise, leave this blank.

NPI (national provider identification) is preprinted in the unshaded area of block 24I.

Block 24J: Rendering Provider ID # (shaded area)

Enter the provider's identification number as assigned by the insurance carrier. Otherwise, leave this blank.

Block 24J: Rendering Provider ID # NPI (unshaded area)

If the provider who performed the service is a member of a group practice, enter the provider's 10-digit NPI. Leave this blank if the provider is a solo practitioner. Other NPIs may be required, such as the NPI for an outside laboratory or durable medical equipment providers.

REINFORCEMENT EXERCISES 8–3

Use the following information to complete block 24A–24J of the CMS-1500 (Figure 8–13). Use June 12, 20YY, as the date of service.

OFFICE VISIT CODE: Established patient office visit, 99212

PLACE OF SERVICE: Provider's office, 11

DIAGNOSIS CODE: Streptococcal pharyngitis, 034.0 (ICD-10-CM J02.0)

CPT CODE: Throat culture, 87081

CHARGES: Office visit, $45; throat culture, $25

PROVIDER NPI: 2345678901

Blocks 25–33: Provider and Billing Entity Identification; Charges

Blocks 25 through 33 are used to record provider and billing identification information and the total charges for services rendered. Accurate information is essential for prompt and adequate reimbursement. Figure 8–14 shows the CMS-1500, blocks 25 through 33.

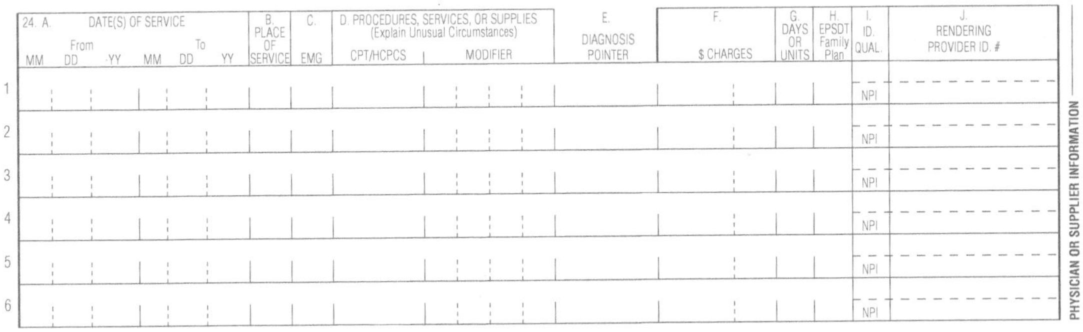

Figure 8–13 CMS-1500 Block 24A–J

For instructional use only. Courtesy of the Centers for Medicare and Medicaid Services, www.cms.hhs.gov.

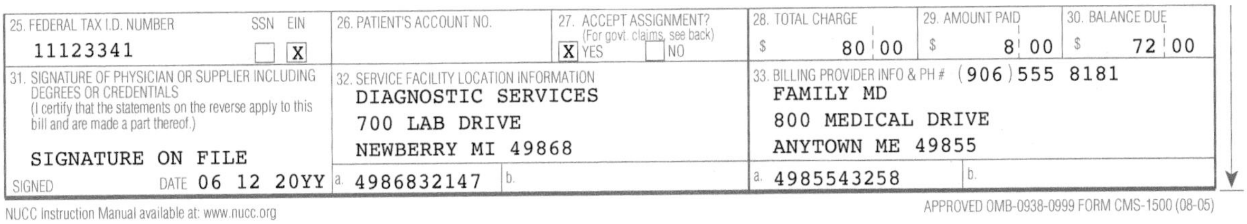

Figure 8–14 CMS-1500 Blocks 25–33

For instructional use only. Courtesy of the Centers for Medicare and Medicaid Services, www.cms.hhs.gov.

Block 25: Federal Tax I.D. Number

Enter the provider's SSN or employer (tax) identification number (EIN). Do not enter hyphens or spaces in the number. Enter an X in the appropriate box.

Block 26: Patient's Account No.

Enter the patient's account number as assigned by the provider. This block is sometimes left blank.

Block 27: Accept Assignment?

Enter an X in the YES box if the provider accepts the insurance payment as payment in full. Enter an X in the NO box if the provider does not accept the insurance payment as payment in full.

Block 28: Total Charges

Enter the total amount for all charges listed in block 24F on one claim form. If more than one claim is submitted for the same patient, each form must have its own total charge entered in block 28.

Block 29: Amount Paid

Enter the total amount the patient or another payer paid toward services covered by the insurance plan. If no payment was made, leave this blank.

Block 30: Balance Due

Balance Due may not be required for electronic claims submission. The NUCC recommends that block 30 not be used.

If a specific payer requires this information, subtract the amount paid (block 29) from the total charges (block 28) and enter the difference in block 30. Do not enter a negative amount or a credit due to the patient.

Block 31: Signature of Physician or Supplier

Enter the provider's first name, last name, and credentials without punctuation. Enter the six-(MMDDYY) or eight-digit (MMDDYYYY) date that the claim was completed. Many insurance companies also accept the statement SIGNATURE ON FILE or SOF.

When using SIGNATURE ON FILE, the practice or facility must maintain a current signature file that has the written signature of every provider or physician. Signature stamps may be used when an arrangement has been made with the insurance carrier to accept the stamps.

Blocks 32–32b: Name and Address of Facility Where Services Were Rendered

Enter the name and address where procedures or services were provided, if the location is other than the provider's office or patient's home. Other locations include a hospital, outside laboratory, skilled nursing facility, or durable medical equipment providers. Otherwise, leave this blank. Enter the name of the facility on the first line, the address on the second line, and the city, state, and zip code on the third line. For a nine-digit zip code, enter a hyphen between the first five digits and the last four digits.

Block 32a (unshaded)

Enter the 10-digit NPI for the facility entered in block 32a.

Block 32b (shaded)

When a third-party payer assigns a unique identification number for the entity named in block 32, enter that number in block 32b. Otherwise, leave this blank.

Block 33: Billing Provider Info & PH

Enter the provider's billing name, address, and telephone number as follows:

- For all providers, enter the phone number in the space to the left of the block title. Do not enter parentheses for the area code; the area code may automatically fill the preprinted parentheses.
- For a solo practitioner, enter the provider's first name, middle initial (if known), last name, and credential on the first line (do not use punctuation); enter the provider's address on the second line; enter the city, state, and zip code on the third line. For a nine-digit zip code, enter a hyphen between the first five digits and the last four digits.
- For practitioners in a group practice, enter the name of the practice or agency on the first line; enter the address on the second line; and enter the city, state, and zip code on the third line. For a nine-digit zip code, enter a hyphen between the first five digits and the last four digits.

Block 33a (unshaded)

Enter the 10-digit NPI of the billing provider. For a solo practitioner, enter the practitioner's NPI number; for a group practice, enter the 10-digit NPI of the group practice (e.g., clinic, agency).

Block 33b (shaded)

When a third-party payer assigns a unique identification number for the entity named in block 33, enter that number in block 33b. Otherwise, leave this blank.

25. FEDERAL TAX I.D. NUMBER		SSN EIN	26. PATIENT'S ACCOUNT NO.	27. ACCEPT ASSIGNMENT? (For govt. claims, see back) YES NO	28. TOTAL CHARGE $	29. AMOUNT PAID $	30. BALANCE DUE $
31. SIGNATURE OF PHYSICIAN OR SUPPLIER INCLUDING DEGREES OR CREDENTIALS (I certify that the statements on the reverse apply to this bill and are made a part thereof.)			32. SERVICE FACILITY LOCATION INFORMATION		33. BILLING PROVIDER INFO & PH # ( )		
SIGNED DATE	a.		b.		a.	b.	

NUCC Instruction Manual available at: www.nucc.org

APPROVED OMB-0938-0999 FORM CMS-1500 (08-05)

Figure 8–15 CMS-1500 Blocks 25–33

For instructional use only. Courtesy of the Centers for Medicare and Medicaid Services, www.cms.hhs.gov.

REINFORCEMENT EXERCISES 8–4

Use the following information to complete blocks 25–33 of the CMS-1500 (Figure 8–15).

PROGRESS NOTE 6/12/20YY: Viola is seen today for a sore throat that first presented three days ago. The patient has a low-grade fever of 100.2°F. Physical examination was essentially normal, with the exception of an inflamed throat. Swab culture was taken and confirmed the presence of streptococcus for a diagnosis of streptococcal pharyngitis. Erythromycin was prescribed. The patient is to return in 10 days for follow-up. Office visit code is 99212. Signed by: Roberta Pharyngeal, MD.

DIAGNOSIS CODE: Streptococcal pharyngitis, 034.0 (ICD-10-CM J02.0)

CPT CODE: Throat culture, 87081

CHARGES: Office visit, $50.00; throat culture, $20.00 (office lab)

GROUP PRACTICE: Family MD; 800 Medical Drive; Anytown, MI 49855. Phone: (906) 555-8181

PHYSICIAN FEDERAL TAX ID NUMBER: EIN 49-2134726

PHYSICIAN NPI: 0051551500

GROUP PRACTICE NPI: 4985543258

The physician accepts assignment

The patient paid the 20% co-pay

COMMON ERRORS MADE WHEN COMPLETING THE CMS-1500

The insurance billing specialist must take great care to ensure the accuracy of all CMS-1500 data fields (blocks). Even the simplest mistake can cause delayed or denied reimbursement. Some common errors associated with CMS-1500 completion are:

- Incorrect patient insurance identification number
- Incorrect CPT code or failure to use a modifier
- Incorrect ICD code
- Diagnoses do not support the services rendered
- Absence of referring physician name and identification when required
- Mathematical errors related to charges and total amount due
- Incorrect, missing, or duplicate dates of service
- Incomplete provider information

Figure 8–16 is an example of a completed CMS-1500.

Figure 8–16 Completed CMS-1500 Form

ABBREVIATIONS

Table 8–2 lists the abbreviations presented in this chapter.

TABLE 8–2

Abbreviations and Meanings	
Abbreviation	**Meaning**
AMA	American Medical Association
CHAMPUS	Civilian Health and Medical Program of the Uniformed Services
CHAMPVA	Civilian Health and Medical Program of the Department of Veterans Affairs
CMS	Centers for Medicare and Medicaid Services
EIN	employer identification number
FECA	Federal Employees' Compensation Act
LMP	last menstrual period
NPI	national provider identifier
NUCC	National Uniform Claim Committee
PIN	physician/provider identification number
POS	place of service
SOF	signature on file
SSN	Social Security number

 ## SUMMARY

This chapter presents a detailed review of the guidelines for the CMS-1500, a universal insurance claim form. Optical scanning guidelines and common errors associated with CMS-1500 completion are listed and described.

 ## REVIEW EXERCISES

Select the Correct Answer

Circle the italicized term or phrase that accurately completes each statement.

1. *Do* or *Do not* include titles in block 2, Patient's Name.

2. The national provider identification number (NPI) was developed by the *Social Security Administration* or *CMS*.

3. The NPI will always apply to *government* or *nongovernment* health insurance programs.

4. Prior authorization numbers are most often associated with *primary care physicians* or *managed care plans.*

5. Block 21 has room for up to four diagnostic codes that are recorded as *current ICD* codes or *CPT/HCPCS* codes.

6. Block 24H, EPSDT, is associated with the *Medicare* or *Medicaid* health insurance program.

True or False

Write True or False on the line following each statement.

1. Note all monetary entries with the appropriate dollar or cents symbol. _____

2. Compound names may be hyphenated. _____

3. Do not use any punctuation in the patient's name. _____

4. Use two zeros in the cent column when the fee is listed in whole dollars. _____

5. Separate the patient's last name, first name, and middle initial with commas. _____

6. Use both lowercase and uppercase letters for alphabetic characters. _____

 CHALLENGE EXERCISE

Interview the billing specialist at a local physician's office about CMS-1500 completion do's and don'ts. Based on the information from the interview, develop a handout to share with the other students in your class.

WEBSITE

National Uniform Claim Committee: http://www.nucc.org

CHAPTER 9

Electronic Claims Submission

LEARNING OBJECTIVES

Upon successful completion of this chapter, the reader should have the knowledge to:

1. Define all key terms and abbreviations.
2. Describe the difference between carrier-direct and clearinghouse electronic claims submission.
3. List five considerations for establishing an electronic data interchange.
4. Discuss the advantages of electronic claims submission.
5. List four confidentiality safeguards related to electronic claims submission.

KEY TERMS

Batch
Carrier-direct
Centers for Medicare and Medicaid Services (CMS)
Clean claim
Clearinghouse
Compliance monitoring
Dirty claims
Electronic claim

Electronic claims submission (ECS)
Electronic data interchange (EDI)
Error-edit
Health Insurance Portability and Accountability Act (HIPAA)
Interactive communication and transactions

Noncovered benefit
Protected health information (PHI)
Reimbursement
Remittance
Third-party administrator (TPA)
Turnaround time
Unauthorized service

OVERVIEW

Electronic claims submission is accomplished by electronic data interchange (EDI). Electronic data interchange is a process that sends information back and forth between two or more individuals by computer linkages. The individuals or organizations can function as both sender and

Figure 9–1 Electronic Data Interchange

receiver. An **electronic claim** is submitted to the insurance carrier by using the following transmission methods:

- *Dial-up:* a dedicated telephone line or digital subscriber line (DSL)
- *Internet:* secure transmission of claims over the Internet
- *Magnetic tape, disk, or compact disc media:* claims are stored on electronic media

Large hospitals have used electronic claims submission since the 1960s. Figure 9–1 illustrates EDI.

This chapter is an introduction to **electronic claims submission (ECS)**, which has been the method of choice for filing insurance claims since the 1980s. During the implementation of the Health Insurance Portability and Accountability Act (HIPAA) regulations and rules, Medicare insurance carriers were encouraged to develop HIPAA-compliant ECS policies and practices. As a result of this effort, 98% of all Medicare claims in 2004 were electronically submitted according to the regulations set forth in HIPAA. In fact, the standard format adopted for national use under HIPAA meets the billing requirements for all U.S. health care payers.

The **Centers for Medicare and Medicaid Services (CMS)** is one of the driving forces behind ECS. CMS promotes the advantages of using ECS. According to CMS publications, the advantages include:

- Faster payment. Electronic claims submitted in the HIPAA standard format can be paid as early as the 14th day after the date of receipt, whereas paper claims and electronic claims submitted in a non-HIPAA format cannot be paid earlier than the 27th day after the date of receipt.

- Reduced opportunity for errors.
- Lower administrative, postage, and handling costs than paper claims.
- Online and immediate acknowledgment that the insurance carrier received the claim.
- The standard format meets billing requirements for all U.S. health care payers who must comply with HIPAA.
- Electronic remittance (payment for services rendered) can be sent to a provider-preferred location (e.g., the provider's/facility's business bank account).

There are disadvantages to ECS, most of which relate to the electronic part of the process. Power outages and computer hardware and software problems will bring ECS to a halt. Because ECS is a two-way street, problems on either end of the connection may affect both the provider and the insurance carrier. A reliable backup system for electronic records is a necessity. ECS poses unique challenges concerning health information security, confidentiality, and privacy. Regardless of the disadvantages or challenges, the electronic exchange of information is a fact of life for the insurance billing specialist. In today's health insurance environment, most claims are filed electronically. Paper claims are submitted as requested or required by the insurance carrier.

 ## ELECTRONIC CLAIMS SUBMISSION OPTIONS

There are two options for ECS:

- Carrier-direct: This option allows the billing specialist to submit claims directly to the insurance carrier.
- Clearinghouse or third-party administrator (TPA): Under this option, insurance claim information is submitted to an organization that in turn distributes the claims to the appropriate insurance company.

There are advantages and disadvantages to both options.

Carrier-Direct Claims Submission

To implement the carrier-direct option, the provider must establish electronic claims processing agreements with each insurance carrier associated with the provider's practice. The agreements or contracts must clearly identify provider/agency and insurance carrier responsibilities regarding the following: information security, compliance monitoring, equipment and software, staff training, and turnaround time.

The Health Insurance Portability and Accountability Act (HIPAA) privacy and security rules mandate that electronic protected health information (PHI) must be secure. To comply with HIPAA, electronic claims processing agreements must describe how insurance information is submitted; who has access to the information; the security features or software that protect information when a wireless network is used; non-rediscolsure policies; and the storage and retention policies for information once the insurance claim is processed.

Compliance monitoring activities include coding accuracy, verification of services provided, and accountability to regulatory agencies when errors are made. Because billing errors can result in charges of insurance fraud or abuse, the electronic claims processing agreement must identify provider and insurance carrier responsibilities related to compliance monitoring.

The agreement must include provisions for teaching the provider's staff how to use the claims submission software and whether there is a training fee. The agreement must also include answers to questions such as these: Where is training conducted—onsite or offsite? Is there a limit on the number of staff who can participate in training? Will retraining be offered when the software is updated?

Turnaround time is the length of time from claims submission to claims payment. As stated earlier, Medicare claims submitted electronically by using the HIPAA standard format can be paid as early as the 14th day after the date of receipt. The agreement should describe the turnaround time for clean claims and the provider's recourse when the expected turnaround time is not met.

The advantages of carrier-direct ECS are that (1) the provider retains control of claims submission; (2) patient medical records are readily available when needed; and (3) the billing specialist can immediately respond to error-edit messages. The carrier-direct claims submission software includes an error-edit feature that identifies errors that cause a claim to be rejected or denied. Error-edit messages flag incomplete required data fields, invalid health insurance claim numbers, discrepancies between a patient's sex and diagnoses, and incompatible diagnosis and procedure or treatment codes. The billing specialist is able to make corrections before the claim is transmitted.

The disadvantages of carrier-direct ECS are (1) the costs associated with purchasing or leasing equipment and software; (2) hiring and training staff to process the claims; and (3) establishing claims processing agreements with each insurance carrier.

Clearinghouse Claims Submission

Under clearinghouse claims submission, the provider sends insurance claims to a processing center, also known as a TPA. The clearinghouse or TPA redistributes the claims to the appropriate insurance carriers. Clearinghouses charge a fee for processing insurance claims. The fee can be assessed per claim or as a percentage of the dollar amount of all processed claims.

Insurance claims are submitted to the clearinghouse via electronic files. A unique identifier is assigned to each insurance company. The unique identifier tells the clearinghouse which insurance company (carrier) must receive the claim. Claims are submitted to the clearinghouse periodically depending on the volume of claims or provider preference. Once claims are submitted, the clearinghouse edits the claims for accuracy; reformats the claims according to the current HIPAA guidelines; and transmits the claims to the appropriate insurance carrier. When a claim clears the editing process, commonly called a clean claim, the insurance carrier sends the payment to the provider or the patient.

When a claim fails to pass the clearinghouse edits, an electronic report is sent to the provider. These reports are commonly called error-edit messages. Claims may fail due to format issues, coding inaccuracies, or other missing or incorrect information. The billing specialist corrects the error and resubmits the claim to the clearinghouse.

In addition to submitting insurance claims via electronic files, a clearinghouse also handles paper claims for the provider. When the provider is required to submit a paper claim, the billing specialist completes the CMS-1500 and sends it to the clearinghouse. As with ECS, the clearinghouse transmits paper claims to the appropriate insurance carrier.

As with carrier-direct claims submission, the provider must have a written contract that identifies provider/agency and clearinghouse responsibilities regarding information security, compliance monitoring, equipment or software, and staff training.

The two main advantages of using a clearinghouse for ECS are: (1) Only one contract is needed, and (2) costs for equipment, software, and additional staff is usually less than the costs associated with the carrier-direct option.

The disadvantages of contracting with a clearinghouse are: (1) The initial set-up of insurance company format requirements may create problems if the clearinghouse has not previously submitted claims to the company; (2) the provider does not have direct control of claims submission; and (3) cash flow is directly affected by the efficiency of the clearinghouse.

INTERACTIVE COMMUNICATION

One of the greatest benefits of ECS is the capacity for interactive communication and transactions. Interactive communication, which is the ability to share information online, is an efficient way to correspond with a clearing house or insurance carrier.

> **EXAMPLE**
> The billing specialist can query the clearinghouse or insurance carrier's electronic files regarding the status of any claim that was submitted. The billing specialist enters necessary information—usually the patient's name, claim number, date of submission, and the office or agency's unique and secure identification number. The billing specialist receives immediate feedback that may allow the billing specialist to resolve the problem.

Interactive communication is an efficient way to monitor the following claims information:

- Delayed payment of claims
- Reasons for claims denial
- Verification of insurance eligibility
- Status of patient's deductible

When a query is made, the insurance billing specialist may be able to correct any inaccurate information and immediately resubmit the claim. If this is not possible, the billing specialist prints a hard copy of the status of the claim, tracks down the problem, and resubmits the claim when the error is corrected.

Some of the more common problems with insurance claims are incomplete diagnostic codes, missing data items, obsolete codes, and insufficient information to justify the services rendered to the patient. When coding and data item errors are corrected, the claim can be electronically resubmitted. If the insurance carrier needs additional documentation to justify the services rendered, the billing specialist can send the required medical reports. In either situation, electronic communication reduces the amount of time it takes to identify and correct insurance claims problems.

REINFORCEMENT EXERCISES 9–1

Fill in the blank.

1. A(n) _____ is submitted to the insurance carrier via the Internet.

2. A(n) _____ distributes claims to the appropriate insurance carrier.

3. The _____ ECS method allows the provider to communicate directly with the insurance company.

4. _____ is a process that checks the claim for accuracy and completeness.

5. The clearinghouse assigns a(n) _____ to each insurance company (carrier).

6. The ability to share information online is known as _____.

Provide a short answer for each item.

1. Briefly describe two components of an electronic claims processing agreement.

_____

_____

_____

2. List three components of an electronic claims processing agreement required by HIPAA.

_____

_____

_____

3. Describe the differences between carrier-direct and clearinghouse ECS options.

_____

_____

_____

PROCESSING ELECTRONIC HEALTH INSURANCE CLAIMS

When a provider contracts with a clearinghouse, the billing specialist may not complete the CMS-1500 insurance claim form. Insurance claim information is transmitted to the clearinghouse via an electronic file. Under carrier-direct contracts, the insurance claim is

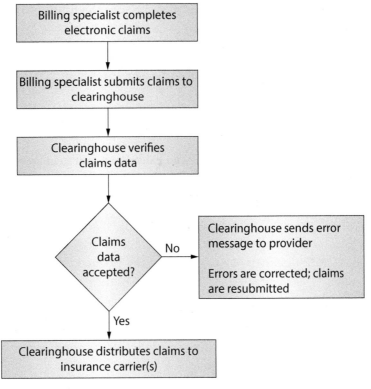

Figure 9–2 Electronic Claims Submission

transmitted to each insurance carrier. Processing electronic health insurance claims includes these steps:

- Retrieving insurance information
- Editing the information
- Submitting the claim
- Responding to clearinghouse or insurance carrier error-edit messages

Figure 9–2 illustrates electronic claims processing and submission.

Retrieving, Editing, and Submitting Insurance Claims

The billing specialist retrieves information from the patient's database or from source documents, such as the encounter form, patient registration documents, and the patient's record. When patient information is maintained in an electronic database or electronic medical record, information is retrieved from those sources. Although all carriers require much of the same information—such as patient demographic information, insurance program information, and treatment or clinical information—there may be data items mandated by an individual insurance carrier as well. The billing specialist must have access to and comply with the requirements of a specific insurance carrier. As with paper claims submission, attention to detail and accuracy are the keys to successful claims submission.

As the billing specialist completes the electronic claim, the billing software may identify general errors such as:

- Invalid diagnoses and treatments related to gender (prostatitis for a female patient)
- Invalid diagnoses and treatments related to age (pregnancy-related diagnosis for a 92-year-old woman)
- Invalid diagnosis and treatment codes
- Discrepancies between diagnosis and treatment codes

Billing software may also include edits that identify evaluation and management (E/M) *Current Procedural Terminology* (CPT) codes that are not justified by the diagnosis and treatment codes.

> EXAMPLE
>
> The physician assigns E/M code 99215, which is the highest level office visit code for an established patient, after seeing a patient for strep throat.
>
> The billing software may flag or highlight the E/M code and the diagnosis code. The billing specialist reviews the patient record for additional information or asks the physician for clarification of the E/M code before submitting the claim.

Even without these automatic edits, the billing specialist must monitor data entries and try to resolve questions before submitting the claim.

Claims are submitted as they are completed or as a batch. Batch submission means a set of claims are filed at one time. Batches are sorted by insurance program, date, or both (see examples). Batch processing is commonly associated with carrier-direct ECS.

> EXAMPLE: PROCESSING BY INSURANCE PROGRAM
>
> The billing specialist completes Medicare claims. Billing software options allow the specialist to select all Medicare claims and send them to the clearinghouse or insurance carrier as one submission.

> EXAMPLE: PROCESSING BY DATE
>
> The billing specialist submits insurance claims for a specified time frame. Billing software options allow the specialist to select the range of dates. Claims that fall in that time frame are sent to the clearinghouse or insurance carriers.

> EXAMPLE: PROCESSING BY INSURANCE CARRIER AND DATE
>
> The billing specialist submits insurance claims, sorted by insurance carrier and date. Billing software options allow the specialist to select the insurance carrier and range of dates. Claims for the specific insurance carrier that fall within the time frame are sent to the clearinghouse or insurance carrier as one submission.

The billing specialist saves the claims and submits them to the clearinghouse or insurance carrier. Billing software may automatically save claims when they are submitted.

Patient and Physician Signature Requirements

ECS makes it impossible to have a written physician signature on each claim. Most insurance carriers accept the statement SIGNATURE ON FILE in fields that require a signature. The health care agency must maintain a current file that includes the written signatures of all individuals who provide services to patients.

The patient's signature is required for assignment of benefits and release of confidential health information to insurance carriers. To accommodate this requirement for ECS, the health care agency must obtain a signed authorization from the patient. The authorization is updated at each visit—monthly, annually, or as frequently as required by the insurance plan, the insurance carrier, or other regulatory agency.

In the physician office setting, the authorizations are obtained when the patient registers for an appointment or when the patient presents the encounter form to the billing specialist at the conclusion of the appointment. In the inpatient or outpatient hospital setting, the authorizations are obtained as part of the registration/admission process. Once the patient has signed the necessary authorization, the phrase SIGNATURE ON FILE may be entered in fields that require the patient's signature.

Clearinghouse/Insurance Carrier Error-Edit Messages

Once claims are submitted, the clearinghouse or insurance carrier software edits the claims for errors. Clearinghouses distribute clean claims, those with no errors or questions, to the appropriate insurance carrier for reimbursement (payment). Under the carrier-direct method, clean claims are reimbursed directly to the provider.

In the case of dirty claims, those with errors or questions, the provider receives an electronic notification about discrepancies or inconsistencies. These notifications are commonly known as error-edit messages. The error-edit message is a list of claims that cannot be reimbursed until the error is resolved or corrected. The messages may be sorted by insurance carrier.

The billing specialist retrieves the claim and corrects errors such as discrepancies between the diagnosis and gender, age-related discrepancies, and data entry (typographical) errors. Corrected claims are resubmitted to the clearinghouse or insurance carrier. The billing specialist may not be able to correct the following types of errors:

- Invalid diagnoses or treatment codes
- Noncovered benefit, which is a service that is not included, or *covered,* by the insurance plan
- Unauthorized service, which is a service that requires preauthorization from the payer
- Services provided to an individual who is not included in the insurance plan

To resolve problems regarding invalid diagnoses or treatment codes, the billing specialist communicates with coding staff or the physician. Invalid codes may lack specificity or be outdated. Coding staff can correct these problems by reassigning valid codes. The physician or other clinical staff may need to provide additional documentation to resolve coding problems. It's worth remembering that a pattern of coding errors may trigger a fraud or abuse investigation.

> **EXAMPLE: INVALID DIAGNOSIS OR TREATMENT CODES**
> An insurance claim with the diagnosis code for strep throat must also include a code for the diagnostic test, such as a rapid strep test, that identifies the streptococcus bacteria as the cause of the problem.

The billing specialist may review the patient's record for the results of a rapid strep test. If the test was done, the CPT code for the test is added to the resubmitted claim. If the test wasn't done, the physician must provide another diagnosis before the claim can be resubmitted.

The billing specialist may not be able to correct error-edit messages related to noncovered benefits, unauthorized services, and services provided to an individual not included in the insurance plan. In these circumstances, the patient is notified that the claim is not covered by insurance, and the reason for noncoverage. The patient, or responsible party, is billed for the service.

REINFORCEMENT EXERCISES 9–2

Provide a short answer for each item.

1. List three types of information required by nearly all insurance carriers.

_____

_____

_____

2. Describe two edits associated with insurance billing software.

_____

_____

_____

3. Identify sources and source documents used to retrieve information for ECS.

_____

_____

_____

4. Briefly describe batch processing and include one example.

_____

_____

_____

continued on the next page

continued from the previous page

5. What is the purpose of an error-edit message?

_____

_____

_____

Write True or False for each statement.

1. ECS software programs edit insurance claims for accuracy. _____

2. A pattern of coding errors can trigger an investigation of fraud or abuse.

_____

3. The billing specialist is responsible for assigning accurate diagnostic and procedure codes. _____

4. The physician must provide an electronic signature on electronic claims. _____

5. The billing specialist must monitor the accuracy of insurance claims data items.

_____

CONFIDENTIALITY AND ELECTRONIC CLAIMS PROCESSING

Confidential information is not open to public inspection. In the age of electronic communication, confidentiality laws and guidelines that apply to the paper medical record may seem outdated. Nothing could be further from the truth. The agency's policies and procedures that govern release of confidential information must include safeguards related to any form of electronic communication. Review Chapter 2 for a complete discussion of confidentiality and release of information. Additional confidentiality safeguards related to ECS and electronic records include the following:

- Assign a unique identifier (password) to staff members who submit or access electronic claims and records.
- Change passwords periodically.
- Delete passwords of individuals who are no longer employed by the agency.
- Enforce written policies and disciplinary actions that address sharing passwords among staff.
- Never save confidential information on the computer hard drive.
- Store media containing backup files in a locked and fireproof location.

These safeguards are reasonable and relatively easy to implement. Whatever steps are taken to ensure confidential treatment of patient-specific insurance information, the insurance billing specialist should insist on a written policy that addresses ECS and confidentiality. The billing specialist could even take the initiative and draft the policy. Figure 9–3 lists some of the items to include in an ECS policy. The policy must be updated as technology changes.

ELECTRONIC CLAIMS SUBMISSION POLICY

A. CONFIDENTIALITY

- Information submitted electronically is subject to the same confidentiality policies as all other patient information.
- Passwords are assigned to individuals who submit claims, and they are changed every three months.
- Do not share your password or allow other staff access to the ECS program with your password.
- Computer monitor privacy screens will be used at all times.

B. SECURITY

- Close the ECS program when you are away from the workstation. NO EXCEPTIONS.
- Visitors are not allowed in the billing department.

C. STAFF TRAINING

- Employees working with ECS must attend training sessions as directed by the supervisor.
- Administrative leave with pay is granted to employees who attend ECS training.

D. ECS CONTRACTS

- The billing department supervisor maintains ECS contracts.
- The billing department supervisor is responsible for sharing contract changes with the billing staff.

Figure 9–3 Electronic Claims Submission Policy Components

 ## ELECTRONIC RECORD MANAGEMENT

Components of a record management system for paper files include filing, storage, retrieval, retention, and protection. Electronic record management addresses these same components—but with a different twist.

EXAMPLE

Paper records are stored as is, usually in a file cabinet or on a shelf. There is no need to make a second copy. Electronic records can be stored on a variety of electronic media that become obsolete. For example, "floppy" and "hard" disks commonly used in the past are nearly useless now. Electronic records should be backed up regularly. Some hospitals maintain two servers: one for current or active records and one that is used as a backup. The University of Utah Health Science Center maintains this type

TABLE 9–1

Record Management Components		
Type	Record Management	Electronic Record Considerations
Filing	• Alphabetic by patient name • Numeric by medical record number	Electronic records are usually filed by a unique patient identification number and patient name.
Storage	• Paper or electronic storage • Location of storage area • Storage area security	Electronic records are stored on electronic media. The storage area must have appropriate safeguards against natural disasters and theft.
Retrieval	• Retrieval is the key to record management • Active vs. inactive records • Twenty-four-hour access or limited access • Information that cannot be retrieved is useless	Electronic records must have a reliable backup system. Active and inactive records need not be separated because electronic media hold large amounts of data.

of backup system. According to a recent medical student's experience, one server "went down," and within 15 minutes, the backup server had restored all electronic records.

Table 9–1 summarizes the components of a record management system and lists some considerations unique to electronic records.

REINFORCEMENT EXERCISES 9–3

Write True or False for each statement.

1. Confidentiality laws for paper records do not apply to electronic records. _____

2. Staff members may share a common password for efficient access to insurance files. _____

3. Confidential information should never be stored on a computer's hard drive. _____

4. A written policy should address ECS and confidentiality. _____

5. Electronic records management systems include the same components as a record management system for paper files. _____

continued on the next page

continued from the previous page

Fill in the blank.

1. _____ must be backed up regularly.

2. All records—either electronic or paper—must be stored in a(n) _____ area.

3. Computer monitor _____ are one of the tools available to protect confidential information.

4. _____ assigned to previous employees should be deleted from all electronic or computer program files.

ABBREVIATIONS

Table 9–2 lists the abbreviations presented in this chapter.

TABLE 9–2

Abbreviations and Meanings	
Abbreviation	**Meaning**
CMS	Centers for Medicare and Medicaid Services
CPT	*Current Procedural Terminology*
ECS	electronic claims submission
EDI	electronic data interchange
E/M	evaluation and management
HIPAA	Health Insurance Portability and Accountability Act
PHI	protected health information
TPA	third-party administrator

SUMMARY

Electronic claims submission (ECS) is an efficient way to submit health insurance claims. A carrier-direct electronic claims submission program means the provider establishes ECS contracts with each insurance company or carrier. A clearinghouse electronic claims submission program means the agency or provider contracts with a third party who receives claims information from the provider and transmits the claim to the appropriate insurance carrier.

Electronic claims submission and interactive communication allow the billing specialist to edit insurance claim information and make corrections via the Internet. The status of insurance claims can be monitored online. Denied and delayed claims can be accessed, and problems can be corrected immediately. Confidentiality and record management issues related to electronic records are similar to those related to paper records. Patient information is confidential, no matter how it is transmitted or stored. The agency should have a written policy that complies with Health Insurance Portability and Accountability Act (HIPAA) security rules related to electronic health information.

REVIEW EXERCISES

Multiple Choice

Circle the correct answer from the choices provided.

1. Which of the following is not included in compliance monitoring?

    a. coding accuracy

    b. non-redisclosure policies

    c. verification of services provided

    d. accountability to regulatory agencies

2. The length of time from claims submission to claims payment is known as

    a. wait time.

    b. real time.

    c. time sharing.

    d. turnaround time.

3. In order to establish electronic claims submission, the provider must

    a. receive approval from the practice manager.

    b. hire an electronic claims processor.

    c. execute a contract with insurance carriers or a clearinghouse.

    d. execute a contract with CMS.

4. Confidentiality safeguards for electronic claims submission include

    a. creating a paper backup for each electronic claim.

    b. assigning and periodically changing passwords.

    c. filing electronic records by patient name.

    d. hiring an electronic claims processor.

5. The process of sending information between two or more individuals via computer linkage is called

    a. electronic data interchange.

    b. carrier-direct ECS.

    c. clearinghouse ECS.

    d. electronic claims submission.

Fill in the Blank

1. Another name for clearinghouse is _____.

2. For electronic claims submission, the phrase _____ is printed in place of the patient or provider signatures.

3. As with paper claims submission, _____ is the most important factor in ECS.

4. The _____ function of electronic claims processing software identifies invalid procedure codes.

5. _____ is defined as the ability to share information online.

Short Answer

Provide a brief definition for each term or a short answer for each question.

1. Identify four advantages of ECS. Explain why you believe your choices are advantages.

    _____

    _____

    _____

    _____

2. Discuss HIPAA's impact on electronic claims submission.

    _____

    _____

    _____

    _____

CHALLENGE ACTIVITY

Using the Internet, find a software company that sells electronic claims processing or billing software. What keywords should you use for the search? Use the online demo if one is available.

 WEBSITE

Centers for Medicare and Medicaid Services: http://www.cms.hhs.gov

CHAPTER 10

Common UB-04 (CMS-1450) Completion Guidelines

LEARNING OBJECTIVES

Upon successful completion of this chapter, the reader should have the knowledge to:

1. Accurately describe key terms and abbreviations.
2. Discuss a brief history of the UB-04.
3. Describe information reported in five sections of the UB-04.
4. Accurately complete UB-04 data fields.
5. Discuss the role of the health insurance billing specialist.

KEY TERMS

Accommodation code
Admitting diagnosis
Ambulatory payment
classification (APC)
Ancillary services code
Assignment of benefits
Attending physician
Centers for Medicare and
Medicaid Services (CMS)
Chargemaster
Clean claim
Clearinghouse
CMS-1450
Co-insurance days
Complication/co-morbidity
(CC)
Condition code
Covered days
Critical access hospital
(CAH)
*Current Procedural
Terminology* (CPT)

Department of Health and
Human Services (HHS)
Diagnosis-related group
(DRG)
Dirty claim
Electronic claims submission
(ECS)
Electronic health record
(EHR)
Encoder
Florida Shared System (FSS)
Form locator (FL)
*Healthcare Common
Procedure Coding System*
(HCPCS)
Health Care Finance
Administration (HCFA)
Health insurance claim
number (HICN)
Health Insurance Portability
and Accountability Act
(HIPAA)

Inpatient prospective
payment system (IPPS)
Insured
Intermediate care
facility (ICF)
*International Classification of
Diseases, Ninth Revision,
Clinical Modification*
(ICD-9-CM)
Length of stay (LOS)
Lifetime reserve days
Major complication/
co-morbidity (MCC)
Medicare-severity diagnosis-
related group (MS-DRG)
National Provider
Identification (NPI) number
National Uniform Billing
Committee (NUBC)
Occurrence code
Outpatient prospective
payment system (OPPS)

Primary payer
Principal diagnosis
Principal procedure
Prospective payment
   system (PPS)

Secondary payer
Skilled nursing facility (SNF)
Subscriber
Taxonomy code
Tertiary payer

UB-04
Uniform Hospital Discharge
   Data Set (UHDDS)
Value code

 ## OVERVIEW

This chapter is an introduction to the complex world of hospital insurance claims processing. Major topics include hospital reimbursement, developing the insurance claim, and guidelines for completing the hospital claims submission form. The universal hospital claims submission form is the CMS-1450, commonly called the UB-04.

Since 1974, the Department of Health and Human Services (HHS), then known as the Department of Health, Education, and Welfare, has required hospitals to report a minimum, common core of information for all hospital discharges. The Uniform Hospital Discharge Data Set (UHDDS) was implemented in 1974 and is periodically revised. The original purpose of the UHDDS was to capture uniform and comparable information related to hospital services provided to Medicare and Medicaid beneficiaries. Because the UB-04 includes data elements required by the UHDDS, all health insurance programs capture uniform and comparable information related to hospital services. Table 10–1 lists the UHDDS elements that are captured on the UB-04.

TABLE 10–1

Uniform Hospital Discharge Data Set	
Data Set	Explanation
Personal identification	A unique number assigned to each patient that distinguishes the patient and the patient's health record from all others
Date of birth	Patient's date of birth
Sex	Patient's sex (male, female, or unknown)
Residence	Zip code or code for foreign residence
Hospital identification	A unique number assigned to each facility
Admission and discharge dates	Dates the patient was admitted and discharged from the hospital
Physician identification	A unique number assigned to each physician; attending physician and operating physician, if applicable
Disposition of patient	The condition or way in which the patient left the hospital (e.g., discharged home; left against medical advice; died)
Expected payer for most of the bill	The major source that the patient expects to pay the bill (e.g., Blue Cross/Blue Shield, Medicare, Medicaid, workers' compensation)
Diagnoses	All diagnoses affecting the current hospital stay

continued on the next page

continued from the previous page

Principal diagnosis	The condition determined after study to be chiefly responsible for the patient's admission to the hospital
Secondary or other diagnoses	Diagnoses that affect the length of stay, develop during the length of stay, or affect the treatment received
Complication	An additional diagnosis that arises after the beginning of hospital care that modifies the course of the patient's illness or required medical care
Co-morbidity	A pre-existing condition that because of its presence with a specific principal diagnosis will cause an increase in the patient's length of stay
Procedures and dates	All significant procedures identified as surgical in nature, carrying a procedural risk, carrying an anesthetic risk, or requiring specialized training
Principal procedure	Procedure performed for definitive treatment rather than for diagnostic or exploratory purposes or procedure deemed necessary to take care of a complication. When two procedures appear to be principal, the procedure most closely related to the principal diagnosis should be selected as the principal procedure.

HOSPITAL REIMBURSEMENT

In the past, insurance companies paid the hospital based on the patient's length of stay (LOS) and the charges associated with the LOS. The LOS is defined as the number of days of service from admission to discharge date. Payment was usually a percentage of the total charges, and the patient was held responsible for the balance. This type of reimbursement is known as per-diem or fee-for-service payment. Under per diem and fee-for-service, there was little incentive to control the cost of hospital care.

During the 1970s, rising health care costs threatened the financial stability of the Medicare program. As a result of this threat, the Centers for Medicare and Medicaid Services (CMS), then called the Health Care Finance Administration (HCFA), established a new hospital reimbursement system. In 1983, CMS implemented a prospective payment system (PPS) for hospital inpatient services provided to Medicare beneficiaries. Under the original PPS, hospital reimbursement was based on diagnosis-related groups (DRGs). DRGs categorized or grouped diagnoses that were medically related, required similar treatments, and had similar lengths of stay. Each DRG had a preset reimbursement amount that the hospital received for each case that fell into a specific DRG. Under the original PPS, the patient's diagnosis determined the amount a hospital received for providing treatment. This payment system is called the inpatient prospective payment system (IPPS).

On October 1, 2007, CMS approved an extensive restructuring of the diagnostic-related groups for the IPPS. The original DRGs were replaced with Medicare-severity diagnosis-related groups (MS-DRGs). Implementation of MS-DRGs was phased in between October 1, 2007, and October 1, 2009. MS-DRGs are based on the patient's principal diagnosis, secondary

TABLE 10–2

MS-DRGs for Heart Failure		
MS-DRG	MS-DRG Title	Reimbursement Rate
MS-DRG 291	Heart failure w (with) MCC	$6246.00
MS-DRG 291	Heart failure w CC	$5030.00
MS-DRG 292	Heart failure w/o (without) CC/MCC	$4350.00

© 2014 Cengage Learning, All Rights Reserved.

diagnosis, procedures performed, sex, discharge status (alive or expired), the presence of a complication/co-morbidity (CC) or a major complication/co-morbidity (MCC), or the absence of a CC or MCC. For purposes of MS-DRG assignment, a CC is defined as a condition that substantially increases the use of hospital resources. An MCC is a more severe CC. Each MS-DRG has a preset reimbursement amount that the hospital receives for each case that falls into a specific MS-DRG. Table 10–2 lists three MS-DRGs for heart failure and a sample reimbursement rate based on CCs and MCCs.

Note the difference between the reimbursement rates for heart failure with or without a CC or MCC. Accurate MS-DRG assignment is dependent on accurate diagnosis and procedure codes, and accurate medical coding depends on the documentation in the patient's medical record. Other factors that affect MS-DRG assignment include the patient's gender and discharge status (e.g., alive or expired).

Several *International Classification of Diseases, Ninth Revision, Clinical Modification* (ICD-9-CM) diagnosis and procedure codes are related to each MS-DRG. For example, ICD-9-CM codes 428.0 through 428.9, with fifth digits as appropriate, represent about 15 different diagnoses and codes related to heart failure. Each of these codes would be grouped into an MS-DRG for heart failure. Encoders—computer programs used to assign diagnostic and procedure codes—are able to assign MS-DRGs based on the diagnostic and procedure codes and other data entered into the program.

In addition to hospital inpatient prospective payment, the CMS have implemented an outpatient prospective payment system (OPPS). This system applies to hospital outpatient/ambulatory procedures and ambulatory surgery centers (ASCs). Under OPPS, outpatient/ambulatory services provided to Medicare patients have a preset reimbursement rate. The payment rates are based on the ambulatory payment classification (APC) system. The APC system groups diagnostic and therapeutic procedures that are similar in nature and that consume similar resources. There are more than 9000 APC categories, and each APC is assigned a unique number. Several *Current Procedural Terminology* (CPT) codes are related to each APC. For example, APC 154, "Hernia/Hydrocele Procedures," includes the CPT codes for over 30 hernia repairs, ranging from reducing a hernia present in a premature infant to repairing a hernia with mesh placement. As with the IPPS, accurate coding is crucial to accurate APC assignment. Table 10–3 lists a few APCs and the procedures associated with the APC.

In a hospital, medical coders are responsible for assigning the appropriate ICD-9-CM, CPT, and level II *Healthcare Common Procedure Coding System* (HCPCS) codes for both inpatient and outpatient services. Medical coders are usually part of the health information or medical record department. Billing specialists and medical coders work together to ensure that insurance claims are filed in a timely manner.

TABLE 10–3

APCs with Procedures	
APC	**Procedures**
APC 105, "Revision/Removal of Pacemakers"	Removal of pacemaker system; removal of pacemaker electrode; removal of pulse generator
APC 113, "Excision, Lymphatic System"	Excision of lymph channels; removal of lymph nodes, neck; removal of lymph nodes, groin; biopsy/removal of lymph nodes
APC 142, "Small Intestine Endoscopy"	Endoscopy, including duodenum; endoscopy, including ileum; endoscopy, removal of polyps; endoscopy, removal of foreign object
APC 154, "Hernia/Hydrocele Procedure"	Repair of inguinal hernia; repair/reduction of umbilical hernia; repair/reduction of epigastric hernia; repair/reduction of inguinal hernia, premature infant; repair/reduction of ventral hernia
APC 254, "Level IV Ear, Nose, Throat Procedures"	Excision of mouth lesion; excision of tongue lesion; reconstruction of the mouth; partial removal of the tongue

© 2014 Cengage Learning, All Rights Reserved.

DEVELOPING THE INSURANCE CLAIM

Developing an insurance claim for inpatient and outpatient services includes the following activities:

- Registering the patient
- Capturing charges for services provided to the patient
- Assigning diagnosis and procedure codes

All activities associated with developing the insurance claim are equally important. The billing specialist is usually the last person to review and edit insurance claim information. When information is missing, incomplete, or inaccurate, the billing specialist works with other departments to resolve the problem.

Patient Registration

Developing an insurance claim begins when the patient comes to the facility for services. The admission staff is responsible for registering the patient. The registration process begins with a valid order for services that includes a diagnosis and physician signature. Admission staff collects the patient's demographic and insurance information, makes a copy of the patient's insurance identification card (both front and back), and enters the information into the hospital's database. For an electronic health record (EHR), the insurance card may be scanned, front and back, into the database. The information is entered with the patient's hospital or billing identification number. Registration information is the foundation for the health insurance claim.

When the patient is covered by more than one insurance plan, the admitting staff collects information that is used to determine the primary or secondary payer. A primary payer is the health insurance plan that is billed first. A secondary payer is the health insurance plan that is billed after payment is received from the primary payer.

When a Medicare beneficiary presents for hospital inpatient services and there is a question as to whether the services will be covered by Medicare, the admitting staff must give the beneficiary written notification of noncoverage. The notification must include the service(s) that may not be covered; the patient's responsibility for the cost of the noncovered services; the name and address of the organization for the beneficiary to appeal the notice; the time frame for an appeal; the beneficiary's signature; and the date and time that the beneficiary received the notification. The beneficiary's legal representative, such as a guardian, may act on behalf of the beneficiary. Figure 10–1 is a sample notice of noncoverage admission or preadmission.

Capturing Charges for Services Rendered

The charges for services provided to the patient must be entered into the hospital's database with the patient's hospital or billing identification number. Each hospital department enters the type of service or supply provided to the patient. For an EHR, supply items such as medications, special dressings, and catheterization kits have a bar code identification number that is scanned. If there is no bar code for the service or supply, the identification number is keyed (typed) into the database. All entries for a specific patient must include the patient's hospital or billing identification number. Once the entry is made, the hospital's chargemaster adds the correct charge for the service or supply. The chargemaster is a computer program or database that contains the charges and CPT and HCPCS codes for services and supplies. Charges range from the room rate for a specific hospital unit to the price for a blood test.

> **EXAMPLE**
>
> On March 10, 20YY, Rosa is admitted to Mercy Hospital for a radical mastectomy. During preoperative preparation, an intravenous line is placed, preoperative sedation is administered, and a urinary catheter is placed. The bar codes for the intravenous line, sedation medication, and catheter line are scanned, and Rosa's patient identification number is entered into the database. After surgery, Rosa is returned to her hospital room. Twenty-four hours later, Rosa develops a fever, and the surgeon orders a postoperative complete blood count (CBC), with a white blood cell differentiation. Once the blood test is completed, the identification code for the test and Rosa's patient identification number are entered into the database. Rosa is discharged on March 15, 20YY.

At the end of the hospital inpatient or ambulatory/outpatient stay, the discharge date is entered into the database. The admission and discharge dates are used to determine the patient's LOS. The LOS is determined by the number of days that the patient was an inpatient at midnight. The LOS is used to calculate the total room charges for the number of days the patient occupied a hospital bed. The discharge date is *not* included in the LOS. The LOS can be calculated by subtracting the admission date from the discharge date or by counting each day from the admission date to the day before the discharge date. If a patient dies or is transferred to another facility on the day of admission, the facility may bill for one day of service.

> **EXAMPLE**
>
> Rosa was admitted on March 10 and discharged on March 15. Rosa occupied a hospital bed from March 10 through March 14, which is five days. The discharge day, March 15, is not counted as an occupied bed. Therefore, Rosa's LOS is five days.

Superiorland Hospital
835 Marquette Drive
Blueberry, ME 49855
(906) 312-9446

NOTICE OF NONCOVERAGE ADMISSION OR PREADMISSION

March 21, 20YY
Date of Notice

March 21, 20YY
Admission Date

Akiko Park
Patient/Representative Name

491884766A
Health Insurance Claim Number

15 High Place, Blueberry ME 49855
Address

Elmer Mattson, MD
Attending Physician

Superiorland Hospital finds that your admission for bronchopneumonia is not covered under Medicare because inpatient treatment for bronchopneumonia is medically unnecessary or could be safely rendered in another setting. This determination was based on Superiorland's understanding and interpretation of available Medicare coverage policies and guidelines. You should discuss other arrangements with your physician. If you decide to be admitted to Superiorland Hospital, you will be financially responsible for all charges related to your inpatient treatment.

This notice, however, is not an official Medicare determination. Maine Peer Review, Inc., is authorized by the Medicare program to review inpatient hospital services provided to Medicare beneficiaries. **If you disagree with our conclusion, you should contact** Maine Peer Review, Inc., **to have your case reviewed**. The following options are available:

1. **Preadmission Review:** Within three days of receipt of this notice, or if you choose to be admitted at any point during the stay, request an *immediate review* of the facts in your case. You may make this request through the hospital or directly to Maine Peer Review.

2. **Admission Review:** Immediately, or at any point during your hospital stay, request an *immediate review* of the facts in your case. You may make this request through the hospital or directly to Maine Peer Review, Inc., at the address listed below.

3. **If you do not wish for an immediate review, you may still request a review within 30 calendar days from the date of receipt of this notice. You may contact** Maine Peer Review **by telephone or in writing.**

MAINE PEER REVIEW 336 BAGGS ROAD BLUEBERRY, ME 57446 1-800-555-5900

1. Maine Peer Review will send you a **formal determination** of the medical necessity and appropriateness of your hospitalization, and will inform you of your reconsideration and appeal rights.

2. If Maine Peer Review **disagrees with the hospital**, you will be refunded any money you paid the hospital except for any amounts for deductible, coinsurance, and convenience services or items normally not covered by Medicare.

3. If Maine Peer Review **agrees with the hospital**, you are responsible for payment for all services beginning on (fill in the date when the patient is responsible for the bill).

ACKNOWLEDGEMENT OF RECEIPT OF NOTICE

I understand that my signature does not indicate that I agree with this notice of noncoverage of benefits. It indicates only that I have received a copy of the notice.

Signature of Beneficiary or Legal Representative

Date

Time

Figure 10–1 Notice of Noncoverage Admission or Preadmission

Assigning Diagnosis and Procedure Codes

As stated previously, medical coders are responsible for assigning the appropriate diagnosis and procedure codes related to hospital services. The patient's medical record is the source document for this activity. In the past, medical coders manually assigned the appropriate ICD-9-CM, CPT, or HCPCS level II codes. In today's electronic age, hospitals have invested in high-quality computer-assisted coding programs called encoders. Several commercial vendors market encoders, and the hospital is able to select the product that best meets its needs.

Encoders are valuable tools, but they cannot replace qualified medical coders. The medical coder carefully reviews the patient's record for the principal diagnosis, the principal procedure, and additional diagnoses and procedures that affect the current hospital stay. Documentation in the patient's record *must* clearly support every code assigned to the case. If the documentation is incomplete or questionable, the medical coder communicates with the appropriate physician or hospital department for additional information.

The medical coder enters diagnostic and procedure information into the encoder. The encoder program delivers on-screen prompts that provide the coder with instructional notes similar to those available in the coding reference books. The medical coder must also follow all coding conventions and regulatory guidelines. Diagnosis and procedure codes are entered into the hospital's database by using the patient identification number. After the codes are entered, patient information is released to the billing department for insurance claim processing.

REINFORCEMENT EXERCISES 10–1

Spell out each abbreviation and write a brief description for the term or phrase.

1. APC

_____

_____

_____

2. CC

_____

_____

_____

3. CMS

_____

_____

_____

continued on the next page

continued from the previous page

4. HHS

_____

_____

_____

5. LOS

_____

_____

_____

6. MCC

_____

_____

_____

7. MS-DRG

_____

_____

_____

8. OPPS

_____

_____

_____

9. IPPS

_____

_____

_____

10. UHDDS

_____

_____

_____

continued on the next page

continued from the previous page

11. EHR

_____

_____

_____

Briefly define or describe the following terms.

1. Chargemaster

_____

_____

_____

2. Co-morbidity

_____

_____

_____

3. Complication

_____

_____

_____

4. Disposition of patient

_____

_____

_____

5. Encoder

_____

_____

_____

continued on the next page

continued from the previous page

6. Primary payer

_____

_____

_____

7. Principal diagnosis

_____

_____

_____

8. Principal procedure

_____

_____

_____

9. Secondary payer

_____

_____

_____

10. Uniform Bill 04 (UB-04)

_____

_____

_____

UB-04 Completion Guidelines

The UB-04 is a universal claims submission form that is accepted by nearly all health insurance companies. The UB-04 was developed and is revised by the National Uniform Billing Committee (NUBC). The NUBC was established to develop a claims submission form that could replace the many billing forms hospitals were required to use. The UB-04 is designed to capture information for reimbursement and statistical purposes. The most current information about the UB-04 form can be found on the NUBC or CMS websites.

General guidelines for completing the UB-04 include the following:

- All information should be keyed or typed.
- Dates are usually entered using eight digits to represent the month, day, and year.

- Key all alphabetic characters in uppercase letters.
- Leave one blank space between last name, first name, and middle initial.
- Do not key the letter O for the number zero.
- Do not use punctuation in the patient/policyholder's name, except for a hyphen in a compound name.
- Do not use designations such as Sr. or Jr.
- Do not use dollar signs, decimals, or commas in any monetary field. Two zeros in the cents column are acceptable.
- Do not include the decimal in medical codes.
- Do not add a dash in front of a procedure code modifier.

Insurance carriers provide guidelines for completing the UB-04 by way of manuals, newsletters, e-mails, and online instruction guides. Guidelines for Medicare claims processing are found in the *Medicare Claims Processing Manual,* Chapter 25, "Completing and Processing [the] UB-04." These guidelines are available at the CMS website. The completion guidelines in this chapter are based on Medicare guidelines and interviews with several billing specialists. The information relates primarily to hospital claims submission.

There are 81 fields on the UB-04. Each field, known as a **form locator (FL)**, has a number, and most fields have a name or title. Instructions for completing the UB-04 are divided into five general sections: (1) patient and provider information; (2) conditions, events, and additional information that may affect claims payment; (3) services provided and related charges; (4) insurance company (payer), insured, and employer information; and (5) medical codes and physician identification information. Each section is presented in a figure that corresponds to the discussion of the section. Refer to the figures as you read the explanations. All fields are keyed in uppercase letters.

UB-04 Patient and Provider Information (FL 1–17)

The first 17 fields capture information about the hospital and the patient. Figure 10–2 shows FL 1 through FL 17. Refer to the figure as you learn about these fields.

FL 1: Provider Name, Address, and Telephone Number (Untitled)

Enter the following hospital information on four lines: (a) hospital name; (b) street address or post office box number; (c) city, state, and zip code; (d) telephone number with area code, fax number, and the country code, if applicable. Lines a–c are required by all insurance carriers.

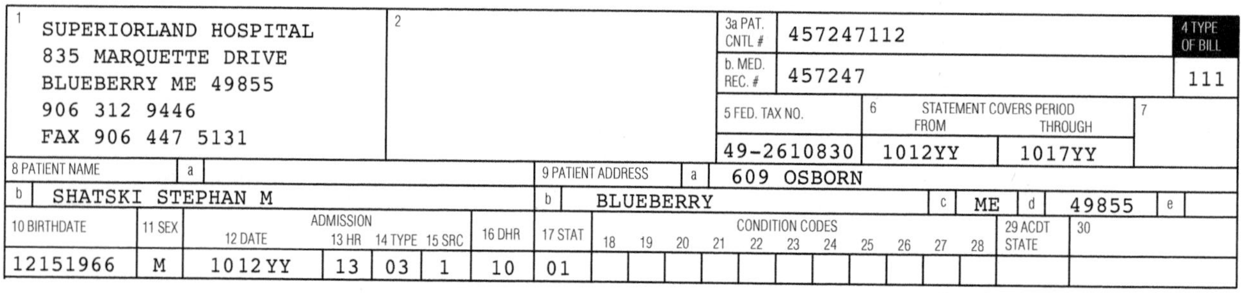
1
SUPERIORLAND HOSPITAL
835 MARQUETTE DRIVE
BLUEBERRY ME 49855
906 312 9446
FAX 906 447 5131

2

3a PAT. CNTL # 457247112
b. MED. REC. # 457247
4 TYPE OF BILL 111
5 FED. TAX NO. 49-2610830
6 STATEMENT COVERS PERIOD FROM 1012YY THROUGH 1017YY
7

8 PATIENT NAME a
b SHATSKI STEPHAN M
9 PATIENT ADDRESS a 609 OSBORN
b BLUEBERRY c ME d 49855 e

10 BIRTHDATE	11 SEX	12 DATE (ADMISSION)	13 HR	14 TYPE	15 SRC	16 DHR	17 STAT	18–28 CONDITION CODES	29 ACDT STATE	30
12151966	M	1012YY	13	03	1	10	01			

Figure 10–2 UB-04 FL 1–17

For instructional use only. Courtesy of the Centers for Medicare and Medicaid Services, www.cms.hhs.gov.

FL 2: Pay-to Name, Address, (Untitled)

If the claim is paid to an entity other than the billing provider named in FL1, enter the name, address, city, state, and zip code of the pay-to entity. Medicare does not require this field.

FL 3a: Patient Control Number (PAT CNTL #)

The patient control number is assigned by the hospital and is also known as the "account number" or "billing number." An account number is assigned each time a patient is admitted. This number is referenced on the remittance advice form that is received from the insurance carrier. The patient control number may consist of alphanumeric or only numeric characters. This field is required.

FL 3b: Medical Record Number

Enter the patient's medical record number, which is assigned by the provider. This number is not the same as the patient control number in FL 3a. This field is optional.

FL 4: Type of Bill (TOB)

This field is required by all third-party payers. The type of bill is a three-digit number, and each digit has a specific meaning. The first digit tells the insurance carrier where the service was provided (type of facility). Table 10–4 lists the type of facility associated with the first digit.

TABLE 10–4

FL 4 TOB First Digit/Type of Facility	
TOB First Digit	**Type of Facility**
1	Hospital—facility licensed to provide inpatient treatment
2	**Skilled nursing facility (SNF)**—facility or distinct part of a hospital that is licensed to provide skilled nursing care or rehabilitation services
3	Home health agency (HHA)—provider licensed to provide skilled nursing and other therapeutic services, usually in the patient's home
4	Religious nonmedical hospital
5	Reserved for national assignment
6	**Intermediate care facility (ICF)**—facility that provides services to patients who do not need skilled nursing care
7	Clinic or hospital-based renal dialysis facility—an outpatient facility that provides scheduled diagnostic, treatment, rehabilitative, and educational services for ambulatory patients
8	Specialty facility or ambulatory surgery center (ASC)—facility that provides some type of specialty services or is licensed to perform surgical procedures that do not require inpatient hospitalization
9	Reserved for national assignment

TABLE 10–5

FL 4 TOB Second Digit for Hospitals	
TOB Second Digit	**Description**
1	Inpatient—services provided from admission to discharge. For Medicare, this applies to services covered by Part A (hospital) insurance.
2	Inpatient—services provided from admission to discharge that are covered by Medicare Part B insurance
3	Outpatient—services including outpatient/ambulatory surgeries, diagnostic tests or procedures, and various therapies
4	Other—diagnostic tests provided as a result of a referral from a provider/physician not directly associated with the hospital or skilled nursing facility (e.g., a family physician orders a mammography and the individual has the test done at the hospital's radiology department)
8	Swing bed—skilled or intermediate nursing care provided in an acute care hospital. This applies to Medicare cases; the hospital must have a swing bed agreement with the Medicare fiscal intermediary.

© 2014 Cengage Learning, All Rights Reserved.

The second digit represents the type of care provided, such as inpatient or outpatient. This digit is also known as the *billing classification*. Table 10–5 includes a brief description for each second digit associated with services provided by a hospital.

The third digit, which is called the "frequency of bill," identifies special conditions related to the claim, such as a series of services; late charges; replacement of a prior claim; or a cancellation of a prior claim. When a patient is scheduled to receive a series of services, such as physical therapy treatments, the facility may submit interim claims from the date the therapy begins until the date it ends. Third digits 2, 3, and 4 tell the insurance carrier that the bill is related to a series of services. The number 4 is used to identify the final interim claim related to a series of services. More than one unit of service may be reported on each interim claim. Table 10–6 provides a brief description of commonly used third digits.

TABLE 10–6

TOB Frequency of Bill/Special Conditions	
TOB Third Digit	**Description**
1	Hospital inpatient from admission through discharge
2, 3	Interim claim for a series of services
4	Final interim claim for a series of services
5	Late charge claim
7	Replacement claim—applies to claims submitted for under- or overpayment adjustments; original claim is null and void
8	Void/cancel of a prior claim—used to change the provider identification number, or health insurance claim number, or to refund a duplicate payment

© 2014 Cengage Learning, All Rights Reserved.

EXAMPLE: TYPE OF BILL THIRD DIGIT FOR A SERIES OF SERVICES

Following a stroke, Martha is scheduled for rehabilitative physical therapy as a hospital outpatient. She participates in a variety of physical therapy treatments three days per week for 12 weeks, for a total of 36 treatments. The hospital submits three claims (about once a month or every four weeks) for the physical therapy services. The TOB first and second digit for each claim is 13, which indicates that the services were provided in a hospital outpatient setting. The type of bill code on the first claim is 132. The third digit (2) indicates that the claim is an interim claim related to a series of services or treatments. The type of bill code on the second claim is 133. The third digit (3) identifies the claim as an interim claim related to a series of treatments. The type of bill code on the third claim is 134. The third digit (4) identifies the claim as the final interim claim related to a series of treatments.

Each interim claim includes the number of treatments provided during the specific time frame of the claim. In this example, 12 treatments are entered on the UB-04 each time an interim claim is submitted.

For Medicare claims, the TOB is a four-digit code that always begins with a *zero*. The CMS ignores the zero, and essentially treats the TOB as a three-digit code.

FL 5: Federal Tax Number

Enter the facility's nine-digit federal tax identification number with a hyphen between the second and third digits (xx-xxxxxxx). Some insurance carriers do not allow a hyphen between the second and third digits. This field is required.

FL 6: Statement Covers Period

This field captures the beginning and ending dates of service, usually the admission and discharge dates. Dates are entered with six or eight digits. The eight-digit form is MMDDYYYY. Enter the admission date under the word "from" and the discharge date under the word "through."

FL 7: Untitled

Reserved for future use.

FL 8: Patient Name

FL 8a: This field is completed when the patient has a unique identification number assigned by the insurance plan, such as a case number for a workers' compensation claim.

FL 8b: Enter the patient's last name, first name, and middle initial (if known).

FL 9: Patient Address

FL 9a: Enter the patient's street address. Enter an apartment number, if applicable.

FL 9b: Enter the name of the city, town, or other municipality.

FL 9c: Enter the two-character state abbreviation.

FL 9d: Enter the zip code.

FL 9e: Enter the country code, when applicable.

FL 10: Patient's Birth Date

Enter the patient's birth date in the eight-digit format (MMDDYYYY).

FL 11: Sex

Enter an M for male or an F for female. Some insurance companies allow U for unknown.

REINFORCEMENT EXERCISES 10–2

Provide a brief explanation for each term or abbreviation.

1. Form locator (FL)

_____

_____

_____

2. NUBC

_____

_____

_____

3. Patient control number

_____

_____

_____

4. TOB

_____

_____

_____

5. TOB first digit

_____

_____

_____

6. TOB second digit

_____

_____

_____

continued on the next page

continued from the previous page

7. TOB third digit

_____

_____

_____

FL 12: Admission Date

Enter the date the patient was admitted for inpatient care or outpatient services or enter the home health care start date. The date is entered in a six- or eight-digit format. Do not use any punctuation between the year, month, and day.

FL 13: Admission Hour

When the insurance plan requires this field, enter the hour the patient was admitted to the facility. Hours are reported in military time, sometimes called the 24-hour clock. Midnight is noted as 00; 1 a.m. as 01; 2 a.m. as 02; and so forth. Noon is noted as 12; 1 p.m. as 13; 2 p.m. as 14; and so forth. The hospital's registration/admission software may automatically enter the hour of admission.

FL 14: Type of Admission

Enter the number that identifies the *priority* of the admission as follows:

> **01: Emergency:** The patient required immediate medical intervention as a result of severe, life-threatening, or potentially disabling conditions.
> **02: Urgent:** The patient required immediate attention.
> **03: Elective:** The patient's condition permitted adequate time to schedule the admission.
> **04: Newborn**
> **05: Trauma Center:** Admission to a licensed trauma center.
> **06–08: Reserved for local use**
> **09:** Information not available.

Codes for this field are supplied by the insurance company or fiscal intermediary.

FL 15: Source of Admission (SRC)

This field is required by Medicare, except for TOB codes as 14X (hospital other Part B). Codes in this field identify the source of the referral for the admission or visit, such as transfers from a hospital or nursing home. This field may be required by other insurance carriers. Table 10–7 lists some source of admission codes with descriptions.

FL 16: Discharge Hour (DHR)

Enter the time that the patient was discharged. When this field is required, hours are reported in military time, as described in FL 13.

TABLE 10–7

Code	Description
1	Physician referral—inpatient admission because of the recommendation of the personal physician; outpatient services requested by personal physician or by self-referral
2	Clinic referral—admission on the recommendation of the facility's clinic physician
3	Managed care plan referral—admission on the recommendation of a managed care plan physician
4	Hospital transfer—admission because of the transfer from an acute care facility
5	Skilled nursing facility transfer—admission because of the transfer from a skilled nursing facility
6	Transfer from another health care facility—admission because of the transfer from a facility other than an acute care hospital or skilled nursing facility
7	Emergency room—admission on the recommendation of the facility's emergency room/ department physician
8	Court/law enforcement—admission because of the action of a court or law enforcement agency representative (e.g., psychiatric inpatient admission)
9	Information not available—means by which the patient was admitted to this facility is not known
A	Transfer from a critical access hospital (CAH)—admission because of the transfer from a critical access hospital, usually to a larger hospital or regional medical center

Source of Admission Codes

FL 17: Patient Status (STAT)

Enter the status of the patient at the time of discharge. This two-digit code is required by all payers. Table 10–8 lists the codes with their meanings. Codes 08; 10–19; 21–29; 31–39; 44–49; 52–50; and 67–99 are reserved for national assignment or for use by states or other reporting agencies.

REINFORCEMENT EXERCISES 10-3

Complete FL 1 through FL 17 in Figure 10–3 using the information in the following paragraph.

Alex Franks was admitted to Memorial Hospital at 1 p.m. on March 20, 20YY. He underwent scheduled surgery for total knee replacement, as recommended by his family physician. His medical record number is 381509 and his account number is 492618. He was discharged at 10 a.m. on March 25, 20YY, and went home. He lives at 825 Maplewood Avenue in Huntsville, Texas 59855. Alex was born on June 5, 1956. Alex has Blue Cross health insurance through his employer, Texas Software Corporation. His hospital stay is covered, and there are no co-insurance days. Memorial Hospital is located in Huntsville at 101 International Drive; phone number is (919) 555-1010. Memorial's federal tax number is 50-3729492. The type of bill code for this admission is 111, which means hospital (1) inpatient (1) from admission to discharge (1).

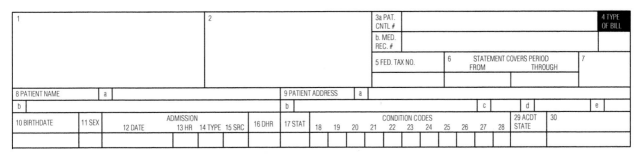

Figure 10–3 UB-04 FL 1–17

For instructional use only. Courtesy of the Centers for Medicare and Medicaid Services, www.cms.hhs.gov.

TABLE 10–8

Discharge Status Codes and Descriptions	
Code	**Description**
01	Discharged; home, self
02	Discharged/transferred; other inpatient hospital
03	Discharged/transferred to a Medicare certified SNF
04	Discharged/transferred to an ICF
05	Discharged/transferred to another type of institution not defined elsewhere
06	Discharged/transferred; home health agency
07	Discharged against medical advice
20	Expired or did not recover (religious nonmedical health care facility)
40	Expired, home; hospice claims only
41	Expired in a medical facility, such as a hospital, SNF, ICF, or freestanding hospice; hospice claims only
42	Expired, place unknown; hospice claims only
43	Discharged/transferred to a federal health care facility
50	Discharged; home hospice care
51	Discharged; medical facility hospice care
61	Discharged/transferred; swing bed, same facility
62	Discharged/transferred; rehabilitation facility
63	Discharged/transferred; long-term care hospital
64	Discharged/transferred to a Medicaid certified nursing facility
65	Discharged/transferred to a psychiatric hospital or psychiatric distinct unit of a hospital
66	Discharged/transferred to a **critical access hospital (CAH)**

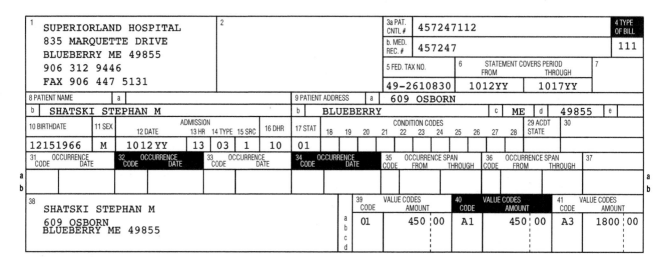

Figure 10–4 UB-04 FL 18–41

For instructional use only. Courtesy of the Centers for Medicare and Medicaid Services, www.cms.hhs.gov.

UB-04 Condition and Event Information (FL 18–41)

Fields 18 through 41 capture additional information about conditions and events that affect payment of the claim. There are three major categories in this section: (1) condition codes (FL 18–28), which relate to the patient's insurance eligibility and primary or secondary insurance coverage; (2) occurrence codes (FL 31–36), which identify specific events that determine liability for paying the claim, including coordinating health insurance benefits; and (3) value codes and amounts (FL 39–41), which identify actual dollar amounts that affect the patient's insurance benefits. Fields 29, 30, 37, and 38 are also described in this section. Figure 10–4 illustrates FL 18 through 41. Refer to the figure as you read about these fields.

FL 18–28: Condition Codes

This section of the UB-04 should be labeled "financial condition codes" because the information is used to determine the patient's insurance benefits, primary and secondary insurance coverage, and insurance liability other than the patient's health insurance carrier. These codes are usually associated with determining whether Medicare is the primary or secondary payer. There are literally hundreds of condition codes. It is beyond the scope of this text to define all of them. Some of the more commonly used condition codes are listed here:

02: Condition is employment related; workers' compensation may be the primary payer.

09: Neither the patient nor spouse is employed; required by Medicare when the patient and spouse are not employed and do not have insurance coverage with an employer.

10: Patient or spouse is employed, but no employer-sponsored group health insurance program coverage exists; required by Medicare when the patient or spouse is employed but does not have health insurance with the employer.

21: Billing for denial notice; hospital knows that the service is not covered but needs a denial notice from Medicare in order to bill another insurance carrier.

28: Patient and/or spouse's employer-sponsored group health plan is secondary to Medicare.

39: Private room medically necessary; most insurance coverage pays for a semiprivate room (two patients per room); medical necessity must be documented, and the insurance carrier may require such documentation.

Enter as many codes as necessary to accurately describe the patient's financial condition related to health insurance coverage.

FL 29: Accident State (ACDT STATE)

If the admission is a result of an automobile accident, enter the two-character abbreviation for the state where the accident took place. Medicare does not require this field.

FL 30: (Untitled)

This is reserved for future use.

FL 31–34: Occurrence Codes and Dates

Occurrence codes define a specific event, such as an auto accident, that affects payment of the claim. The date of the occurrence must also be reported. FL 31a through FL 34a must be used before entering additional codes and dates in FL 31b through FL 34b. Dates are entered in a six- or eight-digit format. Some of the more commonly used occurrence codes are listed here:

01: Auto accident

02: No-fault insurance

03: Other accident, non-auto accident

04: Accident, employment related

06: Crime victim

11: Onset of symptoms/illness; required when outpatient therapy services, such as physical therapy, are provided; include the date that the patient first became aware of the symptoms

16: Date of last therapy; indicates the last day of therapy services such as physical, occupational, or speech therapy

18: Date of retirement of the patient/beneficiary; required by Medicare

19: Date of retirement of spouse; required by Medicare

24: Date insurance denied; date that an insurance carrier other than Medicare denied payment of the claim

32: Date beneficiary is notified of intent to bill for procedures or treatments; required by Medicare when the patient is covered by Medicare and elects to undergo a procedure or treatment that is not covered by Medicare. The patient must be given a written Advance Beneficiary Notice that describes the procedure and the cost and tells the patient that Medicare will not pay for the procedure.

If there are more than eight occurrences, use FL 35 and FL 36 to enter additional codes and dates. Leave the "through" block blank.

FL 35 and 36: Occurrence Span

FL 35 and FL 36 are used to identify occurrences that happen over a period of time (e.g., a series of outpatient services, such as physical therapy). The beginning and ending dates of the occurrence are entered in the *From* and *Through* fields.

FL 37: (Untitled)

This is reserved for future use.

FL 38: Responsible Party (Untitled)

Enter the name and address of the person who is responsible for paying the bill. Patients who have reached the age of majority or who are emancipated minors are responsible for the bill, regardless of insurance coverage. When the patient is covered by health insurance, the responsible party pays the amount not covered by insurance. This field does not apply to individuals who are covered by Medicaid. All providers must accept Medicaid payment and are not allowed to bill the patient for the remaining balance.

FL 39–41: Value Codes

FL 39 through FL 41 capture the actual monetary value associated with insurance payment and room rates. The value code is a two-character numeric, alphabetic, or alphanumeric code that identifies the following information:

- An estimated amount that will be paid by the patient's insurance carrier
- The semiprivate room rate
- Co-insurance, co-payments, and deductibles that are the patient's responsibility
- Services that are not covered by the patient's health insurance

When more than one value code is needed, enter data in lines 39a through 41a first; in lines 39b through 41b second; and so forth. The value code is entered in the *Code* field and the associated dollar amount is entered in the *Amount* field. Insurance carriers, fiscal intermediaries, and Medicare contractors may require a specific order for entering value codes. Table 10–9 lists and describes commonly used value codes.

EXAMPLE: ENTERING VALUE CODES

Stephan was admitted for a total hip replacement and was in the hospital for five days. The semiprivate room rate for an orthopedic bed is $450 per day.

The billing specialist enters the value codes and dollar amounts as follows:

FL 39a: 01 under *Code*; 450 00 under *Amount*. 01 is the code for the most common semiprivate room rate; 450 00, is per day actual dollar amount

FL 40a: A1 under *Code*; 450 00 under *Amount*. A1 indicates the estimated deductible; 450 00 is the deductible actual dollar amount

FL 41a: A3 under *Code*; 1800 00 under *Amount*. A3 indicates the estimated payment from the primary payer; 1800 00 is the estimated payment actual dollar amount

There are hundreds of value codes representing services ranging from units of blood to co-insurance days. Requirements for completing FL 39 through FL 41 vary by insurance carrier. However, nearly all insurance carriers require information related to the semiprivate room rate, the estimated payment from the insurance carrier, co-insurance, co-payments, and deductibles. Secondary payers require value codes and amounts that are paid by a primary payer.

TABLE 10–9

Value Codes with Descriptions	
Code	**Description**
01	Most common semiprivate room rate
14	No-fault auto or other insurance
15	Workers' compensation
32	Multiple patient ambulance transport (more than one patient, single ambulance)
37	Pints of blood furnished
47	Any liability insurance (accident, lawsuit, product liability suit)
50	Physical therapy visits
80	**Covered days**; number of days covered by health insurance; for Medicare claims, the admission staff or billing specialist can determine how many covered days are available to a Medicare beneficiary by accessing a regional Medicare Common Working File (CWF) database. The **Florida Shared System (FSS)** is one of the regional databases that serves this purpose.
81	Noncovered days; number of days not covered by health insurance
82	**Co-insurance days**; number of days that the patient must pay a co-insurance fee. Medicare co-insurance days are counted from the 61st hospital day to the 150th hospital day; the co-insurance amount from the 61st day to the 90th day is 25% of the Medicare deductible; the coinsurance amount from the 91st day to the 150th day is 50% of the Medicare deductible. Other insurance plans may also have co-insurance day requirements.
83	**Lifetime reserve days**; number of days from the patient's Medicare lifetime reserve days (60 days maximum) for inpatient hospital care. The number of lifetime reserve days for a Medicare beneficiary is available by accessing one of the nine regional CWF databases. Lifetime reserve days can be used after the 90th day of hospitalization.
A1	Estimated deductible, Payer A (primary payer) (patient's responsibility)
A3	Estimated payment from Payer A (primary payer)
B3	Estimated payment from Payer B (secondary payer)

REINFORCEMENT EXERCISES 10–4

Write a brief description of the following terms.

1. Condition codes

_____

_____

2. Occurrence codes

_____

_____

continued on the next page

continued from the previous page

3. Value codes

_____

_____

4. Occurrence span codes

_____

_____

5. Common working file

_____

_____

6. Co-insurance days

_____

_____

7. Lifetime reserve days

_____

_____

Identify each of the following codes and descriptions as a condition code, an occurrence code, or a value code.

1. A3: Estimated payment from the primary payer _____

2. 01: Auto accident _____

3. 01: Most common semiprivate room rate _____

4. 06: Crime victim _____

5. 09: Neither patient nor spouse is employed _____

6. 15: Workers' compensation _____

7. 16: Date of last therapy _____

8. 21: Billing for denial _____

9. 39: Private room medically necessary _____

10. 83: Lifetime reserve days _____

FL 42 and FL 43: Revenue Code (REV. CD.) and Description

Revenue codes are three- or four-digit numbers that identify services provided to the patient. When the insurance carrier requires a four-digit entry in this field, the first digit is always 0. Each revenue code has a narrative description that is entered in FL 43. The last entry in FL 42–43 is *always* revenue code 001, with the description "total charges" in FL 43. The total charges must equal the sum of both covered and noncovered charges. There are nearly 1000 revenue codes used by all insurance carriers.

Revenue codes are divided into two categories: accommodation codes and ancillary services codes. Accommodation codes identify the type of bed—such as medical/surgical, pediatric, or psychiatric—that the patient occupies in a hospital room. A hospital room is classified as follows: "private," a single-bed room; "semiprivate," two beds per room or three and four beds per room; and "ward," five or more beds per room. Room and board charges/rates vary by room classification and type of bed. A private room in an intensive care unit (ICU) has a higher room rate than a ward in a medical/surgical unit. The room and board rate includes items and services such as routine linens, towels, nightgowns, meals, and routine nursing care associated with the specific unit. Table 10–10 lists some of the accommodation revenue codes with descriptions.

Ancillary services codes identify services and supplies that are not included in the room and board charges. Items and services such as an egg-crate mattress, pharmacy, laboratory tests, and

TABLE 10–10

Accommodation Revenue Codes (FL 42)	
Code	Definition
114	Psychiatric, private room
116	Detoxification unit, private room
120	General medical, semiprivate room
121	Medical/surgical, gynecology (GYN), semiprivate room
122	Obstetrics (OB), semiprivate room
123	Pediatric, semiprivate room
124	Psychiatric, semiprivate room
151	Medical/surgical, gynecology, ward
171	Newborn nursery, Level I, routine newborn care
174	Newborn nursery, Level IV, newborn intensive care
201	Intensive care unit (ICU), surgical care
206	Intermediate intensive care unit, post ICU, also called step down
211	Coronary care unit (CCU), myocardial infarction care
212	Coronary care unit, pulmonary care
213	Coronary care unit, heart transplant care

TABLE 10–11

Ancillary Services Revenue Codes (FL 42)	
Ancillary Services Code	**Description**
250	Pharmacy, general
258	Intravenous (IV) solutions
261	IV therapy, infusion pump
264	IV therapy/supplies
274	Prosthetic device
275	Pacemaker
276	Intraocular lens
301	Laboratory, blood chemistry tests
306	Lab/bacteriology and microbiology blood tests
311	Lab/pathological, cytology; laboratory tests on cells
312	Lab/pathological, histology; laboratory tests on tissue
314	Lab/pathological, biopsy
321	Radiology/diagnostic, angiocardiography
322	Radiology/diagnostic, arthrography
324	Chest x-ray
331	Radiology/therapeutic, chemotherapy—injected
333	Radiology/therapeutic, radiation therapy
341	Nuclear medicine, diagnostic procedures
342	Nuclear medicine, therapeutic procedures
352	Computerized tomography (CT) scans, whole body
360	Operating room services
370	Anesthesia, general
402	Other imaging services, ultrasound
421	Physical therapy visit
710	Recovery room
730	EKG/ECG (electrocardiogram)

radiology services are separate entries in FL 42 and FL 43. Table 10–11 lists some of the ancillary services revenue codes with descriptions.

When a UB-04 is generated, the hospital's billing software (chargemaster) enters the revenue codes in FL 42. A narrative description of the revenue code is simultaneously entered in FL 43.

The billing specialist reviews the revenue codes and descriptions to determine if entries are complete and accurate.

> **EXAMPLE: REVENUE CODE REVIEW**
>
> Jane Li reviews the UB-04 for a patient who underwent a total hip replacement. She notes that a general anesthesia revenue code (370) and an operating room service code (360) are listed in FL 42 and FL 43. A code for recovery room services is not included on the UB-04. Jane knows that a recovery room code (710) is billed with a general anesthesia code. Jane puts a hold on the claim and notifies the surgical department that a recovery room revenue code is needed. Surgical department staff enters the revenue code. Jane retrieves the UB-04, completes the editing process, and releases the claim for submission.

FL 44: HCPCS/Rates

FL 44 is used to report three types of information: (1) the CPT or HCPCS code for the services identified in FL 42 and FL 43; (2) the per-day room rate for inpatient care for the type of accommodation identified in FL 42 and FL 43; and (3) the Health Insurance Prospective Payment System (HIPPS) rate that apply to skilled nursing facilities.

For inpatient hospital claims, the first line of FL 42 is the accommodation code, the FL 43 is a narrative description of the accommodation (Figure 10–5), and the per-day room rate is entered in FL 44. For inpatient ancillary services identified in FL 42 and 43, such as pharmacy and IV solutions, FL 44 is left blank (see Figure 10–5).

For outpatient (ambulatory) claims, FL 44 is used to report either the CPT codes or the HCPCS codes that apply to the ancillary services revenue codes identified in FL 42 and FL 43. The CPT or HCPCS codes identify the *specific* service provided to the patient. For example, there are about 50 blood chemistry tests associated with revenue code 301 (laboratory, chemistry). When different blood chemistry tests are done, the revenue code is always 301, and the CPT or

42 REV. CD.	43 DESCRIPTION	44 HCPCS / RATES	45 SERV. DATE	46 SERV. UNITS	47 TOTAL CHARGES	48 NON-COVERED CHARGES	49	
120	R/B SEMI	350 00		5	1750 00			1
250	PHARMACY				750 00			2
258	IV SOLUTIONS				5 00			3
274	PROSTHETIC DEVICE				400 00			4
301	LAB / CHEMISTRY				350 00			5
324	DX CHEST / XRAY				75 00	75 00		6
360	OR SERVICES				1500 00			7
370	ANESTHESIA				200 00			8
421	PHYS THERAP / VISIT				75 00			9
710	RECOVERY ROOM				120 00			10
730	EKG/ECG				95 00			11
								12
								13
								14
								15
								16
								17
								18
								19
								20
								21
								22
001	TOTAL CHARGES			5	5320 00	75 00		23

Figure 10–5 UB-04 FL 42–49

HCPCS code tells the insurance carrier exactly which tests the patient received. CPT or HCPCS codes are required entries for Medicare outpatient claims.

FL 45: Service Date (SERV. DATE)

For inpatient services, FL 45 may not be required and is left blank. Some insurance carriers require this field for outpatient services, such as diagnostic tests. If required, enter the date each service identified in FL 42–44 was provided.

FL 46: Service Units (SERV. UNITS)

FL 46 is used to report the number of services identified in FL 42–44 that were provided. Units of service include items such as the number of days in the type of accommodation (hospital room), pints of blood, number of tests performed, and number of therapeutic activities or treatments. Therapeutic activity units of service are measured in 15- or 30-minute increments, which means that every 15 or 30 minutes of therapy is equal to one unit of service. For example, if a patient spends 38 minutes in physical therapy and a unit of service is 30 minutes, enter 1 in FL 46.

FL 47: Total Charges

Enter the total charges for the services identified in FL 42.

FL 48: Noncovered Charges

Enter the charges for the services identified in FL 42 that are *not* covered by the insurance carrier. The noncovered charges are included in the dollar amount entered in FL 47.

FL 49: Untitled

This is for future use.

REINFORCEMENT EXERCISES 10–5

Fill in the blank.

1. _____ is the description for the last entry in FL 43.

2. The type of bed occupied by the patient is identified by a(n) _____.

3. _____ identify services and supplies not included in the room and board rates.

4. _____ identify a specific service that was provided during an outpatient episode of care.

5. Therapeutic activity units of service are measured in _____.

Insurance and Employer Information (FL 50–65)

This section of the UB-04 captures information related to insurance plans, the patient or insured, and employer identification. Accurate insurance information ensures that the primary payer is billed first and that all other payers, especially Medicare, are subsequently billed in the correct order. Insurance information is captured at the time of registration and is entered into

50 PAYER NAME		51 HEALTH PLAN ID	52 REL INFO.	53 ASG BEN.	54 PRIOR PAYMENTS		55 EST. AMOUNT DUE		56 NPI	8901234567	
A B C	AETNA	9101003777	Y	Y			5245	00	57 OTHER PRV ID		A B C
	58 INSURED'S NAME	59 P. REL.	60 INSURED'S UNIQUE ID		61 GROUP NAME			62 INSURANCE GROUP NO.			
A B C	SHATSKI STEPHAN M	18	MSB 902332438		NMU			8100			A B C
	63 TREATMENT AUTHORIZATION CODES			64 DOCUMENT CONTROL NUMBER			65 EMPLOYER NAME				
A B C							NORTHERN MAINE UNIVERSITY				A B C

Figure 10–6 UB-04 FL 50–65

For instructional use only. Courtesy of the Centers for Medicare and Medicaid Services, www.cms.hhs.gov.

the hospital's database. Figure 10–6 illustrates FL 50–65. Refer to this figure as you read the descriptions.

FL 50: Payer Name

Enter the name(s) of the health insurance plan(s) that provide payment for services. The primary payer's (first billed) name is entered on line A; the secondary payer's name is entered on line B; and the tertiary payer's (third billed) name is entered on line C. If Medicare is the primary payer, enter MEDICARE on line A.

FL 51: Health Plan No.

Enter the plan number for the payer named in FL 50. The health plan number, which is on the insurance card, is captured during the patient registration process.

FL 52: Release of Information (REL INFO)

This field tells the payer that the provider has the patient's signature on file to authorize the release of information necessary to process the insurance claim. The patient signs the release of information authorization at the time of registration/admission. Enter one of the following:

- **Y** for "yes": The patient agrees to release information
- **R** for "restricted": The patient places some restrictions on the release
- **N** for "no": The patient refuses to release information

The patient may restrict the release of certain types of information, such as HIV status, substance abuse, or any information not related to the current admission. When the patient refuses to release information, registration staff informs the patient that an insurance claim cannot be submitted and the patient must pay the bill.

FL 53: Assignment of Benefits (ASG BEN)

Assignment of benefits means that the patient authorizes the insurance carrier to send payment to the facility. The patient may choose not to assign benefits, and in that case, payment is sent to the patient. Admission staff enters Y for "yes" or N for "no," depending on the patient's choice.

FL 54: Prior Payments

Payments received before the claim is submitted to an insurance plan are entered in FL 54. This includes deductibles and co-payments collected from the patient. When a claim is submitted to more than one payer, the billing specialist enters the payment received from other payers. For example, a claim submitted to the secondary payer must include the payment received from the primary payer. Claims submitted to a tertiary payer must include the payments received from the primary and secondary payers. Use FL 54 lines A, B, and C to record payments received from the insurance carriers identified in lines A, B, and C in FL 50.

FL 55: Estimated Amount Due

Enter the amount that represents the estimated payment expected from a payer listed in FL 50 A, B, or C. The amount(s) entered in FL 55 A, B, or C must correspond to the insurance carriers noted in FL 50.

FL 56: NPI

Enter the billing provider's 10-digit National Provider Identification (NPI) number. The billing provider is the agency that submits the claim and receives payment for services rendered.

FL 57: Other Provider ID

In some cases, the insurance company assigns a unique identification number to providers. If the payer identified in FL 50 A, B, or C has assigned an identification number to the billing provider, enter that number in FL 57 A, B, or C. The identification number in FL 57 must correspond to the insurance company name in FL 50.

FL 58: Insured's Name

Enter the full name—last, first, and middle initial (if required)—of the insured or subscriber, defined as the individual who has the insurance. If more than one insurance plan is listed in FL 50, enter the subscriber's name on FL 58 A, B, and C that corresponds to the insurance company in FL 50 A, B, and C. When the patient is the subscriber, the names are the same. If the patient is covered by another individual's insurance, the subscriber's name is different from the patient's name. For Medicaid claims, the patient is always the subscriber because all Medicaid recipients have their own ID card. For Medicare claims, enter the name that appears on the patient's Medicare ID card.

FL 59: Patient's Relationship to Insured (P. REL)

Enter the code that accurately reflects the patient's relationship to the individuals named in FL 58 A, B, and C. In October 2003, Medicare implemented Health Insurance Portability and Accountability Act (HIPAA) security codes for this field. Other insurance carriers require either the HIPAA or previous relationship codes. Some frequently used relationship codes are listed in Table 10–12.

FL 60: Insured's Unique ID

Enter the insured's ID number *exactly* as it appears on the patient's health insurance identification card. Medicare beneficiaries are assigned a health insurance claim number (HICN) as the insured's ID number. If more than one insurance plan is listed in FL 50, enter the insured's ID number in FL 60 A, B, and C that corresponds to the insurance plans in FL 50 A, B, and C.

FL 61, 62: Group Name, Insurance Group Number

Enter the name of the group or plan in FL 61 and the insurance group number in FL 62. FL 61 may be the name of the insured's employer, a fraternal or professional association, or other organization. If more than one insurance plan is listed in FL 50, enter the group or plan name on FL 61 A, B, and C that corresponds to the insurance plans in FL 50 A, B, and C. Likewise, enter the

TABLE 10–12

Relationship Codes		
HIPAA Code	Explanation	Previous Code
01	Spouse	02
10	Foster child	06
15	Ward (patient is ward of insured)	07
17	Stepchild (son or daughter)	05
18	Self (patient is the insured)	01
19	Child (patient is natural child of the insured)	03
20	Employee (patient is an employee of the insured)	08
22	Handicapped dependent (dependent child whose coverage extends beyond usual termination age limits)	10
41	Injured plaintiff (patient is claiming insurance as a result of injury covered by the insured)	15
53	Life partner; domestic partner; significant other	20

insurance group number on FL 62 A, B, and C that corresponds to the insurance plans in FL 50 A, B, and C. When Medicare is the primary payer, leave FL 61 and FL 62 blank.

> **EXAMPLE: FL 61 GROUP NAME; FL 62 INSURANCE GROUP NUMBER**
> Rhonda is employed by UP University (UUU), which provides health insurance for over 6000 employees. Rhonda's insurance identification number is XYZ123456. UUU's health insurance plan is administered through the Teacher's Health Insurance Company (THIC), and the plan number is UU5559. In this example, the group or plan name, UP University, is entered in FL 61 and the insurance plan number, UU5559, is entered in FL 62.

FL 63: Treatment Authorization Codes

When the insurance plan requires prior authorization for services, enter the authorization code assigned by the payer or insurance plan. The primary payer's authorization code is entered on line FL 63A. Secondary and tertiary payer authorization codes may be entered on lines FL 63B and FL 63C, respectively, or in the Remarks section (FL 80).

FL 64: Document Control Number

This field is used when the current claim is related to or a replacement for a previous claim that was submitted to a payer. The previous claim number is entered in FL 64. The entry in FL 64A should refer to the payer identified in FL 50A; FL 64B to FL 50B; and FL 64C to FL 50C.

FL 65: Employer Name

If required by the insurance plan, enter the name of the employer(s) of the insured individual(s) entered in FL 58 A, B, and C in FL 65. For FL 65, line A corresponds to the primary payer identified in FL 50A; line B corresponds to the secondary payer (FL 50B); and line C corresponds to the tertiary payer (FL 50C). The employer's name is often required for workers' compensation claims.

REINFORCEMENT EXERCISES 10–6

Write a brief description for each term.

1. assignment of benefits

_____

_____

_____

2. HICN

_____

_____

_____

3. relationship code

_____

_____

_____

4. billing provider

_____

_____

_____

5. treatment authorization code

_____

_____

_____

Medical Codes and Physician Identification (FL 66–81)

This section of the UB-04 captures the diagnosis and procedure codes that identify the patient's medical condition(s) and related treatment(s). At a minimum, inaccurate coding has a negative impact on reimbursement. Intentional coding errors can lead to charges of insurance fraud, whereas unintentional coding errors can lead to charges of insurance abuse. As previously stated, documentation in the patient's record must clearly support all medical codes submitted with the insurance claim.

Diagnoses codes from the current version of the *International Classification of Diseases, Clinical Modification* (ICD-CM), either ICD-9-CM or ICD-10-CM, are used for hospital inpatient and outpatient insurance claims. The codes must be assigned to the highest level of specificity.

Depending on the requirements of the insurance carrier, procedures are reported using either the current ICD-CM procedure codes or HCPCS codes. For inpatient claims, procedures are reported using the current ICD-CM procedure codes. For outpatient claims, Medicare and Medicaid require HCPCS procedure codes, which are entered in FL 44. Other payers (insurance carriers) may also require HCPCS procedure codes for outpatient procedures.

HCPCS codes are divided into two categories: level I and level II. Level I HCPCS procedure codes are the same as the CPT codes. Therefore, outpatient procedures for Medicare, Medicaid, and other payers as required are reported by CPT codes. Level II HCPCS codes, also called "national codes," are used to report services such as ambulance services, chiropractic services, dental procedures, drugs and medications, and durable medical equipment.

Figure 10–7 illustrates FL 66–81. Refer to this figure as you learn about these fields.

FL 66: DX (Diagnosis and Procedure Code Qualifier)

Enter the number that identifies the version of the ICD-CM used to report medical codes. Enter 9 to denote ICD-9-CM or 10 to denote ICD-10-CM.

FL 67: Preprinted 67 (Principle Diagnosis Code)

For inpatient claims, the principal diagnosis is the condition established after study to be chiefly responsible for the patient's admission. Enter the ICD-CM code for the condition or diagnosis that meets the definition of "principal diagnosis." The ICD-CM diagnosis code must be reported to the highest level of specificity. Physicians and medical coders are responsible for identifying the principal diagnosis. The billing specialist works closely with the medical coder—and the physician if necessary—to resolve any questions concerning the principal diagnosis.

For outpatient claims, enter the ICD-CM code that identifies the diagnosis or symptom that is chiefly responsible for the outpatient service. If the outpatient service results in a definitive diagnosis, enter the ICD-CM code for the definitive diagnosis.

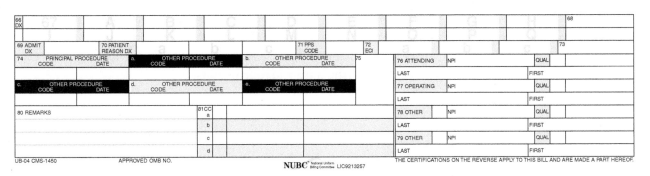

Figure 10–7 UB-04 FL 66–81

EXAMPLE A: OUTPATIENT CLAIM

Chiquita is admitted as an outpatient for a colonoscopy to evaluate the cause of frequent episodes of cramping and diarrhea. The colonoscopy is negative, and the physician tells Chiquita to increase fiber in her diet. In this example, the principal diagnosis is diarrhea, and the appropriate ICD-CM code is entered in FL 67.

EXAMPLE B: OUTPATIENT CLAIM

Chiquita is admitted as an outpatient for a colonoscopy to evaluate the cause of frequent episodes of cramping and diarrhea. The colonoscopy reveals ulcerative colitis. The physician prescribes medication and tells Chiquita to call her if the symptoms do not subside in three days. In this example, ulcerative colitis is the definitive diagnosis, and the appropriate ICD-CM code is entered in FL 67.

FL 67A–Q: Preprinted (Other Diagnosis Codes)

Enter the ICD-CM diagnosis codes for additional problems or conditions that either coexist at the time of admission or develop during the patient's LOS and affect the treatment and services provided.

FL 68: Untitled

This is for future use.

FL 69: Admitting Diagnosis (Admit Dx)

The admitting diagnosis is the diagnosis, condition, symptom, or other reason that required hospitalization. The admitting diagnosis is identified by the physician and may be noted as the chief complaint or the provisional diagnosis. Third-party payers use the admitting diagnosis to determine if the inpatient admission or outpatient service was justified. Enter the ICD-CM code for the admitting diagnosis.

FL 70a–c: Patient's Reason for Visit (Patient Reason Dx)

These fields are used for unscheduled outpatient visits. Enter the diagnosis code for the patient's reason for seeking treatment.

FL 71: Prospective Payment System Code (PPS Code)

If required by the insurance plan, enter the MS-DRG or the APC code in this field.

FL 72: External Cause of Injury Code (ECI)

E codes, which are part of the ICD-9-CM coding system, identify external causes of injury, such as accidents, poisonings, or other adverse affects. FL 72 is an optional field and is completed according to facility policy or insurance carrier requirements. When this field is used, enter the E code, and do not use a period or decimal point between the third and fourth digits.

FL 73: Untitled

Reserve this for future use.

FL 74: Principal Procedure Code and Date

For inpatient claims, the principal procedure is the procedure performed for definitive treatment rather than for diagnostic or exploratory purposes. If two or more procedures appear to meet this definition, the procedure most closely related to the principal diagnosis is selected as the principal procedure. The hospital's medical coders are responsible for identifying the principal procedure and assigning the correct code. The billing specialist works closely with the medical coder to resolve any questions concerning the principal procedure. Enter the ICD-CM procedure code that identifies the principal procedure. Enter the date of the procedure in the six- or eight-digit format.

For outpatient claims, the principal procedure is the procedure performed during the outpatient encounter. Medicare, Medicaid, and other third-party payers do not require the ICD-CM procedure code for outpatient procedures. The CPT codes listed in FL 44 identify outpatient procedures.

The provider may capture the ICD-CM procedure code for internal use. However, electronic claims submission software automatically deletes the ICD-CM codes *before* the claim is sent to the Medicare or Medicaid insurance carrier.

FL 74a–e: Other Procedure Code and Date

This field is used to report additional significant procedures related to the current episode of care. Both diagnostic and treatment procedures that relate to the principal diagnosis are included on the UB-04. For inpatient claims, enter the ICD-CM code for the additional diagnostic and treatment procedures. For outpatient claims, the HCPCS (level I CPT or level II) code *must* be listed in FL 44.

FL 75: Untitled

This is reserved for future use.

FL 76: Attending Physician (Provider) Name and Identification (Attending NPI; QUAL)

Enter the NPI number for the physician (provider) with overall responsibility for the patient's care and treatment. The NPI is required by most insurance carriers. When another identification number is required, a two-digit qualifier is entered to the right of the QUAL box, and the corresponding number is entered to the right of the qualifier.

The two-digit qualifiers identify the type of identification number. Qualifier 0B (State License Number) is used when the provider's state license number is required; qualifier 1G (Unique provider number-UPIN) is used when the insurance carrier assigns a provider identification number; and qualifier G2 (Provider Commercial Number) is used when another entity has assigned a provider identification number. The state license number and UPIN are the most commonly required additional provider identification numbers.

Enter the physician's last and first name in the blocks below the identification numbers.

FL 77: Operating Provider Name and Identification Number (Operating)

Enter the surgeon's name and identification number following the same guidelines for the attending physician (provider) as described in FL 76.

FL 78–79: Other Provider Name and Identification Number (Other)

These fields are used to report the name and identification number of other physicians who provided services to the patient. Enter the other physician/provider name and identification number, as described in FL 76.

EXAMPLE: FL 78–79 OTHER

Carlos is admitted for coronary bypass surgery. During the postoperative period, he develops four-limb paresis, and a neurologist is called in to evaluate Carlos's condition. The surgeon and neurologist both provide treatment until Carlos is discharged. In this example, the neurologist's ID number and name are entered in FL 78 or FL 79.

FL 80: Remarks

This field is used to report additional information required by the payer to assist in claims processing. The information may include the address of the insured when it is not the same as the patient's address; narrative description of unlisted procedure codes; date a Medicare beneficiary received an Advance Beneficiary Notice; reason for billing Medicare prior to receiving payment from the primary payer; reasons that a claim is canceled or voided; or other comments required by the payer.

FL 81a–d: Code-Code (CC)

This field is used to report additional codes related to an FL, such as FL 39 value codes. FL 81 is also used to report the hospital's taxonomy code. A taxonomy code is a 10-digit alphanumeric number that identifies the provider's specialty or provider type. These codes were developed to facilitate electronic claims processing that comply with HIPAA requirements. According to the CMS website, health care providers, including hospitals, select a taxonomy code that most closely represents the services offered by the individual practitioner or facility. For example, taxonomy code 282N00000X identifies a general acute care hospital. Some insurance plans require the taxonomy code for insurance claims processing. Figure 10–8 is an example of a completed UB-04.

REINFORCEMENT EXERCISES 10–7

Fill in the blank.

1. _____ codes are used to report all diagnoses.

2. Level I HCPCS procedure codes are the same as _____ codes.

3. The _____ diagnosis is the reason that caused the patient to seek treatment.

4. _____ identify external causes of injury and may or may not be included on the UB-04.

5. The _____ is performed for definitive treatment rather than for exploratory purposes.

6. The _____ is primarily responsible for the patient's medical care and treatment.

7. Level II HCPCS codes are also called _____ .

8. For Medicare outpatient claims, the _____ must be listed in FL 44.

9. A _____ code is an alphanumeric number that is used to facilitate electronic claims processing.

10. ICD-9-CM codes must be reported to the highest level of _____ .

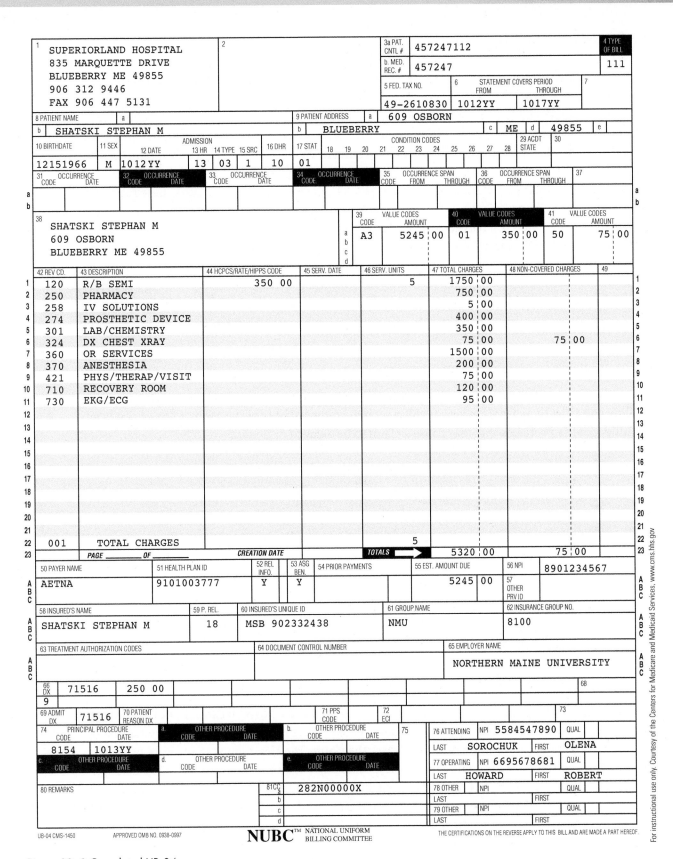

Figure 10–8 Completed UB-04

SUBMITTING THE INSURANCE CLAIM

Most insurance claims are submitted electronically. The hospital may use direct claims submission, which means the billing specialist sends the claim directly to the insurance carrier. Many health care providers, including hospitals, use a clearinghouse for electronic claims submission. A clearinghouse is an organization that accepts electronic claims, edits the claims, provides the billing specialist with error-edit messages, and subsequently distributes the claims to the appropriate insurance carriers. Chapter 9 includes a more detailed discussion of direct and clearinghouse electronic claims submission (ECS). The information presented here relates to clearinghouse ECS.

Once the patient is discharged and medical codes are assigned, patient information is released or downloaded to the electronic billing system. The billing specialist can access the claims by payer type, service type, or individual claim with the patient's name and patient control number. The UB-04 for the individual patient is displayed. The billing specialist checks the UB-04 to determine if all required fields are completed. Special attention is given to the following information:

- The patient's name and sex appear to be consistent.
- ICD-CM and HCPCS codes are properly located on the UB-04.
- Insurance/payer information is present.

Billing specialists are often assigned one or two payers for insurance claims processing. The billing specialist then becomes very familiar with the requirements of the assigned payers and can readily identify problems that may cause a claim to be delayed or denied.

> **EXAMPLE**
>
> Marcus is the billing specialist for Aetna, and he is reviewing a claim for a patient who received outpatient physical therapy treatments. Marcus knows that when the patient receives outpatient physical therapy services, Aetna requires occurrence code 11 and a corresponding date in FL 32. Occurrence code 11 indicates that outpatient physical therapy services were provided, and the date identifies when the patient first became aware of the symptoms. As Marcus checks the UB-04, he notes that FL 32 is not completed, and there are charges for physical therapy treatments in FL 42 through FL 47. Marcus puts a hold on the claim, which prevents the claim from being sent to the clearinghouse. He also phones or e-mails the physical therapist and requests the needed date. When Marcus receives the date, he brings up the patient's UB-04, adds the occurrence code and date, and releases the claim for further processing.

When the billing specialist releases the insurance claim, the hospital can submit the claim to the clearinghouse. Some hospitals submit claims in batches at regular intervals; others allow submission at the time the billing specialist releases the claim. The clearinghouse software programs review and edit the claim for compliance with specific payer requirements and for HIPAA compliance as well. A clean claim has no errors and is submitted to the appropriate insurance company. A dirty claim has errors or omissions that would cause the claim to be delayed or denied. The clearinghouse places a hold on dirty claims and sends error messages to the billing department.

The billing specialist receives the error messages for all claims that have errors or omissions. The error message lists the claims by patient control number and name and includes a detailed list of problems for each claim. More than one claim is included on the error message. The billing specialist retrieves each claim and makes the corrections, if possible. More often than not, the billing specialist can readily correct errors related to the following:

- The patient's age, sex, and marital status
- Simple data entry (typographical) mistakes
- Health Plan ID number(s) (FL 51)
- The provider NPI or ID number (FL 56 or FL 57)
- The insurance group number (FL 62)
- Physician NPI or other ID numbers (FL 77–79)

When the error messages relate to invalid codes, the billing specialist contacts the health information (medical record) department or medical coders and requests the correct codes for the claim.

EXAMPLE: INVALID CODE

Hannah is a billing specialist for Blueberry Memorial Hospital. She works primarily with Medicare inpatient claims and is in the process of reviewing error messages from the insurance carrier. The error message for Mr. Smith's claim states "invalid code, principal procedure." Mr. Smith was hospitalized for a total proctocolectomy due to severe universal ulcerative colitis. Hannah checks FL 67 for the principal diagnosis code and discovers that *diarrhea* was coded as the principal diagnosis. The principal procedure, total proctocolectomy, is invalid when diarrhea is the principal diagnosis. A total proctocolectomy is valid with the diagnosis severe, universal ulcerative colitis.

Hannah contacts a medical coder and requests clarification of the principal diagnosis. The medical coder reviews the patient's record and notes that the code for ulcerative colitis was omitted. Ulcerative colitis is the principal diagnosis and is consistent with the principal procedure. The coder enters the code for universal ulcerative colitis into the database. After the code is entered, Hannah releases the claim for resubmission.

In some cases, an experienced billing specialist knows that a specific treatment is included in an overall code and cannot be billed separately.

EXAMPLE: INCLUDED TREATMENT

Katka is a billing specialist for Superiorland Hospital. She handles all Blue Cross claims and recently received an error message for a patient who had several outpatient physical therapy treatments. The error message states "invalid code, physical therapy services." Katka retrieves the claim and reviews the charges. She notes that the claim includes six entries for physical therapy services and six entries for "cryotherapy." Cryotherapy is a specific type of physical therapy. Katka knows that cryotherapy cannot be billed separately and is included as part of the charge for the physical therapy service. Katka edits the claim, and the separate charges for cryotherapy are deleted. Katka releases the claim for resubmission.

The insurance carrier may also reject claims and send error messages to the billing department. The error message, sometimes called a "facility claim correction message," for a given date or time period lists all claims that need corrections. The billing specialist clicks on the claim identification number, and a window opens that describes the error. As with clearinghouse errors, the billing specialist is often able to correct the errors and resubmit the claim. At times, the billing specialist must contact the insurance carrier to resolve issues related to rejected or denied claims.

Billing specialists rely on nearly every department in the hospital to capture accurate information for insurance claims processing. Although the information is electronically stored, retrieved, and submitted, it is initially entered by people—and people can make mistakes. In order to correct data entry errors, mistakes, and omissions, the successful billing specialist must be detail-oriented and able to communicate and work with others.

 ## ABBREVIATIONS

Table 10–13 lists the abbreviations presented in this chapter.

TABLE 10–13

Abbreviations and Meanings	
Abbreviation	Meaning
APC	ambulatory payment classification (system)
ASC	ambulatory surgery center
CAH	critical access hospital
CC	complication/co-morbidity
CCU	coronary care unit
CBC	complete blood count
CMS	Centers for Medicare and Medicaid Services
CPT	*Current Procedural Terminology*
CWF	Common Working File (Medicare)
DRG	diagnosis related group
ECS	electronic claims submission
EHR	electronic health record
FL	form locator
FSS	Florida Shared System
GYN	gynecology
HCFA	Health Care Finance Administration
HCPCS	*Healthcare Common Procedure Coding System*
HHA	home health agency
HHS	Department of Health and Human Services
HICN	health insurance claim number

continued on the next page

continued from the previous page

HIPAA	Health Insurance Portability and Accountability Act
HIPP	Health Insurance Prospective Payment system
HIV	human immunodeficiency virus
ICF	intermediate care facility
ICU	intensive care unit
IPPS	inpatient prospective payment system
LOS	length of stay
MCC	major complication/co-morbidity
MS-DRG	medicare-severity diagnosis related group
NPI	National Provider Identification (number)
NUBC	National Uniform Billing Committee
OB	obstetrics
OPPS	outpatient prospective payment system
PPS	prospective payment system
SNF	skilled nursing facility
UB-04	Uniform Bill (2004 revision)
UHDDS	Uniform Hospital Discharge Data Set

 ## SUMMARY

This chapter introduces the student to the UB-04, which is the universal hospital claims submission form. The UB-04 is used for hospital inpatient and outpatient claims, skilled nursing facility (SNF) claims, and home health agency (HHA) claims. There are 81 fields on the UB-04, and completion requirements vary by third-party payers, also known as insurance carriers. Although most insurance claims are filed electronically, there are times when a paper claim must be submitted. The billing specialist is usually the last—and sometimes the only—person to review and edit the complete UB-04 before it is submitted. In addition, the billing specialist works with various hospital departments and staff to correct or resolve erroneous or inaccurate claims information.

 ## REVIEW EXERCISES

Abbreviations

Spell out each abbreviation and write a brief description of the term or phrase.

1. APC _____

2. CMS _____

3. CPT _____

4. HHS _____

5. MS-DRG _____

6. DCN _____

7. FL _____

8. HCPCS _____

9. HICN _____

10. LOS _____

11. NUBC _____

12. OPPS _____

13. UHDDS _____

14. NPI _____

Short Answer

Write a brief description for each term.

1. Admitting diagnosis

_____

_____

_____

2. Chargemaster

_____

_____

_____

3. Primary payer

_____

_____

_____

4. Principal diagnosis

_____

_____

_____

5. Principal procedure

_____

_____

_____

6. Florida Shared System

_____

_____

_____

7. Clean claim

_____

_____

_____

8. Dirty claim

_____

_____

_____

Multiple Choice

Circle the best answer from the choices provided.

1. The universal hospital claims form is called the

   a. CMS-1450.

   b. CMS-1500.

   c. UB-04.

   d. a and c

   e. none of the above

2. Diagnosis-related groups were developed as part of the

   a. outpatient prospective payment system.

   b. inpatient prospective payment system.

   c. CMS discharge data set.

   d. ICD-9-CM coding system.

   e. all the above

3. Ambulatory payment classifications were developed as part of the

   a. outpatient prospective payment system.

   b. inpatient prospective payment system.

   c. CMS discharge data set.

   d. CPT coding system.

   e. all the above

4. Developing an insurance claim includes all *except* one of the following:

   a. patient registration

   b. capturing charges for services provided to the patient

   c. completing the UB-04

   d. assigning diagnosis and procedure codes

   e. making a copy of the patient's insurance card

5. The "patient control number" is

   a. assigned by the hospital.

   b. used to enter charges and services provided to the patient.

   c. known as the account or billing number.

   d. referenced on the insurance company's remittance advice form.

   e. all the above

6. "Lifetime reserve days" apply to

   a. Medicare beneficiaries.

   b. outpatient treatment days.

   c. Medicaid beneficiaries.

   d. military treatment centers.

   e. a and c

7. A "condition code" identifies which of the following?

   a. actual dollar amounts that affect the patient's insurance benefits

   b. the condition of the patient at the time of admission

   c. the condition of the patient at the time of discharge

   d. specific events that determine health insurance liability

   e. primary and secondary insurance coverage

8. "Occurrence codes" include all *except* one of the following:

   a. auto accidents

   b. admission date

   c. onset of symptoms/illness

   d. date insurance payment was denied

   e. employment-related accident

9. A "value code" is used to identify which of the following?

   a. the semiprivate room rate

   b. primary payer

   c. secondary payer

   d. lifetime reserve days

   e. b and c

10. "Ancillary services" codes include which of the following patient services?

    a. routine nursing care

    b. operating room services

    c. room and board

    d. intensive care unit services

    e. none of the above

11. Submitting an insurance claim includes all *except* which of the following?

    a. reviewing the UB-04

    b. correcting data entry errors

    c. responding to error-edit messages

    d. making a copy of the patient's insurance card

    e. b and d

Figure 10-9 UB-04

APPLICATION EXERCISE

Review the UB-04 in Figure 10–9. Complete FL 18 through FL 81, as necessary, using the information provided. Refer to Table 10–8, Table 10–9, and Table 10–10 for value and revenue codes.

PATIENT NAME: Alex Franks; Health Insurance ID: FA22306

EMPLOYER: Texas Software Corporation; Huntsville, Texas 59855

INSURANCE: Blue Cross; health plan, ID BC999; group name, Texas Software; insurance group number, 881

HOSPITAL: Memorial Hospital; provider NPI, 1234567890

ATTENDING PHYSICIAN: Takeesha Johnson, MD; NPI, 2345678901

SURGEON: Enrique Shaver, MD; NPI, 3456789012

SERVICES: Semiprivate room, $540 per day; operating room services, $1500; blood chemistry tests, three (3), $50 each; chest x-ray, $90; general anesthesia, $200; recovery room, $50; pharmacy, $250; prosthetic device, $150.

ADMITTING AND PRINCIPAL DIAGNOSIS: Degenerative joint disease, knee, 715.16

PROCEDURE: Total knee replacement, 81.54; Done on March 21, 20YY

NOTE: Mr. Franks has signed a release of information for insurance payment and assignment of benefits.

 CHALLENGE EXERCISES

1. Interview a billing specialist at your local hospital. Ask about the challenges related to hospital billing, such as frequent changes to UB-04 guidelines, the most common insurance claim errors, and the length of time between the patient's discharge and submitting the insurance claim.

2. Visit the National Uniform Billing Committee website at http://www.nubc.org or the Centers for Medicare and Medicaid Services website at http://www.cms.gov for current information about the UB-04. Does either website provide a sample of the UB-04?

 WEBSITES

Centers for Medicare and Medicaid Services: http://www.cms.hhs.gov
National Uniform Billing Committee: http://www.nubc.org

CHAPTER 11

Blue Cross/Blue Shield

LEARNING OBJECTIVES

Upon successful completion of this chapter, the reader should have the knowledge to:

1. Define all key terms and abbreviations presented in the chapter.
2. Describe three pieces of information provided by Blue Cross/Blue Shield insurance identification cards.
3. Define Blue Cross/Blue Shield provider reimbursement methods.
4. List three differences between a participating provider and a nonparticipating provider.
5. Accurately complete the CMS-1500 data fields.

KEY TERMS

Allowable charge/fee
Blue Cross and Blue Shield Association (BCBSA)
Blue Cross/Blue Shield (BC/BS)
Cafeteria plan
Customary fee
Durable medical equipment (DME)
Employer-sponsored health insurance plan
Enrollee

Enrollee ID number
Group number
Health maintenance organization (HMO)
Individual health insurance plan
Insured
Medigap plan
Member
Participating provider (PAR)
Personal care physician (PCP)
Plan code

Preferred provider organization (PPO)
Primary care provider
Reasonable fee
Relative value scale (RVS) fee
Relative value unit (RVU)
Subscribers
Usual fee
Usual, customary, and reasonable (UCR) fee
Write-off

OVERVIEW

Blue Cross/Blue Shield (BC/BS) is a nationwide federation of nonprofit health insurance companies. Blue Cross/Blue Shield is often called the "Blues." Blue Cross health insurance usually covers hospital charges, and Blue Shield health insurance usually covers physician or provider charges. However, between the two plans, services such as outpatient surgery, long-term care, durable medical equipment (DME), and prescription medications are also often covered. DME is nondisposable medical devices such as crutches, prostheses, and wheelchairs. A patient may be enrolled in one or both of the Blues plans.

Blue Cross traces its history to a 1933 St. Paul, Minnesota, hospitalization insurance plan—the first insurance plan to use the blue cross symbol. In 1933, the American Hospital Association (AHA) adopted the symbol when the AHA became the agency for accrediting new prepaid hospitalization plans. In 1978, the AHA deeded the right to both the Blue Cross name and symbol to the Blue Cross Association. The symbol was updated at that time and is a registered trademark.

Blue Shield traces its history to a 1938 American Medical Association (AMA) meeting. At this meeting, the AMA House of Delegates passed a resolution supporting the concept of voluntary health insurance that encouraged physicians to cooperate in prepaid health plans. The first such plan, established in Palo Alto, California, in 1939, was called the California Physicians' Service. Individuals who enrolled in the plan were called subscribers. Physician fees for subscribers with an annual income of less than $3000 were paid in full by the insurance plan. Subscribers with an annual income in excess of $3000 paid a small percentage of the physician fee, and the insurance plan paid the rest. This practice was the forerunner of patient co-insurance. Individuals enrolled in BC/BS plans are called subscribers or enrollees.

The blue shield was first used as a trademark in 1939 by the Buffalo, New York, medical care plan. In 1948, the symbol was formally adopted by the Associated Medical Care Plans, which was the approving agency for accreditation of new physician prepaid health insurance plans. In 1951, the Associated Medical Care Plans changed its name to the National Association of Blue Shield Plans and retained the blue shield symbol.

In 1977, the membership of both Blue Cross and Blue Shield voted to combine their two staffs under one president. By 1986, the board of directors for each association had merged to form the Blue Cross and Blue Shield Association (BCBSA). Although the BCBSA represents the Blues on a national level, some Blue Cross and Blue Shield plans maintain separate corporate identities. In most states, however, Blue Cross and Blue Shield plans function as a single corporation.

Whether they function as separate corporations or as a single corporation, both Blue Cross and Blue Shield are bound by state laws and insurance regulations. Blue Cross and Blue Shield of Michigan operates according to the Michigan laws and regulations that apply to health insurance companies; BC/BS of Hawaii operates according to the laws and regulations of that state; and so forth.

Blue Cross/Blue Shield offers a wide variety of health insurance plans. Therefore, this chapter is limited to general information related to BC/BS plans. The insurance billing specialist must follow the specific state or local BC/BS guidelines that apply to the provider's patient population.

Some state BC/BS offices offer an electronic inquiry system that gives providers online access to information related to BC/BS subscribers and other claims processing information. For example, Blue Cross/Blue Shield of Michigan developed Web-DENIS, which allows providers immediate access to subscriber information such as deductible and co-payment amounts. BC/BS manuals, publications, and insurance claims tracking are also available via Web-DENIS.

This chapter covers the following topics: general types of Blue Cross/Blue Shield health insurance plans; participating versus nonparticipating providers; payment methods; and general insurance claims procedures. Because state or regional Blue Cross/Blue Shield plans may have unique requirements for claims submission, always check with the local BC/BS office for current guidelines.

BLUE CROSS/BLUE SHIELD GENERAL INFORMATION

Blue Cross/Blue Shield is one of the largest health insurance companies and offers a variety of health insurance plans, ranging from individual insurance to large group health plans. Blue Cross/Blue Shield plans are available in all 50 states as well as the District of Columbia. Each state's insurance commission regulates the companies that sell health insurance policies in that state. The Centers for Medicare and Medicaid Services (CMS) regulate and monitor all Medicare and federal employee health plans offered by private health insurance companies. While each state BC/BS organization may offer plans unique to that state, most offer similar products, such as health maintenance organization (HMO) plans, preferred provider organization (PPO) plans, individual and group plans, Medigap plans, and Medicare Advantage plans.

Blue Cross/Blue Shield Medigap and Medicare Advantage plans are regulated by CMS and are available to Medicare beneficiaries. These plans are covered in Chapter 12, "Medicare." Blue Cross/Blue Shield HMO and PPO plans are managed care plans. Detailed information about managed care plans is covered in Chapter 3, "Introduction to Health Insurance."

The individual enrolled with the BC/BS plan is called the subscriber or enrollee. The subscriber or enrollee is usually named on the health insurance identification (ID) card. A member is usually the subscriber's spouse or dependent who is eligible for insurance coverage. Members are not named on the health insurance ID card. BC/BS managed care plans usually require the subscriber and members to have a personal care physician (PCP), also called a primary care provider. The PCP is responsible for the overall management of an individual's medical care.

REINFORCEMENT EXERCISES 11–1

Spell out the abbreviations or write a definition for the terms.

1. BCBSA

_____

2. DME

_____

3. PCP

_____

4. HMO

_____

5. PPO

_____

continued on the next page

continued from the previous page

6. subscriber

_____

7. enrollee

_____

8. member

_____

BLUE CROSS/BLUE SHIELD HEALTH INSURANCE PLANS

It is well beyond the scope of this text to cover every BC/BS plan offered throughout the United States! General information about individual and group plans is included in this chapter.

Blue Cross/Blue Shield Individual Plans

Blue Cross/Blue Shield individual health insurance plans are available to individuals and families who are not covered by a group insurance plan. All individual or family plans are based on the age of the subscriber and family members. For most plans, adults must be under 65 and children must be under 19. BC/BS also has several Medigap plans available to individuals with Medicare.

Individual and family plans have a monthly premium, deductible, and co-payments. Benefits range from basic coverage for hospital and physician services to comprehensive coverage, which usually includes dental and vision insurance. Premiums range from around $50 per month for basic coverage for a healthy, 19-year-old, nonsmoker to around $1500 per month for more comprehensive coverage for a family. Premiums are lower for nonsmokers.

Deductibles can range from $2500 to $5000 per year for an individual and $5000 to $10,000 per year for a family. Premiums are lower for plans with a high deductible. Co-insurance, which usually applies to hospital care, ranges from 30% to 50%. Co-pays, which usually apply to office and emergency room visits, range from $40 per office visit to $250 per emergency room visit. Example A illustrates insurance coverage for a mid-range individual health insurance plan. Example B illustrates coverage for a mid-range family plan.

EXAMPLE A: INDIVIDUAL HEALTH INSURANCE COVERAGE

Erika is a 25-year-old healthy female who does not smoke. She works for a small business that does not offer any type of group health insurance plan. Erika purchases a BC/BS mid-range health insurance plan for herself. The premium is $125 per month, the deductible is $2500 per year, co-insurance is between 20 and 50%, and the co-pay for office visits is $40. Her out-of-pocket expenses are limited to $5000 per year. To get maternity and contraceptive coverage, Erika had to enroll in an HMO. The maternity deductible is $3000.

Erika's insurance coverage begins once she meets the $2500 annual deductible. Simply put, Erika must spend $2500 out-of-pocket each year before her insurance is billed. Because Erika's plan has a $5000 maximum out-of-pocket limit, she can pay an additional $2500 in co-insurance and co-pays. Erika's insurance premiums total $1750 per year. Between the premium cost ($1750) and deductible ($2500), Erika could spend at least $4250 every year for as long as she carries the insurance. In a year when Erika received enough services to meet the $5000 maximum out-of-pocket threshold, she would spend a total of $6750 on health care related expenses.

Should Erika get pregnant, her out-of-pocket expenses must reach $3000 before her insurance is billed for maternity care.

EXAMPLE B: FAMILY HEALTH INSURANCE COVERAGE

Nu and his wife Tae have two children, ages 8 and 10. Nu works full-time for a manufacturing company that has 45 employees and does not offer any type of group health insurance plan. He earns $14 per hour. Tae works about 15 hours per week at a local craft store and earns $8 per hour. Their combined income is about $45,000 per year. After meeting with an insurance company representative, Nue and Tae have three viable choices for purchasing health insurance.

1st Choice: The premium is $240 per month; the annual family deductible is $10,000; the annual maxim out-of-pocket cost is $17,000; and the co-pay is 30%.

2nd Choice: The premium is $330 per month; the annual family deductible is $5000; the annual maximum out-of-pocket cost is $12,000; and the co-pay is 30%.

3rd Choice: The premium is $450 per month; the annual family deductible is $5000; the annual maximum out-of-pocket cost is $10,000; and the co-pay is 30%.

Nue and Tae decide to purchase the health insurance plan described in the second choice. The $5000 family deductible must be met before the insurance is billed. With an annual premium cost of $3960 and an annual $5000 deductible, Nue and Tae could spend at least $8960 each year. In a year when the family receives enough services to meet the $12,000 maximum out-of-pocket threshold, their total cost is $15,960.

In both of the examples, the out-of-pocket costs also depend on whether or not a service is covered by the plan. Under most plans, pre-existing conditions, which often includes pregnancy, are not covered for the first 180 days. The plan may identify exclusions, which are specific conditions not covered by the plan.

Medigap Plans

Medigap insurance plans are designed to cover some health care costs not covered by Medicare. Medigap plans are regulated and approved by the Centers for Medicare and Medicaid Services. There are 10 approved Medigap plans designated by letters A, B, C, D, F, G, K, L, M, and N. The plans cover Medicare Part A co-insurance and co-pays for hospital, hospice, and skilled nursing facility care; Part B co-insurance or co-pays; and emergency care during foreign travel. Medigap plans are offered by private insurance companies. Insurance companies can decide which, if any, of the plans they will offer. For example, in 2012 BC/BS of Michigan offered Medigap Plans A and C. Chapter 12, "Medicare" includes more information about Medigap plans.

Blue Cross/Blue Shield Group Plans

Group health insurance plans operate under the assumption of "savings in numbers." Under a group plan, the cost of the insurance is spread over a large number of subscribers. Some subscribers use more benefits than others, but everyone in the group has the same insurance. Think of it like two families buying a vacation property together because neither family could afford one on their own. The vacation property is available to both families, but there may be times when one family actually uses the property more than the other family.

A group health insurance plan is a contract between an employer or other organization and the health insurance company. The employer or other organization purchases the plan and then offers the plan to members of the defined group. The employee may pay all or a portion of the premium. Premiums for group health insurance are usually lower than individual plan premiums.

Employer-Sponsored Health Insurance Plans

Employer-sponsored health insurance plans are usually offered to employees and their dependents. The employer is often called the insured and the employees are called enrollees. PPOs and HMOs are common for employer-sponsored health insurance plans. Under a PPO, enrollees and dependents are encouraged to obtain services from providers who contract with the plan. Enrollees are rewarded with lower out-of-pocket expenses. Under an HMO, enrollees and dependents have fewer provider choices than those offered by a PPO.

Figure 11–1 illustrates a health insurance identification card. The first three letters identify the plan as a PPO, as does the PPO logo at the top. The enrollee ID number is a unique identifier assigned by the insurance carrier. Since the implementation of the Health Insurance Portability and Accountability Act, the enrollee's Social Security number is not used as an ID number. The group number identifies the name of the employer or group and the plan code identifies the local or state insurance plan.

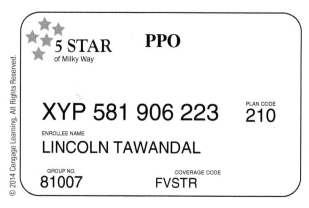

Figure 11–1 A group plan, PPO Identification Card

Some plans include defined benefits for all employees, and others offer employees benefit choices. Plans with benefit or coverage choices are often called cafeteria plans. For example, an employee without children may not select coverage related to childhood conditions.

Other Group Health Insurance Plans

Other groups, such as religious or fraternal organizations, unions, and professional associations may offer their members a group health insurance plan. In these situations, the member usually pays the entire premium. Some professional organizations secure agreements with a health insurance company that allow members of the association to purchase health insurance at a reduced rate.

 ## PARTICIPATING AND NONPARTICIPATING PROVIDERS

Blue Cross/Blue Shield managed care and group health insurance plans often have a network of participating providers (PARs). Contracts are negotiated between the provider and BC/BS. Benefits of becoming a BC/BS PAR include the following:

- Insurance payments are sent directly to the provider.
- Claim-filing assistance is made available to the provider's staff.
- Training seminars, manuals, and newsletters are furnished to the provider's staff.
- The provider's name, address, and specialty are published in the BC/BS PAR directory, which is distributed to all BC/BS subscribers and PARs.

In return for these benefits, PARs agree to do the following:

- Submit claims for all BC/BS subscribers.
- Adjust the difference between the amount charged by the provider and the BC/BS usual and customary fee.
- Base the patient's deductible or co-pay on the BC/BS usual and customary fee.

When a provider agrees to adjust his or her fees, the difference is called an adjustment or write-off. Write-offs have important business and income tax implications. Patient accounts must clearly document all fee adjustments and write-offs. The billing specialist is often responsible for entering adjustments or write-offs into the patient's account. The provider's business manager or accountant is responsible for reporting adjustments and write-offs in accordance with local, state, and federal tax laws.

Nonparticipating providers are health care providers who do not have a contract with a BC/BS plan. Nonparticipating providers charge the patient the provider's full fee for services rendered. The patient may be expected to pay all or part of the fee at the time of service. Either the nonparticipating provider or the patient files an insurance claim. For nonparticipating providers, the patient may receive the payment, and the provider must bill the patient. Many providers sign participation agreements because they receive the insurance payment directly.

For nonparticipating providers, the billing specialist should make every effort to collect deductibles and co-payments when services are rendered. Many providers expect payment in full for charges up to a specific amount. When charges exceed the provider's threshold, the billing specialist sets up a payment schedule with the patient.

REINFORCEMENT EXERCISES 11–2

Write a short answer for each item.

1. List three benefits of being a participating provider.

_____

_____

_____

2. List three obligations of being a participating provider.

_____

_____

_____

3. What is an enrollee ID number?

_____

_____

_____

4. What is the difference between the group number and the plan code on an insurance identification card?

_____

_____

_____

5. Give an example of a write-off.

_____

_____

_____

PROVIDER REIMBURSEMENT

Provider reimbursement or payment is often based on the usual, customary, and reasonable (UCR) fee, the relative value scale (RVS) amount, or a combination of both.

Usual, Customary, and Reasonable (UCR) Fees

UCR fees are defined as follows:

- Usual fee: The fee the provider usually charges for a given service.
- Customary fee: The fee other providers, in the same geographic area and with similar training, charge for the same service. The customary fee is an average of the fees charged by other providers or the fee that falls in the 90th percentile of the fees charged by other providers.

TABLE 11–1

Usual, Customary, and Reasonable Fees
Usual Fee
Dr. Pedal, a dermatologist, charges all patients $250 for the removal of three skin tags.
Customary Fee
The other dermatologists in Dr. Pedal's geographic area have a range of fees for the removal of three skin tags. The 90th percentile of all the fees for this service is $290. Under the 90th percentile rule, $290 is the customary fee for removal of three skin tags.
Reasonable Fee
Dr. Pedal removes three skin tags. The patient has a reaction to the local anesthetic, which requires additional medical attention. Dr. Pedal charges $300, which is $50 more than his usual fee and $10 more than the customary fee. Due to the complication, the insurance carrier determines that $300 is a reasonable fee.

- **Reasonable fee:** A fee that is higher than the usual or customary fee and can be justified by the patient's condition. The insurance carrier determines whether there is sufficient justification for the higher fee.

Insurance companies often use UCR fees as a basis to determine provider reimbursement. If the provider's fee exceeds the usual and customary fee, the insurance carrier reviews all documentation related to the service. The information in the patient's medical record must clearly identify the extenuating circumstances related to the increased fee. Review Table 11–1 for examples of UCR fees. As stated earlier, BC/BS PARs adjust their fees to the BC/BS usual and customary fees. The adjusted fees apply to individuals covered by the BC/BS insurance plan.

Like most insurance plans, BC/BS plans pay a percentage of the UCR. The maximum amount paid by insurance is called the allowable charge or allowable fee. The difference between the UCR fee and the allowable charge is the patient's co-pay. The following Example illustrates the allowable charge and patient co-pay for a PAR.

> **EXAMPLE**
> The BC/BS UCR fee for an established patient office visit is $100. Marta's physician charges $125 for this service. Because Marta's physician is a BC/BS PAR, the charge is adjusted to $100. Marta's BC/BS plan pays 80% of the UCR as the allowable charge and Marta pays 20% as a co-payment. When Marta sees her physician, she pays the $20 co-pay and the billing specialist submits a claim to BC/BS for $80.

Figure 11–2 is an example of a patient account ledger that illustrates this fee sharing for a PAR.

BC/BS enrollees who receive services from a nonparticipating provider have higher out-of-pocket expenses. Nonparticipating providers do not adjust their fees to the BC/BS UCR fee. The patient must pay the difference between the provider's fee and UCR fee. In addition, the co-pay for nonparticipating providers may be higher than the co-pay for PARs. Insurance payment is still based on the BC/BS UCR. The following Example illustrates the patient's out-of-pocket expenses with a nonparticipating provider.

A. PARTICIPATING PROVIDER

ACCOUNT NO. 456789112		PATIENT NAME SMITH PHILIP M.		DOB 10/15/1957	INSURANCE BCBS XYZ44442121		MED REC NO. 456789	
PATIENT ADDRESS		909 DAISY LANE FLOWERS MD 20000		HOME 906 555 8800		WORK 906 555 5678		

DOS	PRVD	CPT CODE	DESCRIPTION	CHARGE		CREDIT		BALANCE	
05/20/20YY	007	99213	OFFICE VISIT	125	00				
05/20/20YY			BCBS ADJUSTMENT			25	00	100	00
05/20/20YY			PT CHK 10234			20	00	80	00
05/22/20YY			INS. FILED						

Figure 11–2 Patient Account Ledger Participating Provider

EXAMPLE

Marta's physician is a nonparticipating provider and charges $125 for an established patient office visit. The co-pay for receiving services from a nonparticipating provider is 25%. After a recent appointment, Marta was asked to pay $50 to cover the $25 difference between the UCR fee and the physician's fee and the $25 co-pay.

It cost Marta more than twice as much to receive services from a nonparticipating provider.

Figure 11–3 is an example of a patient account ledger that illustrates this fee sharing for a nonparticipating provider.

Relative Value Scale (RVS) Amount

The relative value scale (RVS) amount is a calculation that insurance companies use to establish provider fee schedules. The calculation takes into account the provider's time, skill, and overhead costs. These factors are expressed in numerical units called relative value units (RVUs). An RVU is assigned to every covered service. Services that require more time, skill, and overhead costs receive higher RVUs. For example, a pre-employment physical may be assigned an RVU of 0.5, and a comprehensive physical may be assigned an RVU of 1.

B. NONPARTICIPATING PROVIDER

ACCOUNT NO. 456789112		PATIENT NAME SMITH PHILIP M.		DOB 10/15/1957	INSURANCE BCBS XYZ44442121		MED REC NO. 456789	
PATIENT ADDRESS		909 DAISY LANE FLOWERS MD 20000		HOME 906 555 8800		WORK 906 555 5678		

DOS	PRVD	CPT CODE	DESCRIPTION	CHARGE		CREDIT		BALANCE	
05/20/20YY	007	99213	OFFICE VISIT	125	00				
05/20/20YY			PT. CHK 10234			45	00	80	00
05/22/20YY			INS. FILED						

Figure 11–3 Patient Account Ledger Nonparticipating Provider

The second part of the RVS calculation is a fixed dollar amount. Insurance companies maintain extensive databases of provider charges for services rendered. These charges are used to establish a fixed dollar amount per RVU. Once the fixed dollar amount is established, it is multiplied by the RVU assigned to a given service, which results in the RVS fee for that service. The following Example illustrates how the RVU affects the fee.

EXAMPLE

The fixed dollar amount for ABC Insurance Plan PARs is $100. A pre-employment physical has an RVU of 0.5. When you multiply the fixed dollar amount of $100 by 0.5, the fee is $50. A comprehensive physical has an RVU of 1. When you multiply the fixed dollar amount of $100 by 1, the fee is $100.

Each CPT code—a five-digit code assigned to physician and provider services—is assigned an RVU. Table 11–2 lists fees associated with select CPT codes. Note how the RVU affects each fee. The amounts used in the table are for illustration purposes only.

The insurance company furnishes providers with the RVS fees. As with UCR fees, most insurance plans pay a percentage of the fee, and the patient is responsible for the remainder. The following Example illustrates the insurance payment and patient co-pay for CPT 44150, total abdominal colectomy without proctectomy.

EXAMPLE

Marie's BC/BS individual insurance plan pays 70% of the RVS fee for covered procedures. Marie undergoes a total abdominal colectomy without proctectomy. The RVS fee for this procedure is $3000. Marie's insurance pays $2100 (70% of the RVS fee) and her co-pay is $900 (30% of the RVS fee).

In this example, the billing specialist discusses the co-pay with Marie and establishes a payment plan. If the surgeon is a PAR, the billing specialist submits a claim for $2100, and payment is sent directly to the provider. The billing specialist for a nonparticipating provider establishes a payment plan for the $900 co-pay and may submit the claim for the patient. If the patient assigns benefits to the provider, payment is sent to the provider. If the patient does not assign benefits to the provider, payment is sent to the patient. The $2100 is added to the patient's account.

TABLE 11–2

CPT Code Descriptions and Fees				
CPT Code	Description	Fixed Dollar Amount/RVU	RVU	Fee
45380	Colonoscopy with biopsy	$100	10	$1000
54150	Newborn circumcision	$100	2	$200
44150	Total abdominal colectomy w/o proctectomy	$100	30	$3000
19101	Open incisional breast biopsy	$100	6	$600
58260	Vaginal hysterectomy, uterus	$100	15	$1500

Some providers require full payment of the co-pay before the service is performed. In the case of nonparticipating physicians, it is not unusual for the patient to prepay up to 50% of the cost of the service. These payment arrangements are especially important when the service—usually some type of elective surgery—has a high cost. The billing specialist discusses the provider's payment policy with the patient.

REINFORCEMENT EXERCISES 11–3

Fill in the blank with the correct term or phrase.

1. A _____ fee is described as the fee for a service that falls in the 90th percentile of the fees charged by those who provide the service.

2. A(n) _____ fee is the maximum amount insurance will pay for a covered service.

3. BC/BS enrollees have higher _____ when they receive services from a nonparticipating provider.

4. The _____ is a calculation that is used to establish provider fee schedules.

5. A(n) _____ is a numerical unit, based on time, skill, and overhead costs, that is assigned to a covered service.

BLUE CROSS/BLUE SHIELD CLAIMS SUBMISSION

Most Blue Cross/Blue Shield insurance claims are filed electronically. Providers use either the carrier-direct or clearinghouse electronic claims submission method. The CMS-1500 claim form is used for nonelectronic claims submission. Check with the local BC/BS carrier or plan representative if there is any doubt that the CMS-1500 is the correct form. BC/BS will not process an insurance claim submitted on the wrong form. BC/BS plans set time limits for claim submission that range from 90 days to one year. To ensure prompt reimbursement, claims should be submitted within 30 days.

General CMS-1500 completion instructions for Blue Cross/Blue Shield claims are presented here. Claims submission requirements are revised regularly. The local or regional BC/BS office can provide the billing specialist with the most current requirements. General guidelines for completing the CMS-1500 for Blue Cross/Blue Shield plans include the following:

- Enter all insurance identification numbers exactly as they appear on the insurance card.
- The word "insured" on the CMS-1500 form is the same as "subscriber" or "enrollee." BC/BS identification cards use the term "subscriber" or "enrollee" for "insured."
- Prior to the year 2000, birth dates were entered as MM/DD/YY. Many insurance carriers now require four digits for the year: MM/DD/YYYY.
- When entering monetary information, always include both dollars and cents, even if the cents notation is 00. Do not use decimals or dollar signs.

Figure 11–4 is an example of a completed claim form when BC/BS is the primary payer. The health insurance card in Figure 11–1 is the source document for information in blocks 1a, 2, and 11.

(1500)

HEALTH INSURANCE CLAIM FORM

APPROVED BY NATIONAL UNIFORM CLAIM COMMITTEE 08/05

☐☐ PICA | PICA ☐☐☐

1. MEDICARE MEDICAID TRICARE CHAMPVA GROUP HEALTH PLAN FECA BLK LUNG OTHER	1a. INSURED'S I.D. NUMBER (For Program in Item 1)
☐ (Medicare #) ☐ (Medicaid #) CHAMPUS ☐ (Sponsor's SSN) ☐ (Member ID #) ☐ (SSN or ID) ☐ (SSN) ☒ (ID)	XYP581906223

2. PATIENT'S NAME (Last Name, First Name, Middle Initial)	3. PATIENT'S BIRTH DATE MM DD YY SEX	4. INSURED'S NAME (Last Name, First Name, Middle Initial)
LINCOLN TAWANDA L	12 15 1948 M ☐ F ☒	LINCOLN TAWANDA L

5. PATIENT'S ADDRESS (No., Street)	6. PATIENT RELATIONSHIP TO INSURED	7. INSURED'S ADDRESS (No., Street)
714 HENNEPIN ROAD	Self ☒ Spouse ☐ Child ☐ Other ☐	714 HENNEPIN ROAD

CITY CHICAGO	STATE IL	8. PATIENT STATUS Single ☐ Married ☒ Other ☐	CITY CHICAGO	STATE IL

ZIP CODE 49855	TELEPHONE (Include Area Code) (806) 2263336	Employed ☒ Full-Time Student ☐ Part-Time Student ☐	ZIP CODE 49855	TELEPHONE (Include Area Code) (806) 226 3336

9. OTHER INSURED'S NAME (Last Name, First Name, Middle Initial)	10. IS PATIENT'S CONDITION RELATED TO:	11. INSURED'S POLICY GROUP OR FECA NUMBER 81007

a. OTHER INSURED'S POLICY OR GROUP NUMBER	a. EMPLOYMENT? (Current or Previous) ☐ YES ☒ NO	a. INSURED'S DATE OF BIRTH MM DD YY 12 15 1948 SEX M ☐ F ☒

b. OTHER INSURED'S DATE OF BIRTH MM DD YY SEX M ☐ F ☐	b. AUTO ACCIDENT? PLACE (State) ☐ YES ☒ NO	b. EMPLOYER'S NAME OR SCHOOL NAME

c. EMPLOYER'S NAME OR SCHOOL NAME	c. OTHER ACCIDENT? ☐ YES ☒ NO	c. INSURANCE PLAN NAME OR PROGRAM NAME BCBS MI

d. INSURANCE PLAN NAME OR PROGRAM NAME	10d. RESERVED FOR LOCAL USE	d. IS THERE ANOTHER HEALTH BENEFIT PLAN? ☐ YES ☒ NO If yes, return to and complete item 9 a-d.

READ BACK OF FORM BEFORE COMPLETING & SIGNING THIS FORM.

12. PATIENT'S OR AUTHORIZED PERSON'S SIGNATURE I authorize the release of any medical or other information necessary to process this claim. I also request payment of government benefits either to myself or to the party who accepts assignment below.

SIGNED _____ DATE _____

13. INSURED'S OR AUTHORIZED PERSON'S SIGNATURE I authorize payment of medical benefits to the undersigned physician or supplier for services described below.

SIGNED _____

14. DATE OF CURRENT: MM DD YY 01 04 20YY ILLNESS (First symptom) OR INJURY (Accident) OR PREGNANCY (LMP)	15. IF PATIENT HAS HAD SAME OR SIMILAR ILLNESS, GIVE FIRST DATE MM DD YY	16. DATES PATIENT UNABLE TO WORK IN CURRENT OCCUPATION MM DD YY FROM ___ TO ___

17. NAME OF REFERRING PROVIDER OR OTHER SOURCE LILY ROBERTS MD	17a. 17b. NPI 9012345678	18. HOSPITALIZATION DATES RELATED TO CURRENT SERVICES MM DD YY FROM ___ TO ___

19. RESERVED FOR LOCAL USE	20. OUTSIDE LAB? ☐ YES ☒ NO	$ CHARGES

21. DIAGNOSIS OR NATURE OF ILLNESS OR INJURY (Relate Items 1, 2, 3, or 4 to Item 24E by Line)

1. 786 50
2. ____
3. ____
4. ____

22. MEDICAID RESUBMISSION CODE ORIGINAL REF. NO.
23. PRIOR AUTHORIZATION NUMBER

24. A. DATE(S) OF SERVICE From To MM DD YY MM DD YY	B. PLACE OF SERVICE	C. EMG	D. PROCEDURES, SERVICES, OR SUPPLIES (Explain Unusual Circumstances) CPT/HCPCS MODIFIER	E. DIAGNOSIS POINTER	F. $ CHARGES	G. DAYS OR UNITS	H. EPSDT Family Plan	I. ID. QUAL.	J. RENDERING PROVIDER ID. #
1	01 04 YY	11		99212	1	30 00	1		NPI	0123456789
2									NPI	
3									NPI	
4									NPI	
5									NPI	
6									NPI	

25. FEDERAL TAX I.D. NUMBER SSN EIN 495245837 ☒	26. PATIENT'S ACCOUNT NO.	27. ACCEPT ASSIGNMENT? (For govt. claims, see back) ☒ YES ☐ NO	28. TOTAL CHARGE $ 30 00	29. AMOUNT PAID $	30. BALANCE DUE $ 30 00

31. SIGNATURE OF PHYSICIAN OR SUPPLIER INCLUDING DEGREES OR CREDENTIALS (I certify that the statements on the reverse apply to this bill and are made a part thereof.) RONALD W GERVAIS MD SIGNED _____ DATE 01 06 20YY	32. SERVICE FACILITY LOCATION INFORMATION a. b.	33. BILLING PROVIDER INFO & PH # (806) 7529118 MEDICAL CLINC 6 GREENWAY DRIVE CHICAGO IL 49855 a. 8901234567 b.

NUCC Instruction Manual available at: www.nucc.org

APPROVED OMB-0938-0999 FORM CMS-1500 (08-05)

For instructional use only. Courtesy of the Centers for Medicare and Medicaid Services, www.cms.hhs.gov

Figure 11–4 BC/BS Primary Payer CMS-1500

For purposes of illustration, Other is used for Block 1 and all dates are entered as eight digits. Refer to Figure 11–4 as you review the following instructions:

Block 1	Enter X in Other **or** Group Plan as required by the plan.
Block 1a	Enter the subscriber's identification number as it appears on the insurance card.
Block 2	Enter the patient's name—last, first, middle initial—in uppercase letters.
Block 3	Enter the patient's eight-digit birth date. Enter an X in M or F. If the gender is unknown, leave this blank.
Block 4	Enter the subscriber/enrollee's name as it appears on the insurance card.
Block 5	Enter the patient's permanent mailing address and telephone number.
Block 6	Enter an X in the box that describes the relationship of the patient to the subscriber (insured). If the patient is an unmarried domestic partner, enter an X in Other.
Block 7	Enter the subscriber/enrollee's address and telephone number, including the area code.
Block 8	Enter an X in the appropriate box to indicate the patient's marital status. If the patient is an unmarried domestic partner, enter an X in Other. Enter an X in the appropriate box to indicate the patient's employment or student status. If the patient is unemployed and/or not a full- or part-time student, leave this blank.
Blocks 9–9d	**NOTE:** Complete Blocks 9–9d when the patient is covered by more than one insurance plan.
Block 9	Enter the other insured person's name—last, first, and middle initial—in uppercase letters.
Block 9a	Enter the other insured person's policy or group number.
Block 9b	Enter the other insured person's eight-digit birth date.
Block 9c	Enter the other insured person's employer or school name.
Block 9d	Enter the other insured person's insurance plan or program name.
Blocks 10a–10c	Enter X in Yes or No as applicable. If the patient's condition is the result of an auto accident (10b), enter the two-character abbreviation of the state where the accident occurred.
Block 10d	Leave this blank.
Block 11	Enter the subscriber/enrollee's group number exactly as it appears on the insurance card.
Block 11a	Enter the subscriber's eight-digit date of birth. Enter an X in the appropriate box to indicate the subscriber's gender. If the gender is unknown, leave this blank.
Block 11b	Leave this blank.

continued on the next page

continued from the previous page

Block 11c	Enter the subscriber's insurance plan name, including the name of the state (e.g., BCBS MI).
Block 11d	Enter an X in the appropriate box to indicate if there is another health insurance plan. If YES, complete blocks 9 through 9D.
Block 12	Leave this blank.
Block 13	Leave this blank.
Block 14	Enter an eight-digit date, usually the date of service. For injury, accident, or trauma follow-up care, enter the date of the injury, accident, or trauma. For end-stage renal disease, enter the date of the kidney transplant or first maintenance dialysis. For pregnancy-related services, enter the date of the last menstrual period or the estimated date of conception.
Block 15	Enter an eight-digit date, if applicable. Otherwise, leave this blank.
Block 16	Enter an eight-digit date, if applicable. Otherwise, leave this blank.
Block 17	If there is a referring physician/provider, enter the first name, middle initial (if known), last name, and credential. Otherwise leave this blank.
Block 17a	Leave this blank.
Block 17b	Enter the 10-digit NPI number for the referring physician/provider named in block 17.
Block 18	Enter the eight-digit admission and discharge dates if services were provided during a hospital inpatient episode of care.
Block 19	Leave this blank.
Block 20	Enter an X in the NO box if all laboratory services reported on the claim were performed in the provider's office. Enter an X in the YES box if laboratory services were performed by an outside laboratory. Enter the total amount charged by the outside laboratory.
Block 21	Enter the ICD-9-CM (ICD-10-CM when implemented) diagnosis codes to the highest level of specificity. Enter the primary (first-listed) diagnosis in line 1.
Block 22	Leave this blank.
Block 23	Leave this blank.
Block 24A	Enter the date the service was performed, in the eight-digit format, in the FROM column. If the service was performed on consecutive days during a range of dates, enter an eight-digit date in the TO column. **EXAMPLE** Hilda visits the physician on September 7, 8, and 9, 20YY, for a series of prednisone injections. Enter 090720YY in the FROM column and 090920YY in the TO column.
Block 24B	Enter the two-digit code that identifies where the service was provided. (See "Place of Service Codes" in Chapter 8.)

continued on the next page

continued from the previous page

Block 24C	Enter Y for YES if the service was an emergency. Otherwise, leave this blank.
Block 24D	Enter the CPT/HCPCS code and applicable modifier(s) for procedures and services.
Block 24E	Enter the diagnosis reference code from block 21 that relates to the procedure/service performed on the date of service.
Block 24F	Enter the total charge for the service(s) listed on each line.
Block 24G	Enter the number of days or units for procedures or services reported in Block 24D. If just one procedure or service was performed, enter 1 in block 24G.
Block 24H	Leave this blank.
Block 24I	Leave this blank.
Block 24J	Enter the 10-digit NPI number in the unshaded area of block 24J for the provider who performed the service or procedure.
Block 25	Enter the provider's Social Security number (SSN) or employer identification number (EIN). Do not enter hyphens or spaces in the number. Enter an X in the appropriate box to identify which number is reported.
Block 26	Enter the patient's account number as assigned by the provider. Otherwise, leave this blank.
Block 27	Enter an X in YES for providers who accept assignment. Otherwise, enter an X in NO.
Block 28	Enter the total charges for all services on lines 1 through 6.
Block 29	Enter the amount paid by the patient. Do not enter any amount paid by Medicare or other insurance.
Block 30	Enter the difference between the total charges and the amount paid. Otherwise, leave this blank.
Block 31	Enter the provider's name and credential (e.g., LETIA JOHNSON MD) and the date the claim was completed (MMDDYYYY). Do not enter spaces in the date.
Block 32	Enter the name and address where procedures or services were provided, if at a location other than the provider's office. If YES is checked in block 20, enter the name and address of the facility that performed the laboratory service.
Block 32a	Enter the 10-digit NPI number of the facility entered in block 32.
Block 32b	Leave this blank.
Block 33	Enter the provider's billing name, address, and phone number, including the area code. Enter the phone number in the area next to the block title. Do not enter parentheses for the area code. Enter the name on line 1, the address on line 2, and the city, state, and zip code on line 3. For a nine-digit zip code, enter the hyphen.
Block 33a	Enter the 10-digit NPI number of the billing provider. If the provider is a solo practitioner, enter the individual's NPI number. If the provider is part of a group practice, enter the group practice NPI number.
Block 33b	Leave this blank.

Completed claim forms are submitted to the BC/BS claims processing center.

 ABBREVIATIONS

Table 11–3 lists the abbreviations presented in this chapter.

TABLE 11–3

Abbreviations and Meanings	
Abbreviation	**Meaning**
AHA	American Hospital Association
AMA	American Medical Association
BC/BS	Blue Cross/Blue Shield
BCBSA	Blue Cross and Blue Shield Association
DME	durable medical equipment
HMO	health maintenance organization
PAR	participating provider
PCP	personal care physician; primary care provider
PPO	preferred provider organization
RVS	relative value scale
RVU	relative value unit
UCR	usual, customary, and reasonable (fee)

© 2014 Cengage Learning. All Rights Reserved.

 SUMMARY

Blue Cross/Blue Shield (BC/BS) is recognized in all countries that deal with private health insurance plans. In the past, Blue Cross plans covered hospital services, and Blue Shield covered physician or provider services. Today, the two companies cover services such as outpatient surgery, long-term care, and prescription medication.

BC/BS identification cards are a source of important information. The billing specialist needs a copy, both front and back, of the patient's current ID card. The insured's name, identification number, insurance group number, and plan code are found on the ID card.

BC/BS offers several benefits to participating providers (PARs), including sending the insurance payment directly to the provider. Staff training and claims-filing assistance are other services available to participating providers' staff.

BC/BS uses two payment methods: usual, customary, and reasonable (UCR) fees and relative value scale (RVS) fees. BC/BS calculates an allowed charge for covered services. Insurance claims for provider services are submitted electronically or manually by using the CMS-1500 form.

REVIEW EXERCISES

Use the following information to complete a CMS-1500 for submission to BC/BS as the primary payer. Your instructor will tell you how to obtain the form.

PATIENT NAME: Charles Wu

DOB: 11/12/46

ADDRESS: 507 East Osborn; Blueberry, ME 49855

HOME PHONE: (906) 555-6997

WORK PHONE: (906) 555-1234

SPOUSE: Janis Wu

ADDRESS: 507 East Osborn; Blueberry, ME 49855

EMPLOYER: Sawyer Lumber Mill, County Road 550, Blueberry, ME 49855

INSURANCE INFORMATION: ID: XYP 692107334; GROUP #: 92118

PLAN: 421

OTHER INSURANCE: No

SUPERIORLAND CLINIC

714 Hennepin Ave.

Blueberry, ME 49855

TAX ID # 49-4134726

SUPERIORLAND CLINIC PHONE: (806) 555-6060

SUPERIORLAND CLINIC NPI: 4567890123

PROGRESS NOTE

DATE: March 15, 20YY

Mr. Wu is seen today for recurrent pain in the right shoulder. On examination, there is moderate range of motion accompanied by pain with movement. CBC was essentially normal. Right shoulder x-ray taken two days ago revealed changes consistent with bursitis. He is to take 600 mg of ibuprofen q.i.d. and return in three weeks for follow-up. He should call the office if the pain worsens. SIGNED BY: Henry Romero, MD. NPI: 2311287891.

OFFICE VISIT/ESTABLISHED PATIENT: 99212

CBC: 85025

DIAGNOSIS: Bursitis, code 727.3 (ICD-10-CM code: M75.51)

CHARGES: Office visit, $45; CBC, $24

NOTE: Dr. Romero is a participating physician and accepts assignment.

Multiple Choice

Circle the correct answer from the choices provided.

1. Individuals enrolled in a BC/BS plan are called

   a. recipients.

   b. insurees.

   c. subscribers.

   d. members.

2. Blue Cross insurance plans usually cover

   a. hospital charges.

   b. physician charges.

   c. prescription medication charges.

   d. home health charges.

3. Blue Shield insurance plans usually cover

   a. hospital charges.

   b. home health charges.

   c. prescription medication charges.

   d. physician charges.

4. The maximum amount an insurance company pays for a specific service is called the

   a. covered fee.

   b. allowable fee.

   c. UCR fee.

   d. user fee.

5. BC/BS provider payments are often based on the

   a. UCR fee.

   b. physician's fee.

   c. prevailing fee.

   d. customary fee.

6. A write-off is best described as

   a. a bad debt.

   b. a letter informing the patient of an insurance denial.

   c. the difference between the UCR fee and the provider's charge.

   d. a handwritten progress note.

7. BC/BS managed care plans often require the subscribers and members to have

   a. a personal care physician.

   b. an annual physical examination.

   c. supplemental insurance coverage.

   d. random drug screening.

8. BC/BS participating provider benefits include

   a. enhanced reimbursement rates.

   b. inclusion in national advertising campaigns.

   c. guaranteed number of patient visits.

   d. direct payments from the insurance company.

9. "Covered services" refers to

   a. services provided by a physician.

   b. services identified in the insurance plan.

   c. services that are medically necessary.

   d. services requested by the patient.

 CHALLENGE ACTIVITY

Schedule an interview with a BC/BS customer representative. Prior to the interview, develop questions that will help you gather information about the training or education needed to work as a customer representative, the most rewarding aspects of the job, the least rewarding aspects, regulatory pressures from the state and federal governments, working with providers, and working with subscribers. Share the information, as a paper or presentation, with your class or instructor.

 WEBSITE

Blue Cross and Blue Shield Association: http://www.bcbs.com

CHAPTER 12

Medicare

LEARNING OBJECTIVES

Upon successful completion of this chapter, the reader should have the knowledge to:

1. Describe the difference between Medicare Parts A, B, C, and D.
2. Identify the eligibility requirements for Medicare.
3. List 10 examples of services covered by Medicare Part B.
4. Define all key terms and abbreviations.
5. Describe the differences between a participating and a nonparticipating provider.
6. Discuss the incentives for becoming a participating provider.
7. Differentiate between Medicare as the primary and the secondary payer.
8. Successfully complete the CMS-1500 according to Medicare guidelines.

KEY TERMS

Advance Beneficiary Notice (ABN)
Assistant surgeon
Balance-bill
Benefit period
Centers for Medicare and Medicaid Services (CMS)
Conditional primary payer status
Diagnostic service
Durable medical equipment (DME)
Durable medical equipment Medicare Administrative Contractor (DME MAC)
Elective surgery
Formulary

Geographic adjustment factor (GAF)
Health Insurance Claim Number (HICN)
Lifetime reserve days
Limiting fee
Medical savings account (MSA)
Medicare
Medicare Administrative Contractor (MAC)
Medicare Advantage (MA)
Medicare Advantage Prescription Drug Plan (MA-PDP)
Medicare fee schedule (MFS)

Medicare-Medicaid Crossover Program
Medicare Part A
Medicare Part B
Medicare Part C
Medicare Part D
Medicare Summary Notice (MSN)
Medicare supplemental plan, Medicare secondary payer (MSP)
Medicare special needs plan (SNP)
Medigap
National conversion factor (CF)
National Correct Coding Initiative (NCCI)

Nonparticipating provider (NonPAR)
Ordered/referred services
Ordering/performing physician
Out-of-pocket expenses
Participating provider (PAR)

Physician extender
Prescription drug plan (PDP)
Private fee-for-service (PFFS)
Qualified Medicare Beneficiary (QMB)
Qualifying Individual (QI)
Referring physician

Relative value unit (RVU)
Remittance notice
Resource-based relative value scale (RBRVS)
Specified Low-Income Medicare Beneficiary (SLMB)

 OVERVIEW

Medicare is a federal health insurance program created in 1965 as Title 18 of the Social Security Act (SSA). It is managed by the Centers for Medicare and Medicaid Services (CMS). Medicare is the nation's largest health insurance program and covers millions of Americans. Medicare benefits are divided into Medicare Part A, Medicare Part B, Medicare Part C, and Medicare Part D. Medicare Part A helps pay for care received in hospitals and skilled nursing facilities and for home health and hospice care. Medicare Part B helps pay for physician services, outpatient hospital care, and other medical services, such as clinical laboratory services; physical, occupational, and speech therapy; and durable medical equipment (DME). Medicare Part C, also known as Medicare Advantage (MA), is an alternative to the original Medicare fee-for-service plan. Under Medicare Part C, private insurance companies pay for health services that would be covered by Medicare Parts A, B, and D. Medicare Part D is a prescription drug (medication) plan that offers insurance benefits for prescription drugs. Medicare Part A is usually premium-free. Other Medicare plans are available for a monthly premium.

Medicare is generally available to individuals who are:

- Age 65 years and older
- Citizens or permanent residents of the United States
- Retired or who have worked at least 10 years in Medicare-covered employment
- The spouse or widow(er) of an individual who has worked for at least 10 years in Medicare-covered employment

Individuals younger than age 65 may qualify for Medicare if they are:

- Disabled and have received Social Security Disability Insurance (SSDI) benefits for two years
- Diagnosed with end-stage renal disease (ESRD)
- Kidney donors when the donated kidney is transplanted to an individual with ESRD

Medicare beneficiaries with incomes below the federal poverty level may be eligible for the Qualified Medicare Beneficiary (QMB) program. The QMB program is a Medicaid program for beneficiaries who need help paying for Medicare services. The QMB program pays Medicare Part A and Part B premiums, deductibles, and co-insurance amounts.

Medicare beneficiaries with incomes slightly above the federal poverty level may be eligible for the Specified Low-Income Medicare Beneficiary (SLMB) program or the Qualifying Individual (QI) program. The SLMB is a Medicaid program that pays Medicare

Part B premiums for beneficiaries who are enrolled in Medicare Part A. The QI program is a Medicaid program that pays all or a portion of the Medicare Part B premiums for beneficiaries who are enrolled in Medicare Part A and who are not otherwise eligible for Medicaid.

The Medicare Health Insurance Program is constantly changing. Insurance billing specialists must keep up with the changes. The local Social Security office has current Medicare information. Several government websites offer nearly up-to-the-minute changes. The CMS can be reached online at http://www.cms.gov, and the Medicare website is http://www.medicare.gov.

Although CMS manages the Medicare program, it does not directly process the insurance claims for services rendered to Medicare patients. Companies that process insurance claims for Medicare are called Medicare Administrative Contractors (MACs), formerly known as insurance carriers or fiscal intermediaries. MACs provide updated information about Medicare changes and regulations.

This chapter covers information related to Medicare Part A, Part B, Part C, and Part D. Topics include services covered, reimbursement issues for participating (PAR) and nonparticipating (NonPAR) providers for Medicare Part B, the MFS, Medicare as the primary and secondary payer, MA plans, and claim submission procedures.

MEDICARE PART A

An individual is eligible for premium-free Medicare Part A if the person meets the general requirements listed in the previous section.

Enrollment in Medicare Part A is handled in two ways: automatically or by application. Individuals who are not yet 65 and are already receiving Social Security or Railroad Retirement benefits are automatically enrolled in Medicare Part A. A Medicare card is mailed to these individuals about three months before their 65th birthday. Disabled individuals are also automatically enrolled in Medicare Part A beginning in the 25th month of their disability. A Medicare card is mailed to these individuals about three months before they are entitled to Medicare benefits or three months before the 25th month of their disability. Retired and disabled individuals are also automatically enrolled in Medicare Part B, but they may refuse this insurance.

Individuals who are not receiving Social Security or Railroad Retirement benefits must apply for Medicare three months before their 65th birthday. Individuals on kidney dialysis or who are waiting for a kidney transplant must also apply for Medicare.

Individuals enrolled in Medicare or Railroad Retirement Medicare receive an identification card. Figure 12–1 shows a sample Medicare card. The Railroad Retirement Medicare card is nearly identical to the standard Medicare ID card. The toll-free number for the Social Security Administration is replaced with the heading Railroad Retirement Board. The number for the board is on the back of the card.

Note that the Medicare identification card includes the beneficiary's name, sex, type of coverage (Part A, Part B, or both), effective date, and Medicare claim number. The Medicare claim number is called the health insurance claim number (HICN). This number is the Social Security number (SSN) of the wage earner. A one- or two-character suffix follows the SSN. The suffix identifies the beneficiary status of the individual named on the ID card. For example, an HICN that ends with the letter A means that the beneficiary is the wage earner;

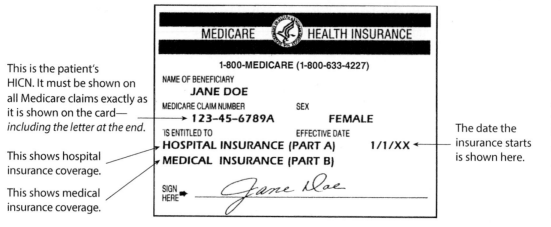

This is the patient's HICN. It must be shown on all Medicare claims exactly as it is shown on the card— *including the letter at the end.*

This shows hospital insurance coverage.

This shows medical insurance coverage.

The date the insurance starts is shown here.

Figure 12–1 Sample Medicare Card

the letter B indicates the wife of the wage earner; B1 is the husband of the wage earner; and D is the widow of the wage earner. Other HICN suffixes are available on the Medicare website.

Medicare Part A: Covered Services

Medicare Part A, commonly known as hospital insurance, provides health insurance coverage for care provided by hospitals, skilled nursing homes, home health care, and hospice. Services covered by Medicare Part A include:

- *Hospital Stays:* Semiprivate room, meals, usual nursing care, and ancillary services and supplies that are medically necessary. Medicare does cover a private room, such as an intensive care unit, if medically necessary.
- *Skilled Nursing Facility (SNF):* Semiprivate room, meals, and skilled nursing and rehabilitative services. SNF care includes services such as intravenous injections and physical therapy that cannot be provided on an outpatient basis.
- *Home Health Care:* Covered services must be ordered by a physician and are limited to reasonable and necessary intermittent skilled nursing care, physical therapy, occupational therapy, speech-language therapy, and home health aide services. Wheelchairs, hospital beds, oxygen, and other medical supplies and services may also be covered.
- *Hospice Care:* For the terminally ill, Medicare covers medications for symptom control and pain relief; physician care; nursing services; and medical supplies.

It is impossible to list every service covered by Medicare Part A. However, in order for any service to be covered, the service must be medically necessary. This means the service must be appropriate for the diagnosis and treatment of the beneficiary's medical condition.

Medicare Part A: Deductibles and Co-payments

Like any health insurance plan, Medicare Part A has deductibles and co-payments. In 2012, the deductible for the first 60 days of inpatient hospital care was approximately $1156. From the 61st to 150th day of inpatient hospital care, the beneficiary is responsible for daily co-payments. The 2012 co-payment for the 61st to 90th day of inpatient hospital care was $289 per day and $578 per day from the 91st to 150th day. The deductible for the 91st to 150th hospital day applies only when the beneficiary uses his or her lifetime reserve days to help pay for an extended hospitalization. Lifetime reserve days are described later in this section. The beneficiary is responsible for all charges after the 150th day of care.

For SNF care, the beneficiary pays nothing for the first 20 days. In 2012, the co-payment for skilled nursing care from the 21st to 100th day of care was about $144.50 per day. After the 100th day, the beneficiary is responsible for all charges.

Medicare Part A deductibles and co-payments are based on the beneficiary's benefit period. A benefit period begins when an individual is admitted to a hospital or SNF and ends 60 days after discharge. Benefit periods are important because the beneficiary must pay the inpatient hospital deductible and the skilled nursing care co-payments for *each* benefit period. There is no limit to the number of benefit periods available to Medicare Part A beneficiaries. Example A illustrates how the benefit period affects inpatient hospital deductibles, and Example B illustrates how the benefit period affects SNF co-payments.

EXAMPLE A: INPATIENT HOSPITAL DEDUCTIBLE

David Brindley, a 70-year-old retired teacher, is admitted to Blueberry Medical Center on June 1 and discharged on June 15. He returns to his home and does well until October, when he trips over a scatter rug, fractures a hip, and is hospitalized from October 12 through October 30. Because 60 days elapsed between hospitalizations, Mr. Brindley received services during two (2) benefit periods and is responsible for $1068 of the hospital bill for June and $1068 of the hospital bill for October. Medicare Part A would cover the remainder of each hospital bill.

EXAMPLE B: SKILLED NURSING FACILITY CO-PAYMENTS

After hip surgery, Mr. Brindley is transferred to an SNF for postoperative rehabilitation. He stays at the facility for two weeks (14 days). Because Mr. Brindley's skilled nursing stay was less than 20 days, Medicare Part A covers the entire 14 days, and he does not pay a deductible. After being home for a week, he is readmitted to the SNF for further rehabilitative care. This time, Mr. Brindley's length of stay is 21 days. Because 60 days did not elapse between the two admissions, Mr. Brindley is in the same benefit period. His first length of stay, 14 days, is deducted from the co-payment-free 20 days, which leaves 6 days in Mr. Brindley's benefit period. Medicare Part A pays for the 6 days of his second episode of care. For the remaining 15 days, Mr. Brindley must pay the deductible for each day. In 2012, the deductible was $144 per day, which means Mr. Brindley is responsible for $2160 of the second episode of care.

The benefit period concept may seem complicated. Simply put, Medicare Part A beneficiaries must have a 60-day break between hospital inpatient or SNF episodes of care to trigger a new benefit period.

The benefit period formula does not apply to Medicare-approved home health care services, such as physician and nursing services. When a beneficiary qualifies for home health care, there is no deductible. There is a 20% co-payment of the Medicare-approved amount for durable medical equipment (DME). DME includes items such as a wheelchair or hospital bed.

Lifetime Reserve Days

Lifetime reserve days are a fixed number of days that Medicare will cover when a beneficiary is hospitalized for more than 90 days during a benefit period. Under the original Medicare plan, beneficiaries are allowed 60 lifetime reserve days that may be used only once during the beneficiary's lifetime. For each lifetime reserve day used, Medicare pays all covered services *except* the per-day deductible, which was $578 in 2012. Lifetime reserve days apply only to inpatient hospital care. The following example illustrates Medicare coverage when using lifetime reserve days.

EXAMPLE

Violet is a 79-year-old woman who has several health problems but is able to live in her own home. She was admitted to Blueberry Memorial Hospital on August 1, 20YY, with necrotizing cellulitis. She was placed on intravenous therapy and other appropriate treatments. She did not respond well to medical therapy and underwent several debridements of necrotic tissue. Gangrene became a problem, and she had three toes amputated. Violet was discharged on September 2, 20YY. Her length of stay was 32 days. Medicare Part A covered all approved charges except the $1156 deductible. Within two weeks, Violet had a setback, and she returned to the hospital. The cellulitis continued to worsen, and she developed several life-threatening complications. Violet was hospitalized from September 14 through November 23, 20YY—a 70-day length of stay. She was discharged to her daughter's home and continued with antibiotic treatment. Violet had a total of 102 hospital days between the two episodes of care.

Because Violet returned to the hospital within two weeks, her benefit period continued from her first admission in August. Medicare Part A covered the cost of the first 28 days of her second admission. There was no deductible because Violet met the deductible for the benefit period during her first hospitalization. On the 61st hospital day, Violet was responsible for the $289 -per-day co-payment until her 90th hospital day.

The hospital social worker visited Violet on November 18 to discuss the possibility of using lifetime reserve days, should the need arise. Violet agreed, and from her 91st hospital day until her discharge, she used 11 of her lifetime reserve days. During this time, Violet paid a $578 co-payment for each of the 11 lifetime reserve days. Medicare Part A paid the cost of all covered services except the per-day deductible.

By the time Violet was discharged on November 23, she had received 102 days of inpatient hospital care in one benefit period and had used 11 of her lifetime reserve days. Her deductibles and co-payments totaled $16,184.00.

Violet recovered and was able to return to her own home after spending Christmas with her daughter's family. On March 15 of the following year, Violet fell in the shower and sustained a femoral neck hip fracture. She was admitted to Blueberry Memorial Hospital and underwent a total hip replacement. Because 60 days had elapsed since her last hospitalization, Violet began a new benefit period. She was in the hospital for 10 days. Medicare Part A paid the cost of all covered services, and Violet was responsible for the $1156 deductible.

Additional information about Medicare Part A is available on the Medicare website at http://www.medicare.gov. Another good resource is the annual publication *Medicare and You,* which is sent to Medicare beneficiaries and is available at your local Social Security Administration office.

REINFORCEMENT EXERCISES 12–1

Write a short answer for each question or statement.

1. Name the government agency that manages Medicare.

   _____

   _____

   _____

2. Who is eligible for Medicare?

   _____

   _____

   _____

3. Briefly describe the differences between Medicare Part A, Part B, Part C, and Part D.

   _____

   _____

   _____

4. Define the term "benefit period."

   _____

   _____

   _____

5. Explain the purpose of Medicare Part A "lifetime reserve days."

   _____

   _____

   _____

Write out each abbreviation.

1. CMS

   _____

2. QMB

   _____

3. SLMB

   _____

4. MAC

   _____

5. HICN

   _____

MEDICARE PART B

Individuals who qualify for Medicare Part A also qualify for Medicare Part B. Participation in Medicare Part B is optional. Beneficiaries pay a monthly premium based on income. In 2012, the standard Medicare Part B premium was $99.90 and the annual deductible was $140. The monthly premium increases according to an individual's or couple's annual income. For example, an individual with an annual income over $85,000 but less than $107,000 pays $139.90 per month. A couple with an annual income between $170,000 and $214,000 pays $139.50 per month each, for a total of $279.80. Part B premiums are deducted from an individual's monthly Social Security check. If an individual does not receive Social Security, the monthly premium is billed to the individual.

In addition to the annual deductible, beneficiaries are required to pay co-insurance for Part B covered services. The co-insurance for most services is 20% of the Medicare-allowed charge. Some services have a higher co-insurance. For example, co-insurance for most outpatient mental health services is 50%. Federal law obligates providers to collect the deductible and co-insurance payment.

Medicare Part B: Covered Services

Like most health insurance plans, Medicare Part B does not pay for every available medical treatment or service. Medicare is only required to pay for services and supplies that are reasonable, medically necessary, and consistent with the patient's diagnosis. Medicare does not pay for procedures or treatments that are considered experimental or still in the investigative or trial stage.

Medicare Part B is intended to help defray the cost of a variety of diagnostic, treatment, and preventive health care services. Table 12–1 describes examples of diagnostic and treatment services, and Table 12–2 describes examples of preventive services.

TABLE 12–1

Diagnostic and Treatment Services	
Medical and Other Services	Physicians' services except for routine physical exams; outpatient medical and surgical services and supplies; diagnostic tests; ambulatory surgery center facility fees for approved procedures; DME such as wheelchairs, hospital beds, oxygen, and walkers; outpatient physical and occupational therapy, including speech-language therapy and mental health services
Clinical Laboratory Service	Blood tests, urinalysis, and more
Home Health Care	Part-time skilled care, home health aide services, DME when supplied by a home health agency while getting Medicare-covered home health care, and other supplies and services as approved by Medicare
Outpatient Hospital Services	Services for the diagnosis or treatment of an illness or injury
Diabetes Supplies	Blood sugar testing monitors, blood sugar test strips, lancets, and more; insulin and certain medical supplies used to inject insulin may be covered by Medicare Part D
Blood	Pints of blood needed as an outpatient or as a component of a Part B-covered service

TABLE 12–2

Preventive Services and Eligible Beneficiaries

Preventive Service	Eligible Beneficiaries
Annual Wellness Visit (AWV) Initial wellness visit to establish Personalized Prevention Plan Services (PPPS) that includes referrals, health education, or counseling aimed at reducing identified health-risk factors; subsequent AWVs to monitor and update PPPS	All Medicare beneficiaries; no deductible or co-pay for the first AWV
Abdominal Aortic Aneurysm (AAA) Screening A one-time screening ultrasound. Medicare only covers this screening if you get a referral as a result of your "Welcome to Medicare" physical	Beneficiaries at risk for having an AAA
Bone Mass Measurement (Bone Density) Once every 24 months or as indicated by the patient's condition	Beneficiaries at risk for losing bone mass
Cardiovascular Screening Monitoring plasma cholesterol, lipid, and triglyceride levels, as indicated by the patient's condition	All beneficiaries
Colorectal Cancer Screening • Fecal occult blood tests every 12 months • Flexible sigmoidoscopy every 48 months • Colonoscopy generally once every 120 months; every 24 months for high-risk individuals • Barium enema once every 48 months when substituted for sigmoidoscopy or colonoscopy	All beneficiaries age 50 and older; no age limit for colonoscopy
Diabetes Screening	Medicare beneficiaries with any of the following risk factors: • high blood pressure • history of abnormal cholesterol and triglyceride levels • obesity • history of high blood sugar
Flu Shots	All beneficiaries
Glaucoma Screening Once every 12 months	Medicare beneficiaries at risk for glaucoma
Mammogram Screening • Once every 12 months • One baseline screening mammogram	All women with Medicare age 40 and older Women between 35 and 39
Pap Smear and Pelvic Exam • Once every 24 months • Once every 12 months for high-risk individuals or women of child-bearing age with an abnormal Pap smear in the past three years	Medicare beneficiaries

continued on the next page

continued from the previous page

Preventive Services and Eligible Beneficiaries	
Preventive Service	**Eligible Beneficiaries**
Physical Examination—(one-time "Welcome to Medicare" Physical) One preventive physical examination within the first 12 months of the date of enrollment	All Medicare beneficiaries
Pneumococcal Shot Pneumonia shot; once in a lifetime	All beneficiaries
Prostate Cancer Screening • Prostate-specific antigen (PSA) test once every 12 months	Beneficiaries age 50 and older
Smoking Cessation Eight face-to-face visits in a 12-month period	Medicare beneficiaries diagnosed with an illness caused or complicated by tobacco use
"Welcome to Medicare" Preventive Visit Also called the "Welcome to Medicare" physical examination	All Medicare beneficiaries; a one-time benefit

In addition to the services listed in Table 12–1 and Table 12–2, Medicare Part B helps cover the cost of artificial limbs and eyes, breast prostheses following mastectomy, and one pair of eyeglasses after cataract surgery with an intraocular lens.

The Medicare co-insurance payment may vary depending on the type of service. Many services require a 20% co-insurance/co-payment, but mental health, physical, and occupational therapy services may have a higher co-payment. Billing specialists receive current information via the MAC and Medicare bulletins and transmittals.

Although Medicare pays only for services and supplies that are considered reasonable and medically necessary, there may be situations in which the provider believes a service is necessary, but payment for the service may be denied by Medicare. When this situation occurs, the insurance billing specialist must have the patient sign an Advance Beneficiary Notice (ABN). The ABN must be completed *before* the service is performed. The notice must contain information that is clear and accurate so the patient can make an informed choice about accepting the service and paying for it. According to CMS guidelines, the ABN must include the following:

- Date of service
- Cost of service
- Narrative of the particular service in a language the patient understands
- Provider's statement that Medicare is likely to deny payment
- Reason(s) the provider believes payment will be denied
- Patient's signature and date of signature

Figure 12–2 is a sample ABN form.

(A) Notifier(s):

(B) Patient Name: **(C) Identification Number:**

ADVANCE BENEFICIARY NOTICE OF NONCOVERAGE (ABN)

NOTE: If Medicare doesn't pay for **(D)**_____ below, you may have to pay.

Medicare does not pay for everything, even some care that you or your health care provider have good reason to think you need. We expect Medicare may not pay for the **(D)**_____ below.

(D)_____	**(E) Reason Medicare May Not Pay:**	**(F) Estimated Cost:**

WHAT YOU NEED TO DO NOW:

- Read this notice, so you can make an informed decision about your care.
- Ask us any questions that you may have after you finish reading.
- Choose an option below about whether to receive the **(D)**_____ listed above.
   Note: If you choose Option 1 or 2, we may help you to use any other insurance that you might have, but Medicare cannot require us to do this.

(G) OPTIONS: **Check only one box. We cannot choose a box for you.**

☐ **OPTION 1.** I want the **(D)**_____ listed above. You may ask to be paid now, but I also want Medicare billed for an official decision on payment, which is sent to me on a Medicare Summary Notice (MSN). I understand that if Medicare doesn't pay, I am responsible for payment, but **I can appeal to Medicare** by following the directions on the MSN. If Medicare does pay, you will refund any payments I made to you, less co-pays or deductibles.

☐ **OPTION 2.** I want the **(D)**_____ listed above, but do not bill Medicare. You may ask to be paid now as I am responsible for payment. **I cannot appeal if Medicare is not billed.**

☐ **OPTION 3.** I don't want the **(D)**_____ listed above. I understand with this choice I am **not** responsible for payment, and **I cannot appeal to see if Medicare would pay.**

(H) Additional Information:

This notice gives our opinion, not an official Medicare decision. If you have other questions on this notice or Medicare billing, call **1-800-MEDICARE** (1-800-633-4227/**TTY:** 1-877-486-2048).
Signing below means that you have received and understand this notice. You also receive a copy.

(I) Signature:	**(J) Date:**

According to the Paperwork Reduction Act of 1995, no persons are required to respond to a collection of information unless it displays a valid OMB control number. The valid OMB control number for this information collection is 0938-0566. The time required to complete this information collection is estimated to average 7 minutes per response, including the time to review instructions, search existing data resources, gather the data needed, and complete and review the information collection. If you have comments concerning the accuracy of the time estimate or suggestions for improving this form, please write to: CMS, 7500 Security Boulevard, Attn: PRA Reports Clearance Officer, Baltimore, Maryland 21244-1850.

Form CMS-R-131 (03/08)   Form Approved OMB No. 0938-0566

Courtesy of the Centers for Medicare and Medicaid Services, www.cms.hhs.gov

Figure 12–2 Advance Beneficiary Notice

Even though the provider believes Medicare will deny a service, a claim is submitted and a copy of the Advanced Notice agreement is sent with the claim. There is always a chance that payment may be approved. Failure to have the patient complete the notice *before* providing the service results in the following:

- Physicians who do not accept Medicare payment must refund any denied charges collected from the patient.
- Physicians who accept Medicare will not receive payment for denied services and must refund any money collected from the patient.

Medicare Part B: Providers

Health care providers may choose whether to participate in Medicare. Physicians who elect to be Medicare participating providers (PARs) contract with Medicare and agree to accept the Medicare-approved payment rate for services rendered to all Medicare patients. A nonparticipating provider (NonPAR) does not contract with Medicare and therefore does not agree to accept the Medicare-approved payment rate for services rendered to all Medicare patients.

Participating Providers

Under Medicare Part B, a PAR agrees to be enrolled in the Medicare program. The MAC remits payment directly to the provider's office and not to the beneficiary. PARs agree to accept assignment for Medicare patients. The provider files claims for services and accepts the Medicare-approved payment rate for services rendered to Medicare patients. The provider receives 80% of the approved rate from Medicare and 20% of the approved rate from the patient. The PAR also collects the deductible, if applicable. As a PAR, the physician or provider cannot balance-bill the patient for the difference between the Medicare-approved amount and the provider's usual fee for the service. Table 12–3 is an example of a PAR fee and payment rate.

To increase the number of PARs, Congress has mandated several incentives:

- Claims are paid directly to PARs
- PAR payment rate is 5% higher than for NonPAR physicians
- Medicare recipients receive a directory that lists all PARs

TABLE 12–3

Participating Provider Payment	
PAR fee	$125
PAR Medicare-approved rate	$100
PAR receives 80% from Medicare	$80
Patient pays PAR 20%	$20
PAR adjusts/writes off the difference	$25

- A message included on the Medicare Summary Notice (MSN) sent to patients treated by NonPAR providers states that out-of-pocket expenses (the amount of money the patient must pay for a service) are reduced if services are received from a PAR

The MSN, also called an explanation of benefits (EOB) or remittance advice, provides detailed payment information. Figure 12–3 is a sample of an MSN.

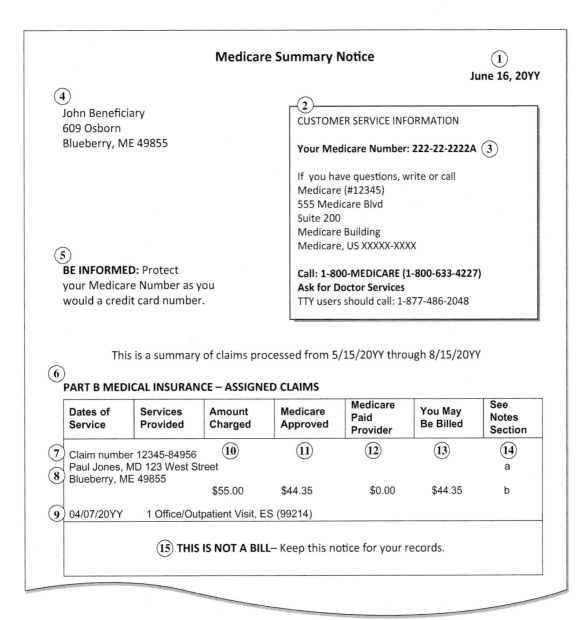

Medicare Summary Notice   ①

June 16, 20YY

④

John Beneficiary
609 Osborn
Blueberry, ME 49855

②

CUSTOMER SERVICE INFORMATION

Your Medicare Number: 222-22-2222A ③

If you have questions, write or call
Medicare (#12345)
555 Medicare Blvd
Suite 200
Medicare Building
Medicare, US XXXXX-XXXX

Call: 1-800-MEDICARE (1-800-633-4227)
Ask for Doctor Services
TTY users should call: 1-877-486-2048

⑤

BE INFORMED: Protect
your Medicare Number as you
would a credit card number.

This is a summary of claims processed from 5/15/20YY through 8/15/20YY

⑥

PART B MEDICAL INSURANCE – ASSIGNED CLAIMS

Dates of Service	Services Provided	Amount Charged	Medicare Approved	Medicare Paid Provider	You May Be Billed	See Notes Section
⑦ Claim number 12345-84956 ⑧ Paul Jones, MD 123 West Street Blueberry, ME 49855		⑩	⑪	⑫	⑬	⑭ a
		$55.00	$44.35	$0.00	$44.35	b
⑨ 04/07/20YY	1 Office/Outpatient Visit, ES (99214)					

⑮ **THIS IS NOT A BILL**– Keep this notice for your records.

1. **Date:** Date MSN was sent.
2. **Customer Service Information:** Who to contact with questions about the MSN. Your Medicare number (3).
3. **Medicare Number:** The number on your Medicare card.

Figure 12–3 Medicare Summary Notice

continued on the next page

continued from the previous page

(16) Notes Section:

a This information is being sent to your private insurer(s). Send any questions regarding your benefits to them.

b This approved amount has been applied toward your deductible.

(17) Deductible Information:

You have now met $44.35 of your $XXX.XX Part B deductible for 20xx.

(18) General Information:

Please notify us if your address has changed as shown on this notice.

(19) Appeals Information – Part B

If you disagree with any claims decision on this notice, your appeal must be Received by **November 1, 20xx.**

Follow the instructions below:

1) Circle the item(s) you disagree with and explain why you disagree.

2) Send this notice, or a copy, to the address in the "Customer Service Information" box on Page 1.

3) Sign here_____ Phone Number _____

4. **Name and Address:** If incorrect, contact the company listed in (2), and the Social Security Administration immediately.

5. **Be Informed:** Messages about ways to protect yourself and Medicare from fraud and abuse.

6. **Part B Medical Insurance = Assigned Claims:** Type of service. See the back of MSN for Information about assignment. (**Please note:** For unassigned services, this section is called **"Part B Medical Insurance – Unassigned Claims."**)

7. **Claim Number:** Number that identifies this specific claim.

8. **Provider's Name and Address:** Doctor (may show clinic, group, and/or referring doctor) or Provider's name and billing address. The referring doctor's name may also be shown if the service was ordered or referred by another doctor. The address shown is the billing address and may be different from where you received the services.

9. **Dates of Service:** Date service or supply was received. You may use these dates to compare with the dates shown on the bill you receive from your doctor.

10. **Amount Charged:** Amount the provider billed Medicare.

11. **Medicare Approved:** Amount Medicare approves for this service or supply.

12. **Medicare Paid Provider:** Amount Medicare paid to the provider. (**Please Note:** For unassigned services, this column is called "**Medicare Paid You.**")

13. **You May be Billed:** The total amount the provider may bill you, including deductibles, coinsurance, and noncovered charges. Medicare supplement (Medigap) policies may pay all or part of this amount.

14. **See Notes Section:** Explains letters in (14) for more detailed information about your claim.

15. **This is not a bill:** This is not a bill.

16. **Notes Section:** Explains letters in (14) for more detailed information about your claim.

17. **Deductible Information:** How much of your yearly deductible you have met.

18. **General Information:** Important Medicare news and information.

19. **Appeals Information:** How and when to request an appeal.

Figure 12–3 *continued*

Nonparticipating Providers (NonPARs)

A NonPAR is a physician or other health care provider who does not enroll in the Medicare program. NonPARs can accept assignment on a claim-by-claim basis, but they are subject to several restrictions:

- Medicare does not send payments directly to NonPARs. Payments are sent to the patients.
- On nonassigned claims, NonPARs are restricted to charging the patient no more than the limiting fee, defined as a maximum of 15% above the NonPAR Medicare-approved rate.
- On assigned claims, only the deductible and co-insurance due at the time of service can be collected.
- Balance-billing the patient is against the law in some states.
- NonPARs must accept assignment on clinical laboratory charges.
- NonPARs must file all Medicare claims regardless of assignment status.

Computing the NonPAR approved rate and limiting fee appears complicated. Basically, the NonPAR approved rate is set at 5% below the PAR approved rate. However, a NonPAR physician who does not accept assignment may charge a maximum of 15% above the NonPAR approved rate. The NonPAR physician must then collect the difference from the patient. The Example shows the difference between the NonPAR approved rate and the limiting fee.

EXAMPLE

The Medicare PAR approved rate for a routine office visit is $100. The Medicare NonPAR approved rate for the same visit is $95, which is 5% less than the PAR approved rate.

The NonPAR is allowed to charge Medicare beneficiaries up to 15% above the NonPAR approved rate ($95 × 0.15 = $14.25). The limiting fee is calculated by adding the dollar amount of the approved rate and 15% of the approved rate, which is $109.25.

In this example, Medicare pays the NonPAR $76, which is 80% of the NonPAR approved rate. The NonPAR collects the co-pay, which is 20% of the NonPAR approved rate ($19.00), *and* the difference between the limiting fee and approved rate ($109.25 − $95.00 = $14.25) from the patient. In summary, Medicare pays $76 and the patient pays $33.25.

Patients who receive services from NonPAR have higher out-of-pocket expenses than patients who receive services from PARs. As illustrated in the previous example, the patient's out-of-pocket expenses are $33.25. If the patient received the same service from a PAR, the co-pay is 20% of the PAR approved rate. Therefore, the out-of-pocket expense is $20.

Nonparticipating physicians who do not accept assignment for elective surgery must provide the patient with a Medicare Surgical Financial Disclosure Statement. Elective surgery is a surgical procedure that is not an emergency and is scheduled in advance and where failure to have the surgery is not life-threatening. The financial disclosure statement must include the following:

- Type of surgery
- Estimated charges
- Medicare estimated payment
- Estimated balance due from the patient

Practice Letterhead

Dear Patient:

As previously discussed, I do not plan to accept assignment for your surgery. The Medicare law requires that I give a Surgery Financial Disclosure Statement to all Medicare patients who are having elective surgery. These estimates assume that you have met the $135.00 annual Medicare Part B deductible.

Type of surgery: *Cholecystectomy*

Estimated charge: $ *1000.00*
Medicare estimated payment: $ *750.00*
Your estimated payment: $ *250.00*

Date: *3/31/20xx*   Beneficiary Signature *Viola Baril*

Figure 12–4 Medicare Disclosure Statement

A sample disclosure statement is shown in Figure 12–4.

Failure to provide the disclosure statement may result in a substantial fine. In addition, assistant surgeon fees may be limited to a specific percentage rate. Check with the local MAC for the current rate.

NonPARs who do not accept assignment collect fees from Medicare patients the same way that they collect fees from other patients. Co-pays and deductibles, if known, are collected at the time of service. If the practice's billing policy requires payment at the time of service up to a certain dollar amount, the policy applies to Medicare patients.

EXAMPLE

A nonparticipating physician who does not accept assignment treats Regina, a 68-year-old Medicare patient. The billing policy states that any balance due of $50 or less is expected at the time of service. Regina's bill is $110, the NonPAR limiting fee. The NonPAR approved fee is $95. Regina pays the 20% co-pay of the NonPAR approved rate ($19) as well as the $15 difference between the limiting fee and the approved rate, for a total of $34. Regina's balance is $76. The billing specialist submits the claim to the MAC. Since Regina will receive the Medicare payment, the billing specialist sends Regina a statement for the remaining $76.

Additional information about Medicare Part B is available on the Medicare website at http://www.medicare.gov. Another good resource is the annual publication *Medicare and You*, which is sent to Medicare beneficiaries and is available at your local Social Security Administration office.

REINFORCEMENT EXERCISES 12–2

Write out the abbreviations.

1. PAR

_____

2. NonPAR

_____

3. ABN

_____

4. MSN

_____

5. AAA

_____

Identify each service with D for diagnostic/treatment or P for preventative.

1. Flu shot _____

2. Pints of blood _____

3. Oxygen _____

4. Pneumococcal shot _____

5. Wheelchair _____

Write a short answer for each question.

1. What is the purpose of an ABN?

_____

_____

_____

2. List three advantages of being a PAR.

_____

_____

_____

3. Define the term "limiting fee."

_____

_____

_____

MEDICARE PART C

Medicare Part C, also known as Medicare Advantage (MA), is an alternative to the original fee-for-service Medicare program. Medicare sponsors MA plans and pays private insurance companies to provide health insurance products to individuals who qualify for Medicare. Individuals enrolled in an MA plan receive an insurance identification card from the insurance company that administers the plan. MA plan enrollees are still on Medicare and retain full rights and protections entitled to all Medicare beneficiaries. Under an MA plan, the individual:

- Must be enrolled in Medicare Part A and Part B
- Must continue paying the monthly premium for Medicare Part B
- May pay a monthly premium for additional benefits offered by the MA plan
- May have prescription drug coverage through the MA plan

Three common types of MA plans are Health Maintenance Organizations (HMO), Preferred Provider Organizations (PPO), and Medicare private fee-for-service (PFFS) plans.

Medicare Advantage Health Maintenance Organizations and Preferred Provider Organizations

Medicare Advantage HMOs and PPOs function in the same way that non-Medicare HMOs and PPOs function. The federal government provides funds for these plans. Table 12–4 lists the features of HMOs and PPOs.

TABLE 12–4

Medicare Advantage HMO and PPO Features	
Medicare HMO Features	Medicare PPO Features
Primary care physician manages health care; makes referrals to specialists (except for OB/GYN)	May or may not assign a primary care physician
Must receive services from providers who contract with the HMO; exception: emergency care, out-of-area urgent care, or preapproved referral	Lower co-payment for receiving services from a provider in the PPO network (preferred or in-network provider)
Does not cover services received from providers outside of the plan, unless exceptions noted above apply. Note: Enrollees must pay for these services.	Covers services received from an out-of-network provider; enrollee has a higher co-pay for out-of-network provider services. Note: Emergency care may be exempt from an out-of-network penalty.
May offer PDP Note: If the HMO does not offer a PDP, enrollees generally cannot get other prescription drug coverage.	Generally no referral is necessary for a specialist Note: Enrollees have a lower co-pay for in-network specialists.
May offer an option that allows enrollees to receive services from providers outside the plan; there is usually a charge for this option, and limits may be set for using the option.	Enrollees may be required to meet a deductible before coverage begins.

Medicare Private Fee-for-Service (PFFS) Plans

A Medicare PFFS plan is an MA plan offered by a private insurance company. The federal government supports these private plans by sending a set amount of money each month to the insurance company. The money is taken from the Medicare Trust Fund. The private insurance company, not the Medicare program, decides how much to pay providers for services, and the co-pay amount for enrollees. Enrollees pay a monthly premium, which is based on the deductible and co-payment. An individual who chooses a high deductible has a lower monthly premium.

Under an MA PFFS, the enrollee is allowed to receive services from any provider or hospital, as long as the provider or hospital accepts the payment terms established by the insurance plan. PFFS plans do *not* contract with health care providers and do *not* distinguish between participating and NonPARs. The enrollee must be sure that the provider will accept the plan's payment terms *before receiving services*. Enrollees may not use a Medicare supplemental insurance plan to cover the cost of co-payments and deductibles. MA PFFSs may include a PDP. If not, the enrollee is allowed to join a separate Medicare PDP.

Providers can choose to accept the insurance plan on a case-by-case basis. When a provider agrees to accept the insurance plan, the enrollee is responsible for any co-payment or deductible. Providers submit the insurance claim to the private insurance company that manages the PFFS plan.

The Medicare Part C information presented in this text is a brief overview of MA insurance plans. Additional and updated information is available on the Medicare website at http://www.medicare.gov.

MEDICARE PART D: PRESCRIPTION DRUG BENEFIT

Under Medicare Part D, Medicare beneficiaries regardless of income, health status, or current prescription expenses have the opportunity to enroll in a prescription drug plan (PDP) to help defray the cost of prescription medications. Beneficiaries will generally have two main options for receiving the prescription drug benefit:

- Beneficiaries who stay with the traditional Medicare health plan may choose to join a stand-alone PDP, and drug benefits are added to their regular Medicare coverage.
- Beneficiaries who choose to receive their medical and drug benefits from one source may join an MA plan and choose a PDP associated with the MA plan. The Medicare Advantage prescription drug plan (MA-PDP) provides integrated benefit coverage for hospital, physician, and medication costs.

PDPs are available from many health-related companies. Beneficiaries can learn about the plans available in their state from the following resources: the local Social Security Administration office, notices sent to them by the CMS, information provided by their Medicare insurance carrier, visiting the Medicare PDP Finder website, or attending one of the many informational meetings hosted by various groups and organizations.

Prescription Coverage

All PDPs are required to offer basic drug coverage, which is also called "standard prescription drug coverage." Some PDPs offer additional coverage for an additional premium.

Medicare PDPs cover generic and brand-name medications. Each PDP has a list of medications that are covered by the plan. This list of medications is called a formulary. The PDP formulary must always meet Medicare requirements. However, Medicare does not require any PDP to include all prescription medications. Medicare beneficiaries must research the PDPs in their area to learn which plans cover their specific medications. If a plan decides to remove a drug from its formulary, it must provide 60 days' notice to beneficiaries affected by the change. In this situation, beneficiaries have the following options: (1) with the help of their physician, apply for an exception that allows beneficiaries to continue to use the medication as part of their covered drug benefits; (2) ask their physician if another medication from the PDP formulary can be substituted for the current drug; or (3) continue taking the medication and pay for it out of pocket.

Prescription Drug Plan Enrollment

Enrollment in a PDP is entirely voluntary. Beneficiaries who already have prescription drug coverage through a former employer, union, or other source may keep that coverage and choose not to enroll in the Medicare drug plan. Beneficiaries are allowed to join, change, or withdraw from a Medicare drug plan when they are first eligible for Medicare or between November 15 and December 31 each year. In most cases, a beneficiary remains enrolled for the entire calendar year. There are circumstances under which a beneficiary is allowed to change a Medicare drug plan, such as moving out of the service area or losing other credible drug coverage. A late enrollment penalty may be added to the monthly premium if a beneficiary does not join a PDP when first eligible.

Medicare beneficiaries can enroll in a PDP by completing an application form provided by the company that offers the plan, completing the company's online application, or calling the company that offers the plan.

Prescription Drug Plan Premiums, Deductibles, and Co-payments

Beneficiaries who enroll in a prescription drug plan pay premiums, deductibles, and co-payments. Monthly premiums vary according to the coverage offered by the plan. According to CMS, the average monthly premium in 2012 was about $32, and the annual deductible was about $320. The beneficiaries' co-payment is usually 25%. The Example explains these fees.

EXAMPLE

Juanita, a Medicare beneficiary, has a Medicare Part D prescription drug insurance plan. Her monthly premium is $32. She has an annual $300 deductible and a 25% co-payment. Juanita's prescription medication costs $300 per month, which equals $3600 per year. Juanita pays the first $300 as a deductible. Once the deductible is met, Juanita pays 25% for her prescriptions and her insurance pays 75%.

In this example, Juanita's annual cost for prescription medication is $1509. This includes $384 for the premium, $300 for the deductible, and $825 in co-payments (25% of the cost once the deductible is met). Medicare Part D saves Juanita about 40% of her prescription medication costs.

Most PDPs limit the total benefit amount for each year. Once the limit is met, beneficiaries pay more for their medications. Monthly premiums, deductibles, and co-payment rates are usually adjusted annually. Increases in these out-of-pocket expenses affect the beneficiary's overall savings.

Individuals with limited income and resources may be eligible for additional help to pay the out-of-pocket expenses of a PDP. Working together, the Social Security Administration and CMS have developed criteria that allow qualified individuals to receive about $2000 to pay premiums, annual deductibles, and co-payments. Medicare Part A or Part B beneficiaries must meet the income criteria and live in the United States to qualify for this assistance.

The information presented here is a brief overview of Medicare Part D. Additional and updated information is available on the Medicare website at http://www.medicare.gov.

OTHER MEDICARE HEALTH PLAN CHOICES

Other Medicare health plans include Medicare special needs plans (SNPs) and Medicare medical savings account (MSA) plans.

Medicare SNPs are a type of MA plan that usually limits membership to individuals with specific diseases or conditions. Medicare SNPs offer benefits that apply to the diseases or conditions covered by the plan; choose providers; and create drug formularies to best meet the specific needs of the individuals enrolled in the plan. Medicare SNPs serve the following:

- Individuals with specific diseases such as diabetes, HIV/AIDS, or congestive heart failure
- Individuals who require nursing care, either in a facility or in their own home
- Individuals who qualify for Medicare and Medicaid

Medicare SNPs are administered by private health insurance companies that establish the criteria for joining the plan. Medicare beneficiaries who enroll in an SNP continue to pay the Medicare Part B premium as well as a monthly premium for the SNP, if required.

Medicare MSAs have been available since November 1998. Under an MSA, the Medicare beneficiary chooses a Medicare-approved insurance policy that has a high annual deductible. Medicare pays a set amount of money to private health insurance companies that contract with Medicare to offer the plan. At the beginning of each year, the private company deposits money from Medicare into the savings account. Individuals enrolled (member or enrollee) in the plan cannot deposit their own money into the account. The enrollee uses the account to pay for medical services until the deductible is met. Once the deductible is met, the MSA insurance plan is billed for medical expenses during the remainder of the calendar year.

Once enrolled in a MSA plan, the Medicare beneficiary must stay in the plan for a full year. If the MSA is exhausted before the deductible is met, the beneficiary pays the rest of the deductible out of pocket. Any balance left at the end of the year can be carried over to the next year, and the Medicare deposited amount is added to the balance. The beneficiary also has the option of withdrawing MSA money for nonmedical reasons, but that money is then taxed.

REINFORCEMENT EXERCISES 12–3

Write out each abbreviation.

1. HMO

_____

2. MA

_____

3. PDP

_____

4. PFFS

_____

5. PPO

_____

Write a short answer for each statement.

1. Describe three differences between an MA HMO and PPO.

_____

_____

_____

2. List three features of a Medicare PFFS plan.

_____

_____

_____

3. Define the term "formulary."

_____

_____

_____

continued on the next page

continued from the previous page

4. What is a Medicare special needs plan?

_____

_____

_____

5. Describe three features of a Medicare medical saving account.

_____

_____

_____

MEDICARE FEE SCHEDULE (MFS)

The Medicare fee schedule (MFS), a list of Medicare-approved fees for physician/ provider services, is based on a fairly complex calculation called the resource-based relative value scale (RBRVS). The RBRVS system calculates approved fees based on the following variables:

- A relative value unit (RVU), which includes physician work, practice expenses, and malpractice costs
- A geographic adjustment factor (GAF), which adjusts the fees according to variations in regional costs
- A national conversion factor (CF), a figure that is multiplied by the RVU to convert the RVU into a payment amount

The MFS is calculated on an annual basis. MACs send the revised schedule to physicians in the region covered by the contractor. The fee schedule includes the Medicare payment rates for participating physicians and nonparticipating physicians and the limiting fee or charge for approved services. Figure 12–5 is an illustrative example of an MFS.

Note that the sample MFS includes the physician's usual fee and three Medicare fees. For purposes of this example, fees are calculated as follows:

- The Medicare fee for PARs is 80% of the physician fee.
- The Medicare fee for NonPARs is 5% less than the PAR fee.
- The limiting fee/charge for NonPARs who do not accept assignment is 15% above the NonPAR fee.

The NonPAR limiting fee is the maximum amount a NonPAR can legally charge a Medicare patient.

SERVICE	PHYSICIAN	MEDICARE FEE		
CODE/DESCRIPTION	USUAL FEE	PAR APPROVED	NonPAR APPROVED	LIMITING* FEE
EVALUATION AND MANAGEMENT				
Office Visit, New Patient				
99201 Level I	30.00	24.00	22.80	26.22
99202 Level II	50.00	40.00	38.00	43.70
99203 Level III	75.00	60.00	57.00	65.55
99204 Level IV	125.00	100.00	95.00	109.25
99205 Level V	150.00	120.00	114.00	131.10
Office Visit, Established Patient				
99211 Level I	20.00	16.00	15.20	17.48
99212 Level II	40.00	32.00	30.40	34.56
99213 Level III	65.00	52.00	49.40	56.81
99214 Level IV	80.00	64.00	60.80	69.92
99215 Level V	100.00	80.00	76.00	87.40

*Maximum amount NonPAR provider may charge Medicare patients

Figure 12–5 Sample Medicare Fee Schedule

Considering the complexity of figuring out Medicare fees and that RBRVS are calculated annually, insurance billing specialists appreciate receiving an updated MFS from the CMS or the MAC.

NATIONAL CORRECT CODING INITIATIVE (NCCI)

The Medicare insurance program pays nearly half a million physicians about $60 *billion* per year for services provided to Medicare beneficiaries. Because diagnosis and procedure codes have a direct impact on physician and provider payment, the CMS has a financial incentive to ensure coding accuracy.

In 1996, CMS implemented the National Correct Coding Initiative (NCCI). The NCCI has two major goals:

- To promote physician and provider compliance with Medicare diagnosis and procedure coding guidelines
- To ensure appropriate payment (reimbursement) for physician and provider services

All claims submitted to Medicare insurance carriers are edited by an electronic screening process that verifies the following: (1) the patient is a Medicare beneficiary; (2) all co-payments and deductibles have been met; (3) Medicare is the primary payer; and (4) diagnosis and procedure codes are accurate.

NCCI edits identify invalid diagnosis codes, such as (ICD-9-CM) E codes, and discrepancies between the diagnosis code and the patient's age or sex. For example, a claim submitted for a male patient with the code for ovarian failure or a claim submitted for a female patient with the code for prostate hypertrophy will be returned to the provider without payment.

NCCI edits identify the following types of procedure coding errors:

- *Mutually exclusive procedures:* Reporting two procedures that cannot possibly be performed at the same time, such as a laminectomy (removal of the bony arches of a vertebra) and a total hip replacement
- *Component part coding:* Submitting separate or multiple codes for a procedure that is covered by a single code, such as reporting a separate code for a laparotomy (incision into the abdomen) that was done as part of an appendectomy
- *Unbundling:* Submitting separate or multiple codes for services that are part of a global surgery package, such as routine postoperative services
- *Invalid modifier:* Assigning the wrong modifier to a *Current Procedural Terminology* (CPT) code or a *Healthcare Common Procedure Coding System* (HCPCS) level II code. For example, CPT modifier -52, "Reduced Services," applies only to procedures or services provided on an inpatient basis and may not be assigned to outpatient or ambulatory surgery center procedure codes.

When NCCI edits identify coding errors, the provider is notified that the claim is rejected. A pattern of coding errors may prompt the MAC to audit a significant sample of all Medicare claims. A consistent pattern of coding errors may lead to charges of Medicare insurance fraud or abuse. The implications of fraud and abuse are discussed in Chapter 2.

Many commercial billing software programs are equipped with edit features that identify errors before the claim is submitted. The billing specialist can prevent claims submission errors by:

- Accurately completing all required fields of the electronic or paper insurance claim form.
- Following Medicare claims submission guidelines.
- Updating insurance billing references, which are sent to providers via bulletins or transmittals.
- Attending training sessions related to changes for submitting Medicare claims.
- Checking all CPT and HCPCS level II modifiers.
- Reviewing the patient's medical record or asking the physician for clarification for questions related to diagnosis and procedure codes.
- Alerting the office manager or physician when there is a concern related to coding accuracy.

Because insurance billing specialists are actively involved in insurance claims submission, they have a vested interest in the accuracy, validity, and legality of that process.

REINFORCEMENT EXERCISES 12–4

Write out each abbreviation.

1. MFS

_____

2. NCCI

_____

3. RBRVS

_____

Briefly define each term or phrase.

1. Mutually exclusive procedure

_____

_____

_____

2. Component part coding

_____

_____

_____

3. Unbundling

_____

_____

_____

4. Invalid modifier

_____

_____

_____

continued on the next page

continued from the previous page

Provide a short answer for each question.

1. Describe three steps the insurance billing specialist can take to prevent claims submission errors.

_____

_____

_____

2. What is the purpose of the NCCI?

_____

_____

_____

MEDICARE CLAIMS SUBMISSION

CMS provides extensive guidelines for submitting health insurance claims in the *Medicare Claims Processing Manual,* which is available on the CMS website. Providers receive current guidelines via Medicare transmittals and communication with the regional MAC. MACs are responsible for processing Medicare claims in a specific jurisdiction. Table 12–5 lists the CMS jurisdictions, states and U.S. territories included in each jurisdiction, and the MAC in effect at the time of publication. Information about the MACs is available on their respective websites. The MACs for the 15 jurisdictions process Medicare Part A and Part B claims and are also known as A/B MACs.

TABLE 12–5

CMS Jurisdictions, States/U.S. Territories, and MACs		
Jurisdiction	States/U.S. Territories	MAC
1	American Samoa, California, Guam, Hawaii, Nevada, Northern Mariana Islands	Palmetto Government Benefits Administrator
2	Alaska, Idaho, Oregon, Washington	National Heritage Insurance Corp.
3	Arizona, Montana, North Dakota, South Dakota, Utah, Wyoming	Noridian Administrative Services
4	Colorado, New Mexico, Oklahoma, Texas	Trailblazer Health Enterprises
5	Iowa, Kansas, Missouri, Nebraska	Wisconsin Physician Services

continued on the next page

continued from the previous page

Jurisdiction	States/U.S. Territories	MAC
CMS Jurisdictions, States/U.S. Territories, and MACs		
6	Illinois, Minnesota, Wisconsin	Noridian Administrative Services
7	Arkansas, Louisiana, Mississippi	Trailblazer Health Enterprises
8	Indiana, Michigan	National Government Services
9	Florida, Puerto Rico, U.S. Virgin Islands	First Coast Service Options, Inc.
10	Alabama, Georgia, Tennessee	Cahaba Government Benefit Administrators
11	North Carolina, South Carolina, Virginia, West Virginia	Palmetto Government Benefits Administrator
12	Delaware, District of Columbia, Maryland, New Jersey, Pennsylvania	Highmark Medicare Services
13	Connecticut, New York	National Government Services
14	Maine, Massachusetts, New Hampshire, Rhode Island, Vermont	National Heritage Insurance Corp.
15	Kentucky, Ohio	Highmark Medicare Services

CMS has identified four DME jurisdictions and awarded Medicare administrative contracts for processing claims related to DME. The contractors are known as durable medical equipment Medicare Administrative Contractors (DME MACs). Table 12–6 lists the CMS jurisdictions, states and U.S. territories included in the jurisdictions, and the DME MAC in effect at the time of publication.

Information about the DME MACs is available on their respective websites.

General Guidelines for Medicare Claims Submission

The majority of Medicare claims are filed electronically. Providers can purchase insurance billing software from a vendor, contract with a billing service or clearinghouse that provides software, or use software provided by MACs.

An electronic claim must pass at least two edits before the claim is submitted for payment. The first edit determines if the claims in a specific batch meet the required standards set forth in the Health Insurance Portability and Accountability Act (HIPAA). When errors are detected, the entire batch is rejected and returned to the provider for correction and resubmission. Claims that pass the first edit are edited against additional HIPAA claim standards. If errors are detected, the individual claims with the errors are rejected and returned to the provider for correction and resubmission.

Once the claims successfully pass the first two edits, each claim is edited for compliance with Medicare coverage and payment policy requirements. Claims with errors identified at this level are either rejected and returned to the provider for correction and resubmission or denied.

TABLE 12–6

CMS Jurisdictions, States/U.S. Territories, and DME MACs		
CMS Jurisdiction	States/U.S. Territories	DME MAC
A	Connecticut, Delaware, District of Columbia, Maine, Maryland, Massachusetts, New Hampshire, New Jersey, New York, Pennsylvania, Rhode Island, Vermont	National Heritage Insurance Corp.
B	Illinois, Indiana, Kentucky, Michigan, Minnesota, Ohio, Wisconsin	National Government Services
C	Alabama, Arkansas, Colorado, Florida, Georgia, Louisiana, Mississippi, New Mexico, North Carolina, Oklahoma, Puerto Rico, South Carolina, Tennessee, Texas, U.S. Virgin Islands, Virginia, West Virginia	CIGNA Government Services
D	Alaska, American Samoa, Arizona, California, Guam, Hawaii, Idaho, Iowa, Kansas, Missouri, Montana, Nebraska, Nevada, North Dakota, Northern Mariana Islands, Oregon, South Dakota, Utah, Washington, Wyoming	Noridian Administrative Services

© 2014 Cengage Learning, All Rights Reserved.

The provider receives a reason for the denial or rejection and has an opportunity to correct the error or appeal the denial.

Claims that are neither rejected (returned for correction and resubmission) nor denied are paid. The provider can opt for electronic funds transfers or receive an actual check. In either case, the provider also receives a detailed notice of the amount paid for each claim.

General guidelines apply to all Medicare claims submission activities. The guidelines include:

- All providers are required to file claims for Medicare beneficiaries.
- Birth dates are entered in an eight-digit format (MMDDYYYY).
- Other dates are entered in either a six- or eight-digit format. Use one of these formats for all other dates.
- Claims must be filed within specified deadlines, usually one year from the date of service or December 31 of the year following the date of service.

There are times when a paper claim is submitted. The CMS-1500 is used for Medicare Part B claims. Learning how to accurately complete the CMS-1500 is a good way to improve data entry skills. CMS-1500 completion instructions depend on Medicare's status as primary or secondary payer.

Medicare as Primary Payer

Medicare is the primary payer for nearly all provider services. Insurance coverage information is captured during the patient registration process. If there is any question about Medicare payer status, the insurance billing specialist clarifies the status *before* submitting a claim. Billing Medicare as primary when the status is secondary can result in sanctions ranging from an audit of the provider's billing practices to charges of Medicare fraud or abuse.

Medicare is considered the primary payer when the following circumstances exist:

- The individual is eligible for an employer-sponsored group health plan but has declined to enroll or recently dropped coverage.
- The individual is currently employed but is not yet eligible for employer-sponsored group plan coverage or has exhausted benefits under the group plan.
- The individual is covered by TRICARE/CHAMPUS.
- The individual is under age 65 and has Medicare due to disability or ESRD and is not covered by an employer-sponsored plan.
- The patient has both Medicare and Medicaid.

Certain situations do allow Medicare to be billed as the primary payer for a temporary period of time. This is known as Medicare conditional primary payer status. Conditional primary payer status may be appropriate under the following conditions:

- Another insurance plan that is normally considered primary to Medicare issues a denial of payment that is being appealed.
- A physically or mentally impaired individual does not file a claim to the primary insurance plan.
- A workers' compensation claim is denied and moving through the appeal process.
- The primary payer does not respond within 120 days of filing a claim.

Conditional primary payer status allows the provider to be reimbursed for services rendered. If payment is received from the primary carrier at a later date, the billing specialist must immediately return payments made by the MAC.

REINFORCEMENT EXERCISES 12–5

Fill in the blank.

1. The _____ is used for Medicare Part B claims.

2. The regional _____ furnish providers with an up-to-date Medicare fee schedule.

3. Medicare is the _____ payer when an individual qualifies for Medicare and Medicaid.

4. CMS has identified _____ MAC jurisdictions.

5. A/B MACs process claims for _____ and _____.

Provide a short answer for each question.

1. What is the difference between A/B MACs and DME MACs?

_____

_____

2. Describe two situations that allow Medicare to be billed as a conditional primary payer status.

_____

_____

Completing the CMS-1500: Medicare as Primary Payer

The following block-by-block instructions for completing the CMS-1500 apply when Medicare is the primary and only payer. All dates are entered in the eight-digit format.

Block 1	Enter an X in the Medicare box.
Block 1a	Enter the patient's HICN exactly as it appears on the Medicare ID card.
Block 2	Enter the patient's last name, first name, and middle initial in uppercase letters exactly as they appear on the Medicare ID card.
Block 3	Enter the patient's eight-digit birth date (MMDDYYYY); enter an X in M or F.
Block 4	Leave this blank.
Block 5	Enter the patient's current mailing address and telephone number. On the first line, enter the street address; the second line, the city and state; the third line, the zip code and phone number.
Blocks 6, 7	Leave this blank.
Block 8	Enter an X in the appropriate box for the patient's marital, employment, and student status.
Blocks 9–9d	Leave this blank.
Block 10a	Enter an X in YES or NO. If YES, another insurance may be primary to Medicare.
Block 10b	Enter an X in YES or NO. If YES, enter the two-character abbreviation for the state where the accident occurred. If YES, another insurance may be primary to Medicare.
Block 10c	Enter an X in YES or NO. If YES, another insurance may be primary to Medicare.
Block 10d	Leave this blank.
Block 11	Enter NONE and then go to Block 12.
Blocks 11a–11d	Leave this blank.
Block 12	Enter SIGNATURE ON FILE.
Block 13	Enter SIGNATURE ON FILE.
Block 14	Enter the eight-digit date of current illness/service, the date an injury first occurred, and the last menstrual period or estimated date of pregnancy. When the patient is being treated by a chiropractor, enter the date that treatment was initiated. In block 19, enter the date of the x-ray that justifies the course of treatment.
Block 15	Leave this blank.
Block 16	Enter the eight-digit dates that indicate the time frame the patient is unable to work. Otherwise, leave this blank.
Block 17	Enter the last name, first name, and middle initial of the referring or ordering physician if the service or item was ordered or referred by a physician. (See Special Notes.)

Special Notes:

- The term "physician" includes a doctor of medicine, osteopathy, dental surgery, dental medicine, podiatric medicine, optometry, and chiropractor.
- Referring physician: A physician who requests an item or service for a beneficiary that will be provided by another physician, and the item or service may be covered under the Medicare program.
- Ordering physician: A physician or, when appropriate, a nonphysician practitioner, who orders nonphysician services, such as diagnostic laboratory tests, pharmaceutical services, or DME.
- Ordered/Referred services: Diagnostic, laboratory, and radiology services; consultant services; DME; parenteral and enteral nutrition; immunosuppressive drug claims; physical and occupational therapy; prosthesis; and orthotic devices. Enter the ordering physician's name in block 17.
- Physician extenders: A physician's assistant, nurse practitioner, or other limited-license practitioner. When these individuals refer a patient for consultant services, the name of the supervising physician is entered in block 17.
- Surgeon: When a physician refers the patient to a surgeon, enter the referring physician's name in block 17. If there is no referring physician, enter the surgeon's name in block 17.
- Assistant surgeon: When the claim is filed for an assistant surgeon, enter the surgeon's name in block 17.
- Ordering/performing physician: When the ordering physician is the performing physician, which is often the case with intra-office clinical laboratory tests, enter the performing physician's name in block 17.
- Diagnostic service: When a physician refers the patient to another physician who then orders and performs a diagnostic service, a separate claim form is required for the diagnostic service. On the first claim form, enter the original ordering/referring physician's name in block 17. On the second claim form, enter the performing physician's name.

Block 17a	Leave this blank.
Block 17b	Enter the NPI of the referring/ordering physician listed in block 17.
Block 18	Enter the dates of hospitalization in an eight-digit format.
Block 19	Information entered in this block may include physical therapy, occupational therapy, and podiatry dates of service; name of dosage of certain medications; descriptions of unlisted procedures; modifiers associated with block 24D when more than one modifier is reported; and other information as described in the Medicare Claims Processing Manual. This block is often left blank.

continued on the next page

continued from the previous page

Block 20	Enter an X in NO when the laboratory tests are performed in the provider's office. Enter an X in YES if an outside laboratory performed the tests listed on the claim and the provider filing the claim was billed for the tests and is passing the fee on to the patient. The total cost is entered in the CHARGES section of block 20. The name and address of the outside laboratory is entered in block 32.
Block 21	Enter up to four ICD-9-CM (ICD-10-CM when implemented) diagnostic codes that describe the patient's condition. Enter the first-listed diagnosis code in 1. Enter other diagnoses in priority order. Do not use any decimal points. All narrative diagnoses for nonphysician specialties must be submitted as an attachment.
Block 22	Leave this blank.
Block 23	Only one condition may be reported in block 23. Enter the Quality Improvement Organization (QIO) prior authorization number, if required. Enter the investigational device exemption (IDE) when an investigational device is used in an FDA-approved clinical trial. Enter the NPI of the home health agency or hospice when CPT code G0181 or G0182 is billed; applies when a physician is providing care plan oversight services. Enter the 10-digit Clinical Laboratory Improvement Act (CLIA) certification number for laboratory services billed by an entity performing CLIA covered tests. For ambulance claims, enter the zip code of the ambulance trip's point-of-pickup. Otherwise, leave blank.
Block 24A	Enter the eight-digit date for each procedure, service, or supply. When from and to dates are shown for a series of identical services, enter the number of days or units in column G.
Block 24B	Enter the place of service code. (See Chapter 8.)
Block 24C	Leave this blank.
Block 24D	Enter the CPT or HCPCS codes and required modifiers. Enter the specific procedure code without narrative description. Exception: When reporting an unlisted procedure code or not otherwise classified (NOC) code, include a narrative description in block 19 or submit an attachment. Do not place a hyphen before the modifier.
Block 24E	Enter one diagnosis reference number (1 through 4) for the ICD-9-CM (ICD-10-CM, when implemented) diagnosis code in block 21 that best justifies the medical necessity for services identified in block 24D. Use only one reference number per line.

continued on the next page

continued from the previous page

Block 24F	Enter the fee for each listed service. Do not use dollar signs or decimal points; always include cents. If the same service was performed on consecutive days, enter the fee for one service in block 24F and the number of times the service was performed in block 24G.
Block 24G	Enter the number of days or units. This block is most commonly used for multiple visits, units of supplies, or anesthesia minutes of oxygen volume. If only one service is performed, enter 1.
Block 24H	Leave this blank.
Block 24I	Enter the ID qualifier 1C in the shaded portion.
Block 24J	Leave the shaded portion blank. Enter the rendering physician's NPI number in the unshaded portion.
Block 25	Enter the provider's Federal Tax ID number (Employer Tax Identification Number [EIN]) or SSN. Enter an X in the appropriate box.
Block 26	Enter the patient account number, as assigned by the provider, if applicable.
Block 27	Enter an X in YES if the physician accepts assignment of benefits. Enter an X in NO if the physician does not accept assignment.
Block 28	Enter total charges for all services submitted on a claim.
Block 29	Enter the total amount the patient paid on the covered services only.
Block 30	Leave this blank.
Block 31	Enter SIGNATURE ON FILE or a computer-generated signature. Electronic claims submission software may automatically enter the date the claim is completed or submitted.
Block 32	Enter the name, address, and zip code of the location where the service was rendered. As of January 1, 2011, this block is required for *all* POS (place of service) codes entered in block 24B.
Block 32a	Enter the NPI of the service facility, as required by Medicare claims processing policy. Otherwise, leave this blank.
Block 32b	Leave this blank.
Block 33	Enter the provider's billing name, address, zip code, and telephone number.
Block 33a	For solo-practice providers, enter the NPI of the provider/physician. For group-practice providers, enter the NPI of the group practice.
Block 33b	Leave this blank.

Figure 12–6 Medicare Primary Payer CMS-1500

Figure 12–6 is a sample of a completed CMS-1500 form when Medicare is the primary payer and the patient has no supplemental insurance.

REINFORCEMENT EXERCISES 12–6

Using the patient and provider information given here, complete a CMS-1500 for a Medicare as primary payer claim. Your instructor can tell you how to obtain the CMS-1500.

Patient Information

Name: Matthew Mattson—married, male, birth date January 3, 1927
Address: 109 Spruce Street, Blueberry, ME 49966
Phone: (906) 555-3336
Insurance: Medicare 388579728A
Employment Status: Retired
Diagnosis/Code: Pleurisy, 511.0 (ICD-10-CM; R09.1); atrial tachycardia, 427.89 (ICD-10-CM; R00.0)
Services/Code: Office visit, 99212; chest x-ray, two views, 71020
Date of Service: March 3, 20xx
Charges: Office visit, $50; chest x-ray, $50

Provider Information

Superiorland Clinic
714 Hennepin Ave.
Blueberry, ME 49966
Phone: (906) 337-8778
Superiorland Clinic NPI : 4567890123
Sara M. Gervais, MD
Physician NPI : 0987654321
EIN: 11-234567
Dr. Gervais is a participating provider.

Medicare as Primary with Supplemental Insurance

Because Medicare does not cover all medical services, some people choose to supplement their Medicare insurance with additional health insurance. There are a number of insurance companies that advertise Medicare supplemental policies. As with any advertised product, the consumer must carefully scrutinize these plans before entering into a contractual arrangement.

There are three general types of Medicare supplemental insurance plans:

- Medigap
- Employer-sponsored Medicare supplemental health insurance
- Medicare-Medicaid Crossover Program

These plans, called Medicare supplemental plans (MSPs), cover the patient's Medicare deductible and co-insurance costs.

Medigap Insurance Plans

Medigap insurance is specifically designed to supplement Medicare benefits and is regulated by federal and state law. A Medigap insurance plan is clearly identified as Medicare supplemental insurance, and it provides specific benefits that fill in the gaps of Medicare coverage. Most private health insurance companies offer Medigap insurance plans. These plans cover various costs ranging from co-pays and deductibles to emergency care while traveling outside the United States. Although the federal government regulates the Medigap benefits, insurance companies set the cost or premium for the policy. Premiums are based on the terms of the policy, services covered, and geographic location. Tobacco use, age, and gender also affect the premium. A 65-year-old female who does not use tobacco often pays a lower premium than her male counterpart. Premiums range from about $125 to $275 per month.

The CMS approve 10 standard Medigap plans, identified by letters A, B, C, D, F, G, K, L, M, and N. Benefits offered by each plan are listed in Table 12–7. A check mark in a column means that the Medigap policy pays 100% of the described benefit. A percentage in the column indicates the percentage of the described benefit paid by the Medigap plan. A blank means the plan does not cover that benefit.

TABLE 12–7

Medigap Plans

Medigap Benefits	Medigap Plans									
	A	B	C	D	F	G	K	L	M	N
Medicare Part A co-insurance and hospital costs up to an additional 365 days after Medicare benefits are used up	√	√	√	√	√	√	√	√	√	√
Medicare Part B co-insurance or co-pay	√	√	√	√	√	√	50%*	75%*	√	√**
Blood, first three pints	√	√	√	√	√	√	50%	75%	√	√
Medicare Part A hospice care co-insurance or co-pay	√	√	√	√	√	√	50%	75%	√	√
Skilled nursing facility care co-insurance			√	√	√	√	50%	75%	√	√
Medicare Part A deductible		√	√	√	√	√	50%	75%	√	√
Medicare Part B deductible			√		√					
Medicare Part B excess charges					√	√				
Foreign travel emergency care (up to plan limits)			√	√	√	√			√	√

*After out-of-pocket yearly and yearly Plan B deductible is met, plan pays 100% of covered services for the rest of the calendar year.

**$20 co-pay for some office visits; $50 co-pay for some emergency room visits.

Processing Medigap Claims

Medigap claim processing depends on the status of the provider. PAR Medigap claims are electronically transferred from the Medicare insurance carrier to the Medigap insurance carrier. The insurance billing specialist enters Medigap carrier and policyholder information in the CMS-1500 blocks 9 through 9d and block 13 when filing the Medicare claim. If the Medigap carrier is not able to process claims electronically, the insurance billing specialist makes a copy of the Medicare remittance or summary notice and attaches it to the claim that is sent to the Medigap insurance carrier.

Nonparticipating (NonPAR) providers are not required to include Medigap information on the claim form. If the NonPAR provider agrees to file a Medigap claim, the patient must provide a copy of the MSN to the provider.

Completing the CMS-1500: Medicare Primary with Medigap

The patient must sign an authorization to release Medigap benefits to the provider so the insurance billing specialist can properly complete the CMS-1500 Medicare claim. When the patient is a Medicare beneficiary and has Medigap supplemental insurance and the provider participates in Medicare, the insurance billing specialist completes the CMS-1500 claim according to the following instructions. These instructions do not apply to employer-sponsored Medicare supplemental plans or to NonPARs.

Blocks 1 through 8	No change from Medicare as primary payer
Block 9	Enter SAME if the patient is the Medigap insured. Enter the last name, first name, and middle initial of the Medigap insured if the name is different from the name in Block 2.
Block 9a	Enter MEDIGAP, MG, or MGAP followed by the policy number and group number. If there is no group, enter the policy number only.
Block 9b	Enter the Medigap insured's eight-digit birth date. Enter an X in M or F.
Block 9c	Leave this blank if the Medigap claim-based identification number is entered in 9d. Otherwise, enter the claims processing address of the Medigap insurer. Use an abbreviated street address, two-letter postal code, and zip code found on the Medigap identification card. For example: 714 Hennepin Road Blueberry, ME 49966 is entered as: 714 HENNEPIN RD ME 49966
Block 9d	Enter the COBA (coordination of benefits administrator) Medigap claim-based ID number. The COBA ID, a five-digit number that begins with a 5, allows the beneficiary's claim to be electronically sent to the Medigap insurer. This service is available to PARs.
Blocks 10–12	No change from Medicare as primary payer
Block 13	Enter SIGNATURE ON FILE. Note: The provider must obtain an authorization that specifically includes the name of the Medigap insurance plan so payment is sent to the provider.
Blocks 14–33	No change from the instructions for Medicare as primary payer

Figure 12–7 is an example of a completed CMS-1500 for Medicare patients with Medigap insurance.

(1500)

HEALTH INSURANCE CLAIM FORM

APPROVED BY NATIONAL UNIFORM CLAIM COMMITTEE 08/05

| | | PICA | | | | | | PICA | | |

1. MEDICARE MEDICAID TRICARE CHAMPUS CHAMPVA GROUP HEALTH PLAN FECA BLK LUNG OTHER
[X] (Medicare #) [ ] (Medicaid #) [ ] (Sponsor's SSN) [ ] (Member ID #) [ ] (SSN or ID) [ ] (SSN) [ ] (ID)

1a. INSURED'S I.D. NUMBER (For Program in Item 1)
11234980A

2. PATIENT'S NAME (Last Name, First Name, Middle Initial)
PUBLIC JOHN Q

3. PATIENT'S BIRTH DATE MM | DD | YY   SEX
09 | 25 | 1930   M [X] F [ ]

4. INSURED'S NAME (Last Name, First Name, Middle Initial)

5. PATIENT'S ADDRESS (No., Street)
108 SENATE AVE

6. PATIENT RELATIONSHIP TO INSURED
Self [ ] Spouse [ ] Child [ ] Other [ ]

7. INSURED'S ADDRESS (No., Street)

CITY
ANYWHERE
STATE
US

8. PATIENT STATUS
Single [X] Married [ ] Other [ ]
Employed [ ] Full-Time Student [ ] Part-Time Student [ ]

CITY
STATE

ZIP CODE
12345
TELEPHONE (Include Area Code)
(101) 201 7891

ZIP CODE
TELEPHONE (Include Area Code)
( )

9. OTHER INSURED'S NAME (Last Name, First Name, Middle Initial)
SAME

10. IS PATIENT'S CONDITION RELATED TO:

11. INSURED'S POLICY GROUP OR FECA NUMBER

a. OTHER INSURED'S POLICY OR GROUP NUMBER
MEDIGAP 486901

a. EMPLOYMENT? (Current or Previous)
[ ] YES [X] NO

a. INSURED'S DATE OF BIRTH MM | DD | YY   SEX
M [ ] F [ ]

b. OTHER INSURED'S DATE OF BIRTH MM | DD | YY SEX
09 | 25 | 1930   M [X] F [ ]

b. AUTO ACCIDENT? PLACE (State)
[ ] YES [X] NO

b. EMPLOYER'S NAME OR SCHOOL NAME

c. EMPLOYER'S NAME OR SCHOOL NAME

c. OTHER ACCIDENT?
[ ] YES [X] NO

c. INSURANCE PLAN NAME OR PROGRAM NAME

d. INSURANCE PLAN NAME OR PROGRAM NAME
59999

10d. RESERVED FOR LOCAL USE

d. IS THERE ANOTHER HEALTH BENEFIT PLAN?
[ ] YES [ ] NO **If yes,** return to and complete item 9 a-d.

READ BACK OF FORM BEFORE COMPLETING & SIGNING THIS FORM.
12. PATIENT'S OR AUTHORIZED PERSON'S SIGNATURE I authorize the release of any medical or other information necessary to process this claim. I also request payment of government benefits either to myself or to the party who accepts assignment below.

SIGNED **SIGNATURE ON FILE**   DATE _____

13. INSURED'S OR AUTHORIZED PERSON'S SIGNATURE I authorize payment of medical benefits to the undersigned physician or supplier for services described below.

SIGNED **SIGNATURE ON FILE**

14. DATE OF CURRENT: MM | DD | YY   ILLNESS (First symptom) OR INJURY (Accident) OR PREGNANCY (LMP)
04 | 12 | 20XX

15. IF PATIENT HAS HAD SAME OR SIMILAR ILLNESS. GIVE FIRST DATE MM | DD | YY

16. DATES PATIENT UNABLE TO WORK IN CURRENT OCCUPATION MM | DD | YY   MM | DD | YY
FROM   TO

17. NAME OF REFERRING PROVIDER OR OTHER SOURCE
17a.
17b. NPI

18. HOSPITALIZATION DATES RELATED TO CURRENT SERVICES MM | DD | YY   MM | DD | YY
FROM   TO

19. RESERVED FOR LOCAL USE

20. OUTSIDE LAB?
[ ] YES [X] NO
$ CHARGES

21. DIAGNOSIS OR NATURE OF ILLNESS OR INJURY (Relate Items 1, 2, 3, or 4 to Item 24E by Line)
1. 540 . 0
2. ____
3. ____
4. ____

22. MEDICAID RESUBMISSION CODE
ORIGINAL REF. NO.

23. PRIOR AUTHORIZATION NUMBER

24. A. DATE(S) OF SERVICE		B. PLACE OF SERVICE	C. EMG	D. PROCEDURES, SERVICES, OR SUPPLIES (Explain Unusual Circumstances)		E. DIAGNOSIS POINTER	F. $ CHARGES	G. DAYS OR UNITS	H. EPSDT Family Plan	I. ID. QUAL.	J. RENDERING PROVIDER ID. #
From MM DD YY	To MM DD YY			CPT/HCPCS	MODIFIER						
1	04 12 20XX 04 12 20XX	11		99213		1	75 00	1		IC NPI	7865432107
2	04 12 20XX 04 12 20XX	11		71020		1	50 00	1		IC NPI	7865432107
3										NPI	
4										NPI	
5										NPI	
6										NPI	

25. FEDERAL TAX I.D. NUMBER SSN EIN
11-123441 [ ] [X]

26. PATIENT'S ACCOUNT NO.

27. ACCEPT ASSIGNMENT? (For govt. claims, see back)
[X] YES [ ] NO

28. TOTAL CHARGE
$ 125 00

29. AMOUNT PAID
$ 25 00

30. BALANCE DUE
$

31. SIGNATURE OF PHYSICIAN OR SUPPLIER INCLUDING DEGREES OR CREDENTIALS (I certify that the statements on the reverse apply to this bill and are made a part thereof.)
SIGNATURE ON FILE
SIGNED   DATE

32. SERVICE FACILITY LOCATION INFORMATION
MEDICARE EAST
1201 MEDIC DRIVE
ANYWHERE US 12345
a. 5687812403 b.

33. BILLING PROVIDER INFO & PH # (101) 111 1234
MEDICARE EAST
1201 MEDIC DRIVE
ANYWHERE US 12345
a. 5687812403 b.

NUCC Instruction Manual available at: www.nucc.org

APPROVED OMB-0938-0999 FORM CMS-1500 (08-05)

CARRIER

PATIENT AND INSURED INFORMATION

PHYSICIAN OR SUPPLIER INFORMATION

For instructional use only. Courtesy of the Centers for Medicare and Medicaid Services, www.cms.hhs.gov

Figure 12–7 Medicare/Medigap CMS-1500

REINFORCEMENT EXERCISE 12–7

Use the patient information from Reinforcement Exercises 12–6 for Matthew Mattson, with the addition of Medigap group and COBA ID numbers, and the following provider information to complete a CMS-1500 for Medicare with Medigap. Your instructor can tell you where to get the form.

Medigap Numbers

Group # 23110; COBA ID: 50505

Provider Information

Superiorland Clinic
714 Hennepin Ave.
Blueberry, ME 49966
Phone: (906) 337-8778
Superiorland Clinic NPI: 4567890123
Sara M. Gervais, MD
Physician NPI: 0987654321
EIN: 11-234567
Dr. Gervais is a participating provider.

Employer-Sponsored Medicare Supplemental Plans

Some employers offer their retired employees an insurance plan that is intended to supplement the retiree's Medicare coverage. These plans do not qualify for designation as a Medigap policy. Employer-sponsored plans are not regulated by the federal government and are subject to the same conditions established in the employer's employee health insurance plans. Premiums for an employer-sponsored supplemental plan are paid by or through the employer.

Health care providers are not required to file employer-sponsored Medicare supplemental insurance claims. Because these plans are not designated as Medigap policies, the insurance billing specialist does not include the plan's insurance information in blocks 9 through 9d on a Medicare claim.

Some employers provide the Medicare insurance carrier with monthly information about retirees who are covered by Medicare supplemental plans. When this is the case, information is electronically transferred from the Medicare insurance carrier to the supplemental plan insurance carrier. If electronic transfer is not an option, the patient must file for benefits after receiving the MSN.

Medicare-Medicaid Crossover Program

The Medicare-Medicaid Crossover Program, a combination of the Medicare and Medicaid health insurance plans, is available to these groups:

- Medicare-eligible individuals with incomes below the federal poverty level, the QMB program
- Individuals who are eligible for Medicare's SLMB program

Crossover program claims are also known as Medi/Medi claims, Care/Caid claims, or 18/19 claims, which refers to Title 18 and Title 19 of the Social Security Act Amendments of 1965.

Processing Medicare-Medicaid Crossover Claims

All health care providers must accept assignment on Medicare-Medicaid crossover claims. If assignment is not accepted, the Medicare payment is likely to be sent to the patient, and the Medicaid payment is either sent to the patient or denied.

The insurance billing specialist enters the designation MCD in block 10d of the CMS-1500 claim that is submitted to the MAC. The MAC electronically transfers the Medicare claim and payment information to the Medicaid insurance carrier. The Medicaid carrier processes payment for the patient's Medicare deductible and co-payment and services covered by Medicaid. The payments are sent directly to the provider.

Completing the CMS-1500: Medicare-Medicaid Crossover Claims

Medicare-Medicaid crossover claim completion guidelines apply to Medicare patients who have Medicaid coverage that is not part of an HMO. In other words, the following CMS-1500 instructions apply to patients who receive services on a fee-for-service basis.

Patients with Medicaid must present a current Medicaid identification card. The billing specialist or receptionist makes a copy of the card, front and back, so the Medicaid ID number is available for inclusion on the CMS-1500.

Block 1	Enter an X in the Medicare and Medicaid boxes.
Blocks 1a–10c	No change from the instructions for Medicare as primary payer
Block 10d	Enter the abbreviation MCD followed by the patient's Medicaid ID number.
Blocks 11–26	No change from the instructions for Medicare as primary payer
Block 27	Enter an X in YES. All providers must accept assignment.
Blocks 28–33	No change from the instructions for Medicare as primary payer

© 2014 Cengage Learning, All Rights Reserved.

Figure 12–8 is an example of a Medicare-Medicaid crossover claim.

REINFORCEMENT EXERCISE 12–8

Using the following patient and provider information, complete a CMS-1500 for a Medicare-Medicaid crossover claim. Your instructor can tell you where to get the form.

Patient Information

Name: Joline Pellitier, single, female
Birth Date: January 4, 1928
Address: 609 Osborn, Blueberry, ME 49966
Phone: (906) 338-2612
Insurance: Medicare 499680839A; Medicaid 212345602XT
Employment Status: Retired
Diagnosis/Code: Gastritis, 535.50 (ICD-10-CM; K29.70)

continued on the next page

continued from the previous page

Service/Code: Office visit, 99212; CBC 85025
Date of Service: March 4, 20YY
Charges: Office visit, $50; CBC, $45

Provider Information

Superiorland Clinic
714 Hennepin Ave.
Blueberry, ME 49966
Phone: (906) 337-8778
Superiorland Clinic NPI: 4567890123
Barbara Dollar, MD
Physician NPI: 9876543210
EIN: 50-3816934
Dr. Dollar accepts assignment.

Medicare as Secondary Payer (MSP)

Medicare is the secondary payer when a Medicare patient is covered by one or more of the following health insurance plans:

- An employer-sponsored group health plan with more than 20 covered employees
- Disability coverage through an employer-sponsored health plan with more than 100 covered employees
- Liability coverage when a person is involved in an automobile or another type of accident
- Illness or injury that falls under workers' compensation
- ESRD covered by an employer-sponsored group health plan of any size during the first 18 months of the patient's eligibility for Medicare
- Veterans Administration (VA) preauthorized services for an individual eligible for both VA benefits and Medicare
- Coal miners, either currently or formerly employed, who have problems that are directly related to black lung disorder and other disorders on the Department of Labor's list of acceptable diagnoses

All primary insurance plans must be billed before Medicare claims are submitted. Providers who routinely bill Medicare as primary when Medicare is the secondary payer may be subject to disciplinary fines and/or penalties. Providers are not required to file Medicare secondary claims unless the patient specifically requests this service.

To identify whether a Medicare patient has an insurance plan that is primary to Medicare, the billing specialist may ask the patient to complete a detailed questionnaire related to other insurance coverage. The questionnaire is incorporated into patient registration procedures, and the information is updated at each subsequent encounter. Figure 12–9 is an example of a detailed insurance coverage questionnaire.

When Medicare is the secondary payer, a copy of the EOB from the primary plan must be attached to the Medicare claim. For the provider to receive payment and an EOB from the primary insurance company, the patient must assign the primary payer benefits to the provider. Once the patient assigns benefits, the billing specialist is able to submit the insurance claim to the primary payer.

(1500)

HEALTH INSURANCE CLAIM FORM

APPROVED BY NATIONAL UNIFORM CLAIM COMMITTEE 08/05

☐☐ PICA

1. MEDICARE [X] (Medicare #) **MEDICAID** [X] (Medicaid #) **TRICARE CHAMPUS** ☐ (Sponsor's SSN) **CHAMPVA** ☐ (Member ID #) **GROUP HEALTH PLAN** ☐ (SSN or ID) **FECA BLK LUNG** ☐ (SSN) **OTHER** ☐ (ID) **1a. INSURED'S I.D. NUMBER** (For Program in Item 1) 00128743D

2. PATIENT'S NAME (Last Name, First Name, Middle Initial) PATIENT MARY S

3. PATIENT'S BIRTH DATE MM 03 | DD 08 | YY 1933 **SEX** M ☐ F [X]

4. INSURED'S NAME (Last Name, First Name, Middle Initial)

5. PATIENT'S ADDRESS (No., Street) 91 HOME STREET

6. PATIENT RELATIONSHIP TO INSURED Self ☐ Spouse ☐ Child ☐ Other ☐

7. INSURED'S ADDRESS (No., Street)

CITY NOWHERE   **STATE** US

8. PATIENT STATUS Single ☐ Married [X] Other ☐

CITY   **STATE**

ZIP CODE 12367 **TELEPHONE (Include Area Code)** (101) 201 8989

Employed ☐ Full-Time Student ☐ Part-Time Student ☐

ZIP CODE   **TELEPHONE (Include Area Code)** ( )

9. OTHER INSURED'S NAME (Last Name, First Name, Middle Initial)

10. IS PATIENT'S CONDITION RELATED TO:

11. INSURED'S POLICY GROUP OR FECA NUMBER

a. OTHER INSURED'S POLICY OR GROUP NUMBER

a. EMPLOYMENT? (Current or Previous) ☐ YES [X] NO

a. INSURED'S DATE OF BIRTH MM | DD | YY **SEX** M ☐ F ☐

b. OTHER INSURED'S DATE OF BIRTH MM | DD | YY **SEX** M ☐ F ☐

b. AUTO ACCIDENT? **PLACE (State)** ☐ YES [X] NO

b. EMPLOYER'S NAME OR SCHOOL NAME

c. EMPLOYER'S NAME OR SCHOOL NAME

c. OTHER ACCIDENT? ☐ YES [X] NO

c. INSURANCE PLAN NAME OR PROGRAM NAME

d. INSURANCE PLAN NAME OR PROGRAM NAME

10d. RESERVED FOR LOCAL USE MCD1012345XT

d. IS THERE ANOTHER HEALTH BENEFIT PLAN? ☐ YES [X] NO *If yes,* return to and complete item 9 a-d.

READ BACK OF FORM BEFORE COMPLETING & SIGNING THIS FORM.

12. PATIENT'S OR AUTHORIZED PERSON'S SIGNATURE I authorize the release of any medical or other information necessary to process this claim. I also request payment of government benefits either to myself or to the party who accepts assignment below.

SIGNED SIGNATURE ON FILE   DATE

13. INSURED'S OR AUTHORIZED PERSON'S SIGNATURE I authorize payment of medical benefits to the undersigned physician or supplier for services described below.

SIGNED SIGNATURE ON FILE

14. DATE OF CURRENT: ILLNESS (First symptom) OR INJURY (Accident) OR PREGNANCY (LMP) MM 01 | DD 28 | YY 20XX

15. IF PATIENT HAS HAD SAME OR SIMILAR ILLNESS, GIVE FIRST DATE MM | DD | YY

16. DATES PATIENT UNABLE TO WORK IN CURRENT OCCUPATION MM | DD | YY FROM   TO   MM | DD | YY

17. NAME OF REFERRING PROVIDER OR OTHER SOURCE   17a. 17b. NPI

18. HOSPITALIZATION DATES RELATED TO CURRENT SERVICES MM | DD | YY FROM   TO MM | DD | YY

19. RESERVED FOR LOCAL USE

20. OUTSIDE LAB? ☐ YES [X] NO **$ CHARGES**

21. DIAGNOSIS OR NATURE OF ILLNESS OR INJURY (Relate Items 1, 2, 3, or 4 to Item 24E by Line)

1. 511 . 10   3. V12 . 51
2. 427 . 89   4. ___ . ___

22. MEDICAID RESUBMISSION CODE ORIGINAL REF. NO.

23. PRIOR AUTHORIZATION NUMBER

24. A. DATE(S) OF SERVICE From MM DD YY — To MM DD YY	**B. PLACE OF SERVICE**	**C. EMG**	**D. PROCEDURES, SERVICES, OR SUPPLIES** (Explain Unusual Circumstances) CPT/HCPCS | MODIFIER	**E. DIAGNOSIS POINTER**	**F. $ CHARGES**	**G. DAYS OR UNITS**	**H. EPSDT Family Plan**	**I. ID. QUAL.**	**J. RENDERING PROVIDER ID. #**
01 28 20XX 01 28 20XX	11		99248	1	150 00			IC NPI	6878901234
01 28 20XX 01 28 20XX	11		71020	1	50 00			IC NPI	6878901234
01 28 20XX 01 28 20XX	11		93000	1	50 00			IC NPI	6878901234
								NPI	
								NPI	
								NPI	

25. FEDERAL TAX I.D. NUMBER 11-123391 SSN ☐ EIN [X]

26. PATIENT'S ACCOUNT NO.

27. ACCEPT ASSIGNMENT? (For govt. claims, see back) [X] YES ☐ NO

28. TOTAL CHARGE $ 250 00

29. AMOUNT PAID $ 25 00

30. BALANCE DUE $

31. SIGNATURE OF PHYSICIAN OR SUPPLIER INCLUDING DEGREES OR CREDENTIALS (I certify that the statements on the reverse apply to this bill and are made a part thereof.)

SIGNATURE ON FILE SIGNED DATE

32. SERVICE FACILITY LOCATION INFORMATION MEDICARE EAST 1201 MEDIC DRIVE NOWHERE US 12367 a. 5432109897 b.

33. BILLING PROVIDER INFO & PH # (909) 555 8888 MEDICARE EAST 1201 MEDIC DRIVE NOWHERE US 12367 a. 5432109897 b.

NUCC Instruction Manual available at: www.nucc.org

APPROVED OMB-0938-0999 FORM CMS-1500 (08-05)

For instructional use only. Courtesy of the Centers for Medicare and Medicaid Services, www.cms.hhs.gov

Figure 12–8 Medicare-Medicaid Crossover CMS-1500

Practice Letterhead

All Medicare Patients:

In order for us to comply with the Medicare as Secondary Payer laws you must fill out this Medicare Data Sheet before we can properly process your insurance claim.

Please complete this questionnaire and return it to the desk. We will also need to make photocopies of all your insurance identification cards. Do not hesitate to ask for clarification of any item on this form.

CHECK ALL ITEMS THAT DESCRIBE YOUR HEALTH INSURANCE COVERAGE

1. I am working full-time _____ part-time _____ I retired on ___/___/___.

_____ I am enrolled in a Medicare HMO plan.

2. _____ I am entitled to black lung benefits.

_____ I had a job-related injury on ___/___/___.

_____ I have a fee service card from the VA.

_____ I had an organ transplant on ___/___/___.

_____ I have been on kidney dialysis since ___/___/___.

_____ I am being treated for an injury received in a car accident _____

_____ other vehicle. Other type of accident (please identify) _____

_____

3. _____ I am employed/My spouse is employed and I am covered by an employer-sponsored health care program covering more than 20 employees. Name of policy:

_____

4. _____ I/My spouse has purchased a private insurance policy to supplement Medicare. Name of policy:

_____

5. _____ I have health insurance through my/my spouse's previous employer or union. Name of previous employer or union:

_____

6. _____ I am covered by Medicaid and my ID number is: _____

7. _____ I am retired and covered by an employer-sponsored retiree health care plan. Name of plan:

_____

8. _____ I am retired but have been called back temporarily and have employee health benefits while I am working. Name of plan:

_____

Patient Signature _____ Date ___/___/___.

Figure 12–9 Detailed Insurance Questionnaire

If the patient does not assign the primary plan benefits, the billing specialist explains the provider's payment policy, collects fees due at the time of service, and informs the patient that he or she must file the insurance claim. The billing specialist also informs the patient that Medicare cannot be billed as a secondary payer until the patient provides the office with a copy of the primary payer's EOB.

Completing the CMS-1500: Medicare Secondary

After payment is received from the primary payer—either directly through assignment of benefits or from the patient when the patient receives the insurance payment and then passes it on to the provider—the billing specialist completes a CMS-1500 for Medicare, secondary payer. As previously stated, a copy of the EOB from the primary payer is attached to the CMS-1500. Guidelines for CMS-1500 completion are listed here.

Block 1	Enter an X in the Medicare box.
Block 1a	Enter the patient's Medicare ID number.
Block 2	Enter the patient's name as instructed.
Block 3	Enter the patient's birth date and sex.
Block 4	Enter the name of the insured for the policy that is primary to Medicare. If the patient is the insured, enter SAME.
Block 5	Enter the patient's address, phone number, and zip code.
Block 6	Enter an X in the box that identifies the patient's relationship to the person named in block 4.
Block 7	Enter the address and phone number of the person named in block 4. If the person in block 4 is the patient, enter SAME.
Block 8	Enter an X in the boxes that describe the patient's marital and employment status.
Block 9–9d	Leave this blank.
Blocks 10a–10c	Check YES or NO as appropriate. If 10b is YES, enter the two-character abbreviation for the state where the accident occurred.
Block 10d	Leave this blank.
Block 11	Enter the insured's policy or group number.
Block 11a	Enter the birth date and sex of the person who has the primary insurance if different from block 3.
Block 11b	Enter the name of the employer who provides the primary insurance. If there is no employer, leave this blank. If the insured is retired, enter RETIRED and the eight-digit date of retirement.
Block 11c	Enter the PAYERID number of the primary insurance plan. If the PAYERID number is not known, enter the name of the primary insurance plan.
Block 11d	Leave this blank.
Blocks 12–28	No change from the instructions for Medicare as primary
Block 29	Enter only the amount the patient has paid. Attach the primary insurance plan's EOB to show the amount paid by the primary payer.
Blocks 30–33	No change from the instructions for Medicare as primary

Figure 12–10 is an example of a CMS-1500, Medicare as secondary payer claim.

Figure 12–10 **Medicare as Secondary Payer CMS-1500**

REINFORCEMENT EXERCISE 12-9

Using the following patient and provider information, complete a CMS-1500 for a Medicare as secondary payer claim. Your instructor can tell you where to get the form.

Patient Information

Name: Viola Baril, married, female
Birth Date: January 5, 1929
Address: 301 West Spruce, Blueberry, ME 49966
Phone: (906) 338-3943
Insurance: Medicare 511919402B
Other Insurance: Husband's BC/BS
Employment Status: Retired
Date of Service: June 20, 20YY
Diagnosis/Code: Colon polyp, 211.3 (ICD-10-CM; K63.5)
Service/Code: Office visit, 99214; Sigmoidoscopy, 45330
Charges: Office visit, $90; Sigmoidoscopy, $150

Spouse

Name: Eugene Baril
Birth Date: May 20, 1935
Employed by: Westland Community College
Insurance: BC/BS R2345678 214
PAYERID: 446543712

Provider Information

Superiorland Clinic
714 Hennepin Ave.
Blueberry, ME 49966
Phone: (906) 337-8778
Superiorland Clinic NPI: 4567890123
Mark Beckwith, MD
Physician NPI: 4444098765
EIN: 61-4927045

 PROCESSING MEDICARE PAYMENTS

Once the billing specialist submits claims to the MAC, PARs receive payments directly from CMS on a regular basis. Payments are not claim-specific; rather, the provider receives a remittance check that covers several claims. A remittance notice is included with the payment. The provider's Medicare remittance notice is a document that recaps, by patient, the services rendered, the amount billed, the allowed amount, co-insurance, and the amount the provider was paid. Figure 12–11 is a sample Medicare remittance notice.

(1) MEDICARE INSURANCE CARRIER
    PROVIDER # G1616 (2)
(3) CHECK # 10298   (6)   (7)   09/21/2000 (8)   (9)   (10)   (11)   MEDICARE
                                                    (4)   REMITTANCE
                                                                                                     NOTICE (12)

NAME	SERVICE DATE	PROCEDURE	BILLED	ALLOWED	COINS	ADJUST.	PROV PD
ACE, Wm. (5)	09032000	99214	62.87	62.87	12.57		50.30
	09032000	93000	27.68	27.68	5.54		22.14
	09032000	85025	36.75	10.73	0.00	26.02	10.73
	09032000	84153	57.75	25.42	0.00	32.33	25.42
	09032000	81000	21.00	4.37	0.00	16.63	4.37
	09032000	G0001	6.04	3.00	0.00	3.04	3.00
		CLAIM TOT	212.09	134.07	18.11	78.02	115.96
DEUCE, M	09032000	80054	51.45	11.45	0.00	40.40	11.05
	09032000	80061	68.25	14.65	0.00	53.60	14.65
		CLAIM TOT	119.70	25.70	0.00	94.00	25.70
TREY, R	09022000	99214	62.87	62.87	12.57		50.30
	09022000	85025	36.75	10.73	0.00	26.02	10.73
	09022000	84439	36.75	12.46	0.00	24.29	12.46
	09022000	85651	25.20	4.91	0.00	20.29	4.91
	09022000	84443	80.32	23.21	0.00	57.11	23.21
	09022000	G0001	6.04	3.00	0.00	3.04	3.00
		CLAIM TOT	247.93	117.18	12.57	130.75	104.61
QUIP, L	09022000	80058	35.40	6.35	0.00	29.05	6.35
	09022000	80051	31.50	5.65	0.00	25.82	5.65
		CLAIM TOT	66.90	12.00	0.00	54.90	12.00
RAYS, P	09022000	99213	41.08	41.08	8.22		32.86
		CLAIM TOT	41.08	41.08	8.22	0.00	32.86
SETH, M	09022000	45330	106.27	106.27	21.25		85.02
	09022000	85025	36.75	10.73	0.00	26.02	10.73
	09022000	G0001	6.04	3.00	0.00	3.04	3.00
	09022000	80054	51.45	14.39	0.00	37.06	14.39
		CLAIM TOT	200.51	134.39	21.25	66.12	113.14
BEST, T	09022000	85027	26.25	6.43	0.00	19.82	6.43
	09022000	G0001	6.04	3.00	0.00	3.04	3.00
		CLAIM TOT	63.79	9.43	0.00	22.86	9.43
WURST, L	09022000	84153	57.75	25.42	0.00	32.33	25.42
	09022000	G0001	6.04	3.00	0.00	3.04	3.00
		CLAIM TOT	63.79	28.42	0.00	35.37	28.42
LOVE, I	09022000	85025	36.75	10.73	0.00	26.02	10.73
	09022000	81000	21.00	4.37	0.00	16.63	4.37
	09022000	G0001	6.04	3.00	0.00	3.04	3.00
		CLAIM TOT	63.79	18.10	0.00	45.69	18.10
HART, C	09032000	99211	16.36	16.36	3.27		13.09
		CLAIM TOT	16.36	16.36	3.27	0.00	13.09

Figure 12–11 Sample Medicare Remittance Notice

continued on the next page

continued from the previous page

1. Name of Medicare insurance carrier.
2. Provider number.
3. Check number for the check included with the remittance notice.
4. Date remittance notice was generated.
5. Beneficiary name.
6. Date the service was rendered.
7. CPT code.
8. Amount the provider billed Medicare for the service.
9. Medicare-approved or -allowed amount for the service.
10. Beneficiary's coinsurance responsibility.
11. Adjustment amount a participating provider takes on the beneficiary's bill.
12. Amount the Medicare insurance carrier paid the provider.

Figure 12–11 *continued*

The billing specialist enters or posts payment information to each patient's account. For PARs, the difference between the amount charged and the amount allowed is written off as an adjustment. If the patient has not already paid the co-insurance or deductible, a statement is generated and sent to the patient.

The remittance notice may include information about denied claims. The billing specialist pulls the financial and medical records for each denied claim, reviews this information, and resubmits the claim as appropriate. For example, the insurance billing specialist may discover a coding error, correct the error, and resubmit the claim.

ABBREVIATIONS

Table 12–8 lists the abbreviations presented in this chapter.

TABLE 12–8

Abbreviations and Meanings	
Abbreviation	Meaning
AAA	abdominal aortic aneurysm
ABN	Advance Beneficiary Notice
A/B MAC	Part A and Part B Medicare Administrative Contractor
AWV	annual wellness visit
CF	(national) conversion factor
CLIA	Clinical Laboratory Improvement Act
CMS	Centers for Medicare and Medicaid Services

continued on the next page

continued from the previous page

Abbreviations and Meanings

Abbreviation	Meaning
COBA	coordination of benefits administrator
DME	durable medical equipment
DME MAC	durable medical equipment Medicare Administrative Contractor
EIN	employer (tax) identification number
EOB	explanation of benefits
ESRD	end-stage renal disease
FDA	Food and Drug Administration
GAF	geographic adjustment factor
HICN	health insurance claim number
HIPAA	Health Insurance Portability and Accountability Act
HMO	health maintenance organization
IDE	investigational device exemption
MA	Medicare Advantage
MAC	Medicare Administrative Contractor
MA-PDP	Medicare Advantage Prescription Drug Plan
MFS	Medicare fee schedule
MSA	medical savings account (Medicare)
MSN	Medicare Summary Notice
MSP	Medicare as secondary payer Medicare Supplemental Plan
NCCI	National Correct Coding Initiative
NOC	not otherwise classified
NonPAR	nonparticipating provider
PAR	participating provider
PDP	prescription drug plan
PFFS	private fee-for-service
POS	place of service
PPO	preferred provider organization
PPPS	Personalized Prevention Plan Services

continued on the next page

continued from the previous page

PSA	prostate-specific antigen
QI	Qualifying Individual (Medicare)
QIO	Quality Improvement Organization
QMB	Qualified Medicare Beneficiary (Medicare)
RBRVS	resource-based relative value scale
RVU	relative value unit
SLMB	Specified Low-Income Medicare Beneficiary (Medicare)
SNF	skilled nursing facility
SNP	special needs plan (Medicare)
SSDI	Social Security Disability Insurance
SSN	Social Security number
VA	Veterans Administration

 SUMMARY

Medicare is the nation's largest health insurance program, covering millions of Americans. Hospital, institutional, home health, and hospice costs are paid under Part A. Physician services, outpatient hospital care, laboratory tests, and other medical costs are paid under Part B. In general, Medicare Part A is available to people (and their spouses) who have worked for at least 10 years in Medicare-covered employment, are 65 years old, and are citizens or permanent residents of the United States. Most people do not pay for Medicare Part A.

Medicare Part B is voluntary, and individuals who choose to enroll pay a monthly premium. The premium is adjusted annually. Medicare Part B covers a wide variety of medical services that are reasonable, necessary, and consistent with the patient's diagnoses or problems. In addition to the monthly premium, Medicare Part B beneficiaries pay an annual deductible and 20% of the allowed charge on all covered services.

Medicare Part D, the prescription drug benefit, provides all Medicare beneficiaries with the opportunity to voluntarily enroll in a prescription drug plan. The purpose of all prescription drug plans (PDPs) is to help defray the costs associated with prescription medications. The plans cover generic and brand-name drugs. Individuals who enroll in a PDP pay premiums, deductibles, and co-payments. Additional financial assistance is available for individuals with limited resources and incomes.

Health care providers can choose whether to participate in Medicare Part B. Participating providers (PARs) agree to accept the Medicare-approved payment rate as payment in full. PARs collect the 20% co-payment from the beneficiary, are obligated to submit Medicare claims to the insurance carrier, receive payment directly from the insurance carrier, and may not bill the beneficiary for any amount that exceeds the approved payment rate. Nonparticipating providers (NonPARs) must also submit Medicare claims to the insurance carrier, are not paid directly, and are restricted to charging fees that are 15% above the NonPAR approved fee.

The Centers for Medicare and Medicaid Services (CMS) developed the National Correct Coding Initiative (NCCI) program. The purpose of the program is to promote accurate coding and appropriate insurance claims payments. The NCCI edits Medicare insurance claims and identifies errors that have a direct impact on reimbursement.

Medicare can be either the primary or the secondary payer for beneficiaries' medical expenses. Medicare is usually the primary payer, even when the patient has Medigap, other Medicare supplemental insurance, or Medicaid. Medicare is the secondary payer when the patient is covered by an employer-sponsored group health plan with more than 20 covered employees, by an employer-sponsored disability insurance plan, by other insurance due to an accident or workers' compensation, by Veterans Administration preauthorized services, or by the FECA black lung insurance plan.

Medicare offers additional health plan choices called Medicare Advantage (MA) plans, which include managed care, preferred provider organizations, private fee-for-service, special needs plans, and medical savings accounts. The goal of the plans is to provide Medicare beneficiaries with quality health care in a cost-effective manner. MA plans are also called Medicare Part C.

REVIEW EXERCISES

Fill in the Blank

1. Medicare _____ covers care received in hospitals and nursing homes.

2. Medicare _____ covers physician services and outpatient hospital care.

3. Medicare beneficiaries with low incomes and limited resources may be eligible for the _____ program.

4. Health insurance companies that handle payments for Medicare Part B are called _____.

5. _____ contract with Medicare and agree to accept the Medicare-approved payment rate.

6. _____ are limited in the amount they can charge for rendering services to Medicare beneficiaries.

7. The _____ is a list of Medicare-approved fees for provider services.

8. A(n) _____ is sent to the provider and recaps services rendered and payments received.

Covered Services

Place an X next to services covered by Medicare.

1. Annual physical exams. _____

2. Breast augmentation. _____

3. Clinical laboratory tests. _____

4. Cosmetic surgery. _____

5. Flu shots. _____

6. Physical therapy. _____

7. Prostate cancer screening. _____

8. Wheelchair. _____

Abbreviations

Spell out the following abbreviations.

1. DME _____

2. MFS _____

3. MSN _____

4. MSP _____

5. NonPAR _____

6. PAR _____

7. QI _____

8. QMB _____

9. RVU _____

10. SLMB _____

11. NCCI _____

12. MA _____

13. DME MAC _____

14. ABN _____

15. PFFS _____

True or False

Write True or False on the line following each statement.

1. Individuals age 65 or older qualify for Medicare. _____

2. Enrollment in Medicare Part B is automatic. _____

3. Most retirees are eligible for premium-free Medicare Part A. _____

4. Medicare beneficiaries must pay a premium for Medicare Part B. _____

5. Providers are allowed to waive the deductible and co-pay for Medicare beneficiaries.
   _____

6. Participating providers may not balance-bill Medicare beneficiaries. _____

7. The limiting fee applies to both PARs and NonPARs. _____

8. Elective surgery is defined as surgery that is scheduled in advance. _____

9. The RBRVS system is used to calculate Medicare-approved fees. _____

10. Medicare is the primary payer when the patient has both Medicare and Medicaid coverage. _____

Multiple Choice

Circle the correct answer from the choices provided.

1. Which governmental agency manages the Medicare program?

   a. CMS

   b. Social Security Administration

   c. Department of Health and Human Services

   d. Medicare Integrity Program

2. The Medicare Summary Notice is also known as the

   a. Advanced Notice Medicare Beneficiary Agreement.

   b. Medicare Surgical Financial Disclosure Statement.

   c. explanation of benefits.

   d. Medicare fee schedule.

3. The deadline for filing Medicare claims is

   a. one year from the date of service.

   b. December 31 of the year following the date of service.

   c. six months from the date of service.

   d. one year from the date the patient expires.

4. Conditional primary payer status may apply when

   a. a workers' compensation claim is being appealed.

   b. the patient's 65th birthday is within three days of the date of service.

   c. the billing specialist submits the claim within six months of the date of service.

   d. the patient's disability determination is pending.

5. The ordering physician is the one who

   a. oversees or manages the patient's treatment plan.

   b. orders nonphysician services.

   c. requests an item or service covered by Medicare.

   d. treats the patient.

6. Medicare is the secondary payer when the patient is covered by

   a. Medigap.

   b. Medicaid.

   c. VA-preauthorized services.

   d. TRICARE.

7. Medicare Advantage plans include all but one of the following:

   a. PDPs.

   b. HMOs.

   c. PFFSs.

   d. PPOs.

8. Prescription drug plans are required to cover

   a. all prescription medications.

   b. generic and brand-name medications.

   c. medications listed on the Medicare formulary.

   d. 75% of the cost of prescription medications.

9. A PDP's list of medications is known as

   a. the formulary.

   b. covered drugs.

   c. standard prescription coverage.

   d. basic prescription coverage.

10. NPIs were developed by the

   a. AMA.

   b. AHA.

   c. NCCI.

   d. CMS.

CHALLENGE ACTIVITIES

1. With the instructor's permission, invite a billing specialist from a local physician's office to talk to your class about Medicare claim submission.

2. Prepare a reference booklet that includes a sample of a CMS-1500 that is correctly completed for each type of Medicare claim presented in this chapter.

 WEBSITES

Cahaba Government Benefit Administrators: http://www.cahabagba.com
CIGNA Government Services: http://www.cignagovernmentservices.com
First Coast Service Options, Inc.: http://www.fcso.com
Highmark Medicare Services: http://www.highmarkmedicareservices.com
Medicare: http://www.medicare.gov
National Government Services: http://www.adminastar.com
National Heritage Insurance Corp.: http://www.medicarenhic.com
Noridian Administrative Services: http://www.noridianmedicare.com
Palmetto Government Benefits Administrator: http://www.palmettogba.com
Trailblazer Health Enterprises: http://www.trailblazerhealth.com
Wisconsin Physician Services: http://www.wpsmedicare.com

CHAPTER 13

Medicaid

LEARNING OBJECTIVES

Upon successful completion of this chapter, the reader should have the knowledge to:

1. Define all terms and abbreviations presented in the chapter.
2. Describe three differences between Medicare and Medicaid.
3. Identify two pieces of federal legislation that apply to Medicaid.
4. Accurately complete the CMS-1500 according to Medicaid guidelines.
5. List two circumstances under which Medicaid is the secondary payer.

KEY TERMS

18/19
Care/Caid
Early and Periodic Screening, Diagnostic, and Treatment Services (EPSDT)
Enrollee
Fiscal agents
Medi/Medi
Medicaid

Medicaid expansion program
Medicare/Medicaid Crossover Program (MCD)
Participant
Payer of last resort
Qualified Medicare Beneficiary (QMB)
Recipient

Remittance advice (RA)
State Children's Health Insurance Program (SCHIP)
Supplemental Security Income (SSI)
Temporary Assistance for Needy Families (TANF)
Title 19
Title 21

OVERVIEW

In 1965, Congress passed Title 19, an amendment to the Social Security Act that established a federal medical assistance program called Medicaid. Medicaid is a joint venture between federal and state governments. Coverage and benefits vary from state to state, but basic Medicaid eligibility requirements apply to all programs. The purpose of Medicaid is to provide health insurance for specific populations. Medicaid services can be covered under health maintenance organization (HMO) or preferred provider organization (PPO) programs. Individuals enrolled in Medicaid programs are known as recipients, participants, and enrollees. Medicaid eligibility

TABLE 13–1

Medicaid Populations	
Population	**Description**
Medically indigent, low-income individuals and families	• Individuals and families who meet the income levels established by the state in which they live • Individuals and families without health insurance
Aged and disabled persons covered by **Supplemental Security Income (SSI)**	• Individuals who qualify for SSI, the federal income assistance program that provides cash payments to blind, disabled, or aged individuals
Persons covered by the **Qualified Medicare Beneficiary (QMB)** Program	• QMB pays Medicare premiums, deductibles, and patient co-payments for Medicare-eligible persons with low incomes—usually a percentage of the federal poverty guidelines
Persons covered by **Temporary Assistance for Needy Families (TANF)**	• TANF provides financial assistance to children and families who meet specific income levels and to pregnant women who meet the income requirements and would qualify if their babies were already born
Persons receiving institutional or other long-term care	• Long-term care facilities, including nursing homes, adult foster care homes, and state psychiatric facilities

does not depend on age, except for programs that are intended to provide services to children and pregnant women. Income is the primary screening tool. Table 13–1 lists the populations eligible for Medicaid.

In the past, the federal government imposed many requirements on states in order to qualify for Medicaid funds. In 1997, Title 21 of the Social Security Act was amended to allow states to create a health insurance program for children of low-income working families, who are often described as "the working poor." The amendment is known as the State Children's Health Insurance Program (SCHIP). Under SCHIP, the federal government provides additional Medicaid funds to states that are willing to expand their Medicaid program health insurance options or develop new health insurance plans to cover more children. Families do not have to qualify for TANF in order to participate in SCHIP programs.

Individual states have different names for Medicaid programs, such as MediCal in California. In Michigan, MICHILD is a Medicaid program for individuals aged 19 and younger and pregnant women of any age. MICHILD is a Medicaid expansion program, which is any federal/state health insurance program that is funded by Medicaid legislation with the specific intent of providing additional or expanded services to Medicaid recipients.

 MEDICAID COVERAGE

Although Medicaid coverage varies from state to state, basic health care services include the following:

- Hospitalization; preauthorization for nonemergency hospitalization usually required
- Outpatient hospital services
- Diagnostic tests

- Skilled nursing care
- Home health care
- Physician's office visits; specialist referrals by the patient's primary care physician required
- Surgical care
- Dental care
- Obstetric and prenatal care provided by a midwife or certified nurse practitioner

Individual states may offer Medicaid coverage for additional services, such as these:

- Vision screening and glasses
- Mental health care
- Prescription medication benefits
- Hearing screening and hearing aids
- Family planning services
- Substance abuse treatment
- Medical supplies and equipment
- Immunizations

An individual who qualifies for Medicaid health insurance receives an identification card. The card is issued monthly, according to changes in the individual's income. Most states require Medicaid participants to report income changes within 10 days of the change. If no change is reported, Medicaid coverage is continued and a new ID card is sent to the individual. The billing specialist carefully checks the date on the identification card to ensure that the services provided fall within the current coverage period.

In 1967, Congress passed the Early and Periodic Screening, Diagnostic, and Treatment Services (EPSDT) Act. EPSDT mandates that states must provide routine pediatric checkups to all children enrolled in Medicaid. In 1989, the EPSDT law was revised to include definitions for terms such as "screening," "vision," "dental," and "hearing services." In addition, a new requirement was added mandating that states provide treatment for any problems identified by the screening services.

Unlike Medicare, Medicaid participants do not pay premiums or deductibles. Over the past several years, Medicaid established a co-payment (co-pay) plan for Medicaid recipients. A co-payment is a fee that the patient pays for services. When this text was published, Medicaid co-payments ranged from $1 to $5. For example, the Medicaid co-pay for a prescription may be $1, and the co-pay for an office visit may be $3.

REINFORCEMENT EXERCISES 13–1

Write True or False on the line following each statement.

1. Medicaid is available to individuals aged 65 and older. _____

2. Medicaid is a social welfare program. _____

3. Title 18 is the section of the Social Security Act that applies to Medicaid.

_____

continued on the next page

continued from the previous page

4. Individuals who receive SSI do not need Medicaid health insurance coverage. _____

5. SCHIP is an amendment to the Social Security Act. _____

Provide a short answer for each item.

1. List four basic health care services included in all Medicaid programs.

_____

_____

_____

_____

2. List four additional health care services offered by individual states.

_____

_____

_____

_____

3. How often is a Medicaid ID card issued?

_____

_____

_____

4. What is the primary screening tool for Medicaid eligibility?

_____

_____

_____

5. What is EPSDT?

_____

_____

_____

MEDICAID BILLING

Providers who treat Medicaid patients are obligated to accept the Medicaid payment as payment in full. By law, the provider may not bill or balance-bill the patient for the cost of a Medicaid-covered service. Medicaid fees are typically much lower than other insurance programs, and reimbursement can be delayed for several months. Because of these issues, many providers limit the number of Medicaid patients they treat. Some providers choose not to participate in Medicaid programs.

When a provider chooses not to participate in Medicaid programs, office staff communicates this information in a nonbiased manner.

> **EXAMPLE**
>
> Part of the screening process for new patients includes questions about insurance coverage. When a prospective patient identifies Medicaid as the health insurance program, the receptionist or billing specialist simply tells the individual that the provider does not participate in Medicaid. It is helpful to have a list of area physicians who do participate and to refer the individual to those physicians.

If the provider agrees to participate in Medicaid programs, the billing specialist and all agency staff must treat Medicaid patients with the same dignity and respect afforded to other patients. Medicaid is a social welfare program; however, the negative stereotypes that may be associated with welfare programs have no place in a professional setting.

Billing specialists who work for providers who participate in Medicaid must have current information about Medicaid coverage and benefits. The information is available from Medicaid insurance carriers, also called fiscal agents, that reimburse the provider for services rendered. Many states have established a website for providers who treat Medicaid recipients. These websites offer information ranging from eligibility verification to claims submission guidelines. Providers who participate in the Medicaid program have access to online information. In fact, several states include their Medicaid policy manual online.

Medicaid is called the payer of last resort. This means that payment for services rendered is collected from all other sources *before* a claim is submitted to Medicaid.

Medicaid Claims Submission

Most states use the CMS-1500 as the insurance claim form. Instructions for completing the CMS-1500 when Medicaid is the only insurance program are given here. These instructions are generic. Each state's Medicaid policy manual has the instructions for that specific state.

Block 1	Enter an X in Medicaid.
Block 1a	Enter the patient's Medicaid identification number.
Block 2	Enter the patient's last name, first name, and middle initial, if known.
Block 3	Enter the patient's eight-digit birth date. Enter an X in the appropriate gender box.
Block 4	Leave this blank. If the patient has insurance coverage that is primary to Medicaid, enter the name of the policyholder.

continued on the next page

continued from the previous page

Block 5	Enter the patient's address and phone number.
Block 6	Leave this blank. If block 4 is completed, check the appropriate box in block 6.
Block 7	Leave this blank. Complete block 7 if blocks 4 and 11 are completed.
Block 8	Enter an X in the box that describes the patient's marital status and whether the patient is employed or a student.
Blocks 9–9d	Leave this blank. If block 11d is YES, complete blocks 9–9d.
Block 10a	Enter an X in YES or NO.
Block 10b	Enter an X in YES or NO. If YES, enter the two-character abbreviation for the state where the accident occurred. Enter the date of the accident in block 14.
Block 10c	Enter an X in YES or NO. If YES, enter the date of the accident in block 14.
Block 10d	Leave this blank.
Blocks 11–11d	Leave this blank. If the patient has insurance primary to Medicaid, complete blocks 11–11d.
Block 12	Leave this blank. The patient's Medicaid application authorizes release of medical information for billing purposes.
Block 13	Leave this blank. Payment is made directly to participating providers.
Block 14	Enter the eight-digit date as appropriate. If YES was answered in block 10b or 10c, enter the eight-digit date of the accident.
Blocks 15 and 16	Leave these blank.
Block 17	Enter the referring/ordering provider's first and last name and professional credential.
Block 17a	Leave this blank.
Block 17b	Enter the national provider identification (NPI) number of the provider named in block 17.
Block 18	Enter the admission and discharge dates in the six- or eight-digit format, if applicable. Otherwise, leave this blank.
Block 19	Enter special remarks, if necessary. Otherwise, leave this blank.
Block 20	Leave this blank.
Block 21	Enter ICD-9-CM diagnoses codes to the highest level of specificity. Enter the first-listed diagnosis code in item 1. Enter other diagnosis codes in items 2, 3, and 4 in descending priority. (Note: Use ICD-10 codes when implemented.)
Block 22	Complete only when resubmitting a Medicaid claim; otherwise, leave this blank. To submit a replacement, voided, or canceled claim, enter the resubmission code in the left side of block 22 and then enter the claim reference number (CRN) of the paid claim being replaced, voided, or canceled. Resubmission codes are available in the Medicaid policy manual.

continued on the next page

continued from the previous page

Block 23	Enter the Medicaid prior authorization number, if applicable. Prior authorization is often required for elective inpatient services, transplant services, and other services described in the Medicaid policy manual.
Blocks 24A–J	Complete the unshaded areas of blocks 24A–24J according to the guidelines given below.
Block 24A	Enter a six- or eight-digit date of service in the From and To columns.
Block 24B	Enter the place of service code. Use the Medicare place of service codes.
Block 24C	Enter a Y if the service was an emergency or an N for nonemergency services.
Block 24D	Enter CPT procedure codes, with modifiers as necessary.
Block 24E	Enter the one diagnosis reference number from block 21 that best justifies the medical necessity for each service listed in block 24D.
Block 24F	Enter the charge for the service rendered.
Block 24G	Enter the number of units of service. If only one service is performed, enter 1.
Block 24H	Leave this blank.
Block 24I	Leave this blank.
Block 24J	Enter the provider's 10-digit NPI number in the unshaded area of this block.
Block 25	Enter the billing entity's Employer's Federal Tax Identification Number. Enter an X in the EIN box.
Block 26	Enter the patient's account number, if one is assigned. This number will be referenced on the remittance advice (RA) form or explanation of benefits (EOB).
Block 27	Leave this blank. Providers treating Medicaid patients must accept assignment.
Block 28	Enter the total charges for services listed on lines 1 through 6.
Block 29	Leave this blank.
Block 30	Enter the balance due from Medicaid by subtracting the amount in block 29 from the amount in block 28.
Block 31	Enter SIGNATURE ON FILE (for electronic claims). The provider's signature or signature stamp may also be required or accepted.
Block 32	Enter the name and address of the facility where services were rendered. Enter the facility's NPI number in block 32a. Leave block 32b blank.
Block 33	Enter the provider's billing name, address, and phone number. Enter the NPI number in block 33a of the individual or entity identified in block 33.
Block 33b	Leave this blank.

Figure 13–1 is an example of a completed claim form when Medicaid is the patient's only insurance plan.

(1500)

HEALTH INSURANCE CLAIM FORM

APPROVED BY NATIONAL UNIFORM CLAIM COMMITTEE 08/05

☐☐ PICA

PICA ☐☐

| 1. MEDICARE ☐ (Medicare #) | MEDICAID [X] (Medicaid #) | TRICARE CHAMPUS ☐ (Sponsor's SSN) | CHAMPVA ☐ (Member ID #) | GROUP HEALTH PLAN ☐ (SSN or ID) | FECA BLK LUNG ☐ (SSN) | OTHER ☐ (ID) | 1a. INSURED'S I.D. NUMBER (For Program in Item 1) 257885301 |

2. PATIENT'S NAME (Last Name, First Name, Middle Initial)
ROZWELL, MARTIN, L

3. PATIENT'S BIRTH DATE MM 10 DD 10 YY 1990 SEX M [X] F ☐

4. INSURED'S NAME (Last Name, First Name, Middle Initial)

5. PATIENT'S ADDRESS (No., Street)
409 CACTUS DRIVE

6. PATIENT RELATIONSHIP TO INSURED
Self ☐ Spouse ☐ Child ☐ Other ☐

7. INSURED'S ADDRESS (No., Street)

CITY DESERT   STATE AZ

8. PATIENT STATUS
Single [X] Married ☐ Other ☐

CITY   STATE

ZIP CODE 69075   TELEPHONE (Include Area Code) (822) 361 6578

Employed ☐ Full-Time Student ☐ Part-Time Student ☐

ZIP CODE   TELEPHONE (Include Area Code) ( )

9. OTHER INSURED'S NAME (Last Name, First Name, Middle Initial)

10. IS PATIENT'S CONDITION RELATED TO:

11. INSURED'S POLICY GROUP OR FECA NUMBER

a. OTHER INSURED'S POLICY OR GROUP NUMBER

a. EMPLOYMENT? (Current or Previous)
☐ YES [X] NO

a. INSURED'S DATE OF BIRTH MM DD YY SEX M ☐ F ☐

b. OTHER INSURED'S DATE OF BIRTH MM DD YY SEX M ☐ F ☐

b. AUTO ACCIDENT? PLACE (State)
☐ YES [X] NO

b. EMPLOYER'S NAME OR SCHOOL NAME

c. EMPLOYER'S NAME OR SCHOOL NAME

c. OTHER ACCIDENT?
☐ YES [X] NO

c. INSURANCE PLAN NAME OR PROGRAM NAME

d. INSURANCE PLAN NAME OR PROGRAM NAME

10d. RESERVED FOR LOCAL USE

d. IS THERE ANOTHER HEALTH BENEFIT PLAN?
☐ YES ☐ NO **If yes,** return to and complete item 9 a-d.

READ BACK OF FORM BEFORE COMPLETING & SIGNING THIS FORM.
12. PATIENT'S OR AUTHORIZED PERSON'S SIGNATURE I authorize the release of any medical or other information necessary to process this claim. I also request payment of government benefits either to myself or to the party who accepts assignment below.

SIGNED _____ DATE _____

13. INSURED'S OR AUTHORIZED PERSON'S SIGNATURE I authorize payment of medical benefits to the undersigned physician or supplier for services described below.

SIGNED _____

14. DATE OF CURRENT: MM 02 DD 03 YY 20YY ◀ ILLNESS (First symptom) OR INJURY (Accident) OR PREGNANCY (LMP)

15. IF PATIENT HAS HAD SAME OR SIMILAR ILLNESS. GIVE FIRST DATE MM DD YY

16. DATES PATIENT UNABLE TO WORK IN CURRENT OCCUPATION MM DD YY FROM   MM DD YY TO

17. NAME OF REFERRING PROVIDER OR OTHER SOURCE

17a.
17b. NPI

18. HOSPITALIZATION DATES RELATED TO CURRENT SERVICES MM DD YY FROM   MM DD YY TO

19. RESERVED FOR LOCAL USE

20. OUTSIDE LAB? $ CHARGES
☐ YES ☐ NO

21. DIAGNOSIS OR NATURE OF ILLNESS OR INJURY (Relate Items 1, 2, 3, or 4 to Item 24E by Line)
1. 782 . 1
2. ___ . ___
3. ___ . ___
4. ___ . ___

22. MEDICAID RESUBMISSION CODE   ORIGINAL REF. NO.

23. PRIOR AUTHORIZATION NUMBER

24. A. DATE(S) OF SERVICE From MM DD YY	To MM DD YY	B. PLACE OF SERVICE	C. EMG	D. PROCEDURES, SERVICES, OR SUPPLIES (Explain Unusual Circumstances) CPT/HCPCS	MODIFIER	E. DIAGNOSIS POINTER	F. $ CHARGES	G. DAYS OR UNITS	H. EPSDT Family Plan	I. ID. QUAL.	J. RENDERING PROVIDER ID. #
1	02 03 YY	02 03 YY	11	N	99212		1	45 00	1		NPI	7890123456
2											NPI	
3											NPI	
4											NPI	
5											NPI	
6											NPI	

25. FEDERAL TAX I.D. NUMBER   SSN EIN
494134726   ☐ [X]

26. PATIENT'S ACCOUNT NO.
277885

27. ACCEPT ASSIGNMENT? (For govt. claims, see back)
☐ YES ☐ NO

28. TOTAL CHARGE $ 45 00

29. AMOUNT PAID $

30. BALANCE DUE $ 45 00

31. SIGNATURE OF PHYSICIAN OR SUPPLIER INCLUDING DEGREES OR CREDENTIALS (I certify that the statements on the reverse apply to this bill and are made a part thereof.)
SIGNATURE ON FILE
SIGNED _____ DATE _____

32. SERVICE FACILITY LOCATION INFORMATION
OUTREACH CLINIC
608 SAGEBUSH
DESERT AZ 69075
a. 7770123456 b.

33. BILLING PROVIDER INFO & PH # (812) 7529118
OUTREACH CLINIC
608 SAGEBUSH
DESERT AZ 69075
a. 7770123456 b.

NUCC Instruction Manual available at: www.nucc.org

APPROVED OMB-0938-0999 FORM CMS-1500 (08-05)

Figure 13–1 Completed CMS-1500 for Medicaid

Medicaid Secondary Payer

It is possible that a Medicaid patient has another health insurance plan. In that case, the other insurance plan is the primary payer and is billed first. The billing specialist completes the CMS-1500 according to the primary payer guidelines and submits the claim to the primary payer. Once payment is received from the primary payer, the billing specialist submits a claim to Medicaid under any one of the following conditions:

- The primary payer denies payment.
- Reimbursement from the primary payer is less than the Medicaid payment.
- Medicaid covers services that are not covered by the primary payer.

The billing specialist completes another CMS-1500 for Medicaid, attaches a copy of the EOB from the primary payer, and submits the claim to the Medicaid fiscal agent. When the Medicaid beneficiary has one private or group health plan, including Medicare, CMS-1500 instructions are as follows:

Blocks 1–3	No change from the instructions when Medicaid is the only payer.
Block 4	Enter the insured's name for the private or group health insurance plan covering the beneficiary. If the insured and the patient are the same, enter the word SAME.
Block 5	No change from the instructions when Medicaid is the only payer.
Block 6	When block 4 is completed, enter an X in the box that describes the patient's relationship to the individual named in block 4.
Block 7	When blocks 4 and 11 are completed, enter the insured's address and telephone number. When the address is the same as the patient's, enter the word SAME.
Blocks 8–10d	No change from the instructions when Medicaid is the only payer.
Block 11	Enter the insured's policy or group number or Medicare health insurance claim number (HICN).
Block 11a	When the insured is not the patient, enter the insured's eight-digit birth date and an X in the appropriate gender box. When the insured is the patient, leave this blank. This information is captured in block 3.
Block 11b	Enter the employer's name or school name, if applicable.
Block 11c	Enter the complete insurance plan or program name.
Block 11d	Enter an X in NO.
Blocks 12–28	No change from the instructions when Medicaid is the only payer.
Block 29	Enter the amount paid by the primary insurance plan.
Block 30–33b	No change from the instructions when Medicaid is the only payer.

Figure 13–2 is a sample CMS-1500 when Medicaid is the secondary payer.

(1500)

HEALTH INSURANCE CLAIM FORM

APPROVED BY NATIONAL UNIFORM CLAIM COMMITTEE 08/05

☐☐ PICA		PICA ☐☐

1. MEDICARE ☐ (Medicare #) MEDICAID ☒ (Medicaid #) TRICARE CHAMPUS ☐ (Sponsor's SSN) CHAMPVA ☐ (Member ID #) GROUP HEALTH PLAN ☐ (SSN or ID) FECA BLK LUNG ☐ (SSN) OTHER ☐ (ID)

1a. INSURED'S I.D. NUMBER (For Program in Item 1)
257885301

2. PATIENT'S NAME (Last Name, First Name, Middle Initial)
ROZWELL, MARTIN, L

3. PATIENT'S BIRTH DATE MM 10 DD 10 YY 1990   SEX M ☒ F ☐

4. INSURED'S NAME (Last Name, First Name, Middle Initial)
ROZWELL, JOHN, M

5. PATIENT'S ADDRESS (No., Street)
409 CACTUS DRIVE

6. PATIENT RELATIONSHIP TO INSURED
Self ☐ Spouse ☐ Child ☒ Other ☐

7. INSURED'S ADDRESS (No., Street)
SAME

CITY DESERT   STATE AZ

8. PATIENT STATUS
Single ☒   Married ☐   Other ☐

CITY   STATE

ZIP CODE 69075   TELEPHONE (Include Area Code) (822) 361 6578

Employed ☐   Full-Time Student ☐   Part-Time Student ☐

ZIP CODE   TELEPHONE (Include Area Code) ( )

9. OTHER INSURED'S NAME (Last Name, First Name, Middle Initial)

10. IS PATIENT'S CONDITION RELATED TO:

11. INSURED'S POLICY GROUP OR FECA NUMBER
81007

a. OTHER INSURED'S POLICY OR GROUP NUMBER

a. EMPLOYMENT? (Current or Previous) ☐ YES ☒ NO

a. INSURED'S DATE OF BIRTH MM 06 DD 04 YY 1960   SEX M ☒ F ☐

b. OTHER INSURED'S DATE OF BIRTH MM DD YY   SEX M ☐ F ☐

b. AUTO ACCIDENT? PLACE (State) ☐ YES ☒ NO

b. EMPLOYER'S NAME OR SCHOOL NAME
DYNAMIC COMPUTERS

c. EMPLOYER'S NAME OR SCHOOL NAME

c. OTHER ACCIDENT? ☐ YES ☒ NO

c. INSURANCE PLAN NAME OR PROGRAM NAME
BCBS

d. INSURANCE PLAN NAME OR PROGRAM NAME

10d. RESERVED FOR LOCAL USE

d. IS THERE ANOTHER HEALTH BENEFIT PLAN?
☐ YES ☒ NO   *If yes*, return to and complete item 9 a-d.

READ BACK OF FORM BEFORE COMPLETING & SIGNING THIS FORM.
12. PATIENT'S OR AUTHORIZED PERSON'S SIGNATURE I authorize the release of any medical or other information necessary to process this claim. I also request payment of government benefits either to myself or to the party who accepts assignment below.

SIGNED _____   DATE _____

13. INSURED'S OR AUTHORIZED PERSON'S SIGNATURE I authorize payment of medical benefits to the undersigned physician or supplier for services described below.

SIGNED _____

14. DATE OF CURRENT: MM 02 DD 03 YY 20YY ILLNESS (First symptom) OR INJURY (Accident) OR PREGNANCY (LMP)

15. IF PATIENT HAS HAD SAME OR SIMILAR ILLNESS, GIVE FIRST DATE MM DD YY

16. DATES PATIENT UNABLE TO WORK IN CURRENT OCCUPATION FROM MM DD YY TO MM DD YY

17. NAME OF REFERRING PROVIDER OR OTHER SOURCE

17a.
17b. NPI

18. HOSPITALIZATION DATES RELATED TO CURRENT SERVICES FROM MM DD YY TO MM DD YY

19. RESERVED FOR LOCAL USE

20. OUTSIDE LAB? ☐ YES ☐ NO $ CHARGES

21. DIAGNOSIS OR NATURE OF ILLNESS OR INJURY (Relate Items 1, 2, 3, or 4 to Item 24E by Line)
1. 782 . 1
2. ___ . ___
3. ___ . ___
4. ___ . ___

22. MEDICAID RESUBMISSION CODE   ORIGINAL REF. NO.

23. PRIOR AUTHORIZATION NUMBER

24. A. DATE(S) OF SERVICE From MM DD YY — To MM DD YY	B. PLACE OF SERVICE	C. EMG	D. PROCEDURES, SERVICES, OR SUPPLIES (Explain Unusual Circumstances) CPT/HCPCS — MODIFIER	E. DIAGNOSIS POINTER	F. $ CHARGES	G. DAYS OR UNITS	H. EPSDT Family Plan	I. ID. QUAL.	J. RENDERING PROVIDER ID. #
02 03 YY 02 03 YY	11	N	99212	1	45 00	1		NPI	7890123456
								NPI	
								NPI	
								NPI	
								NPI	
								NPI	

25. FEDERAL TAX I.D. NUMBER SSN ☐ EIN ☒
494134726

26. PATIENT'S ACCOUNT NO.
277885

27. ACCEPT ASSIGNMENT? (For govt. claims, see back) ☐ YES ☐ NO

28. TOTAL CHARGE $ 45 00

29. AMOUNT PAID $ 0 00

30. BALANCE DUE $ 45 00

31. SIGNATURE OF PHYSICIAN OR SUPPLIER INCLUDING DEGREES OR CREDENTIALS (I certify that the statements on the reverse apply to this bill and are made a part thereof.)
SIGNATURE ON FILE
SIGNED _____   DATE _____

32. SERVICE FACILITY LOCATION INFORMATION
OUTREACH CLINIC
608 SAGEBUSH
DESERT AZ 69075
a. 7770123456   b.

33. BILLING PROVIDER INFO & PH # (822) 7529118
OUTREACH CLINIC
608 SAGEBUSH
DESERT AZ 69075
a. 7770123456   b.

NUCC Instruction Manual available at: www.nucc.org

APPROVED OMB-0938-0999 FORM CMS-1500 (08-05)

Figure 13–2 CMS-1500 Medicaid as Secondary Payer

In the unusual circumstance when the Medicaid recipient has more than one private or group insurance plan, including Medicare, a claim must be submitted to both insurance plans *before* a claim is submitted to Medicaid. Once payment is received from both payers, the billing specialist submits a claim to Medicaid under any one of the conditions previously cited. The billing specialist completes another CMS-1500 for Medicaid, attaches the EOBs from both payers, and submits the claim to the Medicaid fiscal agent. Information for the primary private or group health plan is entered in blocks 11–11d, and information for the second private or group health plan is entered in blocks 9–9d. Complete blocks 9–9d as follows:

Block 9	Enter the insured's name for the secondary commercial or private insurance plan.
Block 9a	Enter the secondary insurance plan policy or group number.
Block 9b	Enter the insured's eight-digit birth date. Enter an X in the appropriate gender box.
Block 9c	Enter the employer name or school name, if applicable.
Block 9d	Enter the plan or program name of the secondary insurance plan.

© 2014 Cengage Learning, All Rights Reserved.

In addition to completing blocks 9–9d, the insurance billing specialist enters the total amount received from both payers in block 29. The remaining CMS-1500 blocks are completed according to Medicaid as secondary payer guidelines.

Medicare/Medicaid Crossover Program

The Medicare/Medicaid Crossover Program (MCD) is a combination of the Medicare and Medicaid programs. This plan is available to Medicare-eligible individuals who also qualify for Medicaid. This program is sometimes called Medi/Medi, Care/Caid, or 18/19 claims. The 18/19 name refers to Title 18 (Medicare) and Title 19 (Medicaid) of the Social Security Act.

When a patient qualifies for both Medicare and Medicaid, the billing specialist submits the claim to the Medicare insurance carrier. The CMS-1500 is completed according to Medicare guidelines, with the following changes:

- Enter an X in Medicare and Medicaid in block 1.
- Enter the initials MCD and the patient's Medicaid ID number in block 10d.

MCD indicates that the claim should be handled as a Medicare/Medicaid crossover. The billing specialist ensures that the claim is filed within the stated deadline. Most Medicare/Medicaid crossover claims follow the Medicare filing deadline, which is December 31 of the year following the date of service. In some states, crossover claims are submitted within the Medicaid filing deadline.

The Medicare insurance carrier pays its portion of the claim and then electronically transfers the claim to the Medicaid fiscal agent. The provider receives payment from Medicare and Medicaid for services covered by each program.

The provider must accept assignment for Medicare/Medicaid crossover claims. If assignment is not accepted, the Medicare payment is usually sent to the patient. The Medicaid payment is either sent to the patient or denied, according to state Medicaid policy.

Processing Medicaid Payments

Medicaid payments are sent directly to the provider. The billing specialist receives a remittance advice (RA), which is a detailed explanation of claims denial or approval, sometimes called an EOB. Many providers still use the term "EOB," although "remittance advice" is more current.

The RA lists the payment activity for several patients. Payment activity falls under these categories: adjustment, approval, denial, suspension, and audit/refund. Most states use these or similar terms to describe how payment decisions are made. Table 13–2 provides a brief description of each payment activity category.

Claims are rarely paid without some of them being adjusted, denied, or suspended. Figure 13–3 is a sample Medicaid RA form.

TABLE 13–2

Medicaid Payment Activities		
Payment Activity	**Description**	**Example**
Adjustment	Adjustments are made to the approved Medicaid fee. Reasons for the adjustment are explained or coded on the RA form.	Provider was overpaid or underpaid for services rendered to a specific patient. The adjustment is made on the next claim submitted for that patient.
Approval	Payment is made at the maximum allowable Medicaid rate.	Provider receives the allowed Medicaid payment, with no adjustments.
Denial	Denial of the approved Medicaid fee is noted, with an explanation, on the RA form.	Reasons for denial include that the service is not covered by Medicaid, claims submission errors, the patient is no longer eligible for Medicaid, and required or requested documentation was not attached to the claim.
Suspension	Payment is suspended while the claim is being reviewed; this is neither an approval nor a denial. An explanation is included on the RA form.	Suspension occurs when a procedure or service is questioned but cannot be summarily denied, additional documentation is needed, or administrative problems prevent the timely payment of claims.

| MEDICAID
REMITTANCE ADVICE | | | | | | Roberta Pharyngeal MD
714 Hennepin Avenue
Blueberry, ME 49855 | |

PROVIDER NUMBER RBP74911	CLAIM TYPE MEDICAL		CHECK NUMBER 490678	DATE 05/01/20xx		PAGE 1 of 2 pages	
RECIPIENT NAME	RECIPIENT MEDICAID ID NO.	SERVICE DATE	PROCEDURE CODE	AMOUNT BILLED	AMOUNT ALLOWED	AMOUNT PAID	EXPL. CODE
APPROVED CLAIMS							
ACE, Wm.	730698276	02/10/20xx	99214	60.00	51.00	51.00	
	730698276	02/10/20xx	93000	20.00	16.22	16.22	
	730698276	02/10/20xx	G0001	3.00	0.00	0.00	0499
			TOTAL	83.00	67.22	67.22	
DUECE, M	841709387	02/11/20xx	99214	60.00	51.00	51.00	
			TOTAL	60.00	51.00	51.00	
			TOTAL FOR APPROVED	140.00	118.22	118.22	
DENIED CLAIMS							
TREY, R	942810498	02/12/20xx	99214	60.00			0401
	942810498	02/12/20xx	85025	36.75			
			TOTAL FOR DENIED	96.75			
SUSPENDED CLAIMS							
QUIP, L	053921309	02/13/20xx	99213	41.00			0399
	053921309	02/13/20xx	85027	26.25			0399
			TOTAL	67.25			
RAYS, P	164032410	02/15/20xx	99213	41.00			0399
SETH, M	275143521	02/15/20xx	45330	106.27			0399
	275143521	02/15/20xx	85025	36.75			0399
			TOTAL	143.02			
			TOTAL SUSPENDED	251.27			

EXPLANATION OF DENIAL, SUSPENSION, ADJUSTMENT CODES

0499 SERVICE NOT COVERED BY MEDICAID
0401 PATIENT NOT ELIGIBLE FOR MEDICAID
0399 ADDITIONAL DOCUMENTATION UNDER REVIEW

Figure 13–3 Medicaid Remittance Advice

REINFORCEMENT EXERCISES 13–2

Write True or False on the line following each statement.

1. Providers who treat Medicaid patients are obligated by law to accept assignment.
   _____

2. Medicaid does not offer coverage under HMOs or PPOs. _____

3. Medicaid is a social welfare program. _____

4. Physicians are obligated to treat a certain number of Medicaid recipients.
   _____

5. Medicaid is the payer of last resort. _____

Provide a short answer for each item.

1. List three situations that prompt a Medicaid claims submission when the patient has other health insurance.

   _____

   _____

   _____

2. Briefly define the Medicare/Medicaid Crossover Program.

   _____

   _____

   _____

3. Describe the unique characteristic of the Medicare/Medicaid Crossover Program.

   _____

   _____

   _____

4. List three reasons a provider may choose not to participate in Medicaid programs.

   _____

   _____

   _____

 ABBREVIATIONS

Table 13–3 lists the abbreviations presented in this chapter.

TABLE 13–3

Abbreviations and Meanings	
Abbreviation	**Meaning**
EOB	explanation of benefits
EPSDT	Early and Periodic Screening, Diagnosis, and Treatment Services
HICN	health insurance claim number (Medicare)
HMO	health maintenance organization
MCD	Medicare/Medicaid Crossover Program
PPO	preferred provider organization
QMB	qualified Medicare beneficiary
RA	remittance advice
SCHIP	State Children's Health Insurance Program
SSI	Supplemental Security Income
TANF	Temporary Assistance for Needy Families

 SUMMARY

Medicaid is a joint venture between federal and state governments that provides health insurance for specific populations, such as individuals and families with low incomes, aged and disabled persons, and persons covered by Temporary Assistance for Needy Families (TANF).

Medicaid coverage varies from state to state, but basic health services are a feature of all Medicaid programs. Medicaid participants pay no premiums for the coverage, and there are usually no deductibles or co-payments. Most Medicaid claims are filed by using the CMS-1500 claim form.

Medicaid is the payer of last resort. Therefore, other insurance programs are billed first. When a patient has both Medicare and Medicaid, information is electronically exchanged between the Medicare and Medicaid insurance carriers.

 REVIEW EXERCISES

CASE STUDY

Read the following case study. From the information provided, complete a CMS-1500 claim form for Medicaid submission. Your instructor can tell you where to obtain the form.

NAME: Ralph English
DOB: 10/3/1952
ADDRESS: 1312 W. Easterday, Blueberry, ME 49855
PHONE: (H) (906) 555-4444; (W) (906) 555-7777
SPOUSE: Rita English

continued on the next page

continued from the previous page

INSURANCE: Medicaid; ID: 3689964123
Superiorland Clinic
714 Hennepin Ave.
Blueberry, ME 49855
PHONE: (906) 336-4600
Tax ID #: 49-4134726
Superiorland Clinic NPI: 4567890123
Elizabeth Foy NPI: 7890123456
PROGRESS NOTE
Date: July 7, 20yy

Ralph is seen today with complaints of difficulty breathing, low-grade fever, and fatigue. On examination, his blood pressure was 140/80, and he appeared to be in some respiratory distress. Chest sounds were consistent with bronchitis. I recommended rest, fluids, and a nonaspirin pain reliever. In addition, I prescribed clarithromycin 300 mg b.i.d. for 10 days. Ralph is to call if his symptoms worsen. Return in two weeks for follow-up.
SIGNED: Elizabeth Foy, MD
OFFICE VISIT: 99212; $40
DIAGNOSIS: acute bronchitis; 466.0 (ICD-10-CM J20)

Abbreviations

Spell out each abbreviation.

1. TANF _____

2. SCHIP _____

3. EPSDT _____

4. QMB _____

5. SSI _____

Fill in the Blank

1. _____ is a joint federal and state government health insurance program.

2. Individuals enrolled in Medicaid programs are known as _____ .

3. A(n) _____ is any federal/state health insurance that is intended to provide additional Medicaid services to Medicaid recipients.

4. Providers who _____ in the Medicaid program must accept Medicaid fees as payment in full.

5. Medicaid insurance carriers are also called _____ .

6. A(n) _____ -digit number is used to enter the patients' birth dates on the CMS-1500.

7. A copy of the primary payer's _____ must be attached to the CMS-1500 when submitting the claim to Medicaid.

8. Medicaid is the _____ of last resort.

9. The initials MCD in block 10d of the CMS-1500 mean the claim is a(n) _____.

10. A detailed explanation of Medicaid claims denial or approval is called a(n) _____.

Multiple Choice

Circle the correct answer from the choices provided.

1. A provider may choose not to participate in Medicaid because

   a. Medicaid is a welfare program.

   b. participation is limited to physicians.

   c. payments are sent directly to the patient.

   d. reimbursement is limited.

2. The Medicaid remittance advice form

   a. is sent to the patient.

   b. lists the payment activity for several patients.

   c. provides claims submission guidelines.

   d. defines eligibility requirements for Medicaid.

3. Titles 18, 19, and 21 are

   a. amendments to the Social Security Act.

   b. a series of references for federal insurance programs.

   c. numeric references to special Medicare guidelines.

   d. Medicaid laws enacted by Congress.

4. Medicaid is the secondary payer

   a. when the primary payer denies payment for services.

   b. never because Medicaid is the payer of last resort.

   c. after the patient pays the first $50 of any charges.

   d. after a claim is submitted to the SCHIP program.

5. Which service is *not* covered under the Medicaid EPSDT program?

   a. pediatric examinations for children

   b. family planning

   c. amniocentesis to detect birth defects

   d. vision screening for children

6. Under the SCHIP program,

   a. patients must chip in to pay for health care services.

   b. families must qualify for TANF.

   c. states are encouraged to expand health insurance programs for children.

   d. parents receive additional funds for child care expenses.

7. Individuals enrolled in Medicaid programs are called

   a. patients.

   b. recipients.

   c. members.

   d. subscribers.

8. Current Medicaid billing instructions are obtained from

   a. other providers who participate in Medicaid.

   b. the Medicaid information center in Washington, D.C.

   c. the state insurance commission.

   d. the Medicaid insurance carrier.

9. Suspension of Medicaid payment occurs when

   a. additional documentation is needed.

   b. the provider's charge exceeds the Medicaid fee.

   c. the service is not covered by Medicaid.

   d. the patient's income exceeds Medicaid limits.

CHALLENGE ACTIVITIES

1. Create a grid that compares how the CMS-1500 is completed block by block for Medicaid and private or commercial insurance programs. What are the main differences? Which blocks are the same?

2. Find out the name of the state agency in your area that administers the Medicaid program. Obtain a copy of the Medicaid application form and fill it out. Is the form complicated? Which questions are the most unusual? Do you think any questions are unnecessary? Ask your instructor if you can discuss the application form in class.

WEBSITES

Centers for Medicare and Medicaid Services: http://www.cms.hhs.gov/Medicaid
MIChild (Michigan): http://www.michigan.gov/mdch

CHAPTER 14

TRICARE and CHAMPVA

LEARNING OBJECTIVES

Upon successful completion of this chapter, the reader should have the knowledge to:

1. Define all terms and abbreviations presented in the chapter.
2. Describe the difference between TRICARE and CHAMPVA.
3. Identify four eligibility requirements each for TRICARE and CHAMPVA.
4. Accurately complete the CMS-1500 according to TRICARE and CHAMPVA guidelines.
5. List three distinguishing characteristics of TRICARE Standard, TRICARE Prime, and TRICARE Extra.

 ## KEY TERMS

Active duty service member
(ADSM)
Allowable charge
Authorized provider
Beneficiary
CHAMPUS Maximum
Allowable Charge
(CMAC)
Civilian Health and Medical
Program of the Uniformed
Services (CHAMPUS)
Civilian Health and
Medical Program of the
Veterans Administration
(CHAMPVA)
Cost sharing
Defense Enrollment Eligibility
and Reporting System
(DEERS)

Department of Defense (DoD)
Durable medical equipment
(DME)
Health Administration Center
(HAC)
Health care finder
Limited charge
Locality code
Maximum allowable charge
Military treatment facility
(MTF)
National Oceanic
and Atmospheric
Administration (NOAA)
North Atlantic Treaty
Organization (NATO)
Other health insurance (OHI)
Primary care manager
(PCM)

Program Integrity Office
Sponsor
TRICARE
TRICARE contractor
TRICARE Extra
TRICARE for Life (TFL)
TRICARE Management
Agency (TMA)
TRICARE Prime
TRICARE Prime Remote
(TPR)
TRICARE Reserve Select
(TRS)
TRICARE Retired Reserve
(TRR)
TRICARE Standard
TRICARE Young Adult (TYA)
Uniformed services
Veteran

OVERVIEW

In 1966, Congress created the Civilian Health and Medical Program of the Uniformed Services (CHAMPUS), a federally funded comprehensive health benefits program for dependents of personnel serving in the uniformed services. Uniformed services include the Army, Navy, Air Force, Marines, Coast Guard, Public Health Service, National Oceanic and Atmospheric Administration (NOAA), and the North Atlantic Treaty Organization (NATO). In 1993, the Department of Defense (DoD) changed the name from CHAMPUS to TRICARE. TRICARE is a health insurance program available to active duty members, retirees, and their dependents. Table 14–1 lists TRICARE programs and includes a brief description for each program.

TABLE 14–1

TRICARE Programs	
Program	Description
TRICARE Prime	A managed care program that allows beneficiaries to receive services from a military treatment facility (MTF) or contracted civilian medical providers in a preferred provider network (PPN)
TRICARE Prime Remote (TPR)	A program for active duty service members (ADSMs) living and working in remote locations and eligible family members living with the active duty member; similar to TRICARE Prime
TRICARE Standard/Extra	A fee-for-service program that allows beneficiaries the most flexibility when choosing a provider; a discount is available for using providers in a PPN
TRICARE Reserve Select (TRS)	A premium-based health insurance plan for qualified National Guard and Reserve members and their families; monthly premiums, annual deductibles, and cost-shares apply
TRICARE Retired Reserve (TRR)	A premium-based health insurance plan for qualified retired Reserve members and their families; monthly premiums, annual deductibles, and cost-shares apply
TRICARE Young Adult (TYA)—**Prime/Prime Remote**	A premium-based, managed care health insurance plan that qualified young adults under the age 26 may purchase; monthly premiums apply; coverage is the same as TRICARE Prime and TPR
TRICARE Young Adult (TYA)—**Standard/Extra**	A fee-for-service health insurance plan that qualified young adults under the age 26 may purchase; monthly premiums apply; coverage is the same as TRICARE Standard/Extra
TRICARE for Life (TFL)	A Medicare supplement program available to beneficiaries who are eligible for Medicare Part A and are enrolled in Medicare Part B

The Civilian Health and Medical Program of the Veterans Administration (CHAMPVA) is a health insurance program for:

- dependent spouses and children of disabled veterans
- surviving spouses and dependent children of veterans who died in the line of duty
- surviving spouses and dependent children of veterans who died as a result of disabilities connected to the uniformed services

Because CHAMPVA and TRICARE are associated with members of the uniformed services and their dependents, the programs are often mistaken for each other. The programs are completely separate and serve totally different beneficiary populations. Information about CHAMPVA is presented later in this chapter. Individuals who are part of TRICARE are not eligible for CHAMPVA.

Dependents eligible for TRICARE or CHAMPVA are called beneficiaries. The ADSM is called the sponsor. A veteran is an individual who served in the U.S. armed forces, is no longer in the service, and was honorably discharged.

 TRICARE HEALTH BENEFITS PROGRAMS

Four TRICARE programs are discussed in this chapter: TRICARE Prime, TRICARE Standard, TRICARE Extra, and TFL.

TRICARE Prime

Under TRICARE Prime, most health care services are provided by a military treatment facility (MTF). Additional services, when necessary, are provided by the TRICARE contractor's PPN. Active duty personnel must enroll in TRICARE Prime. Enrollment is accomplished by registering with the Defense Enrollment Eligibility and Reporting System (DEERS). The DEERS is a worldwide, computerized database of uniformed services members (sponsors), their family members, and others who are eligible for TRICARE and other military benefits. Other individuals who may enroll in TRICARE Prime include:

- Family members and survivors of active duty personnel
- Retirees and their family members and survivors under age 65

Individuals enrolled in TRICARE Prime are assigned a primary care manager (PCM), who coordinates the individual's care, maintains health records, and makes referrals to specialists.

Civilian health care providers can receive reimbursement for treating TRICARE Prime beneficiaries under the following circumstances:

- The civilian health care provider is a member of the TRICARE contractor's PPN.
- The PCM refers the beneficiary to a civilian provider.
- Emergency treatment is needed, and the civilian emergency room is the nearest available facility.
- The beneficiary chooses a civilian health care provider without the PCM's approval.

If a beneficiary seeks treatment from a civilian provider without approval, the beneficiary is responsible for 50% of the cost of the service after the deductible is met.

TRICARE Standard

TRICARE Standard is the basic health insurance plan available to non–active duty beneficiaries. It allows the most flexibility for choosing providers. Under this plan, the beneficiary receives treatment from any authorized provider or preferred provider. An authorized provider is a hospital, institution, physician, or other professional who meets the licensing and certification requirements of TRICARE and is practicing within the scope of that license. A preferred provider is enrolled in TRICARE's PPN. Out-of-pocket expenses are higher with TRICARE Standard than with TRICARE Prime or TRICARE Extra. However, beneficiaries receive a discount for out-of-pocket expenses when they receive treatment from a preferred provider.

TRICARE Extra

Under TRICARE Extra, beneficiaries must choose health care providers who are listed in the TRICARE *Provider Directory*. TRICARE Extra is an option available to all individuals who are eligible for TRICARE Standard. Active duty personnel are not eligible for TRICARE Standard and therefore are not eligible for TRICARE Extra. Civilian health care providers who are listed in the TRICARE *Provider Directory* are reimbursed for providing treatment for TRICARE Extra enrollees.

TRICARE for Life

TFL is a Medicare supplement plan that helps minimize the beneficiary's out-of-pocket expenses. TFL is available to TRICARE beneficiaries who are eligible for premium-free Medicare Part A and who are enrolled in Medicare Part B.

In most cases, Medicare is the primary payer and TFL is the secondary payer. After Medicare pays its portion of a claim, TFL is billed for the remaining portion. Medicare determines whether or not a service is/was medically necessary. If Medicare denies payment based on medical necessity, TFL will not pay for the service.

Services that are covered only by Medicare, such as chiropractic care, cannot be billed to TFL. When services are covered only by TFL, its the primary payer, unless the beneficiary is covered by other health insurance (OHI).

Table 14–2 summarizes the eligibility requirements for TRICARE Prime, TRICARE Standard, TRICARE Extra, and TFL.

TABLE 14–2

TRICARE Program Eligibility	
Program	Eligibility
TRICARE Prime	**Active duty service members (ADSMs)** • Family members and survivors of ADSMs • Retirees and their family members and survivors under age 65 • National Guard and Reserve members called to active duty for more than 30 consecutive days
TRICARE Standard and TRICARE Extra	• Family members and survivors of ADSMs • Retirees and their family members and survivors • Family members of National Guard and Reserve members called to active duty for more than 30 consecutive days
TRICARE for Life (TFL)	TRICARE beneficiaries with Medicare Part A and Medicare Part B

REINFORCEMENT EXERCISES 14–1

Spell out each abbreviation.

1. DoD

_____

2. NATO

_____

3. CHAMPVA

_____

4. MTF

_____

5. PCM

_____

6. DEERS

_____

7. TFL

_____

8. ADSM

_____

Provide a short answer for each item.

1. Describe the difference between TRICARE Prime and TRICARE Standard.

_____

_____

2. Describe the difference between TRICARE Standard and TRICARE for Life.

_____

_____

3. What is the purpose of DEERS?

_____

_____

DEERS ENROLLMENT AND TRICARE REIMBURSEMENT

DEERS is a database used to verify beneficiary eligibility. The billing specialist asks patients with TRICARE coverage if they are enrolled in DEERS. According to the Federal Privacy Act, providers may not access beneficiary information on DEERS. If the patient is not sure about enrollment, the billing specialist makes a telephone available so the patient can call DEERS. TRICARE claims processors (insurance carriers) will verify eligibility via DEERS before reimbursement is sent to the provider.

TRICARE reimbursement is affected by the following:

- Participating versus nonparticipating provider status
- Covered and noncovered services
- Prior authorization for some services
- Durable medical equipment criteria
- Verification of TRICARE eligibility
- Deductibles and cost sharing, which is the same as co-payment and co-insurance
- Allowable charge and CHAMPUS Maximum Allowable Charge (CMAC), which is the maximum amount TRICARE will pay for a service
- Timely claims submission
- Fraud and abuse

These topics are covered throughout the remainder of this chapter.

Participating and Nonparticipating Providers

TRICARE Standard encourages providers to participate in the program and accept assignment. The provider agrees to accept the TRICARE-determined allowable charge as the full fee, even if it is less than the billed amount. TRICARE Standard pays the allowable charge, less the patient cost-share and outpatient deductible. The cost-share is a specific dollar amount or percentage that the patient must pay for the service. Cost-shares and deductibles are called out-of-pocket expenses. Payment is sent directly to the provider. Participation can be on a case-by-case basis. Participating providers may charge the patient for noncovered services.

When a provider agrees to participate, first determine if the service is covered. For covered services, the billing specialist requests that the cost sharing amount be paid at the time of service. The balance is submitted to the TRICARE insurance carrier. For noncovered services, the billing specialist informs the patient that he or she is responsible for the bill.

Nonparticipating providers may or may not submit the insurance claim for TRICARE beneficiaries. If the nonparticipating provider does not submit the claim, payment is sent to the beneficiary. By federal law, nonparticipating providers may charge 15% more than the TRICARE allowable charge, which is called the limited charge. The TRICARE beneficiary pays this charge.

> **EXAMPLE**
>
> Sara's father is a retired army colonel. She is covered by TRICARE Standard and had her tonsils removed as an outpatient. The allowable charge for tonsillectomy is $500. Sara's surgeon is a nonparticipating provider and charges $600 for this service. The surgeon is allowed to charge the TRICARE beneficiary 15% more than the allowable charge, which is $75. Therefore, the limited charge for this service is $575.

In this case, the co-payment is 20% of the allowable charge, which is $100; 15% of the allowable charge is $75. Sara's parents must pay $175 out of pocket. The remaining $400 is billed to TRICARE. The surgeon receives a total of $575 for the procedure and cannot bill Sara's parents for the remaining $25. If the provider's office submits the claim, payment is sent directly to the provider. Otherwise, payment is sent to the beneficiary, and the provider must bill the patient.

By participating in TRICARE, providers have the benefit of collecting payment directly from the insurance carrier. The costs related to billing the patient are minimized.

Covered and Noncovered Services

It is impossible to list all TRICARE covered and noncovered services. Table 14–3 lists examples of covered services. Table 14–4 lists examples of noncovered services. Note that some covered services are limited.

TABLE 14–3

TRICARE Standard Covered Services			
Service	Limits	Service	Limits
Ambulance		Maternity care	
Ambulatory surgery		Medical supplies and dressings	
Anesthesia		Mental health care	Yes
Breast reconstruction	Yes	Morbid obesity	Yes
Chronic renal disease		Outpatient care	
Consultation services		Oxygen	
CT scans		Pap smears	Yes
Diagnostic testing		Percutaneous transluminal coronary angioplasty	
Durable medical equipment		Physical therapy	
Family planning; prescription contraceptives		Prescription drugs and medicines	
Free-standing birthing centers		Prosthetic devices	
Hospice	Yes	Speech therapy	Yes
Immunizations	Yes	Sterilization	
Inpatient care		Radiation therapy services	
In-home cardio-respiratory monitors		Surgery (preoperative and postoperative care)	
Laboratory and pathology		Transplants	Yes
Magnetic resonance imaging	Yes	Well-child care (birth to 17 years)	
Mammograms	Yes	X-ray services	

TABLE 14–4

TRICARE Noncovered Services			
Service	Exceptions	Service	Exceptions
Acupuncture		Naturopaths	
Anesthesia by surgeon		Routine physical exams	Yes
Artificial insemination		Radial keratotomy	
Breast reduction or augmentation (cosmetic purposes)		Routine foot care	
Cosmetic surgery	Yes	Sterilization reversal	
Custodial care		Vitamins	
Domiciliary care		Weight reduction programs	
Electrolysis		Unproven procedures or treatments	
Exercise programs			

© 2014 Cengage Learning, All Rights Reserved.

EXAMPLE

Breast reconstruction: Limited to reconstruction necessary because a mastectomy was performed due to breast cancer. Breast reconstruction for cosmetic purposes would not be a covered service.

There may be limits on the number of services, such as with Pap smears. For a healthy individual, TRICARE may pay for an annual Pap smear. When the initial Pap is abnormal, follow-up exams may be covered. The most current information about covered services, including any limits, is available from the TRICARE regional administrator or in the TRICARE *Provider Manual*.

Noncovered services are not payable by TRICARE. However, there are exceptions. Table 14–4 identifies cosmetic surgery and routine physical exams as noncovered services that may at times be covered by TRICARE.

EXAMPLE

Blepharoplasty, surgical repair of the eyelid, is often done for cosmetic purposes, such as achieving a more youthful appearance. However, if blepharoplasty is done to correct or repair a defect of the eyelid, TRICARE may cover part of the cost.

As with covered services, information about exceptions to noncovered services is available from the TRICARE regional administrator or in the *Provider Manual*. Participating providers receive a copy of and updates to the *Provider Manual*.

Preauthorization

TRICARE Standard requires preauthorization for a number of procedures. Table 14–5 lists examples of some of the procedures requiring preauthorization. The list is not all-inclusive. High-cost procedures usually require preauthorization. The insurance carrier or health care finder—a health

TABLE 14–5

Procedures Requiring TRICARE Preauthorization	
Arthroscopy (shoulder, elbow, wrist, knee, ligament, ankle)	Laparoscopic cholecystectomy
Breast mass or tumor excision	Ligation/transection of fallopian tubes
Cardiac catheterization	Magnetic resonance imaging
Cataract removal	Myringotomy or tympanostomy
Cystoscopy	Neuroplasty
Diagnostic laparoscopy	Rhinoplasty or septoplasty
D&C for diagnostic or therapeutic reasons	Strabismus repair
Hernia repair	Tonsillectomy or adenoidectomy

© 2014 Cengage Learning, All Rights Reserved.

care specialist who assists beneficiaries and providers with preauthorizations—can provide information about the preauthorization status of a specific procedure.

TRICARE Standard does not provide preauthorization for cosmetic, plastic, or reconstructive surgery. These types of surgery are covered when the purpose is:

- To restore function
- To correct a serious birth defect
- To restore body form or structure after an accidental injury
- To improve appearance after severe disfigurement or extensive scarring from surgery or cancer
- For breast reconstruction following a mastectomy

Additional documentation establishing the medical necessity for cosmetic, plastic, or reconstructive procedures may be required when submitting a claim.

Durable Medical Equipment (DME)

According to TRICARE guidelines, durable medical equipment (DME) is equipment that improves function, prevents further deterioration of a physical condition, and provides a medical function and not simply transportation. DME examples include wheelchairs, prostheses, oxygen, and braces.

Items such as eyeglasses, contact lenses, hearing aids, and other communication devices do not qualify for reimbursement as DME. Other noncovered items include exercise equipment, spas, whirlpools, hot tubs, swimming pools, or similar equipment. Air conditioners, humidifiers, dehumidifiers, and air filters are also excluded.

Providers who supply DME as rentals, lease/purchases, or outright purchases may be reimbursed by TRICARE Standard. To receive payment, the DME must meet the following criteria:

- The allowable charge must exceed $100.
- It must be medically necessary for the treatment of a covered illness or injury.

- It must improve the function of a malformed, diseased, or injured body part or prevent further deterioration of the patient's physical condition.
- It must be patient-specific.
- It must be primarily and customarily used to serve a medical purpose. The equipment is not covered if used primarily for transportation, comfort, or convenience.
- It must withstand repeated use.
- It is not for a patient in a facility that provides or can provide the equipment.
- It is not available from a local uniformed service medical facility.
- It cannot be a luxury or deluxe model of the needed equipment.

DME must be prescribed by a physician or an authorized health care professional. TRICARE also shares the cost of repairing a DME already owned by the patient as long as the equipment continues to be medically necessary. The patient's attending physician must provide a signed and dated statement with the claim for DME repair. The statement must include the patient's diagnosis, the nature of the required repair, and the estimated length of time the equipment will be needed. In addition, the cost must be less than the rental or lease/purchase of a new item, and the need for repair must not be due to willful or malicious conduct on the part of the patient.

REINFORCEMENT EXERCISES 14–2

Fill in the blank.

1. _____ providers agree to accept the TRICARE allowable charge as payment in full.

2. Wheelchairs and prostheses are examples of _____.

3. _____ providers are subject to the limited charge for a given service or procedure.

4. Participating providers may charge the patient for _____ services.

Provide a short answer for each item.

1. List three conditions under which TRICARE Standard covers cosmetic surgery.

_____

_____

_____

2. Define "durable medical equipment."

_____

_____

_____

continued on the next page

continued from the previous page

3. Identify five items that do *not* qualify as durable medical equipment.

_____

_____

_____

_____

_____

4. List three items that qualify as durable medical equipment.

_____

_____

_____

TRICARE BILLING

Participating providers are required to file insurance claims for TRICARE beneficiaries. Nonparticipating providers may or may not file the insurance claim. If the nonparticipating provider does not file the claim, the payment is sent to the beneficiary. TRICARE claims must be filed within one year from the date a service is provided or within one year from a patient's discharge from an inpatient facility. Claims received by the TRICARE contractor after the filing deadline are denied, unless there is sufficient evidence to grant an exception. Examples of exceptions to the deadline are listed in Table 14–6.

TABLE 14–6

Exceptions to TRICARE Filing Deadlines	
Exception	**Description/Documentation**
Retroactive eligibility	The uniformed service makes this determination, and the provider submits a copy of the decision with the claim.
Administrative error	The TRICARE contractor delays the claim. A copy of the letter, report, or statement explaining the error must accompany the provider's claim.
Mental incompetency	The patient is or was mentally incompetent and does not have a legal representative. A physician's statement attesting to the mental incompetency must accompany the claim.
Adequate access to care	The patient's access to care, based on procedure code and locality, delayed claims processing.
Primary payer delay	Payment from the primary payer delays the timely submission of the TRICARE claim. The EOB from the primary payer must accompany the provider's TRICARE claim. The TRICARE claim must be submitted within 90 days of the primary payer's final action on the claim.

TABLE 14–7

TRICARE Regions, Contractors, and States		
Region	**Contractor**	**States/Areas**
North	Health Net Federal Services (http://www.hnfs.com)	Connecticut, Delaware, District of Columbia, Illinois, Indiana, Iowa (Rock Island area), Kentucky (except Fort Campbell), Maine, Maryland, Massachusetts, Michigan, Missouri (St. Louis area), New Hampshire, New Jersey, New York, North Carolina, Ohio, Pennsylvania, Rhode Island, Vermont, Virginia, West Virginia, and Wisconsin
South	Humana Military Healthcare Services, Inc. (http://www.humana-military.com)	Alabama, Arkansas, Florida, Georgia, Louisiana, Mississippi, Oklahoma, South Carolina, Tennessee, Texas (excluding the El Paso area), and Fort Campbell, Kentucky
West	TriWest Healthcare Alliance (http://www.triwest.com)	Alaska, Arizona, California, Colorado, Hawaii, Idaho, Iowa (except Rock Island Arsenal area), Kansas, Minnesota, Missouri (except St. Louis area), Montana, Nebraska, Nevada, New Mexico, North Dakota, Oregon, South Dakota, Texas (southwestern corner, including El Paso), Utah, Washington, and Wyoming
Outside the United States	International SOS (http://www.tricare-overseas.com)	Eurasia-Africa Area, Latin America and Canada Area, and Pacific Area

© 2014 Cengage Learning, All Rights Reserved.

The billing specialist submits claims to the TRICARE contractor in the designated TRICARE region. The TRICARE contractor is similar to an insurance carrier. TRICARE contractors are responsible for enrollment, care authorization, and processing claims in one of four regions. Three regions are in the United States and the fourth region covers overseas beneficiaries. The U.S. TRICARE contractors at the time of publication are listed in Table 14–7.

Deductibles, Cost Sharing, and Allowable Charges

Provider reimbursement under TRICARE Standard depends on the patient's deductible, the cost-share amount, and the TRICARE allowable charge. The TRICARE allowable charge is the payment to providers that is the lower amount between the provider's fee and the maximum allowable charge. The maximum allowable charge, also called the CMAC, is the most TRICARE Standard will allow for a procedure or service. Examples A and B illustrate the determination of the TRICARE allowable charge.

> **EXAMPLE A: PROVIDER CHARGE HIGHER THAN ALLOWABLE FEE**
> Dr. Johnson's fee for diabetic testing is $50. The CMAC for diabetic testing is $40. In this example, the TRICARE Standard allowable charge for diabetic testing is $40, which is the lower amount between the provider's fee and the maximum allowable charge.

EXAMPLE B: PROVIDER CHARGE LOWER THAN ALLOWABLE FEE

Dr. McMiller's fee for diabetic testing is $30. The CMAC for diabetic testing is $40. In this example, the TRICARE Standard allowable charge is $30 because the provider's fee is the lower amount.

The billing specialist can find the maximum allowable charge for provider services by using the CMAC System. Carefully read the following example, which is a step-by-step procedure for the CMAC System. If you have access to the Internet, go to http://www.tricare.mil/CMAC/home.aspx and then follow the instructions in the example.

EXAMPLE

1. First Screen: Copyright statement for ASC Public Use and *Current Procedural Terminology* (CPT) codes. Click Accept.
2. Second Screen: Click CMAC Procedure Pricing.
3. Third Screen: CMAC Procedure Pricing and effective dates. Dialog box with five choices: Locality code; State; Catchment Area; Zip Code; Foreign Country. Only one choice is used to search for a procedure price. Enter 49855 in the Zip Code box. Click Search. (Note: In this example, 49855 is a Michigan zip code.)
4. Fourth Screen: Displays the state and a list of **locality codes** on the far left. A locality code is a three-digit number that represents a group of zip codes. If there is more than one locality code, select one for your area. (Note: In this example, there is only one locality code.) Enter the CPT code 30110 in the textbox. Click Show pricing.
5. Fifth Screen: Displays CMAC Search Results. CMAC Detail Screen for Procedure Code 30110. Pricing is listed in four different categories. Category 1: Facility Physician applies to a physician provider in a hospital setting, inpatient, outpatient, and ambulatory surgery center. Category 2: Non-Facility Physician applies to a physician provider in a nonfacility setting such as the provider's office or the patient's home. Category 3: Facility Non-Physician applies to a health care professional in a facility setting who is not a physician. Category 4: Non-Facility Non-Physician applies to a health care professional in a nonfacility setting who is not a physician. Each category has a different fee or reimbursement level.

Estimating TRICARE Payment

By using the information from the CMAC System and computing the cost-sharing percentage, the billing specialist can estimate the TRICARE payment for provider services. Figure 14–1 is an example of estimating the TRICARE payment for a participating physician. The procedure code is 30110, simple excision of nasal polyps.

Figure 14–2 is an example of estimated TRICARE payments for nonparticipating providers. Item B is the estimated payment when the patient has not met the annual deductible.

The billing specialist requests payment for the cost-share amount and the 15% adjustment. Unless the billing specialist can verify the status of the patient's deductible, the deductible cannot be collected until the TRICARE payment is received. If the provider submits the insurance claim, payment is sent to the provider. Otherwise, payment is sent to the beneficiary, and the provider must bill the patient.

Dr. Rhinehard removed nasal polyps from Ms. Wellington, a TRICARE beneficiary.
Dr. Rhinehard is a participating physician and his fee is $200.
The CMAC for excision of nasal polyps, simple (CPT code 30110) is $160.

Estimated TRICARE Payment Calculation

TRICARE allowable charge (Lower amount of physician charge and CMAC)	$160.00
Minus patient cost-share amount (20% of TRICARE allowable charge)	$ 32.00
Estimated TRICARE Payment	$128.00

The patient pays the $32 cost-share.
The billing specialist submits a claim for $128.
The payment is sent to the provider.

The difference between the physician's fee and the TRICARE allowable charge ($40) cannot be billed to the patient.

Figure 14–1 Estimated TRICARE Payment, Participating Provider

---

Procedure: Excision, nasal polyps, simple	CPT: 30110
CMAC: $160	Nonparticipating Provider Fee: $200

A. Estimated TRICARE Payment Calculation: Nonparticipating Provider

TRICARE limited charge, nonparticipating provider (CMAC + 15% of CMAC; $160 + $24 = $184)	$184.00
Minus patient cost-share amount (20% of TRICARE CMAC)	$ 32.00
Minus 15% paid by patient (Patient pays the $24)	$ 24.00
Estimated TRICARE Payment	$128.00

B. Estimated TRICARE Payment Calculation with Deductible (Nonparticipating Provider)

TRICARE limited charge, nonparticipating provider (CMAC + 15% of CMAC; $160 + $24 = $184)	$184.00
Minus patient cost-share amount (20% of TRICARE CMAC)	$ 32.00
Minus 15% paid by patient (Patient pays the $24)	$ 24.00
Minus patient deductible (Patient pays the deductible)	$ 50.00
Estimated TRICARE Payment	$ 78.00

Figure 14–2 Estimated TRICARE Payment, Nonparticipating Provider

REINFORCEMENT EXERCISES 14–3

Fill in the blank.

1. The billing specialist submits TRICARE claims to the _____.

2. The _____ is the most TRICARE Standard will pay for a procedure or service.

3. The TRICARE _____ is the lower of the provider's fee or the maximum allowable charge.

4. A TRICARE _____ code is a three-digit number that represents a group of zip codes.

5. _____ may or may not submit insurance claims for TRICARE beneficiaries.

CMS-1500 Completion for TRICARE

TRICARE claims are submitted via the CMS-1500 form. General instructions for completing the claim form are given here. A specific TRICARE contractor may have some unique variations to the general instructions. The TRICARE contractor provides specific CMS-1500 completion guidelines. When the instructions refer to the "insured," they are referring to the military sponsor. The military sponsor is the active duty, retired, or deceased service member.

Block 1	Enter an X in TRICARE/CHAMPUS.
Block 1a	Enter the sponsor's Social Security number.
Block 2	Enter the patient's name as directed on the form.
Block 3	Enter the patient's eight-digit birth date (MM/DD/YYYY). Enter an X in the appropriate gender box.
Block 4	If the sponsor is *not* the patient, enter the sponsor's name. If the sponsor is the patient, leave this blank.
Block 5	Enter the patient's address, including the zip code. Do not enter a P.O. box number.
Block 6	Enter an X in the box that best describes the patient's relationship to the sponsor.
Block 7	Enter the sponsor's address, including the zip code.
Block 8	Enter an X in the box that applies to the patient's marital, employment, or student status.
Note: Blocks 9–9d are required when the patient has another health insurance plan, as indicated by an X in block 11d.	
Block 9	Must be completed if block 11d is checked Yes. Enter the name of the person with **other health insurance (OHI)** that covers the patient.
Block 9a	Enter the policy number or group number of the other insured's policy.

continued on the next page

continued from the previous page

Block 9b	Enter the other insured's birth date and sex.
Block 9c	Enter the name of the other insured's employer or school.
Block 9d	Enter the name of the insurance plan or program name of the OHI.
Blocks 10–10c	Enter an X in Yes or No as applicable.
	If treatment is related to an automobile accident (10b), enter the two-character abbreviation for the state where the accident occurred.
Block 10d	Leave this blank.
Note: Block 11 through block 11c pertain to the sponsor, named in block 4.	
Block 11	Enter the policy group or Federal Employees' Compensation Act (FECA) number, if applicable. If TRICARE is the only insurance, enter NONE.
Block 11a	Enter the sponsor's date of birth and an X in the gender box if different from block 3.
Block 11b	Enter the sponsor's branch of service.
Block 11c	Enter TRICARE.
Block 11d	Enter an X in Yes if there is another health insurance plan that is primary to TRICARE. If Yes, complete blocks 9a–d. If TRICARE is the only insurance, enter an X in No.
Block 12	Enter SIGNATURE ON FILE if the signature is updated annually.
Block 13	Enter SIGNATURE ON FILE.
Block 14	Enter the date of current illness, injury, or last menstrual period (LMP), for pregnancy.
Block 15	Leave this blank.
Block 16	Enter the date, if applicable.
Block 17	Enter the name and credential of the referring physician or provider.
Block 17a	Enter the referring physician/provider's non-national provider identification (NPI) number with qualifier, if applicable. Use the same codes as for Medicare.
Block 17b	Enter the referring physician/provider's NPI number.
Block 18	Enter the hospitalization dates, if applicable.
Block 19	Enter the referral number for services that require a referral from the PCM.
Block 20	Enter an X in No if lab work was performed in the provider's lab. Enter an X in Yes if lab work was performed outside of the provider's office. When Yes is checked, enter the total amount charged by the outside lab for the services reported on the claim form.
Block 21	Enter up to four ICD-9-CM diagnosis codes. Enter the first-listed diagnosis in 1. Codes must be entered to the highest level of specificity. (Note: Use ICD-10-CM codes, when implemented.)
Block 22	Leave this blank.
Block 23	Enter additional prior authorization number(s), if applicable.

continued on the next page

continued from the previous page

Block 24A	Enter the month, day, and year for each procedure/service or supply. If From and To dates are shown here for a series of identical services, enter the number of services in block 24G.
Block 24B	Enter the place of service code. Use the same codes as Medicare.
Block 24C	Enter a Y for yes if the service provided was an emergency. Enter an N for no if the service was not an emergency.
Block 24D	Enter CPT/*Healthcare Common Procedure Coding System* (HCPCS), code for each service. Enter modifiers, if applicable.
Block 24E	Enter the diagnosis pointer (1–4) for the diagnosis that best justifies the medical necessity for the service.
Block 24F	Enter the charge for each listed service.
Block 24G	Enter the days, units, or number of services for each line item.
Block 24H	Enter an X, if applicable. Otherwise, leave this blank.
Block 24I	In the shaded portion, enter the qualifier that identifies the non-NPI number entered in the shaded portion of block 24J. When only the NPI is reported, leave this blank.
Block 24J	Enter the NPI number (unshaded portion of 24J) of the provider rendering the service in each line. Note that NPI is preprinted in the unshaded portion of Block 24I.
Block 25	Enter the provider's federal tax ID number (employer identification number [EIN]). Enter an X in the EIN box.
Block 26	Enter the patient's account number, if one is assigned by the provider.
Block 27	Enter an X in Yes if the provider accepts TRICARE assignment under TRICARE. Enter an X in No if the provider does not.
Block 28	Enter total charges for the services being reported on the claim.
Block 29	Enter the amount paid by the patient or OHI.
Block 30	Enter balance due by subtracting the amount in block 29 from the amount in block 28.
Block 31	Provider signature and date. SIGNATURE ON FILE acceptable for electronic claims.
Block 32	Enter the name, address, city, state, and zip code of the physical location where services were provided.
Block 32a	Enter the NPI of the facility identified in block 32.
Block 32b	Enter the qualifier and non-NPI number of the facility identified in block 32, if applicable.
Block 33	Enter the name, complete address, and telephone number of the billing provider.
Block 33a	Enter the NPI of the billing provider identified in block 33. For solo-practice physicians, enter the physician's NPI. For group-practice physicians/providers, enter the group practice NPI.
Block 33b	Enter the qualifier and non-NPI number of the billing provider identified in block 33, if applicable.

Figure 14–3 illustrates a completed CMS-1500 when TRICARE is the only payer.

(1500)

HEALTH INSURANCE CLAIM FORM

APPROVED BY NATIONAL UNIFORM CLAIM COMMITTEE 08/05

PICA / PICA

1. MEDICARE / MEDICAID / TRICARE CHAMPUS [X] (Sponsor's SSN) / CHAMPVA / GROUP HEALTH PLAN / FECA BLK LUNG / OTHER	1a. INSURED'S I.D. NUMBER (For Program in Item 1): 698785432
2. PATIENT'S NAME (Last Name, First Name, Middle Initial): COLONEL, SARA, M	3. PATIENT'S BIRTH DATE: 09 05 2005 SEX M F[X]	4. INSURED'S NAME (Last Name, First Name, Middle Initial): COLONEL, ROY, P
5. PATIENT'S ADDRESS (No., Street): 89 CIRCLE DRIVE	6. PATIENT RELATIONSHIP TO INSURED: Self / Spouse / Child [X] / Other	7. INSURED'S ADDRESS (No., Street): 89 CIRCLE DRIVE
CITY: BLUEBERRY STATE: ME	8. PATIENT STATUS: Single [X] Married Other	CITY: BLUEBERRY STATE: ME
ZIP CODE: 49855 TELEPHONE: (906) 228 2612	Employed / Full-Time Student / Part-Time Student	ZIP CODE: 49855 TELEPHONE: (906) 228 2612

9. OTHER INSURED'S NAME (Last Name, First Name, Middle Initial):

10. IS PATIENT'S CONDITION RELATED TO:

11. INSURED'S POLICY GROUP OR FECA NUMBER: **NONE**

a. OTHER INSURED'S POLICY OR GROUP NUMBER:

a. EMPLOYMENT? (Current or Previous) YES / [X] NO

a. INSURED'S DATE OF BIRTH: 08 11 1970 SEX M[X] F

b. OTHER INSURED'S DATE OF BIRTH: MM DD YY SEX M F

b. AUTO ACCIDENT? YES / [X] NO PLACE (State)

b. EMPLOYER'S NAME OR SCHOOL NAME: **USAF**

c. EMPLOYER'S NAME OR SCHOOL NAME:

c. OTHER ACCIDENT? YES / [X] NO

c. INSURANCE PLAN NAME OR PROGRAM NAME: **TRICARE**

d. INSURANCE PLAN NAME OR PROGRAM NAME:

10d. RESERVED FOR LOCAL USE:

d. IS THERE ANOTHER HEALTH BENEFIT PLAN? YES / [X] NO **If yes,** return to and complete item 9 a-d.

READ BACK OF FORM BEFORE COMPLETING & SIGNING THIS FORM.

12. PATIENT'S OR AUTHORIZED PERSON'S SIGNATURE I authorize the release of any medical or other information necessary to process this claim. I also request payment of government benefits either to myself or to the party who accepts assignment below.

SIGNED **SIGNATURE ON FILE** DATE

13. INSURED'S OR AUTHORIZED PERSON'S SIGNATURE I authorize payment of medical benefits to the undersigned physician or supplier for services described below.

SIGNED **SIGNATURE ON FILE**

14. DATE OF CURRENT: ILLNESS (First symptom) OR INJURY (Accident) OR PREGNANCY (LMP): 03 02 20YY

15. IF PATIENT HAS HAD SAME OR SIMILAR ILLNESS, GIVE FIRST DATE MM DD YY

16. DATES PATIENT UNABLE TO WORK IN CURRENT OCCUPATION: FROM TO

17. NAME OF REFERRING PROVIDER OR OTHER SOURCE: **MARY SMITH MD** | 17a. | 17b. NPI 8901234567

18. HOSPITALIZATION DATES RELATED TO CURRENT SERVICES: FROM TO

19. RESERVED FOR LOCAL USE:

20. OUTSIDE LAB? YES / [X] NO $ CHARGES

21. DIAGNOSIS OR NATURE OF ILLNESS OR INJURY (Relate Items 1, 2, 3, or 4 to Item 24E by Line):
1. 599 0
2.
3.
4.

22. MEDICAID RESUBMISSION CODE ORIGINAL REF. NO.

23. PRIOR AUTHORIZATION NUMBER

24. A. DATE(S) OF SERVICE From MM DD YY / To MM DD YY	B. PLACE OF SERVICE	C. EMG	D. PROCEDURES, SERVICES, OR SUPPLIES CPT/HCPCS MODIFIER	E. DIAGNOSIS POINTER	F. $ CHARGES	G. DAYS OR UNITS	H. EPSDT Family Plan	I. ID. QUAL.	J. RENDERING PROVIDER ID. #
1	03 02 YY 03 02 YY	11	N	99212	1	45 00	1		NPI	4567890123
2	03 02 YY 03 02 YY	11	N	81000	1	25 00	1		NPI	4567890123
3									NPI	
4									NPI	
5									NPI	
6									NPI	

25. FEDERAL TAX I.D. NUMBER SSN EIN	26. PATIENT'S ACCOUNT NO.	27. ACCEPT ASSIGNMENT?	28. TOTAL CHARGE	29. AMOUNT PAID	30. BALANCE DUE
22498765 [X]	45678	[X] YES NO	$ 70 00	$ 14 00	$ 56 00

31. SIGNATURE OF PHYSICIAN OR SUPPLIER INCLUDING DEGREES OR CREDENTIALS (I certify that the statements on the reverse apply to this bill and are made a part thereof.)

SIGNATURE ON FILE

SIGNED DATE

32. SERVICE FACILITY LOCATION INFORMATION
MEDICAL CARE SOUTH
809 CIRCLE DRIVE
BLUEBERRY ME 49855
a. 8901234567 b.

33. BILLING PROVIDER INFO & PH # (906) 336 4020
MEDICAL CARE SOUTH
809 CIRCLE DRIVE
BLUEBERRY ME 49855
a. 8901234567 b.

NUCC Instruction Manual available at: www.nucc.org

APPROVED OMB-0938-0999 FORM CMS-1500 (08-05)

For instructional use only. Courtesy of the Centers for Medicare and Medicaid Services, www.cms.hhs.gov.

Figure 14–3 **TRICARE CMS-1500**

TRICARE as Secondary Payer

With the exception of Medicaid and supplemental insurance plans, TRICARE is the secondary payer when the patient is covered by another insurance plan or is eligible for Medicare. The billing specialist first submits a claim to the other insurance company and after receiving payment sends a claim to the TRICARE contractor. When billing TRICARE as the secondary payer, complete blocks 9–9d of the CMS-1500. You may be required to furnish additional information from the OHI program, such as an explanation of benefits (EOB). Remember to include the OHI payment in block 29 of the CMS-1500. The insurance billing specialist should contact the TRICARE contractor if there are any questions about TRICARE primary or secondary payer status.

 ## FRAUD AND ABUSE

The TRICARE Management Agency (TMA) is the agency that administers the TRICARE program. The TMA's Program Integrity Office manages TRICARE's fraud and abuse program. Fraud is defined as the "intent to deceive or misrepresent to secure unlawful gain." The TRICARE Program Integrity Office maintains a website that lists all providers who have been sanctioned for fraud. Sanctions include monetary penalties, criminal convictions, and exclusion from all federally funded health programs. As with Medicare fraud and abuse, the purpose of this program is to reduce or eliminate unnecessary medical costs. Table 14–8 lists examples of fraud.

In addition to fraud, the Program Integrity Office reviews cases of potential abuse, which is defined as practices inconsistent with sound fiscal, business, or medical procedures and as

TABLE 14–8

Examples of Fraud	
Fraudulent Billing Practices	• Billing for services, supplies, or equipment not furnished to the patient • Billing for noncovered services that are disguised as covered services • Billing more than once for the same service—known as duplicate billing • Billing for services provided by another provider—known as reciprocal billing • Billing the beneficiary for amounts that exceed the TRICARE Standard allowable charge or cost
Other Fraudulent Practices	• Misrepresentations of dates, frequency, duration, or description of services rendered • Practicing with an expired or revoked license • Assigning medical codes that reflect a higher level of service than that provided—known as upcoding • Assigning medical codes at a lower level to avoid billing oversight—known as downcoding

TABLE 14–9

Examples of Abuse
• A pattern of waiving beneficiary cost-share or deductible
• A pattern of submitting claims for services that are not medically necessary or, if necessary, not to the extent rendered
• Charging TRICARE beneficiaries higher rates than those charged to other patients or insurance programs
• Providing inferior care
• Failure to maintain adequate clinical or financial records
• Unauthorized use of the term TRICARE

services not considered reasonable and necessary. Abusive activities often result in inappropriate claims for TRICARE payment. Table 14–9 lists examples of abuse.

Fraudulent actions can result in criminal or civil penalties. Fraudulent or abusive activities may result in administrative sanctions, such as suspension or exclusion as an authorized provider.

REINFORCEMENT EXERCISES 14–4

Provide a short answer for each question.

1. When is TRICARE the primary payer?

_____

_____

_____

2. When is TRICARE the secondary payer?

_____

_____

_____

3. What is the purpose of TRICARE's Program Integrity Office?

_____

_____

4. What is upcoding?

_____

_____

continued on the next page

continued from the previous page

> **5.** What is downcoding?
>
> _____
>
> _____
>
> **6.** Describe the difference between fraud and abuse.
>
> _____
>
> _____
>
> _____

CHAMPVA

CHAMPVA is a health care benefits program for the spouse or widow(er) and children of a veteran who meets one of the following criteria:

1. Permanently and totally disabled due to a service-connected disability, as determined by a Veterans Administration (VA) regional office
2. Permanently and totally disabled due to a service-connected condition at the time of death
3. Died from a service-connected disability
4. Died while on active duty

To qualify for CHAMPVA, the dependents *cannot* be eligible for DoD TRICARE benefits. CHAMPVA is administered through the Health Administration Center (HAC) in Denver, Colorado. Table 14–10 provides a list of terms and definitions related to CHAMPVA eligibility.

Except for stepchildren, the divorce or remarriage of the spouse or surviving spouse does not affect the CHAMPVA eligibility of children.

TABLE 14–10

CHAMPVA Eligibility Definitions	
Term	**Definition**
Sponsor	The veteran; CHAMPVA eligibility is based on an individual's relationship to the veteran
Service-connected disability/condition	VA determination that a veteran's illness or injury was incurred or aggravated while on active duty in military service and resulted in some degree of disability
Dependent	Child, spouse, or widow(er) of a qualifying sponsor

Covered and Noncovered Services

In general, CHAMPVA covers most health care services and supplies that are medically and psychologically necessary. There are preauthorization requirements for the following covered services:

- Organ and bone marrow transplants
- Hospice services
- Most mental health/substance abuse services
- Dental care
- DME worth more than $2000

Failure to obtain required preauthorizations results in the denial of the claim.

General exclusions from CHAMPVA payment include the following:

- Services determined by the VA to be medically unnecessary
- Care as part of a grant, study, or research program
- Care considered experimental or investigational
- Care for persons eligible for benefits under other government agency programs, except Medicaid and State Victims of Crime Compensation programs
- Care that is provided free of charge, such as services obtained at a health fair
- Care provided outside the scope of the provider's license or certification
- Custodial, domiciliary, or rest cures
- Dental care, except treatment related to certain covered medical conditions
- Medications that do not require a prescription, except insulin
- Personal comfort and convenience items
- Services rendered by providers who are suspended or sanctioned by other federal entities

Only the VA's Health Administration Center in Denver, Colorado, can authorize benefits and process claims. Therefore, it is strongly recommended that all inquiries for CHAMPVA-related matters are made directly to the center. The address is VA Health Administration Center, CHAMPVA, P.O. Box 469064, Denver, CO 80246-9064. The phone number is 1-800-733-8387.

Providers, Deductibles, and Cost Sharing

Except for certain mental health categories and freestanding ambulatory surgical centers, the HAC does not establish contracts with health care providers or maintain provider listings. Beneficiaries are free to select any provider who is appropriately licensed or certified to perform the services offered.

By law, all health care providers are prohibited from balance-billing beneficiaries for amounts that exceed the CHAMPVA-allowed amount. Once the deductible is met and the cost-share amount is paid, providers must accept the CHAMPVA-allowed amount as payment in full.

With the exception of inpatient services, ambulatory surgery facility services, partial psychiatric day programs, and all hospice services, the annual deductible must be met before CHAMPVA pays its share. At the time of publication, the calendar year deductible was $50 per beneficiary or a maximum of $100 per CHAMPVA-eligible family, whichever is satisfied first.

For most CHAMPVA-covered services, the beneficiary's cost-share is 25% of the allowable charge, and CHAMPVA pays 75%. Remember, balance-billing is not an option for CHAMPVA-covered services. The billing specialist can estimate the CHAMPVA-allowed charge by using TRICARE's CMAC procedure pricing information. Figure 14–4 is an example of beneficiary and CHAMPVA payment amounts for CPT code 30110, Excision, nasal polyps, simple. The patient has met the annual deductible.

CPT CODE: 30110   DESCRIPTION: Excision, nasal polyp(s), simple

PROVIDER FEE: $200   ALLOWABLE CHARGE: $160

Physician Fee	$200.00
Allowable Charge	$160.00
Minus Beneficiary Cost-share Amount (25% of the allowable charge)	$ 40.00
Estimated CHAMPVA Payment	$120.00

The provider collects the $40 cost-share from the patient.

The $40 difference between the Physician Fee and the Allowable Charge cannot be billed to the patient.

Figure 14–4 CHAMPVA Estimated Payment

CHAMPVA BILLING

The billing specialist can verify the eligibility status of CHAMPVA beneficiaries by calling a toll-free number (1-800-733-8387), following the voice-activated instructions, and entering the beneficiary's Social Security number and the provider's federal tax ID number.

Except for Medicaid, insurance policies that supplement CHAMPVA benefits, and State Victims of Crime Compensation programs, CHAMPVA is always the secondary payer. The beneficiary has the option of filing the CHAMPVA claim and receiving the payment. The beneficiary completes the CHAMPVA claim form and attaches a copy of the provider's itemized bill and a copy of any OHI program's EOB. When the beneficiary files the insurance claim, the provider must bill the beneficiary for services rendered.

When the provider files the insurance claim, the beneficiary may be asked to pay the cost-share amount at the time of service. The billing specialist submits the claim to CHAMPVA. If a deductible amount is subtracted from the provider's payment, the provider must bill the beneficiary for the deductible amount.

CMS-1500 GUIDELINES FOR CHAMPVA

Hospitals and ambulatory service centers complete a UB-04. Other providers use the CMS-1500. Each CHAMPVA beneficiary receives his or her own ID card. Under CHAMPVA, when the beneficiary is the patient, the patient is always the insured. Instructions for completing the CMS-1500 follow.

Block 1	Enter an X in CHAMPVA.
Block 1a	Enter the beneficiary's CHAMPVA Authorization Card ID number. (This may be the beneficiary's Social Security number.)
Block 2	Enter the patient's name as directed on the form.
Block 3	Enter the patient's eight-digit birth date (MMDDYYYY). Enter an X in the appropriate gender box.

continued on the next page

continued from the previous page

Block 4	Leave this blank.
Block 5	Enter the patient's address, zip code, and telephone number.
Block 6	Enter an X in Self. (Note: Because each beneficiary has an individual ID card, the patient is the insured.)
Block 7	Leave this blank.
Block 8	Enter an X in the box that applies to the patient's marital, employment, and student status.
Blocks 9–9d are completed when the beneficiary is covered by OHI and YES is answered in block 11d.	
Block 9	Enter the name of the insured with another insurance plan that covers the beneficiary.
Block 9a	Enter the policy or group number of the other insurance plan.
Block 9b	Enter the other insured's eight-digit birth date (MMDDYYYY). Enter an X in the appropriate gender box.
Block 9c	Enter the name of the other insured's employer or school.
Block 9d	Enter the name of the insurance plan or program name of the OHI.
Blocks 10–10c	Enter an X in Yes or No, as applicable. If treatment is related to an automobile accident (10b), enter the two-character abbreviation for the state where the accident occurred.
Block 10d	Leave this blank.
Blocks 11–11c	Leave this blank.
Block 11d	Enter an X in Yes if the patient is covered under another health insurance plan. Complete blocks 9–9d. Enter an X in No if the patient's only health insurance is CHAMPVA.
Blocks 12 and 13	Enter SIGNATURE ON FILE.
Block 14	Enter the date of current illness, injury, or LMP, for pregnancy.
Block 15	Leave this blank.
Block 16	Enter the date, if applicable.
Block 17	Enter the name and credential of the referring physician or provider.
Block 17a	Enter the referring physician/provider's non-NPI number with qualifier. Use the same codes as for Medicare.
Block 17b	Enter the referring physician/provider's NPI number.
Block 18	Enter the hospitalization dates, if applicable.
Block 19	Leave this blank.
Block 20	Enter an X in No if lab work was performed in the provider's lab. Enter an X in Yes if lab work was performed outside of the provider's office. When Yes is checked, enter the total amount charged by the outside lab for the services reported on the claim form.
Block 21	Enter up to four ICD-9-CM diagnostic codes in priority order. The first-listed diagnosis is entered in item 1. Codes must be entered to the highest level of specificity. (Note: Use ICD-10 codes when implemented.)

continued on the next page

continued from the previous page

Block 22	Leave this blank.
Block 23	Enter the authorization number, if applicable.
Block 24A	Enter the month, day, and year for each procedure/service or supply. If From and To dates are shown here for a series of identical services, enter the number of services in block 24G.
Block 24B	Enter the place of service code. Use the same codes as Medicare.
Block 24C	Enter a Y for Yes if the service provided was an emergency. Enter an N for No if the service was not an emergency.
Block 24D	Enter CPT/HCPCS code for each service.
Block 24E	Enter the diagnosis pointer (1–4) for the diagnosis that best justifies the medical necessity for the service.
Block 24F	Enter the charge for each listed service.
Block 24G	Enter the days, units, or number of services for each line item.
Block 24H	Enter an X, if applicable. Otherwise, leave this blank.
Block 24I	In the shaded portion, enter the qualifier that identifies the non-NPI number entered in the shaded portion of block 24J. When only the NPI is reported, leave this blank.
Block 24J	Enter the NPI number (unshaded portion of 24J) of the provider rendering the service in each line. Note that NPI is preprinted in the unshaded portion of block 24I.
Block 25	Enter the provider's federal tax ID number (EIN). Enter an X in the EIN box.
Block 26	Enter the patient's account number if one is assigned by the provider.
Block 27	Enter an X in Yes.
Block 28	Enter total charges for the services being reported on the claim.
Block 29	Enter the amount paid by the patient or OHI.
Block 30	Enter balance due by subtracting the amount in block 29 from the amount in block 28.
Block 31	Provider signature and date or SIGNATURE ON FILE
Block 32	Enter the name, address, city, state, and zip code of the physical location where services were provided.
Block 32a	Enter the NPI of the facility identified in block 32.
Block 32b	Enter the qualifier and non-NPI number of the facility identified in block 32, if applicable.
Block 33	Enter the name, complete address, and telephone number of the billing provider.
Block 33a	Enter the NPI of the billing provider identified in block 33. For solo-practice physicians, enter the physician's NPI. For group-practice physicians/providers, enter the group practice NPI.
Block 33b	Enter the qualifier and non-NPI number of the billing provider identified in block 33, if applicable.

Figure 14–5 illustrates a completed CMS-1500 when CHAMPVA is the only payer.

The provider receives an EOB with the payment. This detailed form explains how reimbursement was determined. Figure 14–6 is a sample CHAMPVA EOB.

Figure 14–5 CHAMPVA CMS-1500

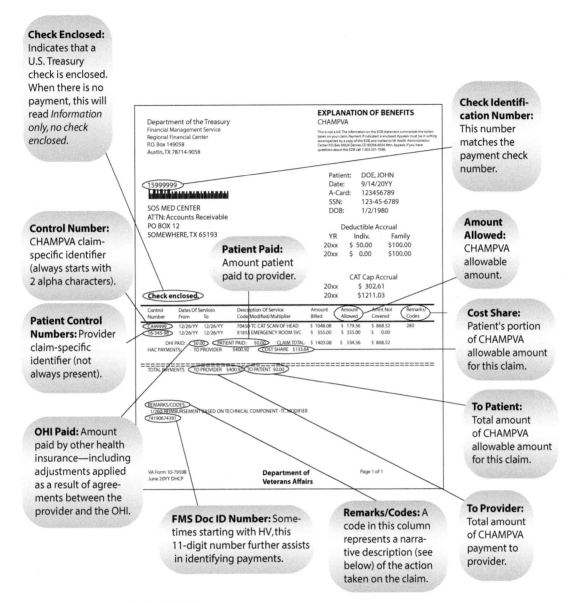

Figure 14–6 Sample CHAMPVA EOB

ABBREVIATIONS

Table 14–11 lists the abbreviations presented in this chapter.

TABLE 14–11

Abbreviations and Meanings	
Abbreviation	**Meaning**
ADSM	active duty service member
BC/BS	Blue Cross/Blue Shield

continued on the next page

continued from the previous page

Abbreviations and Meanings

Abbreviation	Meaning
CHAMPUS	Civilian Health and Medical Program of the Uniformed Services
CHAMPVA	Civilian Health and Medical Program of the Veterans Administration
CMAC	CHAMPUS Maximum Allowable Charge
CPT	*Current Procedural Terminology*
DEERS	Defense Enrollment Eligibility and Reporting System
DME	durable medical equipment
DoD	Department of Defense
EIN	employer identification number
EOB	explanation of benefits
FECA	Federal Employees' Compensation Act
HCPCS	*Healthcare Common Procedure Coding System*
LMP	last menstrual period
MTF	military treatment facility
NATO	North Atlantic Treaty Organization
NOAA	National Oceanic and Atmospheric Administration
NPI	national provider identification
OHI	other health insurance
PCM	primary care manager
PPN	preferred provider network
TFL	TRICARE for Life
TMA	TRICARE Management Agency
TYA	TRICARE Young Adult
VA	Veterans Administration

SUMMARY

TRICARE and CHAMPVA are military services medical benefit programs that serve very different populations. TRICARE is available to active duty and retired members of the uniformed services, their spouses, and their dependents. CHAMPVA has a much narrower scope and is available to the dependents and survivors of totally and permanently disabled veterans and veterans who died in the line of duty, respectively. Cost sharing and deductibles are features of both programs.

TRICARE options include Prime, Extra, and Standard. TRICARE Standard is often referred to as the old CHAMPUS program. TRICARE beneficiaries receive services from military treatment facilities, preferred provider networks (PPNs), and civilian providers of choice. Beneficiary out-of-pocket expenses are highest under TRICARE Standard.

Billing specialists must verify TRICARE and CHAMPVA eligibility. Checking the dates on program ID cards is the most common way to verify eligibility. Under TRICARE, participating providers are paid directly and cannot balance-bill the difference between the TRICARE-allowable charge and the provider's fee. Balance-billing is also prohibited under CHAMPVA regulations.

 REVIEW EXERCISES

CASE STUDY

Read the case study information and complete a CMS-1500 for TRICARE Standard.
   Your instructor will tell you how to obtain the form.

PATIENT NAME: Rebecca Wadsworth

DOB: 03/05/1954

SSN: 503-72-1941

ADDRESS: 92 Specker Drive; Blueberry, ME 49855

PHONE: (H) (906) 336-1313

EMPLOYER: T-Mart, 43 Mall Drive, Blueberry, ME 49855

INSURANCE: TRICARE Standard

SPOUSE: Lt. Colonel John R. Wadsworth (retired, USAF)

DOB: 06/15/1952

SSN: 381-60-2997

PROGRESS NOTE:

DATE: 02/05/20YY

Mrs. Wadsworth is seen today for a follow-up visit related to her diabetes. She has been successful in maintaining her blood sugar within normal limits, but she complains that she "is really hungry all the time." We reviewed her diabetic diet and increased the caloric intake to 1800 calories per day. Her insulin regimen will remain the same. Fasting blood sugar today reveals a blood glucose of 115. Remainder of exam is normal. Mrs. Wadsworth was advised to return in one month unless further problems develop.

SIGNED: Henry Romero, MD

DIAGNOSIS AND TREATMENT CODES: Office visit 99213; insulin-dependent diabetes mellitus, type II 250.00 (ICD-10-CM code E11.9); blood glucose test 82947; venipuncture 36415

SUPERIORLAND CLINIC

714 HENNEPIN AVE.

Blueberry, ME 49855

PHONE (906) 366-4020

TAX ID#: 49-4134726

CLINIC NPI: 4567890123

CHARGES: Office visit $60; blood glucose test $20; venipuncture $6.

Dr. Romero accepts assignment.

Dr. Romero NPI: 2311287891

Fill in the Blank

1. Dependents who are eligible for TRICARE or CHAMPVA are called _____.

2. A(n) _____ is defined as an individual who has served in the armed forces and is honorably discharged.

3. _____ is the term for the ADSM.

4. A(n) _____ is a hospital, an institution, or a provider who meets the licensing and certification requirements of TRICARE.

5. Insurance carriers for TRICARE are called _____.

6. The _____ assists beneficiaries and providers with preauthorizations for specific procedures.

7. The _____ allows the billing specialist to retrieve TRICARE pricing information.

8. CHAMPVA is administered through the _____.

9. CHAMPVA is usually the _____ payer for health care services.

10. CHAMPVA requires preauthorization for _____ worth more than $2000.

Multiple Choice

Circle the correct answer from the choices provided.

1. Under TRICARE Prime, most health services are provided by

   a. a military treatment facility.

   b. the nearest health care provider.

   c. preferred provider organizations.

   d. health maintenance organizations.

2. Individuals enrolled in TRICARE Prime are assigned a

   a. military ID number.

   b. sponsor.

   c. designated health care provider.

   d. primary care manager.

3. TRICARE Extra is

   a. available to all active duty personnel.

   b. an option available to TRICARE Standard beneficiaries.

   c. a health maintenance organization.

   d. administered by the Office of Veterans Affairs.

4. The DEERS program is

   a. a conservation program managed by the armed services.

   b. a database used to verify TRICARE eligibility.

   c. available to active duty personnel only.

   d. available to persons who provide services to TRICARE beneficiaries.

5. Cost sharing under TRICARE programs is the same as

   a. deductibles.

   b. coordination of benefits.

   c. co-payment and co-insurance.

   d. out-of-pocket expenses.

6. Nonparticipating TRICARE providers

   a. are limited in the amount they are allowed to charge.

   b. usually balance-bill the patient.

   c. receive the allowable charge as payment in full.

   d. do not submit insurance claims for TRICARE patients.

7. TRICARE guidelines define "durable medical equipment" by all but one of the following statements:

   a. It improves function.

   b. It prevents further deterioration.

   c. It enhances vision and hearing.

   d. It provides a medical function.

8. TRICARE requires preauthorization for all but one of the following procedures:

   a. tonsillectomy

   b. hernia repair

   c. magnetic resonance imaging

   d. chest x-ray

9. Select the condition that is *not* an exception to TRICARE claims submission deadlines.

   a. adequate access to care

   b. provider's statement was lost

   c. retroactive eligibility

   d. primary payer delay

10. TRICARE is secondary to all other insurance plans except

   a. Medicaid.

   b. BC/BS.

   c. Medicare.

   d. Medicare Supplemental Insurance.

True or False

Write True or False on the line following each statement.

1. CHAMPVA is available to active duty military forces. _____

2. CHAMPVA does not identify participating providers. _____

3. Under TRICARE and CHAMPVA, the beneficiary pays the cost-sharing amount. _____

4. Providers who treat TRICARE beneficiaries are obligated by law to accept assignment. _____

5. CHAMPVA is available to dependents of permanently disabled veterans. _____

6. Military dependents are covered by TRICARE and CHAMPVA. _____

7. High-cost procedures may require CHAMPVA preauthorization. _____

8. The billing specialist collects the cost-share amount only after receiving TRICARE payment. _____

9. Nonparticipating providers can request payment in full prior to receiving TRICARE payment. _____

10. The beneficiary or the provider is allowed to file CHAMPVA insurance claims. _____

CHALLENGE ACTIVITIES

1. Search the Internet for the TRICARE regional office that covers your state. Find the name of the TRICARE contractor for your region. Request a copy of claims filing guidelines from the contractor.

2. Interview a billing specialist at a local physician's office. Ask about the unique problems, if any, associated with TRICARE claims. How does the allowable charge compare with other insurance programs' reimbursement rates?

WEBSITES

CHAMPUS Maximum Allowable Charge: http://www.tricare.mil/CMAC
CHAMPVA: http://www.va.gov/hac
Defense Enrollment Eligibility and Reporting System: http://www.tricare.mil//deers/
Health Net Federal Services: http://www.hnfs.com
Humana Military Health Care Services: http://www.humana-military.com
TriWest Healthcare Alliance: http://www.triwest.com

CHAPTER 15

Workers' Compensation

LEARNING OBJECTIVES

Upon successful completion of this chapter, the reader should have the knowledge to:

1. Define all key terms and abbreviations.
2. Describe four federal workers' compensation programs.
3. Discuss the function and purpose of the Occupational Safety and Health Administration.
4. Compare the four categories of state workers' compensation programs.
5. List the eligibility requirements for workers' compensation benefits.
6. Describe three classifications of work-related injuries.
7. Explain the workers' compensation documentation requirements.
8. Complete the CMS-1500 insurance claim form for workers' compensation.

KEY TERMS

Black Lung Program
CA-7 Claim for
 Compensation
Combination program
Commercial workers'
 compensation program
Department of Energy (DOE)
Department of Labor (DOL)
Division of Coal Mine
 Workers' Compensation
 (DCMWC)
Division of Energy
 Employees Occupational
 Illness Compensation
 (DEEOIC)
Division of Federal
 Employees' Compensation
 (DFEC)

Division of Longshore
 and Harbor Workers'
 Compensation (DLHWC)
Employer self-insured program
Energy Employees
 Occupational Illness
 Compensation Program
 Act (EEOICPA)
Federal Coal Mine Health
 and Safety Act
Federal Employees'
 Compensation Act (FECA)
First report of injury
Longshore and Harbor
 Workers' Compensation
 Act (LHWCA)
Material safety data sheet
 (MSDS)

Medical claim with no
 disability
Occupational Safety and
 Health Administration
 (OSHA)
Office of Workers'
 Compensation Programs
 (OWCP)
Partial disability
Permanent disability
Radionuclides
State compensation board/
 commission
State compensation fund
Temporary disability
Total disability
Vocational rehabilitation

OVERVIEW

Workers' compensation laws are designed to ensure that employees who are injured or disabled on the job are provided with wage replacement and medical and rehabilitation benefits. Prior to 1912, a worker who was injured on the job had to sue his or her employer for compensation. In 1912, as a result of a federal government mandate, most states adopted a Workmen's Compensation Act. Over time and with the advent of women entering the workforce, many states changed the name to Workers' Compensation.

The intent of most workers' compensation acts is to establish a system under which a worker no longer has to prove negligence on the part of the employer. Employers covered by workers' compensation acts are required to compensate a worker for any injury suffered on the job, regardless of fault. State compensation acts do not cover all employees or employers. Some states exclude employers with only three to five employees. Temporary employees, babysitters, domestic help, and volunteers may also be excluded.

 FEDERAL WORKERS' COMPENSATION PROGRAMS

Until 1908, workers injured on the job simply lost their jobs. Employees bore the full responsibility for on-the-job safety, and employers expressed little if any concern for the health or well-being of their workforce.

In 1908, the federal government enacted the Federal Employees' Compensation Act (FECA). FECA is one of four programs administered by the Office of Worker's Compensation Programs (OWCP), a division of the Department of Labor (DOL). The DOL worker's compensation programs include the following:

- Division of Federal Employees' Compensation (DFEC), which manages the FECA, providing workers' compensation coverage to millions of federal and postal workers around the world.
- Division of Energy Employees Occupational Illness Compensation (DEEOIC), which manages the Energy Employees Occupational Illness Compensation Program Act (EEOICPA), providing workers' compensation benefits to the employees of the Department of Energy (DOE) and other employees as defined by the EEOICPA. Other employees include contractors, subcontractors, and vendors associated with the production and testing of nuclear weapons. Uranium miners, millers, and ore transporters may be eligible for EEOICPA benefits due to illnesses caused by radiation exposure.
- Division of Longshore and Harbor Workers' Compensation (DLHWC), which manages the Longshore and Harbor Workers' Compensation Act (LHWCA), providing workers' compensation benefits to employees such as longshore workers, ship-repairers, shipbuilders or ship-breakers, and harbor construction workers.
- Division of Coal Mine Workers' Compensation (DCMWC), which manages the Federal Coal Mine Health and Safety Act, commonly called the Black Lung Program, providing benefits to miners with lung diseases attributable to coal mining.

The DOLs form CA-7 Claim for Compensation must be filed with the OWCP. Figure 15–1 is a sample of this form. Section 1 through Section 7 are completed by the employee, and Section 8

Claim for Compensation

U.S. Department of Labor
Office of Workers' Compensation Programs

SECTION 1		EMPLOYEE PORTION		

a. Name of Employee	Last	First	Middle	OMB No. 1240-0046 Expires: 10-31-2014

b. Mailing Address (*Including City State, ZIP Code*)		c. OWCP File Number

	d. Date of Injury Month Day Year	e. Social Security Number

E-Mail Address *(Optional)*

	f. Telephone No./FAX No.

SECTION 2 Compensation is claimed for:

Inclusive Date Range
From   To   Intermittent?

a. ☐ Leave without pay _____ _____ ☐ Yes ☐ No *Go to Section 3*

b. ☐ Leave buy back _____ _____ ☐ Yes ☐ No *Go to Section 3, and Complete Form CA-7b*

c. ☐ Other wage loss; specify type, _____ _____ ☐ Yes ☐ No *Go to Section 3*
such as downgrade, loss of
night differential, etc. Type: _____

d. ☐ Schedule Award *(Go to Section 4)*

If intermittent, complete Form CA-7a,
Time Analysis Sheet

SECTION 3 You must report **all** earnings from employment (**outside** your federal job); include any employment for which you received a salary, wages, income, sales commissions, piecework, or payment of **any** kind during the period(s) claimed in Section 2. Include self-employment, involvement in business enterprises, as well as service with the military forces. Fraudulent concealment of employment or failure to report income may result in forfeiture of compensation benefits and/or criminal prosecution. *Have you worked outside your federal job for the period(s) claimed in Section 2 ?*

Name and Address of Business:

☐ Yes

☐ No *Go to section 4*

Name	Address	City	State	ZIP Code

Dates Worked: Type of Work:

SECTION 4 Is this the first CA-7 claim for compensation you have filed for this injury?

☐ Yes *Complete Sections 5 through 7 and a Form SF-1199A, "Direct Deposit Sign-up"*

☐ No Has there been any change in your dependents, or has your direct deposit information changed, or has there been a claim filed with U.S. Civil Service Retirement, another federal retirement or disability law, or with the Department of Veterans Affairs since your last CA-7 claim?

☐ Yes - *Complete Sections 5 through 7 or a new SF-1199A to reflect change(s)* ☐ No - *Complete Section 7*

SECTION 5 List your dependents (*including spouse*):

Name	Social Security #	Date of Birth	Relationship	Living with you? Yes No
				☐ ☐
				☐ ☐ *For dependents not living*
				☐ ☐ *with you complete items*
				☐ ☐ *a and b below. ,*

a. Are you making support payments for a dependent shown above? ☐ Yes ☐ No If Yes, support payments are made to:

Name	Address	City	State	ZIP Code

b. Were support payments ordered by a court? ☐ Yes ☐ No If Yes, attach copy of court order.

SECTION 6 a. Was/Will there be a claim made against a 3rd party? ☐ Yes ☐ No

b. Have you ever applied for or received disability benefits from the Department of Veterans Affairs?

☐ Yes ☐ No	Claim Number	Full Address of VA Office Where Claim Filed	Nature of Disability and Monthly Payment

c. Have you applied for or received payment under any Federal Retirement or Disability law?

☐ Yes ☐ No	Claim Number	Date Annuity Began	Amount of Monthly Payment	Retirement System (CSRS, FERS, SSA, Other) ☐ CSRS ☐ FERS ☐ SSA ☐ Other

SECTION 7 I hereby make claim for compensation because of the injury sustained by me while in the performance of my duty for the United States. I certify that the information provided above is true and accurate to the best of my knowledge and belief.

Any person who knowingly makes any false statement, misrepresentation, concealment of fact, or any other act of fraud, to obtain compensation as provided by the FECA, or who knowingly accepts compensation to which that person is not entitled is subject to civil or administrative remedies as well as felony criminal prosecution and may, under appropriate criminal provisions, be punished by a fine or imprisonment, or both. In addition, a felony conviction will result in termination of all current and future FECA benefits.

Employee's Signature _____ Date (*Mo., day, year*) _____

CA-7 (Rev. 05-11)

Figure 15–1 Claim Compensation Form

Employing Agency Portion
For first CA-7 claim sent, complete sections 8 through 15.
For subsequent claims, complete sections 12 through 15 only.

SECTION 8	Show Pay Rate as of	Additional Pay	Additional Pay	Additional Pay
Date of Injury: Date: _____ Grade: _____ step: _____	Base Pay $ _____ per ___	Type _____ $ _____ per _____	Type _____ $ _____ per _____	Type _____ $ _____ per _____
Date Employee Stopped Work: Date: _____ Grade: _____ step: _____	$ _____ per ____	Type _____ $ _____ per _____	Type _____ $ _____ per _____	Type _____ $ _____ per _____

Additional pay types include, but are not limited to: Night Differential (ND), Sunday Premium (SP), Holiday Premium (HP), Subsistence (SUB), Quarter (QTR), etc. (List each separately)

SECTION 9

a. Does employee work a fixed 40-hour per week schedule?   ☐ Yes ☐ No

    1. If Yes, circle scheduled days: ☐ S   ☐ M   ☐ T   ☐ W   ☐ T   ☐ F   ☐ S

    2. If No, show scheduled hours for the two week pay period in which work stopped. Circle the day that work stopped.

FOR EXAMPLE ONLY	S	M	T	W	TH	F	S					S	M	T	W	TH	F	S
WEEK 1 From 5/14 to 5/20		8	4	6	⑥			From ____	To ____									
WEEK From 5/21 to 5/27		8		6	6	4		From ____	To ____									

b. Did employee work in position for 11 months prior to injury?   ☐ Yes ☐ No

If No, would position have afforded employment for 11 months but for the injury?   ☐ Yes ☐ No

SECTION 10 On date pay stopped, was employee enrolled in:

a. Health Benefits under the FEHBP?   ☐ No ☐ Yes Code

b. Basic Life Insurance? ☐ No ☐ Yes

c. Optional Life Insurance? ☐ No ☐ Yes Class _____
    (D-Z only)

d. A Retirement System? ☐ No ☐ Yes Plan _____
    (Specify CSRS, FERS, Other)

SECTION 11 Continuation of Pay (COP) Received (*Show inclusive dates*):

From _____   To _____   Intermittent?   ☐ Yes - Complete Time Analysis Sheet, Form CA-7a   ☐ No

SECTION 12 Show pay status and inclusive dates for period(s) claimed:

			Intermittent?	
Sick Leave From _____	To _____		☐ Yes ☐ No	If intermittent, complete Form CA-7a, Time Analysis Sheet.
Annual Leave From _____	To _____		☐ Yes ☐ No	
Leave without Pay From _____	To _____		☐ Yes ☐ No	If leave buy back, also submit completed Form CA-7b.
Work From _____	To _____		☐ Yes ☐ No	

SECTION 13 Did employee return to work? ☐ Yes ☐ No
    If Yes, date _____

If returned, did employee return to the pre-date-of-injury job, with the same number of hours and the same duties?

☐ Yes ☐ No   If No, explain: _____

SECTION 14 Remarks: _____

SECTION 15 An employing agency official who knowingly certifies to any false statement, misrepresentation, or concealment of fact, with respect to this claim may also be subject to appropriate felony criminal prosecution.

I certify that the information given above and that furnished by the employee on this form is true to the best of my knowledge, with any exceptions noted in Section 14, Remarks, above.

Signature _____   Title _____   Date / /
    (Agency Official)

Name of Agency _____

Date Claim Form Received from Employee ___ / / ___

If OWCP needs specific pay information, the person who should be contacted is:

Name _____   Title _____

Telephone No. _____   Fax No. _____   E-Mail Address _____

CA-7 Page 2 (Rev.05-11)

Courtesy of US Department of Labor, Office of Workers Compensation, www.dol.gov.

Figure 15–1 *continued*

INSTRUCTIONS FOR COMPLETING FORM CA-7

If the employee does not quality for continuation of pay (for 45 days), the form should be completed and filed with the OWCP as soon as pay stops. The form should also be submitted when the employee reaches maximum improvement and claims a schedule award. If the employee is receiving continuation of pay and will continue to be disabled after 45 days, the form should be filed with OWCP 5 working days prior to the end of the 45-day period.

The CA-7 also should be used to claim continuing compensation, when a previous CA-7 claim has been made.

Collection of this information is required to obtain a benefit and is authorized by 20 C.F.R. 10.102 and 20 C.F.R. 10.103.

If you have a substantially limiting physical or mental impairment, Federal disability nondiscrimination law gives you the right to receive help from DFEC in the form of communication assistance, accommodation and modification to aid you in the FECA claims process. For example, we will provide you with copies of documents in alternate formats, communication services such as sign language interpretation, or other kinds of adjustments or changes to account for the limitations of your disability. Please contact our office or your claims examiner to ask about this assistance.

EMPLOYEE (or person acting on the employee's behalf) - Complete sections 1 through 7 as directed and submit the form to the employee's supervisor.

SUPERVISOR (or appropriate official in the employing agency) - Complete sections 8 through 15 as directed and promptly forward the form OWCP.

EXPLANATIONS - Some of the items on the form which may require further clarification are explained below:

Section Number	Explanation
2d. Schedule Award	Schedule awards are paid for permanent impairment to a member or function of the body.
5. List your dependents	Your wife or husband is a dependent if he or she is living with you. A child is a dependent if he, or she either lives with you or receives support payments from you, and he or she: 1) is under 18, or 2) is between 18 and 23 and is a full-time student, or 3) is incapable of self-support due to physical or mental disability.
6a. Was/will there be a claim made against 3rd party?	A third party is an individual or organization (other than the injured employee or the Federal government) who is liable for the injury. For instance, the driver of a vehicle causing an accident in which an employee is injured, the owner of a building where unsafe conditions cause an employee to fall, and a manufacturer who gave improper instructions for the use of a chemical to which an employee is exposed, could all be considered third parties to the injury.
8. Additional Pay	"Additional Pay" includes night differential, Sunday premium, holiday premium, and any other type (such as hazardous duty or "dirty work" pay) regularly received by the employee, but does not include pay for overtime. If the amount of such pay varies from pay period to pay period (as in the case of holiday premium or a rotating shift), then the total amount of such pay earned during the year immediately prior to the date of injury or the date the employee stopped work (whichever is greater) should be reported.
11. Continuation of pay (COP) received	If the injury was not a traumatic injury reported on Form CA-1, this item does not apply.
14. Remarks	This space is used to provide relevant information which is not present else- where on the form.

The authority for requesting this information is 5 U.S.C. 8101 et seq. The information will be used to determine entitlement to benefits. Furnishing the requested information is required for the claimant to obtain or retain a benefit. Information collected will be handled and stored in compliance with the Freedom of Information Act, the Privacy Act of 1974, as amended (5 U.S.C. 552a). Failure to furnish the requested information may delay the process, or result in an unfavorable decision or a reduced benefit.

Public Burden Statement

Public reporting burden forth is collection of information is estimated to average 13 minutes per response including the time for reviewing instructions, searching existing data sources, gathering and maintaining the data needed, and completing and reviewing the collection of information. If you have any comments regarding this estimate or any other aspect of this information collection, including suggestions for reducing this burden, please send them to the Department of Labor, Office of Workers' Compensation Programs, Room S-3229, 200 Constitution Avenue, N.W. Washington, D.C. 20210.

Persons are not required to respond to this collection of information unless it displays a currently valid OMB control number.

DO NOT SEND THE COMPLETED FORM TO THIS OFFICE

CA-7 Page 3 (Rev.05-11)

Figure 15–1 *continued*

through Section 15 are completed by the employing agency. Review the CA-7 and note the instructions in the following sections:

- Section 3: requires the employee to report all earnings
- Section 6: identifies whether reimbursement should be paid by another insurance program
- Section 8: defines additional pay as shift differential, Sunday, or holiday premium

OCCUPATIONAL SAFETY AND HEALTH

Workers' compensation laws provide health insurance for work-related injuries and illnesses. The federal Occupational Safety and Health Administration Act of 1970 was enacted to protect employees from injuries associated with occupational hazards. The act established the federal Occupational Safety and Health Administration (OSHA) and also allowed the states to create an OSHA plan. Once the federal government approves the plan, the state assumes responsibility for carrying out OSHA policies. Compliance with OSHA regulations and guidelines reduces the number of work-related injuries and illnesses.

OSHA regulations have been updated many times since 1970. The Bloodborne Pathogens Act, passed in the early 1990s, has special significance for health care employees. Any employee who comes into contact with human blood or infectious materials must have specific training in handling such materials and must be offered a hepatitis B vaccination. The employer must maintain comprehensive records of all vaccinations and training program attendance. Figure 15–2 illustrates a training session.

OSHA's hazardous-chemical policy mandates that employers must provide employees with the manufacturers' material safety data sheets (MSDSs). An MSDS identifies the risks associated with exposure to specific chemicals or hazardous substances. Health care agencies must provide employees with an MSDS for each hazardous substance associated with the employees' work

Donna Mirco

Figure 15–2 Training Session

environment. Hazardous substances may include oncology drugs or medications, radiation, and radionuclides. Radionuclides are radioactive substances used for nuclear imaging or scanning and for treating tumors and cancer.

REINFORCEMENT EXERCISES 15–1

Spell out each abbreviation and write a brief description for each phrase.

1. DOE

_____

2. DOL

_____

3. FECA

_____

4. MSDA

_____

5. OSHA

_____

STATE-SPONSORED WORKERS' COMPENSATION PROGRAMS

Each state has established some type of workers' compensation program. The state, employer, or private insurance companies may assume responsibility for providing benefits to injured workers. State programs usually fall into one of the following categories:

- State compensation fund: The state identifies a specific agency to function as the insuring body to cover workers' compensation claims. Employers pay premiums to the state fund.
- Employer self-insured programs: Some employers have enough capital and other resources to fund their own workers' compensation program. The employer is obligated by state regulation to set aside a specific percentage of the company's funds to cover medical expenses and wage compensation for work-related injuries.
- Commercial workers' compensation programs: Employers purchase insurance policies that provide benefits for injured employees. Commercial workers' compensation programs must meet state regulations and guidelines related to workers' compensation.
- Combination programs: Some states allow employers to select a combination of state, employer self-insured, and commercial workers' compensation programs.

In addition to workers' compensation programs and regulations, each state has a state compensation board or commission. This government agency is responsible for administering state compensation laws and handling appeals related to workers' compensation claims. Both employer and employee have appeal rights if and when either believes the compensation case was not fairly resolved.

WORKERS' COMPENSATION BASICS

Basic workers' compensation information includes eligibility, classification of work-related injuries, disabilities, and documentation requirements.

Eligibility

To qualify for workers' compensation benefits, the employee must:

- Be injured while working within the scope of the employment agreement or job description
- Be injured while performing a service required by the employer
- Develop a disorder that can be directly linked to employment (e.g., asbestosis, mercury poisoning, or black lung disease)

In some states, work-related stress may also be covered by workers' compensation.

A work-related injury does not have to happen at the primary place of employment. Employees injured while traveling on company business, with the exception of sightseeing activities, are eligible for workers' compensation.

Classification of Work-Related Injuries

According to federal regulations, on-the-job or work-related injuries are classified as follows:

- Medical claims with no disability, temporary disability, or permanent disability
- Vocational rehabilitation claims
- Death

Medical Claims With No Disability

Medical claims with no disability are minor injuries that, once treated, permit the employee to continue working or return to work within a few days. Workers' compensation insurance pays for medical treatment and related follow-up. The employee may use sick time for any days off work or the employer may authorize time off with pay.

Temporary Disability

Temporary disability is a disability that can be overcome by medical treatment or retraining. When an employee becomes temporarily disabled because of a work-related injury, workers' compensation covers medical expenses and lost income. Temporary disability ends when the individual is able to return to gainful employment. Compensation for lost income may be as much as two-thirds of the worker's salary.

Permanent Disability

Permanent disability, as applied to workers' compensation, is not the same as medical disability. In fact, many individuals with a medical disability, such as mobility limitations, are valuable and productive employees. Under workers' compensation regulations, permanent disability refers to the individual's ability to return to the position held before the injury or to the workforce in general.

To meet the legal or workers' compensation definition of permanent disability, the physician or other health care providers must document that the injury is stabilized and the employee is permanently impaired and unable to return to his or her previous position.

Compensation for permanent disability depends on the following:

- Severity of the injury
- Amount of permanent loss of function
- Age of the employee
- Occupation before the injury
- Rehabilitation potential

Based on an assessment of these factors, permanent disability is divided into two groups:

- Partial disability, expressed as a percentage of loss of function
- Total disability, defined as 100% loss of function

Partial disability is exemplified by the loss of a portion or all of a body part (an arm, a leg, or a hand) or the presence of a neurological disorder that prevents full use of the affected body area. Partial disability is described as a percentage of loss—for example 20% loss of the use of a limb or 60% loss of memory capacity. When the loss reaches 100%, the individual is unable to return to work in any capacity.

Workers' compensation insurance carriers and state compensation commissions have developed specific descriptions related to an employee's diminished capacity. Documentation related to an employee's condition should incorporate these accepted descriptions. Table 15–1 through Table 15–3 list the definitions and descriptions associated with the employee's disability.

TABLE 15–1

Pulmonary Disease, Heart Disease, Abdominal Weakness, or Spinal Disabilities	
Category	**Limitations**
Disability resulting in limitation to light work	The individual is capable of working in a standing or walking position that demands minimum effort.
Disability precluding heavy work	The individual has lost approximately 50% capacity to perform bending, stooping, lifting, pushing, pulling, and climbing activities.
Disability precluding heavy lifting, repeated bending, and stooping	The individual has lost 50% capacity to perform the activities listed in the statement.
Disability precluding heavy lifting	The individual has lost 50% capacity for lifting.
Disability precluding very heavy work	The individual has lost 25% capacity for bending, pulling, climbing, or other comparable activities.
Disability precluding very heavy lifting	The individual has lost 25% of lifting capacity.

TABLE 15–2

Disabilities Related to Extremities	
Category	Limitations
Disability resulting in limitation to sedentary work	The individual can work while sitting with minimal demands for physical effort and may do some standing and walking.
Disability resulting in limitation to semi-sedentary work	The individual can work in a position that allows for sitting half the time and standing half the time or walking with minimal demands for physical effort while standing, walking, or sitting.

© 2014 Cengage Learning, All Rights Reserved.

TABLE 15–3

Disability Related to Pain	
Level of Pain	Description
Minimal pain	The pain is an annoyance but will not handicap the performance of the individual's work.
Slight pain	The pain is tolerable, but there may be some limitations in performance of assigned duties.
Moderate pain	The pain is tolerable, but there may be marked handicapping of performance.
Severe pain	The individual is excluded from performing any activity that precipitates pain.

© 2014 Cengage Learning, All Rights Reserved.

Vocational Rehabilitation

Vocational rehabilitation claims cover the cost of retraining employees who have suffered some type of on-the-job injury that results in permanent or temporary disability. Retraining allows the employee to return to the workforce but not necessarily to the same occupation or position held before the injury.

Work-Related Death

Work-related deaths are taken very seriously and usually result in an OSHA investigation. Employee death may also result in civil or criminal litigation and substantial financial settlements to the employee's survivors or dependents.

If the work-related death occurs while the employee is traveling for the employer, other insurance programs may contribute to or bear the full burden of settling financial claims for survivors or dependents. Motor vehicle accidents involving a company car, the employee's vehicle while engaging in work-related activities, and another driver may result in all three automobile insurance programs becoming involved in the claim.

Motor vehicle accidents often include assignment of blame. Police officers are called to the scene and assess contributing factors, such as right-of-way, speed, and condition of the driver. If alcohol or substance abuse impaired the employee's driving ability, the employer may contest any financial settlement.

Common carrier or public transportation accidents (e.g., accidents involving airplane, bus, or train travel) that result in employee death while engaged in work-related travel may involve the common carrier's insurance company. Factors such as the health of the pilot or driver, mechanical failure, pilot or driver negligence or reckless behavior, and acts of war or terrorism may limit the employer's insurance liability.

When a work-related death occurs on company property, there is a state or federal OSHA investigation. The purpose of the investigation is to determine all the facts related to the employee's death and to identify ways to prevent similar occurrences in the future.

REINFORCEMENT EXERCISES 15–2

Provide a brief definition for each term.

1. State compensation fund

   _____

   _____

   _____

2. Employer self-insured program

   _____

   _____

   _____

3. Private or commercial workers' compensation programs

   _____

   _____

   _____

4. Combination program

   _____

   _____

   _____

5. State compensation board/commission

   _____

   _____

   _____

continued on the next page

continued from the previous page

Fill in the blank.

1. _____ refers to the individual's ability to return to the job held before the injury.

2. Loss of all or part of a body part is an example of _____.

3. _____ ends when the individual is able to return to gainful employment.

4. Pain that excludes the individual from performing any task that precipitates pain is called _____.

5. _____ pain does not interfere with the individual's work performance.

Workers' Compensation Documentation Requirements

Physicians and providers who treat patients covered by workers' compensation insurance are required to complete and file a first report of injury form. A first report of injury form is just what its name says it is: a written report of the initial contact with the patient. The report is distributed as follows:

- The original in the employee's medical record or workers' compensation file
- A copy to the state's workers' compensation board or commission
- A copy to the employer-designated workers' compensation insurance carrier
- A copy to the employer

The employer must provide the name and address of the workers' compensation insurance carrier.

Figure 15–3 is an example of a workers' compensation first report of injury form, which can also be used for progress reports and the final report. The employee completes or provides the information for items 1 through 6, and the physician completes items 7 through 23. Item 6 is the employee/patient's description of the accident or cause of disease; item 7 is the medical description of the injury or disease. Worker's compensation cases are one of the few situations that does require patient authorization to release work-related injury information to the workers' compensation board or insurance carrier.

The provider's staff must be aware that, by law, the workers' compensation board or commission and the designated insurance carrier are entitled only to information about the patient's work-related injury. Any other patient information must not be released, even inadvertently, to either of these two entities.

Progress Reports

The physician must file progress reports during the course of treating the patient. Progress reports include enough detail to clearly describe the patient's progress and any significant change in medical or disability status. The first report of injury form may be used for progress reports, or the physician may provide the information in narrative form.

INSTRUCTIONS

1. Type answers to All questions and file original with the Workers' Compensation Commission within 72 hours after first treatment.
2. DO NOT FAIL to forward to the Workers' Compensation Commission PROGRESS REPORTS and FINAL REPORT upon discharge of patient.

WORKERS' COMPENSATION COMMISSION
6 NORTH LIBERTY STREET, BALTIMORE, MD. 21201-3785
SURGEON'S REPORT

This is First Report [X]   Progress Report ☐   Final Report ☐

DO NOT WRITE IN THIS SPACE

WCC CLAIM #

EMPLOYER'S REPORT Yes ☐ No ☐

1. Name of Injured Person: Maureen A. Santega | Soc. Sec. No. 610-98-7432 | D.O.B. 7/19/69 | Sex M ☐ F ☑

2. Address: (No. and Street) 905 Raymond Lane | (City or Town) Atlanta | (State) GA | (Zip Code) 30385-8893

3. Name and Address of Employer: Majors Concrete Company, 238 Leaf Lane, Atlanta GA 30342-3329

4. Date of Accident or Onset of Disease: 4/9/YY | Hour: A.M. ☑ P.M. ☐ | 5. Date Disability Began: 4/9/YY

6. Patient's Description of Accident or Cause of Disease: Concrete truck struck and backed over patient's foot while she was pouring concrete at the job site

7. Medical description of Injury or Disease: massive bruising to left foot, no broken bones, great deal of pain associated with bruises

8. Will Injury result in: (a) Permanent defect? Yes ☐ No ☑ If so, what?   (b) Disfigurement Yes ☐ No ☑

9. Causes, other than injury, contributing to patients condition: None

10. Is patient suffering from any disease of the heart, lungs, brain, kidneys, blood, vascular system or any other disabling condition not due to this accident? Give particulars: No

11. Is there any history or evidence present of previous accident or disease? Give particulars: No

12. Has normal recovery been delayed for any reason? Give particulars: No

13. Date of first treatment: 4/10/YY | Who engaged your services? Patient

14. Describe treatment given by you: Darvon, 100 mg q4h prn for pain

15. Were X-Rays taken: Yes ☑ No ☐ | By whom? — (Name and Address) Edwin Gordon, M.D. 802 Manor Lane, Atlanta, GA 30303 | Date 4/10/—

16. X-Ray Diagnosis: No broken bones

17. Was patient treated by anyone else? Yes ☐ No ☑ | By whom? — (Name and Address) | Date

18. Was patient hospitalized? Yes ☐ No ☑ | Name and Address of Hospital | Date of Admission: Date of Discharge:

19. Is further treatment needed? Yes ☐ No ☑ | For how long? | 20. Patient was ☑ will be ☐ able to resume regular work on: 4/14 Patient was ☐ will be ☐ able to resume light work on:

21. If death ensued give date: | 22. Remarks: (Give any information of value not included above)

23. I am a qualified specialist in: orthopedics | I am a duly licensed Physician in the State of: Maryland | I was graduated from Medical School (Name) Johns Hopkins | Year 1967

Date of this report: 6/21/YY | (Signed) John N. Sparks, M.D.
8504 Capricorn Drive Atlanta, GA 30312 | Phone: (404) 544-0078
Address: | (This report must be signed PERSONALLY by Physician)

Figure 15–3 First Report of Injury

The progress report must include the following information:

- Patient's name and workers' compensation file or case number
- Treatment and progress report
- Work status at the time of the report
- Statement of continued need for treatment and the type of treatment
- Estimate of patient status regarding return to work, disability, or loss of function
- Copies of x-ray, laboratory, or consultation reports related to treatment and progress

The physician signs the report and all copies. The original report is maintained in the patient's record, and a copy is sent to the insurance carrier.

Reimbursement and CMS-1500 Completion

The physician or provider must accept the workers' compensation allowable fee as payment in full for covered services. There is no deductible or co-payment for workers' compensation cases. Workers' compensation claims are submitted via the CMS-1500 form. Completion instructions for the CMS-1500 are presented in two sections: blocks 1–13 and blocks 14–33. Refer to Figure 15–4 for blocks 1–13 and Figure 15–5 for blocks 14–33. The figures represent a generic CMS-1500. Commercial, state, and federal workers' compensation programs have specific guidelines for completing this form. For example, the federal OWCP guidelines in effect at the time of publication required the provider to leave blocks 1, 6, 8 through 10, 11a through 11d, 14 through 20, 22, 23, and 27 blank.

(1500)

HEALTH INSURANCE CLAIM FORM

APPROVED BY NATIONAL UNIFORM CLAIM COMMITTEE 08/05

CARRIER

PICA PICA

1. MEDICARE (Medicare #) MEDICAID (Medicaid #) TRICARE CHAMPUS (Sponsor's SSN) CHAMPVA (Member ID #) GROUP HEALTH PLAN (SSN or ID) FECA BLK LUNG [X] (SSN) OTHER (ID)

1a. INSURED'S I.D. NUMBER (For Program in Item 1): 481608921

2. PATIENT'S NAME (Last Name, First Name, Middle Initial): JOHNSON, MARIE

3. PATIENT'S BIRTH DATE MM DD YY: 04 04 1985 SEX M [ ] F [X]

4. INSURED'S NAME (Last Name, First Name, Middle Initial): PAINTING PLACE

5. PATIENT'S ADDRESS (No., Street): 408 WEST RIDGE

6. PATIENT RELATIONSHIP TO INSURED: Self [ ] Spouse [ ] Child [ ] Other [X]

7. INSURED'S ADDRESS (No., Street): 40 INDUSTRIAL DRIVE

CITY: BLUEBERRY STATE: ME

8. PATIENT STATUS: Single [ ] Married [ ] Other [ ] Employed [X] Full-Time Student [ ] Part-Time Student [ ]

CITY: BLUEBERRY STATE: ME

ZIP CODE: 49855 TELEPHONE (Include Area Code): (609) 422 8190

ZIP CODE: 49855 TELEPHONE (Include Area Code): (609) 555 9999

9. OTHER INSURED'S NAME (Last Name, First Name, Middle Initial)

10. IS PATIENT'S CONDITION RELATED TO:

11. INSURED'S POLICY GROUP OR FECA NUMBER

a. OTHER INSURED'S POLICY OR GROUP NUMBER

a. EMPLOYMENT? (Current or Previous) [X] YES [ ] NO

a. INSURED'S DATE OF BIRTH MM DD YY SEX M [ ] F [ ]

b. OTHER INSURED'S DATE OF BIRTH MM DD YY SEX M [ ] F [ ]

b. AUTO ACCIDENT? [ ] YES [X] NO PLACE (State)

b. EMPLOYER'S NAME OR SCHOOL NAME: PAINTING PLACE

c. EMPLOYER'S NAME OR SCHOOL NAME

c. OTHER ACCIDENT? [ ] YES [X] NO

c. INSURANCE PLAN NAME OR PROGRAM NAME: WORKERS COMPENSATION FUND

d. INSURANCE PLAN NAME OR PROGRAM NAME

10d. RESERVED FOR LOCAL USE

d. IS THERE ANOTHER HEALTH BENEFIT PLAN? [ ] YES [ ] NO *If yes,* return to and complete item 9 a-d.

READ BACK OF FORM BEFORE COMPLETING & SIGNING THIS FORM.

12. PATIENT'S OR AUTHORIZED PERSON'S SIGNATURE I authorize the release of any medical or other information necessary to process this claim. I also request payment of government benefits either to myself or to the party who accepts assignment below.

SIGNED ______ DATE ______

13. INSURED'S OR AUTHORIZED PERSON'S SIGNATURE I authorize payment of medical benefits to the undersigned physician or supplier for services described below.

SIGNED ______

PATIENT AND INSURED INFORMATION

For instructional use only. Courtesy of the Centers for Medicare and Medicaid Services, www.cms.hhs.gov.

Figure 15–4 CMS-1500, Blocks 1–13

14. DATE OF CURRENT: ILLNESS (First symptom) OR INJURY (Accident) OR PREGNANCY (LMP) — MM DD YY: 09 10 20YY

15. IF PATIENT HAS HAD SAME OR SIMILAR ILLNESS, GIVE FIRST DATE MM DD YY

16. DATES PATIENT UNABLE TO WORK IN CURRENT OCCUPATION — FROM 07 10 20YY TO 08 10 20YY

17. NAME OF REFERRING PROVIDER OR OTHER SOURCE — 17a. 17b. NPI

18. HOSPITALIZATION DATES RELATED TO CURRENT SERVICES — FROM MM DD YY TO MM DD YY

19. RESERVED FOR LOCAL USE

20. OUTSIDE LAB? YES [X] NO — $ CHARGES

21. DIAGNOSIS OR NATURE OF ILLNESS OR INJURY (Relate Items 1, 2, 3, or 4 to Item 24E by Line)
1. 807 . 02
2. ___ . __
3. ___ . __
4. ___ . __

22. MEDICAID RESUBMISSION CODE — ORIGINAL REF. NO.

23. PRIOR AUTHORIZATION NUMBER

	24. A. DATE(S) OF SERVICE From MM DD YY	To MM DD YY	B. PLACE OF SERVICE	C. EMG	D. PROCEDURES, SERVICES, OR SUPPLIES (Explain Unusual Circumstances) CPT/HCPCS	MODIFIER	E. DIAGNOSIS POINTER	F. $ CHARGES	G. DAYS OR UNITS	H. EPSDT Family Plan	I. ID. QUAL.	J. RENDERING PROVIDER ID. #
1	07 10 YY		11		99213		1	45 00	1		NPI	1230467891
2											NPI	
3											NPI	
4											NPI	
5											NPI	
6											NPI	

25. FEDERAL TAX I.D. NUMBER — 49811922 — SSN EIN [X]

26. PATIENT'S ACCOUNT NO.

27. ACCEPT ASSIGNMENT? (For govt. claims, see back) [X] YES NO

28. TOTAL CHARGE $ 45 00

29. AMOUNT PAID $

30. BALANCE DUE $

31. SIGNATURE OF PHYSICIAN OR SUPPLIER INCLUDING DEGREES OR CREDENTIALS (I certify that the statements on the reverse apply to this bill and are made a part thereof.)
SIGNATURE ON FILE
SIGNED DATE

32. SERVICE FACILITY LOCATION INFORMATION
UPNORTH MEDICAL
4 MEDICAL DRIVE
BLUEBERRY ME 49855
a. 5678901234 b.

33. BILLING PROVIDER INFO & PH # (609) 555 8888
UPNORTH MEDICAL
4 MEDICAL DRIVE
BLUEBERRY ME 49855
a. 5678901234 b.

PHYSICIAN OR SUPPLIER INFORMATION

NUCC Instruction Manual available at: www.nucc.org

APPROVED OMB-0938-0999 FORM CMS-1500 (08-05)

Figure 15–5 CMS-1500, Blocks 14–33

Block 1	Enter an X in OTHER.
Block 1a	First claim: Enter the patient's Social Security number. Subsequent claims: Enter the insurance carrier's assigned claim number or the patient's Social Security number.
Block 2	Enter the patient's name as directed.
Block 3	Enter the patient's eight-digit birth date (MM/DD/YYYY), and check the appropriate box for gender.
Block 4	Enter the name of the employer at the time of injury. Note: This block may be left blank.
Block 5	Enter the patient's home address and phone number.
Block 6	Enter an X in Other or leave blank.
Block 7	Enter the employer's address and phone number, if known.
Block 8	Leave the patient's marital status blank. Enter an X in Employed.
Blocks 9–9d	Leave this blank.

continued on the next page

continued from the previous page

Blocks 10–10c	Enter an X in Yes for block 10a. Enter an X in Yes or No in box 10b and 10c, as appropriate.
Block 10d	Leave this blank.
Block 11	Enter the workers' compensation insurance carrier's claim number, if known. Otherwise, leave this blank.
Block 11a	Leave this blank.
Block 11b	Enter the employer's name.
Block 11c	Enter the name of the workers' compensation insurance carrier.
Block 11d	Leave this blank.
Block 12	Leave this blank. The patient's signature is not required for workers' compensation claims.
Block 13	Leave this blank.

Review Figure 15–4 for completed blocks 1–13.

Block 14	Enter the date the symptoms started or the injury occurred.
Block 15	Enter the date the provider first rendered services for this injury, if available or applicable.
Block 16	Enter the dates as directed.
Block 17	Enter the name and title of any referring health care provider, if applicable.
Block 17a	Leave this blank.
Block 17b	Enter the national provider identification (NPI) of the provider named in block 17.
Block 18	Enter the hospitalization dates, if applicable.
Block 19	Leave this blank.
Block 20	Enter an X in Yes or No. Enter the total charges, if applicable.
Block 21	Enter up to four ICD-9-CM diagnostic codes in order of priority. (Note: Use ICD-10 codes when implemented.)
Block 22	Leave this blank.
Block 23	Enter any assigned managed care preauthorization number.
Block 24A	Enter the month, day, and year (MM/DD/YYYY) in the From column. Do not enter the To date unless the insurance carrier requests it.
Block 24B	Enter the place of service code.

continued on the next page

continued from the previous page

Block 24C	Leave this blank.
Block 24D	Enter *Current Procedural Terminology* (CPT) codes or *Healthcare Common Procedure Coding System* (HCPCS) codes and modifiers, as applicable.
Block 24E	Enter the diagnosis reference code from block 21 that best proves the medical necessity for each service listed in block 24D.
Block 24F	Enter the charge for the service identified in each line.
Block 24G	Enter the days or units for each line item. Enter 1 if only one service is provided. This block should be used for multiple visits for identical services, the number of miles, the units of supplies, or the oxygen volume.
Block 24H	Leave this blank.
Block 24I	Shaded area: Leave this blank.
Block 24J	Enter the NPI of the physician who provided the service.
Block 25	Enter the provider's employer federal tax ID number (employer identification number [EIN]). If there is not one, enter the provider's Social Security number. Enter an X in the appropriate box.
Block 26	Enter the patient's account number, if one is assigned by the provider.
Block 27	Leave this blank.
Block 28	Enter the total charges.
Blocks 29–30	Leave this blank.
Block 31	Provider's signature or SIGNATURE ON FILE and date.
Block 32	Enter the name, address, city, state, and zip code of the place services were provided.
Block 32a	Enter the NPI for the entity named in block 32.
Block 33	Enter the name, complete address, and telephone number of the billing entity.
Block 33a	Enter the NPI of the entity named in block 33. For a solo practitioner, enter the physician's NPI. For a group-practice practitioner, enter the NPI of the group practice.
Block 33b	Leave blank.

Review Figure 15–5 for completed blocks 14–33.

 ABBREVIATIONS

Table 15–4 lists the abbreviations presented in this chapter.

TABLE 15-4

Abbreviations and Meanings	
Abbreviation	**Meaning**
CPT	*Current Procedural Terminology*
DOE	U.S. Department of Energy
DOL	U.S. Department of Labor
DCMWC	Division of Coal Mine Workers' Compensation
DEEOIC	Division of Energy Employees Occupational Illness Compensation
DFEC	Division of Federal Employees' Compensation
DLHWC	Division of Longshore and Harbor Workers' Compensation
EEOICPA	Energy Employees Occupational Illness Compensation Program Act
EIN	employer identification number
FECA	Federal Employees' Compensation Act
HCPCS	*Healthcare Common Procedure Coding System*
LHWCA	Longshore and Harbor Workers' Compensation Act
MSDS	material safety data sheet
NPI	national provider identification
OWCP	Office of Workers' Compensation Programs
OSHA	Occupational Safety and Health Administration

 SUMMARY

Workers' compensation insurance is intended to ensure that employees who are injured or disabled on the job are provided with wage replacement and medical and rehabilitation benefits. A federal mandate issued in 1912 directed each state to establish a Workers' Compensation Act that established a system for providing these benefits. Different federal workers' compensation programs cover employees who work in the maritime industry, in Washington, D.C., or in the coal mining industry. State-sponsored workers' compensation programs may be managed by the state, the employer, private insurance companies, or a combination of these groups.

Workers' compensation programs identify various levels of disability, ranging from temporary to permanent. Permanent disability is further categorized as partial or total disability. Vocational rehabilitation is an important part of workers' compensation.

REVIEW EXERCISES

Case Study

> Read the following case study and then complete a CMS-1500 by using the workers' compensation guidelines in this chapter. Your instructor will tell you how to obtain the form.
> PATIENT NAME: Dennis Wood
> DOB: 11/11/1960
> SSN: 492-61-0830
> ADDRESS: 80 Visitor Drive; Blueberry, ME 49855
> PHONE: (H) (906) 302-9090
> EMPLOYER: Painting Place, 40 Industrial Drive, Blueberry, ME 49855
> INSURANCE: Workers' Compensation, State Insurance Fund, 300 Capital Ave., Capital ME 42212.
> FECA NUMBER: WCF555000
> PROGRESS NOTE
> DATE: 01/05/20YY
> Mr. Wood is seen today for injuries sustained as a result of a fall from a ladder while painting the window trim on a building. He sustained a closed fracture of the left radius and multiple abrasions on the arms and face. X-rays revealed a Colles's fracture of the left radius that was reduced and a plaster cast applied. He will be unable to work for six weeks. No permanent disability is anticipated. Mr. Wood will return tomorrow for a cast check. A first report of injury was completed.
> SIGNED: Denzel Hamilton, MD
> Superiorland Clinic
> 714 Hennepin Ave.
> Blueberry, ME 49855
> PHONE: (906) 336-4020
> Superiorland Clinic NPI: 4567890123
> Denzel Hamilton NPI: 5567890123
> DIAGNOSIS AND TREATMENT CODES: Colles's fracture, left radius 813.41 (ICD-10-CM 552.532A); abrasion, arms 913.0 (ICD-10-CM 540.819A); abrasion, face 910.0 (ICD-10-CM 500.81A); office visit 99214; forearm x-ray 73090; closed reduction of Colles's fracture 25600; application of plaster cast 29085.
> CHARGES: Office visit $75; closed reduction of fracture $200; application of plaster cast $50; x-ray forearm $60.

Fill in the Blank

1. The _____ provides benefits for employees engaged in maritime work.

2. The Black Lung Program is another name for the _____.

3. _____ work is defined as work while sitting with minimal demands for physical effort.

4. _____ work is defined as work in a position that allows for sitting half the time and standing or walking half the time.

Multiple Choice

Circle the correct answer from the choices provided.

1. Which act is *not* a workers' compensation program?

    a. FECA

    b. LHWCA

    c. Black Lung Program

    d. OSHA

2. An employer self-insured workers' compensation program

    a. sets aside a percentage of the company's financial resources to cover the medical expenses of injured employees.

    b. combines state and federal money for injured employees.

    c. identifies a specific agency to function as an insuring body.

    d. purchases insurance policies from private companies.

3. To qualify for workers' compensation benefits, the employee must

    a. file for benefits within 30 days of the injury.

    b. be injured while working within the scope of the employment agreement.

    c. document the reason the injury occurred.

    d. file a first report of injury form.

4. Under workers' compensation guidelines, permanent disability

    a. is the same as a medical disability.

    b. means the employee will never return to work.

    c. is dependent on the age of the employee.

    d. must be reevaluated on an annual basis.

5. A first report of injury form is completed by the

    a. employer.

    b. employee.

    c. physician.

    d. billing specialist.

6. Compensation for permanent disability depends on all but one of the following:

    a. Assessment by an independent physician

    b. Age of the employee

    c. Amount of loss of function

    d. Occupation before the injury occurred

7. Eligibility for workers' compensation depends primarily on the

   a. occupation of the employee.

   b. location of the injury.

   c. age of the employee.

   d. relationship of the injury to the job.

8. Black lung disease is an example of a

   a. hazard associated with coal mining.

   b. disorder that is directly linked to employment.

   c. temporary disability.

   d. permanent disability.

 CHALLENGE ACTIVITIES

1. Search the Internet for your state's workers' compensation information. Print the guidelines for eligibility.

2. Interview a billing specialist at a local physician's office. Ask about the unique problems, if any, associated with workers' compensation claims.

WEBSITES

Federal Employees' Compensation Act: http://www.dol.gov
Occupational Safety and Health Administration: http://www.osha.gov
Workers' Compensation: http://www.workerscompensation.com

Appendix A

Superiorland Clinic Practice Manual

HOW TO ACCESS APPENDIX A: SUPERIORLAND CLINIC PRACTICE MANUAL AND SIMCLAIM™

The Appendix A Clinic Practice Manual can be found on this text's accompanying Premium Website. Please refer to the information on the printed access card bound in this textbook to access this online asset. Once at the Premium Website, you will find the case studies of Appendix A and additional information on how to use the SimClaim™ software program itself.

GENERAL INSTRUCTIONS AND HINTS FOR SIMCLAIM

Please read the following general instructions before beginning work:

- **Turn on Caps Lock:** All data entered into SimClaim must be in ALL CAPS.
- **Do not abbreviate:** Spell out street, drive, avenue, signature on file, Blue Cross/Blue Shield, and so forth. No abbreviations (other than state abbreviations) will be accepted by the program.
- **Do not use "Same As" or "None" in any block:** Even if patient information is the same as insured information, enter that information again on the claim.
- **More than one Diagnosis Pointer in Block 24E:** For the SimClaim case studies, more than one diagnosis pointer may be required in block 24E.
- **No Amount Paid indicated:** If there is no amount paid indicated on the case study, enter "0 00" in block 29.
- **Secondary Insurance Claims:** If a case study indicates that a patient's primary insurance carrier has paid an amount, fill out a second claim form for the secondary insurance that reflects the amount reimbursed by primary insurance.
- **More than one CMS form:** Remember, if the place of service or the provider changes, another claim form is needed.
- **Fill out Block 32:** Always fill out service facility location information in SimClaim block 32: Superiorland Clinic Practice Manual 551.
- **Enter all dates as given in case study:** For dates that are not given (e.g., signature dates), use MMDDYY. "YY" or "YYYY" is always used in place of an actual year, except for birth dates.
- For additional help using SimClaim, refer to the Block Help within SimClaim.

Appendix B

References

The information in this text is the result of many hours of research. Books, periodicals, and the Internet were invaluable resources that provided the most current data available at the time of publication. Because medical coding and insurance billing guidelines and regulations are frequently revised and updated, the listed references provide students with the opportunity to access professional and governmental organizations that mandate these revisions. Internet sites are also listed in chapters throughout the book.

BOOKS

Basic CPT/HCPCS Coding, Gail I. Smith, MA, RHIA, CCS-P, American Health Information Management Association, Chicago.

Basic ICD-9-CM Coding, Lou Ann Schraffenberger, MBA, RHIA, CCS, CCS-P, American Health Information Management Association, Chicago.

ICD-9-CM, published by the U.S. Department of Health and Human Services, Washington, D.C., 2013.

PERIODICALS

Coding Clinic for ICD-9-CM, Central Office on ICD-9-CM, American Hospital Association, Chicago, IL.

For the Record, Great Valley Publishing Company, Inc., Valley Forge, PA.

Journal of the American Health Information Management Association, American Health Information Management Association, Chicago, IL.

NEWSLETTERS

Briefings on APCs, Opus Communications, Inc., Marblehead, MA.

Coding and Reimbursement for Physicians, St. Anthony's Publishing, Reston, VA.

Physician Practice Compliance Report, Medical Group Management Association, Englewood, CO, and Opus Communications, Marblehead, MA.

WEBSITES

Website	Internet Address
American Academy of Professional Coders	http://www.aapc.com
American Health Information Management Association	http://www.ahima.org

American Medical Billing Association	http://www.ambanet.net
Centers for Medicare and Medicaid Services	http://www.cms.hhs.gov
Department of Health and Human Services, Office of Civil Rights	http://www.dhs.gov/ocr/hipaa
Medical Association of Billers	http://physicianswebsites.com
National Uniform Billing Committee	http://www.nubc.org
ICD-9-CM Official Guidelines for Coding and Reporting	http://www.cdc.gov/nchs/icd9.htm
ICD-10-CM National Center for Health Statistics	http://www.cdc.gov/nchs/icd10cm.htm
ICD-10-PCS (CMS)	http://www.cms.gov//ICD10PCS.asp
TRICARE	http://www.tricare.mil

Appendix C

Abbreviations

A/B MAC	Part A and Part B Medicare Administrative Contractor
AAA	abdominal aortic aneurysm
AAPC	American Academy of Professional Coders
ABN	Advance Beneficiary Notice
ADSM	active duty service member
AHA	American Hospital Association
AHIMA	American Health Information Management Association
AIDS	acquired immunodeficiency syndrome
AMA	American Medical Association
AMBA	American Medical Billing Association
APC	ambulatory payment classification (system)
ASC	ambulatory surgery center
BC/BS	Blue Cross/Blue Shield
BCBSA	Blue Cross and Blue Shield Association
CAH	critical access hospital
CAP	claims assistance professional
CC	chief complaint
CC	complication/co-morbidity
CCA	certified coding associate
CCCC	complex chronic care coordination services
CCS	certified coding specialist
CCS-P	certified coding specialist–physician-based
CDC	Centers for Disease Control
CE	continuing education
CF	(national) conversion factor
CHAMPUS	Civilian Health and Medical Program of the Uniformed Services
CHAMPVA	Civilian Health and Medical Program of the Department of Veterans Affairs
CHIP	Children's Health Insurance Program
CHRS	certified healthcare reimbursement specialist
CMAC	CHAMPUS Maximum Allowable Charge
CMBS	certified medical billing specialist
CMBS-CA	certified medical billing specialist–chiropractic assistant
CMBS-H	certified medical billing specialist–hospital
CMRS	certified medical reimbursement specialist
CMS	Centers for Medicare and Medicaid Services
COB	coordination of benefits
CPC	certified professional coder
CPC-H	certified professional coder–hospital

CPC-P	certified professional coder–payer
CPT	*Current Procedural Terminology*
CVA	cerebrovascular accident
DCMWC	Division of Coal Mine Workers' Compensation
DEEOIC	Division of Energy Employees Occupational Illness Compensation
DEERS	Defense Enrollment Eligibility and Reporting System
DFEC	Division of Federal Employees' Compensation
DLHWC	Division of Longshore and Harbor Workers' Compensation
DME	durable medical equipment
DME MAC	durable medical equipment Medicare administrative contractor
DMEPOS	durable medical equipment, prosthetics, orthotics, and supplies
DoD	Department of Defense
DOE	Department of Energy
DOJ	Department of Justice
DOL	Department of Labor
DRG	diagnosis-related group
E/M	Evaluation and Management
ECS	electronic claims submission
EDI	electronic data interchange
EEOICPA	Energy Employees Occupational Illness Compensation Program Act
EHR	electronic health record
EIN	employer identification number
EMR	electronic medical record
EOB	explanation of benefits
EPHI	electronic protected health information
EPO	exclusive provider organization
EPSDT	Early and Periodic Screening, Diagnosis, and Treatment
ESRD	end-stage renal disease
FBI	Federal Bureau of Investigation
FDCPA	Fair Debt Collection Practices Act
FECA	Federal Employees' Compensation Act
FH	family history
FL	form locator
GAF	geographic adjustment factor
HCFA	Health Care Finance Administration
HCPCS	*Healthcare Common Procedure Coding System*
HHS	Department of Health and Human Services
HICN	health insurance claim number
HIPAA	Health Insurance Portability and Accountability Act of 1996
HIV	human immunodeficiency virus
HMO	health maintenance organization
HPI	history of present illness
ICD	International Classification of Diseases
ICD-10	*International Classification of Diseases, Tenth Revision*
ICD-10-PCS	*International Classification of Diseases, Tenth Revision, Procedure Coding System*
ICD-9-CM	*International Classification of Diseases, Ninth Revision, Clinical Modification*

ICF	intermediate care facility
IDS	integrated delivery system
IPA	independent practice association
IPPS	inpatient prospective payment system
LHWCA	Longshore and Harbor Workers' Compensation Act
LMP	last menstrual period
LOS	length of stay
MA	Medicare Advantage
MAB	Medical Association of Billers
MAC	Medicare Administrative Contractor
MA-PDP	Medicare Advantage Prescription Drug Plan
MCC	major complication/co-morbidity
MCD	Medicare/Medicaid Crossover Program
MCO	managed care organization
MFS	Medicare fee schedule
MRI	magnetic resonance imaging
MSA	(Medicare) medical savings account
MS-DRG	medical-severity diagnosis related group
MSDS	material safety data sheet
MSN	Medicare Summary Notice
MSP	Medicare as secondary payer
MTF	military treatment facility
NATO	North Atlantic Treaty Organization
NCCI	National Correct Coding Initiative
NCHS	National Center for Health Statistics
NEBA	National Electronic Billers Alliance
NEC	not elsewhere classified
NOAA	National Oceanic and Atmospheric Administration
nonPAR	nonparticipating provider
NOS	not otherwise specified
NPI	national provider identifier (number)
NUBC	National Uniform Billing Committee
NUCC	National Uniform Claim Committee
OCR	Office of Civil Rights
OHI	other health insurance
OIG	Office of the Inspector General
OPPS	outpatient prospective payment system
OSHA	Occupational Safety and Health Administration
OWCP	Office of Workers' Compensation Programs
PAR	participating provider
PCM	primary care manager
PCP	primary care provider
PDP	prescription drug plan
PET	positron emission tomography
PFFS	private fee-for-service
PHI	protected health information

PIN	physician/provider identification number
PMH	past medical history
POA	present on admission
POS	place of service; point-of-service plan
PPO	preferred provider organization
QI	Qualifying Individual
QMB	Qualified Medicare Beneficiary
RA	remittance advice
RBRVS	resource-based relative value scale
ROI	release of information
ROS	review of systems
RVS	relative value scale
RVU	relative value unit
SCHIP	State Children's Health Insurance Program
SH	social history
SLMB	Specified Low-Income Medicare Beneficiary
SNF	skilled nursing facility
SNP	special needs plan (Medicare)
SOF	signature on file
SSA	Social Security Act
SSI	Supplemental Security Income
SSN	Social Security number
TANF	Temporary Assistance for Needy Families
TCM	transitional care management
TFL	TRICARE for Life
TMA	TRICARE Management Agency
TPA	third-party administrator
TPR	TRICARE Prime Remote
TRR	TRICARE Retired Reserve
TRS	TRICARE Reserve Select
TYA	TRICARE Young Adult
UB-04	Uniform Bill (2004 revision)
UCR	usual, customary, and reasonable (fee)
UHDDS	Uniform Hospital Discharge Data Set
WHO	World Health Organization

Glossary

A

7th character extension The seventh character of an ICD-10-CM diagnosis code that provides additional information about the patient's condition.

18/19 A combination of Medicare and Medicaid programs available to individuals who are Medicare-eligible and whose incomes fall below the federal poverty level; also called Medi/Medi or Care/Caid.

Abuse Actions that are inconsistent with accepted, sound medical, business, or fiscal practices and that directly or indirectly result in unnecessary costs to the Medicare program through improper payments.

Accept assignment Physicians and providers who accept the benefit paid by the insurance company for a specific service as payment in full for that service; the patient does not have to pay any difference.

Accommodation code A two-character code that identifies the type of hospital bed the patient occupies.

Active duty service member (ADSM) Individual enlisted as a member of the uniformed services of the United States.

Add-on codes CPT codes that must be used with a related procedure code.

Admitting diagnosis The condition that caused the patient to seek treatment.

Admitting physician The physician who arranges for a patient's admission to the hospital.

Adult primary policy The insurance policy that lists the patient as the subscriber or policyholder.

Adult secondary policy The insurance policy that lists the patient as a dependent on a second insurance policy.

Advance Beneficiary Notice (ABN) Written notification provided to Medicare recipients that describes the cost of treatment that may not be covered by Medicare.

Affordable Care Act A federal law enacted in 2010 that is intended to provide access to health insurance to individuals, families, and small businesses; reduce healthcare costs; limit the insurance company's ability to deny, rescind, or restrict coverage. The full title is the Patient Protection and Affordable Care Act.

Allowable charge/allowable fee The payment to a provider that is the lower amount of the provider's fee and the allowed fee; also called the maximum allowable charge.

Alphabetic Index Component of the ICD-9 and ICD-10 coding references; an alphabetic list of diseases, conditions, signs, symptoms, procedures, and other main terms.

Allowed charge The maximum amount the insurance company pays for the service.

Ambulatory Payment Classification (APC) A payment calculation method based on grouping procedures that have similar clinical characteristics and similar costs by CPT/HCPCS codes.

Ambulatory surgery center (ASC) Freestanding facility that specializes in same-day surgery.

American Academy of Professional Coders (AAPC) A professional association that provides education, training, and certification for medical coders.

American Health Information Management Association (AHIMA) One of the Cooperating Parties that provides training and certification for coding professionals.

American Hospital Association (AHA) One of the Cooperating Parties that maintains the Central Office on ICD-9-CM, answers questions about coding, and produces the *Coding Clinic for ICD-9-CM*.

American Medical Association (AMA) The governing body responsible for the development of the procedure codes found in the *Current Procedural Terminology* (CPT).

American Medical Billing Association (AMBA) A professional association that provides education, training, and certification for medical coders.

Ancillary services code A two-character code that identifies services not included in the room and board charges related to an inpatient episode of care.

Approach The technique or method used to reach a given procedure site; a component of ICD-10-PCS procedure codes.

Assignment of benefits Identifies who actually receives the insurance payment.

Attending physician The physician responsible for the patient's care while in the hospital.

Authorized provider A hospital, an institution, a physician, or another professional who meets the licensing and certification requirements of TRICARE and is practicing within the scope of that license.

B

Balance-billing Billing the patient for the amount not covered by insurance.

Batch A process for sending electronic claims based on predetermined criteria.

Beneficiaries Dependents eligible for TRICARE or CHAMPVA; individuals eligible for Medicare.

Benefit period Period of time that begins when an individual is admitted to a hospital or skilled nursing facility and ends 60 days after discharge; used to determine deductibles and co-payments for Medicare Part A.

Benign Noncancerous.

Birthday rule Determines the primary payer when the patient is a child living with both parents and each carries health insurance.

Black Lung Program Act that provides benefits to coal miners; also known as the Federal Coal Mine Health and Safety Act.

Blue Cross and Blue Shield Association (BCBSA) The combined board of directors from the Blue Cross program and the Blue Shield program.

Blue Cross/Blue Shield (BC/BS) A nationwide federation of nonprofit health insurance companies.

Body system The general physiological system or anatomic region involved in a given procedure; a component of ICD-10-PCS procedure codes.

Bullet (•) Symbol used to identify a new addition or new code in the CPT codebook.

C

CA-7 Claim for Compensation A workers' compensation program claims submission form.

Ca in situ Cancerous growth or tumor that is confined to a specific site.

Cafeteria plan A health insurance plan that allows beneficiaries to choose covered services.

California Physicians' Service The first plan to achieve physician cooperation in prepaid health plans.

Capitation A reimbursement method that depends on the number of individuals covered by the health insurance contract.

Carcinoma A growth or tumor that is cancerous or malignant.

Care/Caid A combination of Medicare and Medicaid programs available to individuals who are Medicare-eligible and whose income falls below the federal poverty level; also called Medi/Medi and 18/19.

Carrier-direct A claims submission method that allows the provider to submit claims directly to the insurance carrier.

Carryover line Format used when a complete entry does not fit on one line.

Catchment area A geographic location associated with CMAC procedure pricing.

Categories/subsection Divisions within the CPT codebook sections.

Category A three-digit code that represents a single disease or a group of closely related conditions.

Centers for Disease Control (CDC) A federal government agency responsible for various aspects of disease prevention and control.

Centers for Medicare and Medicaid Services (CMS) A division of the Department of Health and Human Services responsible for managing Medicare and Medicaid health insurance programs; one of the Cooperating Parties that maintains and updates ICD-9-CM procedure codes.

Certification The process that involves successful completion of a professionally recognized exam.

Certified coding associate (CCA) An entry-level medical coding credential offered by the American Health Information Management Association.

Certified coding specialist (CCS) The title given to an individual upon successful completion of the national coding exam of the American Health Information Management Association.

Certified coding specialist–physician-based (CCS-P) A credential offered by the American Health Information Management Association that is appropriate for experienced coders in physician-based settings.

Certified healthcare reimbursement specialist (CHRS) A credential offered by the National Electronic Billers Alliance for individuals with experience in all areas of medical billing.

Certified medical billing specialist (CMBS) An entry-level credential offered by the Medical Association of Billers.

Certified medical billing specialist–chiropractic assistance (CMBS-CA) An intermediate-level credential offered by the Medical Association of Billers that is appropriate for individuals working in a chiropractic agency.

Certified medical billing specialist–hospital (CMBS-H) An intermediate-level credential offered by the Medical Association of Billers that is appropriate for individuals working in a hospital.

Certified medical reimbursement specialist (CMRS) A credential offered by the American Medical Billing Association that is appropriate for individuals with medical billing experience in various health care settings.

Certified professional coder (CPC) The title given to an individual upon successful completion of the national coding exam of the American Academy of Professional Coders.

Certified professional coder–hospital (CPC-H) A credential offered by the American Academy of Professional Coders that is appropriate for experienced coders in hospital outpatient and ambulatory facility settings.

Certified professional coder–payer (CPC-P) A credential offered by the American Academy of Professional Coders that is appropriate for individuals in insurance-related settings.

CHAMPUS maximum allowable charge (CMAC) The highest amount TRICARE will pay for a service.

Chargemaster A computer program or database that contains the charges and medical codes for services and supplies provided to patients.

Charge slip A source document for financial, diagnostic, and treatment information; also called an encounter form, a routing form, or a superbill.

Circle (○) Annotation placed before a CPT code to indicate that the code has been reinstated or recycled.

Circled bullet (☉) Annotation placed before a CPT code to indicate that the service or procedure includes the use of moderate sedation.

Civilian Health and Medical Program of the Uniformed Services (CHAMPUS) A federally funded comprehensive health benefits program for dependents of personnel serving in the uniformed services; now known as TRICARE.

Civilian Health and Medical Program of the Veterans Administration (CHAMPVA) A program to cover medical expenses of dependent spouses and children of veterans with total, permanent service-connected disabilities.

Claims assistance professional (CAP) An individual who assists patients in the completion of paperwork necessary to obtain insurance payment.

Clean claim Claim paid on the first submission.

Clearinghouse A service that distributes claims to the correct insurance carrier.

Closed biopsy A procedure for removing tissue that does not require an incision.

CMS-1450 Alternate name for the UB-04, a universal claims submission form.

CMS-1500 A universal insurance claims submission form; formerly called the HCFA-1500.

Code also Coding instruction that directs the medical coder to assign more than one code to a diagnosis or procedure.

Code first Phrase used to identify the need for two codes.

Code first [the] underlying condition Phrase used to signify that the condition is the result of another underlying disease.

Code, if applicable, any causal condition first Coding instruction that directs the medical coder to assign a medical code for a condition that causes another problem, disease, or condition.

Coding conventions The rules of the ICD-9-CM (or ICD-10-CM) that include instructional notes, abbreviations, cross-reference notes, punctuation marks, and specific usage of the words "and," "with," and "due to."

Co-insurance A specific percentage of the charge the patient must pay the provider for each encounter; also called co-insurance payment.

Co-insurance days Covered days of care that require the patient to pay part of the charges for services rendered.

Co-insurance payment A specific percentage of the charge the patient must pay the provider for each encounter; also called co-insurance.

Colon/comma (:) (,) Punctuation used to identify essential modifiers related to ICD-9-CM and CPT code assignment.

Combination code A single code that is used to classify two diagnoses.

Combination program A combination of state, employer self-insured, and commercial workers' compensation programs.

Commercial workers' compensation program Program in which employers purchase insurance policies that provide benefits to injured employees.

Complex chronic care coordination (CCCC) Services provided by physicians and other qualified health professionals that address one or more chronic health conditions and commonly require the coordination of a number of specialities and services.

Compliance monitoring Identifying provider and insurance carrier responsibilities related to coding accuracy and verification of services provided.

Complication/co-morbidity (CC) A condition that substantially increases the use of hospital resources.

Concurrent condition A problem that exists along with a primary diagnosis and complicates the treatment of the primary diagnosis.

Conditional primary payer status A situation in which Medicare is billed as the primary payer for a temporary period of time.

Condition code A two-character code that relates to the patient's insurance eligibility and primary and secondary payer status; part of the UB-04.

Confidential information Information that is not open to public inspection.

Confidentiality The principle that certain information is not to be shared with others.

Congenital A condition that is present at or since the time of birth.

Connecting words Terms that indicate a relationship between the main term and the associated conditions or causes of disease.

Cooperating Parties Organizations responsible for maintaining and updating the ICD-9-CM or ICD-10-CM; consist of two professional parties—the American Hospital Association (AHA) and the American Health Information Management Association (AHIMA)—as well as two governmental agencies: the Centers for Medicare and Medicaid Services (CMS) and the National Center for Health Statistics (NCHS).

Coordination of benefits (COB) Statement of how benefits are paid when the patient is covered by more than one insurance policy so the total amount of the bill is not exceeded.

Co-pay A specific dollar amount the patient must pay the provider for each encounter; also called co-payment.

Co-payment A specific dollar amount the patient must pay the provider for each encounter; also called co-pay.

Cost sharing Co-payment and co-insurance.

Coverage Statement of the medical conditions that may or may not be paid by the insurance policy.

Covered days The number of hospital days eligible for reimbursement by a health insurance plan.

Covered entities Health plans, health care clearinghouses, and any health care provider who transmits health information in electronic form.

Covered services Services identified as covered by the health insurance plan.

Critical access hospital (CAH) A special designation for Medicare participating hospitals that are a part of a rural health plan.

Current Procedural Terminology (CPT) The coding system used to report physician and ambulatory services and procedures.

Custodial parent The divorced parent the child lives with; the parent responsible for medical bills, unless the divorce decree states otherwise.

Customary fee The fee that other providers in the same geographic area or with similar training charge for a given service.

D

Daily accounts receivable journal A chronological summary of all transactions posted to patient ledgers on a given day; also called a day sheet or daily transaction journal.

Daily transaction journal A chronological summary of all transactions posted to patient ledgers on a given day; also called a daily accounts receivable journal or day sheet.

Dash (-) An ICD-10-CM coding convention that indicates the code is incomplete.

Day sheet A chronological summary of all transactions posted to patients' ledgers on a given day; also called a daily accounts receivable journal.

Defense Enrollment Eligibility and Reporting System (DEERS) A database used to verify TRICARE beneficiary eligibility.

Delinquent claim Claim for which payment is overdue; also called pending claim.

Department of Defense (DoD) Government department that manages the TRICARE program.

Department of Energy (DOE) Government department that provides health insurance benefits for individuals employed in various energy-related industries.

Department of Health and Human Services (HHS) Government department that plays an active role in investigating health insurance fraud and abuse.

Department of Justice (DOJ) Government department that plays an active role in investigating health insurance fraud and abuse.

Department of Labor (DOL) Government department that plays an active role in Workers' Compensation programs.

Dependent Individual who is covered by the insured's health insurance policy.

Device A specific type of material, substance, or implant that is left in place after a procedure or treatment is completed; character 6 of an ICD-10-PCS code.

Diagnosis-related group (DRG) A payment method that pays a fixed amount based on the patient's diagnosis rather than on services provided.

Diagnostic service Services provided to an individual that establish or identify a problem, disease, or diagnosis.

Direct pay The patient pays the physician or health care practitioner for services provided.

Dirty claim Claim that has been denied or rejected.

Divison of Coal Mine Workers' Compensation (DCMWC) Government workers' compensation program related to the coal mining industry.

Division of Energy Employees Occupational Illness Compensation (DEEOIC) Government workers' compensation program for various energy-related industries.

Division of Federal Employees' Compensation (DFEC) Government workers' compensation program for federal employees.

Division of Longshore and Harbor Workers' Compensation (DLHWC) Government workers' compensation program for various shipping-related industries.

Downcoding Selecting codes at a lower level than the service requires.

Durable medical equipment (DME) Devices that improve function or retard any further deterioration of a physical condition; nondisposable medical devices.

Durable medical equipment Medicare administrative contractor (DME MAC) An organization that processes Medicare claims related to durable medical equipment.

Durable medical equipment, prosthetics, orthotics, and supplies (DMEPOS) A company that provided durable medical equipment, prosthetics, orthotics, and supplies to Medicare recipients.

Durable power of attorney Voluntary transfer of decision-making authority from one competent individual to another competent individual that continues after the granting individual's death or loss of ability to make decisions.

Due to A medical coding convention that describes a causal relationship between two conditions.

E

E codes A supplementary classification of the ICD-9-CM: "Classification of External Causes of Injury and Poisoning, Ninth Revision, Clinical Modification."

Early and Periodic Screening, Diagnostic, and Treatment Services (EPSDT) A congressional law mandating that states provide routine pediatric checkups to all children enrolled in Medicaid and provide treatment for any problems identified during these checkups.

Elective surgery A surgical procedure that is not an emergency, that is scheduled in advance, and for which failure to undergo the surgery is not life-threatening.

Electronic claim An insurance claim that is submitted to the insurance carrier by computer, tape, diskette, modem, fax, or personal computer upload or download.

Electronic claims processor (ECP) An individual with experience or training related to electronic claims submission.

Electronic claims submission (ECS) Submission of a claim via computer, tape, diskette, modem, fax, or personal computer upload or download.

Electronic data interchange (EDI) A process that sends information back and forth between two or more individuals by computer linkages.

Electronic health record (EHR) A medical record that is maintained in an electronic format; also called an electronic medical record.

Electronic medical record (EMR) A medical record that is maintained in an electronic format; also called an electronic health record.

Electronic protected health information (EPHI) Protected health information that is maintained or transmitted in electronic form.

Emancipated minor An individual who has not reached the age of majority as established by state law but who lives independently, is self-supporting, and has decision-making rights.

Embezzlement Stealing money that an individual has access to but does not have any legal claim to take, keep, or spend.

Emergency (EMG) Category of patient service that preserves the patient's life or prevents the loss of a limb or sensory functioning.

Employer identification number (EIN) A number that identifies a physician who provides services to patients.

Employer liability The employer is responsible for the actions of employees that are within the context of employment.

Employer self-insured program Program in which the employer sets aside a specific percentage of the company's funds to cover medical expenses and wage compensation for work-related injuries.

Employer-sponsored health insurance plan A health insurance plan in which the employer pays all or part of the fee necessary to purchase health insurance for employees and their dependents.

Encoder A computer-assisted medical coding software program.

Encounter An interaction between a patient and health care provider.

Encounter form A source document for financial, diagnostic, and treatment information; also called a charge slip, a routing form, or a superbill.

Energy Employees Occupational Illness Compensation Program Act (EEOICPA) Federal law that established workers' compensation for employees of various energy-related industries.

Enrollee An individual enrolled in Medicaid programs; an individual enrolled in a health insurance plan; also known as a subscriber.

Enrollee ID number A unique identification number for an individual enrolled in an insurance plan.

Enrollment code A number on an insurance card that identifies the type of plan the subscriber is enrolled in.

Episode-of-care reimbursement Charging a single fee for all services associated with a particular problem, illness, or procedure.

Error-edit feature A feature built into the electronic claims system that edits claims for errors.

Essential modifiers Subterms that are indented under the main term and affect accurate code assignment.

Etiology Cause of disease.

Evaluation and Management (E/M) Section of the CPT coding system that captures information about medical services for office visits, hospital visits, and consultations.

Examination The physical examination of the patient.

Excludes1 An ICD-10-CM notation that indicates the excluded code cannot be coded to a given category.

Excludes2 An ICD-10-CM notation that indicates the excluded condition is not a part of the condition represented by a given code or that more than one code is needed to accurately describe the patient's condition.

Exclusion Statement of the conditions not covered by the health insurance policy.

Excludes note A note that identifies when a medical code cannot be used.

Exclusive provider organization (EPO) A managed care organization that contracts with health care providers to obtain services for members; members are restricted to using the participating providers.

Explanation of benefits (EOB) A document that explains how the reimbursement is determined.

F

Facing triangles (▶ ◀) Symbol used to set off new or revised information in the CPT codebook.

Failed procedure A procedure that does not produce the desired result.

Fair Debt Collection Practices Act (FDCPA) A law that defines acceptable debt collection activities for collection agencies.

Family health insurance coverage Health care policy or program that applies to a family.

Federal Bureau of Investigation (FBI) Governmental body that plays an active role in investigating health insurance fraud and abuse related to federal or private health insurance programs.

Federal Coal Mine Health and Safety Act Act that provides benefits to coal miners; also known as the Black Lung Program.

Federal Employees' Compensation Act (FECA) Act that provides benefits for work-related injuries to all federal employees.

Fee-for-service A price or fee is charged for each individual service.

Final notice A billing statement sent to an individual before the account is sent to a collection agency

First-listed diagnosis The condition that describes the main reason for providing care in health care settings other than hospitals; an ICD-10-CM sequencing guideline.

First report of injury A written statement of the initial contact of the physician with the patient in a workers' compensation claim.

Fiscal agent A health insurance company that handles payments for Medicare Part B and Medicaid; also called insurance carrier.

Fiscal intermediaries Insurance carriers.

Five- and six-character subclassification A letter and two digits followed by a period/decimal point and up to three numbers that provides more information on the description of a condition; applies to ICD-10.

Flash symbol (⚡) An annotation placed before CPT codes that classify products pending FDA approval.

Florida Shared System (FSS) A Medicare database that includes the number of covered days remaining for each Medicare beneficiary.

Form locator (FL) UB-04 data field that captures information needed for insurance reimbursement.

Formulary A list of medications or other drugs available from a pharmacy or pharmacy service.

Four-character subcategory A letter with two digits followed by a period/decimal point and one number that provides more information on the description of a condition; applies to ICD-10.

Fraud An intentional deception or misrepresentation that an individual knows to be false or does not believe to be true and makes, knowing that deception could result in some unauthorized benefit to himself or herself or some other person.

G

General note A note printed in italics or bold in the ICD-9-CM or ICD-10-CM that serves to clarify unique coding situations.

Geographic adjustment factor (GAF) A factor that allows fees to be adjusted to accommodate variations in regional costs.

Global surgery concept Medicare term used to describe the range of services that are included in a surgical intervention.

Government-sponsored health care program A health insurance plan in which the government pays all or part of the fees related to health care services; for example, Medicare, Medicaid, TRICARE.

Group health insurance plan A health insurance plan that covers a defined population or group.

Group model A type of health maintenance organization in which the HMO contracts with physicians who are organized as a partnership, professional corporation, or other association.

Group number Identifies the name of the employer or other group that provides health insurance for the enrollee.

Guardian An individual who is legally designated to act on behalf of a minor or an incompetent adult.

Guardianship The legal authority to act as an individual's guardian.

Guardianship of the estate Responsibility for the financial resources of a minor or an incompetent adult.

Guardianship of the person Responsibility for the nonfinancial decisions related to medical care and other services for a minor or an incompetent adult.

H

HCPCS Level II codes Codes used to report items such as drugs, chiropractic services, dental procedures, durable medical equipment, and other procedures; also known as national codes.

Headings Subdivisions of CPT sections that identify a group of CPT codes.

Health Administration Center (HAC) Agency that administers CHAMPVA.

Healthcare Common Procedure Coding System (HCPCS) System used to code the procedures or treatments a patient receives at a physician or provider's office, at an ambulatory surgery center, or as a hospital outpatient.

Health care claim summary A notice sent to Medicare beneficiaries that describes reimbursement for provided services.

Health Care Finance Administration (HCFA) Former name of the Centers for Medicare and Medicaid Services (CMS).

Health care finder A health care specialist who assists TRICARE beneficiaries and providers with preauthorizations.

Health care fraud Knowingly and willfully executing or attempting to execute a scheme or artifice (1) to defraud any health care benefit program or (2) to obtain—by false or fraudulent pretenses representations or promises—any of the money or property owned by or under the custody or control of a health care benefit program.

Health care provider The generic term for anyone who provides health or medical services to persons who need such services.

Health insurance A contract that provides money to cover all or a portion of the cost of medically necessary care.

Health insurance claim number (HICN) A unique identifier assigned to Medicare beneficiaries.

Health insurance policy Document that describes the conditions related to health insurance, such as covered services, excluded services, and other insurance-related terms.

Health Insurance Portability and Accountability Act of 1996 (HIPAA) A federal regulation that provides extensive protection for the confidentiality and security of an individual's health information; also makes health insurance billing fraud a federal offense.

Health maintenance organization (HMO) A prepaid group practice that can be sponsored and operated by the government, insurance companies, consumer groups, employers, labor unions, physicians, or hospitals.

HIPAA Privacy Rule Federal regulation that gives individuals a federally protected right to control the use and release of their health information.

HIPAA Security Rule Standards set forth by HIPAA that ensure the security of electronic protected health information.

Histological Tissue-related.

History Information about the patient's previous health care encounters, family health, and lifestyle.

Hypertension/Hypertensive Table A table from the *Alphabetic Index* of the ICD-9-CM that provides an arrangement of codes for hypertension.

I

ICD-10-CM *International Classification of Diseases, Tenth Revision, Clinical Modification*; the classification system that will replace the ICD-9-CM.

Includes note A note that identifies lists of conditions that are similar enough to be coded or classified by the same medical code.

Independent practice association (IPA) A type of health maintenance organization in which the HMO contracts directly with physicians, who continue in their existing practices.

Indirect payer The fee for services provided is paid by the insurance company and not by the patient; also known as third-party payer.

Individual health insurance plan An insurance policy or plan that is purchased by an individual or family.

Individual policy A health insurance policy purchased by an individual or a family.

Inpatient prospective payment system (IPPS) Prospective payment system that applies to inpatient hospital services.

Instruction Manual A compilation of rules, guidelines, and coding conventions associated with ICD-10-CM/PCS.

Instructional note Provides the billing specialist with details about code selection; appears at the beginning of a heading, in parentheses before or after a code, or in parentheses as part of the code's description.

Insurance billing specialist An individual who processes health insurance claims in accordance with legal, professional, and insurance company guidelines and regulations.

Insurance collection specialist An individual who works with insurance companies to resolve billing and payment problems.

Insurance counselor An individual who helps the patient identify the amount that health insurance pays for a given service and how much the patient is responsible for paying; also known as a patient account representative.

Insurance policy A legal contract between an individual or organization and the company that provides the insurance.

Insured An individual covered by a health insurance policy or plan.

Integrated delivery system (IDS) A managed care organization that brings together physicians, physician groups, hospitals, HMOs, PPOs, insurance companies, management services, and employers to integrate all aspects of patient care into one comprehensive system.

Interactive communication and transactions The ability to share information online.

Intermediate care facility (ICF) A nonhospital facility that provides inpatient services.

International Classification of Diseases, Ninth Revision, Clinical Modification (ICD-9-CM) The coding system for medical diagnoses.

International Statistical Classification of Diseases and Related Health Problems, Tenth Revision (ICD-10) The coding and classification system for medical diagnoses that will replace the ICD-9.

International Statistical Classification of Diseases and Related Health Problems, Tenth Revision, Clinical Modification (ICD-10-CM) The coding and classification system for medical diagnoses that will replace the ICD-9-CM.

International Classification of Diseases, Tenth Revision, Procedure Coding System (ICD-10-PCS) The coding and classification system developed to replace *Volume 3 ICD-9-CM* procedure codes that will be used to code and report inpatient surgical and diagnostic procedures.

K

Key components Components that are required for *Current Procedural Terminology* (CPT) code assignment.

L

Last menstrual period (LMP) The date of the patient's last menstruation.

Late effect The residual condition that remains after the acute phase of an illness or injury has been resolved.

Laterality A term that refers to the right and left side of the body.

Ledger card Summarizes the financial transactions for each patient.

Length of stay The number of hospital inpatient days from admission to discharge.

Level II codes Codes used to report items such as drugs, chiropractic services, dental procedures, durable medical equipment, and other procedures; also known as national codes or HCPCS Level II codes.

Lifetime reserve days Specific number of days covered by Medicare Part A when a beneficiary is hospitalized for more than 90 days during a benefit period.

Limited charge One hundred fifteen percent of the allowable charge billed by nonparticipating providers.

Limiting fee A fee set at a maximum of 15% above the NonPAR Medicare-approved rate.

Locality A specific geographic area.

Locality code A three-digit number that represents a group of zip codes.

Longshore and Harbor Workers' Compensation Act (LHWCA) Act that provides benefits for private and public employees engaged in maritime work nationwide.

M

Main term Identifies diseases, conditions, or injuries.

Main terms The organizational framework for the CPT *Alphabetic Index*; always printed in bold.

Major complication/co-morbidity (MCC) A more severe complication/co-morbidity.

Malfeasance A category of malpractice in which the wrong action was taken.

Malignant, primary The initial site of a cancerous tumor or growth.

Malignant, secondary The site that identifies the metastasis (spread) of a cancerous tumor or growth.

Malpractice Any professional behavior by one individual that results in damages to another individual.

Managed care Any method of organizing health care providers that provides access to high-quality, cost-effective health care.

Managed care organization (MCO) A type of prepaid health plan.

Manifestations Signs or symptoms associated with a specific disease.

Material safety data sheet (MSDS) A document that identifies the risks associated with exposure to specific chemicals or hazardous substances.

Maximum allowable charge The maximum amount TRICARE or CHAMPVA will pay for a given service.

Maximum allowable fee An amount established by a PPO that a physician may charge for a service.

Medi/Medi A combination of Medicare and Medicaid programs available to individuals who are Medicare-eligible and whose income falls below the federal poverty level; also called Care/Caid and 18/19.

Medicaid A federal/state medical assistance program to provide health insurance for specific populations.

Medicaid expansion program Any federal or state health insurance program that is funded by Medicaid legislation with the intent to provide additional services to Medicaid recipients.

Medical Association of Billers (MAB) A professional association that offers education and certification programs for individuals employed in the insurance billing industry.

Medical claims with no disability Minor injuries that are treated once and after which the individual is able to return to work within a few days.

Medical coder An individual who assigns numeric codes to diagnostic, procedure, and treatment information.

Medical coding The process of assigning numeric codes to medical information.

Medical decision making The complexity associated with establishing a diagnosis or selecting a management or treatment option.

Medical savings account A type of Medicare program that provides a specific amount of money for medical services.

Medical terminology The language of the health care industry.

Medicare A federal health insurance program created in 1965 as Title 18 of the Social Security Act.

Medicare Administrative Contractor (MAC) An organization responsible for processing Medicare claims.

Medicare Advantage (MA) Medicare health insurance plans offered by private insurance companies.

Medicare Advantage Prescription Drug Plan (MA-PDP) Prescription drug plans that are part of a Medicare Advantage plan.

Medicare fee schedule (MFS) A list of Medicare-approved fees for physician/provider services.

Medicare Part A The portion of the Medicare program that pays for care received in hospitals and skilled nursing facilities, home health care, and hospice care.

Medicare Part B The portion of the Medicare program that pays for physician services, outpatient hospital care, and other medical services.

Medicare Part C Medicare health insurance plans offered by private insurance companies.

Medicare Part D A Medicare program that covers some of the costs associated with prescription medications.

Medicare as secondary payer (MSP) A Medicare designation that applies when a beneficiary has an insurance policy that is primary (billed before) to the beneficiary's Medicare insurance.

Medicare special needs plan (SNP) A Medicare Advantage plan that usually limits membership to individuals with specific diseases or conditions.

Medicare-severity diagnosis related groups (MS-DRG) Prospective payment system for hospital inpatient care that replaced the original diagnosis related groups.

Medicare Summary Notice (MSN) An explanation of benefits or remittance advice.

Medicare supplemental plan (MSP) A health insurance plan that supplements the Medicare plan to cover deductibles and co-insurance costs.

Medicare-Medicaid Crossover Program (MCD) A combination of Medicare and Medicaid programs available to individuals who are Medicare-eligible and whose income falls below the federal poverty level; also called Medi/Medi, Care/Caid, and 18/19.

Medigap plan A supplemental insurance plan that provides coverage for services, deductibles, and co-insurance not covered by Medicare.

Member An individual who is enlisted in the armed forces.

Military treatment facility (MTF) Facility where health care services are administered to members of the armed forces.

Minimum necessary Privacy Rule provision of HIPAA that limits the release of protected health information only to that needed to accomplish the intended use, disclosure, or request.

Misfeasance A category of malpractice in which the correct action was done incorrectly.

Modality The method by which a service or treatment is rendered; usually associated with ICD-10-CM/PCS coding.

Moderate sedation Sedation with or without analgesia.

Modifier A two-digit code that may be added to a five-digit CPT code to further explain the service provided; may also be reported as a five-digit code.

Modifier -51 Identifies multiple procedures performed by the same provider during a single encounter.

Modifying term A term that affects the selection of a medical code.

More specific subterm Provides more-specific information about a subterm.

N

National Center for Health Statistics (NCHS) The governmental body responsible for developing the ICD-10-CM.

National codes Medical codes, usually CPT or HCPCS, that apply to physician services.

National conversion factor (CF) A figure that is multiplied by the relative value unit (RVU) to convert the RVU into a payment amount.

National Correct Coding Initiative (NCCI) A medical coding edit process established by the Centers for Medicare and Medicaid Services to promote proper coding methodologies and prevent improper payments related to inaccurate medical coding.

National Electronic Billers Alliance (NEBA) An association that offers a medical billing credential.

National Oceanic and Atmospheric Administration (NOAA) A branch of the uniformed services whose members are eligible for TRICARE benefits.

National provider identifier (NPI) A unique identification number assigned to providers who submit claims to government-sponsored health insurance programs.

National Uniform Billing Committee (NUBC) A committee of health care professionals responsible for revising the UB-04.

National Uniform Claim Committee (NUCC) A committee hosted and chaired by the American Medical Association (AMA) established to develop, promote, and maintain a standard data set submitted to insurance carriers for purposes of reimbursement.

NEC Not elsewhere classified.

Negligence The failure to exercise the standard of care that a reasonable person would exercise in similar circumstances.

Neoplasm Table A feature of the ICD-9-CM and ICD-10-CM Alphabetic Index that organizes neoplasms by site and behavior.

Network model A type of health maintenance organization in which the HMO contracts with more than one physician group and may contract with single-specialty and multi-specialty groups.

New patient A person who is being seen by a physician for the first time or who has not received services within the past three years.

Noncovered benefit A service that is not covered by an insurance plan or policy.

Noncustodial parent The divorced parent who does not have legal custody of the child.

Nonessential modifiers Terms that do not affect code selection.

Nonfeasance A category of malpractice in which no action was taken.

Nonparticipating provider (NonPAR) A physician who does not contract with Medicare and therefore does not agree to accept the Medicare-approved payment rate for services rendered for all Medicare patients.

North Atlantic Treaty Organization (NATO) A branch of the uniformed services whose members are eligible for TRICARE benefits.

NOS Not otherwise specified.

Not elsewhere classified (NEC) Indicates that a diagnosis or condition does not have a separate code.

Not otherwise specified (NOS) Indicates an unspecified diagnosis.

Null zero (ø) Symbol used to identify CPT codes that may or may not be used with modifier -51; also known as the universal no code.

Number symbol (#) A CPT coding notation used to identify codes that are not in numerical order.

O

Occupational Safety and Health Administration Act (OSHA) Act to protect employees from injuries due to occupational hazards.

Occurrence code A two-character code for a specific event that affects the payment of an insurance claim.

Office of Civil Rights (OCR) Federal agency responsible for implementing and enforcing the HIPAA Privacy and Security Rules.

Office of the Inspector General (OIG) A division of the Department of Health and Human Services that plays an active role in investigating insurance fraud and abuse in cases related to Medicare, Medicaid, workers' compensation, and other federal health care insurance programs.

Office of Workers' Compensation Programs (OWCP) A government agency that approves workers' compensation programs.

Omit code A coding convention that instructs the medical coder to omit a code for a service or procedure that is part of another more comprehensive service or procedure.

Open biopsy Removal of tissue via an incision.

Open procedure A procedure that requires an incision or opening into a body part or cavity.

Ordered/referred services A service that is ordered by one provider and performed by a different provider.

Ordering/performing physician A physician or provider who orders or performs a procedure or service.

Other health insurance (OHI) A health insurance plan or policy that is primary to TRICARE or Medicare.

Out-of-pocket expenses The amount of money the patient must pay for a service.

Outpatient Prospective Payment System (OPPS) An outpatient/ambulatory services payment system that establishes a preset reimbursement rate for related procedures and services.

P

Parentheses ( ) Symbol used to enclose nonessential modifiers.

Partial disability A type of permanent disability in which loss of function is expressed as a percentage.

Participant An individual enrolled in Medicaid programs.

Participating provider (PAR) Physicians who contract with Medicare and agree to accept the Medicare-approved payment rate for services rendered to all Medicare patients.

Patient account ledger A permanent record of financial transactions between the patient and the agency.

Patient account representative An individual who helps the patient identify the amount that health insurance pays for a given service and how much the patient is responsible for paying; also known as an insurance counselor.

Patient Protection and Affordable Care Act A federal law enacted in 2010 that is intended to provide access to health insurance to individuals, families, and small businesses; reduce healthcare costs; limit the insurance company's ability to deny, rescind, or restrict coverage; also called the Affordable Care Act.

Payer of last resort A designation associated with Medicaid.

Pending claim Claim for which payment is overdue; also called a delinquent claim.

Per capita Per person.

Perinatal period The period of time that begins before birth and lasts through the 28th day of life.

Permanent disability Designation indicating that the injury has permanently impaired the worker and that the worker is not able to return to his or her previous position.

Personal care physician (PCP) A physician responsible for the overall management of an individual's medical care; also known as a primary care physician.

Personal qualifications Behaviors that define the character or personality of an individual.

Physical status modifiers Additional coding that addresses the overall health status of the patient.

Physician extender A nonphysician who provides services to patients.

Physician/provider identification number (PIN) An identification number assigned by an insurance carrier or other health care entity.

Placeholder x A character used in ICD-10-CM diagnoses codes to create a six-character code when a code with fewer than six characters requires a 7th character extension; also called the dummy x.

Place of service (POS) A two-digit code that identifies where services were provided.

Plan code Part of an insurance card that identifies the insurance plan.

Plus sign (+) Symbol used to identify CPT add-on codes.

Point dash (.–) ICD-10-CM symbol used to indicate that the code is incomplete and an additional digit (or more than one) is needed.

Point-of-service plan (POS) A reimbursement term associated with health insurance claims processing.

Policyholder The purchaser of a health insurance policy.

Power of attorney Voluntary transfer of decision-making authority from one competent individual to another competent individual.

Preauthorization Determines the medical necessity of the treatment.

Precertification Determines if a treatment is covered by the insurance policy.

Predetermination An estimated insurance payment for a given treatment.

Pre-existing condition Statement of the conditions the individual had prior to implementation of the insurance policy.

Preferred provider organization (PPO) A managed care organization that contracts with a group of providers, who are called preferred providers, to offer services to the managed care organization's members.

Premium The cost of the insurance contract; the fee paid by the policyholder at regular intervals.

Prepaid health plan Contract between a specific group of people and local hospitals and physicians, in which each member of the group pays a premium in order to be included in the contract.

Prescription drug plan (PDP) An abbreviation used on an insurance identification card when an individual has prescription drug coverage.

Present on admission (POA) Conditions, diseases, or problems that are present when an individual is admitted to a hospital.

Primary care manager (PCM) An individual who provides or coordinates the member's care, maintains health records, and makes referrals to specialists.

Primary care provider A physician or healthcare provider responsible for the overall management and supervision of a patient's care.

Primary diagnosis The patient's major health problem or the reason for the medical encounter.

Primary insurance The insurance company that is billed first; also called the primary payer.

Primary payer The insurance company that is billed first; also called the primary insurance.

Principal diagnosis The diagnosis determined after study to be the reason for the patient's admission to a hospital.

Principal procedure The procedure that is closely related to the principal diagnosis and is performed for definitive treatment rather than for diagnostic purposes.

Privacy officer An individual employed by a covered entity and responsible for monitoring compliance with HIPAA Privacy and Security Rules.

Private fee for service (PFFS) A Medicare Advantage plan administered by private health insurance companies.

Procedures/services Identification of specific procedures or services rendered by a physician.

Professional component Services provided by a radiologist that include interpreting and writing a report for diagnostic imaging.

Program Integrity Office A branch of the TRICARE Management Agency that analyzes and reviews cases of potential fraud.

Prospective payment system (PPS) A hospital reimbursement system based on the diagnosis, procedure, and treatments provided to a patient.

Protected health information (PHI) Individually identifiable health information that relates to a person's past, present, or future physical or mental health condition; the health care provided to the person; and the past, present, or future payment for the health care provided to the person.

Provider A physician or other individual who provides services to a patient.

Puerperium The period of time that begins at the end of the third stage of labor and continues for six weeks.

Q

Qualified Medicare Beneficiary Program (QMB) Program that pays the premiums, deductibles, and patient co-payments for Medicare-eligible persons with incomes below federal poverty guidelines.

Qualifier The seventh character of an ICD-10-PCS procedure code that defines an additional attribute of the procedure.

Qualifying circumstances Conditions that allow an individual to become part of a Qualified Medicare Beneficiary (QMB) Program.

Qualifying Individual (QI) A Medicare assistance program for beneficiaries with incomes slightly above the federal poverty level.

R

Radionuclides Radioactive substances that are used for nuclear imaging or scanning and treating tumors and cancer.

Reasonable fee A fee that is higher than the usual or customary fee that can be justified by the patient's condition.

Recipient An individual enrolled in Medicaid programs.

Reciprocity health insurance plan A plan that covers expenses for treatment (including nonemergencies) that occur anywhere in the United States.

Referral The transfer of the management of patient care from one physician to another.

Referring physician A physician who requests patient services from another health care provider.

Reimbursement Payment for services rendered.

Relative value scale (RVS) A payment method that establishes fees for services based on the provider's time, skill, and overhead costs associated with providing a service.

Relative value unit (RVU) A numeric unit designating physician work, practice expenses, and malpractice costs.

Release of information (ROI) The written authorization or consent of an individual to release confidential information.

Remittance The amount a provider receives for services rendered.

Remittance advice (RA) A detailed explanation of claim denial or approval; also known as the explanation of benefits (EOB).

Remittance notice A document that recaps, by patient, the services rendered, the amount billed, the amount allowed, co-insurance, and the amount the provider was paid.

Residual effects A temporary or permanent medical problem or condition that results from a treated illness or injury.

Resource-based relative value scale (RBRVS) A calculation of approved fees based on relative value unit, geographic adjustment factor, and national conversion factor.

Respondeat superior Literally, let the master answer; the legal description of employer responsibility.

Root operation A term that identifies the objective of a procedure; a component of ICD-10-PCS procedure codes.

Routing form A source document for financial, diagnostic, and treatment information; also called a charge slip, an encounter form, or a superbill.

S

Secondary condition A condition that coexists with the primary diagnosis but does not directly affect the outcome or treatment of the primary diagnosis.

Secondary insurance An insurance company that is billed after receiving payment from the primary insurance company; also called the secondary payer.

Secondary payer An insurance company that is billed after receiving payment from the primary insurance company; also called the secondary insurance.

Section A group of three-digit categories that represent a single disease or a group of closely related conditions; one of six main parts of the CPT codebook that are preceded by coding conventions.

Section guidelines Provide the billing specialist with information that increases coding accuracy; precede each of the six main CPT sections.

See An ICD-9-CM or ICD-10-CM cross-reference that is a mandatory direction to look elsewhere for the correct code.

See also An ICD-9-CM or ICD-10-CM cross-reference that is a suggestion to look elsewhere if the selected code does not adequately describe the disease or condition.

See category An ICD-9-CM cross-reference that is a mandatory direction and provides a three-digit category code from the *Tabular List*.

See condition An ICD-9-CM or ICD-10-CM cross-reference that identifies when an adjective has been referenced rather than a main term or condition.

Semicolon (;) The symbol used to identify the common part or main entry for indented modifying terms or descriptions in the CPT codebook.

Separate procedure A CPT code description that identifies a procedure that cannot be billed separately from another service or procedure.

Sequela, sequelae A condition or problem that is the result of a previous condition or problem that is or has been resolved.

Sequencing Placing diagnostic codes in the correct order.

Service provider The generic term for anyone providing care.

Signature on file (SOF) Statement or abbreviation used to indicate that an individual's signature is maintained by the health care agency.

Significant procedure A procedure that affects the services provided to a patient.

Single coverage A term related to the Federal Employee Health Benefit Program that means only the employee/retiree is covered by the plan.

Skilled nursing facility (SNF) A facility that meets specific regulatory certification requirements and primarily provides inpatient skilled nursing care and related services to patients who require medical, nursing, or rehabilitative services but does not provide the level of care or treatment available in a hospital.

Slanted square brackets ([ ]) ICD-9 and ICD-10 coding convention that identifies codes for conditions that are manifestations of underlying conditions.

Social Security number (SSN) A personal identification number assigned by the Social Security Administration.

Specified Low-Income Medicare Beneficiary (SLMB) A Medicare program for beneficiaries with incomes slightly above the federal poverty level.

Sponsor An active-duty service member.

Square brackets ([ ]) Punctuation that encloses synonyms, alternate wordings, and explanatory phrases associated with a given code.

Staff model A type of health maintenance organization in which the HMO operates and staffs the facility or facilities where members receive treatments.

State Children's Health Insurance Program (SCHIP) An amendment to the Social Security Act that allows states to create health insurance programs for children of low-income working families; also known as Title 21.

State compensation board/commission A government agency responsible for administering state compensation laws and handling appeals related to workers' compensation claims.

State compensation fund Type of workers' compensation in which the state identifies a specific agency to function as the insuring body to cover workers' compensation claims.

Statute of limitations The period of time in which an agency, business, or individual is vulnerable to civil or criminal proceedings.

Subcategories Divisions within the CPT code book categories.

Subcategory Four digits that provide more information about the disease, such as site, cause, or other characteristics.

Subclassification A fifth digit that allows even more specific information about a disease.

Subpoena A legal document, signed by a judge or an attorney that requires an individual to appear in court as a witness.

Subpoena duces tecum A legal document, signed by a judge or an attorney that requires an individual to appear in court and bring records.

Subscribers Individuals enrolled in a health insurance plan; also known as enrollees.

Subterm Identifies site, type, or etiology for diseases, conditions, or injuries.

Superbill A source document for financial, diagnostic, and treatment information; also called a charge slip, a routing form, or an encounter form.

Supplemental Security Income (SSI) A federal income assistance program that provides cash payments to blind, disabled, and aged individuals.

Surgical package The range of services included in a surgical intervention.

T

Table of Drugs and Chemicals A list of drugs and chemicals included in the ICD-9 and ICD-10 Alphabetic Index

Tables A systematic arrangement of codes included in the ICD-9 and ICD-10 Alphabetic Indices.

Tabular List A component of ICD-9 and ICD-10 coding references that includes medical codes organized by organ systems, etiology, and other criteria.

Taxonomy code A code assigned to a hospital that identifies services provided by the hospital; associated with the UB-04.

Technical component Services provided by a radiology technician.

Technical qualifications Measurable abilities and skills that can be learned through education and experience.

Temporary Assistance for Needy Families (TANF) A program that provides financial assistance to children and families who meet specific income level requirements and to pregnant women who meet the income requirements.

Temporary disability A disability that can be overcome by medical treatment or retraining.

Tertiary payer The insurance company that is billed after payment is received from the primary and secondary payers.

Third-party administrator (TPA) A processing center for insurance claims; also known as a clearinghouse.

Third-party payer The fee for services provided is paid by the insurance company and not by the patient; also known as indirect payer.

Third-party reimbursement Receiving payment from someone other than the patient.

Title 19 An amendment to the Social Security Act that established a federal medical assistance program called Medicaid.

Title 21 An amendment to the Social Security Act that allows states to create health insurance programs for children of low-income working families; also known as State Children's Health Insurance Program (SCHIP).

Total disability A type of permanent disability in which loss of function is 100%.

Transaction journal A list of all items posted to patient accounts for a given time period.

Transitional care management (TCM) Services provided by a physician or qualified health care professional that address any needed coordination of care provided by multiple disciplines and community service agencies.

Triangle (▲) Symbol used to identify a revision in the narrative description of a code in the CPT code book.

TRICARE A federally funded comprehensive health benefits program for dependents of personnel serving in the uniformed services; formerly known as CHAMPUS.

TRICARE contractor An individual who processes claims and sends the provider an explanation of benefits; similar to an insurance carrier.

TRICARE Extra A network of health care providers that dependents can use without required enrollment.

TRICARE for Life (TFL) A health benefit program available to TRICARE beneficiaries who are eligible for Medicare.

TRICARE Management Agency (TMA) The agency that administers the TRICARE program.

TRICARE Prime A managed care program affiliated with a full-service health maintenance organization.

TRICARE Prime Remote (TPR) A TRICARE program for active duty members who are serving outside of the United States.

TRICARE Retired Reserve (TRR) A TRICARE program available to retired members of military reserve organizations.

TRICARE Reserve Select (TRS) A TRICARE program available to retired members of military reserve organizations.

TRICARE Standard Provides all the benefits of the original CHAMPUS, which allows more choice of health care providers but with higher out-of-pocket expenses.

TRICARE [for] Young Adult (TYA) A TRICARE program available certain young adult children of TRICARE beneficiaries or active duty members.

Turnaround time The length of time from claims submission to claims payment.

Type of bill (TOB) A three-digit number that identifies the type of facility where an individual received services; a UB-04 field locator.

U

UB-04 A universal hospital claims submission form; also known as the CMS-1450.

Unauthorized service A service requiring preauthorization that is provided without the preauthorization; a service that is not covered by an insurance plan.

Unbundling Billing separately for procedures that are delivered as a package.

Uncertain behavior A description used when a neoplasm cannot be classified as benign or malignant.

Uniform Hospital Discharge Data Set (UHDDS) A standard set of data that must be reported for all hospital based insurance claims.

Uniformed services Term for organizations such as the army, navy, air force, marines, coast guard, Public Health Service, National Oceanic and Atmospheric Administration, and North Atlantic Treaty Organization.

Universal no code (ø) Symbol used to identify CPT codes that may or may not be used with modifier -51; also known as the null zero.

Unspecified behavior A description used when documentation does not identify or classify a neoplasm as benign or malignant.

Upcoding Selecting codes at a higher level than the service requires.

Use additional code Signifies that it may be necessary to use more than one code to provide the complete picture of the patient's problem.

Usual, customary, and reasonable (UCR) fee (1) The fee the provider usually charges for a given service; (2) the fee that other providers in the same geographic area or with similar training charge for the same service; (3) a fee that is higher than the usual fee and can be justified by the patient's condition.

Usual fee The fee the provider usually charges for a given service; sometimes known as the provider's full fee.

V

V codes A supplementary classification of the ICD-9-CM: "Classification of Factors Influencing Health Status and Contact with Health Services."

Value code A code associated with a charge for a service provided in an inpatient setting; part of the UB-04 claim form.

Veteran An individual who has served in the U.S. armed forces, is no longer in service, and has an honorable discharge.

Vocational rehabilitation The retraining of employees to perform another job duty when they are unable to return to their previous duties because of permanent or temporary disability.

W

Waiver An addendum to the health insurance policy that excludes certain conditions from coverage; also known as a rider.

Workforce members Employees, volunteers, trainees, and other persons under direct control of the covered entity.

Write-off The difference between a full fee and an allowed fee.

Index

A

AAA screening. *See* abdominal aortic aneurysm screening
AAPC. *See* American Academy of Professional Coders
abdominal aortic aneurysm (AAA) screening, 455
abdominal weakness, 561
ABN. *See* Advance Beneficiary Notice
abuse
    examples of, 540
    laws, 37–45
    penalties for, 44
    prevention, 42–44
    reinforcement exercises, 44
    reporting incentives, 42–44
    TRICARE, 539–541
accept assignment, 72
accommodation codes, 403
accurate diagnosis, 39
acute conditions, 111
adaptability, 3
additional codes, CPT, 254
address, patient, 343
admitting diagnosis, 412
admitting physician, 75
ADSM. *See* active duty service members
Advance Beneficiary Notice (ABN), 456, 457
Affordable Care Act. *See* Patient Protection and Affordable Care Act
AHA. *See* American Hospital Association
AHFS. *See* American Hospital Formulary Service
AHIMA. *See* American Health Information Management Association
AIDS
    ICD-9-CM and, 217–218
    ROI, 32
alcohol, 32
allowable charges, 323, 435
    TRICARE, 532–533
allowable fee, 435
alphabetic index, 99–103
alternative codes, CPT, 254
AMA. *See* American Medical Association
AMBA. *See* American Medical Billing Association
ambulatory payment classification (APC) (system), 382, 383
ambulatory surgery, 116, 192
    center modifiers, 288–289
ambulatory surgery center (ASC), 244
American Academy of Professional Coders (AAPC), 11
American Health Information Management Association (AHIMA), 11, 26, 33, 91, 161
    responsibilities of, 92

American Hospital Association (AHA), 91, 161
    responsibilities of, 92
American Hospital Formulary Service (AHFS), 168
American Medical Association (AMA), 244, 339
American Medical Billing Association (AMBA), 11
ancillary services codes, 403
anesthesia section, CPT, 275–280
    add-on codes, 278–279
    code categories, 277
    code selection, 279
    modifiers, 276–278
    reinforcement exercises, 280
annual wellness visit (AWV), 455
anomaly, 173
APC. *See* ambulatory payment classification (APC) (system)
applicant, 66
approach, 138
    artificial opening, 140
    definitions and, 139–140
    endoscopic artificial opening, 140
    endoscopic natural opening, 140
    external, 140, 149
    guidelines, 149
    natural opening, 140
    open, 139
    percutaneous, 139
    percutaneous endoscopic, 140
    percutaneous endoscopic assistance artificial opening, 140
    percutaneous endoscopic assistance natural opening, 140
artificial limb, 209
artificial openings, 208
    approach, 140
    endoscopic, 140
    with percutaneous endoscopic assistance, 140
ASC. *See* ambulatory surgery center
assertiveness, 3
assignment of benefits, 71
    UB-04, 407
assistant surgeon, 478
attending physician, 75, 380
authorized providers, 524
AWV. *See* annual wellness visit

B

balance-bill, 459
batch, 368
BC/BS. *See* Blue Cross/Blue Shield
BCBSA. *See* Blue Cross and Blue Shield Association
beneficiaries, 523

benefit
    assignment of, 71
    coordination of, 71, 72, 73
    extended care benefit, 69
    hospital, 68
    major medical, 69
    surgical, 68
benign, 100
bilateral procedures, ICD-9-CM, 224
billing department supervisor, 12
billing errors, 43
biopsy, 148
    brush, 226
    closed, 226
    coding procedure, 224–228
    needle aspiration, 226
    open, 226
    transbronchial lung, 227
birth date, 343
birthday rule, 316
Black Lung Program, 554
blood, 454
Blue Cross and Blue Shield Association (BCBSA), 428
Blue Cross/Blue Shield (BC/BS), 427–428
    blocks, 440–442
    claims submission, 438–443
    employer-sponsored plans, 432–433
    general information, 429
    group plans, 432–433
    health insurance plans, 430–433
    individual plans, 430–431
    Medigap plans, 431–432
    nonparticipating providers, 433–434
    participating providers, 433–434
    provider reimbursement methods, 434–438
    reinforcement exercises, 429–430
body part, 138–139
    guidelines, 149
body system, 132, 138–139
bone mass measurement, 455
braces, 187
brush biopsy, 226
bullets
    circled, 252
    CPT, 251
burns, 216–217

C

CA-7 Claim for Compensation, 554
cafeteria plans, 433
cancelable policy, 68
canceled procedure, 224–226
CAP. *See* claims assurance professional
capitation, 79–80
carcinoma, 100
cardiovascular screening, 455

career opportunities, 10–14
care plan oversight services, E/M, 260
carrier-direct claims submission, 363–364
carryover lines, ICD-9-CM, 172
case management services, E/M, 260
case manager, 75
category
    CPT, 246
    ICD-9-CM, 165
CC. *See* complication/co-morbidity
CCA. *See* Certified Coding Associate
CCCC. *See* Complex Care Coordination
    Services
CCS. *See* Certified Coding Specialist
CCS-P. *See* Certified Coding
    Specialist–Physician-based
CDC. *See* Centers for Disease Control
CE. *See* continuing education
Centers for Disease Control (CDC), 91
Centers for Medicare and Medicaid
    Services (CMS), 28, 91, 161, 244,
    362, 381, 448
    responsibilities of, 92
certification, 10–14
    medical billing, 11
    medical coding, 11
    reinforcement exercises, 13
    specialty, 11
Certified Coding Associate (CCA), 11
Certified Coding Specialist (CCS), 11
Certified Coding Specialist–Physician-
    based (CCS-P), 11
Certified Healthcare Reimbursement
    Specialist (CHRS), 11
Certified Medical Billing Specialist
    (CMBS), 7, 11
Certified Medical Reimbursement
    Specialist (CMRS), 7, 11
Certified Medical Reimbursement
    Specialist–Chiropractic Assistant
    (CMBS-CA), 11
Certified Medical Reimbursement
    Specialist–Hospital (CMBS-H), 11
Certified Professional Coder (CPC), 11
Certified Professional Coder–Hospital
    (CPC-H), 11
Certified Professional Coder–Payer
    (CPC-P), 11
CF. *See* national conversion factor
CHAMPUS. *See* Civilian Health and
    Medical Program of the Uniformed
    Services
CHAMPVA. *See* Civilian Health and
    Medical Program of the Veterans
    Administration
chargemaster, 384
charge slip, 310
chemicals. *See* drugs and chemicals table
chief complaint, 256
chiropractic, 142
chronic conditions, 190
    coding guidelines, 111
CHRS. *See* Certified Healthcare
    Reimbursement Specialist
circle, 252
circled bullets, 252
Civilian Health and Medical Program of the
    Uniformed Services (CHAMPUS),
    58, 339
Civilian Health and Medical Program of
    the Uniformed Services Maximum
    Allowable Charge (CMAC), 526

Civilian Health and Medical Program
    of the Veterans Administration
    (CHAMPVA), 58, 339, 523
    billing, 543
    CMS-1500, 543–547
    cost sharing, 542
    covered services, 542
    deductibles, 542
    eligibility definitions, 541
    noncovered services, 542
    providers, 542
claims assurance professional (CAP), 8
clean claim, 364, 416
clearinghouse, 363, 364–365, 416
    error-edit messages, 369
clinical examples, 256
closed biopsy, 226
CMAC. *See* Civilian Health and Medical
    Program of the Uniformed Services
    Maximum Allowable Charge
CMBS. *See* Certified Medical Billing
    Specialist
CMBS-CA. *See* Certified Medical
    Reimbursement Specialist–
    Chiropractic Assistant
CMBS-H. *See* Certified Medical
    Reimbursement Specialist–Hospital
CMRS. *See* Certified Medical
    Reimbursement Specialist
CMS. *See* Centers for Medicare and
    Medicaid Services
CMS-1450. *See* UB-04
CMS-1500, 323, 339–340
    amount paid, 355
    balance due, 355
    billing entity identification, 354
    billing provider info, 355
    CHAMPVA, 543–547
    charges, 353
    completed forms, 358
    completion, 482
    Dates of Service, 351
    days or units, 353–354
    diagnosis code, 351
    EPSDT, 353–354
    errors, 357–358
    federal tax ID number, 355
    guidelines, 342
    hospitalization dates, 349
    Medicaid resubmission code, 350
    Medicaid secondary payer, 511–513
    Medicare as primary payer, 477–482
    Medicare as secondary payer, 492
    Medicare-Medicaid crossover program,
        487, 489
    Medicare secondary, 491–493
    optical scanning guidelines, 341
    patient account number, 355
    patient information, 342–347
    physician signature, 355
    Place of Service, 351, 352–353
    prior authorization number, 350
    provider entity identification, 354
    referring provider name, 349
    reinforcement exercises, 482
    rendering provider ID number, 354
    total charges, 355
    treatment and provider information,
        348–357
    TRICARE, 535–538
    workers' compensation, 566–569
    work status, 348

code also note, 107
code causal condition first, 183
code first, 107
    underlying condition, 182
coding conventions
    biopsy, 224–228
    certification, 11
    chronic conditions, 111
    ICD-9-CM, 161
    ICD-10-CM, 103–110
    signs, 111
    symptoms, 111
coding errors, 43
co-insurance, 319
collection manager, 12
colons (punctuation), 187
colorectal cancer screening, 455
combination codes, 111
communicable diseases, 201
complex chronic care coordination
    (CCCC) services, 258
complex chronic care coordination services,
    E/M, 261
compliance monitoring, 363
complication/co-morbidity (CC), 382
complications, 173
component part coding, 471
comprehensive examination, 264
    documentation, 269
comprehensive history, 263
concurrent care, 256
concurrent condition, 123, 198
conditionally renewable, 68
conditional primary payer status, 476
condition codes, 398
confidence, 3
confidential information, 26–36
confidentiality, 3
    electronic claims processing and,
        371–372
congenital anomalies, 164
congenital conditions, 95
connecting words
    in ICD-9-CM, 184
    in ICD-10-CM, 108
consultations, E/M, 259
continuing education (CE), 6
contracture, 217
contrast, 138–141
Cooperating Parties, 91
    responsibilities, 92
cooperation, 3
coordination of benefits, 71, 72, 73
co-payment, 72, 319
    Medicare Part A, 450–451
    PDP, 466
cost sharing, 526
    CHAMPVA, 542
    TRICARE, 532–533
counseling, 256
    risk factor reduction and behavior change
        intervention, 260
county regulation, 20
court-ordered testing, 212
coverage, 67
CPC. *See* Certified Professional Coder
CPC-H. *See* Certified Professional
    Coder–Hospital
CPC-P. *See* Certified Professional
    Coder–Payer
CPT. *See* Current Procedural Terminology
critical care services, E/M, 259

cross-references, 108, 223
  ICD-9-CM, 181
Current Procedural Terminology (CPT), 5, 368, 382
  additional codes, 254
  alphabetic index, 247–248
  alternative codes, 254
  anesthesia section, 275–280
  appendices, 246–247
  bullets in, 251
  categories, 246
  circled bullets in, 252
  circle in, 252
  coding conventions, 249–252
  components, 245
  deleted codes, 254
  descriptions and fees, 437
  Evaluation and Management Section, 255–275
  facing triangles in, 251
  flash symbol in, 252
  heading notes, 253
  instructional notes, 253, 254
  main sections, 245–246
  main terms, 247
  Medicine Section, 291–295
  modifiers, 252
  modifying terms, 247
  notes after codes, 253
  null zero in, 252
  number symbol in, 252
  pathology and laboratory section, 291, 292
  plus sign in, 251
  procedures, 246
  radiology section, 290–291
  reinforcement exercises, 248–249
  section guidelines, 253
  see, 252
  see also, 252
  semicolons in, 249–250
  services, 246
  subcategories, 246
  subsections, 246
  surgery section, 280–290
  triangles in, 251
  universal no code in, 252
custodial care services, E/M, 259
custodial parent, 316
customary fee, 434
cystostomy tube, 209

D

data entry, 5
Dates of Service, 351
DCMWC. *See* Division of Coal Mine Workers' Compensation
deductibles, 71
  CHAMPVA, 542
  Medicare Part A, 450–451
  PDP, 466
  TRICARE, 532–533
DEEOIC. *See* Division of Energy Employees Occupational Illness Compensation
Defense Enrollment Eligibility and Reporting System (DEERS), 523
  covered services, 527–528
  enrollment, 526–531
  noncovered services, 527–528

nonparticipating providers, 526–527
  participating providers, 526–527
  preauthorization, 528–529
definitive diagnosis, 192
deleted codes, CPT, 254
delinquent claims, 328
delivery, 173
Department of Defense (DoD), 522
Department of Energy (DOE), 554
Department of Health and Human Services (HHS), 26, 28, 161, 244, 380
Department of Justice (DOJ), 37
Department of Labor (DOL), 554
dependents, 65, 66
dermatitis late effect, 216
detailed examination, 264
  documentation, 269
detailed history, 263
detail-orientation, 3
device, 141–143
  guidelines, 149
DFEC. *See* Division of Federal Employees' Compensation
DHR. *See* discharge hour
diabetes
  screening, 455
  supplies, 454
diagnosis-related groups (DRGs), 381
diagnostic audiology, 141, 142
diagnostic services, 114, 478
dialysis, 209
direction following, 5
direct pay, 56–57
dirty claims, 328, 369, 416
discharge hour (DHR), 395
Division of Coal Mine Workers' Compensation (DCMWC), 554
Division of Energy Employees Occupational Illness Compensation (DEEOIC), 554
Division of Federal Employees' Compensation (DFEC), 554
Division of Longshore and Harbor Workers' Compensation (DLHWC), 554
DME. *See* durable medical equipment
DME MACs. *See* durable medical equipment Medicare Administrative Contractors
DMEPOS. *See* durable medical equipment, prosthetics, orthotics, and supplies
DoD. *See* Department of Defense
DOE. *See* Department of Energy
DOJ. *See* Department of Justice
DOL. *See* Department of Labor
domiciliary services, E/M, 259
double braces, 187
downcoding, 268
DRGs. *See* diagnosis-related groups
drug abuse, 32
drugs and chemicals table, 102
durable medical equipment, prosthetics, orthotics, and supplies (DMEPOS), 296
durable medical equipment (DME), 296, 328
  Medicare Part A, 451
  TRICARE, 529–530

durable medical equipment Medicare Administrative Contractors (DME MACs), 474
durable power of attorney, 21, 23
duration, 138–141

E

Early and Periodic Screening for Diagnosis and Treatment (EPSDT), 354, 505
E codes, ICD-9-CM, 169, 215–216
ECS. *See* electronic claims submission
EDI. *See* electronic data interchange
educational opportunities, 10–14
  reinforcement exercises, 13
EEOICPA. *See* Energy Employees Occupational Illness Compensation Program Act
EHR. *See* electronic health record
EIN. *See* employer identification number
elective surgery, 461
electronic claims submission (ECS), 362, 416
  interactive communication in, 365
electronic data interchange (EDI), 361
electronic health insurance claims, 362, 366–371
  confidentiality and, 371–372
  editing, 367–368
  reinforcement exercises, 370–371
  retrieving, 367–368
  signature requirements, 368–369
  submission options, 363–365
  submitting, 367–368
electronic health record (EHR), 308, 383
electronic protected health information (EPHI), 28
electronic record management, 372–374
  filing, 373
  reinforcement exercises, 373–374
  retrieval, 373
  storage, 373
electronic release of information, 33–35
electronic remittance, 363
E/M. *See* Evaluation and Management Section
emancipated minor, 21, 22
embezzlement, 21, 22
emergency department services, E/M, 259
employer identification number (EIN), 341
employer liability, 21
employer-sponsored health insurance plans, 58
  BC/BS, 432–433
  cafeteria plans, 433
  plan code, 432
employer-sponsored Medicare supplemental plans, 486
encoders, 386
  ICD-9-CM, 161
  ICD-10-CM, 91
encounters, 110
  form, 310
Energy Employees Occupational Illness Compensation Program Act (EEOICPA), 554
enrollees, 432, 503
  ID numbers, 432
EOB. *See* explanation of benefits
EPHI. *See* electronic protected health information
episode-of-care reimbursement, 78–79

EPO. *See* exclusive provider organization
EPSDT. *See* Early and Periodic Screening for Diagnosis and Treatment
equipment, 141–143
error-edit messages, 369
essential modifiers, 100
established patient, 257
estate, guardianship of, 21
ethics, 3
etiology, 100, 162
Evaluation and Management Section (E/M), 255–275
  care plan oversight services, 260
  case management services, 260
  categories, 255–258, 266
  category guidelines, 259–261
  code component description, 263
  code selection, 272–274
  commonly used terms, 255
  complex chronic care coordination services, 261
  consultations, 259
  counseling risk factor reduction and behavior change intervention, 260
  critical care services, 259
  custodial care services, 259
  definitions, 256
  documentation requirements, 267–270
  domiciliary services, 259
  emergency department services, 259
  examination, 263–264
  history, 262–263
  home services, 260
  hospital observation services, 259
  inpatient neonatal intensive care services, 261
  inpatient services, 259
  key components, 262
  levels of service, 258–262
  medical decision making, 264–266, 269
  modifiers, 274–275
  newborn care services, 260
  non–face-to-face services, 260
  nursing facility services, 259
  other services, 261
  outpatient services, 259
  physician standby services, 260
  preventive medicine services, 260
  prolonged services, 260
  reinforcement exercises, 261–262, 275
  rest home services, 259
  special evaluation and management services, 260
excessive charges, 43
excision, 148
excludes notes, 105, 182
exclusions, 67, 69
exclusive provider organization (EPO), 62, 64
expanded problem-focused examination, 264
  documentation, 269
expanded problem-focused history, 262
explanation of benefits (EOB), 324
  provider, 325
external approach, 140, 149
extracorporeal assistance, 140, 142, 144
extracorporeal therapies, 140, 142
extremities, disabilities of, 562

F

face-to-face time, 257
facing triangles, 251
facsimile release of information, 32–33
failed procedure, 224–226
Fair Debt Collection Practices Act (FDCPA), 332
family history, 257
  V code, 202–203
faxing patient information, 33
fax transmittal cover sheet, 34
FBI. *See* Federal Bureau of Investigation
FDCPA. *See* Fair Debt Collection Practices Act
FECA. *See* Federal Employees' Compensation Act
Federal Bureau of Investigation (FBI), 37
Federal Coal Mine Health and Safety Act, 554
Federal Employees' Compensation Act (FECA), 339, 345, 554
Federal False Claims Act, 39
federal tax ID number, 355
fee-for-service, 78, 79
fetal ultrasound, 205–206
fifth digits, 186
final notice, 330, 332
first-listed diagnosis, 112, 190
first report of injury form, 564, 565
fiscal agents, 507
FL. *See* form locator
flash symbol, CPT, 252
flu shots, 455
follow-up examination, 210
form locator (FL), 390
formulary, 466
fourth digit, 224
fraud
  activities, 38
  billing practices, 539
  health care, 38
  insurance, 37–45
  penalties for, 40–41
  prevention, 39–40
  reinforcement exercises, 41
  reporting incentives, 39–40
  TRICARE, 539–541
function, 141–143

G

GAF. *See* geographic adjustment factor
general medical exams
  with abnormal findings, 116
  V code for, 211
general notes, 105, 182
geographic adjustment factor (GAF), 469
glaucoma screening, 455
global surgery concept, 281
government-sponsored health insurance, 58
grace period, 68
group contract, 66
Group Health Association in Washington, D.C., 61
Group Health Cooperative of Puget Sound, 61
Group Health Plan of Minneapolis, 61
group model, HMO, 63
group number, 432
group plans, BC/BS, 432–433
  ID card, 432

group practice, 75
guaranteed renewable, 68
guardian, 21
guardianship, 22–23
  of estate, 21
  of person, 21

H

HAC. *See* Health Administration Center
HCFA. *See* Health Care Finance Administration
HCPCS. *See Healthcare Common Procedure Coding System*
heading notes, CPT, 253
Health Administration Center (HAC), 541
health care claim summary, 324
Healthcare Common Procedure Coding System (HCPCS), 382
  level II codes, 296, 297, 299
  modifiers, 297
  national codes, 296
  rates, 405–406
  transportation modifiers, 298
Health Care Finance Administration (HCFA), 381
health care finder, 528–529
health care fraud, 38
health care specialist, 76
health insurance
  BC/BS plans, 430–433
  bill payment with, 78–81
  coverage terms, 68
  defining, 56–60
  employer-sponsored, 58, 432–433
  government-sponsored, 58
  history of, 56–59
  policy, 65
  reinforcement exercises, 59–60, 67, 70, 74–75, 77, 79–80
  terminology, 65–77
health insurance claim number (HICN), 408, 449
Health Insurance Plan of Greater New York, 61
Health Insurance Portability and Accountability Act (HIPAA), 48, 267, 308, 363, 408, 474
  administrative safeguards, 29
  organizational requirements, 29
  physical safeguards, 29
  Privacy Rule, 26, 27
  relationship codes, 409
  Security Rule, 28–30
  standards, 30
  summary of, 29
  technical safeguards, 29
Health Insurance Prospective Payment System (HIPPS), 405
Health Insurance Reform: Security Standards, 28
health maintenance organizations (HMOs), 57, 61, 429
  group model, 63
  IPA model, 63
  Medicare Advantage, 464
  reinforcement exercises, 64–65
  staff model, 63
heart disease, 561
heart failure, MS-DRGs for, 382
HHS. *See* Department of Health and Human Services

HICN. *See* health insurance claim number
HIPAA. *See* Health Insurance Portability and Accountability Act
HIPPS. *See* Health Insurance Prospective Payment System
histological type, 167
HIV
    ICD-9-CM and, 217–218
    ROI, 32
HMOs. *See* health maintenance organizations
home health care, 450, 454
home services, E/M, 260
honesty, 3
hospice care, 450
hospital benefit, 68
hospital observation services, E/M, 259
hospital reimbursement, 381–383
hospital stays, 450
hypertension tables, 176–177

I

ICD. *See* International Classification of Diseases
ICD-9-CM. *See* International Classification of Diseases, Ninth Revision, Clinical Modification
ICD-10-CM. *See* International Classification of Diseases, Tenth Revision, Clinical Modification
ICD-10-PCS. *See* International Classification of Diseases, Tenth Revision, Procedure Coding System
ICF. *See* intermediate care facility
IDS. *See* integrated delivery system
ill-defined conditions, 164
includes notes, 105, 182
incomplete procedure, 224–226
independent practice association (IPA), 63
indirect payer, 59
in diseases classified elsewhere, 107
individual contract, 66
individual plans, BC/BS, 430–431
individual policy, 59
injury, 164
in-network provider, 76
inpatient neonatal intensive care services, E/M, 261
inpatient prospective payment system (IPPS), 381
inpatient services, E/M, 259
instructional notes, 104–105, 223
    CPT, 253, 254
    ICD-9-CM, 181–182
insurance billing specialist
    career opportunities, 10–14
    certification, 10–14
    defined, 2
    desirable qualifications of, 7
    educational opportunities, 10–14
    employment opportunities, 6–10
    job description, 7
    minimum qualifications of, 7
    personal qualifications of, 2–3
    reinforcement exercises, 9–10
    responsibilities of, 7, 9
    technical qualifications, 4–6
insurance carrier
    error-edit messages, 369
    private, 66
    procedures, 323–324

insurance claims, 71. *See also* electronic health insurance claims
    BC/BS, 438–443
    carrier-direct, 363–364
    clean, 364, 416
    clinical assessment and treatment, 318
    collections, 330–333
    credit, 330–333
    delinquent, 328
    developing, 308–317, 383–415
    dirty, 328
    editing, 367–368
    electronic, 366–371
    established patient procedures, 313–316
    follow-up, 326–328
    form, 439
    insurance payment posting, 324–326
    Medicare, 473–493
    Medigap, 484
    new patient procedures, 309–310
    numeric code assignment, 321–323
    patient departure procedures, 318–321
    patient registration form, 310–313
    payment posting, 327
    pending, 328
    processing, 323–330
    reinforcement exercises, 316–317
    retrieving, 367–368
    submitting, 367–368, 416–418
    summary, 324
    tracer, 329
    UB-04, 383–418
    workers' compensation, 555
insurance collection specialist, 8
insurance company, 66
insurance counselor, 8
insurance fraud, 37–45
insurance policy, 56
    patient information, 342
    purchaser terminology, 65
insurance questionnaire, 490
insured, 66, 432
insurer, 66
integrated delivery system (IDS), 62, 64
interactive communication, ECS, 365
intermediate care facility (ICF), 391
internal fixation device, 209
International Classification of Diseases (ICD), 5
International Classification of Diseases, Ninth Revision, Clinical Modification (ICD-9-CM), 160, 382
    abbreviations in, 185
    AHFS list, 168
    alphabetic index, 171–180, 218
    alphabetization rules, 173–174
    ambulatory surgery, 192
    appendices, 167
    bilateral procedures, 224
    biopsy coding guidelines, 224–228
    burns, 216–217
    carryover lines, 172
    category, 165
    chronic diseases, 190
    code assignment, 221–224
    coding conventions, 161, 181–188, 219–221
    coding detail levels, 190
    coexisting conditions, 190
    components, 162–188
    connecting words, 184

    contrasting conditions, 193
    cooperating parties, 161
    cross-references, 181
    diagnosis code reporting, 189
    diagnostic code assignment, 196–216
    diagnostic code selection, 196–197
    diagnostic code sequencing, 198
    diagnostic services only, 191
    E codes, 169
    first-listed condition selection, 189
    four-digit tissue codes, 170
    HIV/AIDS, 217–218
    hypertension tables, 176–177
    indentation patterns, 172
    industrial accidents classification, 169
    instructional notes, 181–182
    late effects, 216
    main terms, 172
    M code, 170
    miscellaneous coding guidelines, 216–221
    morphology of neoplasms, 167
    multiple diagnoses, 193
    neoplasm table, 177
    observation unit admission, 194–195
    official coding and reporting guidelines, 188–196
    original treatment plan not carried out, 193–194
    outpatient services diagnostic coding, 189–196
    outpatient surgery admission, 195
    prenatal visits, 192
    preoperative evaluations only, 191–192
    principal diagnosis selection, 192–196
    principal procedure identification, 222
    procedure code sequencing, 222
    procedure coding guidelines, 224–228
    punctuation in, 185–186
    reinforcement exercises, 170–171, 174–175, 179–180, 183, 187–188, 195–196, 198–200, 227–228
    section, 164
    subcategory, 165
    subclassifications, 166
    subterms, 172
    supplementary classifications, 167, 200–216
    surgical complications, 193
    table of drugs and chemicals, 178–179
    tables, 175
    tabular list, 219
    tabular list of diseases and injuries, 162–170
    therapeutic services only, 191
    uncertain diagnosis, 190, 194
    V code, 168, 200–214
International Classification of Diseases, Tenth Revision, Clinical Modification (ICD-10-CM), 90–92
    abbreviations, 108–109
    accurate code reporting, 113
    alphabetic index, 99–102, 109
    ambulatory surgery, 116
    chronic diseases, 114
    code also note, 107
    code ranges, 93
    coding conventions, 103–110
    coding detail levels, 113–114
    coding documented coexisting conditions, 114

International Classification of Diseases, Tenth Revision, Clinical Modification (ICD-10-CM) *(Continued)*
  connecting words, 108
  cross-references, 107
  diagnoses codes assignment, 122–125
  diagnostic services only, 114–115
  encounters for other circumstances in, 113
  essential modifiers in, 100
  etiology, 107
  excludes notes, 105–106
  external cause of injuries index, 101–102
  first-listed condition, 112
  five-character category, 98
  four-character category, 98
  general coding guidelines, 111
  general medical exams with abnormal findings, 116
  general notes, 105
  includes notes, 105
  main terms in, 99
  manifestation notes, 107
  nonessential modifiers in, 100
  official guidelines, 110–121
  preoperative evaluation, 116
  principle diagnosis selection, 117–122
  punctuation in, 103–104, 105
  reinforcement exercises, 92, 99, 106, 110, 113
  routine health screening, 116–117
  routine outpatient prenatal visits, 116
  six-character category, 98
  subterms in, 100
  table of drugs and chemicals, 101–102
  table of neoplasms, 100–101
  tabular list, 93–99
  therapeutic services only, 115
  three-character category, 98
  uncertain diagnosis, 114
International Classification of Diseases, Tenth Revision, Procedure Coding System (ICD-10-PCS), 125
  alphabetic, 128–129
  body system guidelines, 147
  character 4 designations, 138
  code structure, 132–146
  coding guidelines, 147–149
  components, 126–131
  general guidelines, 147
  procedure code assignment, 150–151
  reinforcement exercises, 144–145, 150
  root operations, 134–135
  root operations guidelines, 147–149
  sections, 126–128
  tables, 129–131
internet release of information, 33–35
internet security measures, 35
interrelated conditions in, 192
invalid modifiers, 471
IPA. *See* independent practice association
IPPS. *See* inpatient prospective payment system
isolation, 201–202
isotope, 141–143

K

Kaiser Permanente Medical Care Program, 61

L

labor, 173
laparotomy, 227
last menstrual period (LMP), 348
late effects, 111
  ICD-9-CM, 216
laterality, 111
legal issues, 20–21
legal terms, 21–25
  reinforcement exercises, 25
length of stay (LOS), 381
level II codes, HCPCS, 296, 297
LHWCA. *See* Longshore and Harbor Workers' Compensation Act
lifetime reserve days, 451–452
limited charge, 526
limited license practitioner, 76
limiting fee, 461
LMP. *See* last menstrual period
Longshore and Harbor Workers' Compensation Act (LHWCA), 554
LOS. *See* length of stay

M

MA. *See* Medicare Advantage
MAB. *See* Medical Association of Billers
MACs. *See* Medicare Administrative Contractors
main terms, 99, 222
  additional, 173
  CPT, 247
  ICD-9-CM, 172
major complication/co-morbidity (MCC), 382
major medical benefit, 69
malfeasance, 23
malignant
  primary, 100
  secondary, 100
malpractice, 21, 23–24
mammogram screening, 455
managed care, 60–62
managed care organizations (MCOs), 62–64
manifestation code, 186
manifestation notes, 107
MA-PDP. *See* Medicare Advantage prescription drug plan
material safety data sheets (MSDSs), 558
math skills, 5
maximum allowable fee, 63–64
MCC. *See* major complication/co-morbidity
MCD. *See* Medicare-Medicaid Crossover Program
M code, ICD-9-CM, 170
MCOs. *See* managed care organizations
mediastinoscopy, 227
Medicaid, 58, 503
  adjustment, 514
  approval, 514
  billing, 507–516
  claims submission, 507–513
  CMS-1500, 511–513
  coverage, 504–506
  denial, 514
  expansion program, 504
  payment activities, 514
  payment processing, 514–516

reinforcement exercises, 505–506, 516
  remittance advice, 515
  resubmission code, 350
  secondary payer, 511–513
  suspension, 514
Medical Association of Billers (MAB), 11
medical billing certification, 11
medical claims with no disability, 560
medical coder, 8
medical coding, 5, 39
  certification exams, 11
  errors, 38
medical decision making, 266
  documentation requirements, 269
  evaluation and management code selection, 272–274
  high complexity, 265, 270
  low complexity, 265, 269
  moderate complexity, 265, 270
  straightforward, 264, 269
  types of, 265
Medical Office Manager, 12
Medical Practice Manager, 12
medical savings account (MSA), 467
medical terminology, 5
Medicare, 38, 58
  claims submission, 473–493
  CMS-1500 and, 477–482
  disclosure statement, 462
  Medigap with, 484–485
  payment processing, 493–495
  as primary payer, 475–482
  as primary with supplemental insurance, 482
Medicare Administrative Contractors (MACs), 449
Medicare Advantage (MA), 448
  HMOs, 464
  PFFS plans, 465
  PPOs, 464
Medicare Advantage prescription drug plan (MA-PDP), 465
Medicare as Secondary Payer, 488–493
  CMS-1500, 492
Medicare claims submission, 473–493
  general guidelines, 474–475
  primary payer, 475–482
Medicare fee schedule (MFS), 469–470
Medicare-Medicaid Crossover Program (MCD), 486, 513–514
  CMS-1500, 487, 489
  processing, 487
  reinforcement exercises, 487–488
Medicare Part A, 448, 449–453
  co-payments, 450–451
  covered services, 450
  deductibles, 450–451
  DME, 451
  lifetime reserve days, 451–452
  reinforcement exercises, 453
Medicare Part B, 448, 454–463
  covered service, 454–458
  diagnostic services, 454–456
  NonPAR, 458, 461–462
  PARs, 458
  providers, 458
  reinforcement exercises, 463
  treatment services, 454–456
Medicare Part C, 448, 464–465
Medicare Part D, 448, 467
  prescription coverage, 465–466

Medicare-severity diagnosis-related groups (MS-DRGs), 381
  for heart failure, 382
Medicare special needs plans (SNPs), 467
Medicare Summary Notice (MSN), 459
Medicare supplemental plans (MSPs), 482
  employer-sponsored, 486
Medicine Section, CPT, 291–295
  categories and descriptions, 292–294
Medigap plans, 431–432, 482–483
  claims processing, 484
  Medicare with, 484–485
member, 66, 429
mental health, 141, 142, 144
message documentation, 5
method, 141–143
MFS. *See* Medicare fee schedule
military treatment facility (MTF), 523
minimum necessary, 27
misfeasance, 23
modality, 136
modality qualifier, 138–141
modifiers
  ambulatory surgery center, 288–289
  anesthesia section, 276–278
  CPT, 252
  E/M, 274–275
  essential, 100
  HCPCS, 297, 298
  invalid, 471
  nonessential, 100, 176, 185
  physical status, 276, 277
  surgery section, 285–288
modifying terms
  CPT, 247
  for fracture, 247
morphology of neoplasms, ICD-9-CM, 167
MSA. *See* medical savings account
MS-DRGs. *See* Medicare-severity diagnosis-related groups
MSDSs. *See* material safety data sheets
MSN. *See* Medicare Summary Notice
MSPs. *See* Medicare supplemental plans
MTF. *See* military treatment facility
mutually exclusive procedures, 471

N

National Center for Health Statistics (NCHS), 91, 161
  responsibilities of, 92
national codes, HCPCS, 296
national conversion factor (CF), 469
National Correct Coding Initiative (NCCI), 470–471
  reinforcement exercises, 472–473
National Electronic Billers Alliance (NEBA), 11
National Oceanic and Atmospheric Administration (NOAA), 522
National Provider Identification (NPI), 408
National Uniform Billing Committee (NUBC), 390
National Uniform Claim Committee (NUCC), 340
NATO. *See* North Atlantic Treaty Organization
natural openings
  endoscopic, 140
  with percutaneous endoscopic assistance, 140

NCCI. *See* National Correct Coding Initiative
NCHS. *See* National Center for Health Statistics
NEBA. *See* National Electronic Billers Alliance
NEC. *See* not elsewhere classified
needle aspiration biopsy, 226
negligence, 21, 24
neonatal screening, 206
neoplasms, 100–101
  table, 177
newborn care services, E/M, 260
Nixon, Richard, 61
NOAA. *See* National Oceanic and Atmospheric Administration
noncancelable policy, 68
noncoverage admission, 385
noncovered benefit, 369
noncustodial parent, 316
nonessential modifiers, 100, 176, 185
non–face-to-face physician services, E/M, 260
non–face-to-face time, 257
nonfeasance, 23
nonparticipating provider (NonPAR), 76
  DEERS, 526–527
  Medicare Part B, 458, 461–462
  TRICARE, 526–527
North Atlantic Treaty Organization (NATO), 522
NOS. *See* not otherwise specified
not elsewhere classified (NEC), 108, 109
notes
  code also, 107
  after codes, 253
  exclude, 105, 182
  general, 105, 182
  heading, 253
  includes, 105, 182
  instructional, 104–105, 181–182, 223, 253, 254
  manifestation, 107
not otherwise specified (NOS), 108, 109
NPI. *See* National Provider Identification
NUBC. *See* National Uniform Billing Committee
NUCC. *See* National Uniform Claim Committee
nuclear medicine, 140, 142, 144
null zero, 252
number symbol, 252
nursing facility services, E/M, 259

O

observation unit, 120–212, 194–195
obstetrics, 144
Occupational Safety and Health Administration (OSHA), 558–559
occurrence codes, 398, 399
Office of Civil Rights (OCR), 26, 28
Office of the Inspector General (OIG), 37
Office of Worker's Compensation Programs (OWCP), 554
OHI. *See* other health insurance
OIG. *See* Office of the Inspector General
omit code, 183, 220
open approach, 139
open biopsy, 226
open procedure, 224

OPPS. *See* outpatient prospective payment system
optical scanning guidelines, 341
optionally renewable, 68
oral communication skills, 5
ordered/referred services, 478
ordering physician, 478
OSHA. *See* Occupational Safety and Health Administration
osteopathic, 142, 144
other health insurance (OHI), 524
out-of-network provider, 76
out-of-pocket expenses, 459
outpatient prospective payment system (OPPS), 382
outpatient services, 454
  diagnostic coding and reporting guidelines, 189–196
  E/M, 259
OWCP. *See* Office of Worker's Compensation Programs
Owner, Medical Billing Service, 12

P

pain, disabilities related to, 562
pap smear, 455
PAR. *See* participating provider
parenthesis, 103, 186
partial disability, 561
participants, 503
participating provider (PAR), 76
  BC/BS, 433
  DEERS, 526–527
  Medicare Part B, 458
  reinforcement exercises, 434
  TRICARE, 526–527
past history, 257
pathology and laboratory section, CPT, 291
  categories and codes, 292
patient account ledger, 320, 436
patient account representative, 8
patient departure procedures
  billing, 318–319
  charge posting, 319–321
  payments, 319–321
  scheduling, 318–319
patient information
  address, 343
  authorization, 346
  birth date, 343
  condition, 344–345
  faxing, 33
  insurance plan, 342
  name, 342
  other insured's name, 344
  policy group, 345
  sex, 343
  signature, 346
  status, 343
patient ledger, 328
Patient Protection and Affordable Care Act
  provisions of, 45–47
  2010 Consumer Protections, 45
  2010 Improving Quality and Lowering Costs, 45
  2010 Increasing Access to Affordable Care, 45–46
  2011 Holding Insurance Companies Accountable, 46

Patient Protection and Affordable Care
     Act (*Continued*)
   2011 Improving Quality
     and Lowering Costs, 46
   2011 Increasing Access to Affordable
     Care, 46
   2012 Improving Quality
     and Lowering Costs, 46
   2013 Improving Quality
     and Lowering Costs, 47
   2013 Increasing Access to Affordable
     Care, 47
   2014 Consumer Protections, 47
   2014 Improving Quality
     and Lowering Costs, 47
   2014 Increasing Access to Affordable
     Care, 47
   2015 Improving Quality
     and Lowering Costs, 47
patient registration form, 310–313, 347
patient statement, 331
payer of last resort, 507
payment-related terminology, 71
PCP. *See* personal care physician
PDP. *See* prescription drug plan
pelvic exam, 455
pending claims, 328
percutaneous approach, 139
percutaneous endoscopic approach, 140
percutaneous transluminal angioplasty, 225
performing physician, 478
perinatal period, 94, 164
permanent disability, 560–561
person, guardianship, 21
personal care physician (PCP), 429
personal contract, 66
personal history, 202–203
personal qualifications, 2–3
   reinforcement exercises, 4
PFFS. *See* private fee-for-service
PHI. *See* protected health information
physical examination, 456
physical rehabilitation, 141, 142
physical status modifier, 276, 277
physical therapy, 209
physician
   extender, 76, 478
   signature, 355
   specialist, 76
physician standby services, E/M, 260
placeholder *x*, 98, 99
place of service (POS), 351, 352–353
plan code, 432
plus sign, 251
pneumococcal shot, 456
pneumonectomy, 227
POA. *See* present on admission
point dash, 103
point-of-service plan, 62, 64
poisoning, 164
policyholder, 65, 66
POS. *See* place of service
Posting Detail, 321
postpartum condition, 205
power of attorney, 21, 22–23
PPO. *See* preferred provider organizations
PPS. *See* prospective payment system
preauthorization, 71, 73
precertification, 71, 74
predetermination, 71, 74
pre-existing conditions, 68, 69

preferred provider organizations (PPO),
     62, 63–64, 429
   Medicare Advantage, 464
pregnancy, 173
   high-risk, 204–205
premiums, 56, 68
   PDP, 466
preoperative evaluation, 116
prepaid health plans, 57
prescription drug plan (PDP), 465
   co-payments, 466
   deductibles, 466
   enrollment, 466
   premiums, 466
present illness history, 257
present on admission (POA), 110
preventive medicine services, E/M, 260
primary care manager, 76, 523
primary care physician, 76
primary care provider, 429
primary diagnosis, 112
primary insurance, 310
primary payer, 71, 383
   CMS-1500 and, 477–482
   conditional, 476
   Medicare as, 475–482
   reinforcement exercises, 476
principal procedure, 150, 312
   ICD-9-CM, 222
principle diagnosis, 192–196, 198
   codes, 117–118
   contrasting diagnoses, 118–119
   diagnoses codes selection, 122–123
   diagnoses codes sequencing, 123–124
   interrelated conditions, 118
   multiple diagnoses meeting, 118
   observation unit admission, 120
   original treatment plan not carried
     out, 119
   outpatient surgery admission,
     120–121
   reinforcement exercises, 121
   surgical complications, 119
   UB-04, 411
   uncertain diagnosis, 119–120
Prior Authorization Number, 350
privacy officer, 27
Privacy Rule, HIPAA, 26, 27
private fee-for-service (PFFS), 464
   Medicare Advantage, 465
private insurance carrier, 66
problem-focused examination, 263
   documentation, 269
problem-focused history, 262
procedures
   CPT, 246
   mutually exclusive, 471
professional services, 257
Program Integrity Office, TMA, 539
prolonged services, E/M, 260
prospective payment system (PPS), 381
prostate cancer screening, 456
protected health information (PHI),
     27, 363
provider reimbursement methods, 62.
     See also reimbursement
   BC/BS, 434–438
   capitation, 62
   fee-for-service, 62
   negotiated fee, 62
   salaried, 62

providers, 75, 110. *See also* nonparticipating
     provider; participating provider
   authorized, 524
   CHAMPVA, 542
   CMS-1500 and, 348–357
   EOB, 325
   in-network, 76
   Medicare Part B, 458
   out-of-network, 76
   referring, 349
   service, 75
   UB-04, 390–397
puerperium, 94, 163, 173
pulmonary disease, 561
punctuation, 103–104
   in ICD-9-CM, 185–186

Q

QI. *See* Qualifying Individual
Qualified Medicare Beneficiary (QMB),
     448, 504
qualifier, 143–145
   modality, 138–141
   type, 138–141
qualifying circumstances, 278
Qualifying Individual (QI), 448
questionnaire, 490

R

RA. *See* remittance advice
radiation oncology, 140, 142, 144
radical mastectomy, 222
radiology section, CPT, 290–291
radionuclide, 138–141, 559
reasonable fee, 435
recipient, 66, 503
referring physician, 76, 478
referring provider, 349
reimbursement, 71, 308, 369. *See also*
     provider reimbursement methods
   episode-of-care, 78–79
   hospital, 381–383
   third-party, 78
   TRICARE, 526–531
   workers' compensation, 566–569
relationship codes, HIPAA, 409
relative value scale (RVS), 434, 436–438
relative value unit (RVU), 469
release of information (ROI), 30–36
   AIDS, 32
   alcohol abuse, 32
   authorization of, 31
   drug abuse, 32
   electronic, 33–35
   facsimile, 32–33
   HIV, 32
   internet, 33–35
   items, 30
   reinforcement exercises, 35–36
   telephone, 32
reliability, 3
remittance advice (RA), 324, 514
   Medicaid, 515
remittance notice, 493
   sample, 494
resection, 148
residual effects, 111
responsible party, 400
rest home, E/M, 259
ROI. *See* release of information

root operation, 132
routine health screening, 116–117, 203
routine outpatient prenatal visits, 116
routine prenatal visits, 204
routing form, 310
rule of nines, 217
RVS. *See* relative value scale
RVU. *See* relative value unit

S

SCHIP. *See* State Children's Health Insurance Program
secondary condition, 123, 198
secondary insurance, 312
secondary payer, 71, 383
    TRICARE as, 539
section, 164
    guidelines, 253
    marks, 187
Security Rule, HIPAA, 28–30
see, 108
    in CPT, 252
see also, 108
    in CPT, 252
self-motivation, 3
semicolon, 249–250
separate procedures, 284–285
sequela, 111
sequencing, 123, 198
services, 246
    date, 306
    provided, 39
    provider, 75
    units, 306
7th character extensions, 98, 99
sex, 343
Shadid, Michael, 60
signature, patient, 346
significant procedure, 222
signs, 113, 117–118, 164, 189, 192
    coding guidelines, 111
skilled nursing facility (SNF), 391, 450
slanted brackets, 103, 187
SLMB. *See* Specified Low-Income Medicare Beneficiary
smoking, 456
SNF. *See* skilled nursing facility
SNPs. *See* Medicare special needs plans
social history, 257
Social Security number (SSN), 341
source of admission, 395, 396
special evaluation and management services, E/M, 260
specialty certifications, 11
special report, 257
specificity, highest level of, 190
Specified Low-Income Medicare Beneficiary (SLMB), 448
spinal disabilities, 561
sponsors, 523
sports physical, 211
square brackets, 103, 186
SSI. *See* Supplemental Security Income
SSN. *See* Social Security number
staff model, HMO, 63
State Children's Health Insurance Program (SCHIP), 504
state insurance commission, 328–330
state law, 20
status post, 208

statute of limitations, 21, 24
subcategory
    CPT, 246
    ICD-9-CM, 165
subclassifications, 166
subpoena, 21
    of records, 24
subpoena duces tecum, 21, 24
subscriber, 66, 428
subsections, CPT, 246
substance, 141–143
substance abuse, 141, 142, 144
subterms, 100, 222
    ICD-9-CM, 172
superbill, 310
superficial injury, 217
supplemental insurance, 482
Supplemental Security Income (SSI), 504
support staff job titles, 2
surgeon, 478
surgery section, CPT, 280–290
    categories and codes, 281
    modifiers, 285–288
    separate procedures, 284–285
    surgical package, 281–282
surgical benefit, 68
symptoms, 113, 117–118, 164, 189, 192
    coding guidelines, 111
synonyms, 185
system review, 257

T

tabular list entry, 223
TANF. *See* Temporary Assistance for Needy Families
taxonomy code, 414
TCM. *See* Transitional Care Management
technical qualifications, 4–5
    reinforcement exercises, 6
telephone release of information, 32
Temporary Assistance for Needy Families (TANF), 504
temporary disability, 560
TFL. *See* TRICARE for Life
therapeutic services, 115
third-party administrator (TPA), 363
third-party payer, 59, 66
third-party reimbursement, 78
time limits, 71
Title 19, 503
Title 21, 504
TMA. *See* TRICARE Management Agency
TOB. *See* type of bill
total abdominal hysterectomy, 225–226
total disability, 561
TPA. *See* third-party administrator
TPR. *See* TRICARE Prime Remote
transaction journal, 321
transbronchial lung biopsy, 227
transfer of care, 257
Transitional Care Management (TCM), 258, 261
treatment site, 138–139
triangles
    CPT, 251
    facing, 251
TRICARE, 58, 339
    abuse, 539–541
    allowable charges, 532–533
    billing, 531–539

CMS-1500, 535–538
    contractors, 532
    cost sharing, 532–533
    covered services, 527–528
    deadline exceptions, 531
    deductibles, 532–533
    DME, 529–530
    fraud, 539–541
    noncovered services, 527–528
    nonparticipating providers, 526–527
    participating providers, 526–527
    payment estimation, 533–534
    preauthorization, 528–529
    programs, 522
    regions, 532
    reimbursement, 526–531
    reinforcement exercises, 525, 540–541
    as secondary payer, 539
    states, 532
TRICARE for Life (TFL), 522, 524
TRICARE health benefits programs, 523–525
TRICARE Management Agency (TMA), 540
    Program Integrity Office, 539
TRICARE Prime, 522, 523
TRICARE Prime Remote (TPR), 522
TRICARE Program Eligibility, 524
TRICARE Reserve Select (TRS), 522
TRICARE Retired Reserve (TRR), 522
TRICARE Standard/Extra, 522, 524
    covered services, 527
TRICARE Young Adult (TYA), 522
TRR. *See* TRICARE Retired Reserve
TRS. *See* TRICARE Reserve Select
tubal ligation, 225
turnaround time, 364
TYA. *See* TRICARE Young Adult
type, 136
    qualifier, 138–141
type of bill (TOB)
    first digit, 391
    second digit, 392

U

UB-04, 380
    assignment of benefits, 407
    charge capturing, 384–385
    completed, 415
    completion guidelines, 389–390
    condition and event information, 398–402
    diagnosis assignment, 386
    insurance and employer information, 406–410
    insurance claim development, 383–415
    insurance claim submission, 416–418
    medical codes, 410–415
    patient and provider information, 390–397
    patient registration, 383–389
    physician identification, 410–415
    principal diagnosis in, 411
    procedure codes, 386

UB-04, 380 (*Continued*)
    reinforcement exercises, 386–389, 396, 414
    revenue codes, 403–405
UCR fees. *See* usual, customary,
    and reasonable (UCR) fees
UHDDS. *See* Uniform Hospital Discharge
    Data Set
unauthorized service, 369
unbundling, 283, 471
uncertain behavior, 100
uniformed services, 522
Uniform Hospital Discharge Data Set
    (UHDDS), 380
unit/floor time, 257
universal no code, 252
unlisted service, 257
unnecessary services, 43
unspecified behavior, 100
upcoding, 268
use additional code, 107, 182
usual, customary, and reasonable (UCR)
    fees, 434–436
usual fee, 434

V

VA. *See* Veterans Administration
value codes, 398, 400
    with descriptions, 401
V code, ICD-9-CM, 168, 200–214
    Alphabetic Index main terms leading
      to, 201
    categories and titles, 202
    communicable diseases and, 201
    family history and, 202–203
    general medical examinations, 211
    health status influencing conditions, 208
    for isolation, 201–202
    liveborn infants, 207–208
    personal history and, 202–203
    reinforcement exercises, 206–207,
      210, 214
    reproduction and, 202–206
    specific procedures and aftercare, 208
veterans, 523
Veterans Administration (VA), 488
vocational rehabilitation, 562
voluntary sterilization, 205

W

waiting period, 69
waiver, 69
Web-DENIS, 428
WHO. *See* World Health Organization
workers' compensation, 58
    basics, 560–569
    claim compensation, 555
    CMS-1500, 566–569
    documentation requirements, 564–566
    eligibility, 560
    federal, 554–559
    progress reports, 564–566
    reimbursement, 566–569
    reinforcement exercises, 563–564
    state-sponsored, 559–560
    training session, 558
workforce members, 27
work-related death, 562
work-related injuries, 560
World Health Organization (WHO), 160
write-offs, 433
written communication skills, 5